THE ROUGH GUIDE TO

Guatemala

written and researched by

Iain Stewart

roughguides.com

Contents

Introduction to

Guatemala

Spanning a mountainous slice of Central America immediately south of Mexico, Guatemala is loaded with incredible natural, historical and cultural appeal. As the birthplace and heartland of the ancient Maya, the country is in many ways defined by the legacy of this early civilization. Their rainforest cities were abandoned centuries ago, but Maya people continue to thrive in the Guatemalan highlands, where traditions and religious rituals, mingled with Catholic practices, endure to form the richest and most distinctive indigenous identity in the hemisphere.

Guatemala today is very much a synthesis of Maya and colonial traditions, fused with the omnipresent influences of twenty-first century Latin and North American culture. Baroque churches dating back to the Spanish Conquest coexist with pagan temples that have been sites of worship for millennia. Highland street markets prosper alongside vast glitzy shopping malls, and pre-Columbian festival dances are performed by teenage hip-hop fans.

Guatemala is still a developing nation, a young democracy with a turbulent and **bloody history** that's beset by deep-rooted inequalities. And yet, despite alarming levels of poverty and unemployment, most Guatemalans are extraordinarily courteous and helpful to travellers, and only too eager to help you catch the right bus or practise your Spanish.

It's this genuine and profound hospitality combined with the country's **outstanding cultural legacy** and **astonishing natural beauty** that makes Guatemala such a compelling place for travellers.

Where to go

Guatemala offers a startling range of landscapes, defined by extremes. Most travellers first head for **Antigua**, the delightful former colonial capital, its refined atmosphere and café

ABOVE FROM LEFT SCARLET MACAW; TEXTILES FROM SANTA CATARINA PALOPÓ **RIGHT** CHICHICASTENANGO MARKET

society contrasting with the chaotic fume-filled streets of Guatemala City. Next on your list should be the Maya-dominated **western highlands**, a region of mesmerizing beauty, with volcanic cones soaring above pine-clad hills, traditional villages and shimmering lakes. The strength of Maya culture here is overwhelming with each village having its own textile weaving tradition and unique fiesta celebrations.

Lago de Atitlán, an astonishingly beautiful lake ringed by sentinel-like volcanoes, is unmissable. The shores of the lake are dotted with charming indigenous settlements such as **Santa Cruz La Laguna**, where you'll find some fine places to stay and breathtaking shoreline hikes, and **San Pedro La Laguna**, with its bohemian scene and rock-bottom prices. High up above the lake, the traditional Maya town of **Sololá** has one of the country's best (and least-touristy) markets, a complete contrast to the vast twice-weekly affair at **Chichicastenango**, with its incredible selection of souvenirs, weavings and handicrafts.

To the west, the proud provincial city of **Quetzaltenango** (Xela) is an important language school centre, and also makes an excellent base for exploring the forest-fringed crater lake of **Volcán Chicabal**, the sublime natural spa of **Fuentes Georginas** and some fascinating market towns. Guatemala's greatest mountain range, the **Cuchumatanes**, is a little further distant. In these granite peaks you'll find superb scenery and some of the most isolated and traditional villages in the Maya world, with **Nebaj** and **Todos Santos Cuchumatán** both making good bases for some serious hiking and adventure.

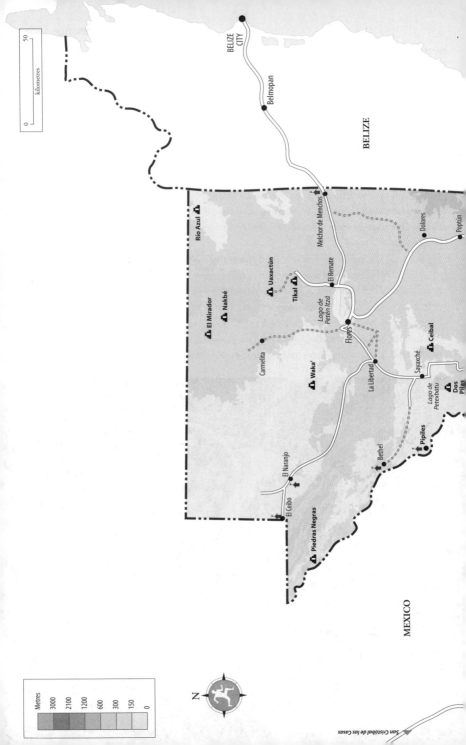

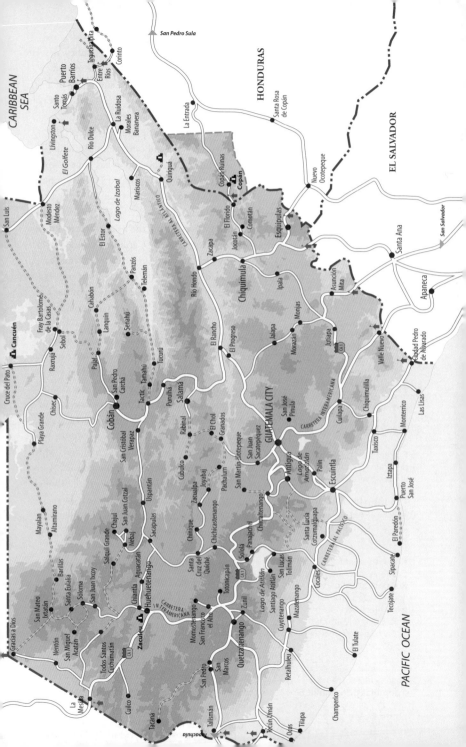

The **Pacific coast** is generally hot, dull and disappointing to visit, with scrubby, desolate beaches backed by a smattering of mangrove swamps. One exception is the relaxed seaside village of **Monterrico**, which has some good accommodation and is part of a wildlife reserve where you can watch sea turtles come ashore to lay their eggs. There's also a small but growing surf scene at **Paredón**, home to a fine new beach lodge.

FACT FILE

- The republic of Guatemala's 108,890 square kilometres include dozens of **volcanoes** (four are active), 328km of **Pacific** coastline and 74km of **Caribbean** coast.

- Guatemala's **population** was estimated at 15.1 million in 2012, with a growth rate of 2.3 percent per annum (the highest in the Western hemisphere).

- Ethnically, the population is almost equally divided between indigenous **Maya** and **ladinos** (who are mainly of mixed race), although there are tiny numbers of black Garífuna (about eight thousand in all), ethnic Chinese and non-Maya Xinca.

- Ron Centenario Zacapa, a fabulously smooth **rum** made in Guatemala, was the first rum to be included in the International Rum Festival's Hall of Fame.

- **Tourism** is the nation's main income earner, followed by coffee, sugar, clothing exports and bananas.

- About sixty percent of Guatemalans are nominally **Roman Catholic** – the lowest figure in Latin America – though many highland Maya practise a unique mix of religions that's heavily dependent on ancient religious ritual.

- Guatemala's 36-year civil war ended in 1996. The nation is now a **democratic republic**, headed by a president who is head of both state and government.

Much of the **east** of the country is **tropical**, replete with banana and cardamom plantations and coconut palms. This region has some stunning lakes, including pristine, jungle-fringed **Laguna Lachúa** and **Lago de Izabal**, whose shores boast plenty of interesting spots, including an amazing hot spring waterfall and the Boquerón canyon. The lake drains into the Caribbean via the **Río Dulce**, which flows through a series of remarkable jungle-clad gorges. At the mouth of the river is the fascinating town of **Lívingston**, an outpost of Caribbean culture and home to Guatemala's only black community, the Garífuna.

Cloudforests cloak the fecund Verapaz hills of central Guatemala, harbouring the elusive quetzal, Guatemala's national symbol. Cultural sites in the east are quite limited, but do include the compact Maya site of **Quiriguá** and the first-class ruins of **Copán**, just over the border in Honduras.

The vast **rainforests** of Petén occupy most of the country's north. This unique lowland area, which makes up about a third of the country, is covered with dense tropical forest and savannah. Though loggers and ranchers have laid waste to large chunks of the terrain, nature reserves alive with wildlife remain, many dotted with outstanding Maya ruins.

From the delightful town of **Flores**, superbly situated on an islet on Lago de Petén Itzá, or the low-key village of **El Remate**, it's easy to reach **Tikal**, the most impressive of all Maya sites, rivalling any ruin in Latin America. The region's forest also envelopes numerous smaller sites, including the striking **Yaxhá**, Aguateca and Uaxactún. For the ultimate adventure in Guatemala the ancient, remote preclassic sites of the extreme north require

CLOCKWISE FROM TOP LEFT LOCALS IN TRADITIONAL DRESS, TODOS SANTOS CUCHUMATÁN; SAN FRANCISCO, ANTIGUA; LA MERCED CLOISTERS, ANTIGUA

VOLCANOES

Overshadowing the southern half of the country, a chain of **volcanoes** extends in an ominous arc from 4220m-high Tajumulco on the Mexican border to the frontier with Honduras. Depending on how you define a volcano – some vulcanologists do not classify lateral cones in the folds of a larger peak to be volcanoes for example – Guatemala has somewhere between 33 and 40. Three of these, **Pacaya**, **Fuego** and **Santiaguito** are highly active, regularly belching soaring plumes of smoke and ash. An ascent up Pacaya (see p.70) rarely fails to disappoint as it's usually possible to get up close and personal with the orange lava flows, but there are myriad other incredible climbs.

Lago de Atitlán is actually the former caldera of a giant volcano that cataclysmically blew its top some 85,000 years ago. So much magma was expelled that most of the vast cone collapsed, and centuries of rainwater filled the depression, creating today's lake.

days of tough hiking to reach. Giant **El Mirador**, in its day a Mesoamerican metropolis, is the main draw but there are dozens of other unrestored sites to explore, situated in the densest rainforest in the country – if you have the time and energy.

When to go

Guatemala has one of the most pleasant climates on earth – the tourist board refers to it as the "land of the eternal spring" – with much of the country enjoying warm days and mild evenings year-round (see box, p.42). The climate is largely determined by **altitude**. In those areas between 1300 and 1600m, which includes Guatemala City, Antigua, Lago de Atitlán and Cobán, the air is almost always fresh and the nights mild and, despite the heat of the midday sun, humidity is never a problem. Parts of the departments of Quetzaltenango, Huehuetenango and El Quiché are above this height, and so have a cooler, damper climate with distinctly chilly nights between early December and late February. Low-lying Petén suffers from sticky, steamy conditions most of the year, as do the Pacific and Caribbean coasts, though here at least you can usually rely on the welcome relief of a sea breeze.

The **rainy season** runs roughly from May to October, with the worst of the rain falling in September and October. In Petén, however, the season can extend into December. Even at the height of the wet season, though, the rain is usually confined to late afternoon downpours with most of the rest of the day being warm and pleasant. Visiting Petén's more remote ruins is best attempted between February and May, as the mud can be thigh-deep during the height of the rains.

The **busiest times** for tourism are between December and March, and again in July and August. Language schools and hotels are fullest during these periods, and many of them hike their prices correspondingly.

Author picks

For the fifth edition of *The Rough Guide to Guatemala*, Iain Stewart travelled every corner of this beautiful country; these are some of his own, personal highlights he discovered along the way:

Wildest fiesta To witness highland-style drink-driving, head to the riotous drunken horse race in remote, unique Todos Santos Cuchumatán (p.164).

Finest coffee Guatemala has some outstanding regional coffees, of which Huehuetenango (p.158) in the western highlands is gloriously complex, Antigua (see p.72) fabulously smooth and Cobán (p.231) in the Verapaces full-bodied and slightly spicy.

Ultimate lake view Lago de Atitlán is outrageously picturesque at any time of day, but at dawn the volcano views from Santa Cruz La Laguna (see p.138) have an ethereal majesty.

Easiest volcano hike The cone of Volcán Chicabal (p.153) is a fairly gentle ascent and contains a magical crater lake encircled by cloudforest.

Sonic boom Howler monkeys are nature's loudest creature; hear them in full force at Yaxhá (p.289), Lago de Petexbatún (p.284) or Tikal (p.265).

Best kayaking Explore the incomparable Río Dulce gorge (p.208) at your leisure, and watch out for manatees.

> Our author recommendations don't end here. We've flagged up our favourite places – a perfectly sited hotel, an atmospheric café, a special restaurant – throughout the guide, highlighted with the ★ symbol.

FROM TOP THE CRATER LAKE OF VOLCÁN CHICABAL; HOWLER MONKEY; A WOMAN SORTS FRESHLY PICKED COFFEE

25

things not to miss

It's not possible to see everything that Guatemala has to offer in one visit, and we don't suggest you try. What follows is a selective taste of the country's highlights, from wildlife-rich nature reserves to colonial cities and indigenous markets. All highlights have a page reference to take you straight into the guide, where you can find out more.

1

1 LAGO DE ATITLÁN
Page 117
Encircled by three volcanoes, the awesome crater lake of Lago de Atitlán was famously described by Aldous Huxley as "the most beautiful lake in the world".

2 QUETZAL
Page 227
Rare and elusive, Guatemala's national bird inhabits the cloudforests of the Verapaces.

3 TODOS SANTOS CUCHUMATÁN
Page 164
A fascinating highland Maya town, home to one of the finest textile traditions in Latin America, which hosts a legendary fiesta, with a rip-roaring horse race.

2

3

4

5

8 RAINFOREST WILDLIFE
Page 356

Guatemala's jungle reserves are ideal places to seek out wildlife including keel-billed toucans, monkeys and, perhaps, a big cat.

9 COFFEE
Page 231

Sample some of the world's finest single estate roasts in Cobán, the easy-going capital of Alta Verapaz.

10 THE IXIL REGION
Page 110

The Guatemalan highlands at their most bewitching: the costume and scenery of this deeply traditional Maya region are astonishing.

11 ANTIGUA
Page 72

The graceful former capital, with an incredible legacy of colonial architecture, is one of the most elegant cities in the Americas.

12 FUENTES GEORGINAS
Page 152

A stunning natural spa, with steaming open-air pools fringed by a dense foliage of ferns.

13 CHICKEN BUSES
Page 27

Garishly painted and outrageously uncomfortable, there's never a dull journey aboard Guatemala's iconic fume-belching camionetas.

12

13

14 SEMUC CHAMPEY
Page 237

Explore the exquisite turquoise pools and river system around Semuc Champey, a natural limestone bridge.

15 NATIONAL ARCHEOLOGICAL MUSEUM
Page 60

A wonderful collection of Maya artistry and breathtakingly carved monuments from many remote Petén sites.

16 CHICHICASTENANGO
Page 101

For souvenir hunters, this twice-weekly highland market is unsurpassed.

17 YAXHÁ
Page 289

This massive Maya site, superbly positioned on the banks of Lago de Yaxhá, has dozens of large temples and impressive monuments.

18 STUDYING SPANISH
Page 39

Guatemala has dozens of excellent language schools that offer one-on-one tuition and home-stay packages at rock-bottom rates.

19 HIGHLAND HIKING
Pages 141 & 110

Explore the beguiling, lofty trails of Guatemala's western highlands: the town of Quetzaltenango and Nebaj are good bases.

17

18

20 TIKAL
Page 265

This unmatched Maya site has it all: monumental temples and palaces set in a tropical forest alive with spider monkeys and chattering parakeets.

21 MAXIMÓN
Page 130

Visit the pagan temple of this liquor-swilling, cigar-smoking evil saint.

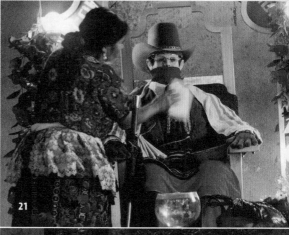

22 COPÁN RUINS
Page 302

There's a plethora of exquisitely carved stelae and altars, a towering hieroglyphic stairway and an outstanding museum at the magnificent ruins of Copán.

23 RON CENTENARIO ZACAPA
Page 32

Indulge in a glass or two of the world's best rum.

24 MONTERRICO
Page 188

A rich nature reserve and village on the Pacific coast, with a sweeping dark sand beach where three species of sea turtle nest.

25 RÍO DULCE
Page 208

Cruise up the jungle-cloaked gorges and estuaries of Guatemala's "sweet river" by boat, and marvel at the scenery and birdlife.

23

24

25

Itineraries

Though compact, Guatemala is a mountainous country and the number of sights is such that you could spend years trying to tick them all off. Our grand tour covers the highlights if you have just a couple of weeks, concentrating on the outstanding attractions. The other two routes focus on ancient Maya ruins (and their rainforest setting) and the western highlands, with its spectacular scenery, fiestas and markets.

GRAND TOUR

A holiday in Guatemala but don't know where to start? Our "Grand Tour" puts you on the right track.

❶ **Antigua** Guatemala's former capital – a mandatory stop – is a heady vision of cobbled streets, colonial mansions, Baroque churches and the nation's best dining scene. **See p.72**

❷ **Chichicastenango** Highland town renowned for its unique blend of Maya and Catholic religion and a huge twice-weekly market. **See p.101**

❸ **Lago de Atitlán** Idyllic lake, surrounded by volcanoes and dotted with Maya villages, with all kinds of activities on offer – from scuba diving to studying Spanish. **See p.117**

❹ **Flores** Refined and very easy on the eye, Flores is a pocket-sized colonial gem that juts into the azure Lago de Petén Itzá. **See p.254**

❺ **Tikal** The Maya World's number one archeological site, the ancient name for this pivotal Classic Maya city may have been the aptly named "Place Where Gods Speak". **See p.265**

❻ **Semuc Champey** Gorgeous kingfisher-blue series of limestone pools in the tropical forests of Alta Verapaz; close by you'll find some impressive cave systems and a forest-fringed river to tube. **See p.237**

❼ **Río Dulce** An astonishing sight, this magisterial gorge system is the highlight of Guatemala's Caribbean region. **See p.208**

❽ **Guatemala City** An untamed capital that gets a bad press, but contains the nation's best museums and a lively cultural life. **See p.50**

ANCIENT MAYA

Guatemala's northernmost department of Petén contains hundreds of astonishing Maya sites; other ruins are scattered around the country.

❶ **Lago de Petexbatún** Stunning jungle-fringed lake ringed with Maya ruins – Aguateca is the main attraction but Dos Pilas also has a fascinating history. **See p.284**

❷ **Yaxhá-Nakúm-Naranjo National Park** This protected reserve harbours the huge Maya site of Yaxhá in a breathtaking location on the banks of an emerald lake, and Nakúm, with well-restored ceremonial buildings. **See p.289**

❸ **Tikal** Lording it above the surrounding rainforest, Tikal's giant temples, palaces, plazas and monuments make it a superstar Maya attraction. **See p.265**

❹ **El Mirador** Two thousand years ago this Preclassic city was approaching its peak, today it's the most enigmatic, remote and ultimately rewarding of all Petén's ruins. **See p.277**

ABOVE FROM LEFT LAGO DE ATITLÁN; MASKS FOR SALE AT CHICHICASTENANGO MARKET

⑤ Cancuén This affluent Maya trading town is little-visited but worthwhile, with a stupendous palace and a lovely location. **See p.242**

⑥ Quirguá A modest site in the south of the country, with a collection of giant, carved stelae out of all proportion to its size. **See p.196**

⑦ Copán Just over the border in Honduras, Copán boasts an astounding hieroglyphic stairway, some exquisite carving and, close by, the lovely town of Copan Ruinas. **See p.302**

WESTERN HIGHLANDS

① Chichicastenango If you've an eye for a souvenir, this market (Thurs & Sun) is bursting with colourful clothing, eye-dazzling textiles, ceramics and leather. **See p.101**

② Ixil An isolated region of evergreen hills and forested mountains, bowl-shaped valleys and some of the most traditional Maya villages in the nation – it's a huge draw for trekkers. **See p.110**

③ Todos Santos Cuchumatán Only reached at the end of a vertiginous journey from Huehuetenango, this Mam village is famous for its textiles, walking trails and breathtaking scenery. **See p.164**

④ Quetzaltenango (Xela) Guatemala's second city is coming into its own with an expanding cultural scene, a great base for forays to the region's sights. **See p.141**

⑤ Laguna Chicabal A short ride from Xela, this near-circular volcanic lake makes a perfect day-trip. **See p.153**

⑥ Fuentes Georginas A high-altitude natural hot-spring spa, half-way up a volcano – the ideal place to soak away an afternoon. **See p.152**

⑦ Sololá Often overlooked, you won't find many souvenirs at this huge Maya market, but its energy and colour is authentic and mesmeric. **See p.118**

⑧ Lago de Atitlán Not only is the volcanic scenery out of this world, this lake is also the ideal place to kick back and paddle a kayak, learn some Spanish or just invest in some hammock time. **See p.117**

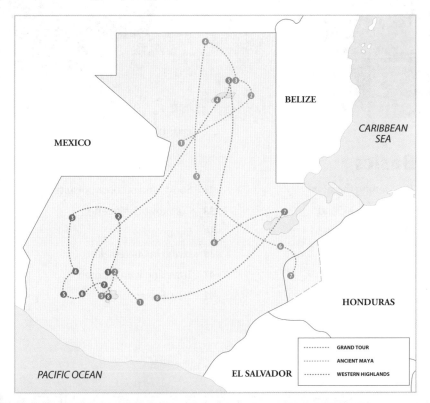

CHICHICASTENANGO MARKET, WESTERN HIGHLANDS

Basics

Getting there

Most people get to Guatemala by plane, arriving in the capital, Guatemala City. Flores airport, near Tikal, also has a few flights from Belize City and Cancún. Guatemalan land and sea entry-points are relatively hassle free, unless you're bringing your own transport, in which case you can expect plenty of red tape, dubious entry fees and delays.

Airfares always depend on the season, with the highest being from Christmas to February, around Easter and in July and August.

Flights from the US and Canada

Most flights to Guatemala are routed through a few **US hub cities**: Atlanta, Chicago, Dallas, Fort Lauderdale, Houston, Los Angeles, Miami and New York. You'll also find several non-direct options via San Salvador (with Taca) and Mexico City (Aeroméxico and Interjet). Prices vary wildly, depending on the season and promotional fares, with return flights starting at around US$330 from Fort Lauderdale with Spirit Airlines or from Miami with Taca, while return fares from either Houston or New York are typically US$460–700.

From Canada, as there are no direct connections to Guatemala, your best bet is to fly via one of the US gateway cities. Return flights from Toronto typically cost Can$700–950, from Vancouver Can$790–950.

Flights from the UK and Ireland

There are no direct flights **from the UK** to Guatemala; most itineraries travel via the US cities of Atlanta, Houston, New York or Miami. Other options include flying via Madrid on Iberia, via Amsterdam and Panama with KLM, or via Mexico with a number of airlines and then on to Guatemala with a Mexican airline. **Prices** for return flights to Guatemala City are around £620 low season/£750 high season, whichever airline and route you take.

From Ireland, it's often cheapest to grab a low-cost airline ticket to one of the London airports and travel on from there, or there are numerous possibilities via gateway cities in the US. Expect to pay around €820 low season/€970 high season.

Flights from Australia, New Zealand and South Africa

There are no direct flights **from Australasia** to Guatemala, so most travellers fly via the US. Tickets cost Aus$1900–2400 (depending on the season) from Sydney via LA or NZ$2800–3300 from Auckland. Delta and United usually have the best fares. If you want to visit Guatemala as part of a longer Latin American trip it often costs only a little more to book an open-jaw ticket flying into Guatemala City and returning from Panama.

From South Africa return flights start at about ZAR15,500; Iberia often have the best rates via London and Madrid, though the total journey time is between 30 and 40 hours.

Buses

From **southern Mexico**, nine daily buses leave Tapachula for Guatemala City (see p.63). One daily minibus connects San Cristóbal de Las Casas with Antigua (see p.81), passing by drop-offs for Huehuetenango, Quetzaltenango and Panajachel. There's also a daily bus route linking Cancún with Flores, with one minibus taking you to the Belize–Mexico border and another connection travelling via Belize City and the Guatemalan border to Flores (see p.256). Shuttle bus connections between Palenque and Flores are another option, (see p.256).

Very regular buses connect **San Salvador** with Guatemala City (see p.64). From **Honduras** there are direct daily links between Copán and Guatemala City/Antigua, and also daily buses from both San Pedro Sula and Tegucigalpa to Guatemala City.

Finally there are buses run by King Quality and Tica Bus between **Panama City** and Guatemala City via Costa Rica, Nicaragua, Honduras and El Salvador. These involve nights in hotels on the way and several days of travel (see p.64).

A BETTER KIND OF TRAVEL

At Rough Guides we are passionately committed to travel. We believe it helps us understand the world we live in and the people we share it with – and of course tourism is vital to many developing economies. But the scale of modern tourism has also damaged some places irreparably, and climate change is accelerated by most forms of transport, especially flying. All Rough Guides' flights are carbon-offset, and every year we donate money to a variety of environmental charities.

Boats

From Punta Gorda, **Belize**, there are three daily boats to Puerto Barrios (see p.202) and twice-weekly connections to Lívingston (see p.202).

You can also arrive in Guatemala from **Mexico** crossing the Usumacinta River at Frontera Corozal (see p.286).

Agents and operators

Booking your tickets online cuts out the costs of agents and middlemen. Check out Momondo (Ⓦ momondo.com), an excellent flight search engine which comes up with some great deals. Discount or auction sites are other possibilities, as are airlines' own websites.

AGENTS AND OPERATORS

The tour prices below do not include airfares to the region, unless stated.

Adventure Life US ☎ 1 800 344 6118, Ⓦ adventure-life.com. Small-group specialists with a choice of seven excellent tours (US$795–2085) in Guatemala, using experienced guides. Well-structured itineraries include many opportunities to visit community-run projects.

Adventures Abroad US ☎ 1 800 665 3998, Ⓦ adventures -abroad.com. Adventure specialists with a selection of comfortable small-group tours; their twelve-day Guatemala tour also includes Copán.

Cayaya Birding Guatemala ☎ 5308 5160, Ⓦ cayaya-birding .com. Resident specialists with unmatched knowledge of birding hot-spots. Great tours including a four-day Quetzal trip and customized itineraries.

Ceiba Adventures US ☎ 1 800 217 1060, Ⓦ ceibaadventures .com. Adventure trips, including rafting, kayaking, caving and archeological tours throughout the Maya region. The ten-day "River of Ruins" (US$2950) tour includes many of the Usumacinta sites, plus Tikal and Aguateca.

eXito US ☎ 1 800 655 4053, Ⓦ exitotravel.com. North America's top specialist for travel to Latin America. Speak to them about open-jaw and multi-stop flights to the region.

Explore Worldwide UK ☎ 0845 013 1537, Ⓦ exploreworldwide .com. Tours include a fifteen-day Guatemala Explorer (from £1275) which covers all the main sites.

Far Horizons US ☎ 1 800 552 4575, Ⓦ farhorizon.com. Superb small-group archeological trips, guided by Mayanists, including a ten-day "Capital Cities of the Maya" tour (US$6895 including airfare) that takes in the sites of Quiriguá and Copán.

Imaginative Traveller UK ☎ 0845 867 5852, Ⓦ imaginative -traveller.com. Offers several affordable tours including Explore Mexico and Guatemala which costs £610 for a 10-day trip between Cancún and Antigua.

Intrepid Travel UK ☎ 0800 781 1660, Ⓦ intrepidtravel.com. Small-group trips with an emphasis on cross-cultural contact and low-impact tourism. Tours have different comfort-level options.

Journey Latin America UK ☎ 020 3432 9271, Ⓦ journeylatinamerica.co.uk. UK-based experts for airfares and all-round travel advice to Guatemala and the region. Also offers a few Central American tours.

Lost World Adventures US ☎ 1 800 999 0558, Ⓦ lostworldadventures.com. A selection of tempting tours (US$1407–4646) including Guatemalan Road Less Travelled, a multi-activity cycling, hiking and kayaking trip.

Maya Expeditions 13 Av 14-70, Zona 10, Guatemala City ☎ 2363 4955, Ⓦ mayaexpeditions.com. Adventure tour specialists offering everything from whitewater rafting day-trips (around US$80) to well-planned archeological expeditions in the Petén.

Toucan Travel US ☎ 805 927 5885, UK ☎ 0800 804 8435; Ⓦ tucantravel.com. Latin America specialists with over a dozen inexpensive, sociable tours through the Maya region and Central America, some using public buses, others mainly camping. The 22-day "Maya Circle" trip from Antigua costs US$2025/£1290.

Trailfinders UK ☎ 020 7368 1200, Republic of Ireland ☎ 01 677 7888; Ⓦ trailfinders.com. One of the best-informed and most efficient flight agencies for independent travellers. Also offer some Central American tours, including Secrets of Guatemala (£1100/€1325).

Wilderness Travel US ☎ 1 800 368 2794, Ⓦ wildernesstravel .com. Well-organized cultural and wildlife adventure trips. The nine-day "Guatemala Private Journey" tour (US$2495) takes in all the main sites.

Wildland Adventures US ☎ 1 800 345 4453, Ⓦ wildland.com. Very well guided and thought-out tours, with "Guatemalan Highlands" (US$1675) and "Great Cities of the Maya" (US$2200) itineraries.

Getting around

With no passenger trains and few people able to afford a car, virtually everyone travels by "chicken bus" in Guatemala. These buses may be decrepit, uncomfortable, fume-filled and overcrowded, but they give you a unique opportunity to mix with ordinary Guatemalans. If you opt only for tourist shuttles, you'll be missing out on one of the country's most essential experiences. More comfortable buses – some of them quite fast and luxurious – ply the main highways, but once you leave the central routes and head off on the byways, there's usually no alternative to a bumpy ride inside a chicken bus or a pick-up truck.

The country's road system has been substantially upgraded in the last few years, but dirt roads are the norm in some rural areas, where the going can be painfully pedestrian. Fortunately, whatever the pace of your journey, you'll always have the spectacular Guatemalan countryside to wonder at.

By bus

Buses are cheap, convenient, and can be wildly entertaining. For the most part the service is extremely comprehensive, reaching even the smallest of villages.

Chicken buses

Guatemala has two classes of bus. **Second-class** or "**chicken buses**", known as **camionetas**, are the most common and easily distinguished by their trademark clouds of thick, black, noxious fumes and rasping exhausts. *Camionetas* are old North American school buses, with limited legroom, and the seats and aisles are usually crammed with passengers. The driver always seems to be a moustachioed ladino with an eye for the ladies and a fixation for speed and overtaking on blind corners, while his helper (*ayudante*) always seems to be overworked and under-age. It's the *ayudante*'s job to scramble up to the roof to retrieve your rucksack, collect the fares and bellow out the destination to all. While travel by second-class bus may be uncomfortable, it is never dull, with chickens clucking, music assaulting your eardrums and snack vendors touting for business.

Almost all chicken buses operate out of public bus terminals, often adjacent to the market; between towns you can hail buses and they'll almost always stop for you – regardless of how many people are already on board.

Tickets are (nearly always) bought on the bus, and whilst they are very cheap, gringos do sometimes get ripped off – try to observe what the locals are paying. Fares cost US$1–1.25 an hour.

Pullmans (first-class buses)

The so-called **pullman**, usually a Greyhound-style bus, is rated as **first-class**, and tickets can be bought in advance. These "express" services are about 25 percent more expensive than the regular buses – around US$1.50 an hour, though there are some very luxurious, more pricey options. Services vary tremendously: some companies' buses are double-deckers, with reclining seats and ice-cold air-conditioning, while other operators use decrepit vehicles. Each passenger is allocated a seat and all pullmans are pretty punctual.

Pullmans usually leave from the private offices of the bus company and they only run the main routes, connecting the capital with Río Dulce and Flores/ Santa Elena, Quetzaltenango, Huehuetenango, the Mexican border, Chiquimula and Esquipulas, Puerto Barrios, Cobán, Copán and the rest of Central America. Note that tickets are often collected by conductors at the end of the journey, so make sure you don't lose yours.

Minibuses and Pick-ups

Non-tourist **minibuses** (*microbuses*) are very common in Guatemala, particularly on paved roads. They usually operate from the main bus station, or use a separate terminal close by. Travel on microbuses costs about US$1.25 per hour.

In remote parts of the country **pick-ups** (*picops*) supplement microbus services, and for sheer joy of travel, you can't beat the open-air views (unless it's raining!). Passengers are charged about the same (around US$1.25/hr).

Shuttle Buses

Providing fast, nonstop links between the main tourist centres, **shuttle buses** are very popular in Guatemala. Conveniently, passengers are picked up from their hotels, so you won't have to lug any heavy bags around. Services are expanding rapidly and now cover virtually everywhere that tourists travel in any number, and it's usually easy to organize an "*especial*" service (for a price) if your destination is not on a regular route. At around US$4–5 an hour, shuttles are expensive, but drivers are almost always more cautious than regular bus drivers.

By plane

The only scheduled internal flight currently operating in Guatemala is from the capital to Flores. Flights cost US$220–250 return (one-way from US$130) and take fifty minutes (as opposed to some eight hours on the bus). Two airlines, Taca and TAG, offer a total of three daily return flights (see p.254). Tickets can be bought from virtually any travel agent in the country.

By car

Driving in Guatemala certainly offers unrivalled freedom, though traffic is incessantly heavy in the capital and always busy along the Interamericana and the highway to Puerto Barrios. Be warned that local driving practices can be alarming, including overtaking on blind corners. All the main routes are

AIR TAXES

Airport departure and airport security taxes are included in the price of your ticket.

ADDRESSES

Almost all addresses are based on the grid system, with **avenidas** (Av) running in one direction (north to south) and **calles** east to west, often numbered. All addresses specify the street first, then the block, and end with the zone. For example, the address "Av la Reforma 3–55, Zona 10" means that house is on Avenida la Reforma, between 3 and 4 calles, at no. 55, in Zona 10. In Antigua calles and avenidas are also divided according to their direction from the central plaza – north, south, east or west (norte, sur, oriente and poniente). Diagonales (diagonals) are what you'd expect – a street that runs in an oblique direction.

paved, but beyond this many roads are often extremely rough. **Filling stations** (gasolineras) are common. Fuel (gasolina) costs US$4.40 per gallon.

Parking and security are an issue, particularly in towns. Always leave your car in a guarded car park and choose a hotel with secure parking. Speed bumps (túmulos) are everywhere, even on main highways.

Local **warning** signs are also worth getting to know. The most common is placing a branch, which indicates the presence of a broken-down car or a hazard ahead. Derrumbes means landslides, and frene con motor (brake with motor) indicates a steep descent.

Renting a car costs from US$40 a day for a tiny hatchback or around US$70 for a 4WD by the time you've added the extras. Always take full-cover insurance and be aware that many companies will make you sign a clause so you are responsible for the first US$1000 of damage in the event of an accident, damage or theft. Local rental companies are listed in the Guide for main towns.

Taking your own car into Guatemala entails a great deal of bureaucracy. You'll be issued a car permit (usually valid for thirty days) at the border, and there are hefty penalties if you overstay. An insurance policy for Central America is necessary. If you plan to continue further south into Central America, expect to pay for more entry permits.

US, Canadian, EU, Australian and New Zealand driving licences are valid in Mexico and throughout Central America.

By taxi and tuk-tuk

Taxis are available in all the main towns, and their rates are fairly low at around US$3 for a short ride (or US$5 in Guatemala City). Outside the capital, metered cabs are non-existent, so it's essential to fix a price before you set off. Local taxi drivers will almost always be prepared to negotiate a price for an excursion to nearby villages or sites (perhaps US$35 for a half-day or US$60 for a full day). If you can organize a group, this need not be an expensive option.

Three-wheeled Thai **tuk-tuks** have proliferated throughout Guatemala in the last few years, operating as taxis, buzzing around the streets, Bangkok-style. They are common in most towns, except in Guatemala City and Quetzaltenango. It's best to fix the fare in advance; a short ride usually costs US$0.75, more in Antigua.

By bike and motorbike

Bicycles are quite common in Guatemala, and cycling has to be one of the most popular sports. You'll be well received almost anywhere if you travel by bike, and most towns will have a repair shop. Be warned that the main roads include plenty of formidable potholes, and it's a rare ride that doesn't involve at least one steep climb – chicken buses will carry bikes on the roof if you can't face the hills.

You can **rent bikes** in towns including Antigua, Panajachel and Quetzaltenango; mountain bikes can be rented by the day (about US$8) or week (US$25). For real two-wheel enthusiasts, Maya Mountain Bike Tours and Old Town Outfitters, both in Antigua (see p.81) and The Bike Shop in Quetzaltenango (see p.146) all offer a range of challenging bike trips.

Motorbikes are not that common in Guatemala, and locating parts and mechanical expertise can be tricky. There's a rental outlet in Panajachel (see p.122) which charges from US$45 a day.

By ferry and boat

In Petén, there are a number of possible boat routes, including tours around Lago de Petén Itzá from Flores. Several terrific boat trips start in the town of Sayaxché, including the trip to Lago de Petexbatún and Aguateca and along the Río de la Pasión to Ceibal.

Along the **Pacific coast**, you can explore the mangroves of the Chiquimulilla canal from Monterrico and Paredón.

Guatemala's most spectacular boat journey is through the **Río Dulce gorge**, either starting in Lívingston or Río Dulce Town. The pubic boats that cover this route will give you a quick glance at the scenery but you can't beat a slow cruise; trips are best organized in Livingston (see p.203). Volcano-framed **Lago de Atitlán** is another idyllic place to experience by boat: public *lanchas* connect all the main villages, or you can charter a boat in Panajachel for about US$12 an hour.

Accommodation

Guatemalan hotels come in all shapes and sizes, and unless you're really off the beaten track there's usually a good range of accommodation to choose from. There are bargains and bad deals at every level. Guatemala really is a budget-travellers' dream, and you should be able to find a clean double room for US$15 (or less) in any town in the country, except the capital. At the top end of the scale, you can stay in some magnificent colonial hotels decorated with real taste. In the mid-price bracket, you'll also find some brilliant places – you can still expect character and comfort, but perhaps without the service and facilities.

Accommodation options have a bewildering assortment of names: *hoteles, hosteles, pensiones, posadas, hospedajes* and *casas de huespedes*. The names don't always mean a great deal, but budget places are usually called *hospedajes* and anything called a *hotel* is usually a bit upmarket. Virtually all the main travellers' centres have backpacker-style hostels with dormitories and a sociable vibe.

Hostels

Most Guatemalan **hostels** tend to be owned and often run by expats, and are geared-up to budget travellers' needs, with excellent travel information, grub and perhaps a bar. Try to avoid huge dormitories; the best places tend to have a maximum of eight beds. Some hostels offer single-sex dorms and also private rooms for couples.

Hotel standards and facilities

The cheapest **hotels** (below US$15) are simple and sparse, usually with a shared bathroom at the end of the corridor. In most towns, upwards of US$20 will give you a private bathroom with hot water. In the midrange (around US$40–60) your room should be comfortable and attractive, while for US$80 and up you can expect high standards of comfort and luxury, with facilities such as swimming pools, gyms and a restaurant.

It's only in Petén, the Oriente and on the coasts that you'll need a fan or **air-conditioning**. In the highlands, some luxury hotels have logwood fires to keep out the winter chill.

Mosquito nets are not that common, so if you plan to spend some time in Petén or by the coast, it's well worth investing in one.

Camping

Campsites are extremely few and far between. It's really not worth bringing a tent as there are only a handful of places in the entire country that offer a designated, secure place to camp.

If you're planning to do a jungle hike or volcano climb, tour agencies will sort out tents (or hammocks and mosquito nets). For **renting camping gear** contact Old Town Outfitters in Antigua (see p.81), or Quetzaltrekkers inside the *Casa Argentina* hotel in Quetzaltenango (see p.147).

Food and drink

Guatemalan food is filling, good value, and can be very flavoursome. The cuisine has evolved from Maya, Latin American

---

ACCOMMODATION PRICES

All accommodation prices in this guide represent the **cheapest double room** available. Many hotels may have more expensive options too. If there's a **dormitory** the price given is per bed.

Hostels and the cheapest hospedajes charge US$3.50–8 per head; a reasonable but basic room with its own bathroom costs US$12–20 (more in the capital and Antigua). Official prices are meant to be displayed in the room, but it's well worth trying to haggle a little.

Prices are highest in Guatemala City and Antigua but extremely cheap in the western highlands. At fiesta and holiday times, particularly Holy Week and Christmas, rooms tend to be more expensive and harder to find, and the July–August tourist season can be busy – book ahead at these times.

and **Western traditions – though they usually overlap now to form what Guatemalans call comida típica. Popular tourist centres tend to have more varied menus and plenty of choice for vegetarians, and in Antigua and Lago de Atitlán you can feast on a wide selection of global dishes.**

In places orientated more to a Guatemalan clientele, you're likely to be offered a lot of simply prepared grilled or fried meat dishes and have much less choice. Off the beaten path the diet can get pretty monotonous, with things revolving around the "three-card trick" of eggs, beans and tortillas for breakfast, lunch and dinner. You'll find that the concept of healthy eating has yet to really penetrate Central America, and a lot of local food tends to be full fat by definition.

Where to eat

Unless you're in a tourist-orientated place, your choice is usually between a **restaurant** and a **comedor**. The latter is like a traditional American diner or an old-school British café; in general, they are simple, often scruffy-looking local eateries serving big portions of food at inexpensive prices (a full meal for about US$2.50–3). In a comedor there is often no menu, and you simply ask what's on offer, or look into the bubbling pots. Restaurants are slightly more formal and expensive and only found in large towns.

Many locals prefer to eat from **street food stalls**, which sell the food of the poor at rock-bottom prices; they're usually clustered around the marketplace.

You'll find **fast-food joints** in towns and on highways. *Pollo Campero* is a *KFC*-style Guatemalan-owned fried chicken chain. While on the road, you'll also come across the local version of fast food: vendors offering a huge selection of drinks, sweets, local specialities and even complete meals. Treat this kind of food with a degree of caution, bearing in mind the potential lack of hygiene.

In every main tourist centre you'll also find gringo-geared **café-restaurants**, often foreign-owned places with cosmopolitan menus featuring sandwiches, curries, stir-fries and the like, and plenty of vegetarian options. There's usually wine by the glass, cappuccinos and lattes, and fresh fruit shakes. Such indulgence does come at a price.

Breakfast

Traditionally, Guatemalans eat a substantial **breakfast** of tortillas, eggs and beans, sometimes with sour cream or fried plantains. Eggs can be served up a myriad of different ways (see p.31), using some superb, often spicy sauces. Pancakes (*panqueques*) are also common, but can be disappointing as they're often made from a mix out of a packet.

Up in the highlands, breakfast often includes a plate of **mosh**, which is made with milk and oats and tastes like porridge – it's the ideal antidote to the early morning chill.

In touristy towns things get a lot more eclectic, with all sorts of granola and muesli options available, with fresh fruit, honey and yoghurt. The bread in these places is often freshly baked.

Lunch

Lunch is the main meal of the day, and this is the best time to fill up as restaurants and comedores offer a *comida corrida*, or *menú ejecútivo*: a set two- or three-course meal (usually soup and grilled meat) that costs about US$2–3 and includes a drink.

Guatemalan cuisine does not vary that much regionally (except on the Caribbean coast) though some areas have famous local dishes (see p.32). **Vegetarians** are rarely catered for specifically, except in tourist-geared restaurants. It is, however, fairly easy to get by eating plenty of beans and eggs (which are always on the menu) and often some guacamole.

In touristy towns, there's a wealth of choice with everything from panini and wraps with imported cheese to sushi and noodles.

Snacks

Guatemalans are fond of their street food **refracciones** (snacks), these include *tostadas* and *tamales*, steamed cornmeal stuffed with chicken or another bit of meat.

For a quick bite, many locals opt for a *shuco* (literally a "dirty", a food cart that sells Guatemalan-style hot dogs), which is a bread bun filled with a sausage (or *chorizo*) and guacamole for US$0.75. Taco stands (often priced at three for Q10 (US$1.30) are also very widespread.

Cakes and pastries are widely available, but tend to be pretty dull and dry.

Dinner

For Guatemalans, **dinner** (taken 7–9pm) is a light meal. Mexican-style dishes, including tacos and enchiladas are popular. In the tourist hot-spots, particularly Antigua, there's a tremendous choice of restaurants, serving cuisine from around the world, with Italian, Japanese, Indian, North American and of course Guatemalan and Mexican food available.

Guatemalan cuisine

Most meals in Guatemala traditionally revolve around the basic staples of beans and maize, though diets are changing due to increased exposure to international cuisine.

Beans (*frijoles*) are usually served in two ways: *volteados* (boiled, mashed, and then refried) or *parados* (served whole with a little onion and garlic).

Maize is the other essential, a food that for the Maya is almost as nourishing spiritually as it is physically – in Maya legend, humankind was originally formed from maize. It appears most commonly as a corn **tortilla**, which is similar to a wrap. Maize is traditionally ground by hand and shaped by clapping it between two hands, a method still in widespread use; the tortilla is then cooked on a *comal*, a flat pan of clay placed over the fire. Guatemalan tortillas should be eaten while warm, usually brought to the table wrapped in cloth. Fresh tortillas have a lovely pliable texture, with a delicate, slightly smoky taste. Maize is also used to make a number of traditional snacks (see below). Squash (*güisquil*) is the main Maya vegetable, often used in dishes along with meat, tomato and onion; *pacaya*, a rather stodgy local vegetable, is another.

Chillies are an essential ingredient of the Guatemalan diet (especially for the Q'ek'chi Maya), usually served as a spicy sauce (*salsa picante*), or sometimes placed raw or pickled in the middle of the table.

Dishes and specialities

Nomenclature is confusing – **cornmeal** wrapped inside banana leaves or corn husks and steamed could take any number of names depending upon flavourings, and these change from region to region. Plain steamed cornmeal is a *tamal blanco*; stuff it with meat and tomato salsa, however, and it becomes either a *chuchito* or a *tamale*. If blended with potato, it's a *pache* – these are common in the Xela area. Up in the Ixil, and around Rabinal, look out for *boxboles*, cornmeal flavoured with spices, almond and a pinch of chilli, and cooked inside a pumpkin leaf. Mixed with *frijoles*, a *tamal* is a *bollo*, *tayuyo* or *tamalito de frijol*. When sweet, it's a *camallito de cambray* (with anise) or an *elote*. Keep an eye out for a **red lantern** outside a house – this indicates the family has fresh *tamales* for sale.

> ## CARIB COOKING
> The eastern coast of Guatemala has a different culinary tradition. Here Creole and **Garífuna** cooking, which incorporates the influences of the Caribbean and Africa, is easy to find in Puerto Barrios and Lívingston. Seafood dominates the scene, along with coconut and plantain. *Tapado* is probably the region's signature dish, a seafood soup that's a superb mix of fish (typically snapper), prawns, coconut milk, peppers, plantain and spices, though you'll also find plenty of grilled fish, lobster, conch fritters and *pan de coco (coconut bread)*.

The **corn tortilla** can also be prepared in a myriad of ways. Fried and topped (typically with guacamole and some salty cheese), it's a tostada, while rolled or folded around a filling – meat-and-cheese is always popular – it may be a taco, enchilada or *doblada*. Usually a salsa, based on a blend of ripe tomato and *miltomates* (green tomatoes), is served with these dishes. A *pupusa* (called a *baleada* in Honduras) is a fresh tortilla stuffed with anything, but usually including refried beans, *repollo* (pickled shredded cabbage leaves) and cheese.

Encasing food in an **egg batter** and frying it either *envueltos* ("wrapped") or *frituras* ("fritter style") is another popular cooking style. *Chiles rellenos*, peppers stuffed with vegetables and meat, are especially delicious. Simpler, often vegetarian variations abound using green bean or cauliflower, but look out for those made with *güisquil* (squash), *flor de izote* (the slightly bitter petals of a palm) or *bledo*, a leaf similar in flavour to spinach.

Salads are often simple, though several variations are well worth trying, including *piloyada*, a hearty affair based on plump red beans with eggs, tomatoes and meat; *iguaxte*, cooked potato or vegetables flavoured with a distinct paste of pumpkin seeds, dried chillies and sometimes tomato; and *chojín*, which is radish-based and often made with cheese and either pork or pork crackling (*chicharrón*). **Fiambre**, a vast salad of pickled vegetables with cured sausage (mixed with beetroot in central Guatemala and often barley in the Quetzaltenango area) is perhaps the country's most celebrated dish; it's eaten on All Saints' Day around a family grave in the cemetery.

Many **traditional dishes** are chunky **soups** or subtly spiced tomato-based **stews** (*caldos, cocidos* or *sopas*). Spicy *pepián* sauce is made throughout the country and usually incorporates chicken and vegetables, but occasionally chocolate. The more lightly spiced *pulique* is flavoured with coriander and capsicum. *Suban-ik*, which hails from Chimaltenango, is a tasty dish with chicken and pork, while Cobán's *kak-ik* is a turkey broth with coriander and mint.

Most large towns have a place that specializes in *ceviche* (raw fish marinated in lime juice), and on the coast it's customary to order fried fish or *camarones* (shrimps), and wash it down with Gallo beer.

Sweets, snacks and desserts tend to be very sweet. *Rellenitos* – cooked, mashed plantain, stuffed with sweetened beans and fried – are widely available, as is *mole de plátano*, which is plantain served in a sweet, spiced cocoa-flavoured sauce. Vegetables – for example, sweet potato, pumpkin or *chayote* – may be simmered in sugar syrups until they are caramelized or stuffed with a sweet mixture. Cake making is generally a specialized business, but *pastel borracho* is one that is soaked in rum syrup before being iced, while *pastel de elote* is made with corn.

Drink

To start off the day most Guatemalans drink a cup of hot **coffee** or tea (both are usually taken with plenty of sugar). Espresso machines are becoming much more widespread in Guatemala and you'll be able to get a cappuccino in most towns. Out in the sticks it's usually instant coffee with powdered milk. Atol, a warm, sweet drink made with either maize, rice (or even plantain) and sugar is also very popular, especially in the highlands.

At other times of day, **soft drinks** are usually drunk with meals. Coca-Cola, Pepsi, Sprite and Fanta (all called *aguas*) are common, as are *refrescos*, thirst-quenching water-based drinks with a little fruit flavour added; *rosa de jamaica* and *tamarindo* are two of the more unusual variants. In many places, you can also get a *licuado*, a delicious, thick, fruit-based drink with either milk or water added (milk is safer).

Tap water in the main towns is purified, and you can usually taste the chlorine. However, this doesn't mean that it won't give you stomach trouble – stick to bottled water, *agua pura* (see box, p.33).

Alcohol

Gallo, a medium-strength lager, is the most popular **beer** in Guatemala, indeed many Guatemalan men consider it the national drink, and the brewer promotes it as "Nuestra Cerveza" (our beer).

Unfortunately it's a pretty bland brew. The main competitor, Brahma, a Brazilian beer, is a little more interesting with a slightly spicy finish. Moza, a dark brew with a slight caramel flavour, is worth trying but rarely available. Other hard-to-come-by brands (all lagers) include the premium beer Montecarlo, Dorada Draft and Cabro. Imported brands are scarce. A 33cl bottle of beer costs about US$1.50–2.75 in a bar, but watch out for litre bottles (around US$3.50), which work out to be very good value.

As for spirits, **rum** (*ron*) and **aguardiente**, a clear and lethal sugarcane spirit, are very popular and cheap. Ron Botran Añejo is a half-decent rum (around US$6 a bottle), while the fabulously smooth Ron Zacapa Centenario (around US$40 a bottle) is one of the world's best; indeed, it regularly wins international prizes.

Hard drinkers will soon get to know Quetzalteca and Venado, two readily available *aguardientes* that fire up many a fiesta. If you're after a real bargain, then try locally brewed alcohol (**chicha**), which is practically given away. Its main ingredient can be anything: apple, cherry, sugarcane, peach, apricot and quince are just some of the more common varieties.

Chilean and Argentinean **wines** are now quite widely available anywhere where tourists gather. A glass of red or white house wine is usually around US$3 in most cafés or restaurants; bottles start at US$10 (or US$6 if purchased in a supermarket).

Health

Most visitors enjoy Guatemala without experiencing any health problems. However, it's always easier to become ill in a country with a different climate, food and germs – still more so in a poor country with lower standards of sanitation than you might be used to.

It's vital to get the best health advice you can before you set off. Consult the websites mentioned on p.34 for health precautions and disease prevention advice. Pay a visit to your doctor or a travel clinic as far in advance of travel as possible, and if you're pregnant or likely to become so, mention this at the outset. Many clinics also sell the latest travel health products, including water filters and medical kits. Finally you'll definitely need health insurance.

Once you're there, what you **eat and drink** is crucial. In addition to the hazards mentioned under "Intestinal troubles" below, contaminated food and water can transmit the hepatitis A virus, which can lay a victim low for several months with exhaustion, fever and diarrhoea, and can even cause liver damage.

Vaccinations, inoculations and malaria precautions

There are no obligatory **inoculations** for Guatemala (unless you're arriving from a "high-risk" area of yellow fever – northern South America and equatorial Africa). Nevertheless, there are several you should have anyway. Make sure you're up to date with tetanus and typhoid vaccinations and consider having hepatitis A and tuberculosis (TB) jabs. Long-term travellers or anyone spending time in rural areas should think about having the combined hepatitis A and B and the rabies vaccines (though see p.34 for a caveat on that).

Malaria is a danger in some parts of the country (particularly in the rural lowlands). It's not a problem in the big cities, or anywhere over 1500m – which includes Antigua, Guatemala City, Chichicastenango, Lago de Atitlán, Quetzaltenango and virtually all of the western highlands. However, if you plan to visit any lowland areas, including Petén, Alta Verapaz and the Pacific or Caribbean coasts, you should consider taking a course of tablets.

The recommended prophylactic is chloroquine (inexpensive, available without prescription and safe in pregnancy); you'll need to begin taking the pills a week before you enter an area where there's a risk of malaria and continue for four weeks after you return. Malarone is an alternative drug, which you need start only two days before you go, though it's not suitable for pregnant women or babies.

Whichever anti-malarial you choose, you should still take **precautions** to avoid getting bitten by insects: always sleep in screened rooms or under nets in lowland areas; burn mosquito coils; cover up arms and legs, especially around dawn and dusk when mosquitoes are most active; and apply insect repellent (with 25–50 percent DEET; but not to children under 2).

Also prevalent in some lowland areas (usually occurring in epidemic outbreaks in urban areas), **dengue fever** is a viral infection transmitted by mosquitoes, which are active during the day. Fever, aches and joint pain (its old name was "break-bone fever") are often followed by a rash. Though most people make a full recovery after a few days, children are particularly at risk. There is no vaccine or specific treatment, so you need to pay great attention to avoiding bites.

Intestinal troubles

Despite all the dire warnings given here, a bout of **diarrhoea** is the medical problem you're most likely to encounter. Its main cause is simply the change of diet: the food in the region contains a whole new set of bacteria, and perhaps rather more of them than you're used to. If you're struck down, take it easy for a day or two, drink lots of bottled water and eat only the blandest of foods – papaya is good for soothing the stomach and is crammed with vitamins. Only if the symptoms last more than four or five days do you need to worry. Finally, if you're taking oral contraception or any other orally administered drugs, bear in mind that severe diarrhoea can reduce their efficacy.

Cholera is an acute bacterial infection, recognizable by watery diarrhoea and vomiting. However, risk of infection is extremely low in Guatemala (and symptoms are rapidly relieved by prompt medical attention and clean water). If you're spending any time in rural areas you also run the risk of picking up various **parasitic infections**: protozoa – amoeba and giardia – and intestinal worms; these are quite common around Lago de Atitlán. These sound hideous, but once detected they're easily treated with antibiotics. If you suspect you may have an infestation, take a stool sample to a good **pathology lab** and go to a doctor or pharmacist with the test results (see p.34).

More serious is amoebic dysentery, which is endemic in many parts of the region. The symptoms are similar to a bad dose of diarrhoea but include bleeding too. On the whole, a course of flagyl (metronidazole) will cure it.

Bites and stings

Taking steps to avoid getting bitten by **insects**, particularly mosquitoes, is always good practice. Ticks, which you're likely to pick up if you're walking or riding in areas with domestic livestock (and sometimes in forests), need careful removal with tweezers. Head or body lice can be picked up from people or bedding, and are best treated with

> ### WHAT ABOUT THE WATER?
> Contaminated water is a major cause of sickness in Guatemala and you should never even brush your teeth with tap water. Stick to bottled water (*agua pura*), which is available everywhere, either in bottles or small plastic bags.

medicated shampoo; very occasionally, they may spread typhus, characterized by fever, muscle aches, headaches and eventually a measles-like rash. If you think you have it, seek treatment from a doctor.

Scorpions are common; mostly nocturnal, they hide during the heat of the day – often in thatched roofs. If you're camping, or sleeping under a thatched roof, shake your shoes out before putting them on and try not to wander round barefoot. Their sting is painful (rarely fatal) and can become infected, so you should seek medical treatment if the pain seems significantly worse than a bee sting. You're less likely to be bitten by a spider, but seek medical treatment if the pain persists or increases.

You're unlikely to see a **snake**, and most are harmless in any case. Wearing boots and long trousers will go a long way towards preventing a bite – tread heavily and they will usually slither away. If you do get bitten, remember what the snake looked like (kill it if you can), immobilize the bitten limb and seek medical help immediately; antivenins are available in most main hospitals.

Swimming and snorkelling might bring you into contact with potentially dangerous or venomous **sea creatures**. If you are stung by a jellyfish, clean the wound with vinegar or iodine.

Finally, **rabies** is present, but rare in Guatemala. The best advice is to give dogs a wide berth and not to play with animals at all. Treat any bite as suspect: wash any wound immediately with soap or detergent and apply alcohol or iodine if possible. Act immediately to get treatment – rabies can be fatal once symptoms appear. There is a vaccine, but it is expensive, serves only to shorten the course of treatment you need anyway and is effective for no more than three months.

Heat and altitude problems

Two other common causes of illness are **altitude** and the **sun**. The best advice in both cases is to take it easy; allow yourself time to acclimatize before you race up a volcano, and build up exposure to the sun gradually. If going to altitudes above 2700m, you may develop symptoms of Acute Mountain Sickness (AMS), such as breathlessness, headaches, dizziness, nausea and appetite loss. More extreme cases might cause vomiting, disorientation, loss of balance and coughing up of pink frothy phlegm. The simple cure – a slow descent – almost always brings immediate recovery.

Tolerance to the sun, too, takes a while to build up. Use a strong sunscreen and, if you're walking during the day, wear a hat and try to keep in the shade.

Avoid dehydration by drinking plenty of water or fruit juice. The most serious result of overheating is heatstroke, which can be potentially fatal. Lowering the body temperature (by taking a tepid shower, for example) is the first step in treatment.

Getting medical help

For minor medical problems, head for a *farmacia* – look for the green cross – there's one in every town and most villages. Pharmacists are knowledgeable and helpful, and many speak some English. They can also sell drugs over the counter that are only available on prescription at home. Every capital city has **doctors** and dentists, many trained in the US, who speak good English. Your embassy will always have a list of recommended doctors, and we've included some in our "Directory" sections for the main towns.

Health insurance is essential and for anything serious you should go to the best **private hospital** you can reach. If you suspect something is amiss with your insides, it might be worth heading straight for the local **pathology lab** before seeing a doctor. Many rural communities have a **health centre** (*centro de salud* or *puesto de salud*), where health care is free, although there may only be a nurse or health worker available and you can't rely on finding anyone who speaks English. Should you need an injection or transfusion, make sure that the equipment is sterile (it might be worth bringing a sterile kit from home) and ensure any blood you receive is screened.

US AND CANADA

CDC ☎ 1 800 232 4636, ⊛ cdc.gov/travel. Official US government travel-health site.
International Society for Travel Medicine ☎ 1 404 373 8282, ⊛ istm.org. Has a full list of travel-health clinics.
Canadian Society for International Health ☎ 613 241 5785, ⊛ csih.org. Extensive list of travel-health centres.

AUSTRALIA, NEW ZEALAND AND SOUTH AFRICA

Travellers' Medical and Vaccination Centre ☎ 1300 658 844, ⊛ tmvc.com.au. Lists travel clinics in Australia, New Zealand and South Africa.

UK AND IRELAND

Hospital for Tropical Diseases Travel Clinic ☎ 020 7388 9600, ⊛ thehtd.org.
MASTA (Medical Advisory Service for Travellers Abroad) ⊛ masta.org or ☎ 0870 606 2782 for the nearest clinic.
Tropical Medical Bureau Republic of Ireland ☎ 1850 487 674, ⊛ tmb.ie.

The media

There are some decent English-language publications available in Guatemala, mainly geared towards the tourist market. It's easy to keep up to date with current affairs online by using internet cafés or wi-fi.

Newspapers and magazines

Guatemala has a number of daily **newspapers**. The best of the dailies is the forthright *El Periódico* (Ⓦelperiodico.com.gt), which has some excellent columnists and investigative journalism. *Siglo 21* (Ⓦs21.com.gt) is also a good read. Guatemala's most popular paper is the *Prensa Libre* (Ⓦprensalibre.com), which features comprehensive national and quite reasonable international coverage. In the Quetzaltenango area, check out the local paper *Quetzalteco* (Ⓦelquetzalteco.com.gt). As for the **periodicals**, *La Crónica* (Ⓦlacronica.com) concentrates on current Guatemalan political affairs and business news with a smattering of foreign coverage.

In theory, the nation's newspapers are not subject to restrictions, though pressures and threats are still exerted by criminal gangs and those in authority. Being a campaigning journalist in Guatemala is a dangerous profession, and every year there are several contract killings.

There are several **free English-language publications**, which can be picked up in hotels and restaurants where tourists congregate. *Revue* (Ⓦrevuemag .com) is a glossy colour magazine with articles about Guatemalan culture and history plus hundreds of advertisements. Based in Antigua, *La Cuadra* (Ⓦlacuadraonline.com) adopts an irreverent, satirical tone and has discursive features about everything from politics to art. In the Quetzaltenango area, *Xela Who?* (Ⓦxelawho.com) concentrates on cultural life in the second city, with bar and restaurant reviews and culture and transport information. For coverage of development issues and Guatemalan society pick up a copy of *Entremundos* (Ⓦentremundos.org), which is widely available in Quetzaltenango.

For really in-depth reporting and analysis, the *Central America Report* (Ⓦcentral-america-report .org.uk) is superb, with coverage of all the main political issues, and investigations. Head to the website Ⓦguatemala-times.com for news about Guatemala in English.

As for foreign publications, *Newsweek*, *Time* and some US newspapers are available in quality bookstores around the country.

Radio and television

Guatemala has an abundance of **radio stations**, though variety is not their strong point. Most transmit a turgid stream of Latin pop and cheesy merengue, which you're sure to hear plenty of on the buses. Try Atmosfera (96.5FM) for rock, Radio Infinita (100.1FM) which is eclectic by nature and strong on indie and electronica, or La Marca on (94.1FM) for reggaeton. Radio Punto (90.5FM) has news and discussions.

Television stations are also in plentiful supply. Most of them broadcast Mexican and US shows (which are subtitled or dubbed into Spanish). Many hotel rooms have cable TV, which often includes (English-language) CNN and sometimes the National Geographic channel.

Sadly the BBC World Service is no longer broadcast in Central America. For Voice of America frequencies consult Ⓦvoa.gov.

Festivals

Traditional fiestas are one of the great excitements of a trip to Guatemala, and every town and village, however small, devotes at least one day a year to celebration. The main day is normally prescribed by the local saint's day, though the celebrations often extend a week or two around that date. With a bit of planning you should be able to witness at least one fiesta – most of them are well worth going out of your way for. A list some of the best regional fiestas appears at the end of each chapter in the Guide.

Until recently fiestas came in two basic models – except Garífuna events (see box, p.36), and were broadly ladino or Maya in style. Ladino towns' fiestas involved fairgrounds and processions, beauty contests and perhaps the odd marching band and nights dancing to Latin music. In the **Maya highlands**, traditional dances with costumes and musicians dominated the celebrations. But

> **DECEMBER 21, 2012**
> On December 21, 2012, there will be events and celebrations all over the country to mark the end of the **Maya Long Count calendar** (see p.350).

today there's a certain blurring of the boundaries between the two and some fiestas in indigenous villages have Latin music and dancing. What they all share is an astonishing energy and an unbounded enthusiasm for drink, dance and fireworks.

One thing you shouldn't expect is anything too dainty or organized: fiestas are above all chaotic, and the measured rhythms of traditional dance and music are usually obscured by the crush of the crowd and the huge volumes of alcohol consumed by participants. If you can join in the mood, there's no doubt that fiestas are wonderfully entertaining and that they offer a real insight into Guatemalan culture, ladino or indigenous.

Fiesta dances

In Guatemala's Maya villages **traditional dances** – heavily imbued with history and symbolism – form a pivotal part in the fiesta celebrations. The most common dance is the **Baile de la Conquista**, which re-enacts the victory of the Spanish over the Maya, while at the same time managing to ridicule the conquistadors. Most are rooted in pre-Columbian traditions (see p.347).

Fiesta music

Guatemalan **music** combines many different influences, but yet again it can be broadly divided between ladino and Maya. For fiestas, bands are always shipped in, complete with a crackling PA system and a strutting lead singer.

Traditional Guatemalan music is dominated by the **marimba**, a type of wooden xylophone that originated in Africa. The oldest versions use gourds beneath the sounding board and can be played by a single musician, while modern models, using hollow tubes to generate the sound, can need as

---

GARÍFUNA FIESTAS

Fiestas in Lívingston, on Guatemala's Caribbean coast, have different traditions and swing to other rhythms. Some of the best dancing you'll ever see is to the hypnotic drum patterns of Garífuna punta, which betrays a distinctive West African heritage. The Garífuna really know how to party, and if you get the chance to attend a fiesta, be prepared for some explosively athletic shimmying and provocative hip movements – nineteenth-century Methodists were so outraged they called it "devil dancing". **Garífuna day** (Nov 26) is the ideal time to see Lívingston really celebrate, though there seems to be a punta party going on most weekends.

---

many as seven players. The marimba is at the heart of traditional music, and marimba orchestras play at every occasion, for both ladino and indigenous communities. In the remotest of villages you sometimes hear them practicing well into the night, particularly around market day. Other important instruments, especially in Maya bands, are the *tun*, a drum made from a hollow log; the *tambor*, another drum traditionally covered with the skin of a deer; *los chichines*, a type of maracas made from hollow gourds; the *tzijolaj*, a kind of piccolo; and the *chirimia*, a flute.

Mainstream ladino music reflects modern Latin American sounds, much of it originating in Miami, Panama, the Dominican Republic and Puerto Rico. The sound on the street is currently **reggaeton**, which uses a dancehall reggae beat, fused with hip-hop vocals and techno. Merengue – fast moving, easy going and very rhythmic – is also very popular, as is salsa.

GUATEMALA'S BEST FIESTAS

Easter Week Semana Santa processions Antigua. See p.73
Easter Week Maximón confronts Christ in Santiago Atitlán. See p.129
July 31–August 6 National Fiesta of Folklore, Cobán. See p.231
August 12–15 Marimba-playing marathon Nebaj, in the Ixil region. See p.111
September 15 Independence Day nationwide, particularly impressive in Guatemala City

October 31 Pagan skull-bearing procession San José, Petén. See p.261
November 1 Kite-flying festival, Santiago, Sacatepéquez and Sumpango. See p.71
November 1 Drunken horse race, Todos Santos Cuchumatán. See p.164
November 26 Garífuna day, Lívingston. See p.203
December 21 Maya-style bungy jump in Chichicastenango. See p.106

Sports and outdoor pursuits

Guatemalans have a furious appetite for spectator sports and the daily papers always devote four or five pages to the subject. Fútbol (soccer) tops the bill, and if you get the chance to see a major game it's a thrilling experience, if only to watch the crowd. There's a great website, ⓦguatefutbol.com (Spanish only), dedicated to the national sport – the two big local teams, both from Guatemala City, are Municipal and Communications. Otherwise, baseball, boxing and basketball are all popular.

Hiking

Guatemala has great **hiking**, particularly volcano climbing, which is certainly hard work but almost always worth the effort – unless you end up wrapped in cloud, that is. There are 37 volcanic peaks; the tallest is Tajumulco in the far west, which at 4220m is a serious undertaking, and should only be tackled when you've been acclimatized to an altitude of over 2000m for a few days. Among the active peaks, Pacaya is a fairly easy climb and a dramatic sight (although not always actively spewing lava, as the tour companies' photographs would have you believe). Trekking trips up volcanoes and along highland trails are organized by a number of tour groups in Antigua, Nebaj, Quetzaltenango, San Pedro la Laguna and Santa Cruz La Laguna.

Sadly, there have been some occasional **attacks** (often armed, but usually non-violent) on hikers climbing volcanoes, and around the shores of Lago de Atitlán. Incidents happen randomly, so take some precautions: it's much safer to walk in a group, and check the security situation before setting out.

Sport-fishing

There's excellent ocean and freshwater fishing in Guatemala. The Pacific coast offers exceptional **sport-fishing**, with some of the best waters in the world for sailfish, as well as dorado, mahi mahi and some blue marlin, jack crevalle, yellow and black tuna, snapper and bonito. Most companies operate out of Puerto Quetzal or Iztapa (see p.187). The Caribbean side, including Lago de Izabal, also offers excellent opportunities for snook and tarpon. In Petén the rivers and lakes are packed with sport fish,

including snook, tarpon and peacock bass, and lakes Petexbatún, Izabal and Yaxhá all offer superb fishing.

A four-night fishing package including an 8m boat, captain, meals, transport connections and accommodation in Iztapa costs from US$2565 (based on four anglers). If this is beyond your budget and you're looking for a more casual arrangement, talk to the local fishermen in Iztapa, Sayaxché or El Estor.

Whitewater rafting

Guatemala's dramatic highland landscape and tumbling rivers also provide some excellent opportunities for whitewater rafting. Trips down the Río Cahabón and seven other rivers are organized by Maya Expeditions, 13 Av 14–70, Zona 10, Guatemala City (☎2363 4955, ⓦmayaexpeditions .com), giving you the chance to see some very remote areas and also visit some of the country's most inaccessible Maya sites. Children as young as 6 can raft some rivers.

Caving and tubing

Caving is another popular activity, especially in the area north of Cobán where you can explore great caverns and tube down underground rivers. The northern Alta Verapaz region (see p.239), particularly Lanquín, Chisec and Candelaria and Finca Ixobel (see p.253) are the places to head for.

Mountain-biking

There are terrific **mountain-bike trails** throughout the highlands and several professional operators organizing trips. Maya Mountain Bike Tours and Old Town Outfitters, both in Antigua (see p.81), have excellent bikes and tours, staring at about US$35 for a half-day escorted ride. Further west, Atitlán Tours (see p.139) organizes excellent mountain-bike excursions around the crater of Lago de Atitlán while The Bike House in Quetzaltenango (see p.147) is a specialist operator in the Xela region.

Kayaking

Two of the best areas for **kayakers** are the Río Dulce region with its stunning gorge and myriad jungle tributaries, and the sublime shoreline around Lago de Atitlán. Hotels in both these places offer kayaks for rent or contact Los Elementos in Santa Cruz La Laguna (see p.139), a kayaking specialist, for expert advice and guided paddles.

Scuba diving

The seas off Guatemala have little to offer compared with the splendours of the neighbouring Belizean or Honduran coastal waters. Nevertheless, there are some diving possibilities, including Lago de Atitlán, where the professional ATI Divers (see p.139) offer instruction, training and fun dives.

Surfing

There is some **surfing** in Guatemala, but with a strong undertow along much of the Pacific coast, conditions are not ideal. Nevertheless there's a growing surf scene at Paredón, near Sipacate, where you'll find a great new surf lodge (see p.186), boards for rent and instructors (US$15/lesson). You'll also find reliable breaks at Iztapa. Global Surf Guatemala (☎7832 1075, ✆globalsurfguatemala .com) offer regular surf trips (US$219) to El Salvador.

Culture and etiquette

Guatemalans have a deserved reputation as some of the most civil, polite people in Latin America. They're nowhere near as upfront as many Ladinos and quite formal in social situations. Mastering an understanding of local social etiquette will greatly enhance your trip.

Greetings

Whether you're clambering aboard a packed public minibus in the country or attending a high-society dinner party in the capital, it's normal to introduce yourself with a polite greeting of "buenos días/tardes" (good morning/afternoon or evening). Up in the highlands, if you're walking a trail or passing through a small village, it's usual to say hello to everyone you meet. It's actually very common for locals, even senior officials, to say "a sus órdenes" (literally "at your orders") as they help you out. If you're introduced to someone, a gentle handshake and a "con mucho gusto" ("pleased to meet you") is appropriate.

Clothing

There's no special dress code for women to consider when visiting Guatemala, though you might want to avoid seriously short skirts or tight tops to avert potential hassle. Generally in indigenous areas, most local women wear a calf-length skirt, but it's fine for foreigners to wear trousers or knee-length short pants. By the coast or around a hotel pool, sunbathing in a swimsuit is perfectly acceptable, though it's best to keep your bikini top on.

Guatemalan men very rarely wear shorts, except on the beach, but foreigners can do as they please without offence – except perhaps to a formal engagement.

You should bear in mind that while most Maya are proud that foreigners find their textiles attractive, clothing has a profound significance, related to their identity and history – it's not wise for women travellers to wear men's shirts or trousers, or for men to wear *huipiles*. Whether you're male or female it's best to dress fairly conservatively when entering a church; knee-length shorts and T-shirts are suitable.

Women travellers

Guatemala is, on the whole, a safe country for female travellers, and it's an extremely popular destination for thousands of solo travellers, most of whom have an amazing experience. It's best to dress fairly modestly (see above) and avoid getting yourself into situations where trouble might arise. In towns, particularly the capital, take a taxi home after dark. Trust your instincts. Most Guatemalan men do not adopt especially macho mannerisms, indeed most are softly spoken and quite deferential to foreign women. That said, if you do encounter hassle it's best to remain firm, assertive and disinterested. As most local men are short in stature, it's possible to adopt an authoritative stance if you're tall. Some hustlers do hang around dance clubs and bars looking to pick up gringas, but most of these guys have a wife and kids at home.

Religion

Guatemala is the least Catholic Latin American country. It's estimated that approaching forty percent of the population now belong to one of several dozen US-based Protestant churches – for more about this evangelical movement, see Contexts. Many of Guatemala's Catholics also continue to practice ancient Maya religious customs in the indigenous villages of the highlands. There has been a resurgence of interest in Maya spiritualism among young, educated Guatemalans since the end of the civil war, and attending "shamanic colleges" has become fashionable. Guatemala City also has tiny Jewish and Muslim communities.

Tipping

In smart restaurants a ten percent tip is appropriate, but in most places, especially the cheaper ones, tipping is the exception rather than the rule. Taxi drivers are not normally tipped.

Toilets

The most common names are *baños* or *servicios*, and the signs are *damas* (women) and *caballeros* (men). Toilets are nearly always Western-style (the squat bog is very rare), with a bucket for your used paper. Standards vary greatly. Public toilets are rare; some are quite well looked after by an attendant who charges a fee to enter and sells toilet paper, others are filthy.

Shopping

Guatemalan crafts, locally known as artesanías, are very much a part of Maya culture, stemming from practices that in most cases predate the arrival of the Spanish. Many of these traditions are highly localized, with different villages specializing in particular crafts. It makes sense to visit as many markets as possible, particularly in the highland villages, where the colour and spectacular settings are like nowhere else in Central America.

Artesanías

The best place to buy Guatemalan **crafts** is in their place of origin, where prices are reasonable and the craftsmen and -women get a greater share of the profit. If you haven't the time to travel to remote highland villages, the best places to head for are Chichicastenango on market days (Thurs and Sun) and the shops and street hawkers in Antigua and Panajachel.

The greatest craft in Guatemala has to be **textile weaving**. Each Maya village has its own traditional designs, woven in fantastic patterns and with superbly vivid colours. All the finest weaving is done on the backstrap loom, using complex weft float and wrapping techniques. Chemical dyes have been dominant in Guatemala for over a century now, but a few weavers are returning to use natural dyes in some areas, including Lago de Atitlán where San Juan La Laguna is something of a hot-spot.

One of the best places to start looking at textiles is in Antigua's Nim Po't (see p.86), a huge store with an excellent collection of styles and designs, and myriad other crafts too. Guatemala City's Museo Ixchel is another essential visit.

Alongside Guatemalan weaving most **other crafts** suffer by comparison. However, if you hunt around, you'll find good ceramics, masks, basketry, blankets, mats, silver and jade. Antigua has the most comprehensive collection of shops, followed by Panajachel.

Markets

For shopping – or simply sightseeing – the markets of Guatemala are some of the finest anywhere in the world. The large markets of Chichicastenango, Sololá and San Francisco el Alto are all well worth a visit, but equally fascinating are the tiny weekly gatherings in remote villages like San Juan Atitán and Chajul, where the atmosphere is hushed and unhurried. In these isolated settlements market day is as much a social event as a commercial affair, providing the chance for villagers to catch up on local news, and perhaps enjoy a tipple or two, as well as sell some vegetables and buy a few provisions. Most towns and villages have at least one weekly event, particularly in the western highlands (see box, p.173) and also the Verapaces.

Living in Guatemala

Plenty of travellers get seduced by Guatemala's natural beauty, inexpensive cost of living and the hospitality of its citizens. Many choose to put down roots for a while to study Spanish. Similarly there are myriad opportunities for voluntary workers, and dozens of excellent projects, though little in the way of paid work.

Studying Spanish

The language school industry is big business, with around sixty well-established schools and many less reliable setups. Most **schools** offer a weekly deal that includes four or five hours one-on-one tuition a day, plus full board with a local family. This all-inclusive package works out at between US$120 and US$310 a week (most are in the US$140–180 bracket) depending on the school and location.

It's important to bear in mind that the success of the exercise is dependent both on your personal commitment to study and on the enthusiasm and aptitude of your teacher – if you are not happy with the teacher you've been allocated, ask for another. Insist on knowing the number of other students that will be sharing your family house; some schools (mainly in Antigua) pack as many as ten foreigners in with one family. Virtually all schools have a **student liaison officer**, usually an English-speaking foreigner who acts as a go-between for students and teachers.

Where to study

The first decision to make is to choose where you want to study. The three most popular choices are Antigua, Quetzaltenango and Lago de Atitlán. Beautiful **Antigua** (see p.87) is undoubtedly an excellent place to study Spanish, though the major drawback is that there are so many other students and tourists here that you'll probably end up spending your evenings speaking English. **Quetzaltenango** (see p.146) has a different atmosphere, with a stronger "Guatemalan" character and far fewer tourists; here students tend to mix more with locals away from school. The third most popular location is now **Lago de Atitlán**, which is popular with young travellers and has very cheap rates. Though standards are not generally as high as the other two places there are decent schools in San Pedro La Laguna (see p.134) and Panajachel (see p.122) and new places now in San Marcos La Laguna (see p.136) and Santa Cruz La Laguna (see p.139). Other towns with schools include Cobán (see p.234), Flores (see p.256), Huehuetenango (see p.160), Monterrico (see p.192), Nebaj (see p.112), San Andrés and San José in Petén (see p.256), Todos Santos Cuchumatán (see p.165) and, in Honduras, Copán (see p.300).

Many schools lay on **after-school activities** like salsa classes, cooking, visits to villages, films and cultural lectures, and even hiking trips. In Quetzaltenango most schools have a social ethos and fund development projects in the region.

Links and resources

You'll find some schools have academic accreditation agreements with North American and European universities. The websites ⓦ guatemala365.com and ⓦ 123teachme.com have feedback from students and some good tips about the relative advantages of different study centres.

Volunteer and paid work

There are dozens of excellent organizations offering voluntary work placements in Guatemala. Medical and health specialists are always desperately needed, though there are always openings in other areas, from work helping to improve the lives of street children to environmental projects and wildlife conservation. Generally, the longer the length of time you can commit to, and the higher your level of Spanish, the more in demand you'll be. The best place to start a search is on the web (or in Guatemala itself).

Two organizations provide links between volunteers and projects in Guatemala. Quetzaltenango-based Entremundos, 6 C 7–31, Zona 1 (☎ 7761 2179, ⓦ entremundos.org), has contacts with about 130 development projects in the Xela area and a few further afield. They charge just US$3 for those already in Xela wanting to volunteer; if you want help in advance there's a US$40 registration fee. Project Mosaic Guatemala (ⓦ promosaico.org) has links to over a hundred projects in Guatemala though you'll be charged a US$270 registration fee.

As for **paid work**, teaching English is your best bet, particularly if you have a recognized qualification like TEFL (Teaching English as a Foreign Language). There are always a few vacancies for staff in the gringo bars of Antigua, and in backpackers' hostels. The *Revue* and noticeboards in Antigua and Quetzaltenango also occasionally advertise vacancies.

VOLUNTEERING PROJECTS

Ak'Tenamit ⓦ aktenamit.org. Health, education, business training and agriculture volunteer positions in a large, established project, working with Q'eqchi' Maya in the Río Dulce region.

Animal Aware ⓦ animalaware.org. Help out in an animal welfare centre for abandoned pets near Sumpango.

Arcas ⓦ arcasguatemala.com. Volunteers needed in Petén to help rehabilitate wild animals including monkeys for release back into forests, and opportunities to help out in a sea turtle reserve at Hawaii on the Pacific coast. You have to pay to volunteer on these programmes.

Casa Alianza ⓦ casa-alianza.org. Charity helping street children in Guatemala and throughout Central America. The work is extremely demanding.

Casa Guatemala ⓦ casa-guatemala.org. Skilled workers (particularly teachers and medical staff) and helpers needed to work with street children and orphans in the Río Dulce region. Long-term volunteers pay a US$300 upfront fee, while helpers are charged US$235 weekly (this includes full board).

Casa Xelajú ⓦ casaxelaju.com/cex/volunteer. Language school with myriad opportunities and links to social projects in the Quetzaltenango region.

Escuela de la Calle Ⓦ escueladelacalle.org. Help educate and mentor street kids in Quetzaltenango. Linked to hiking group Quetzaltrekkers (see p.147).

Habitat for Humanity Ⓦ habitatguate.org. House-building projects; over 25,000 homes have been built in Guatemala since 1979 by this charity.

Hospital de la Familia Ⓦ hospitaldelafamilia.com. Medical staff needed for a remote hospital in the highlands.

Idealist Ⓦ idealist.org. A massive database of links to a wide range of projects in the region – from ecotourism to human-rights work, with both voluntary and paid work opportunities.

NISGUA Ⓦ nisgua.org. Coordinates the Guatemalan Accompaniment Project, which monitors human-rights workers and campaigners deemed to be at risk in Guatemala; minimum commitment of one year.

Proyecto Eco-Quetzal Ⓦ ecoquetzal.org. Opportunities in the Verapaces region for people with experience in ecotourism, environmental education or agriculture. A three-month commitment is necessary.

Safe Passage Ⓦ safepassage.org. Teachers, helpers, admin staff and cooks needed to direct, support and educate children who work on the Guatemala City rubbish dump.

Upavim Ⓦ upavim.org. Community development on the outskirts of Guatemala City, with opportunities for nursery workers and kids' tutors.

Travelling with children

It can be exceptionally rewarding to travel with children in Guatemala. Most locals, particularly in indigenous areas, have large families so your kids will always have some company. By bringing your children along to Guatemala, you'll take a big step toward dismantling the culture barrier and families can expect an extra warm welcome. Hotels, well used to putting up big Guatemalan families, are usually extremely accommodating.

Obviously, you'll have to take a few extra precautions with your children's health, paying particular care to hygiene and religiously applying sunscreen. Dealing with the sticky tropical heat of Petén is likely to be one of the biggest difficulties, but elsewhere humidity is much less of a problem. As young children are rarely enthralled by either modern highland or ancient Maya culture, you may want to plan some **excursions**: the giant Xocomíl water park and Parque Xetulul theme park (see p.182 in the Guide) and Auto Safari Chapín (also see p.193) make great days out for kids. The Museo de los Niños and Aurora zoo in Guatemala City (see p.62) are a lot of fun too. Take extra care if you head for the Pacific beaches, as every year several children (and adults) drown in the strong undertow.

For **babies**, you'll find baby milk and disposable nappies (diapers) are widely available in supermarkets and pharmacies; take an extra stock if you're visiting really remote areas. Every town in the country has at least a couple of pharmacies, and medication for children is available. Breast-feeding in public is fine.

Travel essentials

Climate

Much of the country maintains a warm **climate** year round (see box, p.42), though it is largely determined by altitude, and there are regional variations (see p.10). The **rainy season** runs roughly from May to October, with the worst of the rain falling in September and October.

Costs

Guatemala is one of the cheapest countries in the Americas for travellers, though there are plenty of opportunities for a modest (or serious) splurge if you feel like it. The extremely frugal may be able to get by on around US$140 a week in most parts of the country, or below US$120 in a budget travellers' hub like San Pedro La Laguna. However, if you're after a little more comfort (travelling by shuttle bus and staying in rooms with an en-suite bathroom) you can expect to spend around US$200 per head per week, if you're travelling as a couple, while solo travellers should reckon on perhaps US$260 a week. For US$75 per day you can expect to live quite well. Things are more expensive in regions where the local economy is tourist driven (Antigua in particular). A sales tax (IVA) of twelve percent is usually

---

TRAVEL ADVICE WEBSITES

US State Department Ⓦ travel.state.gov. "Consular information sheets" detailing the dangers of travelling in most countries of the world. The information can be a little alarmist.

British Foreign and Commonwealth Office Ⓦ fco.gov .uk. Constantly updated advice for travellers on circumstances affecting safety in more than 130 countries.

Australian Department of Foreign Affairs Ⓦ dfat.gov .au. Advice and reports on unstable countries and regions.

AVERAGE MONTHLY TEMPERATURES AND RAINFALL

GUATEMALA CITY

	Jan	Feb	Mar	Apr	May	Jun	Jul	Aug	Sep	Oct	Nov	Dec
(°C)	24	25	26	27	26	25	25	25	24	24	23	23
(°F)	75	77	78	81	78	77	77	77	75	75	73	73
Rain (mm)	4	4	6	28	160	275	240	209	328	155	29	6

HUEHUETENANGO

	Jan	Feb	Mar	Apr	May	Jun	Jul	Aug	Sep	Oct	Nov	Dec
(°C)	23	24	25	26	25	25	25	25	24	24	23	22
(°F)	73	75	77	78	77	77	77	77	75	75	73	72
Rain (mm)	4	9	21	36	113	203	114	125	218	137	31	5

PUERTO BARRIOS

	Jan	Feb	Mar	Apr	May	Jun	Jul	Aug	Sep	Oct	Nov	Dec
°C	27	28	29	31	32	31	30	30	30	30	29	28
°F	81	82	84	88	90	88	86	86	86	86	84	82
Rain (mm)	221	113	113	132	193	272	489	322	295	351	318	245

TIKAL

	Jan	Feb	Mar	Apr	May	Jun	Jul	Aug	Sep	Oct	Nov	Dec
°C	27	28	30	31	31	31	30	30	30	29	28	27
°F	81	82	86	88	88	88	86	86	86	84	82	81
Rain (mm)	64	30	62	53	117	222	169	117	183	186	122	41

included in the price you're quoted in most places, except smart hotels. Similarly, the ten percent Inguat accommodation tax is often excluded in luxury places, but rarely elsewhere.

Crime and personal safety

Personal safety is a serious issue in Guatemala. While the vast majority of the 1.8 million tourists who come every year experience no problems at all, general crime levels are high, and it's not unknown for criminals to target visitors, including tourist shuttle buses. There is little pattern to these attacks, but some areas can be considered much safer than others. Warnings have been posted in the Guide where incidents have occurred. It's wise to register with your embassy on arrival, try to keep informed of events, and avoid travelling at night. Officially, you should carry your **passport** (or a photocopy) at all times.

It's important to try to minimize the chance of becoming a victim. Petty theft and **pickpocketing** are likely to be your biggest worry. Theft is most common in Guatemala City's Zona 1 and its bus stations, but you should also take extra care when visiting markets popular with tourists (like Chichicastenango) and during fiestas. Avoid wearing flashy jewellery and keep your money well hidden.

When travelling, there is actually little or no danger to your pack when it's on top of a bus as it's the conductor's responsibility alone to go up on the roof and collect luggage.

Muggings and **violent crime** are of particular concern in Guatemala City. There's little danger in the daylight hours but don't amble around at night; use a taxi. There have also been a few cases of armed robbery in Antigua and on the trails around Lago de Atitlán. The Pacaya and San Pedro volcanoes are now well-guarded and considered safe, though there have been robberies on other volcanoes, including Agua.

Reporting a crime to the police can be a long process, it's best to contact ASISTUR (see box below) first to smooth the process. Most insurance

ASISTUR

If you're a victim of crime, your first port of call should be **ASISTUR** (☎ 1500), a nationwide network of English-speaking staff employed to help tourists. Most ASISTUR employees are extremely helpful and will liaise with local police. Some can also organize a police escort to accompany travellers along highways known for banditry.

companies will only pay up if you can produce a police statement.

Drugs including marijuana and cocaine are readily available in Guatemala. Be aware that **drug offences** can be dealt with severely and even the possession of some weed could land you in jail. If you do get into a problem with drugs, it may be worth enquiring with the first policeman if there is a "fine" (*multa*) to pay, to save expensive arbitration later. At the first possible opportunity, get in touch with your embassy in Guatemala City (see p.69) and negotiate through them; they will understand the situation better than you.

Guatemala's **police** force has a poor reputation. Corruption is rampant and inefficiency the norm, so don't expect that much help if you experience any trouble. That said, they don't have a reputation for intimidating tourists. If for any reason you do find yourself in trouble with the law, be as polite as possible. **Tourist police** forces have been set up in Antigua, Panajachel and Tikal, and English-speaking officers should be available to help you out in these places.

The sheer number of **armed security guards** on the streets and posted outside restaurants and stores is somewhat alarming at first, but after a few days you get used to their presence, even if it is disconcerting to see an 18-year-old with a gun outside *McDonald's*.

Electricity

Power (110–120 volts) and plug connections (two flat prongs) are the same as North America. Anything from Britain or Europe will need a transformer and a plug adapter. Cuts in the supply and fluctuations in the current are fairly common.

Entry requirements

Citizens from most Western countries (including the US, UK, Canada, Australia, New Zealand, South Africa and most, but not all, EU states) need only a valid passport to enter Guatemala for up to ninety days. Passport holders from other countries (including some Eastern European nations) qualify for a Guatemalan visa, but have to get one from a Guatemalan embassy or consulate. Citizens from most developing world nations, including much of Asia and Africa, need to apply for a visa well in advance. If you're wondering whether you'll need a visa, phone an embassy for the latest entry requirements; Guatemala has embassies in all the region's capitals.

> **USEFUL NUMBERS**
> Asistur ☎ 1500 (24hr)
> Police ☎ 120
> Tourism Police ☎ 110
> Red Cross ambulance ☎ 125

Although there's no charge to enter or leave the country, border officials at land crossings commonly ask for a small fee (typically US$2.50), which is destined straight for their back pockets. You might try avoiding such payments by asking for *un recibo* (a receipt); but prepare yourself for a delay at the border.

It's possible to **extend your visit** for a further ninety days, up to a maximum of 180 days. To do this, go to the **immigration office** (*migración*) in Guatemala City at 6 Av 3–11, Zona 4 (☎ 2411 2411; Mon–Fri 8am–4pm). You'll need to present your passport, photocopies of each page of your passport (there's a machine in the office), a photocopy of a valid credit card (front and back), and pay the extension fee (US$15); your extension is usually issued the following day. After 180 days you have to leave Guatemala for 72 hours.

In 2006 a so-called **CA-4 Central American visa system** was set up to facilitate visa-free travel in the four countries of Guatemala, Honduras, El Salvador and Nicaragua. When you entered the region you were issued with a ninety-day visa. However, at the time of research CA-4 appeared to be dead. But to be sure, if your Guatemala visa is coming to an end, extend it by travelling to either Mexico or Belize, which are outside the CA-4, or get an extension in Guatemala City.

Guatemalan embassies and consulates

For a full list of Guatemalan embassies consult ⓦ minex.gob.gt (Spanish only), and click on "directorios", and the link to embajadas.

Australia Contact Tokyo.

Belize 8 A St, King's Park, Belize City ☎ 223 3150, ✉ embbelice1 @minex.gob.gt.

Canada 130 Albert St, Suite 1010, Ottawa ON K1P 5G4 ☎ 613 233 7188, ✉ embaguate-canada.com.

Germany Joachim-Karnatz-Allee 47, Ecke Paulstrasse, 10557 Berlin ☎ 030 206 4363, ⓦ botschaft-guatemala.de.

Honduras Colonia Lomas del Guijaro, c/Londres, Bloque B, casa 0440 Tegucigalpa ☎ 2232 5018, ✉ embhonduras@minex.gob.gt. Consulate: 23 Av & 11 Ca, S.O., Colonia Trejo, San Pedro Sula, ☎ 2556 9550.

Japan 38 Kowa Building, 9th floor, Room 905, 4-12-24, Nishi-Azabu, Tokyo 106–0031 ☎ 380 01830, ✉ embjapon@minex.gob.gt.

Mexico Embassy: Av Explanada 1025, Lomas de Chapultepec 11000, Mexico D.F. ☎ 55 5540 7520, ✉ embaguatemx@minex .gob.gt; Consulates: 1 C Sur Poniente 26, Comitán, Chiapas ☎ 963 100 6816; 5 Av Norte 5, Tapachula, Chiapas ☎ 962 626 1252.
Netherlands Java Straat 44, 2585 AP The Hague ☎ 302 0253, ✉ paisesbajos@minex.gob.gt.
New Zealand Contact Tokyo.
UK 13 Fawcett St, London SW10 9HN ☎ 020 7351 3042, ✉ inglaterra@minex.gob.gt.
US 2220 R St NW, Washington, DC 20008 ☎ 202 745 4952, ✉ estadosunidos@minex.gob.gt. Consulates located in many cities, including Chicago, Houston, LA, Miami, New York, San Diego and San Francisco.

Gay and lesbian travellers

Homosexuality is legal for consenting adults aged 18 or over. However, though Guatemalan society is not as overtly macho as many Latin American countries, it's wise to be discreet and avoid too much affection in public. There's a small, almost entirely male scene in Guatemala City (see p.67).

Insurance

A comprehensive travel insurance policy is essential for visitors to Guatemala. Medical insurance (you want coverage of US$2,000,000) should include provision for repatriation by air ambulance, and your policy should also cover you for illness or injury, and against theft.

Contact a specialist travel insurance company, or consider the travel insurance deal we offer (see box below). A typical **travel insurance policy** usually provides cover for the loss of baggage, tickets and – up to a certain limit – cash or cheques, as well as cancellation or curtailment of your journey. Many of them exclude so-called dangerous sports (this can mean scuba diving, whitewater rafting, windsurfing and kayaking) unless an extra premium is paid. Try to ascertain if your medical coverage will be paid as treatment proceeds or only after return home, and

whether there is a 24-hour medical emergency number.

When securing **baggage cover**, make sure that the per-article limit – typically under US$750/£500 – will cover your most valuable possession. If you need to make a claim, you should keep receipts for medicines and medical treatment, and in the event you have anything stolen, you must obtain an official statement (*una afirmación*) from the police.

Internet

Web services are very well established in Guatemala. Wi-fi is very common in all the main tourist centres, where most hotels, hostels and cafés provide access. You'll find cybercafés everywhere too, even in small towns and villages. Connection speeds are generally fairly swift in the main urban centres but can be painfully pedestrian in more remote areas. **Rates** vary, starting at US$0.80 per hour.

Laundry

Almost every town has at least one laundry; most will wash and dry a load for you for about US$3–4. Self-service laundries are rare. Many hotels and pensiones also offer laundry facilities; the budget places often have a *pila* (sink) where you can wash your own clothes.

Mail

Postal services are quite reliable, though many locals use courier companies to send important packages and documents overseas. The best way to ensure speedy delivery is to use the main **post office** (*correos*) in a provincial capital. Generally, an airmail letter to the US takes about a week, to Europe from ten days to two weeks. **Receiving mail** is not generally a worry as long as you have a reliable address – many language schools and tour operators will hold mail for you. The Poste Restante (*Lista de Correos*) system is no longer operational.

Bear in mind it's very expensive to send anything heavy home. You may want to use a specialized shipping agency instead: see the Antigua and Panajachel "Directory" for recommended companies.

Courier companies (DHL, Federal Express, etc) are establishing more and more offices throughout the region; even small towns now have them.

Maps

Rough Guide's *Guatemala and Belize* map (at a scale of 1:500,000), also covers a sizeable part of western Honduras and most of northern El Salvador. International Travel Maps and Books (ITMB) also publishes a reasonable **Guatemala** map (1:470,000). Both are printed on waterproof, tear-resistant paper.

Locally produced alternatives include an offering by Inguat (US$2) using a scale of 1:1,000,000. Virtually all car rental outlets will provide you with a free map, though most are pretty ropey.

The Instituto Geográfico Militar produces the only **large-scale maps** of the country. At a scale of 1:50,000, these maps are accurately contoured, although many other aspects are now very out of date. You can consult and purchase them at the institute's offices, Av de las Américas 5–76, Zona 13, Guatemala City (Mon–Fri 9am–5pm; ☎2332 2611, ⓦign.gob.gt). Most can be bought for around US$6.

Money

Guatemala's currency, the **quetzal** (Q), has been very stable for over a decade. But because fluctuations can and do take place, we have quoted all prices in US dollars. (At press time, the rate was Q7.80 to US$1, Q12.3 to £1 and Q10.41 to €1.) The **US dollar** is by far the most widely accepted foreign currency in Guatemala; that said, it is not a semi-official one, and you can't get by with a fistful of greenbacks and no quetzals. Euros and other foreign currencies are tricky to cash; try foreign-owned hotels or stores.

Debit and **credit** cards are very useful for withdrawing currency from bank ATMs but are not widely accepted elsewhere, so don't count on paying with them except in upmarket hotels and restaurants (let your bank know in advance that you'll be using it abroad). Beware expensive surcharges (ten percent is sometimes added) if you do want to pay by a card in many stores.

Cashpoints (ATMs) are very widespread, even in small towns. Charges of US$2–3 per withdrawal are

---

ATM SCAM

A number of travellers have reported a ATM scam operating in Guatemala, particularly in Antigua. Cardholders are finding their bank accounts drained of cash, days or even months after they've used a cash machine. It's probable that scammers are "skimming" or using cloned cards. The swindle also possibly involves corrupt bank staff. Check your balance regularly and it's worth changing your pin code when you return to your home country.

---

widespread, but those using the 5B network, including Banrural, did not charge at the time of research. It's important to note that most Central American ATMs do not accept five-digit PIN numbers; contact your bank at home in advance if you have one. You'll probably never have to use them, but it's wise to have a back-up of a few travellers' cheques (American Express is by far the most widely accepted brand, and in US dollars) or US dollar bills in case the ATM network fails or your card gets gobbled by a machine.

Note that all currency exchange counters at Guatemala City airport were offering appalling rates (see p.63). At the main land-border crossings there are usually banks and a swarm of moneychangers who generally give fair rates for cash.

Opening hours and public holidays

Guatemalan opening hours are subject to considerable variation, but in general most offices, shops, post offices and museums are open between 8/9am and 5/6pm, though some take an hour or so break for lunch. Banking hours are extremely convenient, with many staying open until 7pm from Monday to Friday, but closing at 1pm on Saturdays.

Archeological sites are open every day, usually from 8am to 5pm, though Tikal is open longer hours. Principal public holidays, when almost all businesses close down, are listed below, but each village or town will also have its own fiestas or saints' days when many places will be shut.

Phones

There are **no area codes** in Guatemala. To call a number from abroad simply dial the international

PUBLIC HOLIDAYS

January 1 New Year's Day
Semana Santa The four days of Holy Week leading up to Easter
May 1 Labour Day
June 30 Army Day, anniversary of the 1871 revolution
August 15 Guatemala City fiesta (Guatemala City only)
September 15 Independence Day
October 12 Discovery of America (only banks close)
October 20 Revolution Day
November 1 All Saints' Day
December 24 Christmas Eve (from noon)
December 25 Christmas
December 31 New Year's Eve (from noon)

access code, followed by the country code (☎502) and the number (all are eight digit).

The cheapest way to make an international phone call is usually from an internet café. Prices start at around US$0.15 per minute to the US or US$0.25 to Europe via web-phone facilities. Local calls are cheap, and can be made from either a communications office or a phone booth (buy a Ladatel phonecard).

Mobile (cell) phones

Many North American and European mobile phones, if unlocked, will work in Guatemala. To avoid roaming charges all you'll need is a local SIM card (Tigo and Claro are the most popular networks and have excellent coverage). Phones can also be bought locally from as little as US$20 (including around US$15 of calling credit). Keep an eye out for the "*doble*" and "*triple*" offer days, when you can get two to three times the top-up credit you pay for.

Photography

In indigenous areas and the countryside you should avoid taking pictures of children unless you get permission from their parents. Sadly children are stolen from their families every year in Guatemala, and rumours persist that Westerners steal babies for adoption. There's less of an issue in urban areas, where the population is better educated, but even here is sensitive.

Otherwise Guatemala is an exceptionally rewarding destination for photographers with outstanding scenic and human interest. It's polite to ask before taking portraits, but if you're in a marketplace using a zoom it's easy to get shots of people without being too intrusive.

Memory cards for digital cameras are quite widely available; print film and video tapes are getting rarer, but can be bought in most towns. Many internet cafés have card readers and will be able to burn your pictures to a CD for around US$2.

Time

Guatemala is on the equivalent of **Central Standard Time** in North America, six hours behind GMT. Daylight saving is not used. There is little seasonal change – it gets light around 6am, with sunset at around 5.30pm in December, or 6.30pm in June.

Tourist information

Information about Guatemala is easy to come by inside the country, but less available in Europe or North America. In the US, you can call **Inguat**, Guatemala's tourist information authority, on the toll-free number ☎1 888 464 8281, while Guatemalan embassy staff in Europe and Canada can often help out too. The material produced by Inguat is colourful, though much of it is of limited practical use. Often specialist travel agents are excellent sources of information.

Staff at Inguat, at 7 Av 1–17, Zona 4, **Guatemala City** (☎2421 2800, ⓦvisitguatemala.com), are always helpful and English-speakers are available. The organization has smaller branches in Antigua, Flores, Panajachel and Quetzaltenango, and at the airports in Flores and Guatemala City. All branches should have hotel listings and dozens of brochures and leaflets. Generally the main office and the Antigua outpost are the most reliable. Inguat also helps maintain a telephone assistance line for tourists in Guatemala, ☎1500.

If you're in the UK, the Guatemalan Maya Centre, 94A Wandsworth Bridge Rd, London SW6 2TF (☎020 7371 5291, ⓦmaya.org.uk), is one of the finest Guatemalan resource centres in the world. It's open by appointment only, and well worth a visit, with over 2500 books on Guatemala, videos, periodicals and an incredible textile collection.

USEFUL WEBSITES

ⓦ **aroundantigua.com** Dedicated to Guatemala's former colonial capital, with cultural events and listings.

ⓦ **atitlan.com** Concentrates on the Atitlán region, with interesting features plus some hotel and restaurant listings.

ⓦ **copanhonduras.org** Informative site dedicated to the Copán region in Honduras.

ⓦ **famsi.org** Academic reports from Mayanists, maps, and articles about flora and fauna.

Ⓦ **fhrg.org** Website of the Foundation for Human Rights in Guatemala, offering comprehensive coverage of the current human rights situation, plus news reports.

Ⓦ **ghrc-usa.org** Website of the Washington-based Guatemala Human Rights Commission/USA, which publishes regular reports plus urgent action notices.

Ⓦ **guatemala365.com** Good place to begin a search for a Spanish school, with a list of professional schools and plenty of tips.

Ⓦ **guatemalaweb.com** Everything from ATM locations to Maya ceremonies, though some of the practical information is out of date.

Ⓦ **guatemala-times.com** News, features and comment about Guatemala in English.

Ⓦ **lanic.utexas.edu** The Guatemala page on the Latin American Network Information Center's website is a fine place to begin a search; here you'll find a comprehensive set of links to websites for everything from nonprofits and language schools to magazines and museums, as well as various academic and tourism resources.

Ⓦ **maya.org.uk** London-based Guatemalan Maya Centre's site has good articles and links.

Ⓦ **mayadiscovery.com** Strong on art and history of the ancient Maya, plus some wide-ranging cultural essays.

Ⓦ **mayaparadise.com** Dedicated to the Río Dulce and Lago de Izabal area, with useful information for boaters and a busy message board.

Ⓦ **mesoweb.com** All the latest reports about the ancient Maya.

Ⓦ **mimundo-photoessays.org** Superb photojournalism from an independent reporter.

Ⓦ **mostlymaya.com** Useful practical travel information based on first-hand experience and good cultural content.

Ⓦ **revuemag.com** Content from the popular Antigua-based tourism and travel magazine.

Ⓦ **xelapages.com** Concentrates on the Quetzaltenango area, with comprehensive language-school and business listings, plus popular discussion boards.

Ⓦ **xelawho.com** Dedicated to Guatemala's second city, with good cultural information and practical content.

Travellers with disabilities

Guatemalans are extremely helpful and eager to help disabled travellers. Nevertheless, visitors with disabilities are faced with many obstacles. Wheelchair users will have to negotiate their way over cobbled streets, cracked (or nonexistent) pavements and potholed roads in cities, towns and villages. Getting around Guatemala by public transport can be exhausting for anyone, but trying to clamber aboard a packed chicken bus with a wheelchair or walking sticks, even with a friend to help, presents a whole set of other challenges. Plenty of disabled travellers do successfully make their way around the country though. Most of the main sites are connected by tourist shuttle minibuses, which pick you up from your hotel, and have a driver whose job it is to assist passengers with their luggage. Many Guatemalan hotels are low rise (and larger, upmarket places often have lifts and ramps), so it shouldn't be too difficult to find an accessible room. You'll only find disabled toilets in the most expensive hotels.

Guatemala City, Antigua and around

ANTIGUA WITH VOLCÁN DE AGUA LOOMING ABOVE

1

Guatemala City, Antigua and around

Situated just forty kilometres apart, the two cities of Guatemala City and Antigua could hardly be more different. The capital, Guatemala City, is a fume-filled maelstrom of industry and commerce with few attractions to detain the traveller, though a day or two spent visiting its museums and soaking up the (limited) cultural scene won't be wasted. Antigua is everything the capital is not: tranquil, urbane and resplendent with evocative colonial buildings and myriad cosmopolitan cafés and restaurants. Not surprisingly, this is where most travellers choose to base themselves.

Guatemala City sprawls across a huge upland basin, surrounded by craggy hills and volcanic cones. Its shapeless and swelling mass ranks as the largest city in Central America, home to more than four million people, and it's Guatemala's undisputed centre of politics, power and wealth.

The capital has an intensity and vibrancy that are both its fascination and its horror, and for many visitors dealing with the city is an exercise in damage limitation, as they struggle through bus fumes and crowds. For years urban decay has tainted the heart of the city, the **centro histórico**, but new initiatives have revitalized the district as streets have been pedestrianized, buildings restored and new cafés and bars have opened.

Antigua, on the other hand, is the most impressive colonial city in Central America with a tremendous wealth of architectural riches. With just forty thousand inhabitants, the city's graceful cobbled streets, elegant squares, churches and grand houses are ideal to explore on foot. The town's renowned **language schools** also attract students from all over the world, and education and tourism are the city's prime sources of wealth.

The countryside around Antigua and Guatemala City – a **delightful** landscape of volcanoes, pine forests, *milpas* and coffee farms – also begs to be explored. Looming over the capital is **Volcán de Pacaya**, one of the most active peaks in Latin America, while the volcanoes of **Agua** and **Acatenango** are also well worth climbing.

You'll also find countless interesting villages to visit in this area, including **San Andrés Itzapa**, where there is a pagan shrine to the "evil saint" San Simón, and **Jocotenango** which boasts museums dedicated to coffee production and Maya music. The one Maya ruin in the area that can compete with the lowland sites further north is **Mixco Viejo**, which enjoys a breathtaking, remote setting.

Guatemala City

GUATEMALA CITY is not a place to visit for its beauty or architectural charm. First impressions of the centre are pretty grim, with potholed streets choked by pollution

VIEW FROM VOLCÁN DE PACAYA TOWARDS THE PEAKS OF AGUA AND ACATENANGO

Highlights

❶ Museo Nacional de Arqueología y Etnología One of the world's most important collections of Maya sculptures and artefacts. See p.60

❷ Volcán de Pacaya Trek up one of Latin America's active volcanoes and get up close and personal with its lava flows. **See p.70**

❸ Semana Santa Witness the sombre ceremony and processions of the continent's most fervent Easter-week celebrations. **See p.73**

❹ Antigua's colonial architecture A stunning legacy of Baroque churches, colonial mansions and graceful plazas that form a World Heritage Site. **See p.72**

❺ Fine dining Antigua's restaurant scene is vibrant and eclectic, with everything from gourmet French to authentic Guatemalan. See p.84

HIGHLIGHTS ARE MARKED ON THE MAP ON P.53

1

from rasping buses and grinding levels of poverty all too evident. Understandably, few travellers take to *la capital*, and many avoid it completely.

But give it a chance, and you'll find it does offer some metropolitan pleasures. There are three excellent **museums**: the archeological and Popol Vuh (which both concentrate on ancient Maya culture) and the Ixchel, dedicated to the country's terrific textile tradition. **Zona 1** is on the up as landmark buildings are renovated and new venues promoting alternative rock bands and electronic DJs emerge. Dotted around the city you'll also find cinemas and North American-style shopping malls.

That said, the disparities of life in the city are extreme, with glass skyscrapers towering over sprawling slums and shoeless widows peddling cigarettes to designer-clad clubbers. Take a little extra care here as **street crime** is a problem, mainly involving bag snatching – be particularly careful at transport terminals – and use taxis to get around after 8pm. Gang violence is a serious issue in the poor outer suburbs, though this is highly unlikely to concern travellers.

Brief history

The pre-conquest Maya city of **Kaminaljuyú**, its ruins still scattered amongst the western suburbs, was well established here two thousand years ago. In Early Classic times (250–600 AD) it was allied with the great northern power of Teotihuacán (near present-day Mexico City) and controlled key trade routes.

At the height of its prosperity, Kaminaljuyú was home to a population of some fifty thousand and dominated the surrounding highlands. But, following the decline of Teotihuacán around 600 AD, it was surpassed by the great lowland centres, and by around 700 AD it was abandoned.

Colonial era

Eight centuries later, following months of devastating earthquakes, the Spanish were forced to flee Antigua and established a new capital at Guatemala City's present site. Early development was slow: the 1863 census listed just 1206 residences. One of the factors affecting the city's growth was the existence of a major rival, Quetzaltenango, which competed with the capital in both size and importance. But in 1902 Quetzaltenango was razed to the ground by a massive earthquake, and subsequently Guatemala City became unquestionably the country's primary city.

The twentieth century to today

After recovering from more devastating seismic activity in 1917, Guatemala City has grown at an incredible rate, the flight from the fields escalating in the 1970s and 1980s as waves of internal refugees sought an escape from the civil war in the countryside. **Economic migrants** high on hope continue to flock to the capital, the resultant population explosion filling once-uninhabited deep ravines with precariously situated new barrios.

A concerted effort to boost civic pride, improve transport, add greenery and address pollution has been made in the past few years as part of Mayor Arzú's "Guatemala 2020" plan to create a modern, functioning city. Though the overriding issue of security remains a key concern, a more appealing vision of the future is emerging due to successful initiatives like the Transmetro bus system.

Zona 1

The hub of the old city is **Zona 1**, which is also the busiest part of town. This is the **centro histórico**, a world of low-slung, crumbling nineteenth-century town houses and faceless concrete blocks, car parks, noise and dirt. Signs of regeneration are emerging, particularly along newly pedestrianized Sexta Avenida as once-grand edifices are renovated and clusters of cafés are opening, but it's a process that will take decades to achieve.

1

In the far south of the zone the streets broaden and the architecture changes; this part of town contains a mix of buildings (including the impressive Teatro Nacional) from different eras.

Parque Central

An imposing plaza that forms the country's political and religious centre, the **Parque Central** is the point from which all distances in Guatemala are measured. This square, flanked by the grand Palacio Nacional and cathedral, was originally the scene of a huge central market. Today it's a good place to absorb city life as ladino and indigenous *capitaleños* stroll, chat and snack and pigeons, shoe-shiners and raving Evangelicals jostle for space.

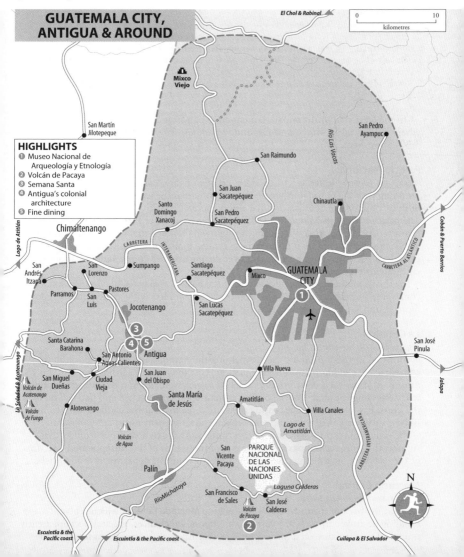

GUATEMALA CITY, ANTIGUA & AROUND

HIGHLIGHTS
1. Museo Nacional de Arqueología y Etnología
2. Volcán de Pacaya
3. Semana Santa
4. Antigua's colonial architecture
5. Fine dining

1

GUATEMALA CITY: ORIENTATION, ZONES AND ADDRESSES

Broadly speaking, the city divides into two distinct halves. The northern section is mainly comprised of **Zona 1**, the historic, if run-down part of town containing the main plaza, the Parque Central, some museums and many of the first-class bus company terminals. **Zona 2** even further north also has a couple of sights.

The modern half of the city is to the south, comprising **zonas 9 and 10**, which are separated by the main artery of Avenida La Reforma. Further south still **zonas 13 and 14** hold wealthy, leafy suburbs, and are home to the airport, a cluster of guesthouses and more museums and cinemas.

Zona 4 serves as a buffer between the two parts of town; here you'll find many civic buildings, the tourist office and the National Theatre.

ADDRESSES

When it comes to finding an address in the city, always check the **zone** first and then the street. For example "4 Av 9–14, Zona 1" is in Zona 1, on 4 Avenida between 9 and 10 calles, house number 14. You may see street numbers written as 1a, 7a etc, rather than simply 1, 7. This is technically more correct, since the names of the streets are not One Avenue and Seven Street, but First (*primera*), Seventh (*séptima*) and so on. A capital "A" used as a suffix indicates a smaller street between two large ones: 1 C A is a short street between 1 and 2 calles.

On the west side of the square is a concrete bandstand, the Concha Acústica, where you'll find marimba and classical music performances (Wed 4–6pm & Sat 3.30–5pm; free).

Palacio Nacional

Parque Central • Entrance by tour daily 10am, 11am, noon, 2pm, 3pm & 4pm in English or Spanish • US$5

Presiding over the entire northern end of the square is the gargantuan **Palacio Nacional**, built in a mixture of Spanish colonial and Neoclassical styles from a green-hued stone. The palace was commissioned in 1939 under the auspices of President Ubico – a characteristically grand gesture from the man who believed that he was a reincarnation of Napoleon. For decades it housed the executive branch of the government, and periodically its steps have been fought over during assorted coups, but now it hosts cultural exhibitions.

The thirty-minute tour includes a look at the palace's two graceful Moorish-style courtyards and the grandiose **Salas de Recepción**, complete with stained-glass windows representing key aspects of Guatemalan history.

La Catedral

Parque Central • Daily 7am–noon & 3–7pm • Free

Completed in 1868, its grand facade merging the Baroque and the Neoclassical, the **cathedral** has a solid, squat form designed to resist the force of earthquakes and, for the most part, it has succeeded. In 1917 the bell towers were brought down and the cupola fell, destroying the altar, but the central structure, though cracked and patched up over the years, has remained intact. Inside there are three main aisles, all lined with arching pillars, austere colonial paintings and intricate altars supporting an array of saints.

The cathedral's most poignant aspect is found outside: etched into the pillars that support the entrance railings are the names of thousands of the "**disappeared**", victims of the civil war, including an astounding number from the department of El Quiché.

Mercado Central

8 C & 8 Av • Mon–Sat 6am–6pm, Sun 9am–1pm

Around the back of the cathedral is the hulking **Mercado Central**, which replaced a building destroyed in the 1976 earthquake. Taking no chances, the architect apparently modelled the structure on a nuclear bunker, sacrificing any aesthetic concerns to the

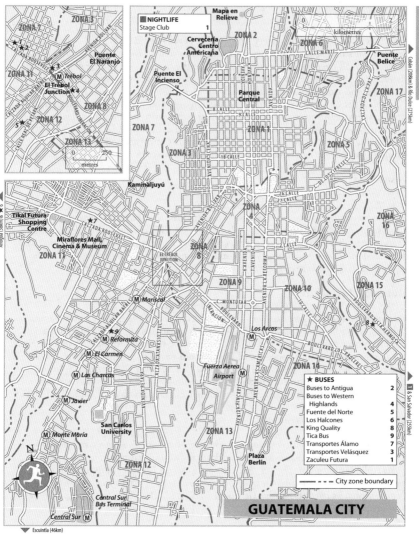

need for strength. On the top floor you'll find a good selection of textiles from across the country, leatherware and trinkets; in the middle is fruit, vegetables, food stalls, flowers and plants; and **handicrafts**, mainly basketry, ceramics and *típica* are in the basement. Prices are fair and traders are willing to bargain.

Museo Nacional de Historia

9 C 9–70 • Mon–Fri 9am–4.30pm, Sat & Sun 9am–noon & 1–4pm • US$6.50

Southeast of the market, the **Museo Nacional de Historia** features a selection of artefacts relating to Guatemalan history, including documents, clothes, paintings and even a conquistador's sword or two, though there's no information in English. Probably the most interesting displays are the photographs by Eadweard Muybridge, who, in 1875, was one of the first people to undertake a study of the country.

1

Sexta Avenida
6 Av between Parque Central & 18 C

The city's main commercial artery for decades, **Sexta Avenida** was lined with glamorous department stores, cinemas and cafés during its heyday in the mid-nineteenth century. People from all over the city would promenade the Sexta to see and be seen. But the character of the street took a downturn in the 1980s, as stalls choked the pavements and the grand stores and cinemas closed.

In 2009, the city authorities implemented a renovation programme, clearing the street traders, planting trees and pedestrianizing the entire avenida (bicycles are permitted) between the Parque Central and 18 Calle, making Sexta a delight to stroll once again. Be sure to stop by the well-kept **Parque Concordia** and take in the fabulously elaborate facade of the **Iglesia de San Francisco** as you explore the street.

Casa Mima
8 Av 14–12 • Mon–Sat 10am–5pm • US$2.50

Casa Mima is an immaculately restored late nineteenth-century town house with original furnishings from various design movements. The decor offers a fascinating glimpse into a wealthy household, with lavish rooms kitted out with gilded mirrors, chandeliers, oriental rugs, hand-painted wallpaper and curios including a gloriously detailed dolls' house and a ninety-year-old "talking machine" (a gramophone). The house even has a private chapel complete with a fabulous wooden altar.

Museo del Ferrocarril
9 Av 18–03 • Tues–Fri 9am–4pm, Sat & Sun 10am–4pm • US$0.25 • ⓦ museofegua.com

Museo del Ferrocarril is an excellent museum dedicated to the history of Guatemalan railways. The splendidly renovated building was Guatemala City's main **train station** until it mysteriously burnt down in 1996. Passenger trains no longer run in Guatemala but you can get a great perspective of how the old network functioned here. You'll find several old steam engines and carriages to clamber over and examine, plus rooms stuffed with railway curiosities including staff uniforms and tickets. Also on show are several lovingly polished classic cars, including a curvaceous chrome-bumpered Jaguar.

Museo de Músicos Invisibles
13 C 9–70 • Mon–Sat 8am–6pm • US$3 including tour

This quirky museum dedicated to the "invisible musician" showcases an incredible collection of automated and wind-up antique musical instruments: organs, music boxes, juke boxes, gramophones, Art Deco radios, mechanical saxophones and harmonicas and even a vinyl-cutting machine. All are in perfect working order, as demonstrated as part of the tour (in Spanish) offered. There's a great little café here too (see p.66).

Teatro National
24 C 3–81, Zone 1 • Daily for theatrical and musical events 9am–9pm • Guided tours of building in Spanish US$5.50, book ahead • ☎ 2232 4041, ⓦ teatronacional.com.gt • Transmetro Centro Cívico

Perched on a hill in the far south of Zona 1, the landmark **Teatro Nacional**, also known as the Miguel Ángel Asturias cultural centre, is one of the city's most prominent and unusual structures. Completed in 1978 and designed by the late Guatemalan architect (and artist) Efraín Recinos, its form evokes a huge ship, painted blue and white, with portholes for windows. The interior is equally impressive: its stunning main theatre complete with balconies finished in gold lacquer is breathtaking. Don't miss the modernist chandelier, which evokes a model of a molecular structure, in the lobby.

The complex, which also includes an open-air theatre and gardens with quirky concrete seating, was built over the ruins of the **San José Fortress**, a nineteenth-century castle that was all but destroyed during the 1944 revolution.

EATING

Altuna	7
Café León	3
Café Música	9
Cafetalito	5
Casa Yurrita	10
El Gran Pavo	8
Kafé Katok	6
Long Wah	1
Rey Sol	4
Rocque Rosito	2

ACCOMMODATION

Chalet Suizo	5
La Coperacha	1
Hotel Ajau	8
Hotel Colonial	6
Hotel Pan American	2
Hotel Santoña	7
Hotel Spring	3
Posada Belén	4

DRINKING & NIGHTLIFE

Bad Attitude	2
Black and White	7
Blanco y Negro	5
La Bodeguita del Centro	8
Las Cien Puertes	3
Eclipse	1
Genetic	9
El Gran Hotel	6
La Luna	5
El Portal	4
Trovajazz	10

★ BUSES

ADN	4
Fuente del Norte and other 1st/2nd class buses to Petén	5
Línea Dorada	3
Litegua	1
Monja Blanca	2
Rutas Orientales	7
Transportes Galgos	6

GUATEMALA CITY: ZONAS 1 & 4

1

Zona 2

North of the old city centre is Zona 2, bounded by a deep-cut ravine that prevents the urban sprawl from spreading any further in this direction. There are a couple of sights in this (mainly residential) district.

Mapa en Relieve

Av Simeón Cañas Final • Mon–Sat 8am–6pm • US$3 • ⓦ mapaenrelieve.org

About 2km north of the Parque Central, the slightly kitsch **Mapa en Relieve**, a relief map of Guatemala, covers 2500 square metres and has a couple of viewing towers. Its vertical scale is out of proportion to the horizontal, making the mountains look incredibly steep. It does nevertheless give you a good idea of the general layout of the country, from the ruggedness of the highlands to the sheer enormity of Petén.

Museo de Cervecería Centroamericana

3 Av Norte Final, Finca El Zapote • Mon–Thurs 8.30am–5pm; tours at 9am, 11am & 2.30pm • Free • ☎ 2289 1555

Cervecería Centroamericana is Guatemala's largest brewery, and has been producing Gallo beer at this factory in the north of the city for 125 years. Today, around a dozen beers are brewed here including Dorada, Victoria, Montecarlo and Gallo. The museum, containing some interesting antique curios and photographs related to the history of beer-making in Guatemala is interesting enough, but the highly informative tour allows you access to the plant so you can gaze into the vast stainless steel vats and view the bottling plant. The tour finishes, appropriately, with a glass or two of complimentary amber nectar.

Zona 4

To the south, Zona 1 merges into Zona 4 around the **Centro Cívico**, which forms a collection of concrete multistorey administrative buildings, mainly dating from the 1960s, including the **Banco de Guatemala** on 7 Avenida, which is bedecked with bold modern murals and stylized glyphs designed by Dagoberto Vásquez recounting Guatemala's history. The zone also contains the main tourist office, Inguat, on 7 Avenida.

Iglesia Yurrita

Ruta 6 8–52 • Sat & Sun 9.30am–1pm • Free • Transmetro Torre del Reformador

An outlandish building designed in an exotic neo-Gothic style, the **Iglesia Yurrita** seems to belong more to a horror movie set than the streets of Guatemala City. The interior contains a fabulous carved wooden altar – just as wild as the exterior. Iglesia Yurrita was finally completed in 1944, forty years after it was originally commissioned as a private chapel by the rich philanthropist Felipe Yurrite Casteñeda. His house, in the same style, stands alongside and is now an excellent restaurant (see p.67).

Zonas 9 and 10

Directly south of Zona 4, these neighbouring zones are split down the middle by Avenida La Reforma: Zona 9 is to the west and Zona 10 on the east. **Zona 9** is a mixed suburb of middle-class housing, a hotel or two and an eclectic assortment of businesses and few sights. **Zona 10** forms one of the smartest parts of town, taking in a couple of excellent museums, the botanical gardens and Zona Viva, an upmarket enclave of hotels, restaurants and bars.

On Sundays (10am–3pm) Avenida La Reforma and its extension to the south, Avenida Las Américas, are closed to motorized traffic and joggers, cyclists, skateboarders and street performers flood the streets in a fiesta-esque atmosphere.

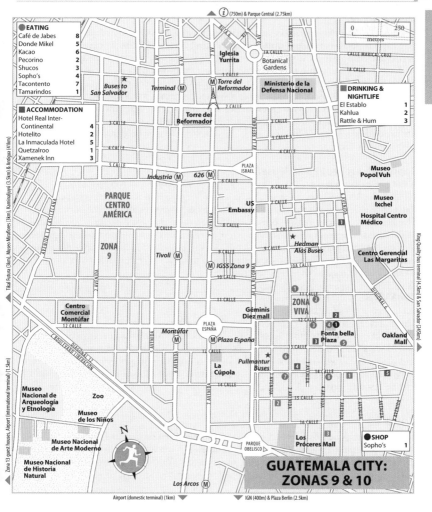

EATING

Café de Jabes	8
Donde Mikel	5
Kacao	6
Pecorino	2
Shucos	3
Sopho's	4
Tacontento	7
Tamarindos	1

ACCOMMODATION

Hotel Real Inter-Continental	4
Hotelito	2
La Inmaculada Hotel	5
Quetzalroo	3
Xamenek Inn	1

DRINKING & NIGHTLIFE

El Establo	1
Kahlua	2
Rattle & Hum	3

SHOP

Sopho's	1

GUATEMALA CITY: ZONAS 9 & 10

Torre del Reformador

7 Av & 2 C, Zona 9 • Transmetro Torre del Reformador

The **Torre del Reformador**, Guatemala's answer to the Eiffel Tower, is a steel structure built along the lines of the Parisian model. It was constructed in honour of President Barrios, who transformed the country between 1871 and 1885; a bell at the top is rung every year on June 30 to commemorate the Liberal victory in the 1871 revolution.

Botanical Gardens

C Mariscal Cruz 1–56, Zona 10 • Mon–Fri 8am–3pm, Sat 9am–noon • US$1.30 • Transmetro Torre del Reformador

These small but pretty gardens contain a selection of species, all neatly labelled in Spanish and Latin. In the grounds, there's also an anachronistic **natural history museum**, with a collection of mouldy stuffed birds, which include a quetzal, and curios such as swordfish swords and some horrific pickled rodents.

1

Museo Ixchel

6 C Final, Zona 10 • Mon–Fri 9am–5pm, Sat 9am–1pm • US$6.50 (includes entrance to Museo Popol Vuh) • ⓦ museoixchel.org

The capital's best-organized museum, the **Ixchel** is dedicated to Maya culture, with particular emphasis on traditional weaving. It contains a stunning array of hand-woven fabrics, including some very impressive examples of ceremonial costumes. There's also information (in Spanish and English) about the techniques, dyes, fibres and weaving tools used, and the way in which costumes have changed over the years. Weavers can usually be seen in action and there's a permanent exhibition of paintings by Guatemalan artists Andrés Curruchich, who painted scenes of rural life around San Juan Comalapa, and Carmen Pettersen, who depicted traditional costumes on canvas.

Popol Vuh Archeological Museum

6 C Final, Zona 10 • Mon–Fri 9am–5pm, Sat 9am–1pm • US$6.50 (includes entrance to Museo Ixchel) • ⓦ popolvuh.ufm.edu

Next to the Museo Ixchel, the small but well-presented **Popol Vuh Archeological Museum** has an outstanding collection of artefacts from sites all over the country. The Preclassic room contains some stunning ceramics and stone masks while highlights of the Classic section include an altar from Naranjo and some demonic-looking incense burners. In the Postclassic room is a replica of the Dresden Codex, one of only three extant pre-conquest Maya books, while the Colonial era is represented by assorted ecclesiastical relics and processional crosses.

Zona Viva

Zona 10, centred around 10 C and 3 Av • Transmetro Plaza España

The swankiest commercial part of town, the **Zona Viva** is a prosperous area of restaurants, nightclubs, boutiques, malls and luxury hotels. It's generally considered safe to walk around here at night, so it's not a bad option if you want to get a meal and hit a bar or two. This area, and the surrounding leafy streets (where the mansions' owners have numerous servants to keep the lawns clipped), is the natural playground for the nation's elite.

Zona 13

South of Zona Viva, Avenida La Reforma becomes **Avenida Las Américas**, a boulevard that divides zonas 13 and 14. Things become even more exclusive here, with many of the large walled compounds belonging to embassies. You'll find a clutch of important state museums, including the archeological museum, the airport, zoo and some excellent guesthouses.

Museo Nacional de Arqueología y Etnología

6 C & 7 Av • Tues–Fri 9am–4pm, Sat & Sun 9am–noon & 1.30–4pm • US$8 • ⓦ munae.gob.gt • Transmetro Acueducto

The **archeological and ethnological museum** has a world-class selection of Maya artefacts, though the displays are very antiquated, and most labels are in Spanish only. The collection has prehistoric sections, some wonderful stelae from Machaquilá and Dos Pilas, a re-creation of a royal tomb from Río Azul, spectacular jade masks from Takalik Abaj and a wonderful replica of a beautifully carved wooden lintel from Tikal's Temple IV. However, it's the exhibits collected from Piedras Negras, one of the most remote sites in Petén, that are most impressive: Stela 12, dating from 672 AD, brilliantly depicts a cowering captive king begging for mercy, while also on display is a monumental carved stone throne (J–6), richly engraved with superb glyphs and decorated with a twin-faced head.

CLOCKWISE FROM TOP KITE FESTIVAL OUTSIDE GUATEMALA CITY (P.71); THE CATHEDRAL, GUATEMALA CITY (P.54); EXHIBIT IN THE ARCHEOLOGICAL MUSEUM (P.60)>

1

Museo Nacional de Arte Moderno

6 C & 7 Av • Tues–Fri 9am–4pm, Sat & Sun 9am–noon & 1.30–4pm • US$7 • Transmetro Acueducto

Opposite the archeological museum, the **Museo Nacional de Arte Moderno**, which also suffers from poor presentation, boasts some imaginative geometric paintings by Dagoberto Vásquez and a collection of startling exhibits by Efraín Recinos, including a colossal marimba–tank sculpture. The permanent collection also holds a selection of bold Cubist art and massive murals by Carlos Mérida, Guatemala's most celebrated artist, which draws strongly on ancient Maya tradition.

Museo Nacional de Historia Natural

6 C & 7 Av • Tues–Fri 9am–4pm, Sat & Sun 9am–noon & 1.30–4pm • US$7 • Transmetro Acueducto

The **natural history museum** has a neglected air about it. It features a range of mouldy-looking stuffed animals from Guatemala and elsewhere as well as a few mineral samples.

Parque Aurora zoo

5 C • Tues–Sun 9am–5pm • US$3, children US$1.50 • ⓦ aurorazoo.org.gt • Transmetro Acueducto

The city's **zoo** is one of the best in Central America, with animals divided into three main geographical zones. You'll find lions, hippos and giraffes in the African section; Bengal tigers, Indian elephants and the reticulated python (the world's longest snake) in the Asian area; tapirs, monkeys, and virtually all the continents' big cats, including some well-fed jaguars, in the Americas region. The zoo is also open on full moon nights, which is an excellent time to see nocturnal animals.

Museo de los Niños

5 C 10-00 • Tues–Thurs 8am–noon & 1–5pm, Fri 8am–noon & 4–6pm, Sat & Sun 10am–1.30pm & 2.30–6pm • US$4.50 • ⓦ museodelos ninos.com.gt • Transmetro Acueducto

The Museum for Children is slightly more recreational than educational, with a huge ball-game room and trampolines as well as an operating theatre display, a hands-on music room and a giant jigsaw puzzle of Guatemala.

Zonas 7 & 11: Kaminaljuyú

Daily 9am–4pm • US$7

Way out on the western edge of the capital, the modest ruins of **Kaminaljuyú** are all that's left of a Maya city that once housed around fifty thousand people and thirteen ball courts. Unlike the massive temples of the lowlands, these structures were built of adobe, and most have been lost to erosion and urban sprawl. Today the archeological site is little more than a series of earth-covered mounds and a favourite spot for footballers and romantic couples. A couple of sections have been cut into by archeologists, but it's virtually impossible to get any impression of Kaminaljuyú's former scale and splendour – for that you'll have to visit the Miraflores museum.

A BRIEF HISTORY OF KAMINALJUYÚ

First settled as far back as around 1000 BC, **Kaminaljuyú** had grown to huge proportions by 100 AD with some two hundred flat-topped **pyramids**. Beneath each of these structures lay entombed a member of the nobility; a few have been unearthed to reveal the wealth and sophistication of the culture. The power of the city faded throughout the second and third centuries, but there was a renaissance after 400 AD when the Guatemalan highlands fell under the domination of Teotihuacán in central Mexico. The invaders prized Kaminaljuyú for its access to nearby obsidian mines and trade routes, but the fall of Teotihuacán around 600 AD weakened the city, resulting in its eventual demise.

Museo Miraflores

Calzada Roosevelt, Zona 11 • Tues–Sun 9am–7pm • US$5.50 • Ⓦ museomiraflores.org

A ten-minute walk south of the ruins, this excellent modern museum details the history of Kaminaljuyú and its importance as a trading centre. Exhibits include striking stone sculptures and stelae pieces, ceramics, impressive jade jewellery and obsidian flints and a scale model of Kaminaljuyú. There's also a permanent exhibition of Guatemalan textiles and the grounds encompass several temple mounds.

ARRIVAL AND DEPARTURE   GUATEMALA CITY

Arriving in Guatemala City is always a bit disconcerting. Wherever you arrive, you should take a taxi to your destination in the city (unless it's a block or two away), or use the Transmetro.

BY PLANE

Aurora airport (☎ 2334 7680) is in Zona 13 some way south of the centre, but close to Zona 10. A huge renovation programme has resulted in a very modern airport with up-to-date facilities including good cafés and duty-free stores.

Transport into the city The easiest way to get to and from the airport is by taxi: you can pre-pay your fare from a taxi desk; Zona 10 costs about US$9, Zona 1 around US$12. Virtually all Guatemala City's four- and five-star hotels, as well as the guesthouses in Zona 13, offer free pick-ups from the airport, if you let them know when you're arriving. Don't risk the city buses that leave from outside the airport because of security concerns.

Getting to Antigua Regular shuttle buses run to Antigua from the airport (US$10/person, three minimum) until about 10pm. A taxi to Antigua from the airport is about US$35.

Currency exchange Note that all the official-looking Global Exchange currency exchange booths offer derisory rates (25 per cent lower than the banks') and represent a total scam. Seek out the Banrural bank (daily 8am–9pm) in arrivals instead, where you can change US dollars and travellers' cheques at fair rates. There are no ATMs currently in the arrivals area, but you'll find two in the departures hall.

Airport taxes are virtually always included in the price of your ticket.

BY BUS

First-class buses Travelling by first-class (pullman) bus, you'll arrive at the private terminal of the company you're using. Zona 1 has the majority of these terminals (see box below), including buses running to Petén, Mexico, Cobán and Quetzaltenango. Note that many of these Zona 1 depots are located in an unsavoury part of the city; be on your guard for petty thieves. Other terminals are scattered around the southern half of the capital in safer areas of zonas 10 and 15.

Second-class buses "Chicken buses" use two main transport hubs. Buses for the western highlands use bus stops (there's no terminal) at 41 C between 7 Av and 11 Av, Zona 8, which is very close to Trébol Transmetro stop. All buses for southern Guatemala (including the border with El Salvador, Monterrico, Retalhuleu and Mexican border) plus Santiago Atitlán use a new terminal called Centra Sur (also known as Centro de Mayorio) in Zona 12. This has a Transmetro stop directly above it and security guards. Note that from Antigua it's far easier, quicker and safer to take a

---

BUS COMPANIES IN GUATEMALA CITY

ADN Mayan World (ADN) 8 Av 16–41, Zona 1 ☎ 2251 0610, Ⓦ adnautobusesdelnorte.com

Fuente del Norte (FN) 17 C 8–46, Zona 1 (for Flores) & Calzada Aguilar Batres 7–55, Zona 12 (for Tecún Uman) ☎ 7447 7070, Ⓦ grupofuentedelnorte.com

Los Halcones (LH) Calzada Roosevelt 37–47, Zona 11 ☎ 2439 4911, Ⓦ transportesloshalcones.com

Hedman Alas (HA) 2 Av 8–73, Zona 10 ☎ 2362 5072, Ⓦ hedmanalas.com

King Quality (KQ) 18 Av 1–96, Zona 15 ☎ 2369 7070, Ⓦ king-qualityca.com

Línea Dorada (LD) 10 Av and 16 C, Zona 1 ☎ 2415 8900, Ⓦ lineadorada.info

Litegua (L) 15 C 10–40, Zona 1 ☎ 2220 8840, Ⓦ litegua.com

Monja Blanca (MB) 8 Av 15–16, Zona 1 ☎ 2238 1409, Ⓦ tmb.com.gt

Pullmantur (P) Based at Holiday Inn, 1 Av 13–22, Zona 10 ☎ 2363 6240, Ⓦ pullmantur.com

Rutas Orientales (RO) 21 C 11–60, Zona 1 ☎ 2253 7282

Tica Bus (TB) Calzada Aguilar Batres 22–55, Zona 12 ☎ 2473 1639, Ⓦ ticabus.com

Transportes Álamo (TA) 12 Av A 0–65, Zona 7 ☎ 2471 8626

Transportes Galgos (TG) 7 Av 19–44, Zona 1 ☎ 2232 3661, Ⓦ transgalgosinter.com.gt

Transportes Velásquez (TV) 0 C 31–70, Zona 7 ☎ 2439 5553

Zaculeu Futura (ZF) Calzada Roosevelt 9–34, Zona 7 ☎ 2473 5081

1

shuttle bus (US$8–10); but it is possible to connect with second-class services at Trébol Transmetro stop.

Domestic destinations Antigua (2nd-class from 21 C & 2 Av, Zona 3, via trébol junction, every 15min until 6.30pm; 1hr); Chichicastenango (2nd-class from 41 C, Zona 8, every 30min; 3hr); Chiquimula (RO, 2 hourly; L, 1 daily at 2.45pm; 3hr 30min); Cobán (AND, 2 daily, MB hourly; 5hr); El Florido border (L, 1 daily at 2.45pm; 4hr 45min); Flores (FN 15 daily, LD 3 daily at 10am 9pm & 9.30pm, ADN 2 daily at 9pm & 10pm; 8–9hr); Huehuetenango (LD 2 daily, LH 6 daily, TV 5 daily, ZF 2 daily; 5–6hr); La Mesilla (LD 3 daily; 7hr); Monterrico (2nd-class from Centra Sur, 2 daily; 3hr 30min; or travel via Iztapa which has hourly onward connections); Nebaj (2nd-class from 41 C, Zona 8, 5 daily; 5hr 15min); Panajachel (2nd-class from 41 C, Zona 8, hourly until 3pm; 3hr); Puerto Barrios (L 19 daily, 5hr 30min–6hr 30min); Poptún (take a Flores bus; 6hr); Quetzaltenango (ADN 2 daily, TA 6 daily, LD 2 daily, TG 3 daily, FD 1 daily; 4hr); Río Dulce (L 5 daily, 5hr, or catch a Flores bus); San Pedro la Laguna (2nd-class from 41 C, Zona 8, 7 daily; 4hr); Santiago Atitlán (2nd-class from Centra Sur; 7 daily); Tecún Umán (FN 6 daily; 6hr).

International destinations Copán, Honduras (HA 2 daily 5am & 9am, FN 1 daily 6.15am; 5hr); La Ceiba, Honduras (HA 2 daily 5am & 9am; 12hr); Managua, Nicaragua (TB 2 daily; 28hr); San Pedro Sula, Honduras (HA 2 daily 5am & 9am, RO 2 daily 5.30am & 1.30pm; 8–9hr); San Salvador, El Salvador (V hourly, TB 2 daily, P 2–3 daily, KQ 2 daily; 5hr); Tapachula, Mexico (KQ 1 daily, LD 1 daily, TB 1 daily, TG 6 daily; 6hr); Tegucigalpa, Honduras (HA 2 daily 5am & 9am; 12–13hr; or the following all involve a stopover in San Salvador, around 36hr in total: KQ 2 daily 7am & 3.30pm, P 1 daily 7am, TB 1 daily 5.30am).

BY CAR

Car rental About a dozen rental agencies have desks at the airport. Two good local companies are Tabarini, 2 C A 7–30, Zona 10 (☎ 2444 4200, ⊛ tabarini.com), and Adaesa, Calzada Aguilar Batres 8–12, Zona 11 (☎ 2472 1122, ⊛ adaesa.com).

GETTING AROUND

It's best to avoid all city buses other than the Transmetro due to security concerns, and always take taxis after dark.

BY BUS (TRANSMETRO)

The good news is that Guatemala City has an excellent new bus network, the Transmetro, which operates on dedicated bus lanes that are closed to all other traffic making it by far the fastest way around the city. The bad news is that there are only two routes (so far). Transmetro articulated buses are modern, air-conditioned, wheelchair-friendly and only stop every kilometre or so. Transport police provide security. The authorities plan to roll out more routes so that by 2020 the capital will have a network of efficient bus services. The next route planned will connect Zona 6 in the north of the city with Zona 4, passing through Zona 1.

Tickets Transmetro tickets cost US$0.15/trip.

The green line (#CC) Runs north–south from Plaza Barrios, 18 C in Zona 1, along 6 Av through zonas 4 and 9 to Zona 13, returning along 7 Av; it operates 5am until 9pm (weekends 5am–8pm).

The orange line (#70) Connects Plaza Barrios and the Centro Cívico with points to the southwest, along Av Bolívar via the Trébol junction and down to the Centra Sur bus terminal. It's useful for passengers on 2nd-class buses to and from the highlands connecting with Zona 1, and operates 4.30am till 10pm (weekends 5am–8pm).

BY TAXI

There are both metered and non-metered taxis. Metered taxis are comfortable and fairly cheap; Amarillo (☎ 2470 1515) is highly recommended and will pick you up from anywhere in the city. The fare from Zona 1 to Zona 10 is about US$5, or a short hop within zones will be around US$2.50. It's best not to risk non-metered taxis, which are not properly regulated.

INFORMATION AND TOURS

Tourist information The main Inguat tourist office (Mon–Fri 8am–4pm; ☎ 2331 1333, ✉ info@inguat.gob .gt) is at 7 Av 1–17, Zona 4 and has English-speaking staff and plenty of brochures.

Tours *Quetzalroo* (see p.65) offers an excellent half-day walking tour of the *centro histórico* for just US$5/person, non-guests are welcome to join. *Hotel Posada Belén* (see p.65) also offers good guided city tours by car for US$35/person (minimum two). Clark Tours offer half-day tours for US$30.

Travel agents Viajes Tivoli, 6 Av 8–41, Zona 9 (☎ 2386 4200, ⊛ viajestivoli.com), is a good all-round agent with competitive rates for international and domestic flights. Clark Tours, 7 Av 14–76, Zona 9 (☎ 2412 4700, ⊛ www .clarktours.com.gt) can organize trips to many parts of the country.

ACCOMMODATION

You'll pay more for a bed in the capital than in the rest Guatemala. Firstly choose the zone where you want to base yourself, each have their advantages. **Zona 1** is not a great area to be hunting for a room late at night, but it's safe enough in the day and early evening. Many travellers stay close to the airport, in **Zona 13**, where there are some good options – virtually all of which offer free airport pick-ups and drop-offs, though be sure to book ahead. The disadvantage with this quiet, suburban location is that there are few restaurants and cafés close by. Guatemala City's upmarket hotels are clustered in a relatively safe part of town, in **zonas 9 and 10**, within reach of the "Zona Viva", where there's a glut of restaurants and bars; there are two good budget Zona 10 options, too.

ZONA 1

★ **Chalet Suizo** 7 Av 14–34 ☎ 2251 8191; map p.57. Resembles a European youth hostel, with large, plain, spotless rooms (with or without private bathrooms), all with pine furniture, good-quality beds and reading lights. The management is friendly and efficient – indeed there's always someone sweeping or cleaning up. Filling meals are available in the dining room. Wi-fi. **US$21**

La Coperacha 4 Av 2–03 ☎ 5526 3422, 🌐 coperacha .org; map p.57. New hostel, in the heart of the city, run by a couple of young Guatemalans and with a sociable vibe. They have bikes for rent and good travel information. Dorms **US$10**, doubles **US$30**

Hotel Ajau 8 Av 15–62 ☎ 2232 0488, ✉ hotelajau @hotmail.com; map p.57. Historic old hotel with an impressive lobby and an old-school ambience – the corridors have lovely original floor tiles. The 41 rooms, all with TVs, are well-scrubbed and many have en-suite bathrooms. There's a comedor for breakfast and evening meals, plus internet is available. **US$15**

Hotel Colonial 7 Av 14–19 ☎ 2232 6722, 🌐 hotel colonial.net; map p.57. Attractive, good-value Spanish-style hotel with a pleasingly prim and proper air created by some classy wrought ironwork and tiling. The three classes of rooms (some without private bathroom) are well kept and have solid dark-wood furniture; most have cable TV. **US$21**

Hotel PanAmerican 9 C 5–63 ☎ 2232 6807, 🌐 hotel panamerican.com.gt; map p.57. Historic hotel a block from the Parque Central, with a strong Guatemalan identity and a formal, civilized atmosphere. The sixty spacious rooms all have cable TV and rates include a filling breakfast in the stately *Restaurante Salón Real*. **US$55**

Hotel Santoña 8 Av 15–13 ☎ 2232 6455; map p.57. If you're using the Monja Blanca bus terminal for Cobán this efficient, welcoming modern hotel is ideal – it's right opposite. Offers spacious, light rooms (though no singles), all with cable TV and firm beds. **US$28**

Hotel Spring 8 Av 12–65 ☎ 2232 2858, 🌐 hotelspring .com; map p.57. Right in the heart of town, this large budget travellers' stronghold is secure and has a pretty courtyard and café for socializing. Rooms vary greatly, some have private bathroom; the budget options can be a tad sparse. There's laundry service, safety boxes and free wi-fi and drinking water. **US$18**

Posada Belén 13 C A 10–30 ☎ 2253 4530, 🌐 posada belen.com; map p.57. A great choice in the historic centre, this peaceful refuge is run by the hospitable and English-speaking Sanchinelli family. Occupies a beautiful old building, with a gorgeous garden patio and plenty of quiet areas for book reading. Excellent home-cooked meals are served in the stately dining room. Tours of the city centre can be arranged. No children under 5. **US$55**

ZONA 10

Hotel Real Inter-Continental 14 C 2–51 ☎ 2379 4444, 🌐 ichotelsgroup.com; map p.59. A fine luxury hotel in the heart of the Zona Viva where the palatial rooms, many with sweeping city views, boast great beds and Egyptian cotton sheets, CD players and preloaded iPods. You'll find French, Japanese and international restaurants, plus a (small) heated outdoor pool. **US$164**

Hotelito 12 C 4–51 ☎ 2339 1811, 🌐 hotelito.com; map p.59. Small, modish hotel with stylish rooms where the soothing cream furnishings are offset with parquet wood floors and tasteful photographs. However, noise is an issue on weekend nights when *Hotelito*'s lounge lobby morphs into something resembling a raucous bar and a neighbouring club fires up. **US$128**

★ **La Inmaculada Hotel** 14 C 7–88 ☎ 2314 5100, 🌐 inmaculadahotel.com; map p.59. The hippest address in the city, this new low-rise boutique place offers modernist decor, an enviable location on the edge of the Zona Viva and high service standards. The thirteen rooms are kitted out in real style with luxury bedding, iPod docks, LCD TVs, L'Occitane toiletries, fast wi-fi and impressive attention to detail. There's a restaurant, peaceful garden to enjoy and rates include airport transfers. **US$122**

★ **Quetzalroo** 6 Av 7–84 ☎ 5746 0830, 🌐 quetzalroo .com; map p.59. Australian/Guatemalan-owned back-packers hostel in an apartment block, with good quality accommodation, three shower rooms, a guests' kitchen, TV lounge, laundry room and a fun, communal vibe. Prices are cheap considering the location and there are some great freebies: a ride from the airport, internet and light breakfast. Excellent city tours can be arranged for just US$5 by the ever-helpful owners, who really understand travellers' needs. Dorms **US$15**, doubles **US$35**

Xamanek Inn 13 C 3–57 ☎ 2360 8345, ✉ xamanek .guatemala@gmail.com; map p.59. Well-run hostel in the heart of the Zona Viva, so there are myriad restaurants and big-city bustle on your doorstep. The rate includes breakfast, internet, wi-fi and use of a DVD library. There's also a kitchen, laundry, huge living room area, rear terrace and reliable hot water in a good shower block. All four dorms are on the large side; of the private rooms no. 5 is a good deal for couples. Dorms **US$14**, rooms **US$26**

1

ZONA 13

Casablanca 15 C C 7–35 ☎ 2261 3129, ⊛ hotel casablancainn.com. A tasteful guesthouse in a tranquil location with very stylish accommodation. All rooms are light, airy and spacious, with bathrooms (most ensuite). There's a well-stocked bar and an attractive sitting room and meals are offered if ordered in advance. Breakfast, airport transfers and wi-fi are included. US$45

★ **Dos Lunas** 21 C 10–92 ☎ 2261 4248, ⊛ hoteldos lunas.com. A very welcoming and efficient guesthouse on a quiet suburban street managed by fluent English speaker Lorena Artola and her Dutch husband Hank, who take great care of travellers. Rooms are spotless, attractively presented and rates include free airport transfers, internet and breakfast.

Excellent evening meals (US$6–10) are also offered and transport and tourist advice is second to none. Very popular, so book well ahead. Dorms US$14, doubles US$28

Hostal Villa Toscana 16 C 8–20 ☎ 2261 2854, ⊛ hostalvillatoscana.com. An immaculate guesthouse with stylish, very well-presented rooms, with neutral colour schemes contrasting with vibrant Maya textiles; all have cable TV, no. 9 has a balcony and the suite has a private terrace. A big breakfast is included and there's ample parking. US$50

Mariana's Petit Hotel 20 C 10–17 ☎ 2261 4105, ⊛ marianaspetithotel.com. A well-managed, welcoming guesthouse very close to the airport with inexpensive rates, a quiet location, free airport transfers and wi-fi. US$37

EATING

Guatemala City offers everything from no-nonsense comedores to high-end dining. In **Zona 1** you'll find a great selection of inexpensive places to eat, with lunchtime a particularly good time for a filling feed. Excellent set-price, three-course menus are available for US$3–4 a head; try the streets west of the Parque Central and around the post office. For more international options – including steak houses, Mexican, Asian and European places – head to **Zona Viva** which has scores of restaurants. Cafés serving espresso-style coffee and snacks are found all over the city.

ZONA 1

★ **Altuna** 5 Av 12–31 ☎ 2232 0669, ⊛ restaurante altuna.com; map p.57. Elegant, formal and expensive Spanish/Basque restaurant rich in ambience and the natural home of Guatemala's Eurocentric elite. Mains include seafood (try the *calamares en su tinta*), great fish dishes and meat choices, all succulent and expertly prepared. Imported Castilian treats like *chorizo ibérico and boquerones* are available. Count on around US$25–30 a head. There's a second branch in Zona 10 at 10 C 0–45. Daily noon–4.30pm & 6–10.30pm.

★ **Café León** 8 Av 9–15 ☎ 2251 0068, ⊛ cafeleon .net; map p.57. A wonderfully atmospheric old-school café of gleaming espresso machines and vintage photographs that's a downtown headquarters for Guatemalan intellectuals and characters. It's all about the coffee and conversation here, with treacle-thick espresso and milky café con leche, though they do sell breakfasts, cakes (*cubiletes*, empanadas) and sandwiches. There's a second Zona 1 branch at 12 C 6–23 which offers more of the same. Mon–Fri 8am–6pm, Sat 9am–1pm.

Café Música 8 Av 10–6 ☎ 2232 2423; map p.57. Inside the wonderful Museo de Músicos Invisibles, this is a very civilized café-restaurant for a filling Guatemala breakfast (US$4.50) or tasty set lunch (US$3.50) of *comida casera*. Tables are grouped around a lovely little grassy patio, and there's a live pianist from noon till 3pm daily. Also good for a coffee or a beer. Daily 7am–6pm.

Cafetalito 8 Av 10–68 ⊛ elcafetalito.com; map p.57. Modern *Starbucks*-style café, with all the familiar coffee combinations, plus granitas and frappuccinos and a few local coffee blends (Antigua, Huehuetenango, Atitlán and

Cobán). Paninis and snacks are also served. Mon–Sat 8am–6pm.

El Gran Pavo 13 C 4–41 ☎ 2232 9912; map p.57. Fairly authentic Mexican food at moderate prices. Things really kick off on weekends when mariachi bands prowl the tables – you'll have to put up with piped ranchero music at other times, though the long tequila list helps ease the pain. Other branches at 6 C 3–09, Zona 9 and 15 Av 16–72, Zona 10. Daily noon–10pm.

Kafé Katok 12 C 6–61 ☎ 7840 3387, ⊛ ahumados katok.com; map p.57. Rustic-style place replete with huge wooden beams and chunky tables that specializes (appropriately enough) in hearty country cooking, especially grilled meats and smoked sausages. Come hungry for the epic set lunch (US$7), or tuck into a sandwich (US$3.50) or a few tapas. There's another branch in Zona 10 at 8 Av 18–01. Mon–Wed 6am–8pm, Thurs–Sun 6am–9pm.

Long Wah 6 C 3–75 ☎ 2232 6611; map p.57. One of the better budget Chinese restaurants in this neighbourhood, consistently recommended by locals with a menu that includes *wontons* and *chow mein*. They also offer food to go. Daily 11.30am–3pm & 6–9.30pm.

Rey Sol 11 C 5–51 ☎ 2232 3516; map p.57. Vegetarian café-restaurant serving pasta, Mexican-style dishes and wholemeal bread sandwiches in slightly uninspiring surrounds. Also acts as a health food store, selling good bread, granola, soya milk, herbal teas and veggie snacks. Mon–Sat 7.30am–7pm, Sun noon–4pm.

Rocque Rosito 8 Av & 9 C ☎ 2232 7343; map p.57. Set in historic premises, this spacious café has banquette seating and stylish sofas. It's ideal for a coffee or juice and a quick bite, and you'll find tasty crêpes and sandwiches on the food menu. Mon–Sat 7.30am–6pm.

ZONA 4

Casa Yurrita Ruta 6 8–52 ☎2360 1615; map p.57. A refined destination for breakfast or lunch that occupies an imposing mansion built in the same Gothic-cum-Baroque style as the Yurrita church next door (see p.57). The interior features oil paintings and stately mirrors that complement the original parquet flooring and building's ornate plasterwork. *Casa Yurrita's* French chef offers a traditional bistro menu that takes in *pâté de campagne* and classics including Provençal-style chicken. Start your meal with a glass of *kir*. Tues–Sun 9am–3pm.

ZONA 10

Café de Jabes 14 C 4–12 ☎2363 4150; map p.59. Classic comedor that offers the best-value set lunch in Zona Viva. The menu changes daily, but there are always four freshly prepared dishes accompanied with vegetables. The price (US$3) includes soup, tortillas and a drink, and you dine in clean surrounds with gingham tablecloths. Daily 7am–3pm.

★ **Donde Mikel** 13 C 5–19 ☎2363 3308; map p.59. Elegant, expensive Spanish restaurant whose authentic food has its regulars dreaming of Iberia, with delicious crispy baby *calamares* (squid) and meats served *a la plancha* (grilled). Always busy, so reserve a table. Mon–Sat 11.30am–3pm & 6–10pm, Sun 11.30am–4pm.

Kacao 2 Av 13–44 ☎2337 4188; map p.59. Beautifully designed place set under a giant *palapa* (thatched) roof; in the evening you enter through a bamboo forest to a dining room illuminated by hundreds of candles. The menu is refined *comida guatemalteca*, with excellent *jocón* (chicken in sauce of tomatillos, coriander, pumpkin and sesame seeds). Around US$20 a head. Daily noon–3pm & 6–11pm.

Pecorino 11 C 3–36 ☎2260 3035, ⒲ristorantepecorino .com; map p.59. Consistently touted by locals as the best Italian in the country. Feast on fresh pasta, pizza from a wood-fired oven and authentic fish, seafood and grilled meats in an elegant interior, or the delightful, sensitively lit garden. Mon–Sat noon–midnight.

Shucos 3 Av & 12 C; map p.59. For bargain-basement nosh in Zona 10, this simple place is perfect: *shucos* (hot dogs with avocado) and taco-style snacks start at US$1.25; a beer costs the same. Daily noon–3pm & 6pm–1am.

Sopho's Fontabella Plaza, 12 C 12–59 ☎2419 7070; map p.59. Inside an upmarket courtyard-style shopping mall, this bookstore café is a delightfully civilized place to browse a book or magazine, sip a café con leche and snack on a sandwich or cake. Daily 8am–7pm.

Tacontento 2 Av & 14 C ☎2363 5028; map p.59. Affordable considering the Zona 10 location; come here to feast on tacos (US$4 for a good feed), wraps and Mexican dishes inside or on the streetside terrace. The lunch special includes soup, three tacos and a drink. Daily 11am–midnight.

★ **Tamarindos** 11 C 2–19 A ☎2360 2815, ⒲tamarindos.com.gt; map p.59. For a decade this has been one of Guatemala City's destination restaurants, with stylish decor, a Japanese-style garden patio and lounge sounds. The East-meets-West menu takes in sushi, lots of seafood and creative house salads as well as fusion dishes like filet mignon served with Thai-style calamari salad. Expect to pay upwards of US$20 a head. Daily noon–3pm & 7pm–midnight.

DRINKING AND NIGHTLIFE

Despite being the capital, Guatemala City isn't a great place for socializing or indulging. Most of the population hurry home in the evening and, apart from a few streets in zonas 1 and 10, there's little nightlife after dark. There are two main areas: **Zona 1**, catering to a young, bohemian crowd, and the **Zona Viva** in Zona 10, which is full of upmarket bars and clubs. For information on Guatemala's club and DJ scene consult ⒲electronik.net.

GAY GUATEMALA CITY

Guatemala City's small **gay scene** is mostly underground and concentrated around a few (almost entirely male) venues; "in" places change quickly: consult ⒲gayguatemala.com for the latest info. After parties are frequent after the 1am curfew.

Black and White 11 C 2–54, Zona 1 ⒲blackandwhitebar.com; map p.57. In the heart of the city since 2006, this bar-club is an intimate space with classy decor and attracts a lively crowd with themed nights, go-go dancers and strippers. Wed–Sat 7pm–1am.

Eclipse 13 Av 4–39, Zona 1; map p.57. A long running gay club where DJs spin house and latin music. Arrive early and the happy hour all-you-can-down drinks specials (US$6) certainly get the party started. Thurs–Sat from 7pm.

Genetic Vía 3 & Ruta 3, Zona 4; map p.57. This is the city's largest (mainly) gay club with three floors and a VIP section, and plays pumping trance and house music. There are themed nights and go-go dancers. Thurs–Sat.

1

1

ZONA 1

Zona 1 has a grungy appeal and is popular with students. Slowly it's once again becoming a focal point for a night out, though at the moment there are only a handful of good venues. In Zona 1, you could do a lot worse than heading to one of the bars on Pasaje Aycinena for a few drinks and then on to *El Gran Hotel* or *La Bodeguita* to see what's on. Note that personal safety can be a concern here, so it's best to get around by taxi late at night.

Bad Attitude 4 C 5–10 ☎ 5206 9510; map p.57. Heavy rock music venue, dripping with death metal banners, where you drink from skull-shaped goblets. Showcases heavy/death/metal/thrash/alternative rock bands on Thurs and Sat, while on Fri it's everything from reggae to trance. Free entrance some nights; maximum cover is US$5 (includes a drink) for popular groups. Thurs–Sat 5.30pm–1am.

Blanco y Negro Pasaje Aycinena, 9 C between 6 & 7 Av; map p.57. This place really jumps on weekends when lovers of Caribbean music descend en masse to soak up Jamaican dancehall, roots reggae, ska and punta sounds.

La Bodeguita del Centro 12 C 3–55 ☎ 2230 2976; map p.57. Large, left-field venue with live music – everything from jazz and ska to alternative and punk rock – most nights plus some comedy and poetry events. Free entry in the week, around US$3–6 on weekends (when a drink is included). Worth a visit for the Che Guevara, Lennon and Marley memorabilia alone. Closed Sun & Mon.

Las Cien Puertes Pasaje Aycinena, 9 C 6–47; map p.57. Guatemala City's definitive bohemian bar is in a beautiful run-down arcade that's popular with artists, students and political activists. Graffiti-splattered walls, good sounds and moderate prices. Mon–Sat 5pm–1am.

El Gran Hotel 9 C 7–64 ⊛ elgranhotel.com.gt; map p.57. Hugely popular new bar-cum-cultural centre that draws a young, studenty crowd with indie, protest rock bands and electronica artists and for its film evenings. On weekends nights, or when a popular band is playing, the atmosphere is raucous and a lot of fun. Cover charge is US$2.50–6, with two or three live bands per week. Mon–Sat 5pm–midnight.

La Luna Pasaje Aycinena, 9 C 8–59 ☎ 2253 8728, ⊛ cafepianolaluna.com; map p.57. Small, sociable little bar in a lovely historic building that has live music (Tues–Sat), mainly *trova*, acoustic and rock. Doubles as a little café in the day when snacks are served. Mon–Wed 10am–midnight, Thurs–Sun 10am–1am.

★ **El Portal** Pasaje Rubio, 9 C between 6 & 7 Av ☎ 2251 6716; map p.57. Said to be one of Che Guevara's old drinking haunts, and the decor (and clientele) has little changed. It's a fantastic place to share a *chibola* of *cerveza mixta*, munch on a few (complimentary) *boquitas* and soak up the scene: hard drinkers glued to bar stools and wandering *trios* of musicians prowling the tables, mariachi-style. Mon–Sat 11am–10pm.

ZONA 4

Trovajazz Via 6 3–55 ⊛ trovajazz.com; map p.57. Intimate venue with a good reputation and loyal clientele that showcases quality jazz, blues, acoustic and *trova* (Latin American folk). Entrance is around US$5 for most acts.

ZONA 10

Zona Viva in Zona 10 is where the wealthy go to have fun. There's a surplus of American-style bars and clubs playing Latino and European dance music, pop hits and salsa – though nothing particularly underground.

El Establo 14 C 5–08 ☎ 2363 3287; map p.59. Large, classy European-owned bar that attracts a wealthy middle-aged crowd. Serves food (including chicken, pizza, goulash) and has two-for-one drinks and dinner specials most days. Sounds range from jazz to bluesy rock music, with live bands on Thurs. Mon–Sat 5.30pm–midnight.

Kahlua 1 Av 15–07 ☎ 4736 2278; map p.59. Well-established club with four levels and a vast main dancefloor that draws a young party-minded crowd. Musically, things very much depend on the night, with sounds ranging from electronica and reggaeton to mainstream Latin dance hits. Thurs–Sat 7pm–1am.

Rattle & Hum 4 Av & 16 C ☎ 2366 6524; map p.59. Snug and stylish Australian-owned bar, popular with expats and locals alike, with lively atmosphere and Western music (mainly rock and indie) on the stereo. Mon 5–10pm, Tues–Sun 5pm–1am.

ZONA 15

Stage Club Km 14.5 Ruta El Salvador ⊛ stage.com. gt; map p.55. Guatemala City's leading club is way down south on the road to El Salvador and hosts eclectic nights, with DJs playing electro, hip-hop, urban Latin and house music. London's Ministry of Sound even hosted a night here in 2011. Cover charges vary from US$5 to US$15 (including a drink) depending on the night. Thurs–Sat 7pm–1am.

CINEMA

Centro Cultural de España Via 5 1–23, Zona 4 ⊛ cceguatemala.org. The Spanish Cultural Centre has an innovative selection of arthouse, European and independent Latin American movies, plus occasional classics. Also hosts plays and cultural events.

Cinépolis Oakland Mall, Diagonal 6 13–01, Zona 10 ⊛ cinepolis.com.gt. This multi-screener has the best-quality audio-visuals in the city, and even offer "butler service" tickets, which get you a leather seat and drinks brought to your seat.

SHOPPING

For souvenirs, foodstuffs and everyday items check out Zona 1's Mercado Central (see p.57). Sexta Avenida in Zona 1 has inexpensive stores selling pirated CDs and DVDs, cellular phones and clothing.

Oakland Mall Diagonal 6 13–01, Zona 10 ⓦoakland mall.com.gt; map p.59. This is the latest and most upmarket mall in Zona 10, and has stores including Diesel, Apple and Zara, a good food court and free wi-fi. Daily 8am–10pm.

Los Próceres 16 C 2–00, Zona 10 ⓦproceres.com; map p.59. This is a conveniently located midrange mall, with four floors and over two hundred stores, including many budget clothes, electrical and phone shops, some food stalls, a multi-screen cinema and a café or two. Daily 8am–10pm.

Sopho's Fontabella Plaza, 12 C 12–59, Zona 10 ⓦsophosenlinea.com; map p.59. Located in a classy shopping mall, Sopho's bookstore has a modest selection of new English titles, including fiction and photographic books, plus thousands of titles in Spanish. There's also a café here. Daily 8am–7pm.

DIRECTORY

Banks and exchange Banks and ATMs are scattered throughout the city, inside all shopping malls and you'll find several at Centro Gerencial Las Margaritas, Diagonal 6 10–01 in Zona 10, where you can also cash travellers' cheques and get cash advances on credit cards. You can exchange euros at Banco Internacional, Av Las Américas 12–54, Zona 13. American Express is inside Clark Tours, 7 Av 14–76, Zona 9.

Dentist Central Dentist de Especialistas, 20 C 11–17, Zona 10 (☎2337 1773), is the best dental clinic in the country and superb in emergencies.

Embassies Most embassies are in the south of the city, along Av La Reforma and Av Las Américas, and they tend to be open weekday mornings only. Australia, contact the Canadian embassy; Belgium (honorary), 6 Av 16–24, Zona 10 ☎2385 5234; Belize, 5 Av 5–55, Zona 14 ☎2367 3883; Canada, 13 C 8–44, Edificio Edyma Plaza, Zona 10 ☎2363 4348, ⓦcanadainternational.gc.ca; Germany, Edificio Reforma 10, Av La Reforma 9–55, Zona 10 ☎2364 6700, ⓦguatemala.diplo.de; Honduras, 19 Av A 20–19, Zona 10 ☎2366 5640; Mexico, 2 Av 7–57, Zona 10 ☎ 2420 3400, ⓦsre.gob.mx/guatemala; Netherlands, 16 C 0–55, 13th floor, Torre Internacional, Zona 10 ☎2381 4300, ⓦguatemala.nlambassade.org; New Zealand (honorary), 13 C 7–85, Zona 10 ☎2431 1705; Norway, Murano Center, 14 C 3–51, Zona 10 ⓦnoruega.org.gt; South Africa (honorary), 11 Av 30–24, Zona 5 ☎2332 6953; Sweden, Edificio Reforma 10, Av La Reforma 9–55, Zona 10 ☎2384 7300, ⓦswedenabroad.com; Switzerland, Torre Internacional, 16 C 0–65, Zona 10 ☎2367 5520; United Kingdom, Torre Internacional, 16 C 0–55, Zona 10 ☎2380 7300, ⓦukinguatemala.fco.gov.uk; United States, Av La Reforma 7–01, Zona 10 ☎ 2326 4000, ⓦguatemala.usembassy.gov.

Immigration The main immigration office (*migración*) is 6 Av & Ruta 3, Zona 4 (Mon–Fri 8.30am–2.45pm; ☎2411 2411). Visas can be extended here for ninety days; you'll need copies of your passport, proof of funds (such as a credit card) and a passport-style colour photograph.

Internet and phones Wi-fi is widespread. There's an internet café at 6 Av 9–43, Zona 1, that does Skype calls. You'll find two internet cafés inside Géminis Diez mall, 12 C & 2 Av, Zona 10, which also have cheap international call rates.

Laundry Lavandería el Siglo 2 C 3–42, Zona 1 (Mon–Sat 8am–6pm), charges US$5 for a wash and dry.

Libraries The Guatemalan American Institute, or IGA, at Ruta 1 and Vía 4, Zona 4, has the best library for English books. There's also the National Library, Parque del Centenario, and specialist collections at the Ixchel and Popol Vuh museums.

Medical care Dr Manuel Cáceres Figueroa, 6 Av 8–92, Zona 9 (☎2332 1506), who speaks English and German, is highly recommended for consultations; your embassy should also have a list of bilingual doctors. For emergency medical assistance, dial ☎125 for the Red Cross or head for the Centro Médico, a private hospital open 24hr, at 6 Av 3–47, Zona 10 (☎2332 3555).

Police The main police station is on the corner of 6 Av and 14 C, Zona 1. In an emergency, dial ☎120.

Post office The main post office is at 7 Av and 12 C, Zona 1 (Mon–Fri 8.30am–5pm, Sat 8.30am–1pm).

Around Guatemala City

The one sight that really warrants a day-trip from the capital is **Volcán de Pacaya**, a highly active cone, though this is actually easier to visit from nearby Antigua, from where most tours leave. From Guatemala City, the highway to the Pacific passes through endless suburbs, a swathe of new housing projects and giant *maquila* (clothing assembly) factories until you glimpse the (polluted waters) of Lago de Amatitlán nestling at the base of the Pacaya volcano.

1

To the northwest of the capital lies a hilly, forested area that, despite its proximity, is little tainted by the influence of the city. The one sight out this way, the **Mixco Viejo ruins**, the ancient capital of the Poqomam Maya, enjoy the most dramatic setting of any archeological site in Guatemala.

Volcán de Pacaya

Rising to a height of 2250m, this volcano regularly spits out clouds of rock and ash in the country's most dramatic sound-and-light extravaganza. The current period of eruption began in 1965, and colonial records show that it was also active between 1565 and 1775. Today it certainly ranks as one of the most accessible and exciting volcanoes in Central America, and a trip to the cone is an unforgettable experience (although sulphurous fumes and very high winds can make an ascent impossible some days). The best time to watch the eruptions is at night, when the volcano often spouts plumes of brilliant orange lava.

It's a steep but steady hour's climb up a good path through *milpas* and thickish forest until you suddenly emerge on the lip of an exposed ridge from where you can see the cone in all its brutal beauty. In front of you is a massive bowl of cooled lava, its fossilized currents flowing away to the right; opposite is the cone itself, a jet-black triangular peak that occasionally spews rock and ash. It's possible to descend, and pick your way carefully across the lava fields until you reach a section that's oozing molten lava. If you've brought a marshmallow along, toast yourself a snack.

Many standard tours don't allow enough time, but it's a further 45 minutes to the summit of the cone itself. The route passes between charred stumps of trees, and then up the slippery ashen sides of the cone itself, a terrifying but thrilling ascent, eventually bringing you face to face with bubbling patches of molten magma and minor eruptions (if conditions permit). A noxious brew of sulphurous fumes (that choke the throat) swirls around the lip of the crater and you'll feel the heat of the ash and lava beneath your feet. The climb certainly shouldn't be attempted when Pacaya is highly active – check with your tour agency about the state of the eruptions before setting out.

TOURS   **VOLCÁN DE PACAYA**

Though it is possible to climb the cone independently, virtually everyone chooses to join a group as part of a **tour**, escorted by a guide. Antigua is the best place to organize things, and there are adventure sports specialists (see p.82) in town which run more comfortable and expensive (from US$50) trips that include food and drink.

Safety and equipment Safety on Pacaya (once the site of regular attacks by bandits) is now much less of a concern since park guards, who accompany groups, were posted on the volcano's slopes. Wear hiking boots if you have them, though people do ascend the peak in all kinds of footwear.

San Francisco de Sales Tour minibuses drop you off in the village of San Francisco de Sales, where you'll be surrounded by dozens of young boys urging you to buy a walking "steek", rent a torch (flashlight) or a horse (US$16 return). Note that in February 2012 villagers here were

charging tourists "entrance fees" of a few dollars to pass through their village; this situation may or may not continue. Once you've paid your US$4 entrance fee to the protected Pacaya area you'll be assigned a local guide to accompany your group on the trail.

Gran Jaguar Tours 4 C Poniente 30 ☎7832 2712, ⓦgranjaguartours.com. Handles virtually all budget trips from Antigua, no matter where you book your ticket. Daily tours leave Antigua around 2pm and return by about 9pm, and include transport in an ageing (often packed) minibus but no entrance fees. US$5–7/person.

Parque Natural Canopy Calderas

Daily 8am–6pm • ☎ 5538 5531, ⓦ canopyguatemala.com.gt

Nestling in the northern slopes of Pacaya is **Parque Natural Canopy Calderas**, a protected zone that encompasses a delightful highland lake and a dense patch of rainforest, close to the *aldea* of San José Calderas. The park is a privately owned nature reserve where you can go horseriding (US$8/hr) or swing through the jungle from professionally built wooden platforms along a 700m network of cable (US$20) which slices through the forest. It's essential to call ahead and book activities.

Mixco Viejo

Daily 8am–4pm • US$7 • Buses (4 daily) to Pachalum from 41 C & 8 Av, Zona 7, in Guatemala City, pass Mixco Viejo

Mixco Viejo was the capital of the Poqomam Maya, one of the main pre-conquest tribes. The site itself is thought to date from the thirteenth century, and its construction, designed to withstand siege, bears all the hallmarks of the troubled times before the arrival of the Spanish. Protected on all sides by deep ravines, it can be entered only along a single-file causeway. At the time the Spanish arrived, in 1525, this was one of the largest highland centres, with nine temples, two ball courts and a population of around nine thousand. Though the Spanish cavalry and their Mexican allies defeated Poqomam forces, the city remained impenetrable until a secret entrance was revealed, allowing the Spanish to enter virtually unopposed and to unleash a massacre of its inhabitants.

Mixco Viejo's **plazas** and **temples** are laid out across several flat-topped ridges. Like all the highland sites the structures are fairly low – the largest temple reaches only about 10m in height – and are devoid of decoration. It is, however, an interesting site in a spectacular setting, and during the week you'll probably have the ruins to yourself, which gives the place all the more atmosphere.

From Guatemala City to Sumpango

Heading west of Guatemala City along the Carretera Interamericana, the serpentine three-lane highway climbs steadily until it reaches **San Lucas Sacatepéquez**, where there's a junction for Antigua and the festival town of **SANTIAGO SACATEPÉQUEZ**. A somewhat scruffy, sprawling highland town some 4km north of the highway, it's only really worth dropping by for the annual kite festival (see box below) though it also hosts a large **market** (Tues & Sun). The neighbouring village of **SUMPANGO**, 6km west along the Interamericana, has an identical Day of the Dead tradition.

ARRIVAL AND DEPARTURE | **SANTIAGO SACATEPÉQUEZ AND SUMPANGO**

Organized tours You'll have no problem reaching either Santiago Sacatepéquez or Sumpango on fiesta day, when travel agencies send fleets of minibuses go up to the villages from Antigua.

By bus To get there by public transport take a Guatemala City-bound bus to San Lucas Sacatepéquez and catch a connection there.

THE DAY OF THE DEAD

Santiago's local fiesta to honour the **Day of the Dead** on November 1 is one of the nation's most spectacular, with massive **kites** flown from the cemetery to release the souls of the dead from their agony. The festival is immensely popular, and thousands of Guatemalans (and tourists) come every year to watch the spectacle. The colourful kites, made from paper and bamboo, are huge circular creations, measuring up to about 3m in diameter. Teams of young men struggle to get them aloft while the crowd looks on with bated breath, rushing for cover if a kite comes crashing to the ground. All in all it's quite a scene, the cemetery lined with even larger kites of up to 10m across that are too heavy to get off the ground but which form an impressive backdrop. Early mornings are often calm, with the wind usually picking up around lunchtime, so you may want to time your arrival accordingly.

1

Antigua

Superbly situated in a sweeping highland valley, **ANTIGUA** is one of the Americas' most enchanting colonial cities. In its day this was one of the great cities of the Spanish empire, serving as the administrative centre for all of Central America and Mexican Chiapas.

Antigua has become Guatemala's foremost tourist destination, a favoured hangout for travellers. The beauty of the city itself is the main attraction, particularly its remarkable wealth of **colonial buildings** – churches, monasteries and grand family homes – that provide an idea of the city's former status. You'll find the ambience unhurried and enjoyable, with a sociable bar scene and superb choice of restaurants adding to the appeal. Antigua's **language schools** are another big draw, pulling in students from around the globe.

Expats contribute to the town's cosmopolitan air, mingling with local villagers selling their wares in the streets, and the middle-class Guatemalans who come here at weekends to eat, drink and enjoy themselves. The downside is that perhaps this uniquely civilized and privileged city, with its café culture and boutiques, can feel at times a little too gringo-geared and isolated from the rest of Guatemala for some travellers' tastes.

You could spend days exploring Antigua's incredible collection of colonial buildings. If you'd rather just visit the gems, make **Las Capuchinas**, **San Francisco**, **Santo Domingo** and **La Merced** your targets.

Brief history

In 1541, after a mudslide from Agua volcano buried the Spanish capital at **Ciudad Vieja**, Antigua was selected as a safer base. Here the new capital grew to achieve astounding prosperity. Religious orders competed in the construction of schools, churches, monasteries and hospitals, while bishops, merchants and landowners built grand town houses and palaces.

The city reached its peak in the middle of the eighteenth century, after the 1717 earthquake prompted an unprecedented building boom, and the population rose to around fifty thousand. By this stage Antigua was a genuinely impressive place, with a university, printing press and a newspaper. But in 1773 two devastating shocks reduced much of the city to rubble and a decision was made to abandon ship in favour of the modern capital. Fortunately, there were many who refused to leave and Antigua was never completely deserted.

Since then the city has been gradually repopulated, particularly in the last hundred years or so, with middle-class Guatemalans fleeing the capital and a large number of foreigners attracted to Antigua's relaxed and sophisticated atmosphere.

The fate of Antigua's ancient architecture has become a growing concern. Efforts are being made to preserve this unique legacy, especially after Antigua was listed as a UNESCO World Heritage Site in 1979. Local **conservation** laws are very strict (extensions to houses are virtually impossible) and traffic reduction initiatives have eased noise and environmental pollution.

FINDING YOUR FEET IN ANTIGUA

Antigua is laid out on a grid system, with **avenidas** running north–south, and **calles** east–west. Each street is numbered and has two halves, either a north and south (*norte/sur*) or an east and west (*oriente/poniente*), with the **Parque Central** regarded as the centre. But poor street lighting and the use of old street names ensure that most people get lost at some stage. If you get confused, remember that the Agua volcano, the one that hangs most immediately over the town, is to the south.

SEMANA SANTA IN ANTIGUA

Antigua's **Semana Santa** (Holy Week) celebrations are perhaps the most extravagant and impressive in all Latin America – a week of vigils, processions and pageants commemorating the most solemn week of the Christian year. The celebrations start with a procession on **Palm Sunday**, representing Christ's entry into Jerusalem, and continue through the week, climaxing on **Good Friday**. On Thursday night the streets are carpeted with meticulously drawn patterns of coloured sawdust, and on Friday morning a series of processions re-enacts the progress of Christ to the Cross. Setting out from the churches of **La Merced** and **Escuela de Cristo** and the village of **San Felipe** at around 8am, groups of penitents, clad in purple or white and wearing peaked hoods, carry images of Christ and the Cross on massive platforms, accompanied by solemn dirges played by local brass bands and clouds of incense. After 3pm, the hour of the Crucifixion, the penitents change into black.

It is a great honour to be involved in the procession but no easy task – the great cedar block carried from La Merced weighs some 3.5 tonnes and needs eighty men to lift it. Some of the images displayed date from the seventeenth century, and the procession itself is thought to have been introduced by Alvarado in the early years of the Conquest.

Check the exact details of events with the tourist office, which should be able to provide you with a map detailing the routes of the processions. During Holy Week virtually every hotel in Antigua is full, and the entire town is packed, but as enterprising locals rent out spare rooms there's always a bed to be had somewhere.

Parque Central

Antigua's focal point has always been its commanding central plaza, the **Parque Central**. In colonial times the plaza held a bustling market, which was cleared periodically for bullfights, military parades, floggings and public hangings. The calm of today's shady plaza, largely isolated from the city's traffic and replete with benches and well-tended flowering shrubs is relatively recent. Don't miss the risqué central fountain, its water jets gushing from the nipples of breast-squeezing mermaids.

La Catedral

Parque Central **Catedral** daily 8am–5pm • Free **Ruins** daily 9am–5pm • US$0.70

Of the structures surrounding the plaza, the **Catedral** is the most arresting, particularly at night when its intricate facade is evocatively illuminated. Built in 1670, the cathedral replaced a poorly built earlier edifice. The new construction was the most spectacular colonial building in Central America – it boasted an immense dome, five aisles, eighteen chapels and an altar inlaid with mother-of-pearl, ivory and silver – but the 1773 earthquake all but destroyed the building. Today only two of the original interior chapels remain; take a peek inside and you'll find several colonial sculptures.

To get some idea of the vast scale of the original building, check out the **ruins** to the rear where there's a mass of fallen masonry and rotting beams, broken arches and hefty pillars, cracked and moss-covered, the great original cupola now just a window to the sky. Buried beneath the floor are some of the great names of the Conquest, including Pedro de Alvarado, his wife, Beatriz de la Cueva, Bishop Marroquín and the historian Bernal Díaz del Castillo. At the very rear of what was once the nave, steps lead down to a burial vault that's regularly used for Maya religious ceremonies – an example of the coexistence of pagan and Catholic beliefs that's so characteristic of Guatemala.

Palacio de los Capitanes Generales

Parque Central • Closed for renovation

Along the entire south side of the Parque Central runs the elegant two-storey colonnaded facade of the **Palacio de los Capitanes Generales**. A structure was built here in 1558, but as usual the first version was destroyed by earthquakes. It was rebuilt in 1761, only to be damaged again in 1773 and finally restored along the lines of the present building. The

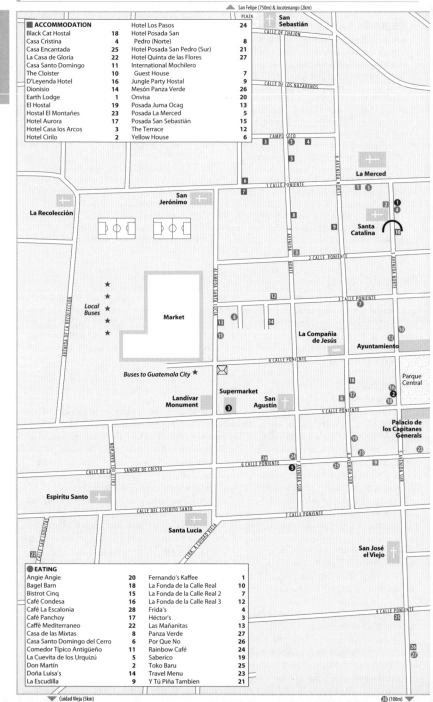

San Felipe (750m) & Jocotenango (2km)

ACCOMMODATION			
Black Cat Hostal	18	Hotel Los Pasos	24
Casa Cristina	4	Hotel Posada San Pedro (Norte)	8
Casa Encantada	25	Hotel Posada San Pedro (Sur)	21
La Casa de Gloria	22	Hotel Quinta de las Flores	27
Casa Santo Domingo	11	International Mochilero Guest House	7
The Cloister	10	Jungle Party Hostal	9
D'Leyenda Hotel	16	Mesón Panza Verde	26
Dionisio	14	Onvisa	20
Earth Lodge	1	Posada Juma Ocag	13
El Hostal	19	Posada La Merced	5
Hostal El Montañes	23	Posada San Sebastián	15
Hotel Aurora	17	The Terrace	12
Hotel Casa los Arcos	3	Yellow House	6
Hotel Cirilo	2		

PLAZA
San Sebastián
CALLE DE CHAJON
CALLE DE LOS NAZARENOS
CALLE DE LOS NAZARENOS
CAMPO SECO
La Merced
1 CALLE PONIENTE
San Jerónimo
La Recolección
Santa Catalina
Local Buses
Market
2 CALLE PONIENTE
3 CALLE PONIENTE
La Compañia de Jesús
Ayuntamiento
Buses to Guatemala City
4 CALLE PONIENTE
Landívar Monument
Supermarket
San Agustín
Parque Central
Palacio de los Capitanes Generals
5 CALLE PONIENTE
Espíritu Santo
CALLE DE LA SANGRE DE CRISTO
6 CALLE PONIENTE
CALLE DEL ESPIRITO SANTO
Santa Lucia
7 CALLE PONIENTE
San José el Viejo
8 CALLE PONIENTE

EATING			
Angie Angie	20	Fernando's Kaffee	1
Bagel Barn	18	La Fonda de la Calle Real	10
Bistrot Cinq	15	La Fonda de la Calle Real 2	7
Café Condesa	16	La Fonda de la Calle Real 3	12
Café La Escalonia	28	Frida's	4
Café Panchoy	17	Héctor's	3
Caffè Mediterraneo	22	Las Mañanitas	13
Casa de las Mixtas	8	Panza Verde	27
Casa Santo Domingo del Cerro	6	Por Que No	26
Comedor Típico Antigüeño	11	Rainbow Café	24
La Cuevita de los Urquizú	5	Saberico	19
Don Martín	2	Toko Baru	25
Doña Luisa's	14	Travel Menu	23
La Escudilla	9	Y Tú Piña Tambien	21

Cuidad Vieja (5km)

(100m)

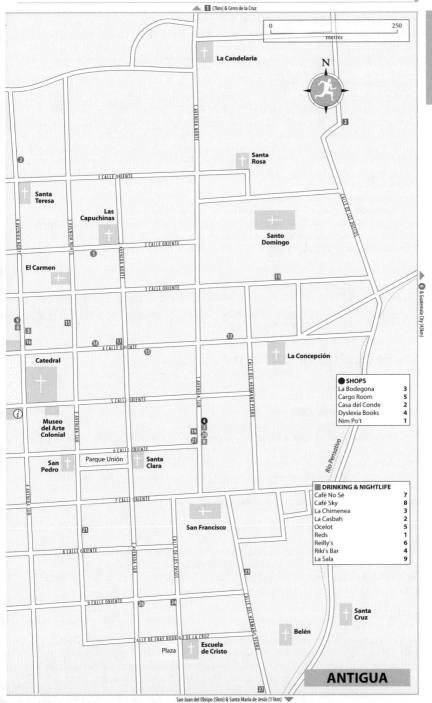

La Candelaria

Santa Rosa

Santa Teresa

Las Capuchinas

Santo Domingo

El Carmen

La Concepción

Catedral

Museo del Arte Colonial

San Pedro

Parque Unión

Santa Clara

San Francisco

San Juan del Obispo (5km) & Santa María de Jesús (11km)

Santa Cruz

Belén

Escuela de Cristo

Plaza

ANTIGUA

& Guatemala City (43km)

Río Pensativo

● **SHOPS**
La Bodegona	3
Cargo Room	5
Casa del Conde	2
Dyslexia Books	4
Nim Po't	1

■ **DRINKING & NIGHTLIFE**
Café No Sé	7
Café Sky	8
La Chimenea	3
La Casbah	2
Ocelot	5
Reds	1
Reilly's	6
Riki's Bar	4
La Sala	9

1

palace was home to the colonial rulers and also housed barracks, stables, the royal mint, law courts, tax offices, great ballrooms and, in recent years, various government offices. It's currently undergoing a major restoration, and its future role the subject of heated debate – many locals oppose one plan to turn part of the structure into a shopping arcade.

El Ayuntamiento

On the north side of the plaza is the **Ayuntamiento**, the city hall. Dating from 1740, its metre-thick walls balance the solid style of the Palacio de los Capitanes Generales. Unlike most others, this building survived earlier rumblings and wasn't damaged until the 1976 earthquake, although it has since been repaired. The city hall was abandoned in 1779 when the capital moved to Guatemala City, but it was later reclaimed for use by the city's administration. The Ayuntamiento also holds a couple of minor museums.

Museo de Santiago

El Ayuntamiento, Parque Central • Tues–Sun 9am–4pm • US$4

The **Museo de Santiago** houses a collection of colonial artefacts, including bits of pottery, a sword said to have been used by Alvarado, some traditional Maya weapons, portraits of stern-faced colonial figures and some paintings of warfare between the Spanish and the Maya. At the back of the museum is the old city jail.

Museo del Libro Antiguo

El Ayuntamiento, Parque Central • Tues–Sun 9am–4pm • US$4

Under the arches of the Ayuntamiento, the **Museo del Libro Antiguo** (Antique Book Museum) is located in the rooms that held the first printing press in Central America. A replica of the press is on display alongside some copies of the works produced on it.

Southeast of the Parque Central

The sights on this side of the city include the vast remains of the convent of Santa Clara and San Francisco.

Museo de Arte Colonial

5 C Oriente 5 • Tues–Fri 9am–4pm, Sat & Sun 9am–noon & 2–4pm • US$6.50

The **Museo de Arte Colonial** is based in the former site of the University of San Carlos Borromeo, an institution founded in 1676. At first only Castilians could study here, but later a broader range of people were admitted. The Moorish-style courtyard, deep-set windows and beautifully ornate cloisters are particularly pleasing. The museum contains a good collection of brooding religious art, sculpture, furniture and murals depicting life on the colonial campus.

San Pedro

Parque La Unión • Open for services

San Pedro church, at the western end of the pretty palm-tree-lined plaza of **Parque La Unión**, dates back to 1662 and also functioned as the city hospital until 1976. Reconstruction was completed in 1991 and the Baroque facade now has a polished perfection that's strangely incongruous in Antigua.

Santa Clara

2 Av Sur 27 • Daily 9am–5pm

At the eastern end of Parque La Union is the convent and church of **Santa Clara**, founded in 1699. This became a popular place for well-to-do young ladies to take the veil, as the hardships were none too hard, and the nuns had earned a reputation for their cooking by selling bread to the aristocracy. The original convent was destroyed in 1717,

as was the second in 1773, and little remains of the church except its ornate facade, which is floodlit at night.

Today you can amble about the ruins of the convent, which cover an entire city block, and pick out the original bread oven, cloisters and huge central courtyard. There's no information on site, but guides are available at the entrance.

In front of Santa Clara are the elegant arches of an impressive open-air *pila*, washing pools where local women gather to scrub, rinse and gossip.

Church of San Francisco

1 Av Sur **Church** 7am–7pm **Ruins and museum** 9am–4.30pm • US$0.70

One of the oldest churches in Antigua, **San Francisco** dates from 1579 and grew into a vast religious and cultural centre that included a school, a hospital, music rooms, a printing press and a monastery. The church originally boasted highly decorative mouldings and sculpture along its nave, but these were ruined by earthquakes. Inside the church is the tomb of **Hermano Pedro de Betancourt**, a Franciscan from the Canary Islands who is credited with powers of miraculous intervention by the faithful – Pope John Paul II made him Central America's first saint in 2002.

The **ruins** of the monastery are among the most impressive in Antigua, with colossal fallen arches and pillars lying strewn over extensive gardens and grassy verges. Don't miss the superb museum here and its astounding "hall of miracles" which contains dozens of crutches and walking sticks left behind by grateful pilgrims, who credit Hermano Pedro with divine healing, and the hundreds of plaques giving thanks for his services.

North of the Parque Central

The essential sights north and east of the centre include the terrific ruins of **Las Capuchinas** and **Santo Domingo**, which both have excellent museums, **La Merced** and the emblematic arch of **Santa Catalina**. Further out to the northeast along 1 Avenida Norte, the badly damaged ruins of the churches of **Santa Rosa**, **Candelaria** and **Nuestra Señora de los Dolores del Cerro** are of interest to ruined-church buffs only.

El Carmen

3 Av Norte • No public access to ruins

The hermitage of **El Carmen** was originally one of the city's great churches, dating back to 1638, but the top half of the facade collapsed in 1976 and today the complex lies in ruins. Today there's a popular artesanias market next to the remains of the church.

Las Capuchinas

2 C Oriente & 2 Av Norte • Ruins Daily 9am–5pm; museum 9am–4pm, Sat & Sun 9am–1pm • US$5 (including museum)

The largest of the city's convents, **Las Capuchinas** are some of the best-preserved but least understood ruins in Antigua. The Capuchin order was the most rigorous in Antigua. Numbers were restricted to 25, with nuns sleeping on wooden beds with straw pillows. Once they had entered the convent it's thought the women were not allowed any visual contact with the outside world; food was passed to them by means of a turntable and they could only speak to visitors through a grille.

The ruins

The convent ruins are the most beautiful in Antigua, with fountains, courtyards and massive earthquake-proof pillars. The tower or "retreat" is the most unusual feature, with eighteen tiny cells set into the walls of its top floor, each having its own independent sewage system. Two of the cells have been returned to their original condition to demonstrate the extreme austerity of the nuns' lives. The lower floor, which functioned as a meat storage room, is dominated by a massive pillar that supports the structure above. The exterior of this architectural curiosity is also interesting, ringed with small stone recesses that represent the Stations of the Cross.

Museum
This new addition, occupying two upper wings of the main courtyard, beautifully showcases some terrific religious art and ecclesiastical artefacts including colonial-era sculptures and portraits. There are information panels in Spanish, English and Chinese.

Santo Domingo
3 C Oriente • Museums all Mon–Sat 9am–6pm, Sun 11.45am–6pm • US$5 to entire complex

Once forming the largest monastery in Antigua, the immense complex of **Santo Domingo** is today largely occupied by a luxury hotel *Casa Santo Domingo* (see p.83). Substantial parts of the gorgeous grounds of the hotel have been sensitively converted into a cultural zone, which includes several small **museums**, the monastery ruins, various subterranean crypts, artisans' workshops, exhibitions of local textiles and crafts, a re-creation of an early pharmacy and an art exhibition space. Together they form a rewarding, highly atmospheric sight well worth half a day of your time.

Museo Colonial and crypts
The **Museo Colonial** harbours an exquisite array of religious artefacts and treasures from the Spanish era including a breathtaking collection of golden crowns, silver lecterns and chalices and sculptures of angels, saints and cherubs. You can then tour the monastery's four **crypts**, including the Calvary crypt which has an impressive mural of Christ and the crucifixion. The crypts are dotted around the ruined remains of Santo Domingo's 68m-long church.

Archeological Museum
Inside the **Archeological Museum** are some impressive Maya ceramics, including intricately painted drinking vessels, funerary urns and incense burners in an exhibition room that has walls painted with scenes from the famous murals of Bonampak.

Museo Arte de Precolombino y Vidrio Moderno
This **museum of Maya art and modern glass** has exhibitions of Maya artefacts and ceramics together with contemporary glassworks that are supposed to have been influenced by them – a slightly bizarre concept.

La Merced
1 C Poniente • Church open for services • Gardens 8am–5.45pm • US$0.75

The church of **La Merced** boasts one of the most intricate and impressive facades in the city. It has been beautifully restored, painted mustard yellow and white, and crammed with plaster moulding of interlaced patterns. Look closely and you'll see the outline of a corn cob, a design not normally seen on Catholic churches and probably added by the original Maya labourers. The church is still in use, but the cloisters and gardens lie ruined, exposed to the sky. In the centre of one of the courtyards is a monumental tiered fountain with four pools, which were used by the Mercedarian brothers for breeding fish.

Santa Teresa
4 Av Norte & 1 C • No public access

The ruined church and convent of **Santa Teresa** was founded by a Peruvian philanthropist for a group of Carmelite nuns from Lima. Until recently part of the structure served as the city jail.

1

Santa Catalina arch

One of Antigua's most emblematic structures, the **arch of Santa Catalina** is all that remains of the original convent founded here in 1609. By 1697 it had reached maximum capacity with 110 nuns and six novices, and the arch was built so that they could walk between the two halves of the establishment without being exposed to the outside world. Restored in the nineteenth century, it's now a favoured spot for photographers as the view to the Volcán de Agua is unobstructed from here.

Cerro de la Cruz

Northeast of Antigua, the **Cerro de la Cruz**, a hilltop with a giant cross, has commanding views of the city and Volcán de Agua. It was something of a mugging hot-spot for years but an increased police presence has meant it's now considered safe. Contact the tourist police (see p.81) and they'll run you up here and back.

West of the Parque Central

The last of the major ruins lie west of the plaza, near the bus station. This is the busiest part of town, the streets humming with traffic and people during the day.

La Compañia de Jesús

6 Av Norte • Mon–Thurs 10am–5pm, Fri 10am–2pm and events • ☎ 7832 1276, ⓦ www.aecid-cf.org.gt

This cultural complex was an educational establishment and church operated by the Jesuits until King Carlos III of Spain, feeling threatened by their growing power, expelled them from the colonies in 1767. Its cloisters and premises have been beautifully renovated by the Spanish government and it now host art exhibitions, lectures and events and is home to an excellent library and courtyard café. The church remains in ruins.

San Jerónimo

C de La Recolección • Daily 9am–5pm • US$5

The spectacular ruined remains of **San Jerónimo**, a school built in 1739 which later functioned as a customs house, boast well-kept gardens woven between huge blocks of fallen masonry and crumbling walls. Parts of the two-storey cloisters and kitchen have been restored, and classical music concerts are regularly performed here.

La Recolección

C de La Recolección • Daily 9am–5pm • US$5

Behind San Jerónimo, a cobbled road leads to the even larger, and more chaotic ruin of **La Recolección**, where the shell of the colossal original church is piled high with the remains of its roof and walls. Friars started building a monastery and church here in 1701 but only months after its completion in 1717, the complex was brought to the ground by a huge earthquake. This second version was destroyed in 1773 and has been steadily decaying ever since.

ARRIVAL AND DEPARTURE — ANTIGUA

By bus The main bus terminal is beside the market. Because of its position off the Interamericana, few bus routes originate in Antigua. Very few travellers now take local buses to Guatemala City as they use an inconvenient terminal in the capital located in Zona 3, 1.5km west of the centre (and also due to security concerns). Shuttle minibuses drop you off at your destination, and represent a more expensive but safer option. If you're heading to the western highlands catch the first bus to Chimaltenango and transfer there. The following buses all leave from the main terminal, except the Panajachel bus and Hedman Alas (ⓦ hedmanalas.com) buses to Copán, Honduras (2 daily, US$65) which leave from *Hotel de Don Rodrigo*, 5 Av Norte 17.

Destinations Chimaltenango (every 20min; 40min); Ciudad Vieja (every 20min; 15min); Escuintla (hourly; 1hr 15min); Guatemala City (every 15min; 1hr–1hr 30min); Panajachel, from 4 Poniente 34 (7am daily; 2hr 30min); San Antonio Aguas Calientes (every 30min; 20min); San Juan Del Obispo (every 30min; 15min); Santa María de Jesús (every 30min; 30min).

By shuttle bus Minibuses can be booked through most travel agents, including Atitrans and Adrenalina Tours (see below). Shuttles cost typically triple the price of public buses, but they are much more comfortable and a bit quicker.
Destinations Chichicastenango (2 daily; 2hr 30min); Cobán (daily; 6hr); Copán, Honduras (daily; 6hr); Guatemala City (8 daily; 1hr–1hr 30min); Lanquín (daily; 8hr 30min); Monterrico (8am daily; 2hr 30min); Panajachel (2–3 daily; 2hr 30min); Quetzaltenango (daily; 3hr 45min), San Cristóbal de las Casas, Mexico (daily; 11hr).

GETTING AROUND

By taxi On the east side of the plaza, or call ☎ 7832 0479. A short trip is about US$3. For a female cab driver, call Chiqui on ☎ 5715 5720.
By tuk tuk Rides cost US$1.30.
Bike rental Guatemala Ventures and Old Town Outfitters (see below) both rent quality mountain bikes for US$20 a day.

Car and motorbike rental Tabarini, 6 Av Sur 22 (☎ 7832 8107, ⓦ tabarini.com), has cars from around US$35/day and 4WD from US$60. CA Tours, 6 C Oriente 14 (☎ 7832 9638, ⓦ catours.co.uk), rent scooters for US$36/day or trail bikes from US$50; contact them about motorbike tours around Guatemala.

INFORMATION

Tourist information Inguat, 2 C Oriente 11 (Mon–Fri 8am–5pm, Sat & Sun 9am–5pm; ☎ 7832 5682, ⓔ info -antigua@inguat.gob.gt). Staff are pretty clued up here, English is spoken and you can pick up a free city map and get advice about monuments.
Tourist police Rancho Nimajay, behind the market ☎ 7968 5303. They will escort visitors up to Cerro de la Cruz. Asistur (☎ 5978 3586) deals with victims of crime and will also escort tourists around Antigua.

Guidebooks Two excellent guidebooks devoted to Antigua are *Antigua Guatemala: The City and Its Heritage* by Elizabeth Bell and *Antigua for You*, by Barbara Balchin De Koose. Both are available from bookshops in town (see p.86).
Notice boards Notice boards in various popular tourist venues advertise everything from salsa classes to apartments and private language tuition. Check those in popular hostels like the *Black Cat* and *El Hostal*, *Doña Luisa's* restaurant and the *Rainbow Café*.

TOURS AND TRAVEL AGENTS

Although guides are often in the plaza hustling for business, it's better to take a **city tour** (see below).

TRAVEL AGENTS

Adrenalina Tours 5 Av Norte 31 ☎ 7832 1108, ⓦ adrenalina tours.com. Good for shuttle buses and organized tours over the western highlands.
Adventure Travel Center Viareal, 5 Av Norte 25B ☎ 7832 0162, ⓦ adventravelguatemala.com. Offers tours to Tikal and across Guatemala, volcano hikes and fishing trips.
Atitrans 6 Av Sur 8 ☎ 7832 3371, ⓦ atitrans.net. This agency runs shuttle bus connections all over Guatemala and has a good reputation for reliability.
Viajes Tivoli 4 C Oriente 10 ☎ 7832 4274, ⓔ antigua @tivoli.com.gt. A recommended all-rounder, contact them for flights and tours of the western highlands or Tikal.

CITY TOURS

Excellent walking tours (US$20) are led by historian Elizabeth Bell, based at *Hotel Casa Santo Domingo* (☎ 7832 5821, ⓦ antiguatours.net).

ADVENTURE SPORTS AND ACTIVITIES

Guatemala Ventures 1 Av Sur 15 ☎ 7832 3383, ⓦ guatemalaventures.com. Has an excellent range of biking trips (from US$25 for a few hours exploring Antigua's villages) to hardcore expeditions, plus bike rental. Horseriding, caving, birdwatching and volcano climbs are also offered.
Old Town Outfitters 5 Av Sur 12 ☎ 5399 0440, ⓦ bike guatemala.com. Runs volcano hikes including Acatenango (US$69), mountain-bike excursions (half-day US$45), rock-climbing trips for all levels, sea kayaking (2 days US$219) and has tent, sleeping bag, pack and bike rental.
Ox Expeditions 1 Av Sur 4B ☎ 7832 0074, ⓦ guatemala volcano.com. Very well set up for volcano hiking. All the main peaks around Antigua are offered, and their Pacaya hikes (US$59–69) offer an unbeatable view of the peak.
Ravenscroft Stables 2 Av Sur 3 ☎ 7832 6229. Horseriding offered in the village of San Juan del Obispo.

TOURIST CRIME IN ANTIGUA

Visitors to Antigua should be aware that crimes against **tourists** – mainly street robberies – do occur infrequently. Pickpockets target the market. Tourist police do patrol the streets but it's still wise to follow the usual **precautions**: avoid quiet areas after dark and take a taxi to get home after 10pm. If you want to visit **viewing spots**, such as the Cerro de la Cruz, join one of the trips organized by the tourist police.

1

VOLCANO TOURS FROM ANTIGUA

Volcán de Pacaya (see p.70) near Guatemala City is a spectacular and very active volcano that spews towering plumes of smoke and brilliant orange sludge – though such fire 'n' brimstone shows only happen sporadically. Gran Jaguar Tours (see p.70) offers basic, inexpensive trips for US$5–7/head, while adventure tour specialists (see p.81) charge from US$50 for a day hike.

Other cones to climb include volcanoes **Agua** (see p.90) and **Acatenango** (see p.88), the toughest climb in this region, which gives a great view of the highly active neighbouring cone of **Fuego**.

ACCOMMODATION

Antigua has an excellent selection of hotels and hostels, and whether you're after a room in a colonial mansion or a bed in a dorm, you shouldn't have a problem, except around **Holy Week** (see p.73) when the place is packed and prices soar. If you're a family, consider renting a house, which can work out to be very reasonable, Guatemala Vacation Rental (☎ 5502 5353, ⊛ guatemala-vacation-rentals.com) has some great houses a short walk from the centre. Another excellent option is a delightful rural guesthouse 7km outside of Antigua, the *Earth Lodge* (see p.84)

BUDGET

Black Cat Hostal 6 Av Norte 1A ☎ 7832 1229, ⊛ blackcathostels.net. One of the first ports of call for young backpackers, this party-minded hostel has decent dorms (some ensuite). There's also a movie room, internet and wi-fi and the breakfast (available for US$2.50 extra) is a satisfying gut buster. Dorms U̲S̲$̲6̲, doubles U̲S̲$̲2̲2̲

La Casa de Gloria C San Luquitas 3B ☎ 4374 1391, ⊖ lacasadegloria@yahoo.com. Sociable guesthouse run by a welcoming young Guatemalan (a salsa and Spanish teacher) with five private rooms and a kitchen. It's a great place for more of a local experience and about a 10min walk southwest of the Parque Central. U̲S̲$̲7̲

Dionisio 3 C Poniente ☎ 5644 9486, ⊛ hoteldionisio antigua.com. Offering a quiet location and great value *Dionisio* has spacious dorms and rooms with good mattresses and lockers. You'll find free wi-fi and coffee, a kitchen, friendly staff, a sunny terrace and a travel agency here too. Dorms U̲S̲$̲6̲, doubles U̲S̲$̲2̲0̲

★ **El Hostal** 1 Av Sur 8 ☎ 7832 0442, ⊛ elhostal .hostel.com. A highly attractive and well-managed hostel with inviting rooms and dorms that have space and style, all with lockers. The shower facilities (with reliable hot water) are spotless, there's a great central courtyard for chilling and socializing, a juice bar and water refills cost just Q1. Rates include breakfast, and it's right by one of the best bars in town: *Café No Sé*. Dorms U̲S̲$̲1̲0̲, doubles U̲S̲$̲3̲1̲

International Mochilero Guesthouse 1 C Poniente 33 ☎ 7832 0520, ⊛ internacionalmochilero.com. This place has cheap rates, especially for private rooms, as well as free wi-fi and a garden. Check out the old musical instruments in the hall, including a marimba. Dorms U̲S̲$̲7̲.̲5̲0̲, doubles U̲S̲$̲1̲8̲

Jungle Party Hostal 6 Av Norte 20 ☎ 7832 0463, ⊛ junglepartyhostal.com. Recently refurbished, this

huge sociable hostel attracts a young backpacking crowd. Offers three "classes" of dorm accommodation – the basic option is a mattress in a room with 21 beds. Bathroom facilities could be improved. The bar/café has a popular happy hour. A good breakfast is included but taxes are not. Dorms U̲S̲$̲6̲–̲1̲1̲

Onvisa 6 C Poniente 40 ☎ 5909 0160, ⊖ onvisatravel @hotmail.com. New place with very cheap, clean and fairly spacious dorms (most with three or four beds) set around a pretty patio. The private rooms, with antique floor tiles and cable TV, are great value too. A guests' kitchen and free internet completes the picture. Dorms U̲S̲$̲5̲.̲5̲0̲, doubles U̲S̲$̲1̲7̲

★ **Posada Juma Ocag** Av Alameda Santa Lucía Norte 13 ☎ 7832 3109, ⊛ posadajumaocag.com. A very well-run little hotel owned by a hospitable family. You'll find eight immaculately presented, if smallish rooms decorated with local fabrics; all have good beds, a wardrobe or clothes rack, private bathroom and reading lights. There's a small patio ideal for relaxing, free drinking water, wi-fi and a laundry room. Book well ahead. U̲S̲$̲2̲1̲

The Terrace 3 C Poniente 24B ☎ 7832 3463, ⊛ terracehostel.com. Sociable new hostel run by helpful staff that has an amazing roof terrace, the perfect spot for barbecues (Wed and Sun) and a glass of ale (microbrew beers are sold). Dorms U̲S̲$̲8̲.̲5̲0̲, doubles U̲S̲$̲2̲6̲

Yellow House 1 C Poniente 24 ☎ 7832 6646, ⊖ yellowhouseantigua@hotmail.com. This welcoming solar-powered hostel is a good choice, boasting a lovely rustic-style roof terrace with hammocks, greenery and views and four bathrooms. Accommodation varies: the three-bed dorms are the best value, while the cabin-like upstairs rooms are lovely (no. 10 has its own little private terrace). Rates include use of kitchen, internet and a good buffet breakfast. Dorms U̲S̲$̲7̲.̲5̲0̲, doubles U̲S̲$̲2̲1̲

MODERATE

★ **Casa Cristina** Callejón Camposeco 3A ☎ 7832 0623, 🖥 casa-cristina.com. This well-run little hotel is superb value for money, with ten very clean and attractive rooms, all with private hot-water bathrooms and some with fridges. They do vary quite a bit, those on the upper floors enjoy more natural light and privacy. There's a rooftop sun terrace, free coffee, drinking water, wi-fi and internet access. It's a 10min walk north of the plaza. **US$27**

D'Leyenda Hotel 4 Av Norte 1 ☎ 7832 6194, 🖥 dleyendahotel.com. Smart new six-room hotel, half a block from the plaza, with high comfort and service levels and a great roof terrace for your complimentary breakfast. **US$80**

Hostal El Montañes C del Hermano Pedro 19 B ☎ 7832 8804, 🖥 hostalelmontanesantigua.com. With beautifully presented rooms, most with private bathroom, this welcoming B&B has character and comfort. There's an elegant guests' lounge, with a piano and TV/DVD player and a pretty front garden. Breakfast is filling, and there's internet access in the lobby. **US$49**

Hotel Aurora 4 C Oriente 16 ☎ 7832 0217, 🖥 hotel auroraantigua.com. Antigua's original hotel occupies a fine colonial building with seventeen spacious rooms grouped around a lovely grassy courtyard and fountain. It's a little old-fashioned, but comfortable and very centrally located. Free wi-fi, and breakfast is included. **US$76**

Hotel Casa los Arcos Callejón Camposeco ☎ 7832 7813, 🖥 casa_losarcos@hotmail.com. With a Guatemalan family atmosphere, this guesthouse is excellent value. Its eleven modern rooms (nine are ensuite) in the compound are spotless, spacious and come with *típica* bedspreads and cable TV. It's a great deal for single travellers or couples who want some privacy. **US$28**

Hotel Posada San Pedro 7 Av Norte 29 ☎ 7832 0718, 🖥 posadasanpedro.net. A fine colonial residence, with immaculate, spacious rooms, all with hand-carved wooden furniture and private bathrooms (with tubs). Accommodation is grouped around two garden patios, and there's a guests' kitchen, roof terrace and it's located on a quiet street. The hotel's second branch, at 3 Av Sur 15 (☎ 7832 3594) is fine, but not as attractive. Both locations **US$44**

Hotel Quinta de las Flores C del Hermano Pedro 6 ☎ 7832 3721, 🖥 quintadelasflores.com. This hotel's spectacular garden – with swimming pool and children's play area – is its real trump card, a wonderful oasis bursting with rare plants, shrubs and trees. The rooms and *casitas* (each sleeping five, with two bedrooms and kitchen) are all attractively decorated, and there's also a restaurant. It's a 10min walk south of town. **US$75**

Posada La Merced 7 Av Norte 43A ☎ 7832 3197, 🖥 merced-landivar.com. Well-run hotel with 23 cheerful rooms (those at the rear are more attractive and overlook a pretty garden patio). There's a well-equipped guests' kitchen, helpful staff and wi-fi. **US$40**

Posada San Sebastián 3 Av Norte 4 ☎ 7832 2621, 🖥 snsebast@hotmail.com. Just a block or so from the Parque Central, this tasteful B&B has nine rooms, each decorated with antiques and artwork. There's also a roof terrace, bar, kitchen and complimentary breakfast. The owners look after their guests well here. **US$68**

EXPENSIVE

Casa Encantada 9 C Poniente 1 ☎ 7832 7903, 🖥 casa encantada-antigua.com. Boutique-style hotel with ten immaculate rooms, most with four-poster beds, and all with delightful bathrooms. There's a small pool, a rooftop bar and full breakfast is included. **US$118**

Casa Santo Domingo 3 C Oriente 28 ☎ 7832 0140, 🖥 casasantodomingo.com.gt. This converted colonial-era convent is a historic and memorable place to stay with corridors bedecked in ecclesiastical art and the grounds (with two pools and a museum) are simply stunning, with ruins illuminated at night by hundreds of candles. However, despite the evocative surrounds there can be a slightly impersonal feel to the place: it's popular with tour groups and wedding parties and many rooms lack a real "wow" factor given the rack rates asked. **US$280**

The Cloister 5 Av Norte 23 ☎ 7832 0712, 🖥 thecloister .com. A real retreat from the streets, this elegant B&B has seven suite-sized rooms around an exquisite tropical garden. The well-stocked private library and reading room, wi-fi and a handy location (almost under Antigua's famous arch) make it excellent value. **US$135**.

★ **Hotel Cirilo** C de los Duelos 11 ☎ 7832 6650, 🖥 hotelcirilo.com. A wonderful hotel, sensitively constructed around the ruined remains of a colonial chapel, with elegant suite-sized rooms that represent exceptional value. The solar-heated lap pool set in idyllic gardens, guests' lounge, café-restaurant and overall air of calm make *Cirilo* a great place to relax. It's about a 15min walk from the centre. **US$100**

Hotel Los Pasos 9 C Oriente 19 ☎ 7832 5252, 🖥 hotellospasos.com. A classy hotel with very inviting accommodation, tastefully presented with exposed stone walls and Maya textiles and some with jacuzzi baths. The gardens and patios are equally attractive, and there's a wonderful beamed restaurant complete with a stately fireplace where your breakfast is served. Rooms **US$104**, suites **US$114**

Mesón Panza Verde 5 Av Sur 19 ☎ 7832 2925, 🖥 panzaverde.com. Antigua's original boutique hotel, with rooms and suites spread over two colonial-style buildings. It's also home to a top-drawer restaurant and an art gallery, while other perks include a lap pool and a healthy complimentary breakfast. Rooms **US$122**, suites **US$196**

1

AROUND ANTIGUA

★ **Earth Lodge** 7km northeast of Antigua ☎5664 0713, ⓦearthlodgeguatemala.com. This spectacular rural retreat high in the hills above Jocotenango has sweeping views of the Panchoy valley and its volcanoes.

Accommodation options include A-frame cabañas, a wood-cabin dorm and tree houses. Wholesome meals are served, and there's a Maya-style sauna and good walking trails. Consult their website for transport information (you can arrange a pick-up from Antigua). Dorm US$5, cabins US$22

EATING

Befitting its decidedly cosmopolitan nature, Antigua has Guatemala's most varied and exciting dining scene with most types of **global cuisine** represented. It's possible to snack well for a few bucks or dine in style for around US$20 a head, and round it off with a perfect espresso or latte. The only thing hard to come by can be authentic Guatemalan **comida típica** – which will be a relief if you've been subsisting on eggs and beans in the mountains.

CAFÉS

Bagel Barn 5 C Poniente 2 & 14 ☎7832 6935. Now with two locations on 5 C, these cafés serve tasty, if a little pricey, filled bagels, including breakfast and combo options. Free wi-fi, and films are also shown here twice daily. Daily 6am–10pm.

Café Condesa West side of Parque Central – go through the Casa del Conde bookshop ☎7832 0038. Café-restaurant with a refined colonial setting, including a cobbled patio and gurgling fountain, that offers excellent (if expensive) breakfasts and lunches, cakes and snacks. Sun–Thurs 7.30am–8pm, Fri & Sat until 9pm.

Café La Escalonia 5 Av Sur 36 C ☎7832 7874, ⓦla escalonia.com. About 800m south of the parque, this lovely café (located inside a plant nursery) is a really peaceful retreat and much of the food is organic. Tuck into healthy breakfasts, *pan de hierbas* sandwiches with salsa dips, pies and salads. They also sell beer and wine. Daily 8am–7pm.

Doña Luisa's 4 C Oriente 12 ☎7832 2578. Still going strong, this is one of Antigua's most renowned café restaurants, set in a historic colonial mansion. A straight-forward menu of sandwiches, burgers and salads, but the in-house bakery (there's a shop next door) really is the best in town. Daily 7.30am–9.30pm.

Fernando's Kaffee 7 Av Norte 43 ☎7832 6953, ⓦfernandoskaffee.com. Fernando, the very hospitable English-speaking Guatemalan owner here, is a complete coffee bean-head who selects and roasts (on the premises) his own arabica coffee from small estates; he also makes gourmet chocolate. Enjoy your breakfast, sandwich or lunch in the pretty courtyard at the back. Daily 8am–8pm.

Por Que No 2 Av Sur & 9 C Oriente. Boho hole-in-wall complete with wacky decor run by a friendly North American and his local wife. Pete cooks a dish or two (like home-made pizza) daily; also good for a casual beer or juice. Daily 10am–9pm.

Rainbow Café 7 Av Sur 8 ☎7832 1919, ⓦrainbow cafeantigua.com. Courtyard café-restaurant that offers a tempting choice of imaginative salads, Mexican and vegetarian dishes with prompt service and tasty grub guaranteed. Prices have crept up recently but there's

always a set lunch for US$4. Hosts live events (music, political and social lectures) most nights. Also home to a good secondhand bookshop. Daily 7am–11pm.

Saberico 6A Av Sur 7 ☎7832 0648, ⓦsaberico.com.gt. Deli-café-restaurant where can you munch away in a lovely walled garden at the rear, which has plenty of shade. On the menu you'll find pancakes, pies, salads, omelettes, pasta and sandwiches with most items US$4–6. Mon & Wed 8am–7pm, Tues 8am–4pm, Thurs–Sat 8am–9pm, Sun 9am–4pm.

Y Tú Piña Tambien 1 Av Sur 10B ⓦytupinatambien .com. Hip café popular with a creative crowd who lap up the near-legendary blended fruit juices (or choose your own mix). Also scores for wraps, waffles, baguettes, omelettes, salads and soups. Free wi-fi, and always an art or photography exhibition to take in on the walls. Mon–Fri 7am–8pm, Sat–Sun 8am–8pm.

RESTAURANTS

★ **Angie Angie** 1 Av Sur 11A ☎7832 3352. A terrific new place with superb Argentinean-style grilled meats, including prime cuts like *entraña*, very flavoursome salads and fresh pasta (try the ravioli in spinach, ricotta and pine nut sauce). Breakfast, sandwiches and light lunches are also served. Pass through the deli section and you'll find a lovely rear garden setting for your meal, with tables set around a log fire at night. Daily 8am–10pm.

★ **Bistrot Cinq** 4 C Oriente 7 ☎7832 5510, ⓦbistrotcinq.com. Delivers on every level, with highly accomplished, technically adept French cooking, atmospheric decor that combines modern and colonial influences and professional, informed service. The menu is short and to the point, with classics (most US$10–16) like *filet mignon au poivre*, and always some excellent daily specials and fish dishes. Daily noon–10.30pm.

Café Panchoy 6 Av Norte 1B ☎7832 6571. Dependable cooking with a Guatemalan flavour, with tables set around an open kitchen. Plenty of grilled meats, plus tacos and local dishes like *chiles rellenos*. Famous for its *horchata* and they serve good margaritas too. Wed–Mon noon–10pm.

Caffè Mediterraneo 6 C Poniente 6A ☎7832 7180. Italian that has enjoyed a good reputation for years with locals for its authentic fresh pasta, *bruschette* and grilled meats. There's always a daily special. Wed–Sat noon–3pm & 6–10pm, Sun noon–4.30pm & 7–9pm.

Casa de las Mixtas 1 Callejón, off 3 C Poniente. For comedor cooking this bright little place is inexpensive and hard to beat. Very extensive breakfast options. Daily 8am–4pm.

Casa Santo Domingo del Cerro ☎7832 3520. On a hilltop directly above Antigua this spectacularly situated restaurant and cultural space (operated by the hotel *Casa Santo Domingo*) makes an extraordinary setting for a meal with the colonial city rolled out below you. After your meal explore the gardens and contemporary sculptures. Signature dishes include pumpkin ravioli and steaks. Connected to Antigua by regular minibuses from the hotel. Tues–Sun 8am–10pm, Mon noon–10pm.

Comedor Típico Antigüeño Alameda Santa Lucía Sur 5 ☎7832 5995. Right opposite the market this huge, down-to-earth place offers reasonably priced Guatemalan grub. The US$3 set lunches include favourites like *pepián* and *carne guisada* which all include a soup starter. Daily 7.30am–6pm.

La Cuevita de los Urquizú 2 C Oriente 9 ☎7832 2493. A good place to try some typical Guatemalan dishes – choose from the bubbling pots at the restaurant entrance. Around US$6/head, including a drink and sweet. Daily 9am–7pm.

Don Martín 4 Av Norte 27 ☎7832 1063. Smallish place that serves up creative, appetizing Guatemalan food-with-a-twist (plus an Italian and French dish or two). The classically trained chef's moderately priced menu includes *pepián* (spicy meat stew), *lomito* and pasta. Tues–Sat 6–10pm & Sun 1–9pm.

La Escudilla 4 Av Norte 4 ☎7832 1327. Given the gorgeous colonial surrounds, the prices at this courtyard restaurant are very moderate. Offers a choice of breakfasts (try the "Kill Hangover" for US$4), Mexican and European dishes. The lunch deal (US$3.50) is a serious bargain. Also home to *Riki's Bar* (see p.86) which is ideal for an aperitif. Daily 8am–10pm.

La Fonda de la Calle Real 3 C Poniente 7 ☎7832 0507, ⓦlafondadelacallereal.com. For flavoursome, authentic Guatemalan food this long-running, moderately priced restaurant is a fine choice, particularly for meat dishes.

Specialities include *caldo real* (chicken soup with rice, spices and lemon). Also two additional branches at 5 Av Norte 5 and 5 Av Norte 12. Daily noon–10pm.

Frida's 5 Av Norte 29 ☎7832 1296. A long-running Mexican restaurant with a dining room festooned with 1950s Americana. There's a familiar line-up of dishes including *flautas*, tacos, fajitas and the like, try the enchiladas with a *mole poblano* sauce for something a little more unusual. Daily noon–10pm.

Héctor's 1 C Poniente 9A ☎7832 9827. One of Antigua's hottest restaurants, this cramped, atmospheric *bistrot*-style place is packed every night with diners eating in every available nook and cranny (including on the bar) such is its popularity. It's easy to understand why, as the chef-patron cooks up a storm in his open kitchen with French classics like *boeuf bourguignon* (US$10) and grilled breast of duck and the wines are well selected. Around US$25 a head. No reservations, so arrive early (before 6.30pm), dine at lunchtime or be prepared to wait. Mon–Wed 6–10pm, Thurs–Sun 12.30–10pm.

Las Mañanitas 4 C Oriente 28 ☎7832 6817. Owned by a friendly Oaxacan couple, this excellent place is located on the edge of town. Cheap and highly authentic southern Mexican dishes, using some terrific *mole* and salsa sauces. You can snack on a few tacos, tamales or tostadas for around US$2.50, or get stuck into the mains (from US$4). Wine is available by the glass. Wed–Mon 8am–10pm.

Panza Verde 5 Av Sur 19 ☎7832 2925. Highly rated, stylish and consistently good European-style restaurant with a well-chosen menu of fish (like *snook marocaine*) and meat mains and desserts to die for. The setting is elegant, too, with tables grouped around a delightful courtyard garden. Expensive, around US$40 a head. Mon–Sat noon–3pm & 7–10pm, Sun 10am–4pm.

Toko Baru 6 C Poniente 21 ☎4079 2092. Tiny, friendly place with just three tables that offers a pretty authentic stab at Middle Eastern favourites like falafel and sharma kebabs, plus Asian dishes including chicken tikka, satay and spring rolls. Tues–Sat noon–9 pm, Sun 1–8pm.

Travel Menu 6 C Poniente 14. This small Dutch-owned candlelit place has very moderate prices and a simple menu catering to both veggies and carne-lovers; try a *plato típico* (US$5), nachos with guacamole or a sandwich. House wine is US$2.25 a glass. Wed–Sat noon–10pm.

DRINKING AND NIGHTLIFE

Antigua has a lively drinking scene with everything from dive bars and Irish pubs to spectacular places in colonial premises, so whether you're after a cold Gallo beer or a glass of Absinthe, it's here. Club culture is pretty limited with only two venues and the nationwide 1am curfew draws the action to a premature end. If you want to learn to dance **salsa**, the teacher Gloria Villata is highly recommended; contact her on ☎4374 1391 or ⓔsalsacongloria@yahoo.com.

BARS

★ **Café No Sé** 1 Av Norte 11C ⓦcafenose.com. Great for conversation, this mighty fine place has grown from a

dive bar into the liveliest joint in town. It's not a touristy hangout as it's located a 10min walk from the parque, but draws a good mix of characters – Guatemalan bohemian

1

types, gringo wasters and wanabes, travellers and boozy expats – plus the odd stray dog. There's good acoustic music virtually nightly, comfort food and a (semi-) secret *mescal* bar serving the house brand: Ilegal. Daily 1pm–1am.

Café Sky 1 Av Sur ☎ 7832 7300. Offers terrific views of Antigua's volcanic surrounds from the upper deck of a three-storey building (there's a restaurant below). With a full cocktail list, this is the perfect place for a sundowner. Daily 8am–11pm.

La Chimenea 7 Av Norte & 2 C Poniente ☎ 7832 4805. This long-running bar has been renovated and now serves food too. It's a good bet for happy hour when there are cocktail specials. Mon–Sat 11am–1am.

Ocelot 4 Av Norte 3 ☎ 5658 9028. Probably Antigua's classiest bar, *Ocelot* is a great place for a relaxed drink with elegant furnishings, gingham floor tiles, seductive cocktails and live music most nights. Tasty tapas are served and there's a quiz (trivia) on Sun evenings. Daily 12.15pm–1am.

Reds 1 C Poniente 3. Large British-owned sports bar with pool tables and a dart board, good beer selection and a pub grub menu that takes in local, Mexican, Indian curries and English comfort food like shepherd's pie. Daily 10am–midnight.

Reilly's (Café 2000) 6 Av Norte 2. Antigua's Irish bar has recently moved premises but the winning formula is unchanged: a gregarious atmosphere, free-flowing beer and lots of drinks promotions. Everyone calls it *Reilly's* but due to silly local laws the sign says *Café 2000*. Daily noon–1am.

Riki's Bar 4 Av Norte 4. Small, stylish place that's a great bet for a relaxed drink due to its excellent location inside *La Escudilla* and extended happy hour (7–9pm). Musically things are often quite interesting with funk, jazz and lounge on the hi-fi. Daily noon–1am.

CLUBS AND LIVE MUSIC

La Casbah 5 Av Norte 30 ☎ 7832 2640, ⊚ lacasbah antigua.com. The only real club in town, and a pretty decent one, with large, airy premises, a terrace and views over the floodlit ruins of a Baroque church. DJs spin Latin house, electro, r'n'b, reggaeton and salsa via a powerful sound system. Doubles as a café in the day. Tues–Sat 9pm–1am.

La Sala 6 C Poniente 9 ☎ 7832 9524. Live music venue (and also a popular bar) that has a strong local flavour and also serves food. Bands (Latin/funk/rock/reggae) play several times a week and there's a big salsa club night on Sundays. Daily noon–1am.

ENTERTAINMENT

A number of small video **cinemas** show a range of Western films on a daily basis, weekly listings are posted on notice boards all over town, one is the *Bagel Barn* (see p.84).

Proyecto Cultural El Sitio 5 C Poniente 15 ⊚ elsitio cultural.org. Has a fairly good choice of Latin American and art-house movies, and also hosts art exhibitions, cultural events including theatre, concerts and lectures. There's a library here too.

SHOPPING

La Bodegona 4 C Poniente and Alameda Santa Lucía. Useful supermarket. Daily 8am–8pm.

Cargo Room 6 C & 7 Av Sur ☎ 7832 2200. Quirky jewellery boutique owned by Lex, a flamboyant Guatemalan designer that showcases his beautiful hand-crafted rings and necklaces. Bizarrely it also doubles as a low key bar-restaurant so it's ideal if you need a shot of liquor to calm the nerves after an expensive purchase. Tues–Thurs noon–10pm, Fri–Sun 1pm–midnight.

Casa del Conde West side of Parque Central ☎ 7832 3322. Bookstore with a good selection of new English-language books about Guatemala as well as travel guides,

novels and photographic books. Daily 8am–7.30pm.

Dyslexia Books 1 Av Sur 11. The best secondhand bookstore in town, with informed staff and lots of interesting fiction and non-fiction in English, Spanish and other European languages. Next to *Café No Sé*, so very handy if you want a beer after browsing.

Nim Po't 5 Av Norte 29 ⊚ nimpot.com. Sells some of the finest textiles in the country at fair prices. The warehouse-like store is something of a museum of contemporary Maya weaving, with a stunning array of complete costumes, plus other *artesanías* including wooden masks and some souvenirs and even Maximón mannequins. Daily 8am–6pm.

DIRECTORY

Banks and exchange Banco Industrial, 5 Av Sur 4, just south of the plaza, has an ATM. There are several more ATMs in town.

Internet and phones Free wi-fi is very common in Antigua's cafés. Internet cafés charge around US$0.75/hr.

Conexión, inside *La Fuente* courtyard at 4 C Oriente 14 (daily 8.30am–7pm) has fast connections. Funky Monkey, 5 Av Sur 6 is another good place for Skype users and cheap international calls.

Laundry Rainbow Laundry, 6 Av Sur 15 (daily 7.30am–8pm).

STUDYING SPANISH IN ANTIGUA

Antigua has around twenty established language schools, and many more or less reliable setups. Whether you're just stopping for a week or two to learn the basics, or settling in for several months in pursuit of total fluency, it's an excellent place to learn Spanish: it's a beautiful, relaxed town, lessons are inexpensive (though tend to cost more than in other areas of Guatemala) and there are several superb schools.

CHOOSING A SCHOOL

The following schools employ experienced teachers and charge between US$180 and US$310/week for four or five hours of one-on-one sessions (Monday to Friday) and full family-based lodging and meals.

Antigüeña Spanish Academy 1 C Poniente 10 ☎ 7832 7241, ⓦ spanishacademyantiguena.com

APPE 1 C Oriente 15 ☎ 7882 4284, ⓦ appeschool.com

Centro Lingüístico Internacional Spanish School Av del Espíritu Santo 6 ☎ 7832 1039, ⓦ spanishcontact.com

Centro Lingüístico Maya 5 C Poniente 20 ☎ 7832 0656, ⓦ clmaya.com

Christian Spanish Academy 6 Av Norte 15 ☎ 7832 3922, ⓦ learncsa.com

Guate Linda Language Center 7 Av Norte 76 ☎ 4360 5238, ⓦ guatelindacenter.com

Ixchel Spanish School 4 Av Norte 32 ☎ 7832 3440, ⓦ ixchelschool.com

Ixquic 7 Av Norte 74 ☎ 7832 2402, ⓦ ixquic.edu.gt

Probigua 6 Av Norte 41B ☎ 7832 2998, ⓦ probigua.org

San José El Viejo 5 Av Sur 34 ☎ 7832 3028, ⓦ sanjoseelviejo.com

Spanish Academy Sevilla 1 Av Sur 17 C ☎ 7832 5101, ⓦ sevillantigua.com

Tecún Umán Spanish School 6 C Poniente 34 A ☎ 7832 2792, ⓦ tecunuman.centramerica.com

Zamora Academia 9 C Poniente 7 ☎ 7832 7670, ⓦ learnspanish-guatemala.com

Medical care There's 24hr emergency service at the Santa Lucía Hospital, Calzada Santa Lucía Sur 7 (☎ 7832 3122). Dr Aceituno, who speaks good English, has an office at 2 C Poniente 7 (☎ 7832 0512).

Pharmacies Farmacia Santa María, west side of the plaza (daily 8am–10pm).

Police The police HQ is on the south side of the plaza (☎ 7832 0251). The tourist police are behind the marketplace (☎ 7968 5303).

Post office Av Alameda Santa Lucía (Mon–Fri 8am–4.30pm).

Swimming pool *Soleil La Antigua*, 9 C Poniente, just south of town on the road to Ciudad Vieja, has two pools (only heated Fri–Sun) that non-guests can use for US$20/day, which also includes a lunch and gives you access to a small gym and sauna.

Around Antigua

The countryside surrounding Antigua is superbly fertile and breathtakingly beautiful, peppered with olive-green coffee bushes and overshadowed by three volcanic cones. The valley is dotted with small villages, ranging from the traditional indigenous settlement of **Santa María de Jesús** to genteel **San Juan del Obispo**, which is dominated by a huge colonial palace. You'll also find two excellent museums in **Jocotenango**, just north of Antigua. No place is more than thirty minutes away.

GETTING AROUND

AROUND ANTIGUA

Buses southwest A steady stream of buses leave the Antigua terminal for Ciudad Vieja, San Antonio and San Miguel Dueñas (for Valhalla); the last ones return around 7pm.

Buses to San Juan del Obispo Hourly buses to San Juan leave from the market in Antigua (7am–6pm; 20min) or you can catch any bus heading for Santa María de Jesús, and it's a 5min walk from the main road.

Buses to Santa María de Jesús Buses run from Antigua to Santa María every 30min or so from 6am to 7pm; the trip takes 30min.

Buses north Hourly buses run between San Andrés Itzapa and Antigua. Any bus heading to Chimaltenango also passes through Jocotenango and via the access roads for the hot springs and San Andrés Iztapa.

1

Southwest of Antigua

Heading out this way you pass between the flanks of Agua volcano to the east and soaring peaks of Acatenango and Fuego on your west side. Sights include a great macadamia farm, a weaving village and of course the volcanoes themselves; hikes are best organized in Antigua (see p.81).

Ciudad Vieja

The first settlement of interest to the southwest of Antigua is **CIUDAD VIEJA**, just east of the highway, a scruffy and unhurried place with a distinguished past: it was near here that the Spanish established their second capital in Guatemala, Santiago de los Caballeros, in 1527. Today, however, there's no trace of the original city, and all that remains from that time is a solitary tree, in a corner of the plaza, which bears a plaque commemorating the site of the first mass ever held in the country. The plaza also boasts an eighteenth-century colonial church that has recently been restored.

San Antonio Aguas Calientes

Three kilometres west of Ciudad Vieja, on the other side of the highway, is **SAN ANTONIO AGUAS CALIENTES**, an indigenous village set on one side of a steep-sided bowl beneath the peak of Acatenango. San Antonio is famous for weaving, characterized by its complex floral and geometric patterns, and there's an indoor textile market next to the plaza where you can find a complete range of the local output.

Valhalla Experimental Station

1km before village of San Miguel Dueñas • Daily 8am–5pm • W exvalhalla.net

Owned by a North American with a passion for the environment, the **Valhalla Experimental Station** is well worth investigating. The farm has thousands of **macadamia nut** trees, using non-grafted stock (which bear bigger crops and are more disease resistant). Blueberries are also grown here. Visitors are very welcome, and a short tour will reveal all the secrets of nut harvesting and roasting, while later there's a chance to sample delicious macadamia pancakes in the café or buy cosmetics and chocolates.

Volcán de Acatenango

Majestic **Acatenango** is the toughest volcano climb in the Antigua region, an exhausting but exhilarating six- to seven-hour hike. Its summit peaks at 3975m, making it the third largest cone in the country. The route is along a trail of slippery volcanic ash that rises with unrelenting steepness through thick forest. Only for the last 50m or so does it emerge above the tree line, before reaching the top of the lower cone. To the south, after another hour's gruelling ascent, is the summit, accessed via a great grey bowl, from where there's a magnificent view out across the valley below. On the opposite side is the Agua volcano and, to the right, the fire-scarred cone of Fuego. Looking west you can see the three volcanic peaks that surround Lake Atitlán and beyond them the Santa María volcano, high above Quetzaltenango.

Several agencies in Antigua run hiking trips (see p.81), usually involving camping halfway up the cone and then an ascent in the early hours of the morning.

Southeast of Antigua

The road southeast of Antigua slaloms up the side of Agua volcano, passing a fascinating colonial palace on its way up to the village of Santa María de Jesús, base camp for hiking the cone.

San Juan del Obispo

The small village of **SAN JUAN DEL OBISPO** is an attractive, quiet little place of cobbled streets with fine views of the great domes of Antigua. San Juan is renowned for its

chocolate production, which is something of a local cottage industry. The excellent, English-owned Ravenscroft stables (see p.81) is also located in the village, a block from the *palacio*.

Palacio de Francisco Marroquín
Beside the church • Daily 9am–noon & 2–4pm • By donation

San Juan's one outstanding sight is the **Palacio de Francisco Marroquín**, who was the first bishop of Guatemala. The palace is currently home to a dozen or so nuns, and if you knock on the great wooden double doors one of them will give you a tour in Spanish. Marroquín arrived in Guatemala with Alvarado and is credited with having introduced Christianity to the Maya, as well as reminding the Spaniards about it from time to time. On the death of Alvarado's wife Marroquín assumed temporary responsibility for the government, and was instrumental in the construction of Antigua. He died in 1563, having spent his last days in the vast palace he'd built for himself here in San Juan.

The palace interior, arranged around two courtyards, is spectacularly beautiful and several rooms still contain their original furniture, as well as a portrait of Marroquín himself. Excellent information panels (in Spanish and English) detail the life of the bishop, who many Guatemalans see as the first father of the nation and credit for introducing the concept of multiculturalism. Attached to the palace is a fantastic church and chapel with ornate woodcarvings, plaster mouldings and austere religious paintings.

Doña Josefa's
200m northeast of church • Mornings

Cacao beans are brought to San Juan from the coast and turned into chocolate bars in several homes, including *Doña Josefa's* – just look out for the "chocolate" sign. You're welcome to drop by and watch the process (mornings only) or buy a bar or two (from US$2) any time; flavours include cinnamon and almond, though beware that local tastes are very sweet.

Santa María de Jesús
Up above San Juan the road arrives in the scruffy indigenous village of **SANTA MARÍA DE JESÚS**, starting point for the ascent of the Agua volcano. Perched high on the shoulder of the great peak, some 500m above Antigua, the village boasts magnificent views of the

---

THE UNLUCKY ONE

After abandoning their short-lived first settlement near the Kaqchikel capital of Iximché, the Spanish founded **Santiago de los Caballeros** on St Celia's Day in 1527. Set amid perfect pastures in the shadow of the Acatenango and Agua volcanoes, the new city quickly flourished, and within twenty years things had really started to take shape, with a school, a cathedral, monasteries and farms stocked with imported cattle. But while most Spaniards were still settling in, their leader, the rapacious **Alvarado**, was off in search of action, wealth and conquest. In 1541 he set out for the Spice Islands, travelling via Jalisco, where he met his end, crushed to death beneath a rolling horse.

When news of Alvarado's death reached his wife, **Doña Beatriz**, she plunged the capital into an extended period of mourning, staining the entire palace with black clay, inside and out. She appointed herself as her husband's replacement, and on September 9, 1541, she became the first woman to govern in the Americas, signing the declaration as *La Sin Ventura* (the unlucky one) – a fateful premonition.

On the night of Beatriz's inauguration, an earthquake shook Volcán de Agua's crater, releasing a great wave of mud that swept away the capital, killing the new ruler and most of her courtiers. Today the exact site of the original city is still the subject of some debate, but the general consensus puts it about 2km to the east of Ciudad Vieja.

1

Panchoy valley and east towards the smoking cone of Pacaya. It was founded at the end of the sixteenth century for Maya transported from Quetzaltenango: they were given the task of providing firewood for Antigua and the village earned the name "Aserradero", lumber yard. Since then it has developed into a farming community where the women wear beautiful purple *huipiles*.

Volcán de Agua

Agua is the easiest and by far the most popular of Guatemala's big cones to climb, and on Saturday nights dozens of people spend the night at the summit. It's an exciting ascent with a fantastic view to reward you at the top. The trail starts in Santa María de Jesús: it's a fairly simple climb on a clear (often garbage-strewn) path, taking five to six hours, and the peak, at 3766m, is always cold at night. There is shelter (though not always room) in a small chapel at the summit, and the views certainly make it worth the struggle.

As there have been (occasional) robberies reported on the outskirts of Santa María it's best to team up with an Antigua adventure sports company (see p.81) and not attempt the hike on your own.

North of Antigua

The route to Chimaltenango passes through a succession of sprawling villages, presenting a scruffy introduction to the western highlands, though there are some interesting attractions on the way including a fine cultural centre, some hot springs and the temple of a pagan saint.

Jocotenango

The grimy suburb of **JOCOTENANGO**, "place of bitter fruit", is set around a huge, dusty plaza where there's a weathered, dusty-pink Baroque church. In colonial times, Jocotenango was the gateway to Antigua, where official visitors would be met to be escorted into the city. Long notorious for its seedy bars, the town's main industries are coffee production and woodcarving. There's an excellent selection of bowls and fruits in the family-owned Artesanías Cardenas Barrios workshop on Calle San Felipe, where they have been working at the trade for five generations.

Centro La Azotea

Mon–Fri 8.30am–4pm, Sat 8.30am–2pm • US$6.50, including tour in English or Spanish • ⓦ centroazotea.com • Special minibuses (US$0.75 return) leave from Antigua's Parque Central hourly to the Centro.

Joco's principal attraction is 500m west of the plaza in the shape of the **Centro La Azotea** cultural centre. **Casa K'ojom**, which forms one half of the compound, is a purpose-built

---

THE WICKED SAINT OF SAN ANDRÉS ITZAPA

San Andrés shares with many other western-highland villages (including Zunil and Santiago Atitlán) the honour of revering **San Simón**, or Maximón, the wicked saint, whose image is housed in a pagan chapel in the village. His abode is home to drunken men, cigar-smoking women and hundreds of burning candles, each symbolizing a request. Curiously this San Simón attracts a largely ladino congregation and is particularly popular with prostitutes. Inside the dimly lit shrine, the walls are adorned with hundreds of plaques from all over Guatemala and Central America, thanking San Simón for his help. For a small fee, you may be offered a *limpia*, or soul cleansing, which involves one of the resident women workers beating you with a bushel of herbs, while you share a bottle of local firewater, *aguardiente*, with San Simón (it dribbles down his front) and the attendant will periodically spray you with alcohol from her mouth. If you are in the region, try to get to San Andrés on **October 28** when San Simón is removed from his sanctuary and paraded through the town in a pagan celebration featuring much alcohol and dancing.

1

FIESTAS AROUND GUATEMALA CITY AND ANTIGUA

The region around Guatemala City and Antigua is not prime fiesta territory; a few villages, listed below, have some firmly established traditions and dramatic celebrations. The following are just a selection of the highlights.

January 1–5 Santa María de Jesús, main day 1st
February First Friday in Lent, Antigua; San Felipe de Jesús has a huge pilgrimage
Holy Week Celebrated with fervour in Antigua (see box, p.73)
May 1 Guatemala City; Labour Day is marked by marches and protests
June 24 San Juan del Obispo and Comalapa have large fiestas
July 25 Antigua, in honour of Santiago

August 15 Jocotenango and Guatemala City
September 29 San Miguel Dueñas; dances include Los Toritos
October 18 San Lucas Sacatepéquez; dances include Moors and Christians
October 28 San Andrés Itzapa; all-nighter with San Simón paraded through the town
November 1 Sumpango and Santiago Sacatepéquez, massive kites flown

museum dedicated to Maya culture, especially music. The history of indigenous musical traditions is clearly presented from its pre-Columbian origins, through sixteenth-century Spanish and African influences – which brought the marimba, bugles and drums – to the present day, with audiovisual documentaries of fiestas and ceremonies. Other rooms are dedicated to the village weavings of the Sacatepéquez department and the cult of Maximón (see box, p.130).

Next door, the **Museo de Café** offers the chance to look around a working organic coffee farm that dates back to 1883. All the technicalities of husking, sieving and roasting are clearly explained, and an interpretive trail leads through the bushes of the finca. If you're here in February or March when the coffee plants flower, there's a wonderfully fragrant scent in the air, a little like jasmine.

San Lorezo El Tejar hot springs
Daily 7am–5.30pm, closed Tues and Fri afternoon • US$0.65
Four kilometres past Jocotenango is **SAN LORENZO EL TEJAR**, which has some superb hot springs; they're a couple of kilometres from the main road. If you want to bathe in the sulphurous waters, you can either use the cheaper communal pool or, for a few bucks rent one of your own – a little private room with a huge tiled tub. Sundays can get very busy with local families.

San Andrés Itzapa
About 10km north of Jocotenango, past Parramos, a side road branches to **SAN ANDRÉS ITZAPA**, famed as a base for the cult of San Simón, or Maximón (see box opposite). The so-called wicked saint's abode is a short stroll from the central plaza, up a little hill – you should spot street vendors selling charms, incense and candles. If you get lost, ask for the Casa de San Simón. San Andrés' Tuesday market is also worth a visit.

The western highlands

TEXTILES FROM NEBAJ, IXIL REGION

The western highlands

Guatemala's western highlands, stretching from the outskirts of Antigua to the Mexican border, are perhaps the most beautiful and captivating part of the entire country. Two main features dominate the area: a chain of awesome volcanoes on the southern side, and the high Cuchumatanes mountain range that looms over the north of the region. Strung between these two natural barriers is a series of spectacular forested ridges, lakes, gushing streams and plunging, verdant valleys. The highland landscape is defined by many factors, but above all altitude. At lower levels the vegetation is almost tropical, supporting dense forests and crops of coffee, bananas and vegetables. Higher up in the hills, pine, cedar and oak forests are interspersed with patchwork fields of maize and potatoes. In the highest terrain, known as the *altiplano*, the land is largely treeless and often wrapped in cloud, suited only to hardy herds of sheep and goats.

This region is predominantly peopled by the **Maya**, who have lived here continuously for the past two thousand years. Maya society, languages and traditions are markedly different from mainstream Latin American culture, and exploring their bewitchingly beautiful highland home is a highlight to any trip in Guatemala.

With stunning mountain scenery yielding colourful market towns and whitewashed colonial churches at every turn, you're spoilt for places to visit. **Lago de Atitlán**, surrounded by volcanoes and with its idyllic shores harbouring some fascinating villages, is absolutely unmissable. To the north is the fabled market town of **Chichicastenango** and the wildly beautiful peaks and remote, intensely traditional communities of the **Ixil**, a region that is excellent for hiking.

Heading west, you'll reach Guatemala's second city, **Quetzaltenango** (Xela), an ideal base for visiting Maya villages, the hot springs of **Fuentes Georginas** and climbing the perfectly proportioned volcanic cone of **Santa María**. Beyond this, you start encountering the massive granite peaks of the Cuchumatanes; you'll find

LAGO DE ATITLÁN

Highlights

❶ **Chichicastenango** Hunt for textiles and souvenirs at this scenic town's legendary market. See p.101

❷ **The Ixil region** Hike the hillside trails of this remote, intensely traditional indigenous region. See p.110

❸ **Lago de Atitlán** An awesome steep-sided crater lake ringed by volcanoes and diminutive indigenous villages. See p.117

❹ **Santa Cruz La Laguna** Idyllic lakeside village with a uniquely relaxed vibe and plenty of great hotels. See p.138

❺ **Quetzaltenango** Guatemala's refined second city enjoys a great highland setting and makes an excellent base for studying Spanish. See p.141

❻ **Fuentes Georginas** The perfect place to kill an afternoon, these sublime hot spring–fed pools are situated halfway up a volcano. See p.152

❼ **Todos Santos Cuchumatán** A sleepy Mam Maya village nestled in a high valley in the mighty Cuchumatanes mountain range, with a famous textile tradition. See p.164

HIGHLIGHTS ARE MARKED ON THE MAP ON PP.96–97

HIGHLIGHTS
1 Chichicastenango
2 The Ixil region
3 Lago de Atitlán
4 Santa Cruz La Laguna
5 Quetzaltenango
6 Fuentes Georginas
7 Todos Santos Cuchumatán

San Cristóbal de las Casas

Gracias a Dios
La Trinidad
Laguna Yolnabaj
Yalambojoch
Río Nacapoxlac
San Mateo Ixtatán
Bulej
Wajxaklajunh
Baril
Nentón
San Sebastián Coatán
Santa Eulalia
Santa Ana Huista
San Miguel Acatán
San Rafael la Independencia
Jacaltenango
Najab
Soloma
San Antonio Huista
Concepción Huista
La Mesilla
San Juan Ixcoy
La Democracia
San Martín
7 Todos Santos Cuchumatán
San Pedro Necta
La Ventosa
Santiago Chimaltenango
San Juan Atitán
Paquix
Chiabal
San Ildefonso Ixtahuacán
Colotenango
Cuilco
CA1
CARRETERA INTERAMERICANA
Chiantla
San Gaspar Ixchil
Zaculeu
Aguac
Motozintla
SIERRA MADRE
Huehuetenango
Tectitán
Concepción Tutuapa
Malacatancito
Tacaná
San José Ojetenan
MEXICO
Ixchiguán
CA1
San Bartolo
Sibinal
Volcán Tacaná
Tejutla
Pologuá
Momoste
Tajumulco
San Carlos Sija
San Francisco El Alto
Volcán Tajumulco
Sibilia
San Cristóbal Totonicapán
Totoni
Talismán Bridge
San Pedro Sacatepéquez
San Andrés Xecul
Cuatro Caminos
San Marcos
Palestina de los Altos
Olintepeque
Nah
El Rodeo
1
Ostuncalco
San Mateo
5
Salcajá
Tapachula
Malacatán
Concepción Chiquirichapa
Quetzaltenango
Almolonga
Cantel
Río Suchiate
El Tumbador
San Martín Sacatepéquez
Zunil
6
Volcán Lacandón
12
Volcán Chicabal
Volcán Santa María
Santa María de Jesús
Coatepeque
Colomba
Volcán Santiaguito
Hidalgo
Tecún Umán
CARRETERA AL PACÍFICO
El Palmar Viejo
CA2
Takalik Abaj
El Asintal
El Zarco
Cuyotenango
Chicaca
Ocós
Tilapa
RESERVA NATURAL EL MANCHÓN
CA2
Retalhuleu
Mazatenango
PACIFIC OCEAN

THE WESTERN HIGHLANDS

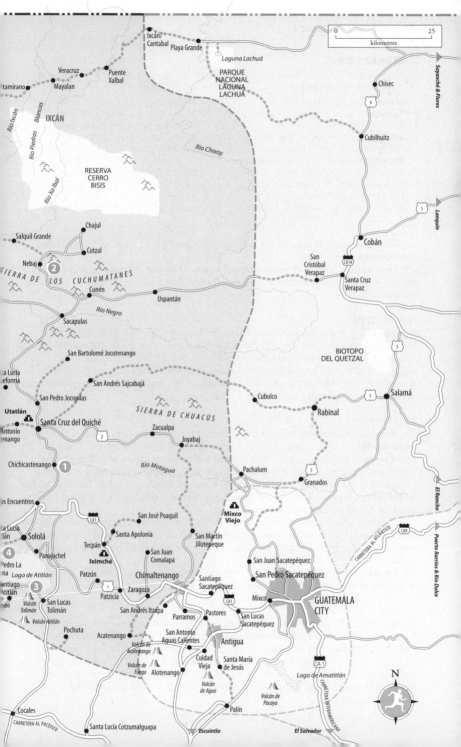

2

MARKET DAYS

Make an effort to catch as many market days as possible – they're second only to local fiestas in offering a rich perspective of Maya life. These are some of the best:

Monday San Juan Atitán; Zunil.

Tuesday Chajul; Comalapa; Olintepeque; Sololá; Totonicapán.

Wednesday Almolonga; Colotenango; Cotzal; Momostenango; Sacapulas.

Thursday Aguacatán; Chichicastenango; Jacaltenango; Nebaj; Panajachel; Sacapulas; San Juan Atitán; San Mateo Ixtatán; San Rafael La Independencia; Soloma; Tajumulco; Uspantán; Zacualpa.

Friday Chajul; San Francisco el Alto; San Martín; Santiago Atitlán; Sololá.

Saturday Almolonga; Cotzal; Todos Santos Cuchumatán; Totonicapán.

Sunday Aguacatán; Chichicastenango; Jacaltenango; Joyabaj; Momostenango; Nahualá; Nebaj; Ostuncalco; Panajachel; Sacapulas; San Juan Comalapa; San Martín Jilotepeque; San Mateo Ixtatán; Santa Eulalia; Soloma; Uspantán; Zacualpa.

excellent hiking trails around the spectacular Mam Maya village of **Todos Santos Cuchumatán**.

Historical sites, such as the pre-conquest cities of **Iximché**, **K'umarkaaj** and **Zaculeu**, are also worthy of your attention – although they don't bear comparison to Tikal and the lowland ruins.

Brief history

A peripheral area during the Classic Maya civilization (250–900 AD), the western highlands were colonized towards the end of the twelfth century by **Toltecs** from central Mexico. With the Toltecs established as overlords, local tribes bitterly contested regional hegemony. The most powerful tribes were the **K'iche'**, based at their capital K'umarkaaj, the **Mam** at Zaculeu and **Kaqchikel** at Iximché. Smaller tribal groups such as the Ixil also occupied clearly defined areas.

The Colonial era

The **arrival of the Spanish** in 1523 was a disaster for the Maya population. Leader **Pedro de Alvarado** and his conquistadors first defeated the K'iche', and by 1527 they had the entire western highlands under their control with a combination of military discipline, stealth and strategic alliances. But the damage done by Spanish swords was nothing compared to the **diseases** they introduced. Waves of smallpox, typhus, bubonic plague and measles swept through the indigenous population, reducing their numbers by as much as ninety percent in the worst-hit areas.

Indigenous labour became the backbone of Spanish rule in Guatemala, with income coming from plantations of **cacao** and **indigo**. The colonists attempted to impose the power of the Catholic Church, but a lack of clergy meant traditional Maya religion could continue.

Independence in 1821 brought little change for the Maya who were still forced (or lured into debt) to work the coastal plantations, often in horrific conditions.

Civil war

Fresh pressures emerged in the 1970s as the Maya were caught up in waves of horrific political violence. **Guerrilla movements** sought support from the indigenous population and established themselves in the western highlands. The Maya became the victims in this process, as they were caught between the guerrillas and the army. Thousands fled the country, 440 villages were destroyed and two hundred thousand died during the conflict, with the highlands by far the worst-affected region.

The highlands today

With the signing of the 1996 **peace accords** political tensions lifted and there is evidence of a new self-confidence within the highland Maya. Grass-roots development groups have prospered, and indigenous organizations have launched land rights campaigns.

Many challenges remain, with poverty levels still some of the worst in the hemisphere, exacerbated by high birth rates and unemployment. The allure of "El Norte" (the US) entices many away. Though many exiles return with money to invest in their communities, centuries-old customs are threatened. The influence of American **evangelical churches** (see p.346) can also undermine local hierarchies, dividing communities and threatening Maya culture.

Despite these pressures, more than a dozen Maya languages are still spoken in the highlands and native costume continues to be worn. Visit on **market** and **fiesta** days when the villages fill to bursting, and you'll clearly sense the values of the Maya world in the subdued bustle and gossip of the market or from the intense joy of celebration.

GETTING AROUND   **THE WESTERN HIGHLANDS**

By bus Buses flow continuously along the Carretera Interamericana between 6am and 7pm, and tourist shuttles serve all the main centres. Many minor roads have been paved in recent years, and transport connections have improved greatly. Often the most practical plan of action is to base yourself in one of the larger places and then make a series of day-trips to village markets and fiestas, although even the smallest settlements will usually offer some kind of accommodation.

The Carretera Interamericana

The serpentine **Carretera Interamericana** forms the main artery of transport in the highlands, and this highway and its junctions will inevitably become very familiar. Most of the route between Guatemala City and the turn-off for Quetzaltenango is now a smooth four-lane highway, though traffic is always heavy. The first of three major junctions you'll get to know is **Chimaltenango**, from where you can make connections to Antigua. Continuing west, **Los Encuentros** is the next main junction, where one road heads off to the north for Chichicastenango and another branches south to Panajachel. Beyond this is **Cuatro Caminos**, from where side roads lead to Quetzaltenango, Totonicapán and San Francisco el Alto. The Carretera Interamericana continues on to Huehuetenango before it reaches the Mexican border at La Mesilla. Virtually every bus travelling along the highway will stop at all of these junctions.

Chimaltenango

Grimy **CHIMALTENANGO**'s main focal point is the Carretera Interamericana, which cuts through the southern side of the town. Frankly it's a traffic-plagued hell-hole, the grossly polluted roadside littered with mechanics' workshops and sleazy bars. There's absolutely no reason to hang around here, and you should take care with your bags if you are changing buses as pickpockets have been known to target disorientated travellers.

ARRIVAL AND DEPARTURE   **CHIMALTENANGO**

By bus Chicken buses to Antigua leave every 15min between 6am and 7pm from the turn-off on the highway. You can also pick up connections to all points west on the highway and Guatemala City (every 20min; 1hr) here.

San Martín Jilotepeque

To the north of Chimaltenango, it's a 19km ride past plunging ravines and pine forests to the village of **SAN MARTÍN JILOTEPEQUE**. San Martín had to be rebuilt following the 1976 earthquake, but its sprawling Sunday market is well worth a visit. The local weaving, women's *huipiles* especially, is some of the finest you'll see, with intricate and ornate patterning, predominantly in reds and purples.

ARRIVAL AND DEPARTURE   **SAN MARTÍN JILOTEPEQUE**

By bus Buses to San Martín leave the market in   30min trip, with many continuing on to Joyabaj.
Chimaltenango every 30min from 5am to 6pm for the

2   San Juan Comalapa

Around 16km west of Chimaltenango, there's a turn-off for the village of **SAN JUAN COMALAPA** which has a collection of eroded pre-Columbian sculptures displayed in its plaza, and a monument to Rafael Alvarez Ovalle, who composed the Guatemalan national anthem. Looking out over the plaza is a fine Baroque church that dates from colonial times.

The villagers of Comalapa have something of a reputation as **folk artists**. The tradition began with **Andrés Curuchich** (1891–1969), who painted simple scenes documenting village life; there's a permanent exhibition devoted to his paintings at the Museo Ixchel, Guatemala City. Several dozen painters continue Curuchich's tradition, and their work can be bought in galleries in the town.

Two blocks from the plaza, **Museo de Arte Maya** (3 C 0–74; Mon–Sat 8am–noon & 2–5pm; US$0.75) has a good collection of folk art as well as Maya ceramics and artefacts and some fascinating old photographs.

As ever, the best time to visit is for the **market**, on Sunday, which brings people out in force.

ARRIVAL AND DEPARTURE   **SAN JUAN COMALAPA**

By bus Buses to Comalapa run hourly from   highway turn-off.
Chimaltenango (45min), and microbuses also wait at the

Iximché

Iximché, the pre-conquest capital of the Kaqchikel, is 5km south of the Interamericana on a beautiful exposed site, isolated on three sides by plunging ravines and surrounded by pine forests. The majority of the buildings, originally built of adobe, have disappeared but the site – which housed a population of about ten thousand – is very atmospheric.

Brief history

Iximché was first established around 1470. From the early days of the conquest the Kaqchikel Maya allied themselves with the Spanish, in order to defeat their tribal enemies the K'iche'. Grateful for the assistance, the Spanish established their **first headquarters** near here on May 7, 1524. The Kaqchikel referred to Alvarado as *Tonatiuh*, the son of the sun, and as a mark of respect he was given the daughter of a Kaqchikel king as a gift.

But within months the Kaqchikel rebelled, outraged by Alvarado's demands for tribute. The conquistador retaliated by burning Iximché and then moved operations to the greater safety of Ciudad Vieja, a short distance from Antigua.

George W. Bush stopped by Iximché in 2007 and was treated to a marimba display and a demonstration of the Maya ball game. Not everyone was pleased with his appearance, and Maya elders later held a ceremony to spiritually cleanse the site and the residual "bad energy".

The ruins

Daily 8am–5pm • US$6.50

The **ruins of Iximché** are made up of four main plazas, a couple of ball courts and several small pyramids. In most cases only the foundations and lower parts of the original structures were built of stone, while the upper walls were of adobe, with thatched roofs supported by wooden beams. You can make out the ground plan of many of the buildings, but it's only the most important all-stone structures that still stand. The most significant buildings were those clustered around courts A and C, and on the sides of **Temple 2** you can make out some badly eroded murals.

It's thought that Iximché was a **ceremonial centre** used for religious rituals, and Maya worship still takes place here down a small trail through the pine trees behind the final plaza. Archeological digs have unearthed the decapitated heads of sacrifice victims, burial sites, grinding stones, obsidian knives, a flute made from a child's femur and large numbers of incense burners.

Iximché's shady location is perfect for a picnic; you can buy drinks at the site.

ARRIVAL AND DEPARTURE IXIMCHÉ

By bus To get here, hop off any bus travelling along the Carretera Interamericana at the turn-off for Tecpán. The centre of Tecpán town is about 500m from the road, from where microbuses leave for the ruins (every 30min; 10min).

El Quiché

At the heart of the western highlands, the department of **El Quiché** encompasses the full range of Guatemalan scenery. The south is fertile and heavily populated while to the north the landscape becomes increasingly dramatic, rising to the massive, rain-soaked peaks of the **Cuchumatanes**. For the traveller, El Quiché has a lot to offer, including **Chichicastenango**, the scene of a vast, twice-weekly market and still a pivotal centre of Maya religion. Beyond here are the ruins of **K'umarkaaj** and, further to the north, the extraordinary scale of the mountain scenery is exhilarating. Isolated villages set in superb highland bowls sustain a wealth of indigenous culture and occupy a misty, mysterious world of their own – above all in the land of the **Ixil**.

Brief history

The department takes its name from the greatest of the pre-conquest tribal groups, the **K'iche'**, who overran much of the highlands by 1450 from their capital at K'umarkaaj. With little in the way of plunder, this remote, mountainous terrain remained an unimportant backwater for the Spanish. The region became a centre of intense guerrilla activity in the late 1970s and was the scene of unrivalled repression, as tens of thousands of villagers were wiped out by the military. Today these highlands remain a stronghold of Maya culture, and El Quiché, dotted with small villages and mountain towns, is the scene of some superb fiestas and markets.

Chichicastenango

North from **Los Encuentros** junction, the road drops down through dense pine forests into a deep ravine before beginning a tortuous ascent around a seemingly endless series of switchbacks until reaching **CHICHICASTENANGO**. Dubbed Guatemala's "Mecca del Turismo", Chichi is a compact and traditional town of cobbled streets, though the charming old adobe houses are now outnumbered by modern concrete structures. Twice a week the town's highland calm is shattered by the Sunday and Thursday **markets**, which attract many tourists, traders and Maya weavers from throughout the central highlands.

The market is by no means all that sets Chichicastenango apart, for it's an important centre of culture and **religion**. Over the years, Maya traditions and folk Catholicism have been treated with a rare degree of respect. Today the town has an important collection of Maya artefacts, parallel indigenous and ladino governments and two churches that make no effort to disguise their acceptance of unconventional pagan worship.

Locals adhere to the ways of **traditional weaving**, the women wearing superb *huipiles* with flower motifs. The men's costume of short trousers and jackets of black wool embroidered with silk is highly distinguished, although it's very expensive to make and these days almost all men opt for Western dress. For Sundays and fiestas, however, a handful of *cofradres* (elders of the religious hierarchy) still wear the *traje* clothing and parade through the streets bearing spectacular silver processional crosses and antique incense-burners.

Santo Tomás church

Main Plaza • Daily 7am–8pm

At the main **Santo Tomás church** in the southeast corner of the plaza, the local K'iche' Maya (called *Maxeños*) have been left to adopt their own style of worship, blending pre-Columbian and Catholic rituals. The church was built in 1540 on the site of a Maya altar and rebuilt in the eighteenth century. It's said that indigenous locals became interested in worshipping here after Francisco Ximénez, the resident priest from 1701 to 1703, started reading their holy book, the **Popol Vuh** (see p.104). Seeing that he held considerable respect for their religion, they moved their altars from the hills and set them up inside the church. Today this ancient, unique hybrid of Maya and Catholic worship still takes place in the church.

Don't enter the building by the front door, which is reserved for *cofrades* and senior church officials, but through the **side door**. It's highly offensive to take **photographs** inside the building – don't even contemplate it.

Before entering the church, it is customary to make offerings in a fire in front of the building and burn *copal* and *estoraque* incense in perforated cans, a practice that leaves a cloud of sweet smoke hanging over Santo Tomas's stone steps.

Inside is an astonishing scene of avid worship. A soft hum of constant murmuring fills the air as the faithful kneel to place candles on low-level stone platforms for their ancestors and the saints. For these people, the entire building is alive with the **souls of the dead**, each located in a specific part of the church: the place of the "first-people", the ancient ancestors, is beneath the altar railing, ordinary folk are to the west in the nave. Equally important are the **Catholic saints**, who receive the same respect and are continuously appealed to with offerings of candles and alcohol. Last, but by no means least, certain areas within the church, and particular patterns of candles, rose petals and *chicha*, are used to invoke specific types of blessings, such as those for children, travel, marriage, harvest or illness.

CHICHICASTENANGO'S MARKET

There's been a **market** at Chichicastenango for hundreds, if not thousands, of years and despite the touristy side of the event, local people continue to come twice a week to trade their wares. On **Sundays** and **Thursdays**, Chichicastenango's streets are lined with stalls and packed with buyers, and the choice is overwhelming, ranging from superb-quality Ixil *huipiles* to wooden dance-masks and everything in between, including pottery, gourds, belts and blankets, plus a gaudy selection of fabrics. You can still pick up some authentic **weaving**, but you need to be prepared to wade through a lot of very average material – and haggle hard. Your chances of getting a good deal are better before the tourist buses arrive at 10am or in the late afternoon once things have started to quiet down. Prices are pretty competitive, but for a real bargain you need to head further into the highlands – or to Panajachel, which is a better bet for *típica* clothing.

For a brilliant vantage point over the **vegetable market**, head for the indoor balcony on the upper floor of the Centro Comercial building on the north side of the plaza. You'll be able to gawk at the villagers below (as well as take photographs without fear of being intrusive) as they haggle and chat over bunches of carrots and onions. It's possible to pick out costumes from all over the highlands, including *huipiles* from the Atitlán villages, and even from as far away as Chajul; the "space cowboy" shirts and pants are worn by men from the neighbouring Sololá area.

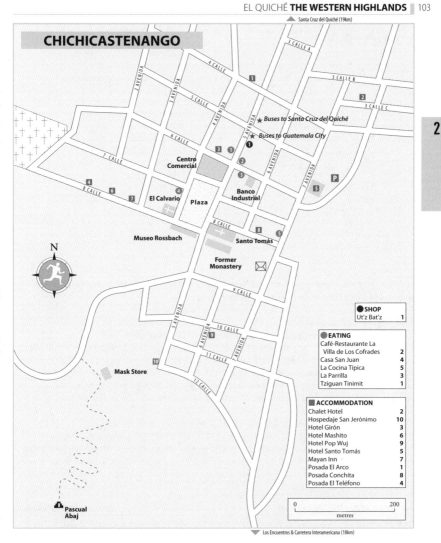

Museo Rossbach

Main Plaza • Tues, Wed, Fri & Sat 8am–12.30pm & 2–4pm, Thurs 8am–4pm, Sun 8am–2pm • US$0.75

On the south side of the plaza, **Museo Rossbach** houses a wide-ranging collection of pre-Columbian artefacts, mostly small pieces of ceramics (including some demonic-looking incense burners), jade necklaces and earrings, and stone carvings (some two thousand years old). A few interesting old photographs of Chichi as well as local weavings and masks are also on display.

El Calvario

Main Plaza • Daily 7am–7pm

On the west side of the plaza, the whitewashed **El Calvario** chapel is like a miniature version of Chichi's main church – its steps also the scene of incense-burning rituals. Inside, the atmosphere is equally reverential as prayers are recited around the

2

THE POPOL VUH

Written in K'umarkaaj shortly after the arrival of the Spanish, the more than nine thousand lines of the **Popol Vuh** detail the cosmology, mythology and traditional history of the K'iche'. The first of the two parts of this sacred poem is an account of the K'iche's **creation** by their god, who is known as **Heart of Sky**. According to the Popol Vuh, at first there was only water and sky; the creator then formed earth and mountains, plants and trees. Heart of Sky turned his attention to animals, and created creatures of the forest including deer, birds and jaguars. Unsatisfied with these animals, the creator fashioned humans from corn paste after twice failing to make man from mud and wood. The Popol Vuh then recounts the adventures of the ancestors of mankind, the **hero twins** (or wizard twins) Hunahpú and Xbalanqué, which culminate in an epic struggle with the death lords of **Xibalbá**, the Maya underworld. The twins ultimately triumph, and the cycle of creation is born.

The Popol Vuh's second half describes the wanderings of the K'iche' ancestors as they migrate south from the Toltec area of Mexico and settle in the highlands of Guatemala. Evidence gathered by archeologists and epigraphers strongly supports the accuracy of this part of the epic. The book concludes with a history of K'iche' royalty, and suggests a shared lineage with these kings and their gods. Dennis Tedlock's translation of the Popol Vuh (see p.361) is regarded as the definitive text.

smoke-blackened wooden altar, and women offer flowers and stoop to kiss a supine image of Christ, entombed inside a glass cabinet.

The shrine of Pascual Abaj

South downhill along 5 Av, then along 9 C; follow the track for 10min past a mask workshop up to the shrine

Churches are certainly not the only scenes of Maya religious activity, and the hills that surround the town are replete with shrines. The closest of these, less than a kilometre from the plaza, is known as **Pascual Abaj**. Although the site is regularly visited by tourists, it's important to remember that the **Maya ceremonies** held here are deeply religious and you should keep your distance and be sensitive about taking any photographs.

The shrine is laid out with several small **altars** facing a stern-looking pre-Columbian sculpture. Ceremonies, usually overseen by a shaman, always incorporate clouds of incense, liquor swilling and incantations, along with offerings of flowers and maybe a sacrificed chicken. In 1957, Pascual Abaj's altars were smashed by reforming Catholics, but traditionalists gathered the scattered remains and patched them together.

ARRIVAL AND INFORMATION   CHICHICASTENANGO

By bus On market days plenty of shuttle services run the route from Antigua to Panajachel via Chichi, allowing you to spend a few hours at the market before continuing on to Lago de Atitlán; the reverse journey is possible from Panajachel too. There's no bus station in Chichi, although the corner of 5 C and 5 Av operates loosely as a terminal. Buses heading between Guatemala City and Santa Cruz del Quiché pass through Chichi; coming from Antigua, you can easily connect with these buses in Chimaltenango. Chicken buses also run from Pana (with extra services on market days) and Quetzaltenango. If you're heading north, it's usually quickest to take the first bus to Santa Cruz del Quiché (every 20min; 30min),

from where buses go to Nebaj and Uspantán.

Destinations Guatemala City (every 20min; 3hr); Panajachel (4–6 buses; 1hr 15min); Quetzaltenango (7 daily; 2hr 30min); Santa Cruz del Quiché (every 20min; 30min).

Shuttle buses If you need a shuttle bus from Chichicastenango, head to Chichi Turkaj Tours, 5 Av 5–24 (☎7756 1579).

Inguat 7 C 5–43 (in theory 8am–6pm; ☎7756 2022). Information is pretty limited and the desk is not always staffed. They have ranks of computers for internet connections.

OPPOSITE CHICHICASTENANGO MARKET>

FIESTA TIME IN CHICHICASTENANGO

Chichicastenango's appetite for religious fervour is especially evident during the **fiesta** of Santo Tomás, from December 14 to 21. It's a spectacular occasion, with attractions including the *Palo Volador*, in which men dangle by ropes from a 20m pole (see p.347), a live band or two, a massive procession, traditional dances, clouds of incense, gallons of *chicha* and deafening fireworks. On the final day, all babies born in the previous year are brought to the church for christening. **Easter** is also celebrated with tremendous energy and piety.

2

ACCOMMODATION

Hotels can be in short supply on Saturday nights before the Sunday market, but you shouldn't have a problem on other days. Some places raise rates on **market days**, though at other times you can usually negotiate a good deal.

Chalet Hotel 3 C 7–44 ☎7756 1360, ⓦwww .chalethotelguatemala.com. A good highland inn, this little hotel has attractive, though smallish rooms decorated with Mayan artesanías and beds with woollen blankets; all are en suite. It's solar-powered, there's free internet and you can eat your breakfast (US$2.50) on the roof terrace overlooking the town. U̲S̲$̲2̲5̲

Hospedaje San Jerónimo 5 Av & 12 C ☎7756 1838. A decent choice, this well-run, quiet hospedaje has clean if simple rooms, all with en-suite hot-water bathrooms, and some with balcony. U̲S̲$̲1̲4̲

Hotel Girón 6 C 4–52 ☎7756 1156. Offers functional, spacious, pine-trimmed rooms with clean bathrooms, wi-fi and safe parking. The hotel is set just off the street and could not be more central. U̲S̲$̲1̲8̲

Hotel Mashito 8 C 1–7 ☎7756 1343. Nothing fancy, but has very cheap rates, and you have a choice of clean rooms, some with cable TV and private bathrooms, others with shared facilities. U̲S̲$̲9̲

Hotel Pop Wuj 6 Av, between 10 & 11 C ☎7756 2014. Pleasantly decorated, spotless rooms, all en suite. The most expensive doubles have huge beds. There's also a restaurant downstairs. U̲S̲$̲2̲2̲

Hotel Santo Tomás 7 Av 5–32 ☎7756 1061, ✉hst @itelgua.com. Attractive hotel built around two courtyards with spacious, modern rooms – though they get chilly at night, make sure you have sufficient blankets. There's a (heated) swimming pool, restaurant and pleasant lounge/bar. Very popular with tour groups, so can feel a little impersonal. U̲S̲$̲1̲1̲0̲

Mayan Inn 8 C & 3 Av ☎7756 1176, ⓦwww.mayaninn .com.gt. Something of a colonial-era timewarp, this historic hotel offers classy rooms with period furniture and fireplaces. The plumbing and fixtures are a bit creaky and the restaurant is overpriced however. Guests are assigned a member of the staff, who all wear mock-traditional dress, to attend you. U̲S̲$̲1̲3̲0̲

★ **Posada El Arco** 4 C 4–36 ☎7756 1255. This solar-powered guesthouse has charm and character, and is run by a hospitable English-speaking Guatemalan who lived in the US for decades. Visitors are looked after well (try the home-made jams and peanut butter). Seven large, attractive rooms with good wooden beds and reading lights; rooms 6 & 7 have access to a pleasant terrace. There's also a beautiful garden with stunning highland views and secure parking. U̲S̲$̲3̲2̲

Posada Conchita 8 C 6–14 ☎7756 1258. On a lane just behind the church, this posada has real charm, with huge, colonial-style rooms, all en suite, that have fireplaces and decorative Maya artefacts. Rates are charged per person, so it's a great deal for solo travellers. U̲S̲$̲2̲6̲

Posada El Teléfono 8 C 1–64 ☎7756 1197. The spartan rooms at this friendly guesthouse are accessed via vertiginous, rickety stairways. Many have fine highland views, and the communal bathrooms are kept pretty tidy. U̲S̲$̲8̲

EATING

Chichi is a good place to indulge in hearty, good-value Guatemalan food – though many restaurants are geared to tourist wallets. The plaza on **market days** is the place to come for authentic, inexpensive highland eating: try one of the makeshift food stalls, where you'll find cauldrons of stews and broths.

Café-Restaurant La Villa de Los Cofrades 6 C & 5 Av, on the first floor ☎7756 1647. Observe local Chichi life from the first-floor balcony while you enjoy great barbecued meats, set meals and breakfasts (US$3). Good quality coffee and wine are available. Daily 7am–9.30pm.

Casa San Juan 4 Av 5–58 ☎7756 2086. The most stylish place in town, this enjoyable restaurant has tables in a pretty patio and there's plenty of artwork on display in the dining room. Dishes start around US$7, expect filling Guatemalan and Mexican cooking plus a few Western options. Tues–Sun 7am–10pm.

La Cocina Típica 7 Av & 7 C. A simple, decent comedor of the plastic chair and no-frills variety that has filling set lunches for US$2.50. Daily 7am–4pm.

La Parrilla 6 C & 5 Av ☎7756 1321. Set in a little courtyard, this is a good place to get away from the market crowds. Meat lovers should try the *especial la parrilla* (US$7), or a steak; all plates come with vegetables, rice and a soup starter. Daily 7am–9pm.

Tziguan Tinimit 5 Av & 6 C ☎7756 1144. A large dining hall, painted with images of the Mayan cosmos. Most of the grilled meat, pasta and pizza dishes are in the US$5–9 range but there's always a good daily special (like *longaniza* sausages) for less than US$4. They serve espresso coffee. Daily 7am–9.30pm.

SHOPPING

Ut'z Bat'z 5 Av 5–24 ☎5008 5193, ⓦwww.enmisalsa .com. An excellent handicraft cooperative that operates on fair-trade principles so female weavers (most are illiterate widows) gain a good price for their beautiful textiles. Also sells quirky bags, purses and scarfs from silk-like *chanel* fibre. Wed 1–5pm, Thurs, Sat & Sun 9am–5pm.

DIRECTORY

Banks Plenty open on Sun including Banrural, 6 C (Tues–Sun 9am–5pm), which has an ATM.

Internet Inguat 7 C 5–43 (US$0.80/hr).

Santa Cruz del Quiché

The capital of the department of El Quiché, **SANTA CRUZ DEL QUICHÉ**, lies half an hour north of Chichicastenango. Quiché, as it is usually called, is a large featureless town, but serves as the jumping-off point for the nearby ruins of K'umarkaaj. It's also a transport hub for the Ixil region. **Market** days are the same as in Chichicastenango – Thursday and Sunday – with stalls sprawling south and east of the plaza down to the bus station.

Dominating the central **plaza** of Santa Cruz del Quiché is a large colonial church and clock tower built with stone from the ruins of K'umarkaaj. In the middle of the plaza, a defiant statue of the K'iche' hero Tecún Umán stands prepared for battle, but his position is undermined somewhat by an ugly urban tangle of shabby stores and streets that surround the square.

ARRIVAL AND DEPARTURE SANTA CRUZ DEL QUICHÉ

By bus The grubby bus terminal is about four blocks south and a couple east of the central plaza.

Destinations Guatemala City, via Chichicastenango (every 20min; 3hr 30min); Joyabaj (hourly; 1hr 45min); Nebaj (7 daily; 2hr 30min); Quetzaltenango (9 daily; 3hr); Totonicapán (4 daily; 1hr 30min); Uspantán (7 daily; 2hr 30min).

Microbuses Microbuses supplement the chicken bus services to Nebaj (hourly until 7pm), Totonicapán (hourly until 6pm) and Uspantán (every 90min until 6pm).

ACCOMMODATION

Hotel Rey Kiche 8 C 0–39 ☎7755 0827, ⓔhotelreykiche@gmail.com. This modern, brick-faced hotel has spacious, plain rooms with firm beds, TVs, desks and wardrobes, and there's free tea, coffee and water. Singles, doubles and triples are available, and there's a comedor too (breakfast and dinner only). US$23

Hotel San Andrés 0 Av 9–04 ☎7755 3057, ⓔhotelsan_andres@hotmail.com. A three-storey hotel with spacious, clean rooms, all with cable TV and private bathrooms with tubs. There's a restaurant and wi-fi. US$17

EATING

Café San Miguel Opposite the church ☎7755 1488. Old-fashioned café-restaurant with filling local food, including *empanadas* and sandwiches (from US$1.50). The pastries can be very dry though. Daily 7am–9pm.

Loven Pastería South side of the Parque. Inside a small shopping centre, this little place serves up good espresso coffee (US$1) as well as burgers, cakes and sandwiches. Daily 8am–7pm.

DIRECTORY

Banks and exchange Banrural at the northwest corner of the plaza has an ATM and might be persuaded to change travellers' cheques.

K'umarkaaj (Utatlán)

4km west of Santa Cruz del Quiché • Daily 8am–5pm • US$6.50

Early in the fifteenth century, riding on a wave of successful conquest, the K'iche' king Gucumatz (Feathered Serpent) founded a new capital, **K'umarkaaj**. A hundred years later the Spanish arrived, renamed the city Utatlán, and then destroyed it, leaving the **ruins** that can be visited today.

K'umarkaaj is nowhere near as grand as the large ruins of Petén, but its dramatic setting, surrounded by deep ravines and pine forests, is impressive, and its historical significance intriguing. Little restoration has taken place and once-grand temples and palaces are today just grassy mounds. The small **museum** has a scale model of what the original city may once have looked like.

Brief history

The splendour of the city, once containing 23 palaces, signified the strength of the K'iche' empire, which at its height boasted a population of around a million.

By the time of the Conquest, however, the K'iche' empire was fractured. Their first encounter with the Spanish was a heavy defeat near Quetzaltenango, resulting in the loss of their leader Tecún Umán. The K'iche' then invited the Spanish to their capital, but on seeing the fortified city, the conquistador feared a trap and captured K'iche' leaders Oxib-Queh and Beleheb-Tzy. His next step was characteristically straightforward: "As I knew them to have such a bad disposition to service of his Majesty, and to ensure the good and peace of this land, I burnt them, and sent [soldiers] to burn the town and destroy it."

The plaza

You'll find three remaining **temple buildings** – the monuments of Tohil, Auilix and Hacauaitz – which were simple pyramids topped by thatched shelters on the central plaza. The Temple of the Sovereign Plumed Serpent once stood in the middle of the plaza, but these days just the foundations of this circular tower can be made out. The only other feature that's still vaguely recognizable is the **ball court**.

Perhaps the most interesting thing about the site today is that *costumbristas* (Maya religious practitioners) still come here to perform sacred rituals. The entire area is covered in small burnt circles – the ashes of incense – and chickens are regularly sacrificed.

La Cueva

Beneath the plaza is a 100m-long **tunnel** (follow the sign for *la cueva*). Inside are nine shrines, the same number as there are levels of the Maya underworld, Xibalbá. Devotees pray at each shrine, but it is the ninth one, housed inside a chamber, that is most actively used for sacrifice, incense and alcohol offerings. Why the tunnel was constructed remains uncertain, but local legends suggest that it was dug by the K'iche' to hide their women and children from the advancing Spanish. Others believe it represents the caves of Tula mentioned in the Popol Vuh (see p.104). Tread carefully inside the tunnel, as some of the side passages end abruptly with precipitous drops. If a ceremony is taking place, you'll hear the mumbling of prayers and smell incense smoke as you enter, in which case it's wise not to disturb the proceedings by approaching too closely.

ARRIVAL AND DEPARTURE   K'UMARKAAJ (UTATLÁN)

By bus or taxi From Santa Cruz del Quiché, you can catch a bus heading to Totonicapán, or take a taxi (around US$14 return trip, with 1hr at the ruins).

On foot It's a pleasant 40min stroll from Santa Cruz del Quiché, heading south from the plaza along 2 Av, then turning right down 10 C, which takes you to the site.

East to Joyabaj

A paved road runs east from Santa Cruz del Quiché, beneath the impressive peaks of the **Sierra de Chuacús**, through a series of villages set in beautiful rolling farmland. The first of these, **Chiché**, is a sister village to Chichicastenango, with which it shares costumes and traditions, though the market here is on Wednesday. Next is **Chinique**, followed by larger **Zacualpa**, which has Thursday and Sunday markets in its imposing plaza. The latter village's name means "where they make fine walls", and in the hills to the north are the remains of a pre-conquest Maya settlement.

Joyabaj

The small town of **JOYABAJ**, the last place out this way, also has a small archeological site to its north. The 1976 earthquake almost totally flattened Joyabaj, killing hundreds of people; the crumbling facade of the colonial church is one of the few physical remains. However, in recent years the town has bounced back, and the Sunday **market** is a huge affair well worth visiting.

It's possible to **hike** from Joyabaj, over the Sierra de Chuacús, to Cubulco in Baja Verapaz. It's a superb but exhausting hike, taking at least a day, though it's perhaps better done in reverse.

ARRIVAL AND DEPARTURE
JOYABAJ

By bus Buses run between Guatemala City's western highlands terminal and Joyabaj (via Santa Cruz del Quiché) about every hour.

By microbus Frequent microbuses (roughly every 30min till 6pm) from Quiché.

ACCOMMODATION

Posada San Rafael 17km northeast of town ☎ 5570 3336, ⓦ www.posada-sr.com. Accessed solely by a rough dirt track, this rural hotel is near the village of San Andrés Sajcabajá, deep in the Quiché hills. The French–Guatemalan owners offer horseriding to the minor Maya ruins of Chijoj, indigenous villages, hot springs and waterfalls, and serve up delicious organic food. If you call first, there's a good chance that someone will pick you up from Joyabaj or Quiché, as few buses run up this way. US$12

DIRECTORY

Banks and exchange There are two banks in town; Banrural in the centre has an ATM.

Sacapulas

The isolated town of **SACAPULAS**, an hour north from Quiché, is set in a spectacular position on the Río Negro beneath the dusty foothills of the Cuchumatanes. Sacapulas has a small colonial church, with some finely carved wooden images of saints, and a good market every Thursday and Sunday, held beneath the two huge ceiba trees in the plaza. Some of the women still wear impressive *huipiles* and tie their hair with elaborate pom-poms, similar to those of Aguacatán.

THE FLYING ANGELS OF JOYABAJ

The town's **fiesta** in the second week of August comprises of five days of unrelenting celebration. There some fantastic traditional dances performed, as also the spectacular *Palo Volador*, in which "flying" men or *ángeles* spin to the ground from a huge wooden pole. Though the fiesta is in many ways a hybrid of Maya and Christian traditions, the *ángeles* symbolize none other than the wizard twins of the Popol Vuh, who descended into the underworld to do battle with the Lords of Death.

2

Since long before the arrival of the Spanish, **salt** has been produced here in beds beside the Río Negro, a valuable commodity that earned the town a degree of importance. It's still collected upstream from the bridge.

ARRIVAL AND DEPARTURE   SACAPULAS

By bus Getting to Sacapulas is straightforward – catch any bus or microbus from Santa Cruz del Quiché heading to Uspantán (hourly; 1hr 45min) or Nebaj (hourly; 1hr 15min).

By microbus Microbuses run to Aguacatán (7 daily; 1hr 30min), from where there are excellent connections to Huehuetenango. The last transport to all destinations is between 6pm and 7pm.

ACCOMMODATION AND EATING

Look out for stalls selling the (very) sweet local snack called *melcocha*, sold all over the country. You'll find cheap comedors and snack vendors dotted around the plaza.

Comedor y Hospedaje Tujaal ☎ 4383 7657. If you do get stuck in Sacapulas, you'll find adequate if uninspiring singles and doubles, some with fine views, at this large concrete structure right on the riverbank. For eating, try the local *mojarra* fish and *papas fritas* (US$5). Food daily 7am–8.30pm. US$16

DIRECTORY

Banks and exchange You'll find both Banrural and an ATM on the plaza.

Uspantán

East of Sacapulas, a dirt road rises steeply, clinging to the mountainside and quickly leaving the Río Negro far below. As it climbs, the views are superb, with tiny Sacapulas dwarfed by the sheer enormity of the landscape. The road eventually reaches **USPANTÁN**, a small town lodged in a chilly gap in the mountains and often soaked in steady drizzle. Rigoberta Menchú (see p.348), the K'iche' Maya woman who won the 1992 Nobel Peace Prize, is from Chimel, a tiny village in this region. Few people hang around long here, but there are some decent hotels.

ARRIVAL AND DEPARTURE   USPANTÁN

By bus and microbus Microbuses leave for Cobán (hourly until 5pm; 3hr) and Santa Cruz del Quiché (every 90min until 6pm; 2hr 30min); regular chicken buses also serve these routes. Note that the road east to Cobán is a hair-raising journey and connections may not be possible when there are heavy rains. Buses do cover this route all year round but the section just past the bridge over the Río Negro is prone to landslides and involves a hair-raising zig-zag up a mountainside.

ACCOMMODATION AND EATING

Cafeteria María Luisa 6 Av & 7 C, Zona 2. This is a pleasant, bright and clean little place run by a friendly lady that serves inexpensive breakfasts, snacks and set lunches for US$2.50. Daily 7am–7pm.
Hotel Posada Doña Leona 6 C 4–09, Zona 1

☎ 7951 8045. An efficiently run hotel with a good selection of very clean rooms, all with TV, and the bathrooms have reliable hot water. There are fair prices for single travellers and you'll find a good comedor and wi-fi here too. US$18

The Ixil region

High up in the Cuchumatanes, in a landscape of steep hills, bowl-shaped valleys and gushing rivers, is the **Ixil region**. Here **Nebaj**, **Chajul** and **Cotzal**, three remote and extremely traditional towns, share a language spoken nowhere else in the country. These lush, rain-drenched highlands are hard to reach and have proved notoriously difficult to control, and today's relaxed atmosphere of highland Maya colour and customs conceals a bitter history of protracted conflict.

The beauty of the landscape and the strength of **indigenous culture** in the Ixil are both overwhelming. When church leaders moved into the area in the 1970s, they found very strong communities in which the people were reluctant to accept new authority for fear that it would disrupt traditional structures, and where women were included in decision-making. Counterbalancing these strengths are the horrors of the **human rights abuses** that took place here during the civil war, which must rate as some of the worst anywhere in Central America. Despite this terrible legacy, however, the fresh green hills are some of the most beautiful in the country, and the towns are friendly and accommodating, with a relaxed and distinctive atmosphere in a misty world of their own.

2

Brief history

Before the arrival of the Spanish, Nebaj was a sizeable centre, producing large quantities of **jade**. The Conquest was particularly brutal in these parts, however. After several setbacks, the Spaniards finally managed to take Nebaj in 1530, by which time they were so enraged that the settlement was burnt to the ground and the survivors enslaved as punishment. Things didn't improve with the coming of independence: the Ixil people were regarded as a source of cheap labour and forced to work on the coastal plantations. Many never returned, and even today large numbers of local people still migrate to the coast, Guatemala City and the US in search of work.

In the late 1970s and 1980s, the area was hit by waves of horrific violence as it became the main theatre of operation for the **Guerrilla Army of the Poor** (see box, p.114). Since the **1996 peace accords**, normality steadily returned to the area, as villagers have returned to their ancestral settlements and rebuilt their homes.

Nebaj

NEBAJ is the centre of Ixil country and the largest of the three settlements. A bustling market town, it's scruffy around the edges, with potholed streets and a dwindling number of attractive old adobe houses that are being steadily replaced by undistinguished concrete structures. Aesthetic grumbles aside, Nebaj has undoubtedly managed to retain its highland charm and is becoming a popular base for adventure-minded travellers drawn by the opportunity to get off Guatemala's main gringo trail. With a temperate climate and gorgeous scenery all around, Nebaj makes a good base for **hiking** – Acul and Cocop are both within striking distance – though some places can also be reached by microbus if you're not feeling so energetic. If you're in town for the second week in August, you'll witness the **Nebaj fiesta**, which includes processions, fireworks, dances, epic drinking sessions and a marimba-playing marathon.

The plaza and market

Nebaj's pretty, recently remodelled **plaza** is the focal point for the community and houses the main municipal buildings and the large whitewashed **Catholic church** – inside its door on the left are dozens of crosses, forming a memorial to those killed in the civil

---

NEBAJEÑO TEXTILES

The **textiles** woven in Nebaj are unusual and intricate, especially the women's *huipiles*, which are a mass of complex geometrical designs. Until very recently, greens, yellows, reds and oranges were omnipresent, worn with brilliant red *cortes* (skirts), though clothes of other hues are now worn. The most spectacular part of Nebaj *traje* is the dramatic women's headcloth, a length of hand-loomed fabric that's decorated with "pom-pom" tassles that they pile up above their heads. Very few men now wear traditional dress, preferring to buy secondhand North American clothes from the market. The scarlet male ceremonial jackets are dusted down for fiestas, however; formal looking and ornately decorated, they're said to have been modelled on those worn by Spanish officers.

war. There's not that much to do in Nebaj itself, though the small **market**, a block east of the church, is worth investigating. It's fairly quiet most days, but on Thursdays and Sundays, the numbers swell as traders sell secondhand clothing from the US, electrical goods from China and fruit and vegetables from all over the Guatemalan highlands.

ARRIVAL AND DEPARTURE   NEBAJ

By bus The bus terminal is two blocks southeast of the plaza. Destinations Guatemala City (3 daily; 6hr); Santa Cruz del Quiché (7 daily; 2hr 30min). There's a daily microbus to Cobán at 5am (6hr), or you can take any bus to the Cunén junction and catch an onward connection there. For Huehuetenango change in Sacapulas. Buses for Acul (25min), Chajul (40min) and Cotzal (50min) leave regularly between 5.30am and 5pm.

INFORMATION AND ACTIVITIES

Tourist information El Descanso, 3 C ☎ 5847 4747, ⓦ nebaj.com. A one-stop shop for Nebaj visitors and easily the best place to go for information on local activities and an internet connection. There's also an information office (in theory daily 8am–5pm) inside the Mercado de Artesanías, 2 Av, but it's frequently closed; however they do stock copies of *Guía de Senderismo*, a superb hiking guide (US$7) to the Ixil region with excellent maps.

GuíasIxiles Inside El Descanso, 3 C ☎ 5847 4747, ⓦ nebaj .com. Inexpensive guided walks (from US$14/head, with a minimum of two people); from day-hikes to Acul and Cocop to a spectacular three-day trek to Todos Santos. Trips across the mountains staying in *posadas comunitarias* (guesthouses) and eating local meals in remote villages can also be arranged.

Language School Nebaj Language School, based at El Descanso, 3 C ☎ 5847 4747, ⓦ nebaj.com. A week of one-on-one tuition and a family homestay with meals is just US$120.

ACCOMMODATION

Nebaj has some good budget places, many with inimitable highland charm, though nothing luxurious. There are also excellent rural lodges in nearby Acul (see p.115).

Gran Hotel Ixil 2 Av 9–15, Zona 5 ☎ 7756 0036. It's not actually very grand, but the owners, the Briz family, are hospitable and helpful and it's a comfortable, relaxed place to stay. All the rooms are spacious and well kept, have a private bathroom and TV, and overlook a central garden. US$15

★ **Hospedaje Ilebal Tenam** Calzada 15 de Septiembre ☎ 7755 8039. An efficient, welcoming hospedaje with dozens of rooms, ranging from the small and functional to the attractive and comfortable – those in the rear block have TVs and private bathrooms. Towels are provided, and the hot water is reliable. It's about 400m north of the plaza, and has a small garden. US$7

Hotel del Centro Naab'a 3 C 3–18, Zona 1 ☎ 7755 8101. This spotless, welcoming place has 24 very clean rooms set around a parking lot, slightly spartan but comfortable, all with bathrooms, TVs and good beds. US$16

★ **Hotel Santa María** 4 Av & 2 C ☎ 4212 7927. Excellent new place that's the best hotel in town, with comfortable accommodation set around a grass courtyard. The spacious rooms all have attractive furniture, including wardrobes and handcarved wooden headboards, as well as good mattresses, TVs and modern en-suite bathrooms. US$21

Hotel Shalom Calzada 15 de Septiembre & 4 C ☎ 7755 8028. A centrally located place with large rooms, some with wood-panelled walls and all with desks, TV and private bathroom. US$16

Hotel Villa Nebaj Calzada 15 de Septiembre 2–37 ☎ 7755 8115, ⓦ villanebaj.com. This garish four-storey construction is something of a blot on the landscape, but the accommodation is extremely comfortable – all the clean, attractive rooms have quality beds, bedside lights, cable TV and phones, and the Ixil fabrics add a splash of colour. Those without private bathroom are a real bargain. US$9

Media Luna Media Sol 3 C 6–15 ☎ 5311 9100. A reasonable hostel-style place with clean dormitory facilities and a private room. There's a TV lounge, ping pong and basic cooking facilities. Dorms US$4.50, rooms US$10

Popi's 5 Av 3–35 ☎ 7756 0092. Popi is a kind, highly informative North American senior citizen and his guesthouse is a good place to meet other travellers, with rooms around a yard. There's a kitchen, or just let your host, an excellent cook, rustle something up. Internet and wi-fi. Dorms US$4, rooms US$12

EATING

This is an isolated highland town so choices are quite limited, but you will find filling local food. If you can, try *boxboles*, a delicious Ixil dish made of maize dough and a little meat that's wrapped and steamed in a *güisquil* leaf. For superb local **cheese**, made in the valley of Acul (see p.115), head to the store Chancol, Calzada 15 de Septiembre or *Rincon del Queso*.

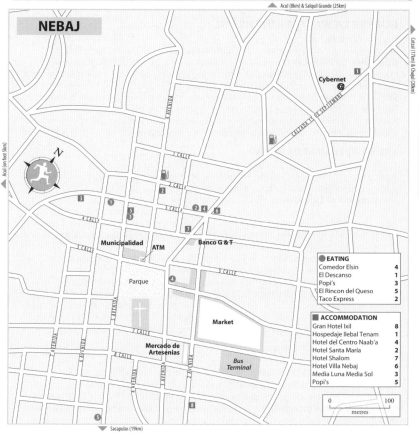

NEBAJ

Acul (8km) & Salquil Grande (25km)

Cybernet @

2

EATING

Comedor Elsin	4
El Descanso	1
Popi's	3
El Rincon del Queso	5
Taco Express	2

ACCOMMODATION

Gran Hotel Ixil	8
Hospedaje Ilebal Tenam	1
Hotel del Centro Naab'a	4
Hotel Santa María	2
Hotel Shalom	7
Hotel Villa Nebaj	6
Media Luna Media Sol	3
Popi's	5

Municipalidad ATM Banco G & T

Parque

Market

Mercado de Artesanías

Bus Terminal

0   metres   100

Sacapulas (19km)

Comedor Elsin East side of the Parque. Classic Guatemalan comedor with humble surrounds, a loyal clientele and hearty portions of *pollo dorado*, chorizo and *longaniza* (sausage) for US$2.50 a plate. No alcohol. Daily 7.30am–9pm.

★ **El Descanso** 3 C ☎ 5311 9100. A barn-like place that's a popular hangout for backpackers and development workers and many locals, with sofas and internet access. There's a long menu, including bowls of granola, fruit and yoghurt for breakfast (U$3), while the mains – pasta, Mexican dishes, sandwiches and grilled meats – are around US$4. There's also cold beer (US$1.75) and wine by the glass. Daily 8am–10pm.

Popi's 5 Av 3–35. Excellent-value food including bacon-and-egg breakfasts (US$3.50), sandwiches on home-baked bread, and dishes like stir-fried veggies with tofu (US$3.50). Everything is freshly cooked to order by the genial owner.

El Rincon del Queso 5 Av ☎ 4006 9678. This is the nearest Nebaj has to a deli, selling treats like smoked chorizo, Ixil coffee, good wholemeal bread, Chancol cheese and home-made jams.

Taco Express 3 C 3–18. Tiny, clean little place ideal for inexpensive Mexican snacks (three tacos cost US$1.50) and there are *gringas* (tortillas and chopped salad), burritos and burgers. Daily 9am–9pm.

SHOPPING

Mercado de Artesanías 2 Av and 7 C. Stocks a good selection of local textiles and other crafts from the region.

DIRECTORY

Banks and exchange Banrural, on the north side of the plaza, has an ATM.

Internet El Descanso, 3 C. Surf (slowly) for US$1.25/hr.

2

GUERRILLA WARFARE IN THE IXIL

The bitter **civil war** of the 1970s and 1980s ravaged the western highlands, and left the Ixil devastated by the conflict between the **Guatemalan army** and the insurgent **Ejército Guerrillero de los Pobres** (the EGP, or Guerrilla Army of the Poor). By 1996, when the guerrilla war officially ended, nearly all of the region's smaller villages had been destroyed and fifteen thousand to twenty thousand people had been killed, with thousands more displaced. Most of the victims were villagers, dying not because of their political beliefs but because they had been caught between the army and the EGP, who saw the creation of a liberated zone in the Ixil as the springboard to national revolution. Investigations later found the Guatemalan military responisble for of over ninety per cent of civilian deaths in the Ixil.

THE 1970S: THE RISE OF THE EGP

The EGP first entered the area in 1972, when a small group of guerrilla fighters crossed the Mexican border and began building links with locals, impressing some villagers with plans for political and social revolution. The guerrillas opened their military campaign in 1975 with the **assassination of Luis Arenas**, a finca owner from near Chajul, who employed hundreds of labourers under a system of debt bondage. The EGP shot Arenas in front of hundreds of his employees as he was counting the payroll. According to the group, workers joined them with cries of "Long live the poor, death to the rich". But other accounts describe how people walked for days to pay their last respects to Arenas.

These actions prompted a huge response from the armed forces, who began killing, kidnapping and torturing suspected guerrillas and sympathizers. The EGP was already well entrenched, however, and by late 1978 was regularly occupying villages, holding open meetings and tearing down debtors' jails. In January 1979 they killed another local landowner, Enrique Brol, of Finca San Francisco near Cotzal. On the same day, the EGP also briefly took control of Nebaj itself, summoning the whole of the town's population, as well as Western travellers, to the central plaza, where they denounced the barbaric inequalities of life in the Ixil.

THE 1980S

The army responded with a wave of horrific attacks on the civilian population. Army units swept through the area, committing atrocities, burning villages and massacring thousands. Nevertheless, the strength of the guerrillas continued to grow, and in 1981 they again launched an **attack on Nebaj**, by then a garrison town. Shortly afterwards the army chief of staff, Benedicto Lucas García (the president's brother), flew into Nebaj to threaten locals that if they didn't "clean up their act" he'd bring five thousand men "and finish off the entire population".

The army changed its tactics under new president Ríos Montt, using anti-Communist propaganda and conscripted **civilian patrols** (PACs) to ensure the loyalty of the people. Villagers were given ancient rifles and told to protect their communities from guerrillas. The army swept through the Ixil, razed fifty villages to the ground and settled the displaced in new "model" communities. With the EGP retreating to more remote terrain, Ixil people began to adapt to the army's newfound dominance, many opting to reject contact with the guerrillas.

Hit hard, the EGP responded with desperate acts. On June 6, 1982, guerrillas stopped a bus near Cotzal and executed thirteen civil patrol leaders and their wives; eleven days later a guerrilla column entered the village of **Chacalté**, where the civil patrol had been particularly active, and killed a hundred people.

The army's offer of **amnesty** soon drew refugees out of the mountains: between 1982 and 1984 some 42,000 people turned themselves in, fleeing a harsh existence under guerrilla protection. Others returned after years spent living like nomads, hunting animals in the jungles of the Ixcán to the north. By 1985 the guerrillas had been driven back into a handful of mountain strongholds.

PEACE ACCORDS

Skirmishes continued until the mid-1990s, but ceased with the signing of **peace accords**. Since then, ex-guerrillas and former civil patrollers have resettled the old village sites and communities have been rebuilt.

Acul

One of the most interesting walks from Nebaj takes you to the village of **ACUL**, an hour and a half away via a steep track. Starting from the church in Nebaj, head east downhill along 5 Calle. At the bottom of the dip, as the road divides, take the right-hand fork and head out of town. Just after you pass the last houses, it's just possible to make out some **pre-Columbian burial mounds** in the corn fields on your right. These are still used for Maya religious ceremonies.

Beyond here the wide track switchbacks up a steep hillside, before dropping down into Acul, one of the original "model villages" into which people were herded after their homes were destroyed by the army. The municipality now has a population of around five hundred Ixil and K'iche' Maya families. Sights are few, but it's fascinating to see how well the place has come on in the past few years; every home has a little plot of land for growing maize and vegetables, and there's a lovely Baroque-style whitewashed **church**.

ARRIVAL AND DEPARTURE   ACUL

By minibus Minibuses (roughly every 30min; 25min) connect Acul with Nebaj until 5pm.

ACCOMMODATION

★ **Finca San Antonio** On the road to Nebaj, 500m from village ☎ 5599 3352, ⓦ quesochancol.com. One of two superb country hotels run by the Azzari family, who have been dairy farming here for generations. This is the original family home, with rustic but comfortable simply furnished rooms that have private bathrooms. Home-cooked meals cost US$6, horseriding is US$20 for a four-hour trip, including a guide. Two varieties of Guatemala's best cheese are made here, and nonguests are very welcome to drop in and buy some produce. **US$38**

Hacienda Mil Amores Next door to Finca San Antonio ☎ 5704 4817, ⓦ haciendamilamores.com. Enjoys a simply breathtaking setting and views over a paradisal valley of rich pastureland and pine trees to a mighty fold in the Cuchumatanes mountains. Very well-built stone cottages, each with fireplaces and verandas with views, and hearty cooking (same rates as the finca) is offered. **US$45**

Posada Doña Magdelena ☎ 5782 0891. This excellent little *posada* in the village has rooms fronting a pretty flowering garden. It's run by a friendly Ixil lady who also serves tasty meals. **US$10**

Cocop

A half-day circular walk climbs up the steep eastern edge of the natural bowl that surrounds Nebaj to the village of **COCOP** and back to the main Nebaj–Cotzal road. Starting in the centre of Nebaj, walk south along 2 Avenida past *Hotel Gran Ixil* until the end of the road, bear right, and then take the first left downhill to the bridge. Cross the bridge and you'll quickly reach the pueblo of **Xemamatzé** on the edge of Nebaj. This village used to be home to a huge internment camp where Ixil villagers who had surrendered to the army were subject to lengthy "repatriation" treatment. In Xemamatzé, take the well-trodden, signposted muddy track uphill to **Cocop** – this trail climbs steadily for about an hour to 2300m. Back across the valley there are spectacular views towards Nebaj. When the trail eventually begins to level out, directly facing a maize field, the path then turns a sharp left and continues round the mountain. The path grips the side of the slope then gradually starts to descend as the small village of Cocop comes into view below.

The village has been rebuilt on old foundations; during the civil war it was razed to the ground and 98 villagers were massacred by the army. Today, however, it's a pretty little settlement in a delightful setting beside a gurgling river. A few stores sell fizzy drinks, or for something stronger ask to see the village's *cusha* liquor distillery. To head back, walk straight ahead from the crossroads in the centre of the village, past the Emmanuel church for a lovely hour's stroll along the V-shaped valley through sheep-filled meadows. At the end of the trail is the village of **Río Azul** on the main Cotzal–Nebaj road, from where you can wait for a microbus or pick-up, or hike back to Nebaj in an hour and a half.

COMMUNITY TOURISM IN SAN JUAN COTZAL

Based just behind the town's market place is an excellent **community tourism** project called Tejidos Cotzal (☎ 5428 8218 or ☎ 4621 9725; ⓦ tejidoscotzal.org). The project aids dozens of local weavers, who use natural dyes and backstrap looms; you can buy their work at the office. Guided tours (US$20–25/head, minimum two people) are offered, taking in visits to the weavers' homes, and to see other craftspeople, such as candlemakers, at work; prices include a great lunch of local food like *boxboles*. Hikes to a Maya hilltop altar to watch a religious ceremony and to local waterfalls are also offered.

San Juan Cotzal

The small town of **SAN JUAN COTZAL** is beautifully set in a gentle dip in the valley, sheltered beneath the Cuchumatanes and often wrapped in a damp blanket of mist. In the 1920s and 1930s, this was the largest and busiest of the three Ixil towns, as it was from here that the fertile lands to the north were colonized. Cotzal is a quiet, friendly little place with a very attractive little plaza. Market days here are Wednesday and Saturday.

ACCOMMODATION AND EATING   SAN JUAN COTZAL

El Maguey Two blocks north of the plaza ☎ 7765 6199. Simple place, where all the clean, basic rooms have TV; bathrooms are shared. The hotel's comedor is also the best in town with large set meals for US$2.50. U̲S̲$̲1̲2̲

Chajul

Last but by no means least of the Ixil settlements is **CHAJUL**, replete with a good stock of old adobe houses, their wooden beams and red-tiled roofs blackened by the smoke of cooking fires. It is also the most traditional and least bilingual of the Ixil towns. The streets are usually bustling with activity: you'll be met by an army of small children, and local women gather to wash clothes at the stream that cuts through the middle of the village. Here boys still use blowpipes to hunt small birds, a skill that dates from the earliest of times. Time your arrival for **market day**, (Tues & Fri) when the town is at its most lively.

Chajul's church

The colonial church on the plaza is fascinating: you enter through a colossal wooden door carved with animal motifs, and the huge old structure is full of gold leaf and topped by a timber ceiling of massive beams. It's home to the **Christ of Golgotha** and the target of a large pilgrimage on the second Friday of Lent – a particularly exciting time to visit.

Museu Maya Ixil

C Principal • Mon–Sat 7am–5.30pm • US$1.30 • ☎ 4236 3149

This modest little museum has a small collection Postclassic Maya ceramics and craftwork from the Chajul region including basketry, carved slingshots, pottery and textiles.

INFORMATION AND TOURS   CHAJUL

Limitless Horizons Ixil By Salón Municipal ☎ 5332 6264, ⓦ limitlesshorizonsixil.org. This excellent development project is immersed in the town, providing funding for schooling and a library and education. Staff here can direct you to local guides for hiking and skilled volunteers are always in need.

ACCOMMODATION AND EATING

Most of the town's (few) pensiones are very run down. Local families also rent out beds in their houses to travellers; you won't have to look for them, they will find you. You'll find a few comedores just off the plaza, of which *Cristina* is the best.

Posada Vetz K'aol 400m south of the plaza ☎ 7765 6114. This charming *posada* is in a gorgeous old historic building which has wood-panelled walls and is kept tidy. The big rooms, with good wooden bunk-beds and blankets, are set up for groups but anyone is welcome. There's a lovely sitting room with a fireplace and inexpensive food and espresso coffee is available. Dorm bed U̲S̲$̲7̲

CHAJUL COSTUME

The women of Chajul are terrific weavers, their *huipiles* richly embroidered with animals and symbols, filling the streets with colour. Until recently, all the textiles created here used to be woven in scarlet thread, though nowadays royal blue is almost as common. Look out, too, for the women's earrings, which are made of old coins strung up on lengths of wool. The traditional red jackets of the men are an extremely rare sight these days. Make sure you visit the shop run by the local **weaving cooperative**, Va'l Vaq Quyol, between the church and the market, where you'll find some of the best-quality handmade textiles in the country at very decent prices.

2

DIRECTORY

Banks and exchange The Banrural on the plaza will change cash dollars.

Lago de Atitlán

Lake Como, it seems to me, touches the limit of the permissibly picturesque; but Atitlán is Como with the additional embellishments of several immense volcanoes. It is really too much of a good thing. After a few days of this impossible landscape one finds oneself thinking nostalgically of the English Home Counties.

Aldous Huxley, Beyond the Mexique Bay (1934)

Whether or not you share Huxley's refined sensibilities, there's no doubt that **LAGO DE ATITLÁN** is astonishingly beautiful, and most people find themselves captivated by the lake's scenic excesses. Indeed its appeal is so intoxicating that a handful of gringo devotees have been rooted to its shores since the 1960s, and today Atitlán rates as the country's number-one tourist attraction.

Hemmed in on all sides by volcanoes and steep hills, the lake is at least 320m deep and measures 18km by 12km at its widest point. Depending on the time of day its waters shift through an astonishing range of blues, steely greys and greens as the sun moves across the sky. Mornings are usually calm, but by early afternoon the *xocomil* wind makes boat travel quite a rock'n'roll experience.

The strength of Maya culture evident here is profound. Many of the villages remain intensely traditional – **San Antonio Palopó**, **Santiago Atitlán** and **Sololá** are some of the very few places in the entire country where Maya men still wear *traje* – despite the tourist presence. Around the southwestern shores, from Santiago to San Pablo La Laguna, **Tz'utujil** is spoken, while from San Marcos La Laguna to Cerro de Oro the **Kaqchikel** language predominates.

Most travellers base themselves in one lakeside village and visit other pueblos from there. **Panajachel** is the main resort, an enjoyable if touristy town that has an

RISING HIGH

Atitlán's beauty remains overwhelming, although recent pressures are decidedly threatening. Sediment analysis has shown that the **lakewater has risen and fallen** in cycles for hundreds of years, but after the tropical storm Stan in 2010 Atitlán rose 5m in eighteen months, an unprecedented event that caused businesses to flood, beaches to disappear and threatened livelihoods. The once-idyllic lakeside pathway in Santa Cruz (a village particularly badly affected) is no more and docks in San Pedro and San Juan have had to be rebuilt. Theories rage as to why the lake has risen so quickly – some reckon landslides caused by Stan have blocked underwater drainage channels – but for Maya with centuries of local knowledge it was less of a surprise; their villages sit high above the shore, and many sold lakefront land to foreigners. For visitors, the impact so far has been pretty minimal, with only a handful of lakefront hotels losing land and Atitlán looks as beautiful as ever. But of course if the lake continues to rise more businesses will be affected.

2

LAGO DE ATITLÁN

abundance of hotels and restaurants. **San Pedro**, with budget digs and a party vibe, is the main backpacker hangout, while those seeking tranquillity head for **Santa Cruz**, **San Marcos** or isolated spots on the north side of the lake. Other possibilities include San Juan, Santiago Atitlán and San Antonio Palopó all of which have a hotel or two.

Sololá and around

Some 12km south of the Los Encuentros junction on the Carretera Interamericana is **SOLOLÁ**, the departmental capital and gateway to the lake. Perched on a natural balcony some 600m above the water, the town itself isn't much to look at, but its huge central plaza is certainly good for people-watching.

TOURIST CRIME AROUND LAGO DE ATITLÁN

It is rare but not unknown for hikers to be robbed in the Atitlán area. Statistically, the chance of you becoming a victim is extremely small, and hundreds of hikers enjoy trouble-free walks around the lakeshore every month. Nevertheless, if you plan to hike any of the volcanoes or the trails between San Pedro and Santa Cruz, check out the security situation first. Guesthouse staff are usually well informed, and some language school teachers in San Pedro can advise you about the situation, as can the tourist office in Panajachel.

Sololá is one of the only places in the country that has parallel indigenous and ladino governments, and is one of Guatemala's largest Maya towns with tradition dominating daily life. The town's symbol, still seen on the back of the men's jackets, is an abstraction of a bat, referring to the royal house of Xahil from pre-conquest times. Several other villages can be reached from Sololá, most of them within walking distance.

The Friday market

Sololá's **Friday market** (there's also a smaller one on Tues) is one of Central America's finest, a mesmeric display of colour and commerce which Aldous Huxley described as "a walking museum of fancy dress". Traders are drawn from all over the highlands, as well as thousands of Sololá Maya, the women covered in striped red cloth and the men in their outlandish "space cowboy" shirts, woollen aprons and wildly embroidered trousers. It's a non-touristy affair, great for people-watching and photographic opportunities, not for souvenir hunting.

Santa María Concepción

About 8km to the east of Sololá is tiny **Santa María Concepción**, an exceptionally quiet farming village with a spectacularly restored, whitewashed colonial church whose altar has some wonderful gilded cherubs. The walk out here, along a dirt track skirting the hills above Panajachel, offers superb views across the lake.

San Jorge La Laguna

Clinging to a hillside below Sololá, **San Jorge La Laguna** is a small hamlet built of cinder block and adobe with sweeping lake vistas. Villagers have suffered a long history of disasters: the settlement was founded by refugees from the 1773 earthquake in Antigua, and its original lakeside incarnation was swept into the water by a landslide, persuading the people to move up the hill (though some land-hungry residents have recently returned to set up a new community there).

ARRIVAL AND DEPARTURE   SOLOLÁ AND AROUND

By bus Buses run from Sololá to both Panajachel (20min) and Los Encuentros (20 min) every 15min or so until 7.30pm; minibuses also run to the nearby *pueblos* of Santa María Concepción and San Jorge La Laguna.

Panajachel

Ten kilometres beyond Sololá, separated by a precipitous descent, is **PANAJACHEL**, Atitlán's main tourism centre. Over the years what was once a small Maya village has become something of a resort, with a sizeable population of long-term foreign residents, whose numbers are swollen by tourists. Panajachel is one of those inevitable destinations for travellers, and although no one ever owns up to actually liking it, most people seem to drop by for a day or two.

Not so long ago (although it seems an entirely different age) Panajachel was a quiet little **Kaqchikel Maya** settlement. The old village has been enveloped by a construction boom, and though most of the new buildings are pretty nondescript, its lakeside setting is superb. Maya people continue to farm in the river delta behind the town, and the Sunday market, bustling with people from all around the lake, remains oblivious to the tourist invasion.

The old village

The **old village** – a handful of narrow lanes grouped around a sombre, stone-faced Catholic church that dates from 1567 – is not particularly picturesque, though its narrow lanes are worth a little exploration. The **market** has recently been revamped, but is still resolutely geared to local needs rather than tourist tastes; it's a block to the north of the church.

2

INTO THE VORTEX

Some of Atitlán's more mystically minded gringos love to talk about Atitlán being one of the world's few **vortex energy fields**, along with the Egyptian pyramids and Machu Picchu. Though you are unlikely to see fish swimming backwards or buses rolling uphill to Sololá, the lake does have an undeniable draw and Panajachel attracts a polyglot population of healers, therapists and masseurs. Indeed, back in the 1960s and 1970s, Panajachel was the premier Central American **hippie hangout**, though it's now fully integrated into the tourism mainstream and is as popular with Guatemalans (and Mexicans and Salvadoreans) as Westerners. The lotus eaters and crystal gazers have not all deserted the town, though – many have simply reinvented themselves as capitalists, owning restaurants and exporting handicrafts. In many ways it's this **gringo crowd** that gives the town its modern character and identity – vortex energy centre or not.

Calle Santander

The main tourist drag of **Calle Santander** cuts a colourful path through the modern heart of Pana. This kilometre-long street boasts dozens of stores and stalls, loaded up with a kaleidoscopic collection of weaving and handicrafts from all over Guatemala, as well as an amazing selection of places to eat, drink and surf the net. **Street hawkers**, weighed down with armfuls of *típica* textile shirts and gaudy trinkets, ply their goods with daunting persistence, and buzzing tuk-tuks weave their way along the lane touting for business.

Museo Lacustre

In the grounds of Hotel Posada de Don Rodrigo, C Santander • Sun–Fri 8am–6pm, Sat 8am–7pm • US$5

This modern **museum** is dedicated to the turbulent geological history that led to the creation of the lake. There's also an interesting collection of Maya artefacts, including Preclassic- and Classic-era ceramics and some terrific ceremonial incense-burners collected from the underwater Maya site of Samabaj (see p.127).

The beach and promenade

There's little left of Pana's **beach** at the southern end of Calle Santander due to rising lakewater, and swimming is not recommended due to poor water quality. However, the promenade is an ideal place to stretch your legs, particularly around sunset.

The Reserva Natural Atitlán

1km west of centre • Daily 8am–5pm • US$6 • ⓦ atitlanreserva.com • US$2.50 tuk-tuk ride, or 15min walk from Pana

The **Reserva Natural Atitlán** is a privately run forest reserve on the steep slopes of the lake. There are several walking trails (20–75min) through dense foliage, and viewing platforms from where spider monkeys and small mammals like possum and kinkajou are often spotted. Inside the reserve there's a **butterfly park** with dozens of species, including golden orange monarch and blue morpho, plus a breeding laboratory; there are also orchid gardens and aviaries. Eight **zip lines** (US$29), ranging between 90m and 320m offer an unparalleled perspective of the forest and lake.

ARRIVAL AND DEPARTURE   PANAJACHEL AND AROUND

By bus Buses to and from Sololá stop on C Principal and continue to the marketplace. The bus to and from Antigua departs from a separate stop on C Principal.

Destinations Antigua (Mon–Sat at 10.45am; 3hr);

Chichicastenango (6 daily; 1hr 30min); Cocales (6 daily; 2hr); Guatemala City (8 daily; 3hr 30min); Quetzaltenango (7 daily; 2hr 30min)

GETTING AROUND

By tuk-tuk or taxi Tuk-tuks (US$0.80/head) are everywhere in Pana, while taxis wait by the Santiago dock, or you can call one on ☏ 7762 1571.

By boat Most lakeside villages are served by *lanchas*

– small, fast boats, which depart when the owner has enough passengers to cover fuel costs. You usually won't have to wait long, but at quiet times of the day you may have to hang around for up to 40min. Panajachel has two piers. The main pier, at the end of C del Embarcadero, serves the villages on the northern side of the lake: Santa Cruz (about 15min), Jaibalito (20min), Tzununá (30min) and San Marcos (40min). This pier is also home to direct (15min) and non-direct (50min) boats to San Pedro, from where you can easily get to San Juan. The second pier, at the end of

C Rancho Grande, is for Santiago Atitlán (1hr by slow boat, or 25min by *lancha*) and lake tours. The last boats on all routes leave around 7.30pm. A semi-official fare system is in place: tourists pay US$1.30–2 for a short trip, or US$2.50–3 for a longer journey. Locals pay less. Some *lancheros* try to charge more for the last boat of the day.

2

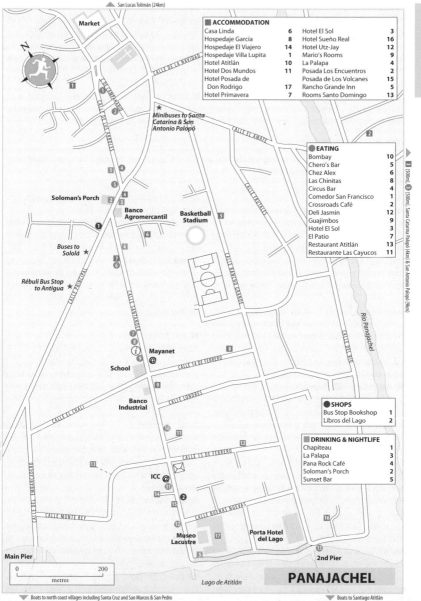

San Lucas Tolimán (24km)

Market

N

■ ACCOMMODATION

Casa Linda	6	Hotel El Sol	3
Hospedaje García	8	Hotel Sueño Real	16
Hospedaje El Viajero	14	Hotel Utz-Jay	12
Hospedaje Villa Lupita	1	Mario's Rooms	9
Hotel Atitlán	10	La Palapa	4
Hotel Dos Mundos	11	Posada Los Encuentros	2
Hotel Posada de		Posada de Los Volcanes	15
Don Rodrigo	17	Rancho Grande Inn	5
Hotel Primavera	7	Rooms Santo Domingo	13

CALLE DE LA NAVIDAD

Minibuses to Santa Catarina & San Antonio Palopó

CALLE EL AMATE

● EATING

Bombay	10
Chero's Bar	5
Chez Alex	6
Las Chinitas	8
Circus Bar	4
Comedor San Francisco	1
Crossroads Café	2
Deli Jasmín	12
Guajimbos	9
Hotel El Sol	3
El Patio	7
Restaurant Atitlán	13
Restaurante Las Cayucos	11

Soloman's Porch

Banco Agromercantil

Basketball Stadium

Buses to Sololá

Rébuli Bus Stop to Antigua

CALLE PRINCIPAL

CALLE SANTANDER

CALLE RANCHO GRANDE

Mayanet @

School

CALLE 14 DE FEBRERO

Banco Industrial

CALLE LONDRES

Río Panajachel

CALLE DEL RIO

CALLE EL CHALÍ

CALLE 15 DE FEBRERO

● SHOPS

Bus Stop Bookshop	1
Libros del Lago	2

■ DRINKING & NIGHTLIFE

Chapiteau	1
La Palapa	3
Pana Rock Café	4
Soloman's Porch	2
Sunset Bar	5

CALLE EMBARCADERO

ICC @

CALLE MONTE REY

CALLE BUENAS NUEVAS

Museo Lacustre

Porta Hotel del Lago

Main Pier

0   200
metres

Lago de Atitlán

PANAJACHEL

2nd Pier

Reserva Natural Atitlán (700m) & Sololá (8km)

(400m),

(500m), ● (500m), Santa Catarina Palopó (4km) & San Antonio Palopó (9km)

2

INFORMATION AND ACTIVITIES

Tourist information Inguat, just off C Santander (daily 9am–5pm; ☎7762 1106, ✉info-panajachel@inguat.gob.gt), has helpful English-speaking staff and hotel information.

Tours Tours of the lake (from US$12) usually visit San Pedro, Santiago Atitlán and San Antonio Palopó and can be booked in travel agencies and hotels; all leave around 9am and return by 4pm.

Travel agents Atitrans, *Anexo Hotel Regis*, C Santander (☎7762 0146, ⓦatitrans.net), are a professional nationwide agency which offers tours of the region and shuttle buses; Adrenalina Tours, C Santander (☎7762 6236, ⓦadrenalinatours.com) is another good agency which has excellent shuttle bus connections and highland tours.

Bike and motorbike rental Motos Maco, C Navidad (☎7762 1192, ✉macobajaj@yahoo.com), rents scooters (US$10/hr; US$46/day) and 200cc trail bikes

(US$14/55); Emanuel, C 14 de Febrero, has mountain bikes for US$9/day.

Watersports Canoes and kayaks (both US$2.50/hr) can be rented on the main beach; note the lake is usually much calmer in the morning. Contact ATI divers for scuba diving or Los Elementos (see p.139) for guided kayak tours, both are in nearby Santa Cruz la Laguna.

Language schools Pana has two language schools where you can study Spanish, though rates are cheaper in San Pedro la Laguna. Escuela Jabel Tinamit, Callejon las Armonias (☎7762 6056, ⓦjabeltinamit.com), and Jardín de América, off C El Chali (☎7762 2637, ⓦjardindeamerica.com) are both professional.

Website The website ⓦatitlan.com has some good historical and cultural information and upmarket accommodation options about the Atitlán area.

ACCOMMODATION

The streets of Panajachel are overflowing with **hotels**, most in the budget and mid-range categories. Many cheap hospedajes are in the lanes of the old village.

BUDGET

Casa Linda Down an alley off the top of C Santander ☎7762 0386. A secure, well-run and friendly place, where all the simple clean rooms (some with private bath) overlook a gorgeous, fecund central garden. US$13

Hospedaje García C 14 de Febrero 2–24 ☎7762 2187. Large, rambling, garish-looking place with tons of basic, clean, spartan rooms in various blocks. There's sure to be space here. US$12

Hospedaje El Viajero C off Santander ☎7762 0128. A peaceful place with an excellent location close to the lakeshore, and all rooms have en-suite bathrooms and cable TV. There's a (basic) guests' kitchen, laundry facilities and free internet access. It's priced per person, so rates are very reasonable for single travellers. US$22

★ **Hospedaje Villa Lupita** Callejón El Tino ☎7762 1201. Excellent-value, family-run place on a quiet lane in the old village. Spotless rooms, all with bedside lights, rugs and mirrors; those with private baths are only a fraction more. Huge sun-terrace and free purified water and coffee. US$14

Hotel El Sol Rd to Santa Catarina Palopó ☎7762 6090, ⓦhotelelsolpanajachel.com. Japanese-owned hotel with super-clean accommodation including a spacious eight-person dorm, singles and doubles. There's delicious Japanese food available (see p.123) and the bathrooms have reliable hot showers. It's 1km from the centre on the other side of the river. Dorms US$7, doubles US$25

Mario's Rooms C Santander ☎7762 2370. A justifiably popular and efficiently run place, close to the lake and in the thick of things. The smallish rooms are well presented, some airy and light with private bath, others more basic,

and the shared balconies overlook a slim courtyard. Free water, light breakfast and wi-fi. US$15

La Palapa C Santander ☎4568 8033. Bunk-bed accommodation in large rooms at the rear of this popular bar; you won't have to stagger far to your bed. Dorms US$7

Rooms Santo Domingo Down a path off C Monterrey ☎7762 0236. Age-old travellers' stronghold with a garden ideal for chilling. A few old clapboard shacks remain, but most rooms here are now modernish, some with en-suite bathrooms. US$10

MODERATE

Hotel Dos Mundos C Santander ☎7762 2078, ⓦhoteldosmundos.com. Set off the main drag, this hotel has spacious comfortable *casitas* set to one side of a palm-filled garden with a swimming pool. Breakfast is included for most rooms, and discounts are often available. US$55

Hotel Primavera C Santander ☎7762 2052, ⓦprimaveraatitlan.com. This attractive hotel has ten smart rooms with magnolia walls, pale wood and a notable absence of *típica* textiles. Expect a little noise in the street-facing rooms. There's a very smart restaurant downstairs, *Chez Alex*. US$42

Hotel Sueño Real C Ramós ☎7762 0608, ✉hotelsuenoreal@hotmail.com. Excellent little family-run guesthouse with ten immaculate rooms, each with ikat curtains and highland blankets. It's located very close to the lakeshore and there's a free breakfast, internet access and wi-fi included. US$26

★ **Hotel Utz-Jay** C 15 de Febrero ☎7762 0217, ⓦhotelutzjay.com. Offering a great garden setting, this fine place has rustic, comfortable rooms and adobe-and-stone *casitas* dotted around lawns, lemon trees a hot tub and *tuj* (sauna). There's good home-cooked food available in the restaurant. US$38

Posada Los Encuentros Callejón Chotzar 0–41 ☎ 7762 2093, ⓦ losencuentros.com. American-owned B&B with seven rooms and an apartment, leafy garden, sauna, thermal pool and gym. Owner Richard Morgan is a knowledgeable, welcoming host. Located a 15min walk from the centre. US$40

Posada de los Volcanes C Santander ☎ 7762 0244, ⓦ posadadelosvolcanes.com. Well-presented, bright rooms, all with good beds, modern bathrooms and cable TV; some have lake aspects. Slightly overpriced so prime those bargaining skills with the helpful management. US$46

Rancho Grande Inn C Rancho Grande ☎ 7762 2255, ⓦ ranchograndeinn.com. One of Pana's original inns, this B&B has spacious chalets and rooms dotted around lovely grassy, shady grounds. Offers local character, in the form of local fabrics and period furnishings, but some rooms are a little dark. There's free wi-fi and a small pool, and the breakfast pancakes are legendary. US$66

EXPENSIVE

Hotel Atitlán 1km west of the centre ☎ 7762 1441, ⓦ hotelatitlan.com. Landmark hotel that enjoys a sublime lakeside location with idyllic gardens of flowering scrubs like heliconias, passion flowers and bougainvillea stretching down to the shore. Rooms boast all mod-cons and volcano views, though the decor could use an update and you have to pay for wi-fi. US$144

Hotel Posada de Don Rodrigo C Santander ☎ 7762 2326, ⓦ posadadedonrodrigo.com. Colonial-style hotel with a lakeside location and outdoor pool. The accommodation is comfortable but a little perfunctory for the price – most rooms lack safes and minibars and don't have lake views – however, those in the new wing (301–311) offer better value and fine vistas. US$124

EATING

Panajachel has an abundance of cafés and **restaurants**, though standards are pretty mediocre. You'll find Italian, Mexican, Asian and some good local places. Cheap comedores can be found close to the market.

Bombay C Santander ☎ 7762 0611. Inviting vegetarian place which, despite the name, has little Indian food, instead featuring global cuisine from Indonesia and east Asia, Mexico and beyond. Wed–Mon 11am–9pm.

Chero's Bar C de los Árboles. Simple *pupusería* where the Salvador-style healthy snacks are made right in front of you, including veggie options with cheese and spinach. A good feed is around US$2.50. Doubles as a low-key bar with cheap drink specials, cocktails and wine by the glass available. Daily 10am–10pm.

Chez Alex C Santander ☎ 7762 0172. High-end dining with a European menu featuring dishes like *wiener schnitzel*, snails, duck and a long wine list. It's expensive and formal, with starched tablecloths and fancy cutlery. Daily noon–3pm & 6–10pm.

Las Chinitas C Santander ☎ 7762 2612. Can be a bit hit-and-miss but worth a try if you're hankering for Asian food: Nonyan (Malay–Chinese) dishes, curries, stir-fries and *sate*. Tues–Sun 8am–9.30pm.

Circus Bar C de los Árboles ☎ 7762 2056, ⓦ circusbar .com.gt. Serving the best pizza (from US$6) in Pana, this atmospheric restaurant is divided into little sections with walls covered in circus memorabilia. Also offers good salads, bruschettas, pasta and grilled meats. Full bar including cocktails (and mocktails) and live latin music most evenings. Daily noon–midnight.

Comedor San Francisco C del Campanario. Come to this good, honest comedor for a filling Guatemalan lunch. Dishes might include *caldo de pollo* or *chuletas*; all are priced at US$2–3 and include rice, salad and a drink. Daily 7am–7pm.

★ **Crossroads Café** C del Campanario 0–27 ☎ 5292 8439. A temple to the arabica coffee bean, this welcoming, humble-looking little place is tucked away on a little lane in the old town. It's run by an American perfectionist who selects, blends and roasts his own beans from the Guatemalan highlands and far beyond. Also offers herbal teas, rich hot chocolate and delicious fresh pastries and cakes. Closed Sun and Mon and for siesta 1–3pm.

★ **Deli Jasmín** C Santander ☎ 7762 2585. Some of the best food in town, this lovely little place has a healthy menu of breakfasts, sandwiches, salads, Mexican dishes and *tempe*; most dishes are priced between US$3–6. It enjoys a great tropical garden setting with a delightful rear patio area – eat your meal surrounded by fluttering butterflies and hovering hummingbirds. There's a second branch, with the same menu, halfway up C Santander (closed Wed; 7am–9pm). Mon & Wed–Sun 7am–6pm.

Guajimbos halfway down C Santander. Ideal for a South American–style feast, all the meat – including kebabs, chorizo and giant steaks – is barbecued on a giant *parrilla*. Well-priced breakfasts too. Mon–Wed & Fri–Sun 8am–10pm.

Hotel El Sol Road to Santa Catarina Palopó ☎ 7762 6090, ⓦ hotelelsolpanajachel.com. Need your fix of Asian flavours? The restaurant at this Japanese-run hotel serves authentic, delicious miso soup, soba, ramen and

2

tempura for between US$5 and US$10 a meal. Note that fresh sushi is not always available (though warm sake is). Daily 7am–9.30pm.

El Patio C Santander ☎ 7762 2041. The pretty street-facing patio is the main appeal here, from where you can relax and watch Pana life pass by. The menu is pretty standard Guatemalan, but portions are massive and the *licuados* (shakes) are cheap (US$1.50). Daily 8am–9pm.

Restaurante Atitlán Lakeside, by the Santiago Pier. A huge palapa-roofed place with fine lake views and a reliable menu offering big portions of Guatemalan favourites: try *camarones especial Atitlán*. Daily 8am–9pm.

Restaurante Las Cayucos C Santander. A large, Maya-owned upper-level restaurant with a good perspective over the main drag. Scores highly for inexpensive local grub, very cheap breakfast deals (from US$2) and lunches (US$3). Daily 7am–9.30pm.

Tal Vez C de los Árboles ☎ 4525 4362. Excellent German-owned vegan café-cum-health food store renowned for its delicious soups (try the spicy eggplant and peanut) and other tasty treats, using *tempe*, soya and tofu. There are particularly good Middle Eastern dishes, including an appealing vegan doner kebab. Mon–Sat 11:30am–4pm & 6–9pm.

DRINKING AND NIGHTLIFE

Panajachel buzzes at weekends and during holidays, when many young Guatemalans head to the lake. Pana's mini Zona Viva is situated around the southern end of C de los Árboles. Many places have happy hours, and either live music or a DJ. *The Circus Bar* (see p.123) also has live music nightly at 7.30pm.

Chapiteau Southern end of C de los Árboles ☎ 7762 2056, ⓦ panajachel.com/chapiteau. Disco with a lively dancefloor on weekend nights. Salsa instructors are often at hand early in the evening to sort out your steps. Cover is around US$3. Wed–Sat 7pm–1am.

La Palapa C Santander ☎ 4568 8033. Huge new bar with live music (blues, rock, *trova* and acoustic) four times a week. Food (everything from breakfasts to a very popular Saturday barbecue) is also served and trivia (quiz) nights are also popular. Daily 7am–1am.

Pana Rock Café C Santander ☎ 7762 2144, ⓦ panarockcafe.com. A kind of *Hard Rock Café* theme bar. It's a popular place to watch sports games, and there are

numerous drinks specials. Live rock music on weekend nights. Daily 8am–1am.

Soloman's Porch C Principal ☎ 7762 6032. Check this barn of a place out for films (you also can choose your own movie), live music and social and environmental lectures, including talks by former gang members and Maya activists. Also has a pool table, café-restaurant and free wi-fi. Tues–Sat noon–10pm.

Sunset Bar By the lake ☎ 7762 0003. This appropriately named bar is worth considering as a spot to enjoy a cocktail or cold cerveza towards the end of the day. Overpriced food is also served. Daily 11am–midnight.

SHOPPING

For Guatemalan textiles, clothes and handicrafts there are dozens of stores along C Santander.

Bus Stop Bookshop C Principal 0–99 ☎ 5297 0138. Inside a little *centro comercial*, this store stocks a great selection of secondhand books and has friendly staff.

Libros del Lago C Santander 9 ☎ 7762 2788. Has a decent choice of books on Maya culture, Central American society and politics, maps and guidebooks. Daily 9am–7pm.

DIRECTORY

Banks and exchange Banco Industrial, C Santander, has an ATM, and there's a 5B ATM at the northern end of the road too.

Internet There are about a dozen or so inexpensive internet cafés around town, with rates around US$1/hr. Mayanet, C Santander, is a good bet.

Laundry Lavandería Santander, C Santander opposite *Pana Rock* (Mon–Sat 7am–8pm), charges US$0.75 for a pound of washing, drying and folding.

Medical care Dr Edgar Barreno speaks good English; his

office is down the first street that branches to the right off C de los Árboles (☎ 7762 1008).

Pharmacy Farmacia La Unión, C Santander.

Police For emergencies, first contact Asistur, Av El Tzalá (☎ 5874 9450), who will help you deal with the police.

Post office C Santander and C 15 de Febrero, or try Get Guated Out on C de los Árboles (☎ 7762 0595) for bigger shipments.

Telephone Get Guated Out, C de los Árboles, has very inexpensive rates to landlines and mobiles worldwide.

2

PARADISE IN PERIL

Cyanobacteria is blue-green algae that occurs in lakes worldwide, feeding on pollution from agricultural run-off and human waste. In September 2009, following a period of warm, settled sunny weather, a smelly gooey green mass of algae began to carpet the surface of Atitlán, at times affecting around thirty percent of the lake, and only fading as the temperature cooled and high winds broke it up. In 2010 and 2011 the climate was far more favourable and there were only tiny patches of algae bloom, but the threat remains for years as phosphorus- and nitrogen-rich nutrients remain in the lake.

Meanwhile, the **fishing industry**, once thriving on the abundance of small fish and crabs, has been crippled by the introduction of **black bass** which eat the smaller fish and water birds.

The eastern shore

There are two roads around the lake's eastern shore from Panajachel. The shoreline road heads as far as **San Antonio Palopó** via **Santa Catarina Palopó** while the other route climbs up to the lip of the crater and heads towards Godínez.

Santa Catarina Palopó

Just 4km from Pana, **SANTA CATARINA PALOPÓ** is a small village with no sights (except a whitewashed colonial church) but an interesting weaving tradition. The *huipiles* worn here have dazzling zigzags in vibrant shades of turquoise or purple, and the women of Santa Catarina have a reputation for being persistent vendors, so expect to be pressed for a purchase if you stop by.

San Antonio Palopó

Continuing along the lakeside road, **SAN ANTONIO PALOPÓ** is a larger and more traditional village, squeezed in beneath a steep hillside. The hillsides above San Antonio are well irrigated and terraced, and older men still wear the village *traje* of red shirts with vertical stripes and short woollen kilts. The central **church** is worth a look; just to the left of the entrance are two ancient bells.

Down by the shoreline you'll find a MayanKe, a small store selling hand-painted **ceramics** made locally and there are two **weaving stores** on the main road selling textiles.

ARRIVAL AND DEPARTURE   THE EASTERN SHORE

Minibuses run along the lakeshore to both villages from C El Amate, Panajachel (6am–7pm, every 20min).

ACCOMMODATION

Much of the shoreline around here has been developed, and great villas and **luxury hotels** have come to dominate the environment.

SANTA CATARINA PALOPÓ

Casa Palopó 2km beyond Santa Catarina ☎ 7762 2270, ⓦ casapalopo.com. The best hotel on this sybaritic strip, the sumptuous and very tasteful *Casa Palopó* offers lovely rooms kitted out with grand furniture and oil paintings, each with million-Quetzal lake views. The restaurant is good (if pricey, meals cost around US$30) and you'll find gorgeous grounds, with a pool area also facing the lake. US$182

Hotel Villa Santa Catarina between village and lakeshore ☎ 7762 1291, ⓦ villasdeguatemala.com.

Colonial-style place with smallish and comfortable, if not exceptional, rooms that face the hotel's large pool. US$92

SAN ANTONIO PALOPÓ

Hotel Terrazas del Lago By the water ☎ 7762 0037, ⓦ hotelterrazasdellago.com. Sitting pretty on a point at the southern end of the village this hotel has comfortable, attractive rooms with stone walls and beautiful views. Tasty meals of local dishes including *empanadas* are also served. US$34

San Lucas Tolimán

Taking the high road from Pana, you pass through the tiny village of **San Andrés Semetabaj** and ramshackle **Godínez** before descending abruptly to **SAN LUCAS TOLIMÁN**. Set apart from the other lakeside settlements in many ways, this largely ladino town, surrounded by coffee fincas, is probably the least attractive of the lot. Both the Tolimán and Atitlán **volcanoes** can be climbed from here, though trips are easier to organize in Pana or San Pedro. The main **market** days are Thursday and Sunday.

ARRIVAL AND DEPARTURE — SAN LUCAS TOLIMÁN

By bus Very regular buses run from San Lucas to Santiago Atitlán and there are hourly buses to Guatemala City via Cocales. There are also six daily buses to Panajachel (1hr) plus occasional boat connections.

ACCOMMODATION

Hotel Tolimán Just above the lakeshore ☎ 7722 0033, ⓦ hoteltoliman.com. Classy, tranquil hotel with lovely grassy grounds overlooking the lake. There's a pool and comfortable rooms that have a colonial feel; the good restaurant serves mains in the US$10 range. U̲S̲$̲5̲0̲

Los Tarrales South of San Lucas at Km164 on the road to Cocales ☎ 5136 3410, ⓦ tarrales.com. This coffee finca and rural lodge borders a nature reserve and offers specialist birding tours (from US$12/head for a half-day guided hike). Transport up to the cloud forest can be arranged, over three hundred species have been recorded in the area. The guides here really know their stuff and the lodge has an engaging old-world charm. U̲S̲$̲5̲2̲

Santiago Atitlán

In the southwest corner of the lake, set to one side of a sheltered horseshoe inlet, **SANTIAGO ATITLÁN** is overshadowed by the cones of the San Pedro, Atitlán and Tolimán volcanoes. It's the largest and most important of the lakeside villages, and also one of the most traditional, being the main centre of the Tz'utujil-speaking Maya. The modest remains of the ancient Tz'utujil fortified capital, **Chuitinamit-Atitlán** are close by, and are easily visited.

Today Santiago is an industrious sort of place in a superb setting, though ugly new concrete and cinder block constructions besmirch its aesthetic appeal. During the day the town becomes fairly commercial, its **main street** (which runs up from the dock)

SAMABAJ

For years scuba divers have come across ceramic fragments and artefacts from Maya times beneath Lago de Atitlán. But in December 2011 news emerged that the remains of an important cermonial Maya settlement, dubbed **Samabaj**, had been discovered offshore from the tiny village of Cerro de Oro on the south side of the lake. (The site had actually been known about since 1997 but its location had been kept secret to deter thieves.)

Samabaj is highly unusual on many fronts. Most of the Maya remains found in the Atitlán region date back five hundred years or so, but Samabaj was a **Preclassic Maya** site that thrived over two thousand years ago. The **condition** of the pieces discovered, including a stela (found still standing upright on the lake bed) and a colossal 1.5m incense burner were remarkable, some displaying their original paint. The number of altars and religious artefacts found indicates that Samabaj was a place of **pilgrimage**.

If it was, pilgrims would have had to travel by boat to reach it, because the site was located on an island. Around 250 AD an abrupt rise in Atitlán's lakewater flooded Samabaj, preserving the monuments around 16m below the surface.

Investigations are ongoing but already tentative links have been established with the Preclassic Maya superpower of El Mirador, way to the north in Petén, which controlled a huge network of trade links throughout Mesoamerica.

In the future it could be possible to dive the remains of Samabaj, so contact ADI Divers (see p.139). Or you can view many of the discoveries for yourself in Panajachel's Museu Lacustre (see p.120).

2

lined with weaving shops and art galleries. Expect to be hustled by hawkers, particularly if you visit during the huge Friday-morning **market**.

The church
The fabulous old colonial Catholic **church** is worth a look for its fascinating Maya religious detail. Its huge central altarpiece, carved when the church was under *cofradía* control, culminates in the shape of a mountain peak and a cross, symbolizing the Maya world tree. Dozens of statues of saints (all bedecked in indigenous attire) line the walls. On the right as you enter, a stone memorial commemorates **Father Stanley Rother**, an American priest who served in the parish from 1968 to 1981. Father Rother was a committed defender of his parishioners in an era when, in his own words, "Shaking hands with an Indian has become a political act". Branded a communist by President García, he was assassinated by a paramilitary death squad like hundreds of his countrymen before and after him.

Chuitinamit
Open access to ruins • Boat from the dock in Santiago US$15 return for 1hr trip

Opposite Santiago Atitlán on the lower flanks of the San Pedro volcano, a steep ten-minute hike up from the lake, are the postClassic Maya ruins of **Chuitinamit**. This small site, originally called **Chiya**, was the fortified capital of the Tz'utujil before the conquistador Alvarado and his Kaqchikel allies laid waste to the place in 1524 – arriving in a flotilla of three hundred canoes. Sadly, the site is in pretty poor shape today as locals have re-carved the stone monuments (and even added a Virgin Mary), creating Disneyesque figures. That said, Chuitinamit is still actively used by shamen for **ceremonies** and its position high above the lake affords panoramic views. The paths around the site are littered with Maya ceramic fragments and obsidian arrowheads.

Maximón
Santiago is one of the main places where Maya pay homage to **Maximón** (see box, p.130), the "evil" saint who can usually be found drinking liquor and smoking a cigarette. It costs a few quetzals to enter his abode, and you'll have to pay extra to take his picture. Local children will lead you to his current residence (Maximón moves every year or so) for a small tip.

Museo Cojolya
100m up from the dock, on the left • Mon–Fri 9am–4pm, Sat 9am–1pm • Free • ⓦ cojolya.org

This small **weaving museum** has excellent displays (in English and Spanish) about the tradition of backstrap weaving in Santiago, natural dyes and types of cotton and methods of spinning and weaving. You can see some of the weavers in action at 11am and 1pm daily. A range of very good quality shirts, bags and souvenirs too are sold too.

SANTIAGO STYLE
The **traditional costume** of Santiago, still worn a fair amount by the older men, is both striking and unusual. The men wear long shorts, which, like the women's *huipiles*, are white- and purple-striped and intricately embroidered with birds and flowers. Some women also wear a **xk'ap**, a band of red cloth approximately ten metres long, wrapped around their heads, which has the honour of being depicted on the 25 centavo coin. Sadly, this headcloth has almost gone out of use, though you may still see it at fiestas and on market days, when it's worn by canny girls eager to attract the eye of tourists (and charge for a photo). The Popol Vuh's second half describes the wanderings of the K'iche' ancestors as they migrate south from the Toltec area of Mexico and settle in the highlands of Guatemala. Evidence gathered by archeologists and epigraphers strongly supports the accuracy of this part of the epic. The book concludes with a history of K'iche' royalty, and suggests a shared lineage with these kings and their gods. Dennis Tedlock's translation of the Popol Vuh (see p.104) is regarded as the definitive text.

HOLY SMOKE

Easter celebrations are particularly special in Santiago, and as Holy Week draws closer the town comes alive with expectation and excitement. **Maximón** maintains an important role in the proceedings. On Monday of Holy Week his effigy is taken to the lakeshore where it is washed, on Tuesday he's dressed, and on Wednesday the idol is housed in a small chapel close to the plaza. Here he waits until **Good Friday**, when the town is the scene of a huge and austere religious procession, the plaza packed with everyone dressed in their finest traditional costume. Christ's statue is paraded solemnly through the streets, arriving at the church around noon, where it's tied to a cross and raised above the altar. At around 3pm the *cofradres* arrive to cut him down from the cross, and Christ is lowered into a coffin. Then pandemonium erupts as dozens of the faithful spray his image with perfume, and the air becomes thick with fragrance and aerosol fumes. Penitents bear Christ out of the church on a vast cedar platform, inching forward and back, taking around two hours to exit the church, before there's a **symbolic confrontation** in the plaza with Maximón, who is carried out of an adjoining chapel by his bearers.

The presence of Maximón (see box, p.130), decked out in a felt hat and Western clothes, with a cigar in his mouth, is scorned by reforming Catholics and revered by the traditionalists.

Activities around Santiago

You can rent a **canoe** and paddle out into the lake – just ask around at the dock. North of Santiago is a small island, surrounded by reeds, which has been designated a **nature reserve**, originally for the protection of the *poc*, or Atitlán grebe, a flightless water bird. However predatory black bass (a species introduced in the 1950s for sportfishing) ate all the young birds and the *poc* is now extinct.

The Tolimán and Atitlán **volcanoes** can both be climbed from Santiago, but it's always best to take a guide to smooth the way as there have been robberies – ask at one of the hotels.

ARRIVAL AND DEPARTURE   SANTIAGO ATITLÁN

By boat *Lanchas* connect Santiago with both San Pedro (15min) and Panajachel (20min); they leave when full. Larger boats also make the odd crossing; there are timetables at the dock.

By bus The town is well connected by bus to Cocales and Guatemala City (7 daily 3am–4pm), and microbuses leave for San Lucas Tolimán.

ACCOMMODATION

Casa de las Buganvillas Opposite Clínica Rxiin Tnamet in Cantón Chechiboy, about 5min east of the church ☎7820 7055. A good choice, this place has spacious, spotless en-suite rooms with attractive wooden furniture and a rooftop restaurant. US$23

Hotel Bambú A 10min walk north of the dock ☎7721 7332, ⓦecobambu.com. A peaceful retreat, *Bambú* has beautiful thatched-roofed stone bungalows and rooms set around a large grassy lakefront, plus an excellent restaurant with Spanish specialities. US$60

Hotel Chi-Nim-Ya On the left uphill from the dock ☎7721 7131. Basic, clean and friendly, with rooms (some with private bathrooms) set around a courtyard. US$12

Hotel Lago de Atitlán Head to the centre from the dock, on the left ☎7721 7174, ⓔhotellagodeatitlan @hotmail.com. Functional concrete block with several floors of clean, plain rooms, all with private bathrooms and cable TV. US$18

Mystical Yoga Farm On shore opposite Santiago ☎4860 9538, ⓦmysticalyogafarm.com. Eco yoga retreat, on the lower flanks of San Pedro volcano with a lakefront plot, run on environmental principles. The ethos is very strict: it's alcohol-, drug- and electricity-free and guests are asked to only bring organic toiletries and "spiritual" books to share. A boat here from the dock in Santiago costs US$5/trip. Rates include all meals, yoga and meditation. Dorms US$45, shared bungalow US$50

★ **Posada de Santiago** 1km south of town ☎7721 7366, ⓦposadadesantiago.com. One of Atitlan's most atmospheric places to stay, this lakeside B&B has delightful rooms, suites and cottages built from volcanic stone. Guests have free access to mountain bikes, canoes, wi-fi, a hot tub, sauna and pool and there's a fine restaurant with very flavoursome cooking and an excellent wine list. US$50

EATING

The hotels *Bambú* and *Posada* both have excellent restaurants with meals costing around US$10.

El Horno 400m up from the dock. A fine bakery with fresh baguette sandwiches, cakes (including macadamia nut pie) and strong coffee. Daily 7am–6pm.

Wach'alal 400m up from the dock. A clean, good-value comedor, with an unpronounceable name but satisfying *comida típica* and lake fish. Daily 7am–7pm.

DIRECTORY

Banks and exchange There's an ATM on the north side of the plaza.

San Pedro La Laguna

Around the other side of the San Pedro volcano from Santiago is the town of **SAN PEDRO LA LAGUNA**, one of Central America's prime places for young travellers to hang out and **party**. San Pedro has a distinctively bohemian feel, and there's plenty of bongo-bashing and bong-smoking counterculture in evidence. Bars pump out reggae and trance till the early hours of the morning, which upsets some locals (most of whom are evangelical Christians). Periodically, crackdowns curtail the party action.

If you've no interest in the high life, you'll still find plenty to do in San Pedro, with **yoga** classes, good **language schools** and plenty of **hiking** trails. It's the kind of place people love or hate – come and make your own mind up.

The setting is simply spectacular. The town sits on the lower slopes of the San Pedro volcano, while to the northwest the steep ridged edge of the Atitlán caldera rises to an irregular peak known as Indian Nose.

San Pedro is a town of two halves. The Maya village sits above the lake, while the gringo zone, replete with bars and cafés, occupies the lower part of town.

The museums

Both museums between the docks • **Museo Tz'unun Ya'** Mon–Fri 8am–5pm • US$5 • ☎ 5846 1923 **Museo Maya Tz'utujil** Mon–Fri 8am–noon • US$1.50

Museo Tz'unun Ya' community museum focuses on the geology of the lake and the history and culture of the Tz'utujil people, and you can arrange guided tours of San Pedro here. Dedicated to Atitlán's Maya culture the modest **Museo Maya Tz'utujil** has examples of traditional weaving from local villages, some interesting old photographs and a small library.

MAXIMÓN

The **precise origin** of Maximón, the evil saint, is unknown, but he's also referred to as San Simón, Judas Iscariot and Pedro de Alvarado in Santiago Atitlán, and always seen as an enemy of the Church. Some say that he represents a Franciscan friar who chased after young indigenous girls, and that his legs are removed to prevent any further indulgence. **"Max"** in the Mam dialect means tobacco, and Maximón is associated with ladino vices such as smoking and drinking; more locally he's known as *Rij Laj or Rilej Mam*, the powerful man with a white beard.

Throughout the year he's looked after by a *cofradía*. Such is Maximón's fame these days, and the number of tour groups visiting Santiago, locals actually use one tourist-geared Maximón house (which outsiders are directed to) and a second location where they can pay their respects to the powerful folk sinner-saint in peace. You'll only likely be invited to the latter – a crepuscular pagan shrine where stuffed animals hang from the ceiling and incense and tobacco fill the air – if you have good local connections. Make a contribution to fiesta funds if you do get an invite.

SAN PEDRO LA LAGUNA

ACCOMMODATION	
Casa Elena	3
Casa Lobo	13
Hotel Gran Sueño	6
Hotel Mansión del Lago	8
Hotel Maria Elena	2
Hotel Mikaso	12
Hotel Nahual Maya	5
Hotel Pinocchio	10
Hotel San Antonio	4
Hotelito El Amanecer Sakcari	11
Jarachik	9
Posada Casa Domingo	1
Zoola	7

EATING	
Café La Puerta	6
D'Noz	3
Hotel Mikaso	8
Hummus-Ya	1
Idea Connection	5
Nick's Place	2
Ventana Blue	7
Zoola	4

DRINKING & NIGHTLIFE	
Alegre Pub	2
El Barrio	4
Buddha Bar	3
Hummus-Ya	1

ARRIVAL AND DEPARTURE
SAN PEDRO LA LAGUNA

By boat There are two docks in San Pedro. All boats from Panajachel and villages on the north side of the lake, including Santa Cruz and San Marcos, arrive and depart from the Panajachel dock on the north side of town. Boats from Santiago Atitlán use a separate dock to the southeast, a 10min walk away.

By bus Buses connect San Pedro with Quetzaltenango (7 daily; 2hr 30min) and Guatemala City (9 daily, last at 2pm; 3hr 45min); all leave from the plaza. Minibuses (about every 20min) connect the town with San Juan, San Pablo and San Marcos, or you can hire a tuk-tuk, which are everywhere in San Pedro. Casa Verde Tours, just above the Pana dock (☏ 5837 9092), run shuttles to Chichicastenango, Quetzaltenango, Antigua, Cobán and Lanquín, Guatemala City, Huehuetenango and San Cristóbal de las Casas in Mexico.

INFORMATION, TOURS AND ACTIVITIES

Information There's no official tourist information office in San Pedro but the website ⓦ tzununya.com offers plenty of online guidance.

ACTIVITIES
Kayaks (US$2/hr) can be rented from the lakeshore west of the Pana dock.
Pools To unwind, head to the thermal pools, between the two docks, for some serious relaxation or just hang out by La Pisina (Tues–Sun 11am–5.30pm, US$2.50) a 15m swimming pool uphill from the Santiago dock.

TOUR OPERATORS
Casa Verde Tours Up from the Panajachel dock ☏ 5837 9092, ⓦ casaverdetours.com. Offers horseriding to Playa Dorada, hikes to Indian Nose and community walks; precise prices depend on numbers but rates are reasonable.

Excursion Big Foot Just left of the Panajachel dock ☏ 7721 8203. Organizes treks up San Pedro volcano and to

2

HIKES FROM SAN PEDRO

The **San Pedro volcano**, which towers above the village to a height of some 3020m, is largely covered with tropical forest; to hike up it get an early start (ideally before 5am) to maximize your chances of a clear view and to avoid the worst of the heat. It can be climbed in around four hours, and takes between two and three hours to descend. The hike is well organized and secure, with all walkers directed via a **base camp** (☎5593 8302) with information 2km south of town. Official **guides** (US$14/head) escort hikers up the volcano along a well-maintained trail with a stop at a *mirador* deck, which has superb lake views. Wildlife you may encounter include wild boar, turkeys and bountiful birdlife. The peak itself is ringed by forest, which blocks the view over San Pedro, although an opening on the south side gives excellent views of Santiago.

An alternative that's possible to arrange with an agency (see p.131) is to climb the peak **Indian Nose**, which arguably provides the best view of the lake and its three volcanoes. You may be asked for an "access fee" to climb this peak of around US$5. This summit is regularly used for Maya religious ceremonies – if you do come across a ritual, it's best not to take photographs.

Indian Nose, horseriding for US$5/hr (guide included) and bicycles for US$7/day.
Atitlán Adventures On the main trail ☎5860 3027, ⓦatitlanadventures.com. Contact Jack for excellent hikes (from US$20), kayak tours to Santiago (US$25) and for mountain biking (US$55) and ziplining.

ACCOMMODATION

San Pedro has an abundance of comfortable, clean **guesthouses** charging around US$7–15 a double per night, though few mid-range options. **Street names** are rarely used in San Pedro, but local children act as guides (for a tip).

Casa Elena Left from the Pana dock ☎5310 9243. A three-storey lakeside place with simple functional rooms; you pay more for a private bath. There's a dock at the rear for swimming. US$7

Casa Lobo Lakeshore 1.5km south of Santiago dock ☎5950 9294, ⓦcasalobo.org. Very tasteful place with stone bungalows, each equipped with huge beds, artwork, kitchenette and verandas set in a lovely garden. The hospitable German owners whip up a mean, healthy breakfast. It's about a 20min walk from town, situated right on the lakeshore so ideal for those who want to get away from it all. US$37

Hotel Gran Sueño Left from the Pana dock ☎7721 8110. Owned by a welcoming family, this efficient, ever-expanding place has clean, attractive if smallish rooms all with private bathrooms and TV. Some have nice touches like wall maps, and those on the upper level have lake views. Free drinking water and wi-fi. US$17

Hotel Mansión del Lago Up from Pana dock ☎7721 8041, ⓦhotelmansiondellago.com. A well-built hotel with light, clean rooms all with pine beds, private bath and balcony areas with lake views. Also has a rooftop hot tub and internet café. US$20

Hotel Maria Elena Left from Pana dock ☎5098 1256. Two-storey block with eleven spacious rooms, all with private bathrooms. The communal balconies have hammocks at the front for quality swinging time. US$14

Hotel Mikaso Close to Santiago dock ☎5973 3129, ⓦmikasohotel.com. San Pedro's best hotel is very Spanish in style, an attractive building with lovely tilework.

Rooms are elegant and comfortable, there's a comfy dorm (with en-suite bathroom) and a great roof-terrace restaurant (see p.133). Dorm US$9, rooms US$35

★ **Hotel Nahual Maya** Left from the Pana dock ☎7721 8158. A smart, whitewashed colonial-style place set back off the road with two floors of very well-kept, attractive rooms; all have plenty of natural light and private bathrooms. Popular, so book ahead. US$16

Hotel Pinocchio Between the docks ☎5845 7018. Yes, it's a large concrete block, but the rooms are kept tidy, the huge garden is lovely, staff are welcoming and there's wi-fi and a guests' kitchen. US$7

Hotel San Antonio Left of the Pana dock ☎5823 9190. A good mustard-coloured place where all the inviting rooms have TVs and bathrooms, and there's wi-fi and a café too. US$15

Hotelito El Amanecer Sakcari 7 Av 2–12, Zona 2 ☎7721 8096. This place has attractive grassy grounds that enjoy fine lake aspects and well-kept rooms with private bathrooms in brightly painted accommodation blocks. The owners are welcoming and there's wi-fi. US$22

Jarachik Between the docks ☎5543 4111. This place has two clean dorms (with shared bathrooms) and plain, spacious en-suite rooms on the upper floor. There's wi-fi and a café here. Dorms US$5, rooms US$12

Posada Casa Domingo Between the docks. Six simple clean rooms, all with tiled floors, lockers and private bath in a block that faces Volcán San Pedro. The location is quiet. US$8

Zoola Between the docks ☎5547 4857. This Israeli-owned lakeside hostel is popular with young travellers and has a great chillout space shaded by canvas and a (tiny) lakeside pool for cooling off. Dorms are pleasant and there's great Middle Eastern food; however, the stoner vibe won't appeal to all. Minimum two-night stay. Dorms US$4, rooms US$13

EATING

San Pedro's **cafés** and **restaurants** have a decidedly international flavour, and most are also excellent value for money. Vegetarians are well catered for, and there are also a few typical Guatemalan comedores in the centre of the village.

★ **Café La Puerta** Between the docks ☎ 5098 1272. The best food in San Pedro, courtesy of an accomplished Guatemalan cook, in a lovely garden setting, with tables under the trees. Offers a freshly prepared, healthy and varied menu, with several dozen delicious breakfast choices (US$2.50–5), delicious snacks and appetizing smoothies and juices. The pasta and bread are home-made, salads are wonderful and wine is available by the glass. Daily 7.30am–9pm.

D'Noz Pana dock ☎ 5578 0201. Something of a San Pedro institution, this refurbished bar/restaurant offers a global menu – bagels, Indian, Guatemalan and Chinese – friendly service, free films (8.30pm every night), wi-fi and a long happy hour (5–8pm). Daily 8am–1am.

Hotel Mikaso Close to Santiago dock ☎ 5973 3129. This hotel's roof terrace restaurant has wonderful elevated lake views. The menu features pasta, fish, grilled meats, salads and bocadillos as well as paella (order a day in advance). Around US$10 for most mains. Daily 7am–10pm.

Hummus-Ya Left at Pana dock ✆ hummusya.com. Come to this big barn of a place for authentic Israeli and Middle Eastern food including shakshuka (US$3.50), falafel (US$3) and tasty kebabs as well as steaks. Free wi-fi; doubles as a bar. Mon, Tues & Thurs–Sun 9am–midnight.

Idea Connection Between the docks. Superb very welcoming Italian-owned garden café with delicious breakfasts (US$3–4), muffins and croissants and fast wi-fi. Doubles as an internet café, and has Wii and fifty games for the X-Box 360. Daily 7.30am–5.30pm.

Nick's Place By the Pana dock ☎ 7721 8065. Popular, locally owned restaurant with a superb-value menu of international and Guatemalan food (most meals cost around US$3) and a fine lakefront location. Daily 7am–11pm.

Ventana Blue Between the docks ☎ 5284 2406. Small, attractive place with just four tables offering creative, delicious food. The menu is split between authentic Guatemalan dishes like jocom, which are brilliantly executed, and Asian cuisine (Thai curries and teriyaki beef) which the chef also makes more than a good stab at. A great selection of Martinis is served. Mon & Wed–Sun 6–10pm.

Zoola between the docks, ☎ 5547 4857. This hotel/restaurant has low tables set under a tent and serves commendable Israeli and Middle Eastern food. Service is very sloooow, so take a good book or play backgammon while you wait. Daily 8am–10pm.

DRINKING, NIGHTLIFE AND ENTERTAINMENT

San Pedro's **bar action** is concentrated on the trail between the docks, and around the Pana dock. There are some great boho bars, and most places have happy hours. Alegre, D'Noz and the Buddha all show **movies**.

Alegre Pub Above Pana dock ☎ 7721 8100, ✆ thealegrepub.com. Pub showing European football, NFL and NBA games, and serving comfort grub such as Sunday roasts, shepherd's pie and burgers. Mon 5pm–1am, Tues–Sat 9am–1am, Sun 9am–11pm.

El Barrio Between the docks ☎ 4424 6941. An intimate little bar with garden, busy for its happy hour (5–8pm) and quiz (trivia) on Wednesdays. Also serves reasonable grub including a good Saturday brunch. Mon–Fri & Sun 5pm–1am, Sat 9am–1am.

Buddha Bar Between the docks ☎ 4178 7979. This three-storey American-owned bar is popular for its live music (everything from cumbia to country), DJ and comedy events, pool tables, dart board, films and general craic. Daily 9am–1am.

Hummus-Ya Left at Pana dock ✆ hummusya.com. Huge bar/restaurant that regularly host live bands and has a lake aspect. Mon, Tues & Thurs–Sun 9am–midnight.

DIRECTORY

Banks and exchange Banrural (Mon–Fri 8am–5pm, Sat 9am–12.30pm) has an ATM, and there's a second ATM by the Pana dock.

Books Zuvuya, between the docks, has a good selection of used titles.

Internet Wi-fi is very widespread in San Pedro. Head to Idea Connection (see above) for fast connections and Skype calls. D'noz is well set up for all your internet needs too.

LANGUAGE LESSONS IN SAN PEDRO

San Pedro has established itself as a **language school** centre in recent years – the beautiful location and inexpensive schools drawing increasing numbers of students. Prices are still extremely cheap, ranging from around US$120 to US$175/week for four hours' one-on-one tuition and full board with a local family. These schools are recommended:

Casa Rosario South of Santiago Atitlán dock ☎ 5613 6401, ⓦ casarosario.com

Cooperativa Spanish School Uphill from the Santiago dock ☎ 5398 6448, ⓦ cooperativeschool sanpedro.com

Corazón Maya 1km south of Santiago dock ☎ 7721 8160, ⓦ corazonmaya.com

San Pedro Spanish School Between the piers ☎ 5715 4604, ⓦ sanpedrospanishschool.com

The northern shore

The **northern side** of the lake harbours a string of isolated, traditional villages. From San Pedro, a rough road runs as far as Tzununá and from there a spectacular path continues all the way to Sololá. Non-direct *lanchas* to Panajachel will call in at any village en route, but the best way to see this string of isolated settlements is **on foot**: it makes a fantastic day's walk, though check the security situation first (see p.118). A narrow strip of level land is wedged between the water and the steep hills most of the way, and where this disappears the path is cut into the slope, yielding dizzying views of the lake below. It takes between five and six hours to walk from San Pedro to Santa Cruz. You can get drinks, snacks and meals at all the villages along the way, which also all have accommodation.

San Juan La Laguna

From San Pedro it's just 2km to the tidy, tranquil little town of **SAN JUAN LA LAGUNA**, at the back of a sweeping bay. The beaches that surrounded the town were until recently swamped by rising lakewater but San Juan remains a pretty place to visit and something of a model for highland Guatemala. Citizens here take a real pride in the appearance of their town; streets are swept and you won't encounter any litter.

The town has developed an excellent **community tourism** project (☎ 5964 0040, ⓦ sanjuanlalaguna.org; tours US$15–18) that allows travellers to visit natural dye-weaving co-ops, local forests for birdwatching, a medicinal plant nursery, coffee plantations and to learn about local crafts (mats called *petates* are made from lake reeds), culture and folklore. Guides can also lead you to some extraordinary **archeological remains** that lie around the fringes of the town, including a huge Olmec head that's buried in coffee bushes and a carved stone monument that depicts a birth.

You'll also find several good artist **galleries** and **weaving co-ops** just up from the dock including Las Artesanías de San Juan and Asociación de Mujeres de Color – all have plenty of goods for sale.

Next door to *Restaurant Chi'nimaya* in the centre of the village is a shrine to **Maximón** (see p.130). Inside you'll find the saintly sinner dressed in local garb – as this shrine attracts fewer visitors than those elsewhere, you may want to bring him some liquor or a cigar.

ARRIVAL AND DEPARTURE   **SAN JUAN LA LAGUNA**

By pick-up/minibus Pick-ups and minibuses run between San Pedro and San Juan about every 20min.

ACCOMMODATION

Pa Muelle 200m up from the dock ☎ 4141 0820. A lovely place consisting of a row of five immaculately presented rooms that share a lake-facing terrace. Staff are kind and helpful and there's a guests' kitchen. <u>US$20</u>

Uxlabil Atitlán 1km southeast of centre ☎ 2366 9555,

ⓦ uxlabil.com. Fine eco-hotel with a strong Maya flavour in stunning gardens. There are wonderful vistas from the top-floor rooms and the restaurant serves excellent local food. It's a 10min walk from town. <u>US$60</u>

EATING

★ **Café El Artesano** In centre of village ☎4555 4773, ⓦcafeelartesano.com. One of the best dining experiences in the country, this delightful garden café-restaurant was established by Ditres, a chef from the capital who tired of city life. His platters of cheese (US$12 for two people) are simply sublime, featuring a dozen or more artisan products that he's sourced from across Guatemala which he serves with olives, nuts, home-made bread and a pickle or two. After you order, allow an hour for the cheese to reach air temperature, uncork a bottle of wine and you're set. The rest of the menu takes in smoked fish, delicious salads (US$3) and grilled meats. Mon–Fri 11.30am–6pm, until 8pm Nov–April.

San Pablo La Laguna

From San Juan, the lakeside road passes below the Tz'utujil settlement of **SAN PABLO LA LAGUNA**. This village's traditional speciality is the manufacture of rope from the fibres of the *maguey* plant; you can sometimes see great lengths being stretched and twisted in the streets.

Santa Clara La Laguna

A precipitous but paved road continues from San Pablo up to **SANTA CLARA LA LAGUNA**, a sprawling town situated in a plateau high above the western shore of the lake, renowned for its basketry. Women use *cañvera*, which is similar to bamboo, to make fine fruit bowls and other household goods; you can check out a good selection at the Copikaj weavers co-op at 4 Avenida 2–71.

Parque Chuiraxamoló

9km north of Santa Clara La Laguna • Daily 8am–5pm • Zip lines US$13 • ☎7927 1859 • All buses running between San Pedro and the Carretera Interamericana pass the entrance

The spectacular **Parque Chuiraxamolós** is a forest reserve and adventure centre with some of Central America's longest zip lines (including a 400m run), hiking and bike trails, and picnic and camping areas. It's professionally managed and a great day out.

San Marcos La Laguna

SAN MARCOS LA LAGUNA is famous for its holistic and healing centres, veggie cafés, yoga and rebirthing classes and all things esoteric. It's home to a merry bunch of foreigners of an artistic and spiritual persuasion so if you're searching for a therapist or masseur this is the place.

The settlement has a decidedly tranquil feel – there's no real bar scene – so it's a perfect place to relax and read a book in your hammock and enjoy the natural beauty of the lake. **Hotels and restaurants** are clustered close to the water under thick forest cover while the **Maya village** is inland on higher ground. Relationships between the two communities remain a little distant. Apart from a huge new stone **church**, built to replace a colonial original destroyed in the 1976 earthquake, there are no real sights in the Maya village.

One of the main draws is *Las Pirámides* yoga and meditation retreat, and there's also a healing centre (San Marcos Holistic Center), which offers acupuncture, reflexology, massages, crystal therapy and natural remedies. You can also **study** Spanish in San Marcos.

Uphill from the village, Cambalacha (ⓦlacambalacha.org) is an arts project that teaches dance, music and theatre to local children; volunteers are always welcome and shows are also performed.

Cerro Tzankujil

500m west of the dock • Mon–Fri 8am–6pm • US$2

This wooded peninsula juts into the lake and has been developed for visitors with paths, a lookout point and trampoline. There's a famous **cliff jump** here where you can plunge six metres or so into the lake (though it's not obligatory). Tzankujil is also a sacred spot used for Maya ceremonies.

2

2

SAN MARCOS LA LAGUNA

San Juan (9km) & San Pedro (11km)

2 (400m) & Tzununá (4km)

Seasonal River

Básico

Parque

Church

Dock

N

CERRO
TZANKUJIL

● EATING	
Blind Lemon	1
Blue Lily	8
Comedor Mi	
Marquensita Susi	2
La Fé	7
Il Giardino	6
Moonfish	3
El Paco Real	5
Seiko's	4
Tul y Sol	9

■ ACCOMMODATION	
Aaculaax	10
Hospedaje Panabaj	1
Hotel La Paz	4
Hotel Quetzal	3
Hotel Silani	2
El Paco Real	6
Las Pirámides	7
Posada del Bosque	
Encantado	5
Posada Schumann	9
Tul y Sol	8

0   100
metres

ARRIVAL AND DEPARTURE
SAN MARCOS LA LAGUNA

On foot San Marcos is a 2hr walk from San Pedro.
By minibus From San Pedro it's a 20min ride in one of the regular minibuses and pick-ups that connect the villages.

ACTIVITIES

Swimming from wooden jetties by the lakeshore has got more troublesome as the lakewater has risen in the last few years, but there are still docks for lake access. Kayaks can be rented from a cabin close to *Aaculaax*.

Spanish Study San Marcos Spanish School, inside *Paco Real* (☎ 5852 0403, ⓦ sanmarcosspanishschool.org), charges US$95/week for four hours of classes, excluding accommodation.

ACCOMMODATION

Most of San Marcos' hotels and guesthouses are best reached from the main dock by *Posada Schumann*.

★ **Aaculaax** 300m west of the dock ☎ 5803 7243, ⓦ aaculaax.com. This fantasy eco-hotel was built by a visionary German craftsman from thousands of recycled bottles and wood, incorporating lots of stained glass and artistic touches including murals and sculptured concrete. Prices vary considerably according to which of the twelve accommodation options you select: "Mirador" (US$120) has a huge deck and a kitchen, but even the budget choices (US$15–25) are very attractive. Breakfast is included. US$15

Hospedaje Panabaj In the village ☎ 5483 1225. Two-storey block in a quiet location, with basic rooms that face a garden. The shared bathrooms are kept tidy. US$7

Hotel La Paz Uphill from dock ☎ 5702 9168, ⊛ sanmarcoslapaz.com. Long-running place with very spacious, rustic cottages, a superior six-bed, two-storey dorm, good home-cooking and yoga classes. Guests get the run of a lovely leafy garden, there's a sauna/massage room and your host Benjamin is amiable. Dorms US$7, rooms US$15

Hotel Quetzal Just off road to San Juan ☎ 4146 6036. Swiss–Guatemalan-owned hotel with attractive, high-quality rooms (some without bathrooms) that are decorated with local textiles. The owner is a baker, so be sure to try his produce. Rates are US$8 or US$16/person (with a bathroom), so it's a good deal for solo travellers. US$16

Hotel Silani Lakeshore on extreme eastern side ☎ 2425 8088, ⊛ silani.net. Enjoys a prime plot with direct lake views and private dock. Accommodation includes a treehouse and charming adobe rooms, and there's a restaurant and sauna. US$10

El Paco Real Uphill from the dock ☎ 3009 5537, ⊛ hotelpacoreal.com. This place has real ambience with very well-built thatched bungalows, some sleeping up to four and many with private bathrooms, dotted around a shady garden. There's a good bar/restaurant and reliable wi-fi. Dorms US$7, rooms US$18

Las Pirámides Uphill from dock ☎ 5205 7302, ⊛ laspiramidesdelka.com. It's not exactly a hotel, but a life experience. This meditation retreat is set in leafy grounds and has monthly courses, which begin the day after the full moon (though you can also enrol on a daily or weekly basis). These include hatha yoga, metaphysics, meditation techniques and an esoteric learning week, followed by a final week of fasting and complete silence. All accommodation is in comfortable, if smallish pyramid cabañas; there's also delicious vegetarian food. The cost is US$22/540/head (per day/month), which includes courses but not food. US$44

★ **Posada del Bosque Encantado** Uphill from dock ☎ 5208 5334, ⊛ hotelposadaencantado.com. Managed by charming staff, this wonderful place has four huge, gorgeous adobe cottages with a shared terrace; they face a lovely garden. You'll find a *temascal* (sauna), hammocks to lounge in and a little café/restaurant serving tasty Guatemalan grub as well. US$20

Posada Schumann By the dock ☎ 5202 2216, ⊛ posadaschumann.com. Established hotel with a selection of attractive, good-value stone-and-timber rooms and bungalows (though due to rising lakewaters some of the pretty lakeside garden has been lost). There's a Maya-style sauna, free use of kayaks and a nice, though slightly pricey restaurant. US$26

Tul y Sol Short walk west at dock ☎ 5293 7997. Two very spacious and superb-value rooms at the rear of a lakeside restaurant. You get a huge bed, nice wooden furniture, private bathrooms, lake views from a shared balcony and even a free breakfast and wi-fi for very little here. It's a total bargain for single travellers. US$15

EATING AND DRINKING

There's a good range of cuisines in San Marcos, where vegetarians are particularly very well catered for; prices don't vary that much in the gringo places (around US$4–6 for a meal). For cheap comedor cooking head to the Maya village.

Blind Lemons On road to San Juan ☎ 5540 0399, ⊛ blindlemons.com. This colonial-style bar/restaurant showcases blues artists (Fri), films (most nights) and offers a familiar US-style menu including burgers, cajun grub and steaks. Daily 11am–10.30pm.

Blue Lili Inland from dock. A great place to pass the day, this quirky boho café is owned by a friendly English traveller with tables scattered around a fecund, shady garden. Popular for breakfasts (from US$2.50), lunches like falafel wrap (US$3.50), juices and shakes. Or just order a pot of tea. Mon–Sat 7am–10pm.

Comedor Mi Marquensita Susi In the village. Simple local place just off the plaza, ideal for your fill of *comida típica* at very reasonable prices. Daily 7am–7pm.

La Fé Inland from dock ☎ 5994 4320. Large restaurant with a keenly priced, eclectic menu that takes in tapas (US$2 each), sandwiches (from US$2.50), home-made

soups and burritos, burgers and kebabs. It's also renowned for its authentic Indian and Thai curries and steak with blue cheese and pepper. Daily 7.30am–midnight.

Il Giardino Inland from dock ☎ 7804 0186. This restaurant has a lovely peaceful garden setting and serves Italian food, Latin American dishes, tapas and addictive honey wine. Daily 4–9pm.

Moonfish On road to San Juan. In a new inland location, the owners of this enjoyable café grow their own leaves for the delicious salads and much of the menu (*tempe*, hummus with panini) is organically sourced. Their dark roast coffee really hits the spot. Daily 8am–6pm.

El Paco Real ☎ 3009 5537. Serves the best pizza in town and also good for gourmet burgers and cocktails including margaritas and mojitos. Daily 4–10pm.

Seiko's By the football field. Quirky, authentic

Japanese-owned garden restaurant ideal for delicious noodle dishes, veggie tempura, sushi, *onigiri*, miso soup and warm sake. Daily 6–10pm.

Tul y Sol Short walk west of dock ☎5293 7997. For a splurge this French-owned lakeside restaurant is worth considering, with fairly expensive mains (fish, shrimps and grilled *lomito*) in the US$10–14 range. Snacks are also served. Daily 7am–10pm.

DIRECTORY

Banks The nearest banks and ATMs are in San Pedro la Laguna.

Internet Wi-fi is pretty common in most hotels and restaurants. There's an internet café (daily 9am–8pm) opposite *Paco Real*.

Tzununá

Beyond San Marcos, the villages feel more isolated. The first one you come to is **TZUNUNÁ**, a scruffy-looking, very traditional place strung up a steep hillside. Originally it sat at the lakeside, but after it was badly damaged by a flood in 1950, the people rebuilt their homes on higher ground. As ever the local costume is striking, the women wearing vivid red *huipiles* striped with blue and yellow on the back.

ACCOMMODATION   TZUNUNÁ

Lomas de Tzununá 800m east of the dock ☎5201 8272, ⊛lomasdetzununa.com. Perched high above the lake with stupendous views, this is a magnificently sited and well-managed solar-powered hotel. The ten lovely cottages all come with huge, sliding glass doors that make the most of the unsurpassed lake vistas. There's a small pool, kayaks and bikes for rent, a good restaurant with a healthy menu and home-made ice cream. The hotel is a very steep climb up from the lakeshore, but if you call in advance, they'll pick you up from the village dock. US$90

Jaibalito

The lakeside road indisputably ends at *Lomas*, giving way to a narrow path cut out of the steep hillside. The next village, **JAIBALITO**, nestling between soaring *milpa*-clad slopes, is another place that was extremely isolated until recent years. It remains resolutely Kaqchikel – little Spanish is spoken, and few women have ever journeyed much beyond Lago de Atitlán – though the opening of four tourist-geared businesses means that outside influence is growing.

ACCOMMODATION   JAIBALITO

La Casa del Mundo A steep 5min walk from the village ☎5218 5332, ⊛lacasadelmundo.com This remarkable place seems to cling to a cliffside, with accommodation (budget rooms, doubles, stone cabins and a suite) that make the most of the dramatic location. There's a great restaurant (dinner is US$10/head), but some of the facilities involve extra charges including kayaks (US$3–7/hr) and the lakeside tub (US$35). US$35

Posada Jaibalito In the centre of the village ☎5192 4334, ⊛posadajaibalito.com. A very inexpensive and fine-value option with a superb six-bed dorm (which has lockers and en-suite bathroom), great private rooms, plus tasty Guatemalan food (US$2–3.50) and very cheap drinks – treat yourself to a shot of 23-year old Ron Zacapa for just US$2.50. Wi-fi. Dorms US$5, doubles US$12

Vulcano Lodge Just off the main pathway ☎5410 2237, ⊛vulcanolodge.com. Lacks lake views, but this fine Norwegian-owned inn has an amazing garden bursting with exotic scrubs to enjoy. All the rooms and cottages are absolutely spotless and very comfortable and there's gourmet European and Guatemalan food in the restaurant. Rooms US$40, suite US$76

EATING

Ven Acá Lakeshore ☎5051 4520, ⊛clubvenaca.com. This upmarket bar-restaurant has a hot tub and pool, a fusion menu and excellent cocktails. Very popular for Sunday brunch. Wed–Sun 11am–10pm.

Santa Cruz La Laguna

Gorgeous **SANTA CRUZ LA LAGUNA**, stretching for about two kilometres in a verdant ribbon along the lakeshore, is a supremely tranquil and beautiful village. With some terrific accommodation, yoga classes, kayaking and hiking, it's not surprising its star is on the rise. Above all, it's the (almost) complete lack of roads that really makes this place – just one little lane snakes up to the Maya village high above the lakeshore, and the only access is by boat. With no traffic to contend with, the lake really comes into its own, and it's very easy to be seduced by the mellow pace of life, watching hummingbirds buzz between exotic flowers or Maya boatmen fish for crabs. You really can get back to nature here.

Most of the **lakeshore** has been bought up by foreigners and wealthy Guatemalans, while the Maya village is high above the water. The two communities coexist well, with many villagers employed in foreign businesses. Unfortunately the rise in Atitlán's lakewater has swamped some shoreline paths, but it's still possible to explore the Santa Cruz bay using a system of gangplanks and trails.

Maya village

Perched on a shelf 150m above the lake, you'll immediately notice the contrast between the affluent shore and the indigenous community in the **Maya village**, who live in rudimentary conditions. There are no real sights in the village itself, though lake views are truly spectacular and there's a sixteenth-century church on the plaza. The charity **Amigos de Santa Cruz** (ⓦamigosdesantacruz.org) does sterling work improving opportunities for the local Maya by funding environmental, educational and health programmes. Visitors are welcome to drop by the highly impressive **Cecap** centre, just below the plaza, which Amigos helped establish, where you can take a look at the library, workshops and have a drink or meal in the **café**, which is staffed by catering students.

ARRIVAL AND DEPARTURE SANTA CRUZ LA LAGUNA

By boat There's no road access to Santa Cruz. Boats (6am–7.30pm) connect the community with Panajachel (15min) and all villages to the west including San Marcos

(20min) and San Pedro (25min) every 20min or so. **Tuk-tuks** (US$0.75/person) buzz between the lakeshore and Maya village, or you can hike it in 15min.

INFORMATION, TOURS AND ACTIVITIES

Swimming is great in Santa Cruz (the lake water is cleaner away from the centre). You can **scuba dive** here with ATI Divers (see below), or there's some excellent **hiking**, including a walk to a waterfall above the village football pitch, and another to Sololá along a spectacular path. Staff at the *Iguana Perdida* will be able to get you on the right track for these walks. **Kayaking** is also very popular and you can **study Spanish** here too.

ATI Divers At the Iguana Perdida ☎5706 4117, ⓦatidivers.com. Dive the lake with this professional scuba school. One fun dive is US$30, while a PADI Open Water course is US$220.
Atitlan Tours ☎5355 8849, ⓦtours-atitlan.com. Local Maya guide and Santa Cruz resident Pedro Juan Solis speaks fluent English, knows the area like the back of his hand and can organize excellent mountain-bike trips (around US$50) in the hills behind Santa Cruz, hikes (from US$23), birdwatching excursions and tours of the highlands.

Los Elementos 400m west of the dock ☎5359 8328, ⓦkayakguatemala.com. Owner Lee Beal offers fine kayak tours (or you can just rent one and explore yourself) plus hiking to the cloud forest (US$50) above the village, and beyond. Recuperate with a massage (US$30) or spa service here afterwards.
Santa Cruz Spanish School 300m inland from dock ☎3047 5583, ⓦatitlanspanishschools.com. Various study packages are available, with twenty hours' one-on-one tuition costing US$90.

ACCOMMODATION AND EATING

Santa Cruz has some wonderful accommodation. The main village **dock** beside the *Iguana Perdida* is at the centre of things but boatmen will drop you off at any of the following places; all have private docks (except *Eggedal*).

Casa Rosa Just east of dock ☎5803 2531, ⓦatitlanlacasarosa.com. Run by a friendly Guatemalan woman and her daughter, this lakefront place offers beautiful, peaceful gardens, spacious bungalows (US$67) and smallish but neat rooms. There's excellent home-style cooking served in the farmhouse-style kitchen or on the

stylish lakefront lounge-café. ̄U̲S̲$̲3̲2̲
La Fortuna 1km east of Santa Cruz ☎4021 8117, ⓦlafortunaatitlan.com. Intriguing new place on the tiny, virtually private bay of Pachisotz – an isolated but wonderful setting. There are two gorgeous Indonesian-style wooden bungalows, complete with outdoor

2

bathrooms and very fine attention to detail. More accommodation is also under construction (rooms will be around US$50/night) and creative global cuisine is offered. Bungalows US$100

Hotel Arca de Noé ☎ 5515 3712, ⓦ arcasantacruz .com. Rustic but comfortable enough stone cottages and rooms, with or without private bathrooms, spread around an expansive, very beautiful, terraced lakeside garden. There's good home-cooking, including a communal set dinner for US$10. US$12

★ **Iguana Perdida** ☎ 5706 4117, ⓦ laiguanaperdida .com. Owned by a very hospitable and knowledgeable English-American couple, the *Iguana* has one of the most convivial atmospheres in Lago de Atitlán. Basic dorms and budget rooms, as well as more luxurious options (US$25–50), but it's the lakefront location and social vibe that really makes this place. Dinner (US$7) is a three-course communal affair. The hotel also offers yoga classes, massage, internet, a TV lounge, book exchange, kayak rental, scuba diving and great travel advice. Dorms US$5, rooms US$10

★ **Isla Verde** 10min walk west of the dock ☎ 5760 2648, ⓦ islaverdeatitlan.com. This little slice of paradise has been beautifully and ecologically designed with lovely A-frame bungalows, rooms and two apartments set high above the lake, below a forest canopy; all have fine views. The cuisine here is as good as it gets in Guatemala, with healthy nutritious meals including exquisite mezze platters, fresh pasta and daily specials; meals are in the US$5–10 range. US$45

Villa Eggedal East side of the bay, above the shore ⓦ villaeggedal.com. Lovely studio apartments and *casas* (one with four bedrooms) all enjoying stunning lake views and complete with kitchens and luxury bathrooms. They're located in a simply gorgeous garden. Managed by the *Iguana Perdida*. Per week: studios from US$300, *casitas* from US$500

Villa Sumaya In Paxanax bay, a 15min walk east of the dock ☎ 4026 1390, ⓦ villasumaya.com. Boutique hotel with a prime lakefront location and sixteen rooms – those in the *torre* are larger – each with a stupendous lake view, plush beds and stylish decor. Also boasts a great restaurant (meals US$6–10), library, hot tub and sauna. Spa treatments and massages are available and there are daily yoga/meditation/ Pilates sessions in a stunning rooftop space. US$78

Along the Carretera Interamericana: Los Encuentros to Cuatro Caminos

Heading west from the Los Encuentros junction to Cuatro Caminos, the **Carretera Interamericana** runs through some fantastic high-mountain scenery. The views alone are superb, and if you have time to spare it's well worth dropping into Nahualá for the market.

Nahualá

NAHUALÁ ("place of sorcerers") is a small and intensely traditional town a kilometre or so north of the highway, at the base of a huge, steep-sided and intensely farmed bowl.

NAHUALÁ RESISTANCE

At the end of the nineteenth century the government confiscated much of the town's **land**, as they did throughout the country, and sold it to **coffee** planters. In protest, the entire male population of Nahualá walked the 150km to Guatemala City and demanded to see **President Barrios** in person, refusing his offers to admit a spokesman and insisting that they all stood as one. Eventually, they were allowed into the huge reception room where they knelt with their foreheads pressed to the floor, refusing to leave until they were either given assurances of their land rights or allowed to buy the land back, which they had done twice before. They saved their land this time, but since then much of it has gradually been consumed by coffee bushes all the same.

On another occasion, during the 1930s under President Ubico, **ladinos** were sent to the town as nurses, telegraph operators and soldiers. Once again the Nahualáns appealed directly to the president, insisting that their own people should be trained to do these jobs, and once again their request was granted. Ubico also wanted to set up a government-run drink store, but the villagers chose instead to ban **alcohol**, and Nahualeños who got drunk elsewhere were expected to confess their guilt and face twenty lashes in the town's plaza.

NAHUALÁ CRAFTS

Nahualá is a major artisan centre and has a fine **weaving** tradition. Men wear outlandish-looking "dayglow" bright yellow and pink shirts with beautifully embroidered collars, kilt-like woollen "skirts" (called *rodilleras* or *ponchitos*) and huge hats and leather sandals similar to those of the ancient Maya. Woollen garments, including *capixay* cloaks and jackets, are also woven locally. The town is also famous for its **woodwork**, and Nahualá carpenters churn out a good proportion of the country's hand-carved wardrobes and bedsteads.

The unique atmosphere of isolation from and indifference to the outside world makes Nahualá one of the most impressive and unusual K'iche' communities.

The town itself is not much to look at, a sprawl of old cobbled streets and adobe houses mixed with newer concrete structures, but the inhabitants of Nahualá have a reputation for fiercely preserving their independence and have held out against ladino incursions with exceptional tenacity (see opposite). There are a few basic pensiones, but it's best to visit the town as a day-trip from the lake or Quetzaltenango.

A self-imposed alcohol ban has now been lifted, and if you're here for the fiesta on November 25 you'll see that the people are keen to make up for all those dry years. Even today only a handful of ladinos live in the town, and the indigenous Maya still have a reputation for hostility, with rumours circulating about the black deeds done by the local shaman.

Sunday market always finds the town full to bursting, and there's also a smaller market on Thursdays.

ARRIVAL AND DEPARTURE   NAHUALÁ

By bus Take any bus along the Carretera Interamericana between Los Encuentros and Cuatro Caminos, and get off at the Puente Nahualá, from where minibuses run the 1km or so uphill to the town centre.

Quetzaltenango (Xela)

Guatemala's second city, **QUETZALTENANGO (XELA)**, is the natural hub of the western highlands. It can't claim to be a tourist attraction in its own right, but the city's ordinariness is in many ways its strength – it's a resolutely Guatemalan place. Off the main gringo trail, it has a hospitality and friendliness that belies its size and a slightly subdued provincial atmosphere. Bizarre though it may seem, Quetzaltenango's character and appearance is vaguely reminiscent of an industrial town in northern England – grey and cool with friendly, down-to-earth inhabitants, who have a reputation for formality and politeness. At an elevation of 2330m, Quetzaltenango is always cold in the early mornings, the city waking up slowly, getting going only once the warmth of the sun has made its mark.

The city is an important **educational centre**, its universities and colleges attracting students from all over the country, while its Spanish schools (see p.146) are internationally renowned. More and more **development** projects are also basing themselves here, and this growing outside influence is steadily adding a cosmopolitan feel to the city's bars, restaurants and cultural life. Many overseas visitors settle easily into the relatively easy-going pace of the city; it also makes an excellent base for exploring this part of the country, making **day-trips** to villages, basking in hot springs like **Fuentes Georginas**, or hiking in the mountains. The city is divided into zones, although for the most part you'll only be interested in **zonas** 1 and 3, which contain the city centre and the area around the Minerva bus terminal respectively. The centre, heavily indebted to Neoclassicism, is a monument to stability, with great slabs of grey stone belying a history of turbulence and struggle. Things deteriorate as you head away from the plaza, with thick traffic and fumes blighting the highland air, particularly around the main bus terminal. Locally, the city is usually referred to as **Xela** (pronounced "shey-la"). Meaning "under the ten", the name is probably a reference to the surrounding peaks.

Brief history

Originally there was a walled city here called **Xelajú**, but it was destroyed during the conquest – Pedro de Alvarado is said to have killed the K'iche' king, Tecún Umán, in hand-to-hand combat. The victorious Spanish founded a new town, Quetzaltenango, "the place of the quetzals", the name probably chosen because of the brilliant green quetzal feathers worn by the K'iche' nobles and warriors.

Under colonial rule Quetzaltenango flourished as a commercial centre, benefiting from the fertility of the surrounding farmland and good connections to the port at

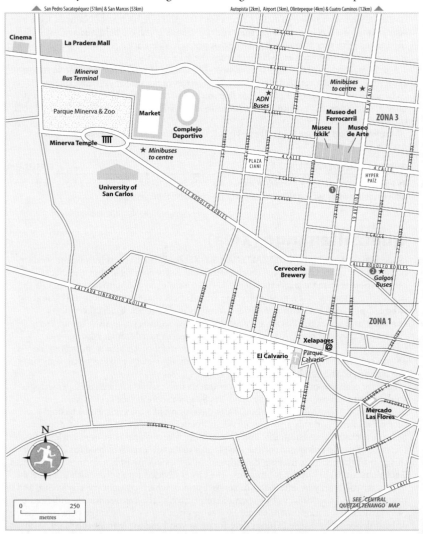

Champerico. When the prospect of independence eventually arose, the city was set on deciding its own destiny. After the Central American Federation broke with Mexico in 1820, Quetzaltenango declared itself the capital of the independent state of **Los Altos**, which incorporated most of the western highlands. But the separatist movement was put down by force and the city had to accept provincial status. Quetzaltenango remained an important centre of commerce and culture however, its wealth and population continued to grow, and it remained a potent rival to the capital.

All this, however, came to an abrupt end when the city was almost totally destroyed by the massive **1902 earthquake**. Rebuilding took place in a mood of high hopes; all the grand Neoclassical architecture dates from this period. A new **rail line** was built to connect the city with the coast, but this was washed out in the early 1930s, and the town steadily fell further and further behind the capital.

2

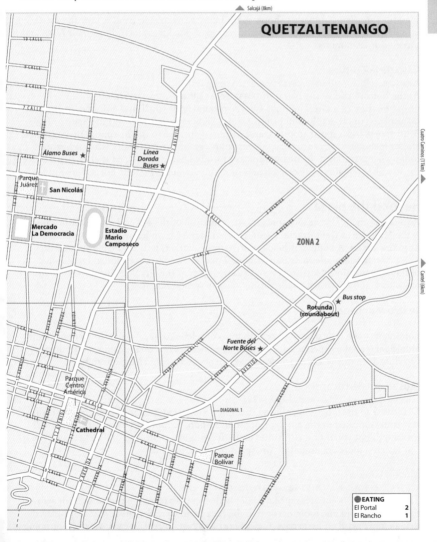

● EATING	
El Portal	2
El Rancho	1

Parque Centro América

The heart of the city is the central plaza, or **Parque Centro América**. Here you'll find the requisite stone benches and well-tended shrubs as well as a monument to former President Barrios – all overshadowed by a mass of Greek columns. With an atmosphere of dignified calm, the plaza is the best place to appreciate the sense of self-importance that accompanied the city's rebuilding after the 1902 earthquake. The buildings have a look of defiant authority, although there's none of the buzz of business you'd expect – except on the first Sunday of the month when it plays host to a good artesanías market, with blankets, basketry and piles of *típica* weavings for sale.

Along the eastern side of the plaza is the **cathedral**, with a new cement version set behind the spectacular crumbling front of the original. There's another unashamed piece of Greek grandeur, the **municipalidad**, or town hall, a little further up.

On the west side, the impressive Neoclassical **Pasaje Enríquez** was planned as a sparkling arcade of upmarket shops, spent many years derelict, and is now the social hub of the city centre. Inside you'll find a crop of good bars, including *Salón Tecún* and some great restaurants.

Casa de la Cultura
Parque Centro América • Mon–Fri 8am–noon & 2–6pm, Sat 9am–1pm • US$0.75

At the bottom end of the plaza, the **Casa de la Cultura** is the city's most blatant impersonation of a Greek temple. On the **ground floor** you'll find a display of assorted documents, photographs and pistols from the liberal revolution and the State of Los Altos (see p.143), sports trophies, and a room dedicated to the marimba. **Upstairs** there are some modest Maya artefacts, historic photographs and a bizarre natural-history room where, amongst the dusty displays of stuffed bats and pickled snakes, you can see the macabre remains of assorted freaks of nature, including a four-horned goat.

Beyond the plaza

Away from the plaza the city spreads out, a mixture of the old and new. Out in Zona 3 is the **Mercado La Democracia**, a vast, covered market complex with stalls spilling out onto the streets. A couple of blocks north of the market, next to the **Parque Juárez**, stands the modern **Iglesia de San Nicolás**, a bizarre and ill-proportioned neo-Gothic building, sprouting sharp arches. In the northwest of the city you'll find three small **museums**, all in the shell of the former railway station building.

Teatro Municipal
14 Av & 1 C

Lording it over a little plaza replete with busts of celebrated local artists and writers, **Teatro Municipal** is another spectacular Neoclassical edifice heavy with grey stone and columns. On clear days, there's a spectacular perspective of Volcán Santa María from here.

Museo del Ferrocarril
4 C & 19 Av, Zona 3 • Mon–Fri 8am–noon & 2–6pm, Sat 8am–1pm • US$0.75

Dedicated to the long-gone **railway** that once connected Xela to the Pacific coast, this museum is located in the city's former **train station**. Exhibits are not particularly well presented, but you'll find curiosities including original train seats and tickets and you can watch a short documentary (in Spanish) about the line.

Museo Ixkik'
4 C & 19 Av, Zona 3 • Daily 9am–1pm & 3–6pm • US$3 • ☎ 7761 6472

This museum concentrates on Maya *traje*, with examples of village **costumes** from across the highlands and one room devoted to the Xela itself. Ceremonial *huipiles* are displayed that are only worn on fiesta days. Guides are often here to explain each weaving's meaning.

CENTRAL QUETZALTENANGO

EATING & DRINKING
Al Natur	10
Café Baviera	6
Cardinali's	4
El Cuartito	9
Dos Tejanos	5
La Luna	8
Panorama	12
El Pasaje Mediterraneo	7
Sabor de la India	1
Sagrado Corazón 1	2
Sagrado Corazón 2	11
Ut'z Hua	3

ACCOMMODATION
Black Cat Hostel	3
Casa Argentina	9
Casa Mañen	6
Casa Renaissance	11
Flora Inn Hotel	4
Hostal Don Diego	7
Hostal Miguel	10
Hostal Siete Orejas	1
Hotel Modelo	2
Pensión Andina	8
Pensión Bonifaz	5

DRINKING & NIGHTLIFE
Bajo La Luna	3
El Cuartito	7
Discoteca La Parranda	1
Pool and Beer	8
Salón Tecún	2
Tilde	4

ENTERTAINMENT
Blue Angel	5
Casa Noj	6

SHOPS
North & South	3
Tilde	2
Vrisa	1

Museo de Arte

4 C & 19 Av, Zona 3 • Mon–Fri 9am–1pm & 3–7pm • US$2

Next door to the railway museum, this **art museum** has an important collection of over two hundred paintings from artists including Efraín Recinos. Local painter Rodrigo Díaz has a studio here and is often at hand to show you around.

Minerva temple, zoo and market

4 C, Zona 3 **Zoo** Tues–Sun 9am–5pm • Free

On the western edge of town, there's another Greek-style monument: the **Minerva temple**. Just behind the temple is a little **zoo**, doubling as a kids' playground. The cages are small but all the animals – including birds, monkeys and pizotes – are well cared for. Below the temple are the sprawling, dusty **Minerva bus terminal** and **market**. It's here that you can really sense the city's role as the centre of the western highlands, with indigenous traders from all over the area doing business, and buses heading to or from every imaginable village and town.

ARRIVAL AND DEPARTURE

QUETZALTENANGO (XELA)

SECOND-CLASS BUSES

Unfortunately, all buses arrive and depart Quetzaltenango from nowhere near the centre. Second-class buses all arrive and depart from the chaotic Minerva Bus Terminal on the city's northwestern edge; to get to the main plaza, walk 300m through the market stalls to 4 C and catch a microbus marked "Parque". Microbuses bound for the terminal leave the centre from the corner of 4 C and 14 Av 'A' in the city centre.

2

Destinations Chichicastenango (7 daily; 2hr 30min); Coatepeque (every 30min; 1hr 45min); Guatemala City (every 30min; 4hr); Huehuetenango (every 30min; 2hr); La Mesilla (6 daily; 3hr 30min); Momostenango (every 30min; 1hr 15min); Panajachel (6 daily; 2hr 45min); Retalhuleu (every 30min; 1hr 15min); San Francisco el Alto (every 30min; 45min); San Pedro la Laguna (7 daily; 2hr 30min); Santa Cruz del Quiché (7 daily; 3hr); Tecún Umán (hourly; 3hr); Totonicapán (every 30min; 1hr); Zunil (from Minerva via 10 C and 9 Av, Zona 1, every 30min; 30min).

FIRST-CLASS BUSES

Five companies operate first-class buses to and from the capital (14 daily in total; 4hr), each with their own private terminal; for the latest schedules check out ⓦxelawho.com. For travel to Guatemala City and beyond it's more comfortable and always cheaper to use first-class buses rather than shuttles (for Antigua change to a local bus at Chimaltenango).

ADN 7 C 23–58, Zona 3 ☎6649 2089, ⓦadnautobuses delnorte.com.

Fuente del Norte 7 Av 3–33, Zona 2 ☎7761 4587, ⓦgrupofuentedelnorte.com.

Línea Dorada 12 Av 5–13, Zona 3 ☎7767 5198, ⓦlineadorada.info.

Álamo 14 Av 5–15, Zona 3 ☎7767 7117.

Galgos C Rodolfo Robles 17–43, Zona 1 ☎7761 2248.

SHUTTLE BUSES

Shuttle buses are offered by travel agents (see below); destinations include Panajachel (US$15–20), Antigua ($30), Cobán (US$50), Guatemala City (US$32), San Pedro la Laguna (US$15) and San Cristóbal de las Casas in Mexico (US$35).

INFORMATION AND TOURS

Tourist information Inguat, Parque Centro América (Mon–Fri 9am–5pm, Sat 9am–1pm; ☎7761 4931) is not very helpful; you'll find travel agencies much better informed.

Listings and websites The English-language magazine *Xela Who* (ⓦxelawho.com), has good listings and features about the city. Check out the website ⓦxelapages.com for hotel and cultural information and discussion forums.

TOUR OPERATORS

Adrenalina Tours Pasaje Enríquez, Parque Centro América ☎7761 4509, ⓦadrenalinatours.com. Recommended for shuttle buses, tours of the Xela region, hikes and volcano climbs.

Altiplano's 12 Av 3–35 ☎5247 2073, ⓦaltiplanos.com .gt. Good, locally owned operator with trekking and tour programmes to villages around Xela and beyond.

STUDYING SPANISH IN QUETZALTENANGO

Quetzaltenango boasts dozens of **language schools**, many of a very high standard, and makes an excellent place to really immerse yourself in Guatemalan culture. Its relatively large population means that you shouldn't have to share a family home with other gringos. Few local people speak much English, so many students find the city is a good place to progress quickly in their language studies. An added benefit of choosing to study in Quetzaltenango is that most schools fund **community development** and environmental projects.

All of the schools listed here are well established and employ professional teachers, but they are only a selection.

Casa Xelajú Callejón 15, Diagonal 13–02, Zona 1 ☎7761 5954, ⓦcasaxelaju.com.

Celas Maya 6 C 14–55, Zona 1 (☎7761 4342, ⓦcelasmaya.edu.gt.

Centro Bilingüe Amerindia (CBA) 12 Av 10–27, Zona 1 ☎7761 8535, ⓦcbaspanishschool.com.

Educación para Todos Av El Cenizal 0–58, Zona 5 ☎5935 3815, ⓦspanishschools.biz.

Inepas 15A Av 4–59, Zona 1 ☎7765 1308, ⓦinepas.org.

Juan Sisay 15 Av 8–38, Zona 1 ☎7765 1318, ⓦjuansisay.com.

Kie Balam Diagonal 12 4–46, Zona 1 ☎7761 1636, ⓦkiebalam.com.

La Paz 2 C Callejon 16 2–47, Zona 1 ☎4018 2180, ⓦxelapages.com/lapaz.

Madre Tierra 13 Av 8–34, Zona 1 ☎7761 6105, ⓦmadre-tierra.org.

Miguel de Cevanates 12 Av 8–31, Zona 1 ☎7765 5554, ⓦlearn2speakspanish.com.

El Nahual 28 Av 9–54, Zona 1 ☎5606 1704, ⓦlanguageselnahual.com.

Pop Wuj 1 C 17–72, Zona 1 ☎7761 8286, ⓦpop -wuj.org.

El Portal 9 Callejón 'A' 11–49, Zona 1 ☎7761 5275, ⓦspanishschoolelportal.com.

Proyecto Lingüístico Quetzalteco de Español 5 C 2–40, Zona 1 ☎7765 2140, ⓦhermandad.com.

Sakribal 6 C 7–42, Zona 1 ☎7763 0717, ⓦsakribal .com.

The Bike House 15 Av 5–22 ☎5292 9399. Expert bike specialists who run some excellent guided mountain bike rides around Xela area and offer bike rental.

Diversity Tours 15 Av 3–86 ☎7761 2545, ⓦdiversitytours.com.gt. Very competitive rates for shuttle buses, and offers tours of sights including the Santiaguito viewpoint (US$15) and Tajumulco (US$70).

Quetzaltrekkers Inside Casa Argentina, 12 Diagonal 8–37 (see p.145) ☎7761 4520, ⓦquetzaltrekkers.com. Offers some outstanding hikes, including a three-day trek from Xela to Atitlán (minimum donation US$75) and a two-day ascent of Tajumulco (US$55), plus rock climbing. All profits go to a charity for street children.

ACCOMMODATION

2

Quetzaltenango cannot boast a huge choice of hotels, but does have some decent **budget places**. All those listed are within a ten-minute walk of the **parque**.

Black Cat Hostel 13 Av 3–33 ☎7761 2091, ⓦblackcathostels.net; map p.145. Set in a historic building just north of the parque this hostel has a sociable vibe, and a hip bar with retro sofas. The dorms are fine, shared bathrooms are clean, but the private rooms are very average. Rates include internet and a massive breakfast, though staff can be a little disinterested at times. Dorms US$7, rooms US$21

Casa Argentina 12 Diagonal 8–37 ☎7761 2470; map p.145. Long-standing backpackers' hangout that has seen better days. Dozens of small rooms (most with TVs and a few with bathrooms), a huge dorm and guests' kitchen. Dorms US$3, rooms US$7

Casa Mañen 9 Av 4–11 ☎7765 0786, ⓦcomeseeit .com; map p.145. A very comfortable and attractive B&B with good selection of spacious rooms, which have plenty of local charm thanks to the use of highland textiles and furnishings. Numbers 8 and 9 have fireplaces, and the two suites offer sofas and fridges. There's also a rooftop terrace and the breakfast (included) is a veritable banquet. Rooms US$62, suites US$84

★ **Casa Renaissance** 9 C 11–26 ☎7761 8005, ⓦcasarenaissance.com; map p.145. Welcoming Dutch-owned place in a fine old town house with five huge rooms, gorgeous original floor files, free tea, coffee and water, sunny patios, fast wi-fi, good bathrooms and a TV lounge stocked with over a thousand DVDs. There are discounted weekly rates. US$26

Flora Inn Hotel 12 Av 3–61 ☎7761 2033, ⓦflorainnhotel.com; map p.145. Just north of the parque, this hotel has been carefully renovated by the helpful young Dutch/Guatemalan owners. The ten modern, uncluttered and immaculately clean rooms face a covered courtyard, all with flat-screen TVs and en-suite bathrooms. Wi-fi is speedy and breakfast is available. US$35

Hostal Don Diego 6 C 15–12 ☎5308 3616, ⓦhostaldondiegoxela.com; map p.145. This secure place has twenty simple, cheap rooms (none with private bathrooms), a pleasant courtyard and guests' kitchen. There's free wi-fi and purified water. Dorm US$5.50, rooms US$14

Hostal Miguel 12 Av 8–31 ☎7765 5554, ⓦlearn2speakspanish.com; map p.145. Welcoming guesthouse within a Spanish language school. The eight rooms, in a slightly ramshackle old house, are basic but you'll find a living room with TV, cooking facilities and free wi-fi. US$11

Hostal Siete Orejas 2 C 16–92 ☎7768 3218, ⓦ7orejas.com; map p.145. A fine new flashpacker place with very high-quality spacious rooms, each with hand-carved beds, good mattresses and a wooden chest-of-drawers. There's an upstairs bar – though few drinkers – as well as wi-fi, and your continental breakfast is gratis. Dorms US$8, rooms US$30

Hotel Modelo 14 Av A 2–31 ☎7761 2529, ⓦhotelmodelo1892.com; map p.145. Classy, historic hotel with elegant dining and reception areas and plenty of character. The rooms are spacious if a little creaky, all have private bathrooms and TVs (note that streetside rooms can be noisy on weekend nights). The annexe is a slightly cheaper, similar alternative. Breakfast and wi-fi included. US$54

Pensión Andina 8 Av 6–07 ☎7761 4012; map p.145. Offers good value, with neat, smallish but well-scrubbed rooms, all with private bathrooms and reliable hot water, set around a covered courtyard. US$13

Pensión Bonifaz 4 C 10–50 ☎7723 1100, ⓦpensionbonifaz.com.gt; map p.145. Landmark hotel, founded in 1935 with a beautiful facade and prime location on the north side of the plaza. Retains an air of faded upper-class pomposity, and has a smart restaurant and small pool. However, make sure you choose your room carefully, all are spacious but some are a little dated. US$75

EATING

Quetzaltenango has a moderate selection of restaurants, but lots of new cafés have opened in recent years. Few places open before 8am.

2

Al Natur 13 Av 8–34 ☎ 7761 9435; map p.145. Ideal for a snack, this café-deli has tasty dishes like *tortas de papas* with grated carrot, and shelves stocked with organic and co-op produce. Try the delicious home-made *limonada*. Wi-fi. Mon–Sat 9am–6pm, Sun 1–6pm.

Café Baviera 5 C 12–50 ☎ 7761 5018; map p.145. Old-fashioned coffeehouse, with plenty of yesteryear photos of Xela on its walls. Serves teas, cakes, sandwiches, soups and has a set lunch for US$5. Wi-fi and a takeaway window. Daily 7am–8.30pm.

Cardinali's 14 Av 3–41 ☎ 7761 0924; map p.145. Long-running Italian restaurant of the gingham tablecloths and hanging Chianti flask school of decor. Good for pizza or pasta with huge portions at (fairly) moderate prices; reckon on US$8–10/person. Daily 11am–10pm.

El Cuartito 13 Av 7–09 ✉ elcuartitocafe.tumblr.com; map p.145. Xela's hippest little café/bar has a simple menu of snacks and delicious, though pricey drinks like strawberry-tinged lemonade (US$3). Wi-fi. Mon & Wed–Sun 11am–11pm.

Dos Tejanos inside the Pasaje Enríquez ☎ 7765 4360, ✉ dostejanos.com; map p.145. The "two Texans" serves toothsome dishes like barbecued ribs, chicken-fried chicken and fajitas. Most mains are US$8–12. Mon–Thurs & Sun 11am–10.30pm, Fri & Sat 11am–midnight.

La Luna 8 Av 4–11 ☎ 5174 6769; map p.145. Crammed with curios and antiques, *La Luna* is famous for its seven different varieties of authentic drinking chocolate, though note that they are (outrageously) pre-sweetened to local tastes. Snacks are also served (around US$3.50). Mon–Fri 10am–9pm, Sat 4–9pm.

★ **El Pasaje Mediterraneo** Inside the Pasaje Enríquez ☎ 5515 6724 or ☎ 5825 1782; map p.145. Classy tapas restaurant with two atmospheric dining rooms and an attractive menu of Mediterranean dishes, including

favourites from Spain, Greece, Turkey and Italy. Portions are very generous – reckon on three or four tapas (most are US$4–6) for two people. There's a decent wine list and excellent service. Mon–Sat noon–10pm.

El Portal C Rodrigo Robles 17–55 ☎ 7761 7681; map pp.142–143. Neighbourhood restaurant highly recommended for very tasty meat dishes: the *parrillada* includes a carnivore's delight of chicken, pork cuts, sausages and ribs all cooked barbecue-style. Also sells draught beer – a jug of *mixta* is the perfect accompaniment. Mon–Sat noon–10pm.

El Rancho 3 Av & 20 C, Zona 3 ☎ 5301 8979; map pp.142–143. Bills itself as *la casa de tilapia*, so not surprisingly it's very popular for fresh fish (US$7/pound), which are kept live in tanks. Also offers huge breakfasts (US$6-ish) and grilled meats. Daily 11am–10.30pm.

Sabor de la India 15 Av 3–64 ☎ 7765 0101; map p.145. This Indian-owned place serves up filling and pretty authentic curries and lots of vegetarian options – including a decent *thali* (US$7). The premises lack atmosphere though. Tues–Sat noon–10pm, Sun 5–9pm.

Sagrado Corazón 1 14 Av 3–08; map p.145. Run by a formidable *señora*, this small, informal place is a great spot to try Guatemalan specialities like *pepián* or *jocón* (meat cooked with peppers and *tomatillos*). Daily 8am–8pm.

Sagrado Corazón 2 9 C 9–00; map p.145. Reliable, authentic comedor with a long menu including Guatemalan-style breakfasts – the *completo* is just US$2 – and set lunches for around US$2.50. Daily 7am–8pm.

Ut'z Hua 12 Av & 3 C ☎ 7768 3469; map p.145. Busy, intimate place specializing in Guatemalan (including highland) cuisine. Mains, costing about US$3–4, include *jocón, quichóm*, local sausages, *mojarra* fish and seven kinds of soup. There's a second branch at 4 C and 13 Av. Daily 7am–9pm.

DRINKING AND NIGHTLIFE

Bars are clustered around Pasaje Enríquez and along 14 Av A; clubs are spread throughout the city. To find **what's on**, pick up a copy of *Xela Who?* (✉ xelawho.com). Salsa Latina Academy (Diagonal 12 6–58; ☎ 5613 7222, ✉ salsalatinaacademy .com) is a professional dance school.

Bajo La Luna 8 Av 3–72 ☎ 7761 2242; map p.145. In an atmospheric cellar, this relaxed wine bar with background tunes is perfect for a quiet drink. You can nibble on a cheese platter (US$4) while you sip. Thurs–Sat 8pm–1am.

El Cuartito 13 Av 7–09; map p.145. Relaxed, happening bar with shabby-chic decor (including lighting made from old beer bottles) and live music and DJs some nights. Doubles as a café in the day. Wed–Mon 11am–11pm.

Discoteca La Parranda 14 Av 4–47; map p.145. In the heart of the city, this bar/club has salsa on Wed (when there are free classes), while from Thurs to Sat it's a mix of reggaeton, Latin, electronica and r'n'b. Wed–Sat 6pm–1am.

Pool and Beer 12 Av 10–21; map p.145. Pool tables and table football are available in this spacious bar with friendly staff. A litre of beer is US$3.50. Tues–Sun 6pm–midnight.

★ **Salón Tecún** Inside the Pasaje Enríquez; map p.145. Xela's most dependable and popular bar, this atmospheric pub-like drinking institution is a favourite of both locals and travellers. There's a sociable interior and bench seating outside in the arcade. Daily 8am–1am.

Tilde 10 Av 5–33 ☎ 4444 7796; map p.145. Part boutique, part-bar this groovy little number is a good bet for a beer and interesting company. It's run by a hip female crew who are into their urban music, and DJs spin hip-hop and electronica (until late) some nights. Tues–Sat 11am–8pm, Sun 11am–4pm.

ENTERTAINMENT

Quetzaltenango is a good place to catch a movie or a play and there's a pretty good cultural programme of events. You'll find a multi-screen cinema by La Pradera mall, near the Minerva bus terminal. Check *Xela Who?* (ⓦ xelawho.com) for the latest schedules.

Blue Angel 7 C 15–79. Offers a daily video programme with a large selection of movies (mainly Hollywood blockbusters and cult films). You can also select a film at most times of day and watch it in a private room. Doubles as a café. Mon–Sat 1–10.30pm, Sun 3–10pm.
Casa N'oj 7 C 12–12 ☎7768 3139. Art exhibitions, films,

lectures and cultural events in a wonderful restored building just off the parque.
Teatro Municipal 14 Av A & 1 C ☎7761 2218. This imposing Neoclassic theatre hosts contemporary and traditional dance, plays, concerts and exhibitions.

SHOPPING

Despensa Familiar 3 Av & 7 C. Supermarket in the centre of town.
North & South 8 C & 15 Av ☎7761 0589. Stocks cultural and political books and guidebooks, and has a café. Daily 8am–7pm.
La Pradera Just behind the Minerva market, the shopping mall La Pradera boasts over a hundred stores.

Tilde 10 Av 5–33 ☎4444 7796. This stylish little boutique/café has customized clothes, vintage wear with a Seventies bent and headgear for both chicks and chaps. Tues–Sat 11am–8pm, Sun 11am–4pm.
Vrisa 15 Av 3–64 ☎7761 3237. Bookstore with thousands of used titles, and buys and trades as well. Mon–Sat 9am–6pm.

DIRECTORY

Banks and exchange There are several banks on the plaza including Banrural which has an ATM.
Bike rental The Bike House 15 Av 5–22, ☎5292 9399. Rents mountain bikes (US$5/24hr or US$13/week). Vrisa bookstore (see above) offers similar rates.
Car rental Tabarini, 9 C 9–21 (☎7763 0418, ⓦtabarini .com), has cars from US$39/day.
Internet and phones There are dozens of internet cafés, most charge around US$1/hr. Xelapages, 4 C 19–48, is very professional and has quick connections, and cheap rates for

phones. Wi-fi is very common in Quetzaltenango's cafés.
Laundry Lavandería Emanuel, 7 C 13–29. Just US$2 for a full wash and dry.
Medical care Hospital San Rafael, 9 C 10–41, Zona 1 (☎7761 4414).
Police If you're in trouble or been the victim of crime first contact Ángel Quiñonez (☎4149 1104), the very efficient Asistur rep for the Xela area.
Post office 15 Av and 4 C (Mon–Fri 8.30am–5.30pm, Sat 9am–1pm).

Around Quetzaltenango

The Xela area offers some of the country's most evocative highland scenery, with volcanic cones soaring above forested ridges, and a number of fascinating indigenous villages to explore. Straddling the coast road south of the city are **Almolonga** and **Zunil**, where you'll find superb hot springs, including **Fuentes Georginas**, a stunning natural spa. Just west of here the **Santa María volcano**, towering above Quetzaltenango, is a terrific if exhausting excursion. The most accessible climb in the area lies southwest of the city, up **Volcán Chicabal** to an exquisite crater lake set in the extinct volcano's cone.

North of the city, the traditional Maya town of **Olintepeque** is renowned for its shrine devoted to the pagan saint of San Pascual. A little further distant are **Totonicapán**, a departmental capital, and the famous market town of **San Francisco el Alto**, perched on a rocky outcrop. Beyond here, in the midst of a pine forest, lies **Momostenango**, the country's principal wool-producing centre.

Almolonga

The most direct route from Quetzaltenango to the coast takes you through a narrow gash in the mountains to the village of **ALMOLONGA**, just 5km from Quetzaltenango. Almolonga is K'iche' for "the place where water springs", and streams gush from the

2

hillside, channelled to the waiting crops. This is the region's market garden: the flat land, far too valuable for houses, is parcelled up into neat, irrigated fields.

In markets throughout the western highlands, the women of Almolonga corner the vegetable trade; it's easy to recognize them, dressed in their bold, orange zigzag *huipiles* and wearing beautifully woven headbands. The village itself has **markets** on Wednesday and Saturday mornings – the latter being the larger one – when the town is crammed with people, while piles of scrubbed radishes and gleaming carrots are swiftly traded.

The village **church** is an arresting banana-yellow-and-white affair that backs onto the plaza. Inside there's a wonderfully gaudy gilded **altar** with a silver statue of a crusading San Pedro, complete with bible, set behind protective bars. Pay the caretaker a quetzal and the whole altar lights up in a riot of technicolour fluorescent tubes, including a halo for the saint.

Los Baños

Daily 5am–10pm • US$2

A couple of kilometres beyond the village lie **Los Baños**, where about ten different operations offer a soak in hot-spring water; Fuentes Saludable and El Recreo are good options. For two or three bucks you get a private room, a sunken concrete tub, and enough hot water to drown an elephant. In a country of lukewarm showers, it's paradise.

ARRIVAL AND DEPARTURE   ALMOLONGA

By bus Buses from Quetzaltenango leave the Minerva terminal every 15min, via a stop at 9 Av and 10 C in Zona 1, to Almolonga and Los Baños on their way to Zunil.

Copavic Glass Factory

1km south of Cantel village • **Factory** Mon–Fri 8am–1pm **Shop** Mon–Fri 8am–5pm & Sat 8am–noon • ⓦ copavic.com • Buses every 20min from Quetazltenango's Minerva terminal

Accessed by a separate road to Zunil that passes the giant Cantel Fábrica textile factory, the **Copavic glass factory** is one of Guatemala's most successful cooperatives. Copavic uses one hundred percent recycled glass and exports the finished product all over the world. Visitors are welcome to see the glass-blowers in action, or visit the factory shop, which sells a fine selection of glasses, vases, jugs and other assorted goods.

Zunil

Down the valley from Almolonga is **ZUNIL**, another centre for vegetable growing. The plaza is dominated by a beautiful white **colonial church** with twin belfries and a magnificent Baroque facade – complete with a quetzal and vines. Inside an intricate silver altar is protected behind bars. The women of Zunil wear vivid purple *huipiles* and carry incredibly bright shawls; during the Monday market the streets are awash with colour. Just below the plaza is a **textile cooperative** (Mon–Sat 8.30am–5pm, Sun 2–5pm), where hundreds of women market their beautiful weavings.

Zunil is also renowned for its adherence to the cult of **San Simón** (or Maximón), the evil saint. You can meet the man himself in his pagan temple (see box, p.130); children will take you to his abode for a small tip.

ARRIVAL AND DEPARTURE   ZUNIL

By bus Buses to Copavic and Zunil (30min) run from Quetzaltenango's Minerva bus terminal every 20min or so; you can also catch a bus from the centre of town beside the Shell gas station at 10 C and 9 Av in Zona 1. Buses bound for Retalhuleu also pass by Zunil.

ACCOMMODATION

Las Cumbres 1km south of Zunil ☎ 7767 1746. This spa hotel has a dozen attractive rooms, all with chunky wooden beds and fireplaces, and most with huge bathtubs fed by hot-spring water and private saunas (room nos. 6–9 enjoy the best views). The restaurant serves tasty *comida típica* (US$5–9 a meal) and there's a gym and squash court. The spa's sauna rooms (US$4/hr) and massage facilities (from US$28) are open to visitors. __US$52__

VISITING SAN SIMÓN IN ZUNIL

Zunil's reputation for the worship of **San Simón** is well founded. Every year on November 1, at the end of the annual fiesta, San Simón (also known as Maximón) is moved to a new house. His effigy sits in a darkened room, dressed in Western clothes, and guarded by several attendants, including one whose job it is to remove the ash from his lighted cigarettes – this is later sold off and used to cure insomnia, while the butts are thought to provide protection from thieves. San Simón is visited by a steady stream of villagers, who come to ask his assistance, using candles to indicate their **requests**: white for the health of a child, yellow for a good harvest, red for love and black to wish ill on an enemy. The petitioners touch and embrace the saint, and just to make sure that he has heard their pleas they also offer cigarettes, money and *aguadiente* liquor. Meanwhile, outside the house, a bonfire burns continuously and more offerings are given over the flames, including whole eggs – if they crack it signifies that San Simón will grant a wish.

If you visit San Simón, you will be expected to **contribute** to his upkeep (US$0.75 or so), and pay to take photographs. While the entire process may seem chaotic and entertaining, it is in fact deeply serious – proceed with respect.   David Dickinson

Fuentes Georginas

8km south of Zunil • Mon–Fri 8am–6pm, Sat & Sun 7am–6pm • US$6 • ☏ 5704 2959, ⓦ lasfuentesgeorginas.com

In the hills above Zunil, reached via a steep road which switchbacks through magnificent volcanic scenery, **Fuentes Georginas** is a spectacular natural spring spa situated on the evergreen slopes of Volcán Pico Zunil. The pools here are surrounded by fresh green ferns, thick moss and lush forest, and to top it all there's a restaurant (meals US$3–8) with a well-stocked bar. It's a blissful place to spend a few hours soaking away the chicken bus blues or recovering from a volcano climb in the heavenly steaming pools. Unfortunately the eco-vibe is spoiled by cheesy piped music. Fuentes Georginas has barbecue and picnic areas.

ARRIVAL AND DEPARTURE
FUENTES GEORGINAS

By bus There's a dedicated shuttle bus service from Xela; buses (US$17 return; daily at 9am & 2pm; 30min) leave from the Fuentes office, 14 Av and 5 C. Otherwise, minibuses (US$10 one-way) head up from Zunil on demand.

ACCOMMODATION

Fuentes Georginas ☏ 5704 2959. Just below the pools, these stone bungalows come complete with bathtub, two double beds and fireplaces (wood is provided). They're a little musty but have a certain rustic charm. US$42

Volcán Santa María

Due south of Quetzaltenango, the perfect cone of **Volcán Santa María** rises to a height of 3772m, towering over most of the Xela valley. It's possible to climb the volcano as a day-trip, but to really see it at its best you need to be on top at dawn, either sleeping on the freezing summit, or camping at a site part of the way up and climbing the final section in the dark by torchlight. Full moon trips are also an option.

The volcano's highest point is marked by an altar where the Maya burn *copal* and sacrifice animals, and on a clear day the **view** will take your breath away – as will the cold if you get here in time to watch the sun rise. In the early mornings the Quetzaltenango valley is blanketed in a layer of cloud, and while it's still dark the lights of the city create a patch of orange glow; as the sun rises, its first rays eat into the cloud, revealing the land beneath.

Below, to the south, is the angry, lava-scarred cone of **Santiaguito**, which has been in constant eruption since 1902. Every now and then it spouts a great grey cloud of rock and dust hundreds of metres into the air. To the **west**, across a chaos of twisting hills, are the cones of Tajumulco and Tacaná, marking the Mexican border. But most impressive is the view to the **east**. Wrapped in the early morning haze, four more volcanic cones can be seen, two above Lago de Atitlán and two more above Antigua – one of which, highly active Fuego, often emits a puff of smoke.

It's highly advisable to climb Santa María with one of the Quetzaltenango **tour operators** (see p.146) who will organize transport, food and water for the trip. You should also be acclimatized to the altitude before attempting the hike.

San Martín Sacatepéquez

Southwest from Xela, the road to the coast winds down to the farming centre of **SAN MARTÍN SACATEPÉQUEZ**, also known as San Martín Chile Verde. This isolated Mam-speaking village is set in the base of a natural bowl and hemmed in by steep, wooded hills. The men here wear a particularly unusual costume made up of a long white tunic with thin red stripes, ornately embroidered around the cuffs and tied around the middle with a red sash; the women wear beautiful red *huipiles* and blue *cortes*.

By bus Buses and minibuses between the Minerva terminal in Quetzaltenango and Coatepeque pass through San Martín every 30min or so. The journey time is 40min.

Make sure you board a bus for the right San Martín as there are several in the Xela area.

Laguna Chicabal

A two-hour hike from San Martín brings you to **Laguna Chicabal**, a spectacular lake set in the cone of the Chicabal volcano that is the site of Maya religious rituals. To reach the start of the hike, get the bus to drop you off at the stop for "la laguna" and head uphill through the outskirts of the village. Follow the steep track for forty minutes until it levels out near the entrance to the Chicabal reserve (US$2.50 entrance) where there's a football field and some rustic **cabins** (US$5–9/person).

A good signposted trail then ascends again through forest to the rim of the cone, before descending to the **lake**. At the water's edge, you enter a different world, eerily still, disturbed only by the soft buzz of a hummingbird's wings or the screech of parakeets. Small **sandy bays** bear charred crosses and bunches of fresh-cut flowers mark the site of ritual sacrifice. On May 3 every year *costumbristas* gather here for ceremonies to mark the fiesta of the Holy Cross; at any time, but around this date especially, you should take care not to disturb any **rituals** that might be taking place. You are welcome to camp at the shore, though you'll have to bring all your own supplies. Swimming is prohibited.

On your return route you can climb some vertiginous steps to a *mirador* from where there are stunning views of the emerald lagoon, and, if the cloud gods permit, the volcanoes of Santa María and Santiaguito, Tajamulco and Tacaná.

Olintepeque

North of Quetzaltenango, perched on the edge of the Xela plain, is the small textile-weaving town of **OLINTEPEQUE**. According to some accounts this was the site of the huge and decisive battle between the Spanish and K'iche' warriors, but these days it's better known as a peaceful little place with an intriguing **pagan shrine** and a great Tuesday **animal market**. The latter gets going soon after daylight, winding down by midday, by which time hundreds of pigs on leads, chickens, goats and cattle have been prodded and poked over, bought and sold.

Capilla de Rey San Pascual

The pagan temple **Capilla de Rey San Pascual**, in the centre of town behind the huge Catholic church, is dedicated to an idol believed by devotees to have supernatural powers. San Pascual is certainly a curious sight: a foot-high effigy with an exposed skull bedecked in gaudy robes, surrounded by hundreds of candles and offerings of flowers. Numerous plaques give thanks for his ability to heal the sick (and bring misfortune to enemies). A flight of steps leads up to an exposed platform known as the *quemadero* ("bonfire") where the faithful whisper incantations through clouds of pungent *copal* (incense) smoke.

By bus Buses for Olintepeque (20min) leave from the Minerva terminal in Quetzaltenango every 30min.

Salcajá

Between the Cuatro Caminos junction and Quetzaltenango, the unappealing ladino town of **SALCAJÁ** is one of Guatemala's main commercial weaving centres.

Salcajá's other claim to fame is that (according to most sources) its modest-looking **Ermita de San Jacinto**, with a simple facade embellished with plasterwork pineapples and bananas, was the first church built in Guatemala. If you drop by the small **museum** (5 Av & 2 C; daily 8am–1pm, 2–5pm; free; ☎7768 8750) behind the church they'll unlock the great doors of the church – inside there's an ornate original altarpiece.

While you're in town it would be silly not to sample some *caldo de fruitas* (fruit-based) or *rompopo* (egg and *aguardiente*) liquor which are both made in Salcajá. Many places can sell you a shot or a bottle, including the museum.

ARRIVAL AND DEPARTURE   SALCAJÁ

By bus Buses from the Minerva terminal run to Salcajá every 20min.

San Andrés Xecul

A few kilometres northwest of Salcajá, the village of **SAN ANDRÉS XECUL** boasts an astonishing canary-yellow Catholic **church**, with a facade that's a riot of vines dripping with plump, purple fruit, and podgy little angels scrambling across the surface. The twin jaguars at the top are said to represent the hero twins of the Maya holy book, the Popol Vuh. Inside there are some fabulously chintzy chandeliers made of glass stones, coins and rosary beads.

The village's other religious activities are less orthodox. It's a centre for Maya worship, and in the 1970s the artist Carmen Petterson claimed that a "university" for shamans was operating in the village; there's also an actively used shrine to **Maximón**, Guatemala's pagan saint (see box, p.130) – locals will direct you there.

ARRIVAL AND DEPARTURE   SAN ANDRÉS XECUL

By bus Hourly buses leave the Minerva terminal in Quetzaltenango for San Andrés; the last returns at around 6pm.

San Cristóbal Totonicapán

One kilometre west of the Cuatro Caminos junction, the ladino town of **SAN CRISTÓBAL TOTONICAPÁN** is generally a quiet place that holds a position of importance as a source of **fiesta costumes**. (It's not to be confused with neighbouring Totonicapán, 12km away, which is in a separate department.) San Cristóbal's colossal Baroque **colonial church** is its main landmark, with a magnificent wood-beamed roof and some fantastic frescoes. Look out too for the extravagant side-altars with images of saints made from ornate silverwork. **Easter week** is an impressive time to visit, when there are huge processions to the church, or you could drop by for the Sunday market.

ARRIVAL AND DEPARTURE   SAN CRISTÓBAL TOTONICAPÁN

By bus Buses from the Minerva terminal run to San Cristóbal every 30min.

San Francisco el Alto

From a magnificent hillside setting, the small town of **SAN FRANCISCO EL ALTO** hosts the largest weekly **market** in the country. Each Friday traders from every corner of Guatemala make the trip, many arriving the night before, and some starting to sell by candlelight from as early as 4am. Throughout the morning a steady stream of buses and trucks fills the town to bursting; by noon the market is at its height, buzzing with activity.

The upper section of the market is an open field used as an **animal market**, where everything from pigs to parrots changes hands. Prospective buyers inspect the animals' teeth and tongues, and at times the scene degenerates into a chaotic wrestling match, with pigs and men rolling in the dirt. Below is the town's plaza, dominated by **textiles**

OPPOSITE THE ANIMAL MARKET AT OLINTEPEQUE>

and clothing, mainly *ropa americana*. Here the streets are filled with vegetables, fruit, pottery and cheap comedores.

For a really good perspective of the market action and surrounding countryside, pay the caretaker a quetzal and climb up to the **church roof**, from where you can fire off frames from a great vantage point.

ARRIVAL AND DEPARTURE	SAN FRANCISCO EL ALTO
By bus Buses connect Quetzaltenango with San Francisco every 20min from the Minerva terminal; many also stop at	the rotunda on the east side of town.

Momostenango

Less than an hour from San Francisco, **MOMOSTENANGO** is a small, isolated highland town renowned for its **wool** production. Momostecos travel throughout the country peddling their blankets, scarves and rugs, and years of experience have made them experts in the hard sell. The wool is also used in a range of traditional costumes, including the short skirts worn by the men of Nahualá and San Antonio Palopó as well as the jackets of Sololá. The ideal place to buy Momostenango blankets is in the **Sunday market**, which fills the town's two plazas, or the smaller Wednesday occasion.

A visit at this time will also give you a glimpse of Momostenango's other feature: its rigid adherence to **Maya tradition**. Opposite the entrance to the church, you may see people making offerings of incense and alcohol on a small fire, muttering their appeals to the gods. While here, you can also take a walk to *los riscos*, a set of bizarre sandstone pillars on the northern edge of town.

ARRIVAL AND DEPARTURE	MOMOSTENANGO
By bus Buses run here from the Minerva terminal in Quetzaltenango, passing through Cuatro Caminos and	San Francisco el Alto on the way, every 45min from 7am (1hr 15min). The last bus returns around 5pm.

ACCOMMODATION AND EATING

You'll find comedores on the main plaza.

Hotel Otoño 3Av A 1–48 ☎ 7736 5078. This good new place has modern rooms, priced per person, all with generous en-suite bathrooms and some with balconies. U$$25

Totonicapán

TOTONICAPÁN, capital of one of the smaller departments, is a pleasant if unremarkable provincial town reached down a direct road leading east from Cuatro Caminos. As you enter Toto you pass one of the country's finest *pilas* (communal washing places), ringed

---

THE TZOLKIN YEAR

Momostenango's religious **calendar** is still based on the 260-day *Tzolkin* year – made up of thirteen twenty-day months – which has been in use since ancient times. The most celebrated ceremony is *Guaxaquib Batz*, "Eight Monkey", which marks the beginning of a new year. Originally, this was a purely **pagan ceremony**, starting at dawn on the first day of the year, but the Church has muscled in on the action and it now begins with a Catholic service the night before. The next morning the people make for Chuitmesabal (Little Broom), a small hill about 2km west of town. Here offerings of broken pottery are made before age-old altars. (Momostenango means "the place of the altars".) The entire process is overseen by shamans responsible for communicating with the gods. At dusk the ceremony moves to Nim Mesabal (Big Broom), another hilltop, where the *costumbristas* pray and burn incense throughout the night.

THE FISCAL KING

The Toto valley has always held out against outside influence, isolated in a world of its own, and in 1820 was the scene of one of the most famous **Maya rebellions**, sparked by demands for tax. The indigenous people expelled all of the town's ladinos and crowned their leader, Atanasio Tzul, the "king and fiscal king". His reign lasted only 29 days, ending when state troops from the capital violently quashed the rebellion – a stone memorial commemorates the event in the town's southern plaza.

2

with Gothic columns. Surrounded by rolling hills and pine forests, the town stands at the heart of a heavily populated and intensely farmed region.

Toto's Tuesday and Saturday **morning markets** fill its two plazas to bursting. The town is an important centre of **commercial weaving**, producing much of the *jasped* cloth worn as skirts by indigenous women throughout the country.

Casa de la Cultura

8 Av 2–17 • ☎ 5630 0554

To take a closer look at the work of local artisans, head for the **visitor centre**, the Casa de la Cultura. It organizes guided walks around the fringes of town (around US$30/head, for 2–6 people) that take in sacred Maya sites, mask and fiesta costume-making workshops and weavers' houses. Lunch is included and funds raised help benefit the community.

El Abrisco

Daily 8am–5pm • US$5 including guide

This forest reserve is 7km north of town on the road to Santa Cruz del Quiché. Trails lead around the protected area and your guide will explain (in Spanish only) the trees and their significance to the local Maya culture. Large owls which the locals call *buho* are common here, and you'll find rustic, basic cabañas (US$10), a campground and kids' play area.

ARRIVAL AND DEPARTURE　　　　　　　　　　　　　　　TOTONICAPÁN

By bus Buses and minibuses for Toto leave Quetzaltenango's Minerva terminal every 30min between 6am and 5pm, passing through Cuatros Caminos; the last minibus returns from Toto at 7.30pm.

ACCOMMODATION AND EATING

For inexpensive **eats**, try one of the comedores scattered around the town's two plazas.

Dino's Upstairs at 6 C and 8 Av, Zona 4 ☎ 7766 2631. Large modern restaurant serving pizza, pasta, steak, sandwiches, seafood and salads for around US$4–8 a meal. Leave some room for a slice of delicious *pie de elote* (corn pie). Mon–Fri 9am–10pm, Sun 11am–10pm.

Hospedaje San Miguel 8 Av & 3 C ☎ 7766 1452. A basic place where the rooms (some with private bathrooms) have a few sticks of furniture and are acceptable for a night. US$11

Hotel Totonicapán 8 C & 8 Av ☎ 7766 4458, ⓦ hoteltotonicapan.com. The best hotel in town, with large, modern, comfortable rooms, a restaurant and parking. US$31

The Department of San Marcos

Leaving Quetzaltenango you can head west to the little-visited department of **San Marcos** – home of the country's highest volcano, **Tajumulco**, and some magnificent highland scenery. The route passes through Ostuncalco and then the **twin towns** of San Marcos and San Pedro Sacatepéquez (these form the main population centre in these parts but hold little interest for visitors).

Northwest of here there's some magnificent high country, and a paved road that fringes the Tajumulco and Tacaná **volcanoes**. Continuing along this remote route you pass through the isolated villages of Tectitán and Cuilco, and can eventually loop up to the Carretera Interamericana.

Volcán Tajumulco

North of San Pedro, the road climbs steeply through thick pine forests and emerging onto a high, grassy plateau. Here it crosses a great boggy expanse to skirt around the edge of **Volcán Tajumulco**, whose 4220m peak is the highest in Central America. It's best climbed from the roadside hamlet of **Tuichán** (the exact drop-off point is called Llana de la Guardia) from where it's about five hours to the summit. It's not a particularly hard climb as long as you're **acclimatized** – the risk of altitude sickness is a serious concern at this height. As there have been land disputes around the volcano it's best to hike with a guide who knows the terrain: Quetzaltrekkers (see p.147) and other tour operators in Quetzaltenango organize trips up Tajumulco.

North to the Carretera Interamericana: Tacaná

Up here the land is sparsely inhabited, with barren rocky ridges soaring over adobe houses and flocks of sheep and goats. After Tuichán you approach the village of **Ixchiguán**, set on an exposed hillside at 3050m, surrounded by bleak rounded hills and in the shadow of the two towering volcanic cones. The road climbs to the **Cumbre de Cotzil**, a spectacular 3400m pass before descending to the scruffy town of **TACANÁ** – less than 10km from the Mexican border. Looming above the village is the active cone of **Volcán Tacaná** (4064m). The volcano is regularly climbed (the last small eruption was in 1986) but do check on its status if you plan a trek.

ARRIVAL AND DEPARTURE	TACANÁ
By bus First catch a bus from Quetzaltenango to San Pedro (every 20min; 1hr 30min). Buses from San Pedro run via Tuichán (1hr 15min) for Tacaná (3hr) hourly until 4pm.	Heading on from Tacaná, minibuses leave roughly hourly for Cuilco (2hr) from where there are regular buses to Huehuetenango.

Huehuetenango and around

At the foot of the mighty Cuchumatanes, **HUEHUETENANGO** is a departmental capital and the focus of trade and transport for a vast area of northwest Guatemala. Its atmosphere is provincial and pretty relaxed, though heavy traffic, much of which thunders through the town centre, reduces this appeal somewhat.

Before the arrival of the Spanish it was the site of one of the residential suburbs that surrounded the Mam capital of **Zaculeu** (the ruins of this site, just a few kilometres from town, are worth a visit). Under colonial rule it was a small regional centre with little to offer beyond a steady trickle of silver and a stretch or two of grazing land. Today the department is famous for its rich, complex high-quality **coffee** – which you'll have ample opportunity to sample in the town's cafés.

The plaza

Huehuetenango is a likeable if unremarkable place, its character best expressed in the unhurried atmosphere of the attractive **plaza**, where shaded walkways are surrounded by grand administrative offices. Overlooking this square are a shell-shaped bandstand, clock tower and a grand Neoclassical church, a solid whitewashed structure with a facade crammed with Doric pillars and Grecian urns. In the middle of the plaza, there's a **relief map** of the department which gives you an idea of the mass of rock that dominates the region, and its deep river valleys, even if the scale is warped.

ARRIVAL AND DEPARTURE HUEHUETENANGO

All **buses** stop at the chaotic bus terminal, halfway between the Carretera Interamericana and town. Each bus company has its own office, at which you should ask for the latest schedule (the timetables painted on the walls are often wrong). Also note that it is standard practice, even for second-class buses, to buy your ticket in advance. Microbuses connect the town centre with the terminal, leaving from 6 Av, between 4 and 5 calles. Buses to Zaculeu leave from the corner of 2 C and 7 Av, and micros (roughly every 40min) to Todos Santos leave from El Calvario, 1 Av and 1 C. If you want to go to Antigua, take a capital-bound bus and change at Chimaltenango; for Lago de Atitlán or Chichicastenango change at Los Encuentros.

SECOND-CLASS BUSES

Destinations Aguacatán (every 30min; 40min); Barillas (9 daily; 6hr 30min); Cuilco (8 daily; 2hr); Gracias a Dios (5 daily; 5hr); Guatemala City (every 30min; 6hr); La Mesilla, Mexican border (every 30min; 2hr); Nebaj – take an Aguacatán or Sacapulas bus; Nentón (5 daily; 3hr 30min); Quetzaltenango (every 30min; 2hr); Sacapulas (2 daily at 11.30am and 12.30pm; 2hr); San Juan Atitán (hourly; 1hr 15min); San Mateo Ixtatán (9 daily; 5hr); San Miguel Acatán (4 daily; 4hr 30min); San Rafael La Independencia (4 daily; 4hr 15min); Todos Santos (12 daily; 2hr 15min – some continuing on to San Martín and Jacaltenango); Yalambojoch (2 daily; 5hr).

FIRST-CLASS BUS COMPANIES

Línea Dorada operates the most comfortable buses to the capital.

Línea Dorada Calzeda Kaibil Balam 8–70 ☎7768 1566, ⓦlineadorada.info; 2 daily pullmans to Guatemala City, 1 daily to La Mesilla.
Los Halcones 10 Av 9–12 ☎7765 7986, ⓦtransportesloshalcones.com; 6 daily to Guatemala City.
Zaculeu Futura 6 C & 9 Av ☎7764 1535; 2 daily to Guatemala City.
Transportes Velásquez main terminal ☎7764 7594; 5 daily to Guatemala City.

SHUTTLE BUSES

Adrenalina Tours (see p.146) organizes shuttle buses to Antigua (US$35); Chichicastenango (US$30); Panajachel (US$30); Quetzaltenango (US$25) and San Cristóbal de las Casas in Mexico (US$35). Services to Todos Santos (US$25) and other destinations are on request.

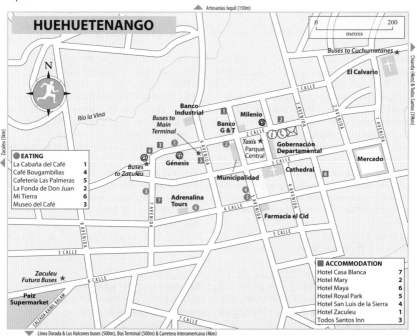

EATING	
La Cabaña del Café	1
Café Bougambilias	4
Cafetería Las Palmeras	5
La Fonda de Don Juan	2
Mi Tierra	6
Museo del Café	3

ACCOMMODATION	
Hotel Casa Blanca	7
Hotel Mary	2
Hotel Maya	6
Hotel Royal Park	5
Hotel San Luis de la Sierra	4
Hotel Zaculeu	1
Todos Santos Inn	3

2

INFORMATION, TOURS AND ACTIVITIES

Tourist information There's no Inguat office in Huehue. Adrenalina Tours are your best source of information.

Adrenalina Tours 4 C 6–54 ☎ 7768 1538, ⓦ adrenalina tours.com. Offers excellent tours throughout the department, including guided walks to a cheese farm and Zaculeu (US$15), Chiabal, San Juan Atitán and two-day trips to Laguna Yalambojoch (US$145).

Language schools Huehuetenango is a good place to learn Spanish as you don't rub shoulders with many other gringos. Academia de Español Xinabajul, 4 Av 14–14, Zona 5 (☎ 7764 6631, ⓔ academiaxinabajul@hotmail .com) receives positive reports from students. Teacher Abesaida Guevara de López gives good private lessons: call ☎ 7764 2917.

ACCOMMODATION

Huehuetenango has a pretty good range of **hotels**, all a short walk from the plaza, but no luxury options.

Hotel Casa Blanca 7 Av 3–41 ☎ 7769 0777. Classy hotel, centred on a colonial-style house and its twin patios, though there is some modern accommodation. Spacious rooms with very attractive furnishings, but those on the lower floor can be a little dark. There's good food served in the gorgeous dining room. US$36

Hotel Mary 2 C 3–52 ☎ 7764 1618. A basic, friendly and secure place where the rooms, all with private bathrooms, are ageing but will suffice for a night; some have a sofa or wardrobe. There's a comedor too. US$17

Hotel Maya 3 Av 3–55 ☎ 7764 0369. Concrete hotel with good-sized rooms, decent beds and private bathrooms. US$24

Hotel Royal Park 6 Av 2–34 ☎ 7762 7774. Flashy place with a gaudy colour scheme, but the impressive rooms, most with two double beds, are all spacious and well equipped – avoid those facing the street which suffer traffic noise. Rates include breakfast and wi-fi. US$33

Hotel San Luis de la Sierra 2 C 7–00 ☎ 7764 9217. A well-run, modern hotel with attractive rooms, all with pine furnishings; some have wonderful views of the mountains. There's ample parking and a restaurant. US$27

Hotel Zaculeu 5 Av 1–14 ☎ 7764 1086, ⓦ hotelzaculeu .com. This fine colonial-style inn has real class, with spacious if old-fashioned rooms set around a lovely leafy courtyard (and a newer section which is far less appealing). Don't miss the fantastic old bar, with piano and elegant chairs. Solo travellers get a great deal here. US$35

Todos Santos Inn 2 C 6–74 ☎ 5432 3421. Run by a hospitable lady, this budget place has clean, well-scrubbed rooms. Those upstairs are fairly bright and cheery, those downstairs less so. The shared bathrooms are clean. US$14

EATING AND DRINKING

Budget places are grouped close to the plaza. There's no real bar scene, but 6 C has a couple of possibilities.

La Cabaña del Café 2 C 6–50. A tiny log cabin-style place with wonderful coffees (from US$0.75); all beans are sourced from the Huehue region. Sandwiches (there's even roast beef), snacks and cakes are also served. Daily 8am–9pm.

Café Bougambilias Opposite the church ☎ 7764 0105. This four-storey pink and lurid green comedor is a good place for breakfast – try the highland-style *mosh*: porridge with cinnamon, wheat and sugar. Daily 7am–9.30pm.

Cafetería Las Palmeras Opposite the church ☎ 5783 2967. This very popular, clean and efficiently run restaurant has been recently renovated, so the large premises are quite smart. You can't go wrong with the set lunch deals (US$3); try the *chiles rellanos*. Also offers lots of tasty meat dishes and *tamales* (Sat only) for US$0.60 a pop. Daily 7am–9.30pm.

La Fonda de Don Juan 2 C 5–35 ☎ 7764 1173. Large restaurant with gingham tablecloths. The menu includes good pizzas, pastas and burgers, though it's quite pricey for Huehue, with most dishes over US$5. Daily 7am–10pm.

Mi Tierra 4 C 6–46 ☎ 7764 1473. Intimate little restaurant, set in a covered patio with a welcoming atmosphere. There's plenty of choice on the menu, with popular Guatemalan dishes like *pollo dorado*, grilled meats and Mexican classics too, most US$3–4. Mon–Sat 7am–9pm, Sun 2–9pm.

★ **Museo del Café** 7 Av 3–24 ☎ 7764 8903. A veritable temple to the arabica and robusta bean where you'll find coffee sacks on the walls, photographs of coffee fincas and tons of café curios. Great cappuccino, espresso and filter coffee served, and it's also a good choice for breakfast (from US$2.50), or lunch and dinner dishes including steamed vegetables (US$3.50), grilled beef (US$6) or the *menu del día* (US$3). And if you have a sweet tooth, don't miss the cakes. Mon–Sat 8am–9pm.

SHOPPING

Artesanías Ixquil 1 C 1–115, Zona 4 ☎ 5736 1415. Superb textiles can be bought here, a 15min walk north of the plaza up 6 Av to the top of a hill, then on the right; both the prices and quality are high.

Paiz Southwest of the town centre at 6 C and 10 Av. You could head to this supermarket to stock up on goodies and groceries if you're heading for the hills.

DIRECTORY

Banks and exchange Banco G&T Continental on the plaza and Banco Industrial on 6 Av both have ATMs.
Internet Milenio, 4 Av 1–54 charges US$0.75 per hour.
Mexican consulate Inside the Farmacia el Cid on the plaza's south side (☎ 7764 1366).
Post office 2 C 3–54 (Mon–Fri 8am–5pm).
Telephone Telgua, Centro Comercial el Triángulo, 10 Av & 6 C.

Zaculeu

Daily 8am–5pm; museum 8am–noon & 2–5pm • US$6.50 • Buses to the "ruinas" every 30min from 7 Av, between 2 and 3 calles in Huehuetenango

A few kilometres to the west of Huehuetenango are the ruins of **ZACULEU**, capital of the **Mam**, who were one of the principal pre-conquest highland tribes. The site includes several large temples, plazas and a ball court, but unfortunately it was restored pretty unsubtly by a latter-day colonial power, the United Fruit Company, in 1946 and 1947. The walls and surfaces were levelled off with a layer of thick white plaster, leaving them stark and undecorated. There are no roof-combs, carvings or stucco mouldings, and only in a few places does the original stonework show through. Even so, the site has a peculiar atmosphere of its own and is worth a look; surrounded by trees and neatly mown grass, with fantastic views of the mountains, it's also an excellent spot for a picnic.

There's a small **museum** on site with examples of some of the burial techniques used – bodies were crammed into great urns, interred in vaults and also cremated – and some interesting ceramics.

Brief history

The site of Zaculeu, first occupied in the fifth century, is thought to have been a religious and administrative centre for the **Mam**, and the home to its elite; the bulk of the population most likely lived in small surrounding settlements. After a period of subjugation under the rival K'iche' tribe in the fifteenth century, the Mam reasserted their independence, only for another expansionist empire, the **Spanish** – a yet more brutal alternative – to arrive. Following a massacre by the Spanish of five thousand Mam warriors to the south, Mam chief Kaibal Balam withdrew to the safety of Zaculeu, which was protected by ravines and walls. The Spanish army prepared for a lengthy siege, giving the Maya a choice: become Christians "peacefully" or face "death and destruction".

Attracted by neither option, the Mam struggled to hold out against the invading force, but after about six weeks under siege, his army starving to death, Kaibal Balam surrendered. With the bitterest of ironies a bastardized version of his name has been adopted by one of Guatemala's crack army regiments – the "Kaibiles", who were responsible for numerous massacres during the 1970s and early 1980s.

Chiantla

The village of **CHIANTLA** is backed right up against the mountains, 5km to the north of Huehuetenango. The main point of interest is the colonial **church**. Built by Dominican friars, it is now the object of one of the country's largest pilgrimages, held annually on February 2 in honour of its image of the **Virgen del Rosario**. She is thought to be capable of healing the sick, and at any time of the year you'll see people who've travelled from all over Guatemala asking for her assistance. A mural inside the church depicts a rather ill-proportioned Spaniard watching over the Maya toiling in his mines, while on the wall opposite the Maya are shown discovering God. The precise connection between the two is left somewhat vague, but presumably the gap is bridged by the Virgin.

By bus Buses from Huehuetenango to Chiantla travel between the bus terminal and Chiantla every 15min until 8pm. You can catch one as it passes the plaza in the town centre, or wait for a bus at the Calvario (by the junction of 1 Av and 1 C).

Aguacatán

East of Huehuetenango, **AGUACATÁN** is a small agricultural town strung out along a very long main street, and the only place in the country where the Akateko and Chalchitek languages are spoken. It's best visited for the huge **Sunday market**, which actually gets under way on Saturday afternoon, when traders arrive early to claim the best sites. On Sunday mornings people pour into town, cramming into the market and plaza, and soon spilling out into the surrounding area. Around noon the tide turns as the crowds start to drift back to their villages, with donkeys leading their drunken drivers home.

The **traditional costume** worn by the women of Aguacatán is unusually simple: their skirts are made of dark blue cotton and the *huipiles*, which hang loose, are decorated with bands of coloured ribbon on a plain white background. This plainness, though, is set off by the local speciality – the *cinta*, or headdress, an intricately embroidered piece of cloth combining blues, reds, yellows and greens, in which the women wrap their hair.

By bus or minibus Minibuses and buses run from Huehuetenango to Aguacatán every 30min until about 7pm (40min). Beyond Aguacatán a paved road runs east out along a ridge, eventually dropping down to the riverside town of Sacapulas 1hr 30min away; minibuses cover this route every 30min until about 5pm.

ACCOMMODATION AND EATING

Hotel y Restaurant Ray 1 Av ☎ 7766 0877. A good place to stay with very clean, well-kept tiled rooms with private bathroom and tasty, inexpensive food. <u>US$18</u>

The Cuchumatanes

The **Cuchumatanes**, rising to a frosty 3837m just to the north of Huehuetenango, are the largest non-volcanic peaks in Central America, stretching from the Mexican border to the highlands of Alta Verapaz.

The mountain **scenery** is magnificent, ranging from wild, exposed craggy outcrops to lush, tranquil river valleys. The upper parts of the slopes are barren, scattered with boulders and shrivelled cypress trees, while the lower levels, by contrast, are richly fertile, cultivated with corn, coffee and some sugar. Between the peaks, in the deep-cut valleys, are hundreds of tiny villages, isolated by the enormity of the landscape.

It's an immensely rewarding area, offering a rare glimpse of Maya life and some of the country's finest **fiestas** and **markets**. The mountains are also ideal for **hiking**, particularly if you've had enough of struggling up volcanoes.

The most accessible of the villages is **Todos Santos Cuchumatán**, which is also one of the most fascinating – its horse-race fiesta on November 1 has to be the most outrageous in Guatemala. North of here a remote road leads to Barillas through some of the most compelling Maya settlements in Guatemala; deeply traditional **San Mateo Ixtatán** is probably the most interesting place on the way. A trip into this mountainous area reveals an exceptional wealth of Maya culture. In this world of jagged peaks and deep-cut valleys Spanish is definitely the second language, and women rigidly adhere to traditional costume, offering you an ideal opportunity to witness Maya life at close quarters, and perhaps undertake a **hike** or two.

Brief history
This area had little to entice the **Spanish**, and they only exercised vague control, occasionally disrupting things with bouts of religious persecution. The people were, for the most part, left to maintain their old ways, and their traditions are still very much evident in the fiestas, costumes and **folk Catholicism**.

In the 1970s and 1980s, the violence and terror of the **civil war** sent thousands fleeing across the border to Mexico. Most families returned from exile in the 1990s, settling back to life in their old communities, but the cycle of **emigration** has repeated itself again in recent years, as thousands of young villagers have sought work in the US.

From Huehuetenango to Paquix
Heading north out of Huehuetenango, the road to the Cuchumatanes – paved until Soloma – passes through Chiantla before beginning the long climb up the vertiginous south face of the mountain chain. Buses sway around endless switchbacks, but the views back across the valley are superb. If you're driving, you can stop at a *mirador* almost at the top of the 1000m ascent for a spectacular vista of the chain of volcanoes away to the south, including the near-flawless coned profile of the **Volcán Santa María**.

Paquix junction
Eventually the road levels out in a *región andina*, a desolate, grassy 3000m-high plateau suspended between the peaks that's usually wrapped in cloud in the late afternoon. At the three-way **Paquix junction** you'll find a couple of comedores, a gas station and the turn-off for Todos Santos.

Directly behind Paquix's *Comedor Amparito* a wonderful **hiking trail** climbs for an hour and a half up the side of Chikox mountain, then descends for 45 minutes to a lookout. From here there's a sublime vista over Huehuetenango to a volcano-studded horizon.

ARRIVAL AND DEPARTURE   PAQUIX
By bus All buses for both Barrillas and Todos Santos to/from Huehuetenango pass through Paquix.

ACCOMMODATION
Unicórnio Azul 6km east of Paquix ☎5205 9328, ⓦunicornioazul.com. A wonderful French–Guatemalan-owned ranch that organizes superb horseriding excursions (an hour's ride is included in the room rate). Accommodation is in very attractive adobe-walled rooms and the food (breakfast is complimentary) is farm-fresh and delicious. <u>US$72</u>

Chiabal
At a lung-challenging 3300m, the lonely livestock-raising settlement of **CHIABAL** is one of the highest villages in all Central America. A good **community tourism** initiative (☎5381 0540, ⓦturismocuchumatanes.com) has been established with guided **hikes,** including one trail up to the 3666m Piedra Cuache *mirador*, homestay accommodation and the chance to herd llama and sheep. The village is 4km west of Paquix and served by all transport between Huehuetenango and Todos Santos.

La Torre
Six kilometres west of Chiabal, **La Ventosa** is another high-altitude village perched between peaks. From here a trail leads north to **La Torre** (at 3837m the highest non-volcanic mountain in Guatemala). It's around an hour and a half to the top, a stunning hike that passes one-room adobe farmsteads and then weaves through a pine- and cedar-tree forest before arriving at the summit, which is topped with antennae. On clear days (mornings are best) a jagged profile of distant volcanoes, from Tacaná to Tolimán, pierces the horizon to the south.

Todos Santos Cuchumatán

West of La Ventosa, the road steadily descends and you'll soon start to see the explosively coloured traditional costume of the Todosanteros.

Spectacularly sited in its own deep-cut river valley, the small town of **TODOS SANTOS CUCHUMATÁN** is strung out along an elongated main street plotted with some venerable old wooden houses. It's a pretty settlement, with a small plaza and a colonial-style whitewashed church, but the village is totally overwhelmed by the looming presence of the Cuchumatanes mountains which insulate Todos Santos from the rest of the world.

The depth of **tradition** evident here is startling. Men fill the streets with colour in their red-and-white-striped trousers, black woollen breeches, brilliantly embroidered shirt collars and natty straw hats; women wear dark blue *cortes* and superbly intricate purple *huipiles*. Todos Santos is one of the few places where people still use the 260-day *Tzolkin* **calendar** (see p.156) which dates back to ancient times. Highland traditions and the epic surroundings have long captivated visitors, and photographers in particular, though you should be wary of taking pictures of people – particularly children. In this isolated community rumours persist that some foreigners steal babies.

Todos Santos is a great place to simply hang out but it would be a shame not to try a traditional **sauna** (*chuc*) while you're here – most guesthouses will prepare one for you. Note that Todos Santos has declared itself a dry town, so **no alcohol** is sold (except during the fiesta); *Casa Familiar* guests are exempt.

Tojcunanchén

Above the village – follow the track that goes up behind the *Comedor Katy* – is the small Maya site of **Tojcunanchén**, where you'll find a couple of grass-covered mounds sprouting pine trees and two large crosses. The site is occasionally used by *costumbristas* for the burning of incense and the ritual sacrifice of animals.

The market

If you can't make it for the fiesta (see below), the Saturday **market** is another good time to see the village come to life. Textile shoppers will also find two excellent co-ops selling quality **weavings**: one is located next to the *Casa Familiar* and the other (named Cooperativa Estrella de Occidente) is just east of the plaza on the main street.

The museum

Just east of the plaza • Daily 9am–5pm • US$0.75

This little **museum** has some fine festival costumes, a marimba or two, a collection of masks, assorted Maya ceramics and archeological finds and some wonderful old photos.

ALL SAINTS FIESTA

One spectacular annual event, which brings emigrants home from as far away as Canada, is the famous November 1 **fiesta** for All Saints (*todos santos*). For three days the village is taken over by unrestrained drinking, dance and marimba music. The festival starts with an all-day **horse race**, which begins as a massive stampede, as riders tear up the course, thrashing their horses, capes flowing behind them. At either end of the run they take a drink before burning back again. As the day wears on some riders retire, collapse, or tie themselves on their mounts, leaving only the toughest to continue.

On the second day, **The Day of the Dead**, the action moves to the cemetery, with marimba bands and drink stalls setting up amongst the graves for a day of intense ritual that combines grief and celebration. By the end of the fiesta, the streets are littered with collapsed villagers and the jail packed with brawlers

Organized trips to the Todos Santos fiesta are offered by tour agencies in Quetzaltenango and Lago de Atitlán.

> ## LEARNING SPANISH OR MAM IN TODOS SANTOS
>
> **Hispano Maya** (☎ 5163 9293, �ⓦ hispanomaya.weebly.com), opposite the *Hotelito Todos Santos*, offers four to five hours' instruction a day – plus accommodation and meals with a local family for US$150 a week. Excursions and activities are run too. As Spanish is the second language here (after Mam), it's as much about the cultural experience as the studying.

ARRIVAL AND INFORMATION

By bus Buses and microbuses from Huehuetenango (2hr 15min) pass right through the centre of town, some carrying on down the valley to Jacaltenango.

Information Roman (☎ 5900 7795, ⓔ romanstopp @yahoo.com), the Swiss owner of the *Casa Familiar*, is a font of knowledge about the village and region. There are two excellent community websites – ⓦ stetson.edu/~rsitler /TodosSantos and ⓦ todossantoscuchumatanes.weebly .com – dedicated to the Todos Santos region.

TODOS SANTOS CUCHUMATÁN

2

ACCOMMODATION AND EATING

★ **Casa Familiar** 100m uphill from the plaza ☎ 5580 9579, ⓔ romanstopp@yahoo.com. Renovated hotel where the rooms have balconies with valley views, TVs, woven bedspreads and private hot-water bathrooms. Warm up in the guests' lounge around the fireplace, enjoy a *chuj* on the roof terrace and tuck into good grub in the café. There's a store selling local weavings here too. US$26

Hotelito Todos Santos On the left just before you reach the Casa Familiar ☎ 7783 0603. A good cheap choice with fifteen small clean tiled rooms, six with bathroom, friendly staff and a comedor. US$12

EATING

Casa Familiar 100m uphill from the plaza ☎ 5580 9579. Popular gringo hangout for its local and western food, including granola and porridge breakfasts, though quite pricey (meals US$3–5) compared to the local places. Wine and beer are available to guests. Daily 7am–9pm.

Comedor Katy below Casa Familiar ☎ 4593 9831.

Cheap and cheerful place serving filling *comida típica*; a typical meal goes for around US$2.50. Daily 6.30am–8pm.

Comedor Martita below Hotelito Todos Santos ☎ 5194 9276. This place is always popular for its fine view across the valley. Serves Guatemalan highland food for around US$3 a plate. Daily 6.30am–8pm.

DIRECTORY

Bank The Banrural bank on the plaza changes dollars.

Internet There's slow internet access available from a couple of places on the main drag.

Around Todos Santos

The scenery around Todos Santos is some of the most spectacular in all Guatemala, and there's no better place to leave the roads and set off on foot. In a day you can walk across to **San Juan Atitán**, and from there loop back to Huehuetenango.

Alternatively, you can travel (on foot or by microbus) down the valley from Todos Santos to **San Martín** and on to **Jacaltenango**, a route that offers superb views.

Hiking to San Juan Atitán

The village of **SAN JUAN ATITÁN** is around a five-hour walk from Todos Santos, across a beautiful, isolated valley. Mondays and Thursdays are the best days to do this hike – if you set out early in the morning (around 6.30am) you can arrive in San Juan before the market there has finished.

The walk follows the track up past the *Casa Familar*, and climbs steeply above the village through endless muddy switchbacks. You reach the top of the ridge after about an hour and, if the skies are clear, you'll be rewarded by an awesome view of the Tajumulco and Tacaná volcanoes. Here the path divides: to the right are the scattered remains of an ancient **cloudforest** and a lovely grassy valley, while straight ahead is the path to San Juan, dropping down past some huts, through beautiful forest. The route takes you up and down endless exhausting ridges, and over a total of five gushing streams.

2

Between the fourth and fifth streams – about three hours on from Todos Santos – you'll find an ideal place for a **picnic** overlooking the valley. Soon after here the path swings up to the left, over another pass, and the village of San Juan, strung out along the steep hillside, comes into view in the distance (though it is still more than an hour's walk away). Bear left here.

San Juan is an intensely traditional place: virtually all the men wear dark-brown woollen *capixayes* (a kind of knee-length poncho) over a scarlet shirt, held in place by a sash, and plain white trousers. The high-backed sandals worn here are a style depicted in ancient Maya carvings.

Like most of these mountain villages, San Juan is a pretty quiet place, active only on market days, Monday and Thursday. The central square has a giant palm tree and a pretty garden, and there are spectacular views across the valley.

ARRIVAL AND DEPARTURE	**SAN JUAN ATITÁN**

By pick-up Microbuses and pick-up connections to Huehuetenango leave (roughly) every hour or so from 6am (1hr).

Hiking to San Martín

Heading down the valley from Todos Santos, **SAN MARTÍN,** a three-hour walk away, is the next place of any size. This village is inhabited almost entirely by ladinos but its Friday market attracts indigenous people from communities far and wide. A little beyond the village the road down the valley divides, with a right fork that leads around the steep western edge of the Cuchumatanes. On a clear day there are spectacular views, reaching well into Mexico. The route continues through the poor and ragged village of **Concepción Huista** from where a road plunges to Jacaltenango.

Jacaltenango

Perched on a plateau overlooking the limestone plain that stretches out across the Mexican border, **JACALTENANGO** is the heart of an area that was once very traditional, inhabited by a small tribe of Akateko-speakers. Several notable **books** about Maya customs were researched here in the early twentieth century, including the classic *The Year Bearer's People* by Douglas Byers. More recently, the village's most famous resident, Víctor Montejo, documented his experiences during the dark days of the civil war in his book *Testimony: Death of a Guatemalan Village.*

Today **coffee** cultivation dominates the local economy and the town has a calm and fairly prosperous feel. **Market day** is Sunday.

ARRIVAL AND INFORMATION	**JACALTENANGO**

By bus and microbus Microbuses and buses connect Todos Santos with Jacaltenango, running roughly every 90min until 4pm. Regular buses also run between the town and the Carretera Interamerica highway just south of the Mexican border.

Bank Banrural 2 C 2–11 has an ATM.

The high road to Barillas

North of the Paquix junction (see p.163), a lonely road, paved until **Soloma**, runs across the mass of the Cuchumatanes, crossing the exposed central plateau before finally dropping into the more temperate coffee country around Barillas. This magnificent, isolated highland area encompasses a network of deeply traditional indigenous villages and three separate **linguistic zones**. Between **San Juan Ixcoy** and **Santa Eulalia**, Q'anjob'al is spoken; around **San Miguel Acatán**, it's Akateko; and in the **San Mateo Ixtatán** region the language is Chuj.

The **road to Barillas** was something of a dead-end until recently but new bridges across the mighty rivers of the Ixcán and road improvements have now opened up a slow, if challenging route east of Barillas to Playa Grande (in neighbouring Alta Verapaz).

2

Paquix to San Juan Ixcoy

Beyond **Paquix** the road runs through a couple of magical valleys, where great grey boulders lie scattered among ancient-looking oak and cypress trees, their trunks gnarled by the bitter winds. A few families manage to survive the rigours of the altitude, collecting firewood and tending flocks of **sheep**.

Continuing north the road gradually winds down off the plateau, clinging to a hillside, the highway cut out of the sheer rock-face and often wrapped in clouds. On your right are two huge incisor-shaped rocky outcrops, known locally as the **Piedras de Captzín**, which are sacred to the Q'anjob'al Maya of these parts.

The first village you come to is **SAN JUAN IXCOY**, an apple-growing centre drawn out along the valley floor. In season, around the end of August, passing buses are besieged by an army of fruit sellers but there's no particular reason to stop at other times.

This innocent-looking village has a past marked by violence. In 1898, following a dispute about pay, the Maya of San Juan murdered the local labour contractor, and in a desperate bid to keep the crime secret they slaughtered all but one of the village's ladino population. The authorities responded mercilessly, killing about ten Maya for the life of every ladino. In local mythology the revolt is known as *la degollación*, the beheading.

Soloma

Over another range of hills, the town of **SOLOMA** is the largest, busiest and richest of the settlements in the northern Cuchumatanes. Its flat valley floor was once the bed of a lake, and the steep hillsides still come sliding down at every earthquake or sustained cloudburst. The long white *huipiles* worn by the women of Soloma are similar to those of San Mateo Ixtatán and the Lacandones, and are probably as close as any in the country to the style worn before the Conquest. These days only a few elderly ladies don them for **market** days (Thurs & Sun), by far the best time to visit.

ARRIVAL AND DEPARTURE SOLOMA

By bus Buses from Huehuetenango pass through Soloma (3hr) about every hour on their way to Barillas; the last bus leaves Huehue at 5pm.

ACCOMMODATION AND EATING

Hotel Don Chico 4 Av 3–65 ☎ 7780 6087. This concrete block north of the plaza may be aesthetically unpleasing but its rooms are fine for a night or two. It's cheap for solo travellers, and there's a restaurant and underground parking. US$18

Restaurante California South side of the plaza. Reliable comedor that serves up hearty portions of highland grub, and filling breakfasts. Daily 7am–8pm.

DIRECTORY

Bank Banrural at 6 C 7–03 has an ATM and will change dollars.

Internet Several places offer internet connections in the streets around the plaza.

Santa Eulalia

Leaving Soloma the paved road soon ends, and you continue over another range of hills to the large village of **SANTA EULALIA**, where highland religious ritual is adhered to very strongly. The **church** here is fascinating: a large, dusty pink-coloured building where the faithful assemble on their knees to recite prayers, and the air is thick with the smoke from hundreds of candles. Many then stop to burn incense at a separate **Maya altar**, choked in smoke, in front of the church.

Beyond Santa Eulalia is the **Cruce Pett** junction, after which the Barillas road pushes on north through pastureland, skirting patches of pine forest, with exhilarating views west into Mexico. The sense of isolation is immense up on this beautiful 3000m-high plateau, and you'll barely see a soul except for shepherd boys and their goats.

THE MAYA PRIESTS OF THE CUCHUMATANES

Ethnographer Krystyna Deuss, author of Shamans, Witches, and Maya Priests: Native Religion and Ritual in Highland Guatemala, has been studying traditions in remote Cuchumatanes communities for decades, focusing her attention on the prayersayers, who occupy a position parallel to that of local priests. Here she explains their role and the key rituals.

THE CALENDAR

Some of the purest **Maya rituals** remaining are found among the Q'anjob'al Maya of northwestern Cuchumatanes. The office of *alcalde resador* (chief prayersayer) still exists here and the 365-day *Haab* calendar is used in conjunction with the 260-day *Tzolkin*. The former ends with the five days of *Oyeb' ku'*, when adult souls leave the body; the return of the souls on the fifth day brings in the new year. As this always falls on a day of *Watan*, *Lambat*, *Ben* or *Chinax*, these four-day lords are known as the "Year Bearers" or "Chiefs". The *Haab* year begins either at the end of February or the beginning of March, coinciding with the corn-planting season.

PRAYERSAYER DUTIES AND TRADITIONS

The **duty of the prayersayer** is to protect his village from evil and ensure a good harvest by praying for rain at planting time and for protection against wind, pests and disease while the corn is maturing. He's usually a man in his 60s or 70s, and his year of office – during which he and his wife must remain celibate – begins on January 1.

In Santa Eulalia, Soloma and San Miguel Acatán, where traditions are particularly strong, he lives in a purpose-built prayermakers' house. Here he's visited by traditionalists and left gifts of corn, beans, candles and money.

On the altar of the house stands the **ordenanza**, a chest that contains religious icons and ancient village documents. This chest serves as a symbol of authority and as a sacred object, and can only be opened by the *alcalde resador*, in private, once a year.

The *resador's* whole day is spent in prayer: at his home altar before the *ordenanza*, in church and at sacred sites marked by crosses. Prayers for rain are often accompanied by the ritual sacrifice of turkeys, whose blood is poured over candles and incense, which is then burned at the sacred places the following day. These ceremonies are not open to the public.

NEW YEAR RITUALS

Festivals more in the public domain happen on **January 1** when the incumbent *alcalde resador* hands over his responsibilities to his successor. In **Soloma**, after an all-night vigil, the *ordenanza* is carried in procession to the middle of the market square and put on a makeshift altar under a pine arch. When the incoming group arrives there are prayers and ritual drinking, and they receive their wooden staffs of office; after this, the outgoing *alcalde resador* is free to leave for his own home. The new prayersayer's group stays in the marketplace, collecting alms and drinking until 3pm, when they carry the *ordenanza* back to the official residence in a somewhat erratic procession. Notwithstanding a further night of vigil and ceremonial drinking, at 7am the following morning the *alcalde resador* sets out on his first prayer-round to the sacred mountains overlooking the town.

In **San Juan Ixcoy** the year-end ceremonies differ in that the new *resador* is not appointed in advance. Here the outgoing group carries the *ordenanza* to a small chapel on the night of the 31st and leaves it in the care of a committee of traditionalists. The usual all-night vigil with prayers, ritual drinking and collecting alms continues throughout the following day while everyone waits anxiously for a candidate to turn up. As the office of *resador* is not only arduous but also expensive, the post is not always filled. The *ordenanza* sometimes stays locked in the chapel for several days before a volunteer takes on the office again rather than let the *ordenanza* and the tradition be abandoned.

– Krystyna Deuss, the Guatemalan Maya Centre, London (Ⓦ maya.org.uk)

Cafetería Margol Next door to the Hotel y Restaurante Eulalense. A humble local place that serves up tasty *comida típica* including some good *caldos*. Daily 7am–8pm.

Hotel y Restaurante Eulalense Just below the church ☎ 7765 9634. Basic, perfectly serviceable highland inn with clean, very cheap rooms and shared bathrooms with hot water. <u>US$9</u>

San Rafael La Independencia

At the **Cruce Pett** junction, 5km north of Santa Eulalia, there are comedores and a branch road that cuts off to the west, curving around the peaks of the Cuchumatanes to the village of **SAN RAFAEL LA INDEPENDENCIA**, 11km away. Perched on an outcrop with magnificent views down towards the Mexican border, this peaceful Akateko-speaking settlement amounts to not much more than a scattering of old timber houses and utilitarian concrete structures. Nevertheless, it makes an enjoyable place to spend a day or two, at the heart of a very traditional region where Maya customs remain very strongly observed.

Centro Cultural Maya Akateko

Above the municipalidad • Mon–Fri 7am–5pm, Sat 7am–noon • ☎ 7779 7239

This **cultural centre** has a fascinating collection of old artefacts, including polychrome ceramics, obsidian flints, a two-metre blowpipe and some interesting photographs. The staff can put you in touch with guides (Pedro Juan Méndez Martinez is recommended) who can lead you to the Maya ruins of **Tenam**, the Chimbam chapel, Xeyatak ceremonial centre and the numerous sacred caves and altars that dot the hills around.

Tienda San Andrés One block downhill from the plaza, no phone. You can stay in the basic rooms above this shop, though there's no hot water here. <u>US$8</u>

San Miguel Acatán

From San Rafael it's just 4km to the larger, much less attractive village of **SAN MIGUEL ACATÁN**. It's less traditional than San Rafael, but has better transport connections and you'll find a couple of hospedajes, plenty of comedores, a lively Sunday market and a branch of Banrural.

By bus Buses leave Huehuetenango for San Miguel, via San Rafael, four times daily (4hr 30min).

San Mateo Ixtatán

On the high road to Barillas, it's 24km from Cruce Pett to **SAN MATEO IXTATÁN**, the most traditional, and quite possibly the most interesting of this string of settlements. Its name derives from the Nahuatl for "abundance of salt", which is still a major industry in the communally owned mines around the village. Little more than a thin sprawl of wooden-tiled houses, the village tumbles down a steep east-facing hillside, occupying the ground between two plunging river valleys. The people here speak **Chuj** and form part of a Maya group who occupy the extreme northwest corner of the highlands and some of the forest beyond; their territory borders that of the Lacandón, a jungle tribe from Mexico. The best time to visit, other than for the fiesta (Sept 17–21), is on a **market day**, Thursday or Sunday – the rest of the week the village is virtually deserted.

Traditional dress is becoming less common, but the older women here still wear unusual and striking *huipiles*, long white gowns embroidered in brilliant reds, yellows and blues, radiating out from a star-like centre. You may also see men wearing short woollen poncho-like tunics called *capixayes*, often embroidered with flowers around the collar and quetzals on the back.

The church

San Mateo's cream-coloured **church**, its wonky facade embellished with niches and the images of saints, is one of the most interesting in Guatemala, with a pagan character that barely offers a passing reference to conventional Catholicism. Smoke from a Maya altar attended by *costumbristas* drifts across the courtyard in front of the church, while inside devotees kneel on the nave floor clutching candles, the stone walls reverberating with the constant murmur of solemn incantations.

Ruins of Wajxaklajunh

Just below the village are the quite substantial unrestored Maya ruins of **Wajxaklajunh**, which enjoy a magical position overlooking the San Mateo valley and down to ridge after ridge of hills on the horizon to the east. Here you'll find several temples, including the pyramid-shaped structure known as **Yolk'u**, a ball court and a couple of weathered stelae shaded by cypress trees.

2

ARRIVAL AND INFORMATION — SAN MATEO IXTATÁN

By bus Nine daily buses leave Huehuetenango for San Mateo (5hr 15min). It's also possible to travel by pick-up from San Mateo northwest to the village of Yalambojoch (see p.172) in around 2hr 30min.

Information The website ⊛ ixtatan.org, run by development project the Ixtatán Foundation, is a great source of information, and you may run into their staff in town. There are a couple of places to surf the internet in town.

ACCOMMODATION AND EATING

Hotel Ixtateco Above the parque ⊕ 7756 6586. Quite fancy for these parts, this modern hotel is the best in town with comfortable rooms that have en-suite bathrooms. <u>US$20</u>

Hotel Magdalena Below the parque ⊕ 5374 3390. A simple place with basic rooms and few guests, but at least it has hot water. <u>US$9</u>

Restaurante Wajxaklajunh Above the police station. For a filling feed, including generous portions of grilled *bistec* and occasional Maya specials, this is clean and cheap. Daily 7am–8pm.

Barillas and around

Beyond San Mateo the road drops steadily east to **BARILLAS**, an unlovely ladino frontier town 28km away in the relative warmth of the tierra templada at 1450m and devoted to coffee production. If you're heading to or from Laguna Lachúa (see p.243) it's an obvious place to break the journey, otherwise it holds few attractions.

About 18km north of Barillas (take the dirt road towards the village of Yolhuitz) is the beautiful hourglass-shaped **Laguna Maxbal**, which is ringed by forest – locals say it's possible to see a quetzal bird here some mornings. You'll need your own transport to get here, or you can visit on a tour from Huehue (see p.158).

ARRIVAL AND DEPARTURE — BARILLAS

By bus Nine daily buses (6hr 30min) connect Barillas to Huehuetenango. Pick-ups to Playa Grande (5–7hr depending on road conditions) leave roughly hourly until 4pm from opposite the *Hotel Arizona*. Microbuses connect the bus terminal with the centre of town.

ACCOMMODATION AND EATING

Hotel Arizona 3 C 7–19, Zona 6 ⊕ 7780 2758. Close to the bus terminal, this well-run place with pleasant rooms is handy if you have an early start to Playa Grande. <u>US$22</u>

Hotel Villa Virginia On the plaza ⊕ 7780 2236. In the heart of town, this dependable hotel offers decent rooms with en-suite bathrooms and has a comedor. <u>US$24</u>

DIRECTORY

Bank Banrural has a bank at 3 Av 2–28, Zona 1, which has an ATM.

West to the Mexican border

From Huehuetenango the Carretera Interamericana runs for 79km through the narrow Selegua valley to the Mexican border at **La Mesilla** (see below). A short distance before here, from the roadside village of **Camoja Grande**, a paved road leads off to the north, paralleling the frontier. The road crosses a dusty white limestone plateau to the village of **Nentón**, then continues up into the extreme northwest corner of the country, where there are a couple of wonderful natural attractions.

El Cimarrón

The first of these attractions is the startling **El Cimarrón** *cenote* (a sink hole in the limestone crust), a near-perfect cylindrical depression measuring about 500m across and around 300m deep. The bottom harbours a lake and dense forest. Locals attest all sorts of legends to the *cenote*, which is about just 5km from the junction of La Trinidad.

Yalambojoch

About 15km east of the border post Gracias a Dios (see box below), the village of **YALAMBOJOCH** is something of a transport hub for these parts. It's also the jumping-off point for the spectacular cobalt-blue waters of **Laguna Yolnabaj** a large lake 5km to the north, that's also known as Laguna Brava. Locals, many of whom are *repatriados* (returned refugees from Mexico), have launched a reforestation programme around the lake and act as guides. Adrenalina Tours (see p.160) runs trips here.

ARRIVAL AND DEPARTURE   **YALAMBOJOCH**

By bus There are two daily buses (both leaving in the early morning) for Huehue and pick-ups for San Mateo Ixtatán.

Finca San Francisco

The recent history of Yalambojoch is bound up with that of **FINCA SAN FRANCISCO**, a smaller village just to the east. In 1982 the army massacred around three hundred people here and the entire population of the surrounding area fled for their lives, crossing the border into Mexico. After more than a decade, people started to return, and today life in the region seems to have returned to normal. Finca San Francisco has some small Maya temples, and also a plaque commemorating those who died in the massacre.

CROSSING THE MEXICAN BORDER

AT LA MESILLA

The two sets of **immigration** are 3km apart and connected by collective taxis (US$0.50). On the **Mexican side** very regular buses run to Comitán (1hr 15min), where you change for San Cristóbal de las Casas. Heading **into Guatemala**, second-class buses to Huehuetenango leave the border every thirty minutes (2hr) until 7pm and there are occasional services to Quetzaltenango (4hr) too. Línea Dorada run a first-class services to Guatemala City at 12.30pm and 9pm. Most travellers use **shuttle bus** connections between San Cristóbal de las Casas and towns in Guatemala including Quetzaltenango, Panajachel and Antigua; consult Adrenalina Tours (🌐 adrenalinatours.com) for the latest schedule. There's a Banrural bank (with ATM) and plenty of moneychangers.

Hotel Maricruz Close to Guatemalan immigration ☎ 7773 8686. This place will suffice for a night. Its clean rooms have private bathrooms and there's a restaurant. <u>US$20</u>

AT GRACIAS A DIOS

This remote border crossing is 8km northwest of La Trinidad junction and has a Guatemalan immigration post, though no Mexican one. The Banrural bank here will changes pesos and dollars but there's no ATM. Just over the border, the village of Carmixán has transport for Comitán where you can get your Mexican entry stamp.

FIESTAS IN THE WESTERN HIGHLANDS

The western highlands are the home of the traditional Guatemalan fiesta. These are some highlights.

JANUARY

18–20 San Sebastián Coatan
22–26 San Pablo La Laguna, main day 25th
23–27 San Pablo, department of San Marcos

FEBRUARY

Jan 28–Feb 2 Chiantla, main day 2nd
Jan 28–Feb 2 Jacaltenango
8 Ostuncalco
8–13 Santa Eulalia, main day 8th

MARCH

Varies Chajul, the second Friday in Lent marked by huge pilgrimages
Holy Week Santiago Atitlán, Maximón paraded through the streets, usually on the Wednesday; San Cristóbal Tonicapán, the biggest processions in the Xela area

APRIL

22–28 San Marcos, main day 25th
24 San Jorge La Laguna
25 San Marcos La Laguna
29–May 4 Barillas
Varies Zacualpa and Aguacatán, fiestas to mark forty days from Holy Week

MAY

6–10 Uspantán, main day 8th
8–10 Santa Cruz La Laguna

JUNE

12–14 San Antonio Palopó, Lago de Atitlán, main day 13th
21–25 San Juan Ixcoy, north of Huehuetenango
21–25 Olintepeque, just north of Quetzaltenango
22–25 Cotzal, main day 24th
22–26 San Juan Atitán, main day 24th
23–26 San Juan La Laguna, main day 24th
24 Comalapa
24–30 San Pedro Sacatepéquez
26–30 Soloma, main day 29th
27–30 San Pedro La Laguna, main day 29th
28–30 Almolonga, main day 29th

JULY

12–17 Huehuetenango
21–Aug 4 Momostenango, the 25th is a very important day in the Maya religious calendar, and the 1st is the main fiesta day
22–27 Chimaltenango, main day 26th
23–27 Santiago Atitlán, main day 25th

AUGUST

1–4 Sacapulas, main day 4th
9–15 Joyabaj, main day 15th. Superb fiesta; traditional dances here include the *Palo Volador*
10–13 Santa Clara La Laguna, main day 12th
11–17 Sololá, main day 15th
12–15 Nebaj, main day 15th
14–19 Santa Cruz del Quiché, main day 18th

SEPTEMBER

12–18 Quetzaltenango, main day 15th
17–21 San Mateo Ixtatán, main day 21st
24–30 Totonicapán, main day 29th
25–30 San Miguel Acatán, main day 29th
26–Oct 5 Tecpán

OCTOBER

1–6 San Francisco el Alto, main day 4th
2–6 Panajachel, main day 4th
15–20 San Lucas Tolimán, Lago de Atitlán, main day 18th

NOVEMBER

1–2 Todos Santos Cuchumatán, a wild, alcohol-infused horse race on the 1st, with everyone heading to the cemetery on the 2nd for All Souls' Day
7–12 San Martín Jilotepeque, main day 11th
22–26 Zunil, main day 25th
23–26 Nahualá, main day 25th
25 Santa Catarina Palopó, Lago de Atitlán
27–Dec 1 San Andrés Xecul, main day 30th

DECEMBER

5–8 Huehuetenango, main day 8th
7 The Burning of the Devil is celebrated in most highland towns with bonfires and men running around dressed as devils
14–21 Chichicastenango, very impressive fiesta, main day 21st

2

The Pacific coast

TILAPITA BEACH

The Pacific coast

A sweltering strip of low-lying, tropical land, some 300km long and 50km wide, Guatemala's Pacific coast is usually known as La Costa Sur. Featureless yet fertile, the coastal plain is a land of vast fincas, dull commerce-driven towns and ramshackle seaside resorts. The main attraction should be the coastline, though as the sand is black and the ocean has a dangerous undertow this region is not a big draw for travellers. But if you're yearning for some ocean air, and pick your spot carefully, the coast does have a couple of attractive beaches and some intriguing attractions dotted along the Pacific highway.

It's certainly not a resort, but the little seaside settlement of **Monterrico** has an unspoilt charm and is well worth a visit. Here you'll find a superb beach (a magnet for sea turtles) and a rich network of mangrove wetlands to explore. In the far west, and the twin villages of **Tilapa** and **Tilapita** also offer sweeping sands, no crowds and relatively safe swimming.

Several ancient Mesoamerican cultures once flourished in the region, leaving some important archeological remains. The one site in the area that comes close to ranking with those elsewhere in the country is **Takalik Abaj**, outside Retalhuleu, which displays both Maya and Olmec heritage.

Steadily the Pacific coast is gaining a reputation as a world-class **sport-fishing** location – offshore waters have stupendous numbers of sailfish, tarpon, tuna and marlin. **Iztapa** and **Puerto Quetzal** are the main bases for excursions. The region also has a couple of world-class **theme parks** on the Pacific slope that represent a huge draw for families.

Brief history

It's generally held that sophisticated **Olmec** influence – emerging first in Mexico and spread along the coast – shaped both **Ocós** and **Iztapa** cultures, which thrived here after 1500 BC. These were small, village-based societies that developed considerable skills in the working of stone and pottery.

Between 400 and 900 AD, parts of the coastal plain were overrun by the **Pipil**, who migrated south from Mexico, bringing new architectural styles and artistic skills. They established settlements with compact ceremonial centres and rubble-filled pyramids and traded cacao. The first **Spaniards** to set foot in Guatemala did so on the Pacific coast. In **colonial times** indigo and cacao were cultivated and cattle ranches established, but the inhospitable climate and accompanying diseases took their toll, and for the most part the region remained a miserable backwater. It was only after **independence** that commercial agriculture began to dominate. By the early twentieth century, the area was important enough to justify the construction of two **railways** to the coast and a line to the Mexican border.

Today the coastal strip is the country's most **intensely farmed** region, with entire villages effectively owned by vast fincas. There's a little domestic tourism but in general it's **agribusiness** – palm oil, bananas and sugar on the coast and coffee on the Pacific slope – that dominates the local economy.

MONTERRICO

Highlights

❶ Tilapa and Tilapita Palm trees line these fine, dark-sand beaches whose gently shelving profile makes this one of the coast's best spots for a swim. **See p.178**

❷ Takalik Abaj This small but rewarding archeological site features well-executed Olmec and Maya carvings. **See p.181**

❸ Xocomil and Xetulul leisure parks The country's largest water-park and its neighbouring amusement complex offer a glut of slides, pools and chutes, plus some thrilling rides. **See p.182**

❹ Surfing Guatemala's best surf beach, Paredón, is beginning to take off with the opening of a hip new surf lodge. **See p.185**

❺ Sport-fishing World-class conditions are offshore Guatemala's Pacific coast: the two main centres are Puerto Quetzal and Iztapa. **See p.187**

❻ Monterrico This oceanside village boasts Guatemala's most enjoyable beach, famous for its nesting sea turtles, plus an extensive network of mangrove swamps to explore. **See p.188**

HIGHLIGHTS ARE MARKED ON THE MAP ON PP.178–179

By bus The Pacific highway is served by a near-constant flow of pullmans and second-class buses. Buses travelling from Guatemala City to the Mexican border (5hr) stop at most of the main towns en route. If you plan to leave the highway, connections are less frequent but still regular to most coastal towns.

Tilapa and Tilapita

Most travellers arriving in Guatemala's extreme west forgo the beaches in these parts and head straight from the border to Quetzaltenango or Guatemala City. But for total relaxation, a day or two in tranquil Tilapita will be time well spent.

Tilapa

South of Tecún Umán (see box, p.180), a paved road paralleling the border passes endless palm-oil and banana plantations to the humble little village of **TILAPA**. The dark-sand beach here has a relatively gently shelving profile compared with many places on this coast, so the undertow is less fierce and it's easier for children to paddle in safety. Lifeguards are only posted on weekends though.

Reserva Natural El Manchón-Guamuchal

The coastline forms part of the **Reserva Natural El Manchón-Guamuchal**, which covers some 30km of prime turtle-nesting beach and extends around 10km inland to embrace a belt of swamp and mangrove, which is home to crocodiles, iguanas, kingfishers, storks, white herons, egrets and an abundance of fish. If you're interested in exploring

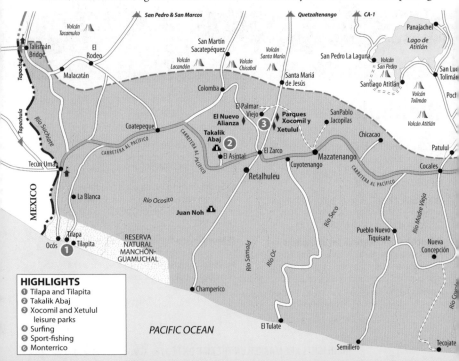

HIGHLIGHTS
1. Tilapa and Tilapita
2. Takalik Abaj
3. Xocomil and Xetulul leisure parks
4. Surfing
5. Sport-fishing
6. Monterrico

the area's **wetlands**, speak to one of the local boatmen in Tilapa or Tilapita about taking a tour (around US$16/hr) of the canals and lagoons.

Tilapita

On the other side of an estuary from Tilapa is the even tinier, and more agreeable, beach settlement of **TILAPITA**. Here there's a real opportunity to get away from it all and enjoy a superb stretch of clean, dark sand and the ocean (with not too much undertow). Just next to the *El Pacífico* hotel is a small **turtle hatchery**, with protected enclosures where eggs are buried until they hatch, and some information boards (the Olive Ridley turtle is the main visitor here).

ARRIVAL AND INFORMATION   TILAPA AND TILAPITA

By bus Regular buses connect Coatepeque and Tilapa (every 30min, last bus returns at 6pm; 2hr). If you're travelling along the Carretera al Pacífico, just wait at the Tilapa junction on the highway for a connection.

By boat Boatmen buzz you up the canal that connects Tilapa and Tilapita. The 10min ride costs US$1.50/head; it's possible to wade over at low tide.

Information Consult the website ⓦ playatilapa.com for more information about the village.

3

ACCOMMODATION AND EATING   TILAPA

There's a row of beach comedores dispensing good, fresh prawns and fried fish (around US$6 a meal), plus cold Gallo beer.

Hotel Tilapa ☎ 4777 9190. All the hospedajes here are extremely basic indeed, but if you're very desperate this place has bare-bones rooms and parking. US$14

TILAPITA

El Pacífico ☎ 5940 1524. Owned by charming local couple Siria and Alex Mata, this hotel has functional,

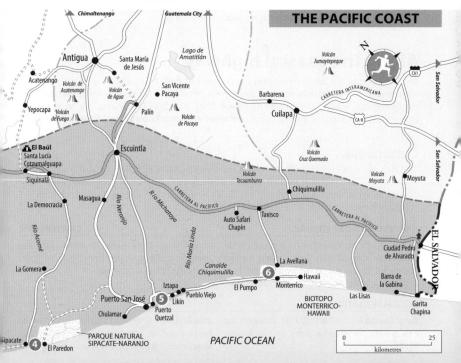

3

CROSSING THE MEXICAN BORDER

The two **border posts**, Talismán and Tecún Umán are both open 24 hours. Minibuses run every twenty minutes or so from Tapachula in Mexico (30min away) to Talismán and Tecún Umán until 9pm. Four companies – Galgos, King Quality, Ticabus and Línea Dorada (see p.64) – run **direct buses** between Tapachula in Mexico, and Guatemala City.

VIA TALISMÁN (EL CARMEN)

Talismán, also referred to as El Carmen, is the more relaxed of the two crossings. There's a regular flow of buses from here to Malacatán, from where buses head along on a slow, mountainous route for San Marcos and Quetzaltenango.

VIA TECÚN UMÁN

This busy border is favoured by most commercial traffic. The town has an authentic frontier flavour with all-night bars, lost souls, contraband and moneychangers. Cycle rickshaws (charging US$1.30 to immigration) snake through the traffic. Pullmans run by three companies (see above) connect Guatemala City with Tecún Umán on their way to Tapachula, and there are additional second-class services from the capital's Centra Sur terminal. Heading into Guatemala, there's a steady stream of buses running along the coastal highway to Guatemala City and direct buses to Quetzaltenango until about 4pm; after this time get the first bus to Retalhuleu ("Reu") and get an onward connection from there.

VISAS

Few nationalities need a visa for Guatemala, but there's a consulate in Tapachula if you don't qualify for a waiver. The same is true for Mexico, though there are Mexican consulates in Retalhuleu, Quetzaltenango, Huehuetenango and Guatemala City for those who do need a visa.

---

large rooms, all with decent mattresses, fans and showers – though you might want to bring your own mosquito net. The 18m swimming pool is filled at weekends. Good food, including fresh fish, is served (a huge meal is about US$6) and the hotel is always well stocked with cold beers. US$10

Along the coastal highway

Heading east of the border you pass a succession of dull, incessantly hot, purely commercial towns. **Retalhuleu** is slightly more attractive than most, close to which are the intriguing Maya-Olmec ruins of **Takalik Abaj**. North of Retalhuleu you're within easy reach of the terrific theme parks of **Parque Acuático Xocomil** and **Parque Xetulul**.

Coatepeque

The first place of any importance along the highway **COATEPEQUE** is a shabby, furiously busy town where coffee is processed. As it's infamous for its street gangs, and the climate is oven hot and perpetually sticky, it's best to avoid hanging around, though you may have to change buses here.

ARRIVAL AND DEPARTURE   COATEPEQUE

By bus From the bus terminal buses run regularly to the two Mexican border crossings, Quetzaltenango (via both Colomba and Zunil) until about 7pm and the capital. Destinations Guatemala City (every 30min; 4hr); Quetzaltenango (every 30min; 1hr 30min); Retalhuleu (every 20min; 50min); Talismán (every 20min; 1hr 30min); Tecún Umán (every 20min; 40min).

ACCOMMODATION

Hotel Baechli 6 C 5–35 ☎ 7775 1483. Family-run and a cheap option, this place has decent fan-cooled rooms. US$21

Villa Real 6 C 6–57 ☎ 7775 1308. If you do get stuck, this hotel is a good bet, with comfortable, if smallish, modern singles and doubles, a restaurant and secure parking US$24

Retalhuleu

Set 6km south of the Carretera al Pacífico, **RETALHULEU** – usually shortened to **Reu** ("Ray-oo") – is a relatively civilized place compared with the chaos evident elsewhere on the coast. Grand-looking palm trees line the entrance road to the town, while the **parque** retains a degree of faded authority: towering Greek columns grace the elegant *municipalidad* and there's an imposing colonial church.

Museo de Arqueología y Etnología

Parque Central • Tues–Sat 8am–5.30pm • US$1.30

This small museum inside the *municipalidad* on the plaza has a collection of Maya anthropomorphic figurines that show a strong Mexican influence and some evocative old photographs of the region.

ARRIVAL AND INFORMATION   RETALHULEU

By bus Most buses running along the coastal highway pull in to the bustling Retalhuleu terminal on 7 Av and 10 C, a 10min walk from the plaza.
Destinations Champerico (every 15min; 1hr); Guatemala City (every 30min; 3hr); Quetzaltenango (every 30min;

1hr 15min); Tecún Umán (every 20min; 1hr 30min); El Tulate (roughly hourly; 1hr 45min).
Adventure trips Reuxtreme (☎5202 8180, ⊛reuxtreme .com), based in *Hotel Casa Santa María*, offers mountain-bike trips to Takalik Abaj and kayaking through mangrove lagoons.

ACCOMMODATION AND EATING

Hotel América 8 Av 9–32 ☎7771 1154. A good bet for an inexpensive place to stay with well-kept rooms with fan and private bathrooms. US$16
Hotel Casa Santa María 4 C 4–23 ☎5202 8180, ⊛hostalcasasantamaria.com. This colonial-style place has a small pool and attractive singles and doubles with

a/c. A continental breakfast is included (weekdays only) and meals (US$5) are also available. The owners run the Reuxtreme tour agency (see above). US$39
Lo de Chaz 5 C 4–65 ☎7771 4649. Just west of the plaza, this café/bar is the best bet for a beer. They also serve snacks, breakfasts and Guatemalan favourites. Daily 7.30am–10pm.

DIRECTORY

Banks and exchange Around the plaza are several banks, including the Banco Agromercantil, with an ATM.

Mexican consulate At the *Posada de Don José* (Mon–Fri 4–6pm).

Takalik Abaj

19km west of Retalhuleu • Daily 7am–5pm • US$6.50, guide US$6.50

The archeological site of **Takalik Abaj** has cast fresh light on the development of early Maya civilization, particularly the influence of **Olmec** culture. The city presided over trade routes along the Pacific littoral, controlling the movement of jade, cacao and obsidian. An unlooted Maya royal grave was uncovered in 2002, and excavations are ongoing. First settled around 1800 BC, early ceremonial buildings and monuments were executed in Olmec style between 800 and 400 BC, including the characteristic pot-bellied humans with swollen eyelids. But by the late Preclassic period, Maya-style carvings of standing rulers were beginning to replace Olmec art. Later in the Classic era

---

UNDERTOW

Most of Guatemala's Pacific coastline is affected by a strong **undertow**, which occurs when big waves break on a shore with a steep profile. Because there's nowhere for the water to escape, it retreats backwards under the next breaking wave, creating a **downward force** close to the shore. Unless you're very confident in the ocean, it's best not to mess around if the surf is big. By not getting out of your depth, you can use your feet to jump up into the oncoming waves and let their force push you toward the shore. If you do get caught in an undertow, don't panic, as the downward force only lasts a second or two and you'll soon surface. Catch a breath, duck under the next breaker, and then work your way steadily back to shore.

some of the Maya World's most exquisite jade masks were created here – they now reside in Guatemala City's Museo Nacional de Arqueología y Etnología (see p.60).

The ruins

You can only access the Olmec's urban centre, while the city's outskirts are spread over five coffee plantations. The first substantial structure you encounter is **Terraza 3**, a low, rectangular stepped temple with three stone Olmec-head statues facing a ceremonial Maya altar. Some of the finest carved stelae are in front of **Temple 12**, which is the site's largest with a 56m-wide base; Monument 67 depicts a jaguar head; Monument 68 is toad-like; Monument 9, a rare representation of an owl; and, most impressive of all, the grouping of **Altar 8** and **Monument 5**, which has a date of 126 AD and shows twin kings presiding over bound captives. Facing Temple 12 is **Temple 11**, resembling a grassy mound, which is mid- to late Classic Maya and has seven more stelae in front of it. More good carvings lie round the back of Temple 12 including Olmec-style Monument 99, which shows a baboon-like creature with a protruding jaw.

Behind Temple 12 is a small building that serves as a **museum**, containing a model of Takalik Abaj along with assorted carvings and ceramics. There are also several fairly miserable animal enclosures that contain pizotes, spider monkeys and porcupines, among other creatures.

ARRIVAL AND DEPARTURE
TAKALIK ABAJ

By bus To get to Takalik Abaj, take a local bus from Reu to El Asintal, a small village 15km to the west, from where you can either hire a pick-up or walk the 4km to the site through coffee and cacao plantations.

By car If you're driving, take the Asintal turn-off from the coastal highway.

ACCOMMODATION

Takalik Maya Lodge 2km north of ruins ☎ 4055 9831, ⓦ takalik.com. This fine eco-resort is one of the best hotels along the Pacific slope, with stylish and attractive accommodation in two separate buildings. Horseriding, birdwatching and boat trips through coastal mangroves can be organized. There's a pool set in lovely grounds. It's managed with the local community as a kind of "fair trade" partnership; check the website for special packages. **US$76**

North of Retalhuleu

The **El Zarco** junction above Reu marks the start of one of the country's most scenic roads, which heads up into the highlands passing two impressive **leisure parks** and the abandoned village of El Palmar Viejo. It then skirts the plunging lower slopes of the Santa María and Zunil **volcanoes** before emerging in the valley of Quetzaltenango.

El Nuevo Alianza

15km north of Zarco junction • Tours US$13 • ☎ 4532 3063, ⓦ comunidadnuevaalianza.org

Reached by a minor (dirt) road north of El Zarco, **Nuevo Alianza** is an organic, fair-trade coffee and macadamia farm run as a cooperative. You can tour the finca's handsome colonial-style mansion and its extensive grounds that lead to a waterfall and learn about coffee cultivation and processing (as well as their micro-hydro-electricity and biodiesel production). Dorm beds (US$8/head), private rooms (US$11/head) and meals (US$2.50–6) are available, and volunteers are welcome. Many Spanish schools and tour operators in Quetzaltenango run trips here.

Parque Acuático Xocomil

6km north of Zarco junction • Mid-Jan till Oct Thurs–Sun 9am–5pm; Nov till mid-Jan Wed–Sun 9am–5pm • US$13, children US$7.50 • ⓦ irtra.org.gt • Buses between Retalhuleu and Quetzaltenango pass the water-park every 30min

On the main road to Quetzaltenango, **Parque Acuático Xocomil** is a superb theme park landscaped into the foothills of the highlands. It's a vast complex containing 1.2km of water slides, wave pools and artificial rivers amidst grounds replete with Maya temples and copious greenery.

ACCOMMODATION	PARQUE ACUÁTICO XOCOMIL
Irtra hotels ☎ 7722 9100, ⓦ irtra.org.gt. Seven excellent, family-friendly hotels – including colonial- and ranch-style places – in the grounds of the theme park. These are very	pricey for foreigners, with many rooms costing well over US$100 on weekends, but the superb facilities (including pools and sports) will help ease your wallet's pain. <u>US$48</u>

Parque Xetulul

6km north of Zarco junction • Mid-Jan till Oct Thurs–Sun 10am–6pm; Nov till mid-Jan Wed–Sun 10am–6pm • US$13, children aged 5–12 US$7, ride packages US$7 extra • ⓦ irtra.org.gt

Neighbouring Parque Acuático Xocomil, **Parque Xetulul** is divided into different zones, with the Plaza Chapina having re-creations of famous Guatemalan buildings, the Plaza España showcasing a galleon, and Plaza Francia boasting replicas of Parisian structures such as the Gare de France. The park has some terrific rides, including the thrilling La Avalancha rollercoaster and, like its sister complex, is clean, well run and extremely popular with Guatemalan families.

El Palmar Viejo

North of parks Xocomil and Xetulul, it's about 14km to a turn-off (on the west side of the road) that leads to the absorbing remains of the village of **El Palmar Viejo**. After torrential rains in 1998, mud-flows swept through the centre of this farming community, cutting the church in two and leaving its western facade hanging over a ravine. Villagers were evacuated to the other side of the highway – leaving an overgrown ghost town that represents a haunting reminder of the destructive powers of Hurricane Mitch, which killed thousands.

ARRIVAL AND DEPARTURE	EL PALMAR VIEJO
By bus Buses heading between Retalhuleu and Quetzaltenango will stop at the El Palmar Viejo turn-off, from	where you can walk or wait for a pick-up to cover the 3.5km route. There are also tours from Quetzaltenango (see p.146).

Champerico

South from Retalhuleu, a good paved road heads to the run-down beach resort of **CHAMPERICO**. Founded in 1872, it was originally connected to Quetzaltenango by rail and enjoyed a brief period of prosperity based on the export of coffee. In 1934 Aldous Huxley passed through but was distinctly unimpressed, pleased to escape "the unspeakable boredom of life at Champerico". Little has improved here except that the rusty old pier has been fixed up a little. Champerico spends most of its time waiting for the weekend, when hordes of weary city-dwellers descend on the coast to gorge on greasy fried fish and cratefuls of cold Gallo. Although the sheer scale of the dark-sand **beach** is impressive, it's essential to watch out for the dangerous **undertow**, even when lifeguards are present. Stick to the main part of the beach; there have been muggings reported in isolated spots.

ARRIVAL AND DEPARTURE	CHAMPERICO
By bus Buses run between Champerico and Retalhuleu very regularly; the last bus leaves Champerico around 8pm.	**Destinations** Quetzaltenango (every 30min; 2hr 15min); Retalhuleu (every 15min; 1hr 20min).

El Tulate

Beyond Retalhuleu the highway runs east through **Cuyotenango**, a featureless town blighted by the thunder of the highway. Another branch road turns off from here to the isolated, palm-lined black-sand beach **EL TULATE**. Here the village and the ocean are separated by a narrow expanse of mangrove swamp; boats ferry passengers across for US$0.75. As it's a small place, you're virtually guaranteed a quiet place to chill once you're away from the strip of shore-side seafood comedores. The beach has a gentle shelving profile, so it's much better for paddling and swimming than most places along the Pacific coast.

ARRIVAL AND DEPARTURE   EL TULATE

By bus Buses (every 30min; 1hr 45min) struggle down here every hour or so from both Retalhuleu and Mazatenango.

ACCOMMODATION AND EATING

The row of beach shacks churning out fresh fried fish shrimp (all US$5–7 a meal) are the best place to eat in town.

Playa Paraíso 1km east of the centre ☎ 5985 0300. Ageing but reasonable beachside place offering comfortable-enough bungalows with verandas. There are two pools and a restaurant. US$48

3

Santa Lucía Cotzumalguapa and around

East along the speedy Carretera al Pacífico past Mazatenango you'll soon approach **SANTA LUCÍA COTZUMALGUAPA**, an uninspiring Pacific town a short distance north of the highway. The only reason to visit the area is to take in some (minor) nearby Pipil and Maya **archeological** sites, scattered in the surrounding cane fields, and the colossal Olmec carved figures at nearby **La Democracia** or the **surf at Sipacate** to the south. Getting to them is not easy unless you rent a taxi however.

Sites near Santa Lucía Cotzumalguapa

It's best not to tour of the **sites** around Santa Lucía Cotzumalguapa on foot as it's easy to get lost and there have been muggings. A round-trip by taxi – you'll find plenty in the plaza in varying degrees of decrepitude – should cost around US$18 to them all.

Bilbao
Uphill from the plaza, along 4 Av

In 1880 more than thirty Late Classic stone monuments were removed from the Pipil site of **Bilbao**, and nine of the very best were shipped to Germany. Four sets of stones are still visible in situ, however, and two of them perfectly illustrate the magnificent precision of the carving, beautifully preserved in slabs of black volcanic rock. Two large stones are carved with bird-like patterns, with strange circular glyphs arranged in groups of three, most of which are recognizable as the names for days once used by the people of southern Mexico. In the same cane field, further along the same path, is another badly eroded stone, and a final set with a superbly preserved set of figures and interwoven motifs.

El Baúl
5km northeast of Santa Lucía • Free

This hilltop site has two **stone monuments**, one a standing figure wearing a skirt and a spectacular headdress, the other a massive half-buried stone head (known as Dios Mundo) with a wrinkled brow and patterned headdress – this is possibly Huhuetéotl, the fire god of the Mexicans. In front of the stones is a set of small altars on which local people make animal sacrifices, burn incense and leave offerings of flowers.

Finca El Baul
7km north of Santa Lucía • Mon–Fri 8am–4pm, Sat 8am–noon • Free

The next stones of interest are in the grounds of **Finca El Baul** a few kilometres further away from town where they're kept under a shelter. The carvings include some superb heads, a stone skull, a massive jaguar and an extremely well-preserved stela of a ball-court player (Monument 27) dating from the Late Classic period. Alongside all this antiquity is the finca's old steam engine, a miniature machine that used to haul sugar cane.

Finca Las Ilusiones
1.5km east of centre Mon–Fri 8am–4pm, Sat 8am–noon • US$1.40

The final site is at **Finca Las Ilusiones**, where another collection of artefacts and some stone carvings has been assembled in the **Museo Cultura Cotzumalguapa**. Two of the most striking figures are an Olmec-style pot-bellied statue (Monument 58), probably from the middle Preclassic era, and a copy of Monument 21, which bears three figures, the central one depicting a ball player. There are several other carved pieces, including a fantastic stela, plus some more replicas and thousands of small stone carvings and pottery fragments. The museum is located 1km east along the highway and 400m up a signposted side road on the left.

ARRIVAL AND DEPARTURE	SANTA LUCÍA COTZUMALGUAPA
By bus Pullmans now use a new bypass that avoids the centre of town. Most second-class buses running along the highway will drop you at the entrance road to Santa Lucía.	From Centra Sur terminal in Guatemala City, second-class buses (every 30min; 1hr 45min) run to Santa Lucia's terminal, which is a few blocks from the plaza.

ACCOMMODATION	
Hotel Internacional Just south of the Carretera al Pacífico ☎ 7882 5504. This is the nearest half-decent	place to the town centre, with clean, large rooms with either fan or a/c. US$18

La Democracia

Just east of Santa Lucía Cotzumalguapa is the run-down settlement of Siquinalá, from where a there's a road south to the coastal resort of Sipacate. Taking this branch road you'll soon arrive in **LA DEMOCRACIA**, an orderly little town that's of particular interest as the home of a collection of archeological relics. To the east of town lies the archeological site of **Monte Alto**; many of the best pieces found there are now spread around La Democracia's renovated plaza, under a vast ceiba tree. These "fat boys" are massive Olmec-style **stone heads** with simple, almost childlike faces, grinning with bizarre, Buddha-like contentment. Some are attached to smaller rounded bodies and rolled over on their backs, clutching their swollen stomachs. They probably date from the mid-Preclassic period, around 500 BC.

On the plaza, the town **museum**, Museum Regional de Arqueología (Tues–Sun 8am–4pm; US$4), houses carvings, ceremonial yokes worn by ball-game players, pottery, grinding stones, a wonderful jade mask and a few more carved heads.

ARRIVAL AND DEPARTURE	LA DEMOCRACIA
By bus Regular buses to La Democracia (every 30min; 15min) leave Siquinalá on the highway.	

Sipacate and Paredón

The low-key village of **SIPACATE** is located inside the Parque Natural Sipacate-Naranjo, a mangrove coastal reserve. The black sand beach here is separated from the village by the black waters of the **Canal de Chiquimulilla**; boats ferry a steady stream of passengers to the waves. The best surf here is about 5km to the east on the empty sands of neighbouring **Paredón beach**, where a great new hotel has kick-started a Guatemalan surf scene. Waves average two metres and are most consistent between December and April, though conditions are usually tough for beginners. There are surf reports posted on the *Paredón Surf House* website (see p.186).

3

ARRIVAL AND DEPARTURE

By bus Regular buses to Sipacate (8 daily; 2hr) leave Siquinalá on the highway. There are also two daily buses from the Centra Sur terminal in Guatemala City to Sipacate (4hr). Once you're in Sipacate village you need to catch a public boat to reach the beach. (It's a little complicated to reach Paredón from Sipacate, but the *Paredón Surf House* website has clear instructions.)

By shuttle bus From Antigua direct shuttles operated

SIPACATE AND PAREDÓN

by *Paredón Surf House* head to El Paredón (2hr; US$15); these tend to run on weekends only. Contact them to book your place.

By car If you've got your own wheels, you can reach Paredón via Puerto San José (see opposite). Take the coast road past Juan Gaviota and El Carrizal; the last section is a dirt track.

ACCOMMODATION AND EATING

El Paredón Surf Camp Beachside in Paredón ☎ 4593 2490, ⊚ surf-guatemala.com. This simple set-up has dorms (with mosquito nets and lockers) and basic accommodation. Food is prepared by a local family and boards and kayaks can be rented; surf lessons are US$15/hr. You must contact them first so they can prepare for your arrival, and transport can be organized from Antigua. Dorms US$6.50, rooms US$20, apartment US$40

★ **Paredón Surf House** Beachside in Paredón ☎ 4994 1842, ⊚ paredonsurf.com. Really putting the Guatemalan surf scene on the map, this fine new place has beautifully designed thatched bungalows with Bali-style outdoor bathrooms and a great loft dorm with quality mattresses. There's a small oceanside pool, tasty grub

(lunch around US$5, dinner is US$8–10), a full bar and lots of smiles from the Guatemalan staff and gringo owners. Surf lessons are US$15/hr and there are boards for rent. Horseriding and canoe tours of the mangroves are offered (US$10/hr) and there's beach volleyball (and occasional yoga classes). Get in touch and transport can be organized from Antigua. Cash only. Dorms US$10, bungalows US$50–67

Rancho Carillo Beachside in Sipacate ☎ 5517 1069, ⊚ marmaya.com. A comfortable place geared towards the local weekending family market. Decent if pricey a/c rooms and cabañas, four small pools and a restaurant; they also run fishing trips and offer surfing lessons on weekends. Rooms US$65, bungalow US$105

Escuintla and around

Southeast of the capital, bustling **ESCUINTLA** ranks as Guatemala's third largest city with a population of around 130,000. Despite its size there's nothing to see here, but you do get a good sense of life on the coast – its heat, pace and energy, as well as the frenetic industrial and agricultural commerce that drives it. The city dominates this stretch of Pacific coast, along with **Puerto San José**, formerly its most important port – though neither place is at all attractive. In the city centre, below the plaza a huge, chaotic **market** sprawls across several blocks, spilling out into 4 Avenida, the main commercial thoroughfare.

ARRIVAL AND DEPARTURE

By bus Buses to Escuintla leave Centra Sur terminal in Guatemala City until about 8pm. There are two terminals in Escuintla: for places en route to the Mexican border, buses run through the north of town and stop by the Esso station opposite the Banco Uno; buses east towards El Salvador

ESCUINTLA

leave from the main terminal on the south side of town, at the bottom of 4 Av.

Destinations Antigua (every 40min; 1hr); Guatemala City (every 20min; 1hr 15min); Puerto San José (every 20min; 1hr).

ACCOMMODATION AND EATING

For a casual atmosphere and fresh seafood, head to the row of *cevicherias* on 1 C near the Plaza Palmeras mall.

A Blanqui 1 C 3–55, Zona 2. A large, efficient place that specializes in fresh seafood, *ceviche* and fried fish – a mixed plate is US$10 and contains conch, shrimp, fish, sea snails and squid. Mariachis prowl the tables, and there's a great atmosphere at lunchtime and during the early afternoon.

Daily 9am–7pm.

Hotel Costa Sur 12 C 4–13 ☎ 7888 1819. It's nothing fancy, but this fair-value hotel has rooms with a/c and secure parking. US$16

Puerto San José

South from Escuintla the coast road heads through acres of cattle pasture to **PUERTO SAN JOSÉ**, the capital's nearest and most popular, if run-down, resort. Everything is geared to extracting as many quetzales as possible from the rowdy day-trippers who fill the beach at weekends. The **hotels** are poor value and not at all enjoyable, catering as they do to a largely drunken clientele. If you want to spend a few days on the coast, head to Monterrico instead.

ARRIVAL AND DEPARTURE   PUERTO SAN JOSÉ

By bus Buses run between San José and Guatemala City's Centra Sur terminal. For Monterrico get the first microbus to Iztapa (also known as Pueblo Viejo) and change there.

Destinations Escuintla (every 20min; 1hr); Guatemala City (every 20min; 2hr 15min); Iztapa (every 30min; 30min); Monterrico (2 daily; 1hr 30min).

Puerto Quetzal

Leaving San José and following the coast in either direction brings you to the beach resorts of Guatemala's wealthy elite, who have established their own enclaves, with holiday homes built in a pale imitation of Miami. Just east of San José, there's a container port and a **marina** at **PUERTO QUETZAL** with good facilities for yachts. It's also one of the main bases for sport-fishing excursions (see p.37) in Guatemala, though there are no hotels, just a restaurant and dozens of berths.

Iztapa and around

East of Puerto San José, it's 13km to **IZTAPA**, a venerable little place that's an important base for **sport-fishing**. Iztapa is Guatemala's oldest port – Spanish leader Pedro de Alvarado built boats here that took him to Peru and back. There's little sense of this historical past in Iztapa today but the sleepy little town does have a vague, faded charm and a nice setting on the bank of the Canal de Chiquimulilla. The sweeping black-sand beach is on the eastern side at a separate village called **Pueblo Viejo** – a bridge (US$2/car) spans the canal. There's pretty reliable **surf** here with right-handers and an occasional hollow, and no crowds, with only a couple of local surfers.

Beyond Iztapa a paved road traces the 25km coastline from Pueblo Viejo to Monterrico through a littoral landscape punctuated with **loofa** farms. Patches of this coastline are being developed but there are still vast empty stretches of clean, dark sand to enjoy if you pull down one of the side tracks.

ARRIVAL AND DEPARTURE   IZTAPA

By bus Buses run from Iztapa to both Guatemala City (6 daily; 2hr 30min) and Monterrico (every 30min; 1hr).

ACCOMMODATION

Hotels in Iztapa are either pretty basic, salt-bitten places that attract domestic tourists or luxury lodges orientated squarely at **sport-fishermen**. The latter work with sport-fishing tour companies, and include accommodation and transport as part of inclusive fishing packages; all have a/c, wi-fi and restaurants.

Buena Vista Resort ☎ 7880 4203, ⓦ buenavista sportfishing.com. Has a spacious grassy canal-side plot with a pool and good facilities though rooms are average. There's plenty of fresh seafood served. Packages (four anglers and four fishing days) start at US$2,565/ person.

Pacific Fins Resort ☎ 7881 4788, ⓦ pacificfins.com.gt. Four attractive two-bedroom villas, a couple of private

rooms and a pool in palm-tree-shaded grounds. All-inclusive packages (based on four anglers and four fishing days) start at US$3,550/person.

Sailfish Bay Lodge ☎ 2426 3909, ⓦ sailfishbay.com. Eight high-quality double rooms right on the beach, with a waveside pool and hot tub. Most guests are on fishing packages. US$125

EATING

El Capitán Facing the canal in Iztapa ☎ 7881 4403. Large *palapa*-roofed restaurant famous for its seafood, including good *ceviche* and fried shrimp. Daily 7am–9.30pm.

Monterrico and around

The setting of **MONTERRICO** is one of the finest on the Pacific coast, with the scenery reduced to its basic elements: a strip of dead-straight sand, a line of powerful surf, a huge empty ocean and an enormous curving horizon. The village is a bit scruffy but steadily being smartened up. It's a friendly and relaxed place fringed by the waters of the Canal de Chiquimulilla, which weaves through a fantastic network of **mangrove swamps**. The atmosphere changes a little on weekends when party-geared visitors from the capital fill up the hotels.

Monterrico sits at the heart of the **Biotopo Monterrico–Hawaii**, a nature reserve that embraces a 20km-long beach-blessed slice of the Pacific coast and includes a vital turtle-nesting ground, abundant wetlands and the small villages of Monterrico and Hawaii. Sadly, however, the reserve's officially protected status does not prevent the widespread poaching of turtle eggs.

The beach

Monterrico's impressive **beach**, a prime turtle-nesting ground (see box opposite), is a wide strip of dark grey sand that's continuously pummelled by the Pacific – with a power that sounds like rolling thunder. The beach's steep profile means there's usually a strong **undertow**. Lifeguards are posted here on weekends, but swimmers regularly get into trouble and drownings occur, so take great care. Squadrons of pelicans – flying in formation and nicknamed the "Monterrico air force" by locals – skim over the ocean, angling their wings to clip the crest of the wave as they glide along the coastline.

Turtle hatchery

Beachside, west of centre • Visitor centre daily 8am–noon & 2–5pm • US$5

Be sure to drop by the headquarters of CECON, which also runs the renowned local **turtle hatchery**. The visitor centre here occupies a large beachside area with a shaded section of sand where **turtle eggs** are reburied after they have been laid. A short trail runs from the headquarters along the edge of the reserve, past enclosures of freshwater

---

EGG COLLECTORS

Watching a turtle lay her eggs at Monterrico should be a memorable experience, but the presence of the local **hueveros** (egg collectors) may ensure that it's not. In season, Baule beach is patrolled by sentries scanning the waves for turtles. After a turtle comes ashore and lays its eggs, these poachers delve straight into the nest. Most foreign witnesses are content to take a photo before the turtle claws its way back to the ocean (note that you shouldn't use flash photography as it can upset and disorient the turtles). Braver souls who have challenged the *hueveros* have been threatened with machetes.

Officially the taking of eggs is outlawed, but an informal deal has been struck so that out of every clutch of eggs collected, a dozen are donated to the reserve's turtle hatchery, from where thousands of baby turtles are released each year. This agreement is designed to ease relations between the local community, who sell the eggs for US$2.50 a dozen, and the conservationists. The ethics may be debatable, but some visitors buy entire clutches from *hueveros* (most of whom are extremely poor) and donate these eggs to the CECON hatchery.

THE TURTLES OF MONTERRICO

The huge, sparsely populated expanses of beach around Monterrico are prime nesting sites for three types of **sea turtle**, including the largest of them all, the giant leatherback. The **reserve** was originally established to protect the turtles from the soup pot and curb the collection of their **eggs**, which are considered an aphrodisiac in Guatemala. Further dangers to the turtles include being hunted for their shells, drowned inside fishing nets and poisoned by pollution, especially plastic bags that resemble jellyfish, a favourite food. Turtles almost always **nest** in the dark, and on a moonless night during egg-laying season, you have a good chance of seeing one in Monterrico.

LEATHERBACK

The gargantuan **leatherback** is by far the largest of the world's turtles, growing up to 3m in length and weighing up to 900kg. Called *baule* in Spanish, the leatherback gives the beach at Monterrico its name. They feed almost exclusively on jellyfish, diving as deep as 1200m below the surface in search of its prey. It's the only turtle not to have a hard exterior shell; instead it has a layer of black, soft, rubbery skin. The leatherback frequents tropical and temperate waters from Malaysia to Scotland and makes one of the longest **migrations** of any creature on earth – one turtle was tracked journeying 20,000km from Indonesia to the US. The species, which has been around for one hundred million years, is in severe danger of **extinction** as a result of long-line fishing and gill netting. It nests at Monterrico between mid-October and late December. Nestings have plummeted in the Monterrico region in recent years, with only a handful recorded now each season.

OLIVE RIDLEY

Spread throughout the tropical waters of the Pacific, Atlantic and Indian oceans, the **Olive Ridley** is the most numerous of the world's eight species of marine turtle and also one of the smallest, typically around 80cm long and weighing around 35kg. Olive Ridleys gather in huge numbers off favoured beaches to mate, after which the females return en masse to nest. They are **omnivores**, feeding on fish and shrimp as well as sea grass and algae. They are common visitors at Monterrico (where they are known as *parlamas*) during their nesting season between July and December.

GREEN TURTLE

Green turtles reach more than a metre in length, typically weigh 200kg and have a characteristic dark heart-shaped shell. They are found throughout the tropics and are mainly herbivores, eating sea grasses. Historically, green turtles have been killed for their fat in many parts of the world. It's this fat, which is green in colour – their shells are usually muddy brown or grey – that gives the turtle its name. The green turtle nesting season in Monterrico is also from July to December.

NESTING

All the species of turtle use similar **nesting techniques**, hauling themselves up the beach, laboriously digging a hole about 50cm deep with their flippers, and then with great effort depositing a clutch of a hundred or so soft, golfball-sized eggs. The turtles then bury the eggs and head back into the ocean. The eggs of the two smaller turtles take about fifty days to hatch, those of the leatherback require 72. When their time comes, the tiny turtles, no larger than the palm of your hand, use their flippers to dig their way out and make a mad dash for the water, desperately trying to avoid the waiting seabirds. Once they are in the water, their existence is still very hazardous for the first few years of life; only one in a hundred makes it to maturity.

turtles, alligators and green iguanas, which are also bred for release into the wild. There are information boards, some in English.

During nesting season, visitors can donate to the project by backing a turtle hatchling in the Saturday "**turtle race**" on the beach. However, most experts are now uneasy about encouraging such races (as well as close contact or "petting" of turtles), as they involve grouping baby hatchlings together in buckets for days, a practice that exhausts and disorients the turtles and could interfere with the natal homing instinct by which they return to their beach of birth.

Mangrove swamp

Behind the beach and village, the extensive **mangrove swamp** is an unusually rich environment. These dark, nutrient-rich waters are superbly fertile, and four distinct types of mangrove form a dense mat of branches, interspersed with narrow canals, open lagoons, bull rushes and water lilies. The tangle of roots acts as a kind of **marine nursery**, offering small fish protection from their natural predators, while above the surface the dense vegetation and ready food supply provide an ideal home for hundreds of species of bird and a handful of reptiles and mammals, including racoon, iguana, alligator and opossum.

You should see a good range of **bird life**, including kingfisher, white heron and several species of duck. The Palmilla lagoon is a particularly good spot. Note if you **tour** the mangrove in a motorized boat you won't see much because the engine noise tends to frighten wildlife.

ARRIVAL AND INFORMATION

MONTERRICO

By shuttle Shuttle buses link Monterrico with Antigua daily (2hr 15min; US$10). Tickets can be bought at most hotels in Monterrico or from travel agents in Antigua.

By bus/minibus By public transport, there are two routes to Monterrico. The quickest way is via Puerto San José and Iztapa (but usually involves a bus change or two on the way). From Guatemala City's Centra Sur terminal buses leave for

Monterrico (2 daily; 3hr 15min), Iztapa (6 daily) and Puerto San José (every 20min). There are very regular microbus links between Puerto San José and Iztapa (every 30min; 30min) and Iztapa and Monterrico (every 30min; 1hr) until 6pm. The other route is complicated and longer, perhaps taking four hours or so. Start by jumping aboard a bus bound for the El Salvador border at Ciudad Pedro de Alvarado (leaving every

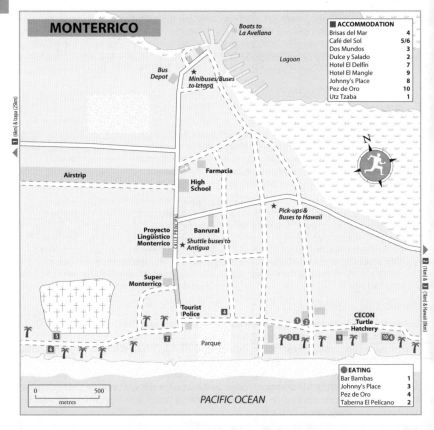

MONTERRICO

■ ACCOMMODATION

Brisas del Mar	4
Café del Sol	5/6
Dos Mundos	3
Dulce y Salado	2
Hotel El Delfín	7
Hotel El Mangle	9
Johnny's Place	8
Pez de Oro	10
Utz Tzaba	1

Boats to La Avellana

Lagoon

Bus Depot

Minibuses/Buses to Iztapa

① (6km) & Iztapa (25km)

Airstrip

Farmacia

High School

Pick-ups & Buses to Hawaii

Proyecto Lingüístico Monterrico

Banrural

Shuttle buses to Antigua

CALLE PRINCIPAL

Super Monterrico

Tourist Police

Parque

CECON Turtle Hatchery

PACIFIC OCEAN

② (1km) & ③ (1km) & Hawaii (8km)

0 500 metres

● EATING

Bar Bambas	1
Johnny's Place	3
Pez de Oro	4
Taberna El Pelícano	2

30min from Centra Sur), jump off at Taxisco, from where buses trundle down to La Avellana and then get a boat to Monterrico.
By boat Boats (8 daily; 40min) shuttle passengers (US$0.75) and cars (US$10) from Monterrico to La Avellana.
Information Check out the community website, ⓦmonterrico-guatemala.com, for hotel and transport information.

Tours Local guides (look for them by the Turtle Hatchery, they have ID badges) can arrange tours of the mangrove. Otherwise hotels can recommend a local boatman, or you could even rent a small *cayuco* (US$1.30/hr) and paddle around yourself from the ferry dock.

ACCOMMODATION

All Monterrico's accommodation is right on or just off the **beach**. Many places increase prices by 20–30 percent at weekends, when it's also best to book ahead. Avoid the *Hotel Baule Beach* as regular thefts have been reported.

Brisas del Mar Turn left just before beach; it's on the left ☎5517 1142. It looks a little soulless and motel-like but these 26 bungalows (with fan or a/c) are in decent condition, have private bathrooms, mosquito nets, good beds and are keenly priced. All face a garden with two pools and there's a restaurant. Fan US$10, a/c US$16
Café del Sol Turn right at the beach, 250m to the west ☎5050 9173, ⓦcafe-del-sol.com. Perhaps the best reason to stay here is the lovely beach-facing frontage, with sunbeds facing the ocean. It's a well-run place with accommodation divided between inland and beachside blocks (avoid rooms in the bar-restaurant which lack privacy). The food is tasty, though quite pricey, and there's a small pool. US$42
Dos Mundos 1.5km east of centre ☎7823 0820, ⓦhotelsdosmundos.com/monterrico. Luxurious place, with stunning minimalist-style, *palapa*-roofed, detached a/c bungalows, each with a huge terrace and swanky bathroom, set in beachfront gardens. There's a fine pool overlooking the rollers, a kids' pool and a good, if pricey, restaurant. Rates include breakfast. US$92
Dulce y Salado 2km east of village centre ☎5579 8477, ⓦdulceysaladoguatemala.com. A beachside location and nice, thatched bungalows that come with good wooden beds, mosquito nets and private bathrooms. There's also a decent-sized pool, plus good Italian and Latin American food. US$48
Hotel El Delfín On the right at beachfront ☎5702 6701, ⓦhotel-el-delfin.com. This once-grim rambling place is being steadily renovated by an enthusiastic, welcoming American-Guatemalan couple. There's a way to go (many rooms remain cell-like) but all have fans and mosquito nets. You'll find a good backpacker vibe, pool, bar and cheap food. US$10

Hotel El Mangle Turn left at beach and walk for 300m ☎5514 6517. This is a relaxed lodge with charming (if small) fan-cooled *casitas*, all with mosquito nets, bathrooms and little front porches with hammocks. There are also various a/c rooms, some with fine sea views, scattered around the property (via dodgy staircases). The central garden area has two small pools. All are a little overpriced; try bargaining. US$28
Johnny's Place Turn left at beach and walk for 150m ☎5812 0409, ⓦjohnnysplacehotel.com. For years this place has been a backpacker centre, and the prime beachside location and chillout zone (a *palapa* with hammocks) are enticing. Offers a well-designed new beachside block (with simple rooms and beach-facing suites), rough'n'ready ancient bungalows, plus some a/c rooms and a family-sized apartment. The party vibe has been turned down a notch but the bar here still rocks on weekends. Dorms US$7.50, rooms US$30, suites US$60
★ **Pez de Oro** Turn left at beach and walk for 350m ☎7920 9785 or ☎2368 3684, ⓦpezdeoro.com. A very well run and attractive place to stay, with lovely, spotless, thatched cottages, all with mosquito nets, wooden furniture, and bedcovers made from Guatemalan textiles (nos. 1 and 13 have sea views). There are two palm-shaded pool areas and the beach-facing restaurant serves fine Italian and international food. US$55
Utz Tzaba About 6km before Monterrico in the pueblo of El Pumpo ☎5318 9452, ⓦutz-tzaba.com. A smart Dutch-owned place with immaculate rooms and bungalows (each with living room and two bedrooms, some with kitchens) on a spacious seafront plot where the lawns are kept well clipped; there's a large pool, hot tub and a bar area. Beware the cheesy music around the pool on weekends though. US$84

EATING AND DRINKING

Eating in Monterrico basically comes down to either dining in one of the village **comedores** on C Principal, which all have near-identical menus (large portions of fried fish and shrimp cost about US$8) or on the beach itself, where the cuisine is more international.

Bar Bambas Behind Johnny's Place. This likeable *palapa*-roofed bar is a good bet for a cold beer and a game of pool. There's a bass-heavy sound system. Mon–Thurs 5–11pm, Fri–Sun 11am–1am.

Johnny's Place Turn left at beach and walk for 150m. This waveside café is renowned for its *ceviche* (US$10 a pound), which is available in three different styles, and also offers sandwiches and the like. Doubles as a bar and there's some DJ and dance action most Saturdays. Daily 7am–10pm.

Pez de Oro Left at beach and walk for 350m ☎ 7920 9785. Has a nice beachfront dining area with checked tablecloths and Italian food like fish cooked in white wine (US$12), salads, pasta and sandwiches (US$5). Daily 7am–9.30pm.

★ **Taberna El Pelícano** Behind Johnny's Place

☎ 4001 5885. The creative Swiss chef here serves up fine European food, including fresh pasta (US$6), seafood and grilled fish (around US$10). The attractive thatched premises have atmosphere (including wonderful wooden dining tables) and make up for the lack of sea views. Wed–Sat noon–2pm & 5–9pm, Sun noon–3pm & 6–9pm.

DIRECTORY

Banks and exchange There are two banks; Banrural has an ATM. The Super Monterrico store on C Principal also has an ATM.
Internet There are a couple of places on C Principal.
Language lessons Proyecto Lingüístico Monterrico

(☎ 5475 1265, ⊕ monterrico-guatemala.com), on the main drag, offers inexpensive one-on-one Spanish instruction (20hr for US$100).
Police The tourist police (☎ 2269 0041) have an office on C Principal.

Hawaii

About 7km east along the beach from Monterrico, isolated **HAWAII** is a tiny, relaxed little fishing village. Other than the turtle sanctuary, the magnificent empty beach is the only sight in town.

Turtle Centre

Beachside, entrance to village • Daily 9am–6pm • Donation expected • ☎ 5849 8988, ⊕ arcasguatemala.com

This large **turtle project**, run by the environmental group ARCAS, releases around thirty thousand turtles each year. There's plenty for the visitor to see, with a couple of trails, egg-count charts and lots of information about turtles and the myths and beliefs associated with them throughout the world. **Volunteers** are always needed (at any time of year, though June to November is the main nesting season). The work is primarily nocturnal, with volunteers walking the beach collecting sea-turtle eggs and assisting in the management of the hatcheries. You can also assist in environmental education, mangrove reforestation, construction and caiman and iguana captive-breeding. Dorm accommodation costs US$60 a week (meals not included).

ARRIVAL AND INFORMATION   HAWAII

By bus Buses (every 1hr 30min; 30min) connect Hawaii with Monterrico.

Information Check out ⊕ hawaiiguatemala.com for more information.

FIESTAS IN THE PACIFIC COAST

Ladino culture dominates on the Pacific coast so fiestas here tend to be more along the lines of fairs, with parades, amusement rides, fireworks, sporting events and heavy drinking.

JANUARY
12–15 Taxisco, events include bullfighting
12–16 Colomba, events include bullfighting

MARCH
11–19 Coatepeque, main day 15th
16–22 Puerto San José, main day 19th
Varies Ocós

APRIL
30–May 4 Chiquimulilla, main day 3rd

JULY
25 Coatepeque, in honour of Santiago Apóstol

AUGUST
4–8 Champerico, main day 6th

OCTOBER
20–26 Iztapa, main day 24th

NOVEMBER
23–26 Siquinalá

DECEMBER
6–12 Retalhuleu, main day 8th
6–15 Escuintla, main day 8th

ACCOMMODATION

Hotel Honolulu Beachside in village ☎ 4005 0500, ⓦ hotelhonolulu.com.gt. This new place offers well-constructed, detached, screened wooden bungalows in neat beachside gardens plus a small pool and restaurant. A little overpriced, but very peaceful (during the week). US$80

From Escuintla to El Salvador

Heading east from Escuintla you skirt a Guatemalan safari park and then the coastal highway passes **TAXISCO**, from where you can access La Avellana, which has boats to Monterrico. Beyond here, lonely side roads lead to isolated beaches, including Las Lisas.

Auto Safari Chapín

Tues–Sun 9.30am–5pm • US$8 • ⓦ autosafarichapin.org

One of Guatemala's most unusual tourist sights, the **Auto Safari Chapín** is Central America's only safari-style park. Here you'll find giraffes, hippos, a pair of black rhinos, tapir and big cats including African lions, pumas and jaguar. There's a superbly comprehensive collection of Central American animals, snakes and birds. The park is clean and well organized with viewing platforms and wildlife trails, and the animals are well cared for. Every species, except for the black rhino, has been successfully bred here in captivity. The entrance fee entitles you to a trip through the park in a minibus, although you can drive yourself if you have a car, and there are swimming pools, a restaurant and picnic areas.

Las Lisas

A short distance before the border with El Salvador a side road runs off to the seashore village of **LAS LISAS**, another good spot for spending time by the sea.

ARRIVAL AND DEPARTURE LAS LISAS

By bus Hourly buses run between Las Lisas and turn-off on the Carretera al Pacífico (7am–5pm; 30min).

ACCOMMODATION

Isleta de Gaia ☎ 7885 0044, ⓦ isleta-de-gaia.com. Located on a sandy offshore islet, this hotel has twelve bamboo-and-thatch bungalows with either ocean or lagoon views (though they're quite pricey for what you get). There's a big pool, food prepared by a French chef and a lovely clean beach – though again watch out for the undertow. You'll have to hire a boat (around US$15) to get to the hotel from the village of Las Lisas. US$92

Ciudad Pedro de Alvarado

The coastal highway finally reaches the border with El Salvador at the small settlement of **CIUDAD PEDRO DE ALVARADO**. Most of the commercial traffic and all of the pullman buses use the highland route to El Salvador, and consequently things are fairly quiet and easy-going here.

ARRIVAL AND DEPARTURE CIUDAD PEDRO DE ALVARADO

By bus Second-class buses run to and from Guatemala City every 30min or so until about 7pm, though minibuses run later to Chiquimulilla.

Crossing the El Salvadorean Border The border at Ciudad Pedro de Alvarado is open 24 hours. The few places to stay on the Guatemalan side are run-down.

The Oriente and Izabal

PILGRIMS AT ESQUIPULAS

The Oriente and Izabal

The region east of Guatemala City is the most disparate part of the country – a mix of near-desert, rainforest, mountains and lakes peopled by ladinos, creoles and isolated pockets of Maya. Close to the capital is a seldom-visited region of dry, sun-scorched hills known as the Oriente, centred on the towns of Chiquimula and Esquipulas. The eastern section of Guatemala, the department of Izabal, could not be more different. Here the climate is always thick with humidity and the land has a decidedly sultry, tropical feel, with rainforest reserves, a Caribbean coastline, a vast lake and a dramatic gorge system to explore.

Densely populated in Maya times, this region served as an important trade route and also was one of the main sources of **jade**. Connecting the capital with the Caribbean, the Motagua valley is a broad corridor of low-lying land between two high mountain ranges. Following the decline of Maya civilization, the area lay virtually abandoned until the end of the nineteenth century when the **United Fruit Company** established huge banana plantations and reaped massive profits. Today bananas are still the main crop, though cattle ranching is becoming increasingly important.

For the traveller, the main draw is exploring idyllic **Río Dulce** and the **Lago de Izabal** area – a vast expanse of freshwater ringed by isolated villages, rich wetlands and hot springs. The most spectacular section is undoubtedly the **Río Dulce gorge,** best experienced on a slow boat from nearby **Lívingston**, a laidback town that's home to Afro-Carib Garífuna people. You could also drop by the fascinating Maya ruins and giant stelae of **Quiriguá**, just off the main highway, the Carretera al Atlántico. South of here, the **Oriente offers** magnificent scenery in places, with the **Ipala volcano** and its crater lake a highlight. **Esquipulas**, home of the famous black Christ and the scene of Central America's largest annual pilgrimage, is another curiosity.

The Motagua valley

Leaving Guatemala City, the main highway descends through a dry and distinctly inhospitable landscape with cacti spiking the barren hillsides. The first place of any note is the **Río Hondo junction** where the road divides: one arm heads south to the Oriente and town of Esquipulas, while the main branch continues on to the coast.

On down the valley the landscape starts to undergo a radical transformation; the flood plain opens out and there's a profusion of tropical growth. It was this supremely rich flood plain that was chosen by both the Maya and the United Fruit Company, to the great benefit of both.

The ruins of Quiriguá

Sitting in an isolated pocket of rainforest, surrounded by an ocean of banana trees, the small archeological site of **Quiriguá** has some of the finest carvings in the entire Maya

RÍO DULCE

Highlights

❶ Quiriguá's carvings Miniature Maya site with colossal stelae and astonishing carved altars. **See p.199**

❷ Lívingston nightlife Party punta-style with the Garífuna in this laidback Caribbean town. **See p.207**

❸ Río Dulce Cruising through this soaring, jungle-clad gorge and exploring its magical tributaries is an exhilarating experience. **See p.208**

❹ Hot spring waterfall Soak away an afternoon or two at the exquisite hot spring-fed waterfall at the Finca el Paraíso. **See p.211**

❺ Volcán de Ipala This remote volcano's summit has a stunning crater lake. **See p.216**

❻ Esquipulas A vast basilica that's home to an ancient carving of a black Christ – the focus for the largest pilgrimage in Central America. **See p.217**

HIGHLIGHTS ARE MARKED ON THE MAP ON P.198

world. Only nearby Copán can match the magnificent stelae, altars and zoomorphs that are covered in well-preserved and superbly intricate glyphs and portraits.

The **ruins** are situated 68km beyond the junction at Río Hondo, and 4km from the main road, reached down a side road that serves the banana industry. Weather conditions are decidedly **tropical**. Indeed, cloudbursts are the rule and the buzz of mosquitoes is almost uninterrupted – bring repellent.

A brief history of Quiriguá

Quiriguás early history is still relatively unknown, but during the Late Preclassic period (250 BC–300 AD) migrants from the north established themselves as rulers here. In the Early Classic period (250–600 AD), the area was dominated by **Copán**, just 50km away, with Quiriguá no doubt valued for its position on the banks of the Río Motagua, an important trade route and as a source of jade. It was during the rule of the great leader **Cauac Sky** that Quiriguá challenged Copán, capturing its leader, Eighteen Rabbit, in 738 AD and beheading him, probably with the backing of the "superpower" city of Calakmul. Quiriguá was then able to assert its independence and embark on a building boom: most of the great stelae date from this period. For a century Quiriguá dominated

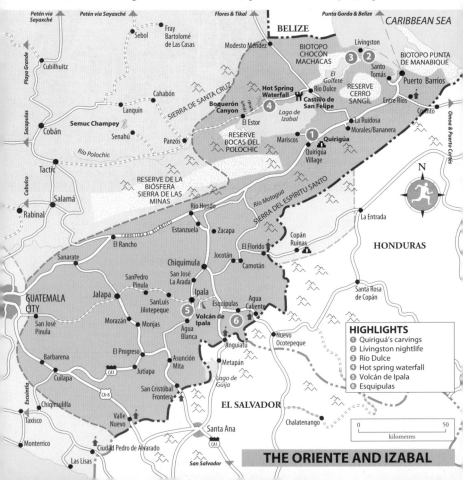

the lower Motagua valley. Under **Jade Sky**, who took the throne in 790, Quiriguá reached its peak, with fifty years of extensive building work, including a radical reconstruction of the acropolis. Towards the end of Jade Sky's rule, in the middle of the ninth century, the historical record fades out, as does the period of prosperity and power.

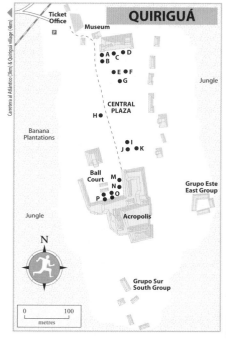

The ruins

Daily 8am–4.30pm • US$10

Entering the site you emerge at the northern end of the **Great Plaza**. On the left is a badly ruined pyramid, directly ahead are the stelae for which Quiriguá is justly famous.

Stelae

The nine **stelae** in the plaza are the tallest in the Maya world and the quality of carving is remarkable. Similar in style in many ways to that of Copán, they feature portraits on the principal faces of the standing monuments and glyphs covering the sides. As for the figures, they represent the city's rulers, with Cauac Sky depicted on no fewer than seven (A, C, D, E, F, H and J). Two unusual features are particularly clear: the vast headdresses, which dwarf the faces, and the beards. Many of the figures are shown clutching a ceremonial bar, the symbol of office. The **glyphs**, crammed into the remaining space, record dates and events during the reign of the relevant ruler.

Largest of the stelae is E, which rises to a height of 8m and weighs 65 tonnes. All the stelae are carved from a fine-grained sandstone. Fortunately for the sculptors the stone was soft once it had been cut, and fortunately for us it hardened with age.

Altars

Another feature that has helped Quiriguá earn its fame is the series of bizarre, altar-like **zoomorphs**: six blocks of stone carved with interlacing animal and human figures. Some, like the turtle, frog and jaguar, can be recognized with relative ease, while others are either too faded or too elaborate to be easily made out. The best of the lot is P, which shows a figure seated in a Buddha-like pose.

Ball court and Acropolis

At the southern end of the plaza, near the main zoomorphs, you can just make out the shape of a **ball court** hemmed in on three sides by viewing stands. The **acropolis** itself, the only structure of any real size that still stands, is bare of decoration. Trenches dug beneath it have shown that it was built on top of several previous versions, the earliest ones constructed out of rough river stones.

Museum

A small site **museum** has informative displays about the site's historical significance and its geo-political role in Maya times as well as a diorama showing the extent of the ruins that remain unexcavated.

Quiriguá village

The **village** – also known as Quiriguá – is just off the highway, about 2km back towards Guatemala City. It's a run-down sort of place, strung out along the railway track, but in the past it was famous for its hospital specializing in the treatment of tropical diseases, run by the United Fruit Company. This imposing building, which still stands on the hill above the track, is now a state-run workers' medical centre; there's a statue of Scottish doctor Neil Macphail (who ran the hospital here for forty years) in front of the structure.

ARRIVAL AND DEPARTURE   QUIRIGUÁ

By bus All buses running between Puerto Barrios and Guatemala City pass by the turn-off for the ruins. From the turn-off, minibuses, motorbikes and pick-ups shuttle passengers back and forth to the archeological site. To get back to the highway, wait until a bus or tuk-tuk turns up.

On foot to the village If you want to walk back to Quiriguá village, you can take a short cut by heading towards the highway for 2km along the access road, then turning left (west) and following the (disused) train track – it's a further 1km to the village.

ACCOMMODATION AND EATING

Hotel y Restaurante Royal In the village ☎ 7947 3639. Offers old rooms downstairs (some are windowless) and better rooms on the upper floor. Will do for a night or a meal of cheap *comida típica*. <u>US$11</u>

Posada de Quiriguá Hillside above village ☎ 5349 5817, ⓦ posadadequirigua.com. Japanese-owned guesthouse, with lovely, immaculately clean accommodation in a fertile garden setting. The four "single" rooms have a double bed and are fine for a couple, while the two doubles are much more spacious. You'll find the food a real highlight, with fine Guatemalan and Japanese meals (dinner is US$10), and good vegetarian choices too. <u>US$15</u>

To the coast: Puerto Barrios

Heading on towards the Caribbean from Quiriguá, the road traverses an evergreen landscape of cattle ranches and fruit trees, passing a junction for the ramshackle twin towns of **MORALES** and **BANANERA** (where non-express buses make a stop). A short distance beyond here you pass another junction, this one known as **La Ruidosa**, where the road splits: the highway to Petén heads north via Río Dulce Town, while if you continue east it's a further 47km to Puerto Barrios. Beyond Barrios, and only accessible by boat, is the **Punta de Manabique** peninsula, home to fine white-sand beaches and wildlife-rich wetlands.

Puerto Barrios and around

Hot and sprawling, **PUERTO BARRIOS** is a pretty forlorn place, its wide, poorly lit streets badly potholed. Barrios' once-fine legacy of old wooden Caribbean-style buildings is disappearing fast, only to be replaced by faceless concrete hotels and stores and an excess of hard-drinking bars. The only reason most travellers come here is to get somewhere else: to Lívingston or Belize by boat or south to Honduras via Corinto.

The town was founded in the 1880s by President Rufino Barrios, but its port facilities soon fell into the hands of the **United Fruit Company**, who used their control of the railways to ensure that the bulk of trade passed this way. Puerto Barrios was Guatemala's main port for most of the twentieth century, and although the UFC was exempt from almost all tax, the users of its port were obliged to pay heavy duties. In the late twentieth century a decline set in as exporters used modern docks elsewhere.

In recent years Barrios has seen something of an upturn in its fortunes as key infrastructure – including the container port – have been modernized.

The market

The main **market**, sprawling around disused railway lines at the corner of 9 Calle and 6 Avenida, is the town's main focus and the best place to start to get a feel for Barrios'

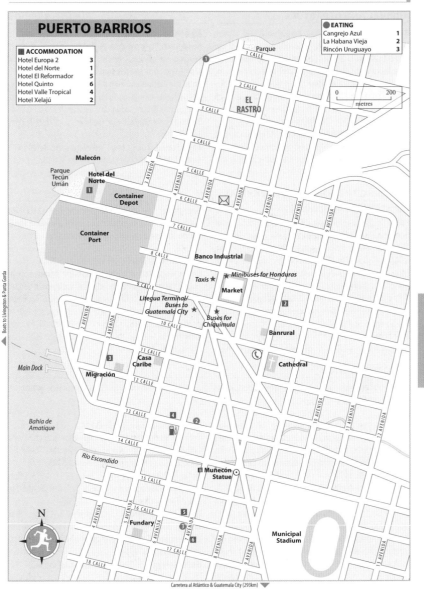

PUERTO BARRIOS

■ ACCOMMODATION

Hotel Europa 2	3
Hotel del Norte	1
Hotel El Reformador	5
Hotel Quinto	6
Hotel Valle Tropical	4
Hotel Xelajú	2

● EATING

Cangrejo Azul	1
La Habana Vieja	2
Rincón Uruguayo	3

modern identity. Lines of ladino vendors furiously whisk up lush fruit *licuado* drinks from a battery of blenders, while Garífuna women swat flies from piles of *pan de coco*.

Hotel del Norte

West along 7 Calle from the market, it's about 800m to the last surviving landmark to Barrios' Caribbean architectural heritage, the elegant **Hotel del Norte** (see p.202), its timber corridors warped by a century of storms and salty air – be sure to take a look inside at the colonial-style bar and dining room.

ARRIVAL AND DEPARTURE

By bus Puerto Barrios lacks a purpose-built bus station. Litegua buses (☎7948 1172, ⓦlitegua.com), some of the best in Guatemala, serve all destinations along the Carretera al Atlántico from a terminal in the centre of town on 6 Av, between 9 and 10 calles. Note that *directos* (some double-deckers) don't leave the highway, but non-direct buses travel via Morales, which adds at least 30min to the journey. Second-class buses to Chiquimula and microbuses to Río Dulce arrive and depart from a stop opposite Litegua's depot. Destinations Chiquimula (hourly; 4hr 30min); Guatemala City (19 daily; 5hr–5hr 30min); Río Dulce Town (every 40min; 2hr).

PUERTO BARRIOS

By boat *Lanchas* leave for Lívingston and Punta Gorda in Belize from the main dock at the end of 12 C. If you're heading to Belize, remember to clear *migración* (7am–7pm) first and pay your US$10 exit tax; the office is on 12 C, a block inland from the dock.
Destinations Lívingston (daily at 6.30am, 7.30am, 9am, 11am, 2pm & 5pm, additional services leave when full; 30min); Punta Gorda, Belize (daily at 10am, 1pm & 2pm; 1hr 15min).

Taxis (called *carreras* here) are everywhere in Barrios – drivers tout for customers as they ply the streets.

CROSSING THE BORDER TO HONDURAS

GETTING TO THE BORDER

Puerto Barrios is the jumping-off point to the north coast of Honduras, a fairly straightforward, if slow, journey. Minibuses depart from the marketplace (every 30min, 6.30am–4.30pm; 1hr; US$2) and pass through the town of Entre Ríos (for *migración*) before continuing on to the border. You may be asked for unofficial border taxes of a dollar or two as you pass through. Note that travellers with their own vehicles have reported lengthy delays and hassles entering Honduras here, including the need to pay a fee of about US$30 for a "custodian" to accompany you to the main immigration office in Puerto Cortés where vehicle

permits (typically US$40/motorbike and around US$125/car, but some have negotiated discounts) are issued. The El Florido border (see p.299) is much less hassle.

ONWARD TRAVEL IN HONDURAS

On the Honduran side, buses leave the border post at Corinto for Puerto Cortés (hourly; 2hr) via Omoa. If you set out early from Puerto Barrios, you should get to San Pedro Sula by lunchtime, from where it's certainly possible to catch an afternoon flight to one of the Bay Islands (or even make it to La Ceiba for the late afternoon boats to the Bay Islands if you're lucky).

ACCOMMODATION

Budget **hotels** are in short supply in Puerto Barrios, and as this is a very hot and humid town, you'll definitely want a fan, if not air conditioning.

Hotel Europa 2 3 Av &12 C ☎7948 1292. This motel-style place is very conveniently located for the dock and has decent (if ageing) clean rooms with two beds and TV with either fan or a/c. It's priced per person so single travellers get a good deal. US$20

★ **Hotel del Norte** 7 C & 1 Av ☎7948 0087. A landmark, highly atmospheric Caribbean hotel, built entirely from wood. Unfortunately the facilities are pretty historic too, and many of the rooms lack bathrooms, but with this much faded style and heritage on offer the comfort levels are adequate enough. There's a swimming pool, and the location, overlooking the Bahía de Amatique and *malecón*, is magnificent. Meals, served in a mahogany-panelled restaurant are disappointing however. There's also a modern block with bland a/c rooms. US$21

Hotel Quinto 7 Av &16 C ☎7948 8553. A new hotel (look out for the arresting blue-and-yellow paint job) with simple, very clean rooms with wooden furniture; bathrooms are cold water only though. US$25

Hotel El Reformador 7 Av & 16 C ☎7948 0533. Offers well-kept, modern rooms set around patios, with either fan or a/c. There's a restaurant here too. US$22

Hotel Valle Tropical 13 C, between 5 & 6 avenidas ☎7948 7084. Large motel-style block where the rooms are all equipped with a/c and private bathrooms. The real appeal is the pool. US$40

Hotel Xelajú 8 Av, between 8 & 9 calles ☎7948 1117. Yes it looks like a prison, but the manager is friendly, rooms are clean (some with bathroom) and it's very secure. US$10

EATING

Puerto Barrios really excels at **fish and seafood**, and you should certainly try some *tapado* (seafood soup with coconut, plantain and spices) while you're here, though it's not a cheap dish to prepare. **Comedores** are around the market – look out for *pan de coco* (coconut bread) and local speciality *tortillas de harina* (wheat tortillas stuffed with meat and beans).

Cangrejo Azul End of 4 Av ☎ 7948 8463. Huge, barn-like seafood restaurant with a good local reputation that also has a dining table or two set on stilts out in the bay. Try the *camarones a la plancha* or *sopa pescado*. Daily 10am–10.30pm.

La Habana Vieja 13 C, between 6 & 7 avenidas ☎ 7948 0695. The most atmospheric place in town, run by very welcoming Cuban exiles, with excellent meat dishes including *chuletas 'baby' del cerdo* (US$7). You can eat a set lunch here for US$3. There's an a/c interior and small street terrace and they also sell Cuban rum, beer and cigars. Mon–Sat 11am–11pm.

Rincón Uruguayo 7 Av & 16 C ☎ 7948 6803. Meat-eaters won't do better than this excellent place which excels at *parrilladas* (South American-style meat barbecues) and has outside seating. About US$8 a head for a serious feast. Mon–Sat 10am–10pm.

DIRECTORY

Banks Banrural at 8 Av & 9 C, and Banco Industrial at 7 Av & 7 C; both have ATMs.

Post office 6 C & 6 Av.

Punta de Manabique

North of Puerto Barrios is **Punta de Manabique**, a hooked peninsula that juts into the Bahía de Amatique and contains many of Guatemala's best beaches. Most of the area has been designated a nature reserve, which is managed by the conservation group **Fundary**. It's one of the richest wetland habitats in Central America, and the swamps, mangroves and patches of flooded rainforest are home to caimen, iguana, spider and howler monkeys, peccary, plus a few manatee, some jaguar, tapir and bountiful birdlife, including the extremely rare yellow-headed parrot (*Amazona oratrix*). The reserve also includes the adjacent coastal water and the only coral-reef outcrops in Guatemalan waters.

About one thousand people eke out a living in Manabique, surviving by subsistence fishing (mainly for sardines, which are then salted), hunting (particularly iguana) and cultivating small rice paddies, though their livelihood is increasingly under threat from cattle ranchers. Most locals are very poor, and Fundary have been busy establishing basic healthcare measures, setting up schools and providing teachers, and raising environmental awareness. They've also been working to develop **ecotourism** in the area.

INFORMATION AND TOURS   PUNTA DE MANABIQUE

Organized trips Trips to Manabique can be organized with Fundary, 17 C between 5 and 6 avenidas, Puerto Barrios (☎ 7948 0435, ⓦ www.guate.net/fundary manabique). This environmental group can arrange transport and accommodation packages (from US$130/ head for two nights including meals), and has good contacts with local guides. The other alternative is to travel to Manabique on a day-trip (around US$50, minimum of six people) from Lívingston; speak to Exotic Travel (see p.204).

ACCOMMODATION

El Saraguate Reservations through Fundary ☎ 7948 0435, ⓦ www.guate.net/fundarymanabique. A rustic lodge with four clean rooms, each with three or four beds, and a restaurant that serves tasty meals: lobster, grilled fish and chicken dishes. From the lodge there's a purpose-built wooden walkway over nearby swampland, jungle paths and coastal walks along stunning palm-fringed white-sand beaches, as well as excellent swimming. Boat trips also can be arranged along the Canal Inglés ("English Channel") – named after British loggers who dug a 10km trench between Laguna Santa Isabel and the Río Piteros – which offers superb birdwatching. Local guides can be hired at the hotel, while sport-fishing in the Bahía la Graciosa or open sea can be organized, too. Beds <u>US$9</u>

Lívingston

Enjoying a superb setting overlooking the Bahía de Amatique, **LÍVINGSTON** offers a unique fusion of Guatemalan and Caribbean culture where marimba mixes with Marley. The town acts as a hub for both the displaced **Garífuna**, or Black Caribs (see box, p.206) and also for the Q'eqchi' Maya of the Río Dulce region.

Lívingston is undoubtedly one of the most fascinating places in Guatemala, but travellers' opinions about it tend to be sharply divided: many enjoy the languid rhythm of life and Lívingston's slightly ramshackle appeal while others just find the town shabby. Whatever your take, Lívingston certainly offers a welcome break from mainstream Ladino culture: **Carib food** is generally excellent and varied, and Garífuna punta rock and reggae make a pleasant change from merengue and salsa. Another excellent reason to come to Lívingston is to take the spectacular trip through the **Río Dulce gorge** (see p.208).

The general atmosphere is pretty chilled, but not unaffected by the pressures of daily life in Central America. Whilst Lívingston is not a threatening place, and there are no particular security concerns, the town does have its share of small-time **hustlers** eager to sell weed to travellers or scrounge a beer.

Beaches

The local palm-fringed **beaches** are slim and, though not of the Caribbean-dream variety, do offer decent swimming once you're away from the centre; you'll find that the sand slopes into the sea very gradually here. On the east side of town, below some cliffs, is **Playa Capitana**, which is usually pretty quiet, though there's not much sand. **Playa Barrique**, on the northeast side of Lívingston, is the town's main beach – if you follow the coconut-studded shoreline north from here there are some nice stretches of sand.

Siete Altares waterfalls

The most popular side-trip is to the **Siete Altares**, an imposing series of waterfalls, much more impressive in the rainy season. Robberies have occurred here occasionally, and though no incidents have been reported for some time, it's best to hire a local guide or visit as part of a **tour**. Boardwalks have recently been constructed so you can access the most impressive upper section easily.

The falls are about 5km northwest of town: head along the shoreline from Playa Barrique and, just before the sands eventually peter out, take a path to the left.

ARRIVAL AND DEPARTURE   LÍVINGSTON

The only way you can get to Lívingston is **by boat**, either from Puerto Barrios, the Río Dulce or Belize. The main dock is on the south side of town.

For the Río Dulce Boats for Río Dulce Town leave daily at 9am and 2pm. Tickets (US$17/person) for the river trip up the *río* can be booked by any travel agent or hotel in Lívingston. The journey takes around 2hr 30min – all boats stop at some hot springs, Isla de los Pájaros (a bird sanctuary) and cruise past the Castillo de San Felipe – but are otherwise eager to get to Río Dulce Town quickly. To really get the most out of the stunning gorge scenery you

need to do a more leisurely cruise (see box, p.208).
For Puerto Barrios *Lanchas* leave for Puerto Barrios (5 daily; additional services leave when full; 30min; US$5).
For Belize Boats run to Punta Gorda in Belize (Tues & Fri at 7am; 1hr; US$26). Combined boat/shuttle-bus tickets are sold by Exotic Travel to Antigua, Copán (both US$41), San Pedro Sula (US$48) and La Ceiba (US$60).

INFORMATION AND TOURS

The most popular tours from Lívingston are the trip to Siete Altares, Playa Blanca and the slow cruise up the Río Dulce. If you want an educative, highly informed walking tour of the Garífuna barrio, contact Philip Flores (also known as Polo) on ☏ 4806 0643.

Exotic Travel At Bahía Azul restaurant, C Principal ☏ 5917 8780, ⊛ bluecaribbeanbay.com. The best travel agent in town. The helpful owners can arrange trips (minimum six people) around the area, including visits to the fine

white-sand beach of Playa Blanca (US$17), the Sapodilla Cayes off Belize for snorkelling (US$55, plus US$20 exit/ entry taxes) and a jungle/culture trek that takes in a Garífuna village and the Siete Altares waterfalls (US$10).

ACCOMMODATION

Lívingston has a pretty good selection of places to stay. Those right on the beach are quite a hike from town. Book ahead on holidays.

★ **Casa de la Iguana** C Marcos Sánchez Díaz ☎ 7947 0064, ⓦ casadelaiguana.com. Party hostel run on a winning formula of drinking games, hedonism and all round merriment. All accommodation – a couple of dorms and attractive private cabañas with private bathrooms – is in well-constructed wooden buildings set around a large grassy plot. There's local and western grub and excellent travel information. Dorms <u>US$5</u>, cabañas <u>US$17</u>

Flowas Beachside, about 800m north of Playa Barrique ☎ 7947 0376, ⓔ infoflowas@gmail.com. Run by a bohemian Spaniard, this beachside place has good two-storey bungalows and a restaurant with local and Spanish food. Enjoys a very relaxing setting, but it's about a 30min walk from the centre. <u>US$21</u>

★ **Hotel Casa Rosada** C Marcos Sánchez Díaz ☎ 7947 0303, ⓦ hotelcasarosada.com. Superb waterfront hotel run by a very hospitable couple from Guatemala and Belgium. The small, cheery wooden cabins are kept immaculately clean and have twin beds, nets and nice hand-painted detailing. Bathrooms are all shared but kept very clean. There's a huge, lush garden to enjoy and a private dock for sunbathing. Excellent, wholesome meals are served (see p.207); wi-fi available. <u>US$21</u>

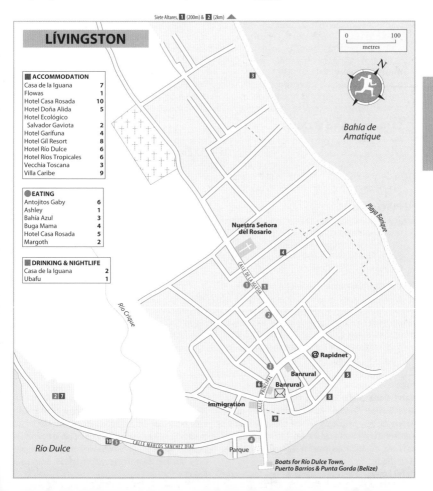

LÍVINGSTON

Siete Altares, **1** (200m) & **2** (2km)

ACCOMMODATION	
Casa de la Iguana	7
Flowas	1
Hotel Casa Rosada	10
Hotel Doña Alida	5
Hotel Ecológico Salvador Gaviota	2
Hotel Garifuna	4
Hotel Gil Resort	8
Hotel Río Dulce	6
Hotel Ríos Tropicales	6
Vecchia Toscana	3
Villa Caribe	9

EATING	
Antojitos Gaby	6
Ashley	1
Bahía Azul	3
Buga Mama	4
Hotel Casa Rosada	5
Margoth	2

DRINKING & NIGHTLIFE	
Casa de la Iguana	2
Ubafu	1

Bahía de Amatique

Playa Barrique

Nuestra Señora del Rosario

Río Crique

@ Rapidnet

Banrural

Banrural

Immigration

Río Dulce

CALLE MARCOS SÁNCHEZ DÍAZ

Parque

Boats for Río Dulce Town, Puerto Barrios & Punta Gorda (Belize)

GARÍFUNA HISTORY AND CULTURE

The Garífuna people trace their history back to the island of **St Vincent** in the eastern Caribbean. In 1635 two Spanish ships carrying slaves from Nigeria were wrecked off the island, and in the following decades the survivors mixed with resident Amerindians, forming an **Afro-Carib** race. In their own language, they are *Garinagu*, or *Garífuna* "cassava-eating people".

For years attempts by the British to gain control of St Vincent were repelled by the Garífuna, who were aided by the French. In 1783 the British imposed a treaty on the Garífuna, but they continued to defy British rule until 1796, when, after a year of bitter fighting, the French and the Garífuna surrendered.

The colonial authorities could not allow a free black society to survive, and a decision was made to deport the Garífuna, who were mercilessly hunted down. Hundreds died of starvation and disease. In March 1797, the remaining 2200 or so Garífuna were loaded aboard ships and sent to **Roatán**, one of the Honduran Bay Islands, where they were abandoned.

SETTLEMENT IN CENTRAL AMERICA

Most Garífuna migrated from Roatán to the mainland where they worked as labourers, farmers and soldiers. In 1802, 150 Garífuna were brought as wood-cutters to southern Belize, from where they moved to Lívingston in 1806.

By the start of the twentieth century, the Garífuna were well established in the Lívingston area, with the women employed in bagging and stacking *cohune* nuts and the men working as fishermen. The Garífuna continued to travel widely in search of work, particularly in the **merchant navy**. Since the 1970s, many have left Central America for the US, where there's now a fifty thousand strong population in New York. Today most Garífuna live in villages along the Caribbean coast of Honduras (where they number more than one hundred thousand) with smaller populations in Belize (around twenty thousand) and Nicaragua.

LANGUAGE AND RELIGION

Most Garífuna speak Spanish (and some English) plus the unique Garífuna **language** that blends Arawak, Carib, French, English, Spanish and a few African words. Though virtually all worship at church, their Afro-Carib **dugu** (religion) – centred on ancestor worship – continues to be actively practiced. *Dugu* is immersed in ritual, and death is seen as the freeing of a spirit, a celebration that involves dancing, drinking and music.

PUNTA MUSIC

Garífuna music, or **punta**, is furiously rhythmic, characterized by mesmeric drum patterns and ritual chanting, and it's very easy to hear its West African origins. The late **Andy Palacio** is the most renowned Garífuna musician; his 2007 album *Wátina* is considered his masterpiece. Critically acclaimed *Umalali: The Garífuna Women's Project* is another superb compilation of Garífuna music.

GARÍFUNA IN GUATEMALA

For many Guatemalans, the Garífuna remain something of a national curiosity. They are not only subjected to **discrimination**, but also viewed with a strange awe that gives rise to a range of fanciful myths, including accusations of voodoo. Such prejudices, and the isolated nature of the community – numbering only around eight thousand in Guatemala – mean many young Garífuna are more drawn to African-American (hip-hop) and Jamaican (rastafari) influences than to Latin culture.

Hotel Doña Alida 150m northeast of C Principal ☎7947 0027. Could do with a makeover, but as the owners are very welcoming and the cliffside situation is excellent it's still worth considering. Rooms are spacious and clean, if dated; many have fine sea (and sunset) views. Wi-fi. US$20

Hotel Ecológico Salvador Gaviota Playa Quehueche ☎7947 0874, ⓦ hotelsalvadorgaviota.es.tl. Right on a slim beach, with good rooms (with or without private bathrooms) and large thatched bungalows in grassy grounds. Tasty, inexpensive local food including fresh fish is available. It's about a 40min walk west of the town centre; take a taxi from the main dock. Rooms US$13, bungalows US$30

Hotel Garífuna Off C de la Iglesia ☎ 7948 1091. Well-managed and secure, locally owned guesthouse with neat, clean and good-value rooms, all with fans and private showers. <u>US$13</u>

Hotel Gíl Resort 150m east of C Principal ☎ 7947 0039, ⊚ gilresorthotel.com. Modern, comfortable and well-run hotel with attractive pine-trimmed rooms that are finished to a high standard (though a little overpriced). There's a sea-view terrace and breakfast is included. <u>US$55</u>

Hotel Río Dulce C Principal ☎ 4022 8680. Gorgeous, old wooden Caribbean-style property with functional, simple rooms and dorms in the main property and more expensive options at the rear. Dorms <u>US$5</u>, rooms <u>US$13</u>

★ **Hotel Ríos Tropicales** C Principal ☎ 7947 0158 or ☎ 5755 7571, ⊚ mctropic.webs.com. An excellent, welcoming place. Very well-presented rooms, some very spacious and with tasteful furniture and art (around US$25), others are much simpler but still a great deal. There's a sunny patio at the rear with sofas and a little espresso bar at the front. Wi-fi. <u>US$8</u>

Vecchia Toscana Beachside, north of Playa Barrique ☎ 7947 0883, ✉ vecchiatoscanan@yahoo.it. Offering the most stylish accommodation in town, this Italian-owned beachside place has immaculate modern rooms, though many are on the small side for the price. There's a large pool and a restaurant with fine cuisine and an extensive wine list. Rarely busy. <u>US$58</u>

Villa Caribe Just off C Principal ☎ 7947 0072, ⊚ villasdeguatemala.com. Resort-style hotel, with spacious modern fan-cooled rooms boasting balconies with views to the bay and a/c bungalows. There's a pleasant bar, swimming pool and gardens stretching to the shore and the location is very central. <u>US$118</u>

EATING

Lívingston is a great place to eat out. For local food, you must try *tapado* (a coconut-based fish soup with plantain and spices): reckon on paying about US$8–10 for a huge bowl. In general, restaurant prices are quite high for Guatemala.

Antojitos Gaby C Marcos Sánchez Díaz. A cheap, clean little comedor with a couple of streetside tables serving good seafood (including *sopa caracol* and *tapado*), fish and pasta. Free wi-fi. Daily 7am–9.30pm.

Ashley C de la Iglesia. Run by a hospitable Garífuna lady, this clean and welcoming place serves tasty, well-prepared local dishes. Order a few hours ahead for specials like *tapado*. Daily 8am–9.30pm.

Bahía Azul C Principal ☎ 7947 0151. A very popular café-restaurant in a fine old Caribbean building, with an inexpensive menu (try the *coco burguesa*) and an excellent terrace for watching the world go by. Daily 7.30am–10pm.

Buga Mama Just left of the jetty ☎ 7947 0981. This lovely wooden Caribbean building also has a huge rear deck – take your pick for either sea or street views. Good shrimp, *tapado*, pasta and salads (in the US$6–12 range). Staff are trained as part of the Ak'Tenamit project (see p.208), a good cause, but service can be spotty. Wi-fi. Daily 7am–10pm.

★ **Hotel Casa Rosada** C Marcos Sánchez Díaz ☎ 7947 0303. This lovely hotel restaurant is a wonderful place for a meal, as you look out over La Buga (the mouth of the Río Dulce). Healthy breakfasts, tasty lunches and near-legendary dinners (US$10–13) and there are always good vegetarian options. There's a cappuccino machine. Book ahead. Daily 7am–9pm.

Margoth C de la Iglesia ☎ 7947 0019. Perhaps the best place to try *tapado*, this large Garífuna-owned place also serves very tasty seafood and a wide array of Garífuna dishes. Daily 7am–10pm.

DRINKING AND NIGHTLIFE

For evening entertainment, Lívingston has lots of groovy hangouts. The beach bars at the end of C Principal have dancefloors and play reggae, punta, r'n'b and Latin sounds.

Casa de la Iguana C Marcos Sánchez Díaz. It may not have a local flavour, but the bar scene here (happy hour 6–8pm) has a lively vibe and can be a riot, with anything from drinking games to mud-wrestling going on if the owners are in the mood. Daily until 1am.

Ubafu C de la Iglesia. This intimate bar is a key place for live music, especially Garífuna punta. Bands play at weekends and the odd weekday too. Daily 6pm–1am.

DIRECTORY

Banks and exchange You'll find two branches of Banrural on C Principal.

Immigration office C Principal (daily 6am–6pm; ☎ 7947 0081). Get your exit stamp for Belize the day before you leave.

Internet Many places have wi-fi. Rapid Internet is 400m north of the dock.

Post office Just off C Principal.

The Río Dulce gorge

Reason enough to come to Lívingston is the spectacular trip through the **Río Dulce gorge**, a roughly 30km journey that eventually brings you to Río Dulce Town. From Lívingston, the river passes through a system of **gorges** with sheer, 100m-high rock faces draped in tropical vegetation and cascading vines. The **birdlife** is exceptional with white herons, sea eagles and squawking parakeets among the stunning tropical scenery. If you're very lucky you may even see a **manatee** – dawn is the best time.

Ak'Tenamit

Some 8km west along the Río Dulce, then up the Río Tatín, is **Ak'Tenamit** (ⓦaktenamit.org), a health and development centre that caters to the needs of over a hundred Q'eqchi' Maya villages. Until the project was started in 1992 the people had neither schools, medical care, nor much else. Now there is a 24-hour clinic, schools and a floating dental clinic. Self-help programmes, a women's craft-making cooperative, an ecotourism centre and Maya cultural initiatives have also been launched. Volunteer doctors, nurses and dentists who can commit themselves for at least three months are needed. Visitors are invited to take a look around, there's a short **interpretive trail** through the rainforest, and some handicrafts for sale.

Biotopo Chocón Machacas

Daily 7am–4pm • US$3

Travel a kilometre or so upriver from Ak'Tenamit and you'll find a spot where warm sulphurous waters emerge from the base of a cliff – a good place for a dip. Just beyond, the gorge opens into a small lake, **El Golfete**, on whose northern shore is the **Biotopo Chocón Machacas**, a nature reserve designed to protect the habitat of the **manatee**, or sea cow, a threatened species that's seen around here from time to time. The manatee is a massive seal-shaped mammal that lives in both sea- and freshwater and, according to some, gave rise to the myth of the mermaid. Female manatees breastfeed their young, clutching them in their flippers, though – tipping the scales at as much as a ton – they're hardly as dainty as fairytale mermaids. The reserve was also set up to protect the area's rich wetlands and lowland rainforests (home to jaguar and tapir and wonderful birdlife) but recent encroachment by campesinos has led to a bitter battle over land use.

ACCOMMODATION   RÍO DULCE GORGE

Around 7km inland from Lívingston, just west of the gorge, there are a trio of fine eco-lodges. Boats travelling between Río Dulce and Lívingston will drop you off at any of these places. All have kayaks available to explore this uniquely beautiful region.

Finca Tatín 400m up the Río Tatín ☎4148 3332, ⓦfincatatin.centroamerica.com. Fine jungle lodge with an eight-bed dorm (above the bar), private rooms and two-storey cabins set in dense rainforest. It's well set up for

---

CRUISING THE RÍO

Most people experience the **Río Dulce** as a fleeting glimpse from one of the public boats that zip between Río Dulce Town and Lívingston, but to experience the río properly invest some time and take it slow. As the most spectacular section is near Lívingston it makes sense to begin a cruise there. Day-trips typically take in several attractions – including some hot springs, swimming spots, jungle tributaries and Ak'Tenamit – but the real pleasure is simply enjoying the spectacular **gorge** itself, with all the time in the world to soak up the idyllic scenery, which can be arranged through tour operators in Lívingston. Kayaking the gorge area and its jungle rivers from one of the hotels nearby (see above) is perhaps the perfect option.

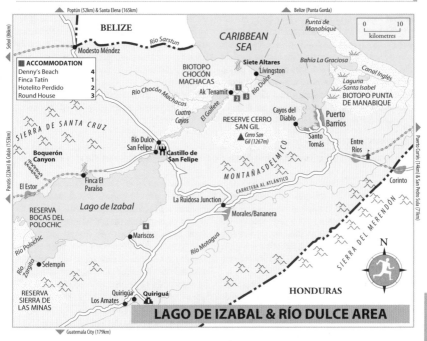

Map labels:
Poptún (52km) & Santa Elena (165km)
Belize (Punta Gorda)
Sebol (86km)
BELIZE
Río Sarstún
Punta de Manabique
CARIBBEAN SEA
0   10   kilometres
Modesto Méndez
Bahía La Graciosa
Siete Altares
BIOTOPO CHOCÓN MACHACAS
Lívingston
Canal Inglés
Laguna Santa Isabel
BIOTOPO PUNTA DE MANABIQUE

■ ACCOMMODATION
Denny's Beach   4
Finca Tatín   1
Hotelito Perdido   2
Round House   3

Río Chocón Machacas
Ak'Tenamit
Río Dulce
Cayos del Diablo
Puerto Barrios
Cuatro Cayos
El Golfete
RESERVE CERRO SAN GIL
Cerro San Gil (1267m)
Santo Tomás
Entre Ríos
SIERRA DE SANTA CRUZ
Río Dulce San Felipe
Castillo de San Felipe
Boquerón Canyon
Pansós (22km) & Cobán (153km)
El Estor
Finca El Paraíso
MONTAÑAS DEL MICO
Corinto
Puerto Cortés (144m) & San Pedro Sula (71km)
CARRETERA AL ATLÁNTICO
La Ruidosa Junction
Lago de Izabal
Morales/Bananera
RESERVA BOCAS DEL POLOCHIC
Mariscos
Río Polochic
Río Motagua
Río Zarquito
Selempín
SIERRA DEL MERENDÓN
N
RESERVA SIERRA DE LAS MINAS
Quiriguá
Los Amates
Quiriguá
HONDURAS
LAGO DE IZABAL & RÍO DULCE AREA
4
Guatemala City (179km)

travellers with healthy food (the communal dinner is US$7.50), table tennis, tubes, hammocks, walking trails, wi-fi and even a gym and yoga space. Dorms <u>US$5</u>, rooms <u>US$15</u>, cabañas <u>US$27</u>

Hotelito Perdido 300m up the Río Lámpara ☎ 5725 1576, ⊛ hotelitoperdido.com. Set in a verdant tropical garden this intimate place has split-level wooden cabañas, dorm beds and a relaxed vibe. Dorms <u>US$6</u>, rooms <u>US$20</u>, cabañas <u>US$27</u>

★ **Round House** 1km west of Río Dulce gorge ☎ 4294 9730, ⊛ roundhouseguatemala.com. Excellent new place, run by a very welcoming, well-travelled English-Dutch couple with high-quality accommodation, a sociable vibe and excellent cooking (a filling, flavoursome dinner is US$7). There's a small pool (ideal for volleyball) and great swimming in the río itself. Manatees are often seen directly offshore in the early morning. Dorms <u>US$6</u>, rooms <u>US$15</u>

Río Dulce Town

Heading on upstream, across the Golfete, the river closes in again and passes several marinas and a monstrous concrete bridge at the squalid settlement of **RÍO DULCE TOWN** (sometimes also known as Fronteras), on the northern side of the river. The waterfront away from Río Dulce Town is a favourite playground for wealthy Guatemalans, with boats and hotels that would look very at home in Monte Carlo or the Hamptons.

Most Petén-bound traffic pauses here for a few minutes, and the town itself is little more than a truck stop. Though initial impressions are terrible it's very easy to escape all this, and the best hotels are in much more tranquil, attractive locations a short boat-ride away.

ARRIVAL AND INFORMATION   RÍO DULCE TOWN

By bus Buses to Petén, Guatemala City and Puerto Barrios leave and depart from bus stops on the highway, just north of the bridge. First-class services are run by Línea Dorada, Litegua and ADN, all of which have offices on the highway, as does Fuente del Norte (whose buses are pretty beat-up and unreliable). Minibuses to El Estor leave from a side

road, just north of the Río Dulce bridge.

Destinations El Estor (every 45min; 1hr 30min); Flores (every 30min; 3hr–3hr 30min); Guatemala City (every 30min; 5–6hr); Lanquín (1 daily at 1.30pm from *Sundog Café*; 5hr); Poptún (every 30min; 1hr 45min); Puerto Barrios (hourly; 2hr).

By boat For Lívingston via the Río Dulce gorge, *colectivo* boats (9.30am & 1.30pm, 2hr 30min; additional services until 4pm; 2hr; US$17) arrive and depart from a designated dock under the north side of the bridge. If you book through your hotel on either the 9.30am or 1.30pm departures a pick-up can usually be arranged. Downstream, the trip takes around two hours, depending on how many stops are made. The boatmen usually cruise up to the Castillo de San Felipe for photographs (but do not stop there), slow down at an islet to see nesting cormorants and pelicans then stop for fifteen minutes at a place where hot springs bubble into the river and at another spot where water lilies are profuse. To explore the lake and river at a more leisurely pace, consider a slow cruise (see box, p.208), rent a kayak or try asking around in *Bruno's* or at your hotel.

Information For tourist information consult ⓦ mayaparadise.com, a comprehensive website covering the Río Dulce region.

ACCOMMODATION

All the following hotels, except *Hostal del Río*, are a short boat-ride away from the main dock. Most offer a free pick-up service.

Casa Perico 3km northeast of the bridge ☎ 5930 5666. Up a small lakeside inlet, this rustic Swiss-owned jungle hideaway has a relaxed atmosphere and is popular with budget travellers, though it's not a party spot. All the buildings are wooden, built on stilts and connected by walkways. Meals cost around US$4, the set dinner is US$7. You'll find kayaks for rent and trips are offered around the río. Dorms US$6, rooms US$15

Hacienda Tijax Just across from the dock ☎ 7930 5505, ⓦ tijax.com. Nicely located on the lakefront, and has a pool. There's a range of accommodation from small A-frame cabins to large bungalows, and the restaurant food is tasty, if a little overpriced. Also offers a canopy jungle walk, hiking trails and horseriding. Cabins US$29, bungalows US$88

Hostal del Río North of bridge, by Sundog Café ☎ 5527 0767. If you just want a bed for the night, this place is fine, with eight clean, functional rooms all with bathrooms and some with a/c. US$16

Hotel Backpackers Underneath the south side of the bridge ☎ 7930 5480, ⓦ hotelbackpackers.com. This huge, rickety wooden structure has large dorms and some mediocre doubles. Unfortunately it lacks atmosphere and is noisy which is a shame as it's owned by the nearby Casa Guatemala children's home, and many of the young staff are former residents. Dorms US$5.50, doubles US$15

Hotel Catamaran On a tiny private island, a 5min lancha east of bridge ☎ 7930 5494, ⓦ catamaranisland .com. Offers pleasant grounds with a smallish pool, restaurant and bar. Most of the a/c cabañas back onto the river and are comfortable enough, but overpriced. US$97

Hotel Kangaroo On a creek opposite the Castillo ☎ 4513 9602, ⓦ hotelkangaroo.com. Sociable place owned by an Australian–Mexican couple with a six-person dorm and attractive wooden rooms, some with private bathrooms. There's a jacuzzi, a fully stocked bar and filling tucker (though meals might be a little pricey for backpackers). Dorms US$7, doubles US$20

Isla Xalajá 3min lancha ride from bridge ☎ 7930 5767, ⓦ xalaja.com. Fine new place, with high service standards and excellent bungalows and houses (with kitchens) that are beautifully finished and offer good value. There's a marina here and a sociable bar-restaurant. US$50

★ **Tortugal** 4min by water taxi from bridge ☎ 5306 6432, ⓦ tortugal.com. A great selection of very good quality accommodation, all attractively presented and well finished. The two dorms have quality mattresses, mosquito nets and lockers. There are also lovely spacious rooms, wood-and-thatch bungalows, a stunning luxury *casita* and even a family-sized finca. Above the river-facing restaurant (meals are in the US$6–10 range) there's a chill-out area with free internet, pool table and library. Free kayaks for guests. Dorms US$10, bungalows US$49

EATING AND DRINKING

Benedición a Dios Down a little side road off the main drag ☎ 5797 1120. Comedor famous for its huge wheat tortillas, topped with cabbage and marinated beef (though there are veggie options) and fine, fruit-packed *licuados*. Daily 7am–9pm.

Bruno's Under north side of the bridge ☎ 7930 5721. The area's most popular yachtie hangout, with a wide menu of local and international grub including sandwiches, seafood (US$7–12) and pasta. The happy hour (4–7pm)

features Victoria beer for less than a dollar. Wi-fi and a pool. Daily 8am–11pm.

★ **Sundog Café** Down a lane on north side of bridge ☎ 5760 1844. Excellent little place run by a friendly Swiss guy that serves great thin-crust pizza (from a wood-fired oven) starting at US$7, baguettes and sandwiches (on delicious home-made bread) and espresso coffee. Also offers wine, and all spirits are double shots. Wi-fi. Mon & Wed–Sun noon–10pm.

DIRECTORY

Banks There are several, including Banrural and Banco Industrial, both with ATM, in Río Dulce Town.

Lago de Izabal

The beautiful tropical area along the lush banks of the **Lago de Izabal** has plenty to keep you occupied for a few days and a genuinely relaxed atmosphere. A road around the northern shore of the lake provides a route up to the Verapaces (see p.299), passing the idyllic **hot spring waterfall** close to the *Finca El Paraíso* and the towering **Boquerón canyon**. On the western side of the lake, the small town of **El Estor** is a good alternative base to explore these sights and the biodiverse wetlands of the **Reserva Bocas del Polochic**.

Castillo de San Felipe

Daily 8am–5pm • US$3 • 3km west of Río Dulce Town; water taxi (US$5) or minibus from Río Dulce bridge

Looking like a miniature medieval castle and marking the entrance to Lago de Izabal, the *castillo* is a tribute to the audacity of British pirates, who used to sail up the Río Dulce to raid supplies and harass mule trains. The Spanish were so infuriated by this that they built the pocket-sized fortress here in 1652 to seal off the entrance to the lake, and a chain was strung across the river. Inside there are a maze of tiny rooms and staircases, plus plenty of cannons and panoramic views of the lake.

Hot spring waterfall

Daily 8am–6pm • US$1.30 • Buses between Río Dulce and El Estor pass the hot spring hourly till 6pm

Beyond the *castillo*, the broad sweep of Lago de Izabal opens before you, with great views of the fertile highlands beyond the distant shores. Some 25km from Río Dulce, a **hot spring waterfall** in land owned by the *Finca el Paraíso*, 300m north of the road, is one of Guatemala's most remarkable natural phenomena. Bathtub-temperature spring water cascades into pools cooled by a separate chilly flow of fresh river water, creating a sublime, steamy spa-like environment where it's easy to soak away an afternoon. Above the waterfall is a series of caves whose interiors are crowded both with bats and extraordinary shapes and colours – made even more memorable by the fact that you have to swim by torchlight to see them (bring your own flashlight).

ACCOMMODATION	HOT SPRING WATERFALL
Finca el Paraíso 2km south of the waterfall ☎ 7949 7122. This hotel enjoys a delightfully peaceful location, sitting on the waterfront, with two rows of large, if ageing,	cabañas. However, rates are steep for what you get, there's little atmosphere and the restaurant is pricey. <u>US$48</u>

Boquerón canyon

Seven kilometres west along the lakeshore from the waterfall is the **Boquerón canyon**, completely hidden yet just 500m from the road. Near-vertical cliffs soar to more than 250m above the Río Sauce, which flows through the bottom of the startling jungle-clad gorge, the riverbed dotted with colossal boulders. To see the canyon, employ one of the local **boatmen** who wait at the end of the signposted track from the main road. They'll paddle you upstream in logwood canoes for a small fee. The round trip takes thirty minutes or so, though it's possible to get your boatman to drop you off and return to pick you up later in the day. The canyon extends for 5km; if you want to explore Boquerón further make sure you have sturdy footwear as it's quite a scramble.

El Estor

Heading west beyond Boquerón, it's just 6km to the sleepy lakeside town of **EL ESTOR**, allegedly named by English pirates who came up the Río Dulce to buy supplies at "The Store". There are no sights in easy-going El Estor itself, though you could easily spend a few days exploring the surrounding area. Keep an eye out for huge green iguanas in the trees around town; locals hunt them with slingshots.

The town is located close to high-grade nickel deposits, the presence of which has provoked bitter disputes between mining companies and locals. **Strip mining** has recently resumed, impacting the vast ecotourism potential of the region, and under new owners, the Russian-owned Solway group, production is set to double by 2014.

ARRIVAL AND INFORMATION   EL ESTOR

By bus Microbuses (every 45min; 1hr 30min) connect Río Dulce Town with El Estor until 6pm.

Information For local information the best contacts are Hugo at *Hugo's Restaurant*, or Óscar Paz, who runs the *Hotel Vista del Lago*. Both can arrange boats and guides to explore any of the region's attractions.

ACCOMMODATION AND EATING

The town has a decent choice of good-quality budget **accommodation**, though nothing much in other price categories.

Chaabil lakeshore on 3 C ☎ 7949 7272. This place is a good choice as the cabaña-style rooms have fans, chunky wooden beds and private bathrooms, and some have fine views. The restaurant (daily 7.30am–9.30pm) offers a lakeside setting for meals (US$5–10) of grilled meats and lots of seafood. US$20

Hotel Ecológico Cabañas del Lago ☎ 7949 7245 or ☎ 4037 6235. Set in a tranquil shady lakeside plot 1.5km east of the centre, these wooden bungalows are functional yet comfortable; some have three beds. There's a private sandy beach, good swimming, a guests' kitchen and bountiful wildlife around (lots of birds, spider monkeys and some iguanas). The restaurant has sweeping views and serves delicious shrimp, *bistek* and *comida chapín* (full meals US$6–10). Hugo, the genial owner, will give you a ride here if you drop by his restaurant ("*Hugo's*") in the plaza. US$26

Hotel Vista del Lago Lakeside ☎ 7949 7205. This beautiful old wooden building by the lakeshore is claimed to be the original "store" that gave the town its name. Small, clean rooms with private bathrooms; those on the second floor boast superb views of the lake. US$22

Posada Don Juan On the main square ☎ 7949 7296. A solid budget choice, this concrete hotel has clean, plain good-value rooms with fans, some with private bathrooms. US$10

DIRECTORY

Banks Banrural, 3 C & 6 Av, has an ATM

Internet There are several internet places in town.

Reserva Bocas del Polochic

Encompassing a substantial slice of lowland jungle on the west side of the lake, the **Bocas del Polochic** nature reserve is one of the richest wetland habitats in Guatemala. The green maze of swamp, marsh and forest harbours at least 224 different species of bird, including golden-fronted woodpecker, Aztec parakeet and keel-billed toucan. It's also rich in mammals, including howler monkeys, which you're virtually guaranteed to see (and hear), plus rarely encountered manatees and tapirs, and alligators, iguanas and turtles. You can explore the reserve from the tiny Q'eqchi' village of **SELEMPÍM** just outside the reserve.

ARRIVAL AND INFORMATION   BOCAS DEL POLOCHIC

By boat To get to Selempím catch a public *lancha* from El Estor (Mon, Wed & Sat at noon; US$7 one-way; 1hr 15min) or hire a private *lancha* (around US$90). *Lanchas* should return to El Estor at 7am the same days, but check schedules at Defensores' office. Day-trips to Bocas cost around US$75; ask Hugo or Óscar in El Estor to recommend a local boatman.

Information Defensores de la Naturaleza, 5 Av & 2 C in El Estor (☎7949 7130, ⓦ defensores.org.gt), manage the reserve and can help with information.

ACCOMMODATION

Selempím Lodge Contact Defensores to book ☎ 7949 7130, ⓦ defensores.org.gt. This large mosquito-screened wooden house has bunk beds and mossie nets. Guides are available to lead you up guided walks up into the foothills of the Sierra de las Minas and conduct kayak tours of the river delta. Rates include three substantial meals. US$18

Mariscos and Denny's Beach

MARISCOS, the main town on the south side of Lago de Izabal, sees very few visitors now that the road around the northern shore of the lake is complete. Travellers only pass through to access Denny's Beach.

ARRIVAL AND DEPARTURE
MARISCOS AND DENNY'S BEACH

By bus and boat There's no road access to Denny's Beach. All buses along the Carretera al Atlántico will stop at La Trinchera junction, the turn-off for Mariscos, from where minibuses (every 30min; 30min) head into the town centre.

ACCOMMODATION

Denny's Beach On the lake 6km east of Mariscos ☎4636 6156 or ☎5171 7477, ⓦdennysbeach.com. This Canadian-run resort is set in a blissfully quiet spot right on Lago de Izabal's best beach. It's an ideal place to get away from it all, with detached cabañas, a dorm above the shore and an open-air restaurant (meals are US$5–12). Kayak use is gratis, while horseriding (US$25) and trips around the lake can be arranged. They'll pick up and drop off guests for free from Mariscos; call ahead. Dorms US$10, bungalows US$50

El Oriente

The eastern highlands, often just called **El Oriente**, connect Guatemala City with El Salvador and Honduras and must rank as the least-visited part of the country. Virtually the entire population is ladino, and only a very few elderly people, in a couple of isolated areas, still speak Poqomam Maya, the region's indigenous language. The ladinos of the east have a reputation for behaving like cowboys, and demonstrations of macho pride – quick tempers, warm hearts and violent responses – are common.

The landscape lacks the immediate appeal of the western highlands – the peaks are lower and volcanoes here are heavily eroded. Close to the border with El Salvador the hills are incredibly fertile and the broad valleys lush with vegetation, but in the north of the area, around the key town of **Chiquimula**, the landscape is very different, with dry rounded hills and dusty fields. From this region it's a short hop to the ruins of Copán in Honduras, while **Esquipulas**, with its famous basilica, and the lovely volcanic crater lake of **Ipala** are also close by. To get to the Oriente you branch off the **Carretera al Atlántico** at the Río Hondo junction, skirt Estanzuela, and head past Chiquimula and Esquipulas to the three-way border with Honduras and El Salvador.

Estanzuela

Three kilometres south of the Río Hondo junction, the small remote town of **ESTANZUELA** is completely forgettable except one curious sight, a small museum of paleontology. If you're passing in a car, it might be worth a quick diversion; the town centre is just a kilometre off the highway. **El Museo de Paleontología Bryan Patterson** (daily 8am–5pm; free) has curious exhibits including the fossil of a blue whale, manatee bones and the entire skeleton of a mastodon said to be some fifty thousand years old. More recent pieces include a small Maya tomb and some stelae.

Chiquimula

Set on the western side of the highway the large town of **CHIQUIMULA** is an ugly, hot, bustling place with a population of around 45,000. If you've just arrived in Guatemala, things only get better from here. Chiquimula's huge plaza area, shaded by ceiba trees, and downtown streets are permanently congested by traffic and sights are slim on the ground. You could take a wander around the **market**, which has a kitsch selection of cowboy gear alongside inexpensive comedores, but for most travellers Chiquimula is just a place to catch a bus to or from the border at El Florido and the ruins of Copán.

ARRIVAL AND DEPARTURE

CHIQUIMULA

By bus The bus terminal is a 10min walk northeast of the plaza on 1 C between 10 & 11 Av.

Destinations Anguiatú (every 30min; 1hr); Esquipulas (every 20min; 1hr); El Florido (every 30min; 1hr 30min); Guatemala City (hourly; 3hr 30min); Ipala (hourly; 1hr); Puerto Barrios (hourly; 4hr 30min); Santa Elena, for Flores (2 daily; 7hr 30min).

ACCOMMODATION

This is a very hot place, so shell out for air-conditioning or make sure you have a good fan in your room.

Hotel Posada Don Adán 8 Av 4–30 ☎7942 0549. A genteel, old-fashioned family-run hotel; if the temperature is soaring the room's a/c will come in handy. Parking. US$22
Hotel Posada Perla de Oriente 2 C & 12 Av ☎7942 0014. Lush tropical gardens, a large pool and restaurant, and the rooms (with or without a/c) are spacious and clean, if a bit garish. Fan-only singles are well priced. US$20

Pensión Hernández 3 C 7–41 ☎7942 0708, ✉chapin54@yahoo.com. Long-standing favourite that's been putting up travellers for years, this warren of a place is run efficiently by a friendly family. Dozens of orderly clean rooms, in several different price categories, spread down long corridors – you pay a lot more for a/c and TV. Safe parking and a small concrete pool for cooling off. US$11

EATING

Jalisco Parque Calvario. Pleasant little café on Parque Calvario, a trendy hangout two blocks south of the main square, with a couple of tables set outside; try the Mexican dishes (from US$2.50). Daily 7.30am–7pm.

Parillada de Calero 7 Av 4–83 ☎7942 5639. For sizzling churrascos, this place excels at barbecued *lomito*, *pollo* and *carne de res*. From US$6. Daily 11am–10pm.

DIRECTORY

Banks Plenty in the centre with ATMs including Banco G&T Continental at 7 Av 4–75.

Internet Powernet for internet connections, on the plaza.

4

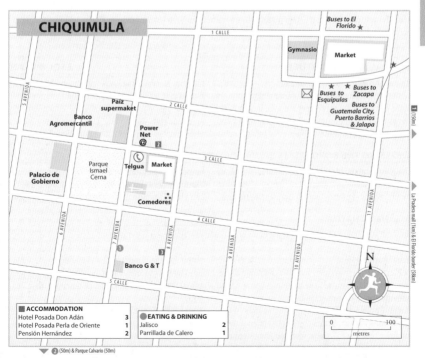

CHIQUIMULA

1 CALLE

Buses to El Florido

Gymnasio
Market

5 AVENIDA

Paíz supermaket

2 CALLE

Banco Agromercantil

Power Net @ 2

Buses to Esquipulas
Buses to Zacapa
Buses to Guatemala City, Puerto Barrios & Jalapa

3 CALLE

Palacio de Gobierno

Parque Ismael Cerna

Telgua   Market

Comedores

11 AVENIDA

4 CALLE

6 AVENIDA
7 AVENIDA
8 AVENIDA
9 AVENIDA
10 AVENIDA

1
3

Banco G & T

5 CALLE

N

0   100
metres

[150m]
La Pradera mall (1km) & El Florido border (58km)

ACCOMMODATION	
Hotel Posada Don Adán	3
Hotel Posada Perla de Oriente	1
Pensión Hernández	2

EATING & DRINKING	
Jalisco	2
Parrillada de Calero	1

2 (50m) & Parque Calvario (50m)

Volcán de Ipala

US$2, pay at visitor centre • Buses between Chiquimula and Agua Blanca (every 45min) pass the trailhead at El Sauce, where there's an Inguat sign

About 20km south of Chiquimula, the **Volcán de Ipala** (1650m) may at first seem a little disappointing – it looks more like a hill than a grand volcano. However, the cone is filled by a beautiful little crater lake and ringed by dense sub-tropical forest. You can walk round the lake in an hour and it's great for swimming or camping. From the trailhead it's a straightforward hour-and-a-half walk to the top, via a visitors' centre.

Esquipulas

The final town on this eastern highway is **ESQUIPULAS**, which has a single point of interest: it is the most important Catholic shrine in Central America, its dark-hued **statue of Christ** the focus of a famous annual pilgrimage. The settlement, and valley, is dominated by the four perfectly white domes of the church, brilliantly floodlit at night. Below, the town is a messy sprawl of cheap hotels, souvenir stalls and overpriced restaurants. The **pilgrimage**, which continues all year, has created a booming religious resort where people come to worship, eat, drink and relax, in a bizarre combination of holy devotion and indulgence. The town also played an important role in modern politics: the first **peace accord** initiatives to end the civil wars in El Salvador, Nicaragua and Guatemala were signed here in 1987.

The Basilica

Inside the **church** there's a constant scurry of hushed devotion amid clouds of smoke and incense. In the nave pilgrims approach the image on their knees, while others light candles, mouth supplications or simply stand in silent crowds. The image itself is most closely approached by a separate side entrance, where you can join the queue to shuffle past beneath it and pause briefly in front before being shoved on by the crowds behind. Back outside you'll find yourself among swarms of souvenir- and relic-hawkers.

ARRIVAL AND DEPARTURE   ESQUIPULAS

By bus and microbus Rutas Orientales runs a superb bus service between Guatemala City and Esquipulas; its office is at the junction of the main street and 1 Av. There are also microbuses from 11 C to the borders with El Salvador and Honduras at Agua Caliente until 6pm. For Copán, catch a microbus towards Chiquimula and change buses at the junction on the highway that leads to El Florido (see p.299). Destinations Agua Caliente (every 30min; 30min); Anguiatú (every 30min; 1hr); Chiquimula (every 20min; 1hr); Guatemala City (every 30min; 4hr 15min).

CROSSING THE BORDERS: EL SALVADOR AND HONDURAS

The Honduran border The 24hr border crossing at Agua Caliente is 10km from Esquipulas. There's a Honduran consulate (Mon–Fri 8am–1pm & 3–6pm) in *Hotel Payaquí,* Esquipulas; most nationalities don't need a visa.
The El Salvador border The border at Anguiatú (24hr) is 33km from Esquipulas; most nationalities don't need a visa.

ACCOMMODATION

Hotels fill up quickly on weekends, when prices (always negotiable) rise. Cheap places are north of the main road, 11 C.

Hotel Payaquí Just west of the church on 2 Av ☎ 7943 2025, ⊛ hotelpayaqui.com. A decent mid-range choice with two pools, restaurant, spa treatments and spacious, well-equipped a/c rooms. US$54
Hotel Portal de la Fe On 11 C ☎ 7943 4124, ⊛ portaldelafe.com. A colonial-style place offering clean, attractive rooms with wrought-iron bed frames and nice decorative touches. US$40

Hotel Posada Santiago 2 Av 11–58 ☎ 7943 2023. Good value at the lower end of the scale; rooms come with private bathrooms and there's a restaurant here too. US$21
Hotel Villa Edelmira 3 Av 8–58 ☎ 7943 1431. This family-run hotel is one of the best budget places, and has excellent rates for single travellers. US$16

THE ESQUIPULAS PILGRIMAGE

The history of the **Esquipulas pilgrimage** probably dates back to pre-conquest times, when the valley was controlled by Chief Esquipulas. Even then the area was the site of an important religious shrine, perhaps connected with the nearby Maya site of Copán.

When the Spanish arrived, the chief was keen to avoid the usual bloodshed and chose to surrender without a fight; the grateful Spaniards named the city they founded at the site in his honour. The famed colonial sculptor **Quirio Cataño** was then commissioned to carve an image of Christ for the church constructed in the town, and in order to make it more likely to appeal to the local people he chose to carve it from **balsam**, a dark wood. (Another version has it that Cataño was hired by the Maya after one of their number had seen a vision of a dark Christ on this spot.) In any event, the image was installed in the church in 1595 and soon was credited with miraculous powers. After the bishop of Guatemala, Pardo de Figueroa, was cured of a chronic ailment on a trip to Esquipulas in 1737 things really took off. The bishop ordered the construction of a new church, which was completed in 1758, and had his body buried beneath the altar.

Although this might seem straightforward, it doesn't explain why this figure has become the most revered in a country full of miracle-working saints. One explanation is that for the **Maya**, who until recently dominated the pilgrimage, it blends pre-Columbian and Catholic worship. The Maya pantheon included several black deities such as Ek Ahau, the black lord, who was served by seven retainers, and Ek'Chuach, the tall black god, who protected travellers.

The principal day of pilgrimage is **January 15**. Even the country's smallest villages will send a representative, their send-off and return marked by religious services. These, plus the thousands who come in their own right, ensure that the town fills to bursting. Buses choke the streets, while the most devoted pilgrims arrive on foot (some dropping to their knees for the last few kilometres). There's a smaller pilgrimage on March 9, and the faithful visit year-round.

4

EATING AND DRINKING

Breakfast is a bargain in Esquipulas, no more than US$2 for a good feed. Cheap places are clustered on 11 C and north.

Hacienda Steak House 2 Av &10 C ☎7943 2328. One of the smartest places in town, head here for chargrilled steaks (around US$8–12) or burritos, sandwiches, burgers or pasta for about half that price. Daily 7.30am–10pm.

Restaurante La Frontera 11 C, opposite the park. There's usually a bustle about this large place which has a good selection of local dishes, including fish and tasty *carne a la plancha*. Daily 7am–9pm.

DIRECTORY

Banks There are plenty of banks with ATMs in town including Banco Industrial at 9 C & 3 Av.

FIESTAS IN THE ORIENTE AND IZABAL

Jan 12–15 El Progreso (near Jutiapa), main day 15th
Jan 15 Esquipulas, the biggest pilgrimage in Central America
Jan 20–26 Ipala, main day 23rd (includes bullfighting)
March 9 Esquipulas, a smaller day of pilgrimage to the Black Christ
March 12–15 Moyuta (near Jutiapa) and Olapa (near Chiquimula)
March (varies) Jocotán
May 2–5 Jalapa, main day 3rd
May 5–9 Gualán (near Zacapa)
July 16–22 Puerto Barrios, main day 19th

July 22–26 Jocotán (near Chiquimula)
July 23–27 Esquipulas, a fiesta in honour of Santiago Apóstol, main day 25th
Aug 11–18 Chiquimula, main day 15th (includes bullfighting)
Aug 25 San Luís Jilotepéque
Nov 7–14 Sanarate
Nov 10–16 Jutiapa, main day 13th
Nov 26 Lívingston, Garífuna day here is a huge celebration
Dec 4–9 Zacapa, main day 8th
Dec 13–16 San Luís Jilotepéque
Dec 22–27 Cuilapa
Dec 24–31 Lívingston, carnival

Cobán
and the
Verapaces

SEMUC CHAMPEY

5

Cobán and the Verapaces

The twin departments of the Verapaces harbour some of the most spectacular mountain scenery in the country, yet attract only a trickle of tourists. Alta Verapaz, in particular, is astonishingly beautiful, with fertile limestone landscapes and craggy, mist-wrapped hills. The highlands here are the wettest and greenest in Guatemala – ideal for the production of the cash crops of coffee, cardamom, flowers and ferns. Locals say it rains for thirteen months a year, alternating between straightforward downpours and drizzle they call the *chipi-chipi*. To the south, Baja Verapaz could hardly be more different: a sparsely populated area of deep valleys dotted with fiesta towns and parched hills that see very little rainfall.

In Baja Verapaz, the towns of **Salamá**, **Rabinal** and **Cubulco** are rightly renowned for their traditional fiestas, while **San Jerónimo** has some interesting historic sights. Guatemala's national bird, the quetzal can occasionally be seen in the cloudforests of this department: the **quetzal sanctuary** is one possible and accessible place to seek them out.

However, the hub of the region is **Cobán** in Alta Verapaz, a fairly attractive mid-sized mountain town with good accommodation and some very civilized coffeehouses and restaurants. Northeast of here, the exquisite natural bathing pools of **Semuc Champey** near **Lanquín** are surrounded by lush tropical forest and are a key travellers' hangout.

North of Cobán, a couple of wonderful natural attractions lie near the town of **Chisec**: the emerald lakes of **Lagunas de Sepalau** and the sink hole of **Bombil Pek**. From Chisec it's a short hop to the extraordinary **Candelaria caves** and the nearby ruins of **Cancuén**. In the extreme northwest of the region, the astonishingly beautiful lake **Laguna Lachúa**, fringed by rainforest, is well worth the detour it takes to get there.

Brief history

Long before the Conquest, local Achi Maya had earned themselves a reputation as the most bloodthirsty of all the tribes, said to sacrifice every prisoner they took. Alvarado's Spanish army was unable to make any headway against them, and eventually he gave up trying to control the area, naming it *tierra de guerra*, the "land of war".

The Catholic church, however, couldn't allow so many heathen souls to go to waste. Under the leadership of **Fray Bartolomé de Las Casas**, the Church made a deal with the conquistadors: if Alvarado would agree to keep all armed men out of the area for five years, the priests would bring it under control. In 1537 Las Casas set out into the highlands, befriended the Achi chiefs and learnt the local dialects. By 1538 they had made considerable progress and converted large numbers of Maya. After five years the famous and invincible Achi were transformed into Spanish subjects, and the king of Spain renamed the province *Verapaz*, "True Peace".

THE RESPLENDENT QUETZAL

Highlights

❶ Quetzal Search for Guatemala's spectacularly plumed national bird in the cloudforests of the Verapaces. **See p.228**

❷ Coffee in Cobán Taste the uniquely smooth, medium-bodied and fragrant coffee for which Cobán is famous in situ. **See p.236**

❸ Semuc Champey Bathe in these sublime turquoise pools at the foot of a plunging river valley. **See p.237**

❹ Chisec Explore the magical lakes of Lagunas de Sepalau and the sacred Maya cave of Bombil Pek near this peaceful little town. **See p.239**

❺ Candelaria caves An extraordinary limestone cave system, extending for more than 20km, with some immense chambers to investigate. **See p.240**

❻ Laguna Lachúa A pristine, near-circular lake rimmed by lowland jungle inhabited by jaguar and tapir. **See p.243**

HIGHLIGHTS ARE MARKED ON THE MAP ON P.223

5

> ## MAYA IN THE VERAPACES
>
> Taken as a whole, the Verapaces are very much **indigenous** country: Baja Verapaz retains a small **Achi** Maya outpost around Rabinal, and in Alta Verapaz the Maya population are **Poqomchi'** and **Q'eqchi'**. The production of **coffee**, and more recently **cardamom** for the Middle Eastern market, has cut deep into their land and their way of life, the fincas driving many people off prime territory to marginal plots. **Traditional costume** is worn less here than in the western highlands, and in its place many indigenous women have adopted a more universal Q'eqchi' costume, wearing the loose-hanging white *huipil* and machine-made *corte*. Maya men do not wear *traje* in the Verapaces.

During the colonial era the Verapaces remained isolated, their trade bypassing the capital by taking a direct route to the Caribbean along the Río Polochic and out through Lago de Izabal.

The twentieth century

The area really started to develop with the **coffee boom** at the turn of the twentieth century, when German immigrants flooded into the country to buy and run fincas.

Around Cobán the new immigrants established an island of European sophistication, the German population reaching around two thousand by the 1930s, with its own schools and clubs (and active Nazi party). A railway was built along the Polochic valley and Alta Verapaz became even more independent. This situation came to an end with World War II, when the US insisted the Guatemalan government expel the German landowners.

Today the Verapaz economy remains dominated by huge coffee fincas, along with cardamom production for the Middle Eastern market and the cultivation of flowers and broccoli for export. Campesinos have been forced to farm more and more marginal plots, and deforestation is a huge issue.

Baja Verapaz

A dramatic mix of dry hills and fertile valleys, **BAJA VERAPAZ** is crossed by a skeletal road network. The small towns of **Salamá** and **San Jerónimo**, situated on a flat-bottomed valley, have some intriguing historic sights, while to the west **Rabinal** and **Cubulco** boast interesting markets and host deeply traditional fiestas. The other big attractions are the **quetzal sanctuary**, on the western side of the Cobán highway, and the forested mountains, waterfalls and wildlife inside the **Reserva Sierra de las Minas** just to the east.

San Jerónimo

At the eastern end of a fertile valley, 18km from the Cumbre junction, lies the small tranquil town of **SAN JERÓNIMO**. In the Conquest's early days, Dominican priests built a church and convent here and planted vineyards, eventually producing a wine lauded as the finest in Central America. In 1845, after the religious orders were abolished, an Englishman replaced the vines with sugarcane and began distilling an *aguardiente* that became equally famous. These days the area still produces sugar, though the cultivation of flowers for export and fish farming are more important.

The church

Parque Central

Presiding over the central plaza, the village's seventeenth-century Baroque **church** contains a monumental gilded altar, brought from France, which was crafted from sheets of eighteen-carat gold.

5

MARKET DAYS IN THE VERAPACES

Monday Senahú; Tucurú.
Tuesday Chisec; El Chol; Cubulco; Lanquín; Purulhá; Rabinal; San Cristóbal Verapaz; San Jerónimo; Tres Cruces.

Saturday Senahú.
Sunday Chisec; Cubulco; Lanquín; Purulhá; Rabinal; Salamá; San Jerónimo; Santa Cruz Verapaz; Tactic.

Museo Regional del Trapiche

Mon–Fri 8am–4pm, Sat & Sun 10am–4pm • Donation • ☎ 5514 6959

Just down the hill from the church, in a wonderful rural setting at the base of the foothills of the Sierra de las Minas, are the remains of the convent complex: the Hacienda de San Jerónimo. Its sugar mill buildings now form the **Museo Regional del Trapiche** with displays that explain the history of the hacienda and refining process, while the extensive grassy grounds make an ideal place for a picnic.

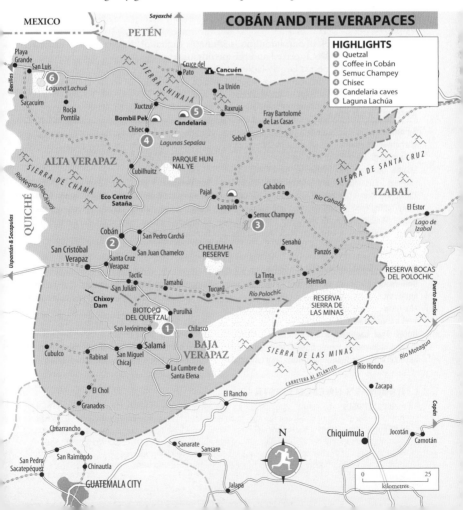

COBÁN AND THE VERAPACES

HIGHLIGHTS
❶ Quetzal
❷ Coffee in Cobán
❸ Semuc Champey
❹ Chisec
❺ Candelaria caves
❻ Laguna Lachúa

5

The aqueduct

Of interest is the colonial **aqueduct**, built in 1679, which once supplied the mill's waterwheels. Many of its 124 original stone arches are still standing on the southern outskirts of town, about ten minutes' walk from the plaza – just ask the way to the *acueducto antiguo*.

ARRIVAL AND DEPARTURE — SAN JERÓNIMO

By minibus Minibuses connect Salamá and San Jerónimo between 6am and 7.30pm, running every 30min.

ACCOMMODATION

Hotel Hacienda Real el Trapiche Western entrance to town ☏ 7940 2542 and ☏ 5649 3479. A colonial-style hotel offering very attractive rooms, all with good beds, and you'll find fair rates for solo travellers. Its restaurant offers home-cooked food. US$25

Hotel Posada de Los Frayles 60m from El Calvario church ☏ 7723 5533. This place runs a close second in town, with a dash of colonial style, comfortable accommodation and the added benefit of a pool. US$28

Salamá

Eight kilometres west of San Jerónimo is **SALAMÁ**, capital of the department of Baja Verapaz. The town has a relaxed and prosperous air, and like many of the places out this way, its population is largely ladino. Sights are slim on the ground, although it's worth checking out the imposing colonial **bridge** on the edge of town, and the old **church**, the gilt of its huge altars darkened by age.

ARRIVAL AND TOURS — SALAMÁ

By bus From Cobán or Guatemala City, you can take any bus between the two and get off at the junction known as La Cumbre de Santa Elena; from here microbuses run to Salamá. There are also microbuses from Cobán. Buses between Guatemala City and Salamá (every 30min; 3hr 15min) run from 11 Av and 17 C, Zona 1, in the capital; many continue on to Rabinal (4hr) and Cubulco (4hr 30min). Minibuses terminate and depart from a dusty car park off 6 Av, one block west of the plaza; there's a steady stream to San Jerónimo and Rabinal.

Destinations Cobán (hourly; 1hr 30min); Cubulco (hourly; 1hr 30min); Guatemala City (every 30min; 3hr 15min); Rabinal (every 30min; 45min); San Jerónimo (every 20min; 15min).

Eco-Verapaz 8 Av 7–12, Zona 1 ☏ 5722 9095, ✉ ecoverapaz@hotmail.com. Offers good mountain-biking, caving, hiking, horseriding and cultural trips throughout the department. Prices are around US$45 a day for most activities.

ACCOMMODATION AND EATING

Deli-Donus 5 C 6–61 ☏ 7940 1121. Attractive café-restaurant ideal for coffee and a slice of home-made cake. Also good for breakfasts (around US$2.50) or a sandwich – try a *bocadillo de jamón y queso*. Daily 7.30am–8pm.

Hotel Real Legendario 8 Av 3–57 ☏ 7940 0501, ⊕ hotelreallegendario.com. A fairly modern, efficiently run hotel where the twenty good rooms have comfortable

beds, private hot-water bathrooms and cable TV. There's a little comedor here for breakfast, as well as internet and wi-fi. US$20

Posada Don Maco 3 C 8–26 ☏ 7940 0083. Hospitable family-run place where the well-scrubbed, neat rooms have private bathrooms, cable TV and nice decorative touches. However, they keep squirrels in cages in the yard here. US$18

RABINAL'S UNESCO FIESTA

Rabinal's **fiesta**, which runs from January 19 to 24, is renowned for its dances, many of them pre-colonial in origin. The most famous is an extended dance drama known as the **Rabinal Achi** which re-enacts a battle between the Achi and K'iche' tribes and is unique to the town, performed annually on January 23 – it's recently been bestowed UNESCO World Heritage recognition. Others include the *patzca*, a ceremony to call for good harvests, using masks that portray a swelling below the jaw, and wooden sticks engraved with serpents, birds and human heads.

RABINAL AND THE CIVIL WAR

The Rabinal region suffered terribly during Guatemala's civil war – there were four **massacres** in 1982 alone. Local people have exhumed several of the mass graves that pepper the hillsides and reburied some of the 4400 victims from the municipality, in an effort to give those killed during *la violencia* a more dignified resting place. In 2004, the Inter-American Court ordered the Guatemalan government to pay US$8 million as compensation to the surviving families of one massacre. The legal battle continues but the army generals who directed the campaign of terror have hitherto escaped justice, though three PUC (paramilitary conscripts) and four Kaibiles (special forces) were jailed in 2011 for their roles in the massacres. In December 2011 President Colom apologized to relatives of the victims of the 1982 Dos Erres massacre near Rabinal, calling it "a stain on Guatemala's history".

DIRECTORY

Banks and exchange Banrural, opposite the church, has an ATM and will cash dollars and travellers' cheques.

Internet Telgua, just east of the plaza, has internet access.

Rabinal and around

Less than an hour from Salamá via a gap in the hills, **RABINAL** is a dusty, isolated farming town where the one-storey adobe and cinderblock houses are dominated by a large colonial church. Founded in 1537 by Bartolomé de Las Casas, Rabinal was the first of the settlements he established in his peaceful conversion of the Achi nation. The proportion of indigenous inhabitants is high here and the fine fiesta (see box opposite) has a uniquely Achi character.

Market days (Tues & Sun) are fascinating in Rabinal – look for some high-quality local artesanías, including carvings made from the *árbol del morro* (calabash tree) and traditional pottery.

Museo Comunitario Rabinal Achi

4 Av and 2 C, Zona 3 • Mon–Sat 8.30am–5pm • US$1.30 • ☎ 7938 8721, ⓦ museo.rabinal.info

The town's small **museum** is worth a visit, with exhibits on traditional medicinal practices, cultural history, local crafts including ceramics and weaving, and a moving room devoted to the impact of the civil war in the region including portraits of the dead.

Cerro Cayup

About 3km northwest of Rabinal, a steep ninety-minute hike away, are the ruins of one of the Achi nation's fortified cities, known locally as **Cerro Cayup**. The hilltop contains the remains of a temple and some fortifications and is actively used by Maya shaman for religious ceremonies. You can organize a guide to lead you here at the museum.

ARRIVAL AND DEPARTURE   RABINAL

By bus Very regular buses connect the town with Salamá (every 30min; 45min). For Guatemala City, there are eight daily buses via La Cumbre (4hr), and three daily via El Chol (6hr).

ACCOMMODATION AND EATING

Cafetería Mishell del Rosario On 1 C behind the church. Count on this reliable place for an inexpensive bite to eat, with filling meals around US$2.50. Daily 7am–8pm.

Hospedaje Caballeros 1 C 4–02 ☎ 7938 8147. Thirteen tidy rooms, some with private bath and TV at this budget hotel. There's a café here too. US$9

Posada San Pablo 3 Av 1–50 ☎ 7938 8025 or ☎ 7848 3343. A decent, well-run budget place, this is the best of Rabinal's several fairly basic hotels. US$10

5

> ## FIESTA TIME IN CUBULCO
>
> Cubulco is best visited for its annual fiesta. This is one of the few places where you can see the **Palo Volador**, a pre-conquest ritual in which men throw themselves from a 30m pole with a rope tied around their legs, spinning down towards the ground as the rope unravels, and hopefully landing on their feet. It's as dangerous as it looks, particularly when you bear in mind that most of the dancers are blind drunk; every few years an inebriated dancer falls from the top of the pole to his death. The fiesta still goes on, though, as riotous as ever, with the main action taking place on July 25. If you're in town at fiesta time be sure to taste the local **chilate** drink, made from corn and spices and served in fruit husks.

DIRECTORY

Banks and exchange Banrural at 2 C and 2 Av, Zona 2, has an ATM.

Cubulco

Leaving Rabinal, a paved road heads west, climbing a high ridge with fantastic views to the left into the uninhabited mountain ranges. The road then descends into the next valley to **CUBULCO**, an isolated town of Achi Maya and ladinos, surrounded on all sides by steep, forested peaks.

ACCOMMODATION AND EATING   CUBULCO

La Fonda del Viajero Marketplace. There are several comedores in the market, but this scores highest marks, serving tasty *comida típica* at reasonable prices. Daily 7am–8.30pm.

Posada Paíz Next to the large farmacia in the centre of town, no phone. Nothing fancy but clean enough and has some rooms with private bathrooms. __US$10__

Reserva Sierra de las Minas

Forming one of Guatemala's largest expanses of **cloudforest**, this misty, thinly populated region, much of which has been designated the **RESERVA SIERRA DE LAS MINAS** harbours abundant wildlife such as howler monkeys, white-tailed deer and coyotes. Birds found here include the emerald toucan, hummingbirds and fairly plentiful numbers of quetzals (see box, p.228).

This mighty mountain range is a tricky place to get to, with few access roads and incredibly steep terrain. For travellers, it's easiest to explore the fringes of the reserve from the village of **San Rafael Chilascó** where the community arranges hikes to two impressive waterfalls.

Salto de Chilascó

12km east of CA-14 highway • Daily 7am–5pm, last entry 1pm • US$4, guide US$4

One of the highest **waterfalls** in Guatemala, **SALTO DE CHILASCÓ** plunges 200m in two drops close to the entrance of Sierra de Las Minas. First stop by the information centre in Chilascó village (see below), where you pay your entrance fee. From here it's a 3km walk along a dirt track to the beginning of the trail to the falls.

The trail begins as a steep, muddy mule path heading down to a ridge flanked by broccoli plantations. Take the footpath to the left for much easier passage. After 1km the path plunges down into the forested valley. The well-maintained trail offers picnic sites with views towards the **Chilascó falls** and information panels on the local flora (rare orchids, giant bromeliads and ferns), liquidambar forest and fauna.

Don't miss the **Saltito**, a delightful smaller waterfall halfway down, where you can bathe in the plunge pool and admire the stunning views. At the base of the main falls, water cascades onto huge boulders and seemingly disappears into the cavernous valley beyond the trail's end. The walk back up to Chilascó village requires a moderate level of fitness (allow at least two hours).

ARRIVAL AND INFORMATION

By microbus From Salamá microbuses (4 daily at 6.30am, 10.30am, noon & 5.30pm; 1hr 45min) run to San Rafael Chilascó, which is 12km east of the Guatemala City–Cobán highway via the turn-off at Km145. There are also random pick-ups from this turn-off. Buses return to Salamá at 5.45am, 8.30am, 12.30pm and 3pm.

RESERVA SIERRA DE LAS MINAS

Information Once in San Rafael, head for the visitor centre (☏ 5301 8928) where you'll be assigned a guide and can also rent waterproofs and boots. Horses (US$13/hr) can be arranged and village accommodation (US$5/person) and meals are also possible.

Biotopo del Quetzal

Daily 7am–4pm • US$3.50

On the highway north to Cobán, just before the village of Purulhá, the **Biotopo del Quetzal** was established to protect the habitat of the endangered quetzal, Guatemala's national bird (see box, p.228). The reserve covers a steep area of dense cloudforest, through which the Río Colorado cascades towards the valley floor, forming waterfalls and natural swimming pools.

Two paths through the undergrowth from the road complete a circuit that takes you up into the woods above the reserve headquarters (where maps are available for US$0.75). Quetzals are occasionally seen here but they're extremely elusive. The best time of year to visit is just before and just after the nesting season (between March & June), and the best time of day is sunrise. In general, the birds tend to spend the nights up in the high forest and float across the road as dawn breaks, to spend the days in the trees below. They can be easily identified by their jerky, undulating flight. A good place to look out for them is at one of their favoured feeding trees, the broad-leaved *aguacatillo*, which produces a small avocado-like fruit. Whether or not you see a quetzal, the forest itself (usually damp with *chipi-chipi*, a perpetual mist) is worth a visit: a profusion of lichens, ferns, mosses, bromeliads and orchids spread out beneath a towering canopy of cypress, oak, walnut and pepper trees.

ARRIVAL AND INFORMATION

BIOTOPO DEL QUETZAL

By bus Buses from Cobán (1hr) and Guatemala City (4hr) pass the entrance (at Km161) every 30min.
Information At the entrance to the reserve, just off the

highway, there's a ticket office where you can get a map (US$0.75) but there's very little other information.

ACCOMMODATION AND EATING

Hacienda Rio Escondido Km144 ☏ 5208 1407. Coming from Guatemala City, the first place you reach is this upmarket rural lodge which has lovely wooden cabañas, some with two bedrooms, and a restaurant with excellent grilled meats. US$52

Hospedaje Ranchito del Quetzal 100m past the entrance to the reserve ☏ 2331 3579. Simple hospedaje offering basic accommodation either in very rustic palapa-roofed huts or in a pretty miserable concrete block. However the home-cooked food and very hospitable family owners help compensate for the no-frills facilities. Quetzals are quite common in the patch of forest around the hotel. US$18

Hotel Posada Montaña del Quetzal Km156.5 ☏ 2332 4969 or ☏ 5800 0454, ⓦ hposadaquetzal.com.

Offers attractive stone and timber bungalows (US$52) with fireplaces and spacious rooms with private bathrooms; many have great forest views and there's a restaurant, bar, swimming pool, walking trails and an orchid garden here. U$37

Ram Tzul Km158.5 ☏ 5908 4066, ⓦ m-y-c.com.ar /ramtzul. The bizarre glass-fronted restaurant here may be a blot on the landscape but the food (most meals US$5–8) is pretty tasty and there's a wide selection of drinks (even cocktails). At the rear there are very attractive, tasteful rooms built from bamboo, timber and stone – many with great views of the Verapaz hills. Ram Tzul sits on the edge of a large privately owned forest reserve, whose trails you are welcome to explore. US$38

5

THE RESPLENDENT QUETZAL

The **quetzal**, Guatemala's national symbol (after which the country's currency and second city are named), has a distinguished past but an uncertain future. The bird's feathers have been sacred from the earliest of times, and in the strange cult of Quetzalcoatl, whose influence once spread throughout Mesoamerica, the bird was incorporated into the plumed serpent, a supremely powerful deity. To the Maya the quetzal was so sacred that killing one was a capital offence; the bird is also thought to have been the *nahual*, or spiritual protector, of the Maya chiefs. When Tecún Umán faced Pedro de Alvarado in hand-to-hand combat, his headdress sprouted the long green feathers of the quetzal, and when the conquistadors founded a city adjacent to the battleground they named it Quetzaltenango, "the place of the quetzals".

In modern Guatemala the quetzal's image saturates the country: it features on the national flag, and citizens honoured by the president are awarded the Order of the Quetzal. The bird is also considered a symbol of freedom, since caged quetzals die from the rigours of confinement. Despite all this, deforestation threatens the very existence of the bird, and the **Biotopo del Quetzal** is about the only serious step that has been taken to save it.

There are six species of the bird, but it's the male **Resplendent Quetzal** (found between southern Mexico and Panama) which is the most exotically coloured. Its head is crowned with a plume of brilliant green, and chest and lower belly are a rich crimson; the unmistakeable iridescent green tail feathers (reaching some 60cm in length) are particularly evident in the mating season. The females, on the other hand, are an unremarkable brownish colour. The birds nest in holes found in dead trees, laying one or two eggs, usually in April or May.

MARIO DARY

The Biotopo del Quetzal is also known as the **Mario Dary Reserve**, in honour of an environmental campaigner who spent years campaigning for a cloudforest sanctuary to protect the quetzal, causing great problems for powerful timber companies in the process. He was murdered in 1988. An ecological foundation, Fundary, has been set up in his name to manage protected areas, including Punta de Manabique on the Caribbean coast.

Southern Alta Verapaz

Heading north of the quetzal sanctuary, the highway crosses into the department of **Alta Verapaz**, and another 13km takes you beyond the forests and into a luxuriant alpine valley of cattle pastures hemmed in by steep, perpetually green hillsides. Most people speed through this region on their way to Cobán, but there are a few interesting attractions to detain you if you have the time to explore these evergreen hills and their towns' curiosities. There's also a possible route east from here to the Caribbean along the **Polochic valley**.

Tactic

The first place of any size is **TACTIC**, a small, mainly Poqomchi'-speaking town, which most buses bypass. The colonial **church** in the plaza is worth noting; it boasts an elaborate facade decorated with mermaids and jaguars.

High above the town up a long flight of steps, the pagan **Chi-ixim** chapel, contains a dark-skinned Christ figure that attracts pilgrims from all over the country, but especially on January 15. Dozens of plaques of thanksgiving for miracles ascribed to the black saint of Chi-ixim, who also goes by the name Dios del Maíz ("Lord of Maíz"), adorn the walls.

ACCOMMODATION AND EATING   TACTIC AREA

Café La Granja Km187 on the highway ☎ 7953 9003, ⓦ cafelagranja.com. For ranch-style food, this café has a menu of Guatemalan favourites plus sandwiches, pasta and salads in a great log-cabin-style setting. There's a kids' play area too. Daily 7am–7.30pm.

Chi'ixim Eco Hotel Km182.5, just off the highway

HIGHWAY TO HELL

Heading west of San Cristóbal towards Uspantán (see p.110) the road passes through an unstable chunk of mountainous terrain that's prone to **landslides**. Hourly Cobán–Uspantán microbuses ply the route, but a hair-raising section involves inching along a precipitous slope; services may not run during heavy rains. West of the Río Negro bridge the highway is paved and in good shape. If you're driving, consider the long detour via Guatemala City.

☎ 7953 9198. The best option near Tactic is this rustic hotel which has comfortable bungalows with fireplaces and a spotless little dining room. US$26

Hotel Villa Linda 4 C 6–25 ☎ 7953 9216. Inexpensive place to stay in town, the *Villa Linda* has decent, clean rooms with private baths. US$14

San Cristóbal Verapaz and around

At the featureless settlement of **Santa Cruz Verapaz** there's a turn-off for **SAN CRISTÓBAL VERAPAZ**, an attractive town surrounded by fields of sugarcane and coffee set on the banks of the **Lago de Cristóbal**. The Poqomchi'-speaking Maya of San Cristóbal are among the last vestiges of one of the smallest highland tribes.

There's an excellent **community tourism** project here which allows visitors to explore the region with expert local guides and really get to grips with Poqomchi' culture. As all the hotels in town are pretty grim, you might want to drop by on a day-trip from Cobán.

Museo Katinamit

C del Calvario 0–03 • Mon–Sat 8am–1pm & 2–5pm, Sun 9am–noon • US$1.30 • ☎ 7950 4039

You can find out more about local culture at this interesting little **museum**, located just off the plaza. The **Museo Katinamit** hosts exhibits on the maguey plant, which is woven into bags, hammocks and rope; Verapaz flora and fauna; and music. Handicrafts are for sale too. The museum also acts as a base for the Centro Comunitario Educativo Poqomchi' (see below).

ARRIVAL, INFORMATION AND TOURS   SAN CRISTÓBAL VERAPAZ

By bus Microbuses and buses connect Cobán with San Cristóbal (30min) until 7pm. They also run west to Uspantán (hourly; 2hr 15min) though the road is prone to landslides (see box above).

Centro Comunitario Educativo Poqomchi' (CECEP) At the museum ☎ 7950 4039, ⦿ cecep.cosmosmaya.info. Organizes ethnotourism trips (from US$10 for half-day

tours) of indigenous communities (where homestays are possible) and sights around San Cristóbal including a hilltop Maya shrine, marimba factory and maguey-weaving villages. Spanish language classes are also offered for US$140 a week, including full board with a local family.
Information online The website ⦿ sancrisav.net has good information about the town and local culture.

The Polochic valley

If you're planning to head towards the Caribbean from Alta Verapaz the route east along the **Polochic valley** is the one to take – head east from the San Julián junction, shortly after Tactic on the Cobán–El Rancho highway. The scruffy towns along the length of this V-shaped valley hold little interest, but you'll witness an immense transformation in scenery as you drop down through the coffee-coated mountains and emerge into lush, tropical lowlands.

SEMANA SANTA IN SAN CRISTÓBAL

San Cristóbal knows how to throw a good **fiesta** – it runs from July 21 to July 26 (the main day is July 25) – and is also an excellent, almost tourist-free place to head for **Semana Santa**, when a kilometre-long coloured sawdust carpet is created between the main church in the plaza and the Calvario chapel to the west.

5

POWER FAILURE

South of San Cristóbal is the billion-dollar disaster known as the **Chixoy dam and hydroelectric plant**. The dam provides Guatemala with about half its electricity needs but the price of the project has been high. Unchecked deforestation in the area has increased sediment in the river thus reducing the efficiency of the power plant, and the cost of constructing the dam accounts for a sizeable chunk of all Guatemala's considerable foreign-debt payments. Villagers displaced by the huge project are still fighting for compensation from the government more than twenty years after it was completed.

The first place at the upper end of the valley is **Tamahú**, 15km below which the town of **Tucurú** marks the point where the valley starts to open out and the river loses its frantic energy. In the hills above Tucurú is the spectacular **Chelemhá forest reserve**, where quetzals are common and there's a fine ecolodge (see p.230).

Continuing down the highway beyond Tucurú the road plunges abruptly, with cattle pastures starting to take the place of the coffee bushes. After 28km you reach **LA TINTA**, a sprawling town with at least one **place to stay**. Continuing east, it's just 13km to **TELEMÁN**, the largest of the squalid trading centres in this lower section of the valley.

Senahú and the Cuevas de Seamay

From Telemán a side road branches off to the north and climbs high into the fecund hills to the town of **SENAHÚ**, an important coffee centre that sits in a steep-sided bowl. Hikes run from here to the nearby **Cuevas de Seamay**, used by Maya shamen for ceremonies, and a track heads north to Semuc Champey and Lanquín, which is passable in dry season by 4WD.

Panzós

Heading on down the Polochic valley from Telemán you soon reach the large town of **PANZÓS**, which was where the old Verapaz railway ended. In 1978 Panzós made international headlines when 53 protesting campesinos (including women and children) were killed by the army and police, one of the earliest massacres of General Lucas García's regime.

ARRIVAL AND DEPARTURE   **THE POLOCHIC VALLEY**

By bus Buses from Cobán for all towns on the Polochic valley leave at least hourly. From the highway, pick-ups and trucks head up side roads to settlements including Senahú and Cahabón. From Panzós buses run to Cobán (hourly; 6hr) via Telemán. Regular buses shuttle between Telemán and Senahú.

ACCOMMODATION AND EATING

CHELEMHÁ

★ **Maya Cloud Forest Lodge** ☎ 5308 5160, ⓦ chelemha.org. A fine Swiss-managed ecolodge with stunning views of the cloudforest that's very popular with birders: quetzals are present in numbers in the area, as are rare warblers, the highland guan (and some very vocal howler monkeys). The main cabin has four comfortable rooms, each with private bathroom, and there's a wonderful observation deck and good meals (US$7–12) in the restaurant. Expert guides are available and there are fine trails to explore. The lodge is 26km north of Tucurú via a dirt road (4WD only). US$100

TELEMÁN

Hotel de los Ralda ☎ 7983 1458. An agreeable family-run place which offers rooms with hot water and fans. US$12

SENAHÚ

Hotel El Recreo Senahú Parque Central ☎ 7983 1779. A pleasant comfortable option where rooms have private bathrooms and hot water. Guides for the Cuevas de Seamay can be arranged here. US$22

Cobán

The heart of this misty alpine land and the capital of the department is **COBÁN**, Guatemala's principal centre for gourmet **coffee** production. Your initial impression of the town may not be that favourable – heavy traffic crawls past the central plaza and the main downtown shopping district is pretty nondescript – but away from here Cobán soon reveals its charms. It's not a large place (the population is around 65,000) and suburbs fuse gently with outlying meadows and pine forests, giving the town the air of an overgrown mountain village.

If the rain sets in, Cobán's atmosphere can become a bit subdued, and in the evenings the air is often damp and cool. The sun does put in an appearance most days, though, and the town certainly makes a useful base for a day or two. Sights include an excellent little Maya archeological museum, an orchid nursery, coffee and tea farms, and you'll find genteel cafés where you can sample a cup made from the world-renowned Verapaz bean. Outside the town, the spectacular mountains and rivers hold all kinds of exciting **ecotourism** possibilities, many of which can be done as day-trips.

Like many other Guatemalan towns, Cobán is divided into a number of **zonas**, with the northeast corner of the **plaza** at 1 Calle and 1 Avenida the dividing point. Zona 1 is to the northwest, Zona 2 to the southwest, Zona 3 to the southeast and Zona 4 to the northeast.

Parque Central

From Cobán's elevated, triangular **parque central**, the town drops away on all sides. The plaza is dominated by the **cathedral**, which is worth peering into to see the remains of a massive, ancient, cracked church bell. A block behind, the **market** bustles with trade during the day and is surrounded by food stalls at night. Cobán's prosperity from coffee (and more recently cardamom and allspice) has built the colonial-style hotels and coffeehouses in the streets around the plaza. Hints of the days of German control are also evident here and there in the town's architecture, which incorporates the occasional suggestion of Bavarian grandeur.

Finca Santa Margarita

3 C 4–12, Zona 2 • Mon–Fri 8am–12.30pm & 1.30–5pm, Sat 8am–noon • US$4 • ☎ 7951 3067

For a closer look at Cobán's principal crop, take the guided tour offered by the **Finca Santa Margarita**, a coffee plantation just south of the centre. The interesting tour (an English-speaking guide is usually available) covers the history of the finca, founded by the Dieseldorff family in 1888, and examines all the stages of cultivation and production, including a walk through the grounds. You also get a chance to sample different low-, middle- and high-altitude arabica coffee blends and, of course, purchase some beans.

Museo El Príncipe Maya

6 Av 4–26, Zona 3 • Mon–Sat 9am–5.45pm • US$2 • ☎ 7952 2809

Several blocks southeast of the plaza you'll find an excellent assembly of Maya artefacts and carvings inside the small **Museo El Príncipe Maya**. The museum has some fine shell necklaces, polychrome bowls, jade earrings and a plethora of clay figurines, including warriors wearing animal masks. Don't miss the eccentric flints, an early Classic urn or the main attraction – a stunning panel from a Cancuén altarpiece, embellished with 160 glyphs.

5

El Calvario

Off 3 C, Zona 1

A short stroll northwest of the centre, the church of **El Calvario** is one of Cobán's most intriguing sights. Steep steps lead up via the Stations of the Cross – blackened by candle smoke and decorated with scattered offerings. There's a commanding view over the town from the whitewashed church, which has a distinctly pagan aura, often filled with candles, incense and corn cobs. The Calvario attracts many Maya worshippers, has both Christian and Maya crosses and the Sundays services are in the Q'eqchi' language.

Parque Nacional Las Victorias

Zona 1 • Daily 8am–4.30pm • US$1

Next to El Calvario, the **Parque Nacional Las Victorias** is Cobán's green lung, and a great place to stroll through the pines along attractive pathways; there's a children's playground too, and you'll find excellent trails for running or walking.

Chirrepeco tea plantation

Km 217 Cobán–San Juan Chamelco rd • Daily 8am–4.30pm • Tour (1hr 30min) including guide US$4 • ☎ 7950 0306, ⓦ techirrepeco.com • Take a micro for San Juan Chamelco and get the driver to stop at Finca Chirrepeco

Coffee is not the only crop in these parts, and this organic tea plantation, about 4km southeast of Cobán, offers highly informative tours of the full process: planting, cultivation techniques, harvesting and packaging. There's a small museum, and the tour also takes in some caves sacred to the Maya and, of course, finishes with a brew.

Vivero Verapaz

2.5km southwest of centre • Daily 9am–noon & 2–4pm • US$1.30 • Taxis charge US$2.50, or jump on a micro heading for Tontem from 3 C, Zona 2

This fascinating nursery, the **Vivero Verapaz** is dedicated to orchids, which flourish in Cobán's damp climate. The farm produces some seven hundred indigenous varieties, as well as a handful of hybrids. The plants are nurtured in a wonderfully shaded environment, and a farm worker will show you around and point out the most spectacular buds, which are at their best between November and February.

To get here on foot take Diagonal 4, turn left at the bottom of the hill, cross the bridge and follow the road.

ARRIVAL AND DEPARTURE   COBÁN

By bus Unfortunately, most public transport arriving in Cobán drops you on the outskirts of town (with the exception of Monja Blanca buses from Guatemala City). The muddy main bus terminal to the north of the city, also known as Campo Dos terminal, has services to Chisec, Sayaxché, Flores, Uspantán, Nebaj, Salamá and Playa Grande. From Campo Dos it's a 20min walk or US$2 taxi ride to the central plaza. Buses for Lanquín use a bus stop at the junction of 3 Av and 6 C on the northeast side of town. Buses down the Polochic valley to El Estor leave from 3 Av and 3 C, Zona 4. For San Juan Chamelco micros leave from the bridge at the bottom of 1 Av A, Zona 3. Monja Blanca pullman buses for Guatemala City have a terminal at 2 C 3–77, Zona 4 (☎7951 1793, ⓦtmb.com.gt); all these buses pass the Biotopo del Quetzal.

Destinations Chisec (every 30min; 1hr 30min); El Estor (hourly; 7hr); Flores (1 daily at 1pm or change in Sayaxché; 6hr); Fray Bartolomé de las Casas (hourly; 2hr 30min); Guatemala City (every 30min; 2am–6pm; 4hr 30min); Lanquín (hourly 6am–6pm; 2hr 15min); Nebaj (1 daily at 5am or travel via Uspantán; 6hr); Playa Grande (every 30min; 4hr); Raxrujá (every 30min; 2hr); San Juan Chalmeco (every 10min; 15min); Sayaxché (hourly; 4hr); Uspantán (hourly; 3hr), though road is prone to landslides (see box, p.230).

By shuttle bus Adrenalina Tours 1 C 5–23, Zona 1 (☎7932 5858, ⓦadrenalinatours.com), offers shuttle buses to Antigua (1 daily; 5hr; US$35); Flores (1 daily; 5hr 30min; US$30); and Guatemala City (1 daily; 4hr 30min; US$35) with other destinations including Panajachel and Quetzaltenango (US$50; 8hr 30min) available with a minimum of two passengers.

COBÁN

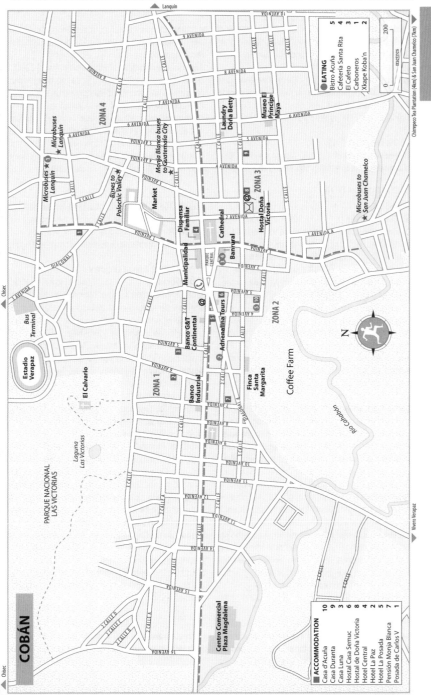

ZONA 4

ZONA 3

ZONA 2

ZONA 1

Lanquín

★ Microbuses Lanquín

★ Microbuses Lanquín

Buses to Polochic Valley ★

Marja Blanca buses to Guatemala City

★ Microbuses to San Juan Chamelco

Chirrepeco Tea Plantation (4km) & San Juan Chamelco (7km)

Vivero Verapaz

Ohisec

Ohisec

Ohisec

Laundry Doña Betty

Museo El Príncipe Maya

Market

Dispensa Familiar

Cathedral

Banrural

Hostal Doña Victoria

Municipalidad

PARQUE CENTRAL

Banco G&T Continental

Banco Industrial

Adrenalina Tours

Estadio Verapaz

Bus Terminal

El Calvario

Laguna Las Victorias

PARQUE NACIONAL LAS VICTORIAS

Finca Santa Margarita

Coffee Farm

Río Cahabón

Centro Comercial Plaza Magdalena

N

	EATING	
Bistro Acuña		5
Cafetería Santa Rita		4
El Cafeto		3
Carboneros		1
Xkape Koba'n		2

0   200
metres

■ ACCOMMODATION	
Casa d'Acuña	10
Casa Duranta	9
Casa Luna	3
Hostal Casa Semuc	6
Hostal de Doña Victoria	8
Hotel Central	4
Hotel La Paz	2
Hotel La Posada	5
Pensión Monja Blanca	7
Posada de Carlos V	1

INFORMATION AND TOURS

Tourist information There is no tourist office in town. Staff at Adrenalina Tours are helpful. Tours to Semuc Champey are offered by most hotels and every agent in town. For remote areas of the Verapaces, contact Proyecto Eco-Quetzal.

Spanish schools Cobán's easy-going atmosphere and relative lack of English-speakers makes it a good place to pick up Spanish. Oxford Language Center, 1 C 14–80, Zona 2 (☎ 5892 7718, ⓦ olcenglish.com) is well regarded.

TOUR OPERATORS

Adrenalina Tours 1 C 5–23, Zona 1 ☎ 7932 5858, ⓦ adrenalinatours.com. Offers trips through the Verapaces including city tours of Cobán, coffee fincas, Candelaria caves, Semuc Champey and the Yalijux mountains for quetzal spotting.

Aventuras Turísticas Inside *Hostal Doña Victoria*, 3 C 2–38, Zona 3 ⓦ aventurasturisticas.com. Trips across both Verapaz departments including Semuc Champey and Laguna Lachúa.

Proyecto Eco-Quetzal 2 C 14–36, Zona 1 ☎ 7952 1047, ⓦ ecoquetzal.org. Adventure and cultural tourism specialist that enables visitors to get off the beaten track. Offers well-priced (around US$50 for two days) ecotourism trips to the Chicacnab cloudforest and beautiful Río Ik'bolay region (see p.244) that benefit poor communities.

ACCOMMODATION

BUDGET

★ **Casa d'Acuña** 4 C 3–11, Zona 2 ☎ 7951 0449, ⓦ casadeacuna.com. A long-running travellers' lodge, this fine place has good four-bed dorms and a couple of private doubles (all with shared bathrooms) set to one side of a simply gorgeous colonial courtyard restaurant (see p.236). As your bed for the night is cheap, make sure you indulge in a meal while you're here. Tours can be booked too. Dorms US$7, doubles US$13

Casa Luna 5 Av 2–28, Zona 1 ☎ 7951 3528, ⓦ cobantravels.com. This backpacker haunt is well run by Lionel, a fluent English-speaker, and his family. There are spacious rooms and a dorm (none with private bathrooms) around a pleasant courtyard garden with hammocks, and there's a TV lounge. Tours and shuttle buses can be booked, and breakfast is included. Dorms US$7.50, doubles US$20

Hostal Casa Semuc 3 Av 2–12, Zona 2 ☎ 7951 4505. Just below the plaza, this excellent new place offers secure, high-quality budget accommodation in a lovely old house. There's a good dorm, plus eleven smallish, very clean private rooms with good mattresses. An airy guests' living room with sofas and internet access (US$0.75/hr) completes the picture. Dorms US$7, doubles US$13

Hotel Central 1 C 1–79, Zona 4 ☎ 7952 1442, ⓔ hotel centraldecoban@yahoo.com. Ageing hotel with decent if plain rooms around a central courtyard. The rooms are a little dark but all have private bathrooms and there's wi-fi. US$23

Hotel La Paz 6 Av 2–19, Zona 1 ☎ 7952 1358. This safe, pleasant budget hotel, run by a very vigilant señora, has clean rooms that face open corridor or courtyard sitting areas. There's a small comedor downstairs. US$11

Pensión Monja Blanca 2 C 6–30, Zona 2 ☎ 7951 1900 or ☎ 7952 0531. Agreeably old-fashioned and has plenty of rooms, many with private bathrooms; the hot water is reliable. The courtyard gardens are lovingly tended, and don't miss the Victorian-style tearoom for breakfast. US$21

MODERATE AND LUXURY

Casa Duranta 3 C 4–46, Zona 3 ☎ 7951 4188, ⓦ casaduranta.com. A lovely, converted colonial house where the bedrooms (7 and 8 are best) are grouped around a wonderful central garden. All rooms have wrought-iron bedsteads and attractive furnishings, though the bathrooms are pretty perfunctory. There's a café and wi-fi; service can be a bit hit and miss though. US$55

Hostal de Doña Victoria 3 C 2–38, Zona 3 ☎ 7951 4213, ⓦ hotelescoban.com. Offering good value, this place is decorated with antiques and artefacts, and oozes character. The bedrooms all have private bathrooms (though avoid the noise-prone streetside rooms). Café/bar, internet and tour agency. US$25

Hotel La Posada 1 C 4–12, Zona 2 ☎ 7952 1495, ⓦ laposadacoban.com. This hotel occupies a four hundred year-old colonial building and boasts a beautiful, antique-furnished interior. Tasteful, comfortable rooms, many with four-poster beds, are set around two leafy courtyards, but traffic noise can be a problem. Good restaurant and café, though no liquors (only beer and wine) are served. US$60

Posada de Carlos V 1 Av 3–44, Zona 1 ☎ 7951 3501, ⓦ hotelcarlosvgt.com. It's set in urban Cobán, but this mountain chalet lookalike would be more at home in the Swiss Alps. The twenty pine-trimmed rooms have cable TV and private bathrooms and there's a restaurant and ample parking. US$30

EATING AND DRINKING

Eating in Cobán comes down to a choice between European-style **restaurants** and local **comedores**. Look out for the local speciality: *kak-ik*, a terrific turkey soup. You'll find the cheapest food at the market, but as it's closed by dusk, head to the street stalls set up around the plaza.

5

★ **Bistro Acuña** 4 C 3–17, Zona 2 ⓦ casadeacuna.com. One of Guatemala's most enjoyable and classy restaurants. It's fantastic for breakfast (a bowl of granola and fruit, or a *desayuno típico*), lunch or dinner – with mains costing US$7 for pasta to around US$12 for exquisite fish and meat dishes. Waiters in starched white uniforms bring out little complimentary appetizers in the evening and the wine list (bottles from US$15) is great. Daily 8am–10pm.

Cafetería Santa Rita 2 C 1–36, Zona 2 ⓣ 7952 1842. An archetypal comedor ideal for cheap, filling *comida típica*, including huge breakfasts, and has friendly service. Daily 8am–8pm.

El Cafeto 2 C 1–36, Zona 2 ⓣ 7951 2850. Right on the plaza, this cosy little place serves coffee (from the local Chijoj finca), including cappuccinos. It's a good bet for breakfast: take your pick from pancakes (US$2), fruit salad,

or a full-on Guatemalan fry-up (from US$2.75). Sandwiches, burgers, hot-dogs and pastas are also served. Daily 7.30am–8pm.

Carboneros 6 C 3–40, Zona 4 ⓣ 5000 9005. This suburban *"Casa de Carne y Más"* serves up delicious grilled meats cooked over charcoal at very moderate prices: plates of chicken, beef or pork are just US$2.50. Daily 10am–9pm.

Xkape Koba'n Diagonal 4 5–13, Zona 2 ⓣ 7951 4152. A wonderful, stylish café/restaurant in a gorgeous old house where the walls are decorated with *huipiles* and local art. There's a very inventive menu with snacks like *tamales* (US$2) and many local recipes including the famous local *kak-ik* turkey soup (US$7.50), and *kakaw-ik* (a chocolate milk drink flavoured with vanilla, chilli and honey). Mon–Sat 8am–6pm.

DIRECTORY

Banks and exchange G&T Continental and Banco Industrial, 1 C west of the plaza; both have ATMs.

Car rental Tabarini, 7 Av 2–27, Zona 2 (ⓣ 7952 1504, ⓦ tabarini.com).

Internet There's an internet café inside *Hostal Doña Victoria*, 3 C 2–38, Zona 3.

Laundry Doña Betty's, 2 C 6–10, Zona 3. Wash and dry service for US$3.50.

Around Cobán: San Juan Chamelco

Seven kilometres southeast of Cobán, **SAN JUAN CHAMELCO** is the most important Q'eqchi' settlement in the area. Some of your fellow bus passengers are likely to be women dressed in traditional costume, wearing beautiful cascades of old coins for earrings. The large **market** around the church sells anything from local farm produce to blue jeans, but very little in the way of crafts.

The church

The town's focal point is a large colonial **church**, whose facade is rather unexpectedly decorated with twin Maya versions of the Habsburg double eagle – undoubtedly a result of the historic German presence in the region. The most significant treasure, the church bell, is hidden in the belfry; it was a gift to the Maya leader Juan Matalbatz from no less than the Holy Roman Emperor Charles V.

Grutas de Rey Marcos

Daily 9am–5pm • US$3.50 including guide service, hard hat and boot rental • Minibuses for the village of Chamil pass close to the caves; they leave regularly from 0 C & 0 Av in Chamelco

Five kilometres east of Chamelco are the **Grutas de Rey Marcos**, a series of **caves** discovered in May 1998. The cave system is more than a kilometre long, though the tour only takes you a little way into the complex – you have to wade across an underground river at one stage to see some of the best stalactites and stalagmites, including one that's a dead ringer for the Leaning Tower of Pisa.

Lanquín and around

Northeast of Cobán, a paved road heads off into the lush hills, connecting a string of coffee fincas. After 46km the road reaches the **Pajal** junction, where a branch road cuts down deep into a valley to **LANQUÍN** (a further 12km away). This sleepy, modest Q'eqchi' village, where Spanish is very much a second language, shelters beneath towering green hills, whose lower slopes are planted with coffee and cardamom bushes. The village itself is very relaxed and quite attractive, but virtually every visitor in town is here to enjoy the extraordinary pools of **Semuc Champey**, a short ride away.

The Lanquín caves

1km west of Lanquín • Daily 8am–6pm • US$4

Just off the road to Cobán, the **Lanquín caves** are a maze of dripping, bat-infested chambers, stretching for at least 3km underground. A walkway has been cut through the first few hundred metres and electric lights have been installed, but it remains dauntingly slippery. Refrain from using flash photography in the cave (it unsettles the bats). It's well worth dropping by the entrance at dusk, when thousands of bats emerge from the mouth of the cave and flutter off into the night. Maya **religious rituals** are held here (particularly at fiesta time and on Dec 5) when the whole village gathers for candlelit ceremonies.

K'anba caves

9km south of Lanquín • US$6.50 • Entrance by guided tour only 8am, 10am, 1pm & 3pm

Just before the entrance to Semuc, the **K'anba cave** system is a lot more fun to explore than Lanquín's caves. Guided spelunking tours involve scrambling and swimming by candlelight through chambers filled with bats and bizarre rock formations. For the brave (or mad) there are the optional additional thrills of climbing a dodgy rope ladder up the side of a 5m waterfall or cliff-jumping into a pool in complete darkness. The tour takes about an hour and a half and finishes with some river tubing.

Semuc Champey

10km south of Lanquín • US$6.50; parking US$1

The region's prime attraction, and one of the most beautiful natural destinations in Guatemala, is **Semuc Champey**, a shallow staircase of sublime turquoise pools suspended on a natural limestone bridge. This idyllic spot sits at the base of a towering jungle-clad valley and makes a wonderful destination for a blissful day's wallowing and swimming. Just a few years ago very few visitors made it to this remote part of Guatemala, but the secret is now definitely out, and the pools are very much a key stop on the backpacking trail between Tikal and the western highlands. That said, you can usually find a peaceful corner without too much difficulty.

If you walk a few hundred metres upstream via a slippery path you come to the river source that feeds Semuc: the fast-flowing **Río Cahabón**, the bulk of which plunges into a cavern, cutting under the pools in an aquatic frenzy before emerging again downstream. For a photo-perfect view of the whole scene, you can hike (and climb a little in sections) for twenty minutes up a slippery, vertiginous trail to a *mirador* high above the pools.

There are security guards at the site, but it's best not to leave your belongings unattended. You'll find a small café (reasonable meals are around US$5) and there are vendors selling drinks and snacks at the entrance.

While you can visit on your own, most travellers choose to visit Semuc as part of a **tour**, which avoids having to wait for infrequent public transport or tackling the terrible dirt access road.

ARRIVAL AND DEPARTURE   **LANQUÍN AND AROUND**

TO LANQUÍN

By bus Public microbuses connect Cobán with Lanquín (hourly 6am–6pm; 2hr 15min). Buses also struggle north

between the Pajal junction and Fray Bartolomé de Las Casas (hourly; 2hr) via a rough road, though ongoing road improvements will speed up this route again in the next

5

few years; check with your hotel for the latest information. Heading east, there are buses to Cahabón (roughly hourly; 1hr 15min), from where one daily bus (at 4am; 4hr) and irregular pick-ups head down to El Estor.

By shuttle bus There are connections from Antigua (2 daily at 2pm; 8hr) and Cobán (3–4 daily; 2hr). Note that service standards on these routes are poor, and minibuses are beat-up and uncomfortable. The Antigua buses are particularly bad and involve travelling at night (which is not recommended). At the time of research *Zephyr Lodge* was about to start up a new Antigua–Lanquín service. On arriving in Lanquín don't listen to what local hustlers tell you about places being full (like *Zephyr*, who don't pay commission); some of these board shuttles buses. There's

also one daily 4WD shuttle pick-up at 7.30am to Río Dulce Town (5 daily; US$20).

TO SEMUC

By truck To get to Semuc Champey without a tour you'll need to catch a pick-up or truck from Lanquín plaza (roughly every 40min until 4pm; 45min). There were direct Cobán-Semuc microbuses until recently but these have been suspended as the Semuc road is in such poor condition.

Tours Tours to Semuc are offered by all the main hotels including *Zephyr* and *El Retiro*, costing US$22 for a full day including tubing and a guide. Several hotels and agencies in Cobán also run trips charging US$45–65 for a day-trip.

ACCOMMODATION AND EATING

Places to stay are both in and around the village of **Lanquín**, and strung out along the road to **Semuc**. Many are hostel-style places geared towards backpackers, but there are also basic guesthouses in the village that will do for a night.

Hostal El Portal 100m from Semuc ☎5319 6848, ⓦhostalelportaldechampey.com. Community-owned lodge, run by a very helpful team, that enjoys a superb elevated plot with fine views down to the Río Cahabón. The accommodation is very inviting, with well-built screened wood cabañas with hammocks and balcony, cosy private rooms and an eight-bed dorm. Bathrooms are well presented. There's good food, they sell wine and cold beers, and you'll find camping space and great birding too. Tubing and other trips are offered. Dorms US$5, rooms US$10

Posada Illobal Past the market and bank in the village centre ☎7983 0014. The best of the village cheapies, with a nice garden and five plain, clean rooms in an old wooden house, some with valley views. Run by the very friendly owner Ramiro Pop. US$11

El Retiro On the banks of the Río Lanquín ☎4513 6396, ⓦelretirolanquin.com. This near-legendary riverside lodge has undergone a change of ownership and standards have slipped a notch or two. The setting is still

lovely, and accommodation is well designed, consisting of four-bed dorms, cabins and rooms, some with private bathrooms. Draws a young backpacker crowd with drinks specials most nights and a gregarious vibe. Buffet-style dinners are served. Dorms US$5, rooms US$10

★ **Zephyr Lodge** Just north of village centre ☎5168 2441, ✉zephyrlodgelanquin@gmail.com. A wonderful lodge, set on a little spur of land that offers stunning views over the Lanquín river valley. A lot of thought has gone into the design, and the bar/restaurant and fine accommodation – dorms, doubles and two-storey cabañas – enjoy a great perspective of the evergreen Verapaz hills. Staff could not be more helpful, the food is great with plenty of veggie choices, cocktails are the best in town, fine tours are offered and there's free wi-fi and purified water. A hot tub and swimming pool are planned too. The British/Dutch owners are very switched on to travellers' needs. Reserve ahead – it's often full. Dorms US$5, doubles US$20, cabañas US$17

DIRECTORY

Banks and exchange Banrural, south of plaza, changes US dollars (but has no ATM).

Internet There's fast wi-fi in *Zephyr Lodge* and a little internet café on the plaza.

Cahabón

Beyond Lanquín the road continues to the small town of **CAHABÓN**, 24km to the east, where there are only basic hospedajes. From here a dirt track spirals around switchbacks to Panzós, cutting high over the mountains then plunging down through spectacular scenery.

ARRIVAL AND DEPARTURE

CAHABÓN

By bus One daily bus (at 4am) makes the 4hr trip to El Estor, while pick-ups ply the route more frequently. There are roughly hourly connections to Cobán via Lanquín (last

bus is 3pm).

Destinations Cobán (about every 90min; 3hr); El Estor (1 daily; 4hr); Lanquín (hourly; 1hr 15min).

Northern Alta Verapaz

In the northern section of Alta Verapaz, the lush hills drop away steeply onto the plain that marks the frontier with the department of **Petén**. The terrain is a beguiling mix of dense patches of rainforest, towering tooth-like outcrops of limestone called karsts, and pastureland. Some of the most extensive **cave systems** in Latin America are located here, particularly in the **Candelaria** region, which is riddled with caverns. The paved highway runs north from Cobán, passing **Parque Hun Nal Ye** and **Chisec**, from where you can explore Bombil Pek cavern and Lagunas de Sepalau, then skirts the ruins of **Cancuén**. Otherwise it's dirt tracks all the way, including a branch road that leads to the spectacular, remote lake of **Laguna Lachúa**.

Parque Hun Nal Ye

Turn-off at km 295 on Cobán–Chisec highway, then 10km east along dirt rd • Wed–Sun 8am–6pm • US$10, children US$5 • ☎ 7951 5921, ⓦ parquehunnalye.com

This well-organized **eco-park** encompasses 135 hectares of rainforest, lagoons, a waterfall and verdant hills rich with wildlife including toucans, amphibians and reptiles. A multitude of activities are on offer: zip-lining, horseriding, hiking, tubing, boating and canopy tours. There's also a small **museum** dedicated to the important Maya relics found here including a highly unusual stone box carved with glyphs. **Accommodation** (around US$80 a double) is in attractive colonial-style rooms, with various packages available.

Chisec and around

Some 60km north of Cobán, **CHISEC** is a quiet, agreeable little town spread out along the highway that's grown quickly in the last few years as land-hungry migrants have moved into the region. It's one of the very few places in Guatemala without a church on its huge central plaza – many of its population are former guerrillas and *repatriados* opposed to religious influence.

Bombil Pek

3km north of Chisec • Daily 8am–3.30pm • Guided tour US$9

Chisec makes the perfect base for visiting two remarkable natural attractions, the nearest being the "painted cave" of **Bombil Pek**. There's a community-run guide office a kilometre north of Chisec, right on the highway, where you pay your entrance fee and collect a flashlight; they also rent **tubes** (US$3; best July–Oct) for river exploration here. A guide leads you along a delightful forty-minute hike through the *milpa* fields and forest, and down a steep, slippery wooden staircase into the sinkhole and its vast 50m-high main cavern. Many ceramics have been found here, and the cave is still used for Maya religious ceremonies.

Your guide will then try to persuade you to squeeze through a tiny hole at the rear to a second, much smaller cave where the faded painted images of two monkeys, possibly representing the hero twins of the Popol Vuh (see box, p.130), adorn the walls.

Lagunas de Sepalau

10km southeast of Chisec • US$5.50 • Pick-ups run all day from the town's plaza, and there's a bus at 11am

The three exquisite jade lakes of **Lagunas de Sepalau**, Chisec's other outstanding attraction, are easily visited. You'll be dropped off at the Q'eqchi' village of **Sepalau Cataltzul**, where entrance fees are collected. While you're here, ask to see the new secondary school which has been built from recycled plastic bottles and inorganic waste.

A local guide will accompany you to the lagoons, 1km further away, where there are *lanchas* for paddling across the water (and lifejackets). **Laguna Paraíso**, the first lake, is ringed by untouched dense jungle and has beautiful turquoise water; the second, **Atsam'ja**, is much smaller. The third and largest lake, **Q'ekija**, another kilometre down the track, is the most remarkable of all – a gorgeous blue-green colour, its near-vertical limestone sides backed by towering jungle. It's perfect for swimming. You'll almost certainly hear howler monkeys and see kingfishers and perhaps toucans, and there are jaguars in the region, too.

ARRIVAL AND INFORMATION

Microbuses Microbuses connect Cobán with Chisec (every 30min; 1hr 30min), and also run to/from Raxrujá via Candelaria (every 30min; 45min).

CHISEC AND AROUND

Tourist information Consult ⓦ puertamundomaya.com for information about this fascinating region.

ACCOMMODATION

Hotel Bombil Pek On highway, 1.25km north of the plaza ☎ 4853 3565, ✉ bombilpek_viavictoria@hotmail .com. This good new place (also known as *Via Victoria*) has eight modern semi-detached cottages, with fan or a/c, and all with two double beds and modern furnishings. They're priced per person so represent a good deal for solo travellers. US$30

Hotel Estancia de la Virgen On highway, 800m north of the plaza ☎ 5514 7444, ⓦ hotelestanciadelavirgen .com. Huge hotel with four floors of plain, functional rooms with cable TV and either a/c or fan. There's a good restaurant and small swimming pool for cooling off. US$20

EATING

Don Miguel About 300m north of the plaza. This place styles itself as a "mini-restaurant", with tasty snacks and Guatemalan staples for US$2.50–5. Daily 8am–9pm.

Restaurant Bombil Pek On highway, at the southern end of the village ☎ 4853 3565. Large, clean, welcoming place, excellent for filling *comida típica*, if a bit pricey at around US$5 a meal, and more for fish. Daily 7.30am–8.30pm.

DIRECTORY

Banks and exchange Banco Agromercantil on the plaza, and has an ATM.

Internet There's a place next door to *Don Miguel*.

Candelaria caves

The limestone mountains in northern Alta Verapaz are full of caves, of which the most impressive and extensive are those at **Candelaria**, northeast of Chisec. Here the Río Candelaria has formed an astonishingly complex system of caverns and passages, occasionally penetrated by skylights from the surface. The Candelaria cave network extends for 22km (though if you include all the subsidiary systems it's more like 80km) and includes some truly monumental chambers.

It's quite straightforward to visit part of this cave network, but rather confusingly, there are four possible entrances. Two are community-run (**Candelaria Camposanto** and **Mucbilhá**) and two are privately owned (**Cuevas de Candelaria** and **Cuevas de los Nacimientos**); the two most impressive sections are the latter two options.

Candelaria Camposanto caves

Km 309 Cobán–Raxrujá highway • US$5.50, tubing US$7

At **Candelaria Camposanto** there are two main caves: Entrada de Sol – measuring some 70m in length and 30m in width – and the smaller Murciélago, where you might see some bats, and perhaps hear the roar of the howler monkeys that live nearby. An interpretive trail leads from the highway to the caves, with information panels about the fruits, plants and trees, wildlife and folklore of the region.

Mucbilhá caves

Km 315 Cobán–Raxrujá highway • US$5.50, tubing US$7

This similar community tourism project provides access to the **Mucbilhá caves** where guides will lead you to the Venado Seco cavern, a return hike of an hour or so. The tubing trip here follows an underground section of the Río Candelaria.

Complejo Cultural de Candelaria

Km 316.5 Cobán–Raxrujá highway • US$3.50 (minimum three people) including a 1hr tour and a guide to the first cave system • ⓦ cuevasdecandelaria.com

This complex includes some of the most spectacular caverns in the entire region, so if you only have time for one cave system pick this one. The largest cave here is the 200m-long, 60m-wide "Tzul Tacca", where skylight shafts create a spectacular light-show on the rocks and cavern water below. Access is via the grounds of the *Candelaria Lodge*; just follow the path from the highway at the "Cuevas de Candelaria" sign and guides will appear.

Cuevas de los Nacimientos

Access by tour only • ⓦ cuevaslosnacimientos.com

The most memorable way to explore the cave system is on one of the full-day **river tours** (US$17; minimum four people) run by *Hotel Cancuén* in Raxrujá (see below), which visit **Los Nacimientos**, where you can take in the crystalline Cueva Blanca, and involve floating for several hours through bat-filled caverns on a tube.

ARRIVAL AND INFORMATION

Organized trips *Hotel Cancuén* in Raxrujá (see below), organizes tours of Los Nacimientos. Many Cobán travel agents (see p.234) also run trips to the Candelaria area.

By bus All buses travelling between Cobán and Raxrujá

CANDELARIA CAVES

(every 30min) pass by the entrances to Candelaria Camposanto, Mucbilhá and Cuevas de Candelaria. All are signposted and just off the highway.

ACCOMMODATION AND EATING

Candelaria Lodge Km 316.5 on the highway ☏4035 0566, ⓦcuevasdecandelaria.com. Very stylish cabins decorated with art and fabrics, but not all have private bathrooms and they're overpriced. The Guatemalan and

French food is excellent, though again very pricey at US$15 for lunch or dinner. Note there are some rather picky hotel rules. US$100

Raxrujá

RAXRUJÁ is little more than a few streets and some ramshackle buildings straggling round a bridge over the Río Escondido, a tributary of the Pasión, but it does function as a gateway to the extensive ruins of Cancuén and the Candelaria caves, and it offers some decent **accommodation**.

ARRIVAL AND DEPARTURE

By bus/microbus Microbuses leave for Chisec and down to Cobán, and also north to Sayaxché. The rough road south to the Pajal junction (for Lanquín) is being slowly upgraded. At the time of research, you had to head for the nearby town of Fray Bartolomé de Las Casas from where microbuses were departing for Pacal (and on to Cobán). Similarly, the road east via Fray to Modesto Méndez is

RAXRUJÁ

being paved and transport links are sure to improve and journey times drop. Check details in Raxrujá before you set off.

Destinations Cobán (every 30min; 2hr); Fray Bartolomé de Las Casas (every 20min; 20min); Sayaxché (every 30min; 2hr 30min).

ACCOMMODATION AND EATING

Doña Reyna Just north of the main junction in the centre. This comedor looks a little dark, but it's busy for a reason as the food (meals from US$2.50) is fresh, tasty and filling. Daily 7am–8pm.

★ **Hotel Cancuén** Towards the western end of town ☏7983 0720, ⓦcuevaslosnacimientos.com. Getting everything right, this expanding hotel has 48 excellent-value, clean, neat rooms around a large car

park. There are some very smart options available for very moderate rates with cable TV and a/c (US$30), but even the basic rooms are perfectly comfortable and have cold-water bathrooms. Dr César, the friendly owner, also offers great tours to the Cuevas de los Nacimientos and to Cancuén ruins. There's a small comedor on site, plus internet access. US$10–30

5

Fray Bartolomé de Las Casas

Sixteen kilometres east of Raxrujá is the isolated settlement of **FRAY BARTOLOMÉ DE LAS CASAS**, referred to as simply "Fray" or "Las Casas" by locals. The town has several accommodation options and comedores, as well as ATMs and a thriving market. Otherwise, there's nothing of interest here. However, it is a transit point between Alta Verapaz and other popular areas, and as the road to Modesto Méndez should be paved by 2013 some intriguing new routes are opening up.

ARRIVAL AND DEPARTURE

FRAY BARTOLOMÉ DE LAS CASAS

By bus Buses leave the market place bus terminal for Cobán via Raxrujá (and also less frequently via Pacal, which is the junction for Lanquín). There are also regular micros east to Chahal, from where buses continue to the town of Modesto Méndez on the main Petén highway. The roads to Pacal and Modesto Méndez are both being upgraded and transport links should speed up in the next few years.

Destinations Chahal (hourly; 1hr 15min); Cobán, via Chisec (every 30min; 2hr 30min); Cobán via Pajal (at least 5 daily; about 5hr); Poptún via San Luis (2 daily; 5hr).

ACCOMMODATION

Hotel y Restaurante Valle del Sol 3 C 1-00, Zona 1 ☎ 7952 0385, ⓦ hotelvalledelsolgt.com. The best place in town, this hotel has dozens of good-value if plain singles and doubles, all with hot-water bathrooms and TV. The restaurant serves tasty grub, including *kak'ik*. US$13

Cancuén

18km north of Raxrujá • Daily 8am–4pm • US$8 including Spanish-speaking guide

North of Raxrujá is the large Maya site of **Cancuén**, where a huge Classic-period palace has been unearthed. Cancuén was discovered in 1907, but the sheer size of the ruins had been underestimated, and investigations in 1999 revealed the vast scale of the royal enclave here. The site is enigmatic in many ways: uniquely, Cancuén seems to have lacked the usual religious and defensive structures characteristic of Maya cities and appears to have existed as an essentially secular merchant city. The vast amounts of jade, pyrite, obsidian and fine ceramics found recently indicate that this was actually one of the greatest trading centres of the Maya world, with a paved plaza (that may have been a marketplace) covering two square kilometres. Cancuén is thought to have flourished because of its strategic position between the great cities of the lowlands, like Tikal and Calakmul, and the mineral-rich highlands of southern Guatemala.

The site

A trail takes you past the ruined remains of workshops where precious materials including jade were fashioned into jewellery by expert artisans. It continues to a **ball court**, where there are replicas of some beautifully carved markers; one depicts ruler Taj Chan Ahk passing the staff of the ruling dynasty to his son Kan Maax in 795 AD.

Before visiting nobility could enter Cancuén's royal enclave, they'd stop to perform ritual cleansing at a highly unusual ten-metre stone **bathing pool**, then climb a hieroglyphic staircase to the entrance of the elite. The vast, almost ostentatious triple-level **palace** (Structure L7-27) itself has 170 rooms and eleven courtyards. Its sides are adorned with dozens of life-sized stucco figures, and it is Cancuén's most impressive structure.

The trail continues past several stricken **stelae**, and returns through some towering hardwood trees to the modest visitor centre, which has information panels (some with English translations) and a model of the site. Cancuén's very finest carvings lie elsewhere; there's an absolutely stunning altar panel in the Maya museum in Cobán (see p.231).

5

FIESTAS IN COBÁN AND THE VERAPACES

Baja Verapaz is famous for its fiestas. In addition, Cobán hosts the **National Fiesta of Folklore** in August, which is attended by indigenous groups from throughout the country.

JANUARY

15 Tactic, large pilgrimage to the town's Chi-ixim chapel
19–24 Rabinal, most important dates are the 23rd (for the Rabinal Achi dance) and the main day, the 24th
22–25 Tamahú, main day 25th

HOLY WEEK

San Cristóbal Verapaz, big religious processions

MAY

1–4 Santa Cruz Verapaz
4–9 Tucurú, main day 8th

JUNE

9–13 Senahú, main day 13th
21–24 San Juan Chamelco, main day 24th (includes spectacular costumed processions)
24–29 San Pedro Carchá, main day 29th
25–30 Chisec, main day 29th

JULY

20–25 Cubulco, includes the Palo Volador on the final day
21–26 San Cristóbal Verapaz, main day 25th

AUGUST

July 31–Aug 6 Cobán, followed by the National Fiesta of Folklore
11–16 Tactic, main day 15th
22–28 Lanquín, main day 28th

SEPTEMBER

17–21 Salamá, main day 17th
25–29 San Miguel Chicaj, main day 29th
27–30 San Jerónimo, main day 30th

DECEMBER

First week Cobán, orchid exhibition held in town's convent (next to the cathedral)
6–8 El Chol, main day 8th

ARRIVAL AND DEPARTURE   CANCUÉN

By minibus/boat To get to Cancuén, pick-ups and minibuses (approximately hourly) leave Raxrujá for the *aldea* of La Unión 12km to the north, where boatmen will take you by *lancha* (reservations ☎ 5978 1465) for the 30min ride (US$45 return trip for up to sixteen people) along the Río de la Pasión to the site.

ACCOMMODATION

Camping There is a camping area at the ruins with showers and shelters. Per person U̲S̲$̲7̲

Parque Nacional Laguna Lachúa

US$5.50 • On public holidays the park can quickly fill to its 84-person limit; call ahead to reserve your place • ☎ 5861 0088

West of Raxrujá a recently paved highway crosses steamy, thinly populated lowlands – the flatness of the landscape broken periodically by soaring forest-topped karst outcrops – to the magical **Parque Nacional Laguna Lachúa**, a near-circular lake surrounded by a dense tropical jungle. One of the least-visited national parks in Central America, this is a supremely beautiful, tranquil spot, with pristine azure-blue waters perfect for swimming. About 2km in diameter and over 200m deep, Lachúa is thought to be a natural sinkhole in the limestone crust, though its circular shape has led to speculation that it could have been formed by a meteorite impact. The rangers are extremely protective of this magnificent national park, and visitors have to carry back all non-biodegradable material.

The reserve is home to tapir and all the main Central American wild cats, including jaguar, but though these creatures usually prove elusive, you're virtually guaranteed to hear howler monkeys, and armadillos and otters are often seen. There's also an abundance of exotic **birdlife** (around three hundred species have been recorded here), including snail kites and flycatchers, but watch out for mosquitoes.

5

ARRIVAL AND DEPARTURE

LAGUNA LACHÚA

By bus Getting to the Lachúa region is obviously easiest if you take a tour from Cobán (see p.234), but it's not that tough under your own steam. Staff at Lachúa can help with local transport schedules and information. From Cobán bus terminal, minibuses leave every 30min for Playa Grande (2hr 45min) via Chisec and the junction of Xuctzul; this route is now all paved. (There are also slower buses for Playa Grande via Cubilhuitz, which use a dirt track through Salacuím and the three-way junction of San Luís.) Coming from Chisec or Raxrujá, there are buses to Playa Grande (roughly every hour; 2hr), or get to the Xuctzul junction and catch a connection there. There's one daily bus (10am) from Cobán's bus terminal to Rocjá Pomtila; it returns at 3.30am.

ACCOMMODATION

Lachúa Lodge Book in advance ☎ 5861 0088. This fine national park lodge is a sweltering 4km-hike through the forest from the information centre/car park on the highway – there's absolutely no access into the reserve by vehicle. The large wood-and-thatch lodge is divided into well-kept rooms, each with good beds and mosquito nets, or you can camp. You'll have to bring all your own supplies, including drinking water, as there's no restaurant or food store, but you will find a fully equipped kitchen. Per person U̲S̲$̲7̲

Peyán canyon

About 25km southwest of Lachúa, there's another wonderful natural attraction where the turquoise waters of the broad Río Chixoy are forced through a narrow gap in a limestone plateau known as the **Peyán canyon**. This canyon, just four metres wide in places, is best explored by boat, but you can walk to a viewpoint above it in thirty minutes from the isolated village of **Salacuím**, which is on the dirt road between Cubilhuitz and Playa Grande. Ask around for a boatman in Salacuím or hire a local guide for the walk.

Río Ik'Bolay

Entrance US$4; half-day boat trip (up to six people) US$30; guide US$10

Twelve kilometres east of Laguna Lachúa along the road to Chisec is the junction known as San Benito, look out for the excellent roadside *Comedor California* at the turn-off. From here a rough dirt track heads south for 12km to the tiny Q'eqchi' *aldea* of Rocjá Pomtila – the jumping-off point for wonderful boat trips up the **Río Ik'Bolay**. The river journey is extremely scenic, passing banks lined with towering tropical trees, and you're sure to see kingfishers skimming across the water. After 45 minutes a slippery trail climbs up the riverbank, past waterfalls to a *nacimiento* (spring), where you can squat down for a jet-powered bidet.

INFORMATION AND TOURS

RÍO IK'BOLAY

Organized trips A community tourism project in Rocjá Pomtila, run with Eco-Quetzal in Cobán (see p.234) organizes trips here, but you can also just drop by; ask for village coordinator Javier Ca'al (☎ 5381 1970). Meals are available in Rocjá Pomtila village homes for US$3, and a bed for the night is US$3.50.

Playa Grande

The transport hub for this region is the sprawling, dusty town of **PLAYA GRANDE** (also referred to as Cantabal or Ixcán), about 12km west of Laguna Lachúa. This is an authentic frontier settlement of scruffy cinder-block-built houses, Mexico-bound migrants and a few rough bars. It is, however, the main administrative centre for the Ixcán region and has a few hotels and a bank with an ATM.

From Playa Grande it's possible to journey west into northern Huehuetenango, via a once-terrible road which should be completely paved by 2013, opening up a spectacular new route to the Cuchumatanes.

ARRIVAL AND DEPARTURE

PLAYA GRANDE

By bus At the time of research several daily pick-ups and the odd chicken bus were making the journey from Playa Grande to Barillas, a journey of five hours or so. As this section will be paved soon and become part of the Franja Transversal del Norte highway (which will stretch west via Raxrujá to Modesto Méndez), transport links should improve considerably in the next few years and journey times drop. There's also very regular transport to Cobán, and less frequent links to Raxrujá.

Destinations Barillas (roughly hourly until noon; 5hr); Cobán (2hr 45min; every 30min).

ACCOMMODATION AND EATING

Hotel España ☎ 7755 7645. This secure place has three classes of rooms, all with firm beds and some with private bathroom and a/c. There's a comedor here too. US$10

Hotel La Reina Vasty Av Principal ☎ 5514 6693. The smartest option in town offers clean, plain rooms some with a/c. US$30

Petén

TIKAL

Petén

The vast northern department of Petén occupies about a third of Guatemala but contains just over three percent of its population. Both the birthplace and heartland of the ancient Maya civilization, the region is peppered with hundreds of sites, and exploring the temples and palaces is an unforgettable experience. The ruins are surrounded by a huge expanse of tropical rainforest, swamps and savannah, with ancient ceiba and mahogany trees that tower above the forest floor. Petén is also extraordinarily rich in wildlife: some 285 bird species have been sighted at Tikal alone, including hummingbirds, toucans, hawks and wild turkeys. Among the mammals are lumbering tapir, ocelots, jaguars and monkeys, plus thousands of species of plants, reptiles, insects and butterflies.

In the past few decades however, swathes of this uniquely biodiverse environment have been ravaged. Waves of **settlers** have cleared enormous tracts of jungle, while oil companies and commercial loggers have cut roads deep into the forest. The population of Petén, just fifteen thousand in 1950, is today estimated to be around five hundred thousand, a number that puts enormous pressure on the remaining forest. Despite forty percent of Petén being officially protected as the **Reserva de la Biósfera Maya** (Maya Biosphere Reserve), regulations are widely ignored and ecological activists are subject to routine threats.

The hub of the department is **Lago de Petén Itzá**, home to the delightful lakeside settlement of **Flores**, which makes a perfect base. An hour or so away are the astonishing ruins of **Tikal**, Petén's prime attraction, located superbly in a rainforest reserve: no trip to Guatemala would be complete without a visit. Other imposing sites include fascinating, accessible **Yaxhá**, while the ruined cities of the **Lago de Petexbatún** region, particularly **Aguateca**, are spectacular. In terms of scale and historical importance, a trip to the jungle-buried monumental remains of **El Mirador**, a 2500-year old city of superpower status, offers a once-in-a-lifetime experience – if you've the time and energy for the trek to get there that is.

Brief history

For almost two thousand years from 1000 BC onwards, Maya culture reached astounding architectural, scientific and artistic achievements (see p.335). Petén was at the heart of this magnificent culture: great cities rose out of the forest, surrounded by huge areas of raised, irrigated fields and connected by a vast network of causeways. But climatic changes provoked the fall of the Preclassic Maya in northern Petén about AD 150, and, incredibly, history repeated itself seven centuries later when high population densities and a prolonged drought provoked the collapse of the Classic Maya. At the close of the tenth century, the great cities of Petén were abandoned, after which some Maya moved north to Yucatán, where their civilization flourished until the twelfth century.

YAXHÁ

Highlights

❶ Finca Ixobel Kick back and enjoy this rural retreat, set in the pine-clad foothills of the Maya Mountains. **See p.253**

❷ Flores Petén's most attractive settlement is a friendly little historic town, with a cosmopolitan choice of restaurants and cafés. **See p.254**

❸ Tikal Explore the spectacular ruins of an ancient Maya metropolis, set in a protected rainforest reserve that's teeming with wildlife. See p.265

❹ Jungle trekking Hike through the virtually untouched forests of northern Petén to the remote jungle ruins of El Mirador and Nakbé. See p.282

❺ Lago de Petexbatún A beautiful remote lake, fringed by thick rainforest, around whose shores are some fascinating Maya ruins. **See p.284**

❻ Yaxhá The ruins of this once-massive Maya city include a glut of imposing temple pyramids, some from the Preclassic era. **See p.289**

HIGHLIGHTS ARE MARKED ON THE MAP ON PP.250–251

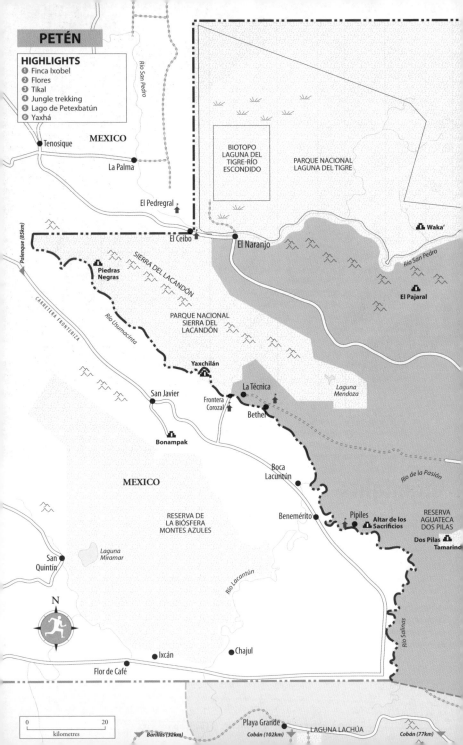

PETÉN

HIGHLIGHTS
1. Finca Ixobel
2. Flores
3. Tikal
4. Jungle trekking
5. Lago de Petexbatún
6. Yaxhá

MEXICO

Tenosique

La Palma

Río San Pedro

Palenque (85km)

CARRETERA FRONTERIZA

El Pedregral

El Ceibo

El Naranjo

BIOTOPO
LAGUNA DEL
TIGRE-RÍO
ESCONDIDO

PARQUE NACIONAL
LAGUNA DEL TIGRE

Waka'

Piedras
Negras

SIERRA DEL LACANDÓN

Río San Pedro

El Pajaral

Río Usumacinta

PARQUE NACIONAL
SIERRA DEL
LACANDÓN

Yaxchilán

San Javier

Frontera
Corozal

La Técnica

Bethel

Laguna
Mendoza

Bonampak

Boca
Lacuntún

Río de la Pasión

MEXICO

RESERVA DE
LA BIÓSFERA
MONTES AZULES

Laguna
Miramar

Benemérito

Pipiles
Altar de los
Sacrificios

RESERVA
AGUATECA
DOS PILAS

Dos Pilas
Tamarind

San
Quintín

Río Lacantún

Río Salinas

N

Ixcán

Chajul

Flor de Café

0   20
kilometres

Barillas (32km)

Playa Grande
Cobán (102km)

LAGUNA LACHÚA

Cobán (77km)

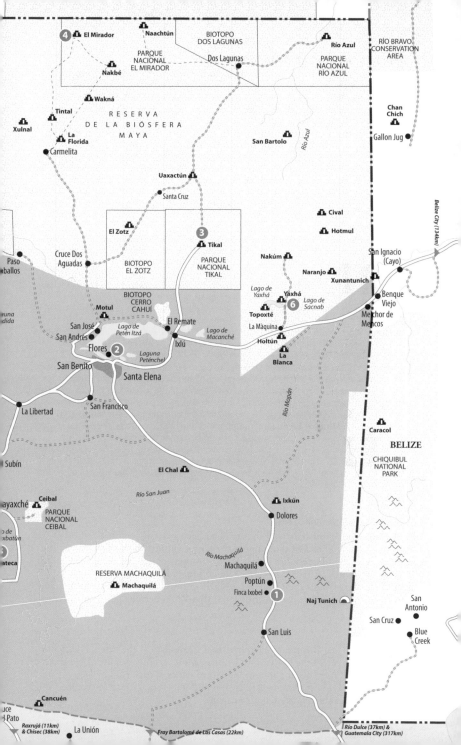

6

THE RESERVA DE LA BIÓSFERA MAYA

In 1974 UNESCO established the idea of **biosphere reserves** in an ambitious attempt to combine the protection of natural areas and the conservation of their genetic diversity with scientific research and sustainable development. The **Reserva de la Biósfera Maya**, created in 1990, covers 16,000 square kilometres of northern Petén: in theory it is the largest tropical forest reserve in Central America.

On the premise that conservation and development can be compatible, land use in the reserve has three designations: **core areas** include the national parks, major archeological sites and the *biotopos*, areas of scientific investigation. The primary role of core areas is to preserve biodiversity; human settlements are prohibited though tourism is permitted. Surrounding the core areas are **multiple-use areas** where inhabitants, aided and encouraged by the government and NGOs, are able to engage in sustainable use of the forest resources and small-scale agriculture. The **buffer zone**, a 15km-wide belt along the southern edge of the reserve, is intended to prevent further human intrusion but contains many existing villages.

Fine in theory, particularly when you consider that much of the reserve borders protected lands in Mexico and Belize. In practice, however, the destruction of Petén's **rainforest** proceeds virtually unchecked in many parts. Less than fifty percent of the original cover remains and illicit logging is reducing it further. Oil exploration is the other industry that has driven the destruction of the forest in the west of the reserve, as petroleum companies have pushed roads deep into the Parque Nacional Laguna del Tigre. Incredibly, successive Guatemalan governments have aided and abetted the oil companies, issuing concessions for exploration. As soon as a road exists, land-hungry migrants follow and slash-and-burn the forest and plant *milpas*, which they farm. After a few years the thin soil is depleted, and cattle ranchers move in. In 2003 the smoke from these fires was so thick that it even affected southern Texas, where children were sent home from school.

Although much has been lost in the west and south of the reserve, environmental groups are fighting to conserve what remains. Foreign funding provides much of the finance for protection, and NGOs are working with settlers to encourage the sustainable use of forest resources. Tourism is an accepted part of the plan and visitors are increasingly getting to remote *biotopos* and national parks – though numbers are still small. The forests and swamps of the **Mirador Basin** (Ⓦ miradorbasin.com) at the core of the reserve are still well preserved and have been spared thanks to the efforts of campaigning archeologists including UCLA's Richard Hansen. In 2008 President Colom announced plans for a Mirador Basin National Park, a proposal that was still in development stage in 2012. It's clear that a wilderness area, with limited or no road access is essential to safeguard what Hansen calls the "Cradle of Maya Civilization".

Colonial and Independence eras

By the time the **Spanish** arrived the area had been partially recolonized by the Itza, a group of Toltec Maya who inhabited the land around Lago de Petén Itzá. The forest proved so impenetrable that it wasn't brought under Spanish control until 1697, more than 150 years after they had conquered the rest of the country, when Tayasal was destroyed. The invaders had little enthusiasm for Petén though, and it remained a backwater. It wasn't until 1970 that Petén became genuinely accessible by road.

Petén today

During the civil war the **guerrilla armies** based themselves in the Petén, and fighting pushed refugees across the border into Mexico. More recently disputes have arisen over land rights, with mass occupations of fincas and national park land by well-organized peasant groups. Drug traffickers have also moved into Petén, flying in cocaine from South America to the region's remote airstrips.

North to Poptún

North of Río Dulce Town, it's 38km to the dull town of **Modesto Méndez** (known as Cadenas locally). Aside from the tempting pools of Las Conchas west of here there's nothing to detain you until you reach Poptún, an area that's home to one of Guatemala's finest rural lodges: **Finca Ixobel**.

Las Conchas

Around 34km west of Modesto Méndez, the huge, broad waterfalls of **Las Conchas** lie at the confluence of the rivers Chiyú and Chahal. These sublime pools are great for swimming, and are well off the tourist trail, so there are no crowds. Minibuses (about every hour) heading west from Cadenas towards Fray Bartolomé de Las Casas pass within 4km of the falls.

6

Poptún

Back on the highway to Flores, the next place of interest is the scruffy town of **POPTÚN**, situated at an altitude of 500m. There's no particular reason to stay here as Finca Ixobel is so close, but there are banks with ATMs and it's served by plenty of buses.

ARRIVAL AND DEPARTURE POPTÚN

By bus and minibus Minibuses shuttle between Poptún and Santa Elena (for Flores) until 6.30pm, while a constant stream of buses and minibuses head south to Río Dulce and on to Guatemala City all day and night.

Destinations Fray Bartolomé de Las Casas (every 2hr; 5hr); Guatemala City (every 30min; 7hr) via Río Dulce Town; Santa Elena (every 30min; 2hr).

ACCOMMODATION

★ Finca Ixobel About 5km south of Poptún ☎ 5410 4307, ⓦ fincaixobel.com. Surrounded by pine forests in the foothills of the Maya Mountains, this farm is a legendary travellers' meeting point. It's a supremely beautiful and relaxing place where you can swim in the pond, walk in the forest and stuff yourself with delicious (mostly organic and home-grown) food. The finca is run ecologically, using solar power and natural composting. You run a tab (dinner costs US$4–8), paying when you leave – which can be a rude awakening. Volunteer workers are usually needed. There are hikes (jungle treks cost US$32/day), horseriding trips (US$13), tubing (US$26) and a famous cave excursion (US$10) as well as internet, wi-fi and a poolside bar. Microbuses and chicken buses will drop you off at the entrance gate from where it's a 15min walk; after dark, take a tuk-tuk here from Poptún (US$2). There's a wide range of accommodation options, from attractive bungalows with two beds and a private bathroom to camping. Bungalows U̲S̲$̲3̲8̲, rooms U̲S̲$̲1̲5̲, rooms with bathroom U̲S̲$̲3̲3̲, dorms U̲S̲$̲5̲, tree houses U̲S̲$̲1̲3̲–̲2̲8̲, camping (per person) U̲S̲$̲4̲.̲5̲0̲

Villa de los Castellanos 6km north of Poptún, on the highway ☎ 7867 4773, ⓦ villadeloscastellanos.com. Offers large, comfortable rustic cabañas with private bathrooms. Speak to Don Placido, the owner, about fascinating excursions to the remote Reserva Machaquilá and its ruins. U̲S̲$̲2̲8̲

Naj Tunich cave

The remote painted cave of **Naj Tunich**, 23km down a rough track from Poptún, has some of the finest cave art of the Maya World, dating back to 100 BC. Due to the fragility of the site, it's not possible to see the original cave paintings, but some excellent replicas can be seen.

Caves were sacred to the ancient Maya, who believed them to be entrances to Xibalbá, the dreaded underworld, and Naj Tunich was one of the most revered sites and a place of pilgrimage. Local artists have re-created some of the extensive hieroglyphic texts, depictions of religious ceremonies and the ball game, as well as the graphic **erotic scenes** thought to be unique to this site.

Tours (around US$36 depending on numbers) of Naj Tunich are organized by *Finca Ixobel* (see p.253) and *Villa de los Castellanos* (see p.253).

Dolores

North of Poptún, it's 26km to **DOLORES**, a dusty, growing town set just east of the highway. There's no reason to stop except to take in the town's impressive **archeological museum** (Mon–Sat 8.30am–4.30pm; US$3.50), which has modern displays, some intricately carved glyph blocks from Ixtutz and artefacts (including some fine incense-burners) from sites including Machaquilá. An hour's walk north of town are the Maya ruins of Ixkún (daily 8am–5pm; US$3.50), a mid-sized site made up of eight plazas.

Flores

Easy-going **FLORES** is a delightfully sedate place with an old-fashioned atmosphere, quite unlike the rest of the region's towns. A cluster of cobbled streets and ageing houses built around a twin-domed church, it sits beautifully on a small island in **Lago de Petén Itzá**, connected to the mainland by a short causeway. The modern emphasis lies across the water in the twin towns of **SANTA ELENA** and **SAN BENITO**, both of which are ugly, chaotic and sprawling places, dusty in the dry season and mud-bound during the rains. Santa Elena, opposite Flores at the other end of the causeway, is strung out between the airport and the market, and takes in a new shopping mall, a few hotels, banks and two bus terminals. San Benito, further west, has even less going for it. The three towns are often lumped together under the single name of Flores.

Today, despite the steady flow of tourists passing through, Flores retains a genteel air, with residents greeting one another courteously in the streets. Though it has little to detain you in itself – a leisurely thirty-minute stroll around the lanes is enough to become entirely familiar with the place – Flores does offer an enjoyable, historic base and has an excellent selection of hotels, restaurants and tour operators.

Brief history

The **lake** is a natural choice for settlement, and its shores were heavily populated in Maya times: the city of **Tayasal**, capital of the Itza, lay on the island that was to become modern Flores. Cortés passed through here in 1525 and left behind a sick horse. In 1618 two Franciscan friars arrived to find the people worshipping a statue of a horse called "Tzimin Chac". Unable to persuade the Maya to renounce their religion, they smashed the image and left the city. The town was eventually destroyed by Martín de Ursúa and an army of 235 in 1697. For the entire colonial period (and indeed up to the 1960s), Flores languished in virtual isolation, having more contact with neighbouring Belize than with the capital.

ARRIVAL AND DEPARTURE	FLORES

BY PLANE

The airport is 3km east of the causeway. Tuk-tuks/taxis charge US$2/3 for a ride between the airport and town. Destinations Guatemala City (3 daily; 50min; from US$235 return), two flights are operated by TACA (☎2470 8222, ☺taca.com) and one by TAG (☎2360 3038, ☺tag .com.gt). Demand is heavy for these flights in peak periods, and over-booking is common. Reserve well in advance and arrive promptly for check-in. Belize City (2 daily; 45min;

US$220 return) with Tropic Air (☎7926 0348, ☺tropicair .com). In early 2012 TAG announced it was to offer direct Flores-Cancun flights; check their website for the latest information.

BY BUS

You'll be dropped off at Santa Elena's large modern Terminal Nuevo on 6 Av about 2km south of the causeway

6

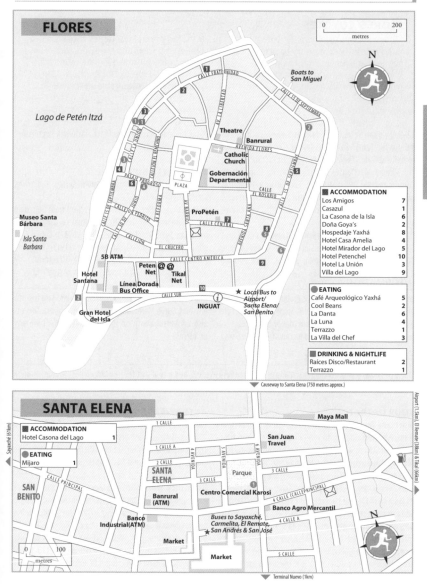

FLORES

0 — 200
metres

N

Lago de Petén Itzá

CALLE FRATERNIDAD

Boats to
San Miguel

Theatre

Banrural

Catholic
Church

AVENIDA FLORES

Gobernación
Departamental

PASEO PROGRESO

PLAZA

Museo Santa
Bárbara

*Isla Santa
Bárbara*

ProPetén

CALLE CENTRAL

CALLE
EL ROSARIO

EL CRUCERO

5B ATM

CALLE CENTRO AMERICA

Hotel
Santana

Peten
Net

@ @

Tikal
Net

Línea Dorada
Bus Office

CALLE SUR

INGUAT

★ Local Bus to
Airport/
Santa Elena/
San Benito

Gran Hotel
del Isla

■ ACCOMMODATION
Los Amigos	7
Casazul	1
La Casona de la Isla	6
Doña Goya's	2
Hospedaje Yaxhá	8
Hotel Casa Amelia	4
Hotel Mirador del Lago	5
Hotel Petenchel	10
Hotel La Unión	3
Villa del Lago	9

● EATING
Café Arqueológico Yaxhá	5
Cool Beans	2
La Danta	6
La Luna	4
Terrazzo	1
La Villa del Chef	3

■ DRINKING & NIGHTLIFE
Raíces Disco/Restaurant	2
Terrazzo	1

▼ Causeway to Santa Elena (750 metres approx.)

SANTA ELENA

Sayaxché (61km)

1 CALLE

Maya Mall

■ ACCOMMODATION
Hotel Casona del Lago	1

1 CALLE A

San Juan
Travel

● EATING
Mijaro	1

2 CALLE A

SANTA
ELENA

Parque

CALLE PRINCIPAL

SAN
BENITO

3 CALLE

Centro Comercial Karosi

Banrural
(ATM)

3 CALLE

4 CALLE (CALLE PRINCIPAL)

Banco Agro Mercantil

Banco
Industrial(ATM)

Buses to Sayaxché,
Carmelita, El Remate,
★ San Andrés & San José

4 CALLE A

Market

5 CALLE

Market

0 — 100
metres

N

Airport (1.5km); El Remate (38km) & Tikal (66km)

▼ Terminal Nuevo (1km)

(though Línea Dorada buses continue on to Flores). Some local buses also use bus stops at the market in Santa Elena, and San Juan Travel use their own private terminal on 6 Av in Santa Elena. Tuk-tuks from Santa Elena to Flores cost US$0.75/ride.

Destinations from Terminal Nuevo Belize City (1 daily at 7am with Línea Dorada; 5hr); Chiquimula (2 daily at 6am & 10am; 7hr 30min); El Ceibo border (12 daily; 4hr);

El Remate (every 30min; 30min); Guatemala City (3 daily at 11am, 9pm & 10pm with ADN; 2 daily at 10am & 9.30pm with Línea Dorada; 16 daily with Fuente del Norte; 2 daily with Rápidos del Sur (8–9hr); La Técnica via Bethel (5 daily); 4hr 30min); Melchor de Menchos (micros every 30min; 2hr 15min); Poptún (hourly; 2hr); San Pedro Sula, Honduras (1 daily at 5.45am with Fuente del Norte; 2 daily at 6am and 10am with María Elena;

6

FLORES' COYOTES

Many travellers experience the hard sell on arrival in Flores from local **ticket touts**, known as **coyotes**. These guys try to get you to book hotel rooms, tours and transport with them, so they can earn a commission. Some lie about hotels being full and even sell fake tickets. Be especially wary on tourist shuttles arriving from Belize and Mexico, when you are likely to be travel-weary and new to the country. Book direct through reputable agencies and hotels.

12–14hr); San Salvador (1 daily at 5.45am with Fuente del Norte; 12hr); Sayaxché (every 30min; 2hr); Tikal (4 daily at 5am, 7am, 9am & 1pm); Uaxactún (2 daily; 2hr 30min). Most buses to Guatemala City stop in both Poptún and Río Dulce en route. For Copán in Honduras catch a bus heading for San Pedro Sula. There are also some services around Lago de Peten Itzá, to San Andrés and San José from here.

Destinations from Market terminal Carmelita (2 daily at 5am & 1pm; around 3hr); San Andrés (every 45min; 30min); San José (every 45min; 35min). There are also

buses to destinations across Petén, including Poptún and Sayaxché, from here.

BY SHUTTLE BUS

You can book shuttle buses through hotels and travel agents.

Destinations Belize City (1 daily at 5am from San Juan Travel terminal; 5hr; US$18); Chetumal (1 daily at 5am from San Juan Travel terminal; 8hr; US$32); Cobán (4hr 30min); Lanquín (1 daily at 9am; 7hr; US$13); Palenque (1 daily at 5am; 8hr; US$30); Tikal (1hr; US$7 return).

INFORMATION

Information *Los Amigos Hostel* is probably the best source of information for budget travellers. Speak to Dieter at *Café Arqueológico Yaxhá* for advice about trips to Maya sites.
Inguat The official tourist board has an office at Av Santa

Ana (daily 8am–4.30pm; ☎7867 5334), and two booths: one on C Sur in Flores and another at the airport. There is also an Asistur booth on the causeway if you have any problems.

TOURS AND ACTIVITIES

Flores has dozens of tour operators, many of them are very average, and lots of coyotes (see box above); you can arrange hikes in El Mirador from here (see p.282).

TOUR OPERATORS

Martsam Travel C 30 Junio ☎7867 5093, ⊛martsam .com. A professional outfit offering well-organized trips to sites including Waka' (El Perú), Yaxhá and Aguateca.
Mayan Adventure Inside *Café Arqueológico Yaxhá*, C 15 de Septiembre ☎5830 2060, ⊛the-mayan-adventure .com. Organizes superb trips to Yaxhá and La Blanca (US$49/head for four people) and ruins including Nakúm, San Clemente and Nixtun Ch'ich'.
San Juan Travel 6 Av, Santa Elena ☎5847 4729. For years this company had a (justifiably) poor reputation for overcharging foreigners. They've recently cleaned up their act somewhat, but it's best to just use them for shuttle services to Tikal, Palenque and Belize City, not other trips. Don't expect service with a smile.
Turismo Aventura 6 Av & 4 C, Santa Elena ☎7926 0398, ⊛toursguatemala.com. A good all-rounder with trips to Maya ruins, tailor-made trips and airline tickets.

ACTIVITIES

Language schools Dos Mundos (C Fraternidad; ☎5830 2060, ⊛flores-spanish.com) has one-on-one, group and crash courses in Spanish. On the other side of the lake, the villages & San José and San Andrés (see p.260) also have schools.
Voluntary work The language schools listed above have programmes for volunteers, including helping women's groups, teaching children and doing environmental work. ARCAS (Asociación de Rescate y Conservación de Vida Silvestre), the Wildlife Rescue and Conservation Association (☎7926 0946, ⊛arcasguatemala.com), runs an inspiring rescue and rehabilitation programme for animals and birds. To volunteer you need to pay $140 a week, which covers food, lodging and transportation.

ACCOMMODATION

There's an excellent range of **hotels** in Flores, including some good budget places, making it unnecessary to stay in noisier, dirtier and traffic-blighted Santa Elena.

FLORES

Los Amigos C Central ☎7867 5975, ⓦamigoshostel
.com. Flores' main backpacker base has plus points
including the courtyard garden, inexpensive room rates,
veggie food, free wi-fi, DVD collection, secure charge points
for cell phones and travel advice. Not so great are the
cramped dorms and rooms, cleanliness (ashtrays are rarely
emptied), slowish service and the 4am Tikal tour exodus
every morning (forget all thoughts of a peaceful lie-in).
Dorms US$5, rooms US$12

Casazul C Fraternidad ☎7867 5451, ⓦcorpetur.com.
Stylishly converted colonial-style house, tastefully
decorated in shades of blue. The large rooms have private
bath, fridge, a/c and TV; some have walk-in wardrobes and
balcony. Free wi-fi. US$46

La Casona de la Isla C 30 de Junio ☎7867 5200,
ⓦcorpetur.com. This gorgeous-looking old hotel has a
decent selection of rooms (those on the upper floors,
particularly 41–43, have the best lake views) with good-
quality beds, a/c and cable TV. Guests have access to a
lakeside terrace, pool, jacuzzi, restaurant/bar and wi-fi.
US$57

Doña Goya's 1 C La Unión ☎7867 5513,
ⓔhospedajedonagoya@yahoo.com. Offers dorm beds
and reasonable, spacious doubles. The rooftop terrace is a
huge bonus, and there's a small breakfast room and internet
facilities downstairs. A second branch of *Doña Goya's* is 20m
around the corner. Dorms US$5, doubles US$12

Hospedaje Yaxhá C 15 Septiembre ☎5830 2060,
ⓦcafeyaxha.com. Fine place above the recommended *Café
Arqueológico Yaxhá* restaurant with well-presented clean
rooms, all with private bathroom and free wi-fi. US$15

Hotel Casa Amelia C La Unión ☎7867 5430,
ⓦhotelcasamelia.com. This four-storey green-and-white
hotel has good-value, very spacious rooms with cable TV,
many with great views of the lake. Single rooms are well
priced here. US$35

Hotel Mirador del Lago C 15 Septiembre ☎7867
5409. You'll find cheap rates and friendly staff here. The
basic rooms have fan, screened windows and bathroom but
no view, while those facing the lake also have cable TV.
There's inexpensive water refills, internet, a laundry service
and a small restaurant. US$10

Hotel Petenchel C Sur ☎7867 5450. On the south side
of the island facing the lake, this little place has a row of
good, clean, double rooms with hot-water bathroom, fan
and TV. There's a little café here too. US$16

Hotel La Unión C La Unión ☎7867 5531. Offering
excellent value, this well-maintained hotel has clean,
bright rooms with private bathroom and fan. Those with
direct lake views cost a bit extra. US$14

Villa del Lago C 15 de Septiembre ☎7867 5181,
ⓦhotelvilladelago.com.gt. Three-storey building with a
great upper-floor terrace with sweeping vistas of the lake.
The rooms are comfortable enough but the decor is
slightly dated; all have a/c and many have great views.
Wi-fi. US$42

SAN MIGUEL

Posada San Miguel San Miguel village ☎7867 5312,
ⓔposadasanmiguel1@gmail.com. A delightful family-
run posada that represents great value, though it's over
the lake in sleepy San Miguel. Large lakeside rooms have
attractive furnishings, private bathroom, TV and stunning
views. There is a small beach directly out front and a
simple comedor downstairs. *Lanchas* (US$0.75) connect
San Miguel with Flores every few minutes. US$16

SANTA ELENA

Hotel Casona del Lago 1 C ☎7952 8700, ⓦcorpetur
.com. Painted in powder blue, this hotel has a colonial feel,
though it's only a few years old. There's a decent-sized pool,
jacuzzi and the 32 rooms all boast two double beds, a/c and
wi-fi. US$98

EATING

Flores has plenty of great places to eat, including many restaurants with lake-facing terraces, though prices are a little
higher than elsewhere in Guatemala.

FLORES

★ **Café Arqueológico Yaxhá** C 15 Septiembre
☎5830 2060, ⓦcafeyaxha.com. An interesting choice,
the menu here boasts many pre-Hispanic dishes of Maya
origin using ingredients like yucca and squash. Most main

dishes are in the US$5–8 range. The walls of the café are
covered with posters and photos relating to local Maya
sites, to which Dieter, the German owner, runs excellent
tours. Evening slide shows about the Maya are well worth
attending too. Daily 7am–9pm.

KNOW YOUR DINNER

Some Flores restaurants serve **wild game**, often listed on menus as *comida silvestre*. Virtually
all this has been taken illegally from reserves and national parks – avoid in particular ordering
items such as *tepescuintle* (paca, a large relation of the guinea pig), *venado* (deer) and *coche de
monte* (peccary, or wild pig).

6

Cool Beans C 15 Septiembre ☎ 5571 9240. This is an atmospheric place, with a thatch-shaded seating area that runs down to a lakeshore garden. The extensive menu features such favourites as pancakes (US$2.75), huge sandwiches (try the shredded carrot, bacon and guacamole) and pasta, as well as mains for US$6–8ish. They also sell draught beer, espresso coffee and cocktails. Free wi-fi. Mon–Fri 7am–10pm, Sat 8am–10pm.

La Danta lakeside ☎ 7926 1993. Stylish new café-restaurant with a lovely lakeside aspect and delicious menu of sandwiches, crêpes, pasta (US$5–6), fish, seafood and meat dishes (try the *chuletas* – chops – barbecued Petén-style). Tues–Sun 1–10pm.

La Luna C 30 de Junio ☎ 7926 3346. Set in a historic building, this classy restaurant has cuisine including carefully prepared fish, French and Italian classics and good vegetarian options like *calebacitas* (stuffed pumpkins). About US$15–20 a head. Daily noon–10pm.

★ **Terrazzo** C La Unión ☎ 7867 5479. Flores' best restaurant boasts an unrivalled upper-level covered deck that catches the breeze, and the cooking is right out the top drawer: chef Juan Pablo has many years of experience. Savour his beef carpaccio (US$6) or fettuccini prepared with grated courgette and shrimps (US$8.50). Get here early for a sundowner. Mon–Sat noon–10pm.

La Villa de Chef C La Unión ☎ 7926 0296. This elegant restaurant has a lovely lookout over the lake from its huge windows and terrace. You'll find lots of vegetarian choices, including Mediterraneo salad (US$4.50), while the beef burgers (US$5.50) are wonderfully flavoursome and filling. However, watch out for annoying extra charges for bread (and even glasses of water). Wi-fi. Daily 7am–10pm.

SANTA ELENA

Mijaro South of the causeway ☎ 7926 1615. Offers good *comida típica* and plenty of meat dishes at local prices, and a daily special for just US$3. Daily 7am–10pm.

DRINKING AND NIGHTLIFE

Raíces Disco/Restaurant Western end of C Sur, Flores. The bar/disco at this lakeside restaurant is the only place in town for dance floor action. Closed Mon. Tues–Sun 8pm–1am.

Terrazzo C La Unión, Flores ☎ 7867 5479. Has a great elevated deck for sunset drinks and the superb cocktails are bargain-priced during happy hour (5–7pm). Mon–Sat noon–10pm.

SHOPPING

La Casa de Jade Inside Café Arqueológico Yaxhá C 15 Septiembre (see p.257). Has excellent jewellery, inspired by classic Maya designs, at fair prices.

DIRECTORY

Banks In Flores there's an ATM on C 30 de Junio. Santa Elena has plenty of banks including two branches of Banrural (both with ATMs) on C Principal. Peten Net (see below) will cash euros, Belizean dollars and Mexican pesos.

Car rental Budget, Hertz, Tabarini (with the widest choice; ☎ 7926 0253, ✉ tabarini.com) operate from the airport. Rates (including insurance) start around US$42 a day for a small car, about US$70 for a 4WD.

Doctor Centro Médico Maya, 4 Av near 3 C in Santa Elena

(☎ 7926 0180) is a professional place, some staff speak a little English here.

Internet and telephone Tikal Net and Peten Net, both on C Centro América in Flores offer fairly quick connections, Skype and discounted international calls.

Laundry Cheapest is Beto's on Av Barrios (wash and dry US$3). Since he runs sunrise tours to Tikal, the shop is often closed until noon.

Post offices In Flores, Av Barrios; in Santa Elena, on C Principal.

Around Flores

The lakeside around Flores has several attractions including a quirky **island museum**, the peaceful villages of **San Andres** and **San José**, the Maya ruins of **Motul**, **Tayasal** and **Nixtun Chi'ch'**, a **zoo** and a **wildlife rehabilitation centre**.

Boatmen in Flores offer **trips around the lake** charging around US$30 to visit two or three of the attractions below. You'll find them waiting for business behind the *Hotel Santana*, in the southwestern corner of Flores and by the public boat dock to San Miguel.

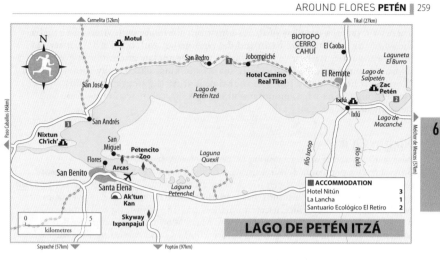

LAGO DE PETÉN ITZÁ

ACCOMMODATION	
Hotel Nitún	3
La Lancha	1
Santuario Ecológico El Retiro	2

Petencito zoo

5km east of San Miguel village • Daily 8am–5pm • US$3

The **Petencito zoo** features a pretty well looked after collection of sluggish local wildlife. Note, though, that the waterslide by the zoo can be dangerous and has caused at least one death. Public boats run to the village of San Miguel (about every 15min; US$0.75) from *Hotel Sabana*, or you can visit on a boat tour.

ARCAS

4km east of San Miguel • Daily 8am–5pm • US$6.50 • ⓦ arcasguatemala.com

ARCAS is a rescue and rehabilitation centre for animals formerly kept as pets or confiscated from wildlife traffickers. There's no public access to the rescue area itself, but there is an environmental education centre, botanical trail and bird observation spot here.

Museo Santa Bárbara

Daily 9am–5pm • US$1.30

Situated on a tiny islet just offshore from *Hotel Santana* in Flores, the **Museo Santa Bárbara** has a small collection of Classic-era Maya ceramics and an incredible assortment of ancient broadcasting equipment (the caretaker's father worked for Radio Petén for years).

Ak'tun Kan

Daily 8am–5pm • US$2.50

This cave is about 2.5km from the Flores causeway, south along 6 Avenida. Otherwise known as *La Cueva de la Serpiente*, the cave is the legendary home of a huge snake. The guard may explain some of the bizarre names given to the various shapes inside, some of which resemble animals and even a marimba.

Skyway Ixpanpajul

10km south of Santa Elena on highway to Poptún • Daily 7am–6pm, plus night safaris • Adults US$25 per activity, children US$15 • ⓦ ixpanpajul.com

At the **Skyway Ixpanpajul**, an amazing system of suspension bridges, cable systems and good stone paths connects 3km of forested hilltops in a private jungle reserve.

There's a monkey's-eye view of the canopy from a *mirador* with views of virtually the whole of the Petén Itzá basin and the zip-line network offers a Tarzan-style jungle encounter. It's best to go in the early morning, late afternoon or even at night, when the wildlife (particularly snakes and kingcacuas) really comes to life; allow a few hours so you can take your time and see the trees and orchids. Horseriding (US$15/hr), mountain biking (US$8), cabin accommodation and camping are offered too.

6

Nixtun Ch'ich'

The only access is via one of the late afternoon boat tours (US$20/person) offered by Mayan Adventure in Flores

Spread over a peninsula about 4km west of Flores, the extensive Maya ruins of **Nixtun Ch'ich'** have barely been touched by archeologists. It's an enormous site, with dozens of small temple mounds and a **triadic temple complex** (ZZ1) over 30m in height that was a magnificent ceremonial centre. The 60m-long ball court ranks as one of the largest ever found in the entire Maya World. A 2007 dig revealed millennia of occupation, beginning before 1000 BC and extending into the early eighteenth century.

Nixtun Ch'ich' is situated on privately owned land (some of which is owned by Manuel Baldizón, Guatemalan presidential candidate in 2012) used for cattle ranching. Virtually all the mounds you see were once temples, but there's been no excavation or restoration so the site looks like a series of grassy hillocks. Wear good boots and expect to encounter cow dung and plenty of mud after heavy rains.

San Andrés

The quiet village of **SAN ANDRÉS** on the north coast of the lake is an interesting traditional settlement where the pace of life is slow and the people courteous and friendly. Most outsiders are students at the two **language schools** (see p.256), and since virtually nobody in the village speaks English, this is an excellent location to immerse yourself in Spanish – though it may be daunting for absolute beginners.

ARRIVAL AND DEPARTURE   SAN ANDRÉS

By bus Microbuses (every 30min; 40min) connect San Andrés with both Santa Elena's market place terminal and Terminal Nuevo.

ACCOMMODATION

Hotel Nitún 3km to the west ☎ 5201 0759, ⓦ nitun .com. Attractive hotel set above the lakeshore with accommodation in stylish stone-and-thatch *casitas*, all with private bathrooms, a restaurant serving superb food (meals are US$20–25 and nonguests are welcome) and a fantastic upper-deck bar/lounge with lake views. Monkey Eco Tours based here organize well-equipped expeditions to remote archeological sites throughout northern Petén. Volunteer workers are accepted from time to time. __US$120__

FOREST GUM

In the past, the mainstay of both San Andrés' and San José's economies was **chicle**, the sap of the sapodilla tree, used in the manufacture of chewing gum. The arduous and poorly paid job of collecting chicle involves setting up camps in the forest, and working for months at a time in the rainy season when the sap is flowing. Today natural chicle has largely been superseded by artificial substitutes, but there is still a demand for the original product, especially in Japan. Other forest products are also collected, including *xate* (pronounced "shatey"), palm leaves used in floral arrangements and exported to North America and Europe; and *pimienta de jamaica*, or allspice. Harvesters (*pimenteros*) use spurs to climb the trees and collect the spice, they then dry it over a fire.

SAN JOSÉ'S SACRED SKULLS

San José is famous for its two **fiestas**. The first, to mark the **patron saint's day**, is held between March 10 and 19 and includes parades and fireworks plus an unusual, comical-looking costumed dance during which a girl (*la chatona*) and a horse skip through the village streets.

The second fiesta is distinctly more pagan, with a unique mass, celebrated in the church on **Halloween** and a festival that continues on into **November 1** – All Saint's Day. For the evening service, one of three venerated human **skulls** (thought to be the remains of early founders of the village, though some claim they were Spanish missionaries) is removed from its glass case inside the church and positioned on the altar for the ceremony. Afterwards, the skull is carried through the village by black-clad skull bearers, accompanied by children dressed in traditional Itza *traje* and hundreds of devotees, many carrying candles and lanterns. The procession weaves through the streets, stopping at around thirty homes, where prayers are said, chants made and the families ask for blessings. In each home, a corn-based drink called *ixpasá* is consumed and special fiesta food is eaten, part of a ceremony that can take over a day to complete.

The exact origin of the event is unclear, but it incorporates a degree of ancestor reverence (or even worship). After all the houses have been visited, the skull is returned to its case in the church, where it remains, and can be seen with the other two skulls, for the rest of the year.

Boats from Flores head across the lake to San José (and back) on the night of the fiesta.

6

San José and around

Just 2km east along the shore from San Andrés, above a lovely bay, **SAN JOSÉ** village is even more relaxed than its neighbour. Take a look at the Catholic **church**, where three sacred skulls are kept in a cabinet: they're paraded through the streets as part of a pagan ceremony on the Day of the Dead each year (see box above). The village is undergoing something of a cultural revival: Itza, the pre-conquest Maya tongue is being taught in the school, and you'll see signs in that language dotted all around.

Asociación Bio-Itzá

Office on C 3 de Mayo • ☏ 7928 8142, ⓦ bioitza.com

The Asociación Bio-Itzá is an excellent community tourism partnership with a well-regarded **Spanish school**, the Bio-Itzá, just above the main dock and parque (US$160 for a week of one-on-one study and homestay with all meals). Students get the chance to help out with the association's projects, which include a **women's cooperative** which sells soaps, creams and shampoos made from natural ingredients like aloe vera. These are produced from plants in the village **botanical garden**, a kilometre inland; visitors are also welcome to drop by for a free tour. One-day tours of the San José area (US$30) are also offered and excursions to a **forest reserve**, rich in wildlife can also be organized (US$40 for two to four people).

ARRIVAL AND DEPARTURE

SAN JOSÉ

By microbus Microbuses (every 45min; 45min) connect San José with both Santa Elena's market terminal and Terminal Nuevo.

ACCOMMODATION AND EATING

Bahía Taitzá ☏ 7928 8125, ⓦ taitza.com. There's only one hotel in San José, but it's a fine one, offering a gorgeous lakeside location including a small beach, and eight lovely airy cottages with exposed stone walls and balconies with fine views. *Taitzá* is owned by a French-Guatemalan couple who look after their guests well; the restaurant (including pizza from a wood-fired oven) is of a high standard. U̲S̲$̲8̲0̲

El Bungalo Right by the lakeshore. For good local meal, this place serves good *comida típica* dishes at fair prices. Daily 7am–8pm.

6

Motul

4km from San José • Free

Some 4km northeast of San José, down a signed track, are the partly restored ruins of the Classic-period settlement of **Motul**. The site, which was historically allied to Tikal, is fairly spread with four plazas, but is little visited. In Plaza B a large stela in front of a looted temple depicts dancing Maya lords. Plaza C is the biggest, with several mounds and courtyards, while Plaza D has the tallest pyramid. It's a tranquil spot, ideal for birdwatching, and probably best visited by bicycle from either of the villages. If you'd rather just chill out for a while by the lake, there are secluded spots east of the village, including a rocky beach with good swimming.

El Remate and around

On the eastern shore of Lago de Petén Itzá, the tranquil village of **EL REMATE** lies midway between Flores and Tikal. The lake is a beautiful turquoise here and swimming is wonderful – an extremely welcome idea after a sweaty morning climbing jungle temples. It's a lovely place to take a break from the rigours of the road, with little traffic and a lot of nature to enjoy, including the adjacent **Biotopo Cerro Cahuí** forest reserve.

There are several high-quality artisan workshops on the lakeshore that sell beautifully carved **wooden handicrafts**; stop by Artesanía Ecológica to see expert carver Rolando Soto at work.

ARRIVAL AND DEPARTURE   EL REMATE

By minibus Getting to El Remate is easy: every minibus to Tikal heads through the village, while minibuses from Santa Elena pass through about every 30min or so. Coming from the Belize border, get off at the Ixlú junction – from here you can walk (it's 2km away) or wait for a ride to El Remate.

ACCOMMODATION

El Remate has an excellent range of budget **hotels** and a few more upmarket options, all strung out around the fringes of the lake. All these places are listed in the order you approach them from the Ixlú junction.

La Mansión del Pájaro Serpiente On right from Ixlú ☏ 5702 9434, ⓦ 30minutesfromtikal.com. This stylish B&B has good, thatched, two-storey stone cabañas, a suite and smaller rooms, all with superb lake views. Wonderful home-cooked food is also available at around US$9/meal, and there's a lovely swimming pool. ̲U̲S̲$̲4̲4̲–̲5̲5̲

Hostal Hermano Pedro On a quiet side road, opposite football pitch ☏ 2261 4181, ⓦ hhpedro.com. This large wooden house has a profusion of good-quality rooms (most with private bath) that open onto a communal decked balcony. There's wi-fi, and a complimentary breakfast. ̲U̲S̲$̲2̲6̲

Hotel Sun Breeze Lakeside, in the centre of the village ☏ 7928 8044, ✉ sunbreezehotel@gmail.com. A fine budget choice as many of the seven good-value, tidy, screened rooms (some with private bathrooms and all with fans) have a lovely perspective over the lake. ̲U̲S̲$̲9̲–̲1̲3̲

Hotel Gardenias By junction for Cerro Cahuí ☏ 5992 3380, ⓦ hotelgardenias.com. This place doesn't look much from the outside but if you pass behind the internet café/travel agency you'll find big, clean rooms with either two or three beds and private hot-water bathrooms; four have a/c. ̲U̲S̲$̲1̲7̲

★ **La Casa de Don David** Centre of village ☏ 7928 8469, ⓦ lacasadedondavid.com. This efficiently run guesthouse, owned by a welcoming Guatemalan-American family, is a beautifully maintained place. Spotless rooms (most with a/c) all face a huge garden that extends down towards the lakeshore, and there are some smart new suites too. Meals are served on an elevated deck that makes the most of the views, and there's excellent independent travel advice and books and magazines to browse. Rates include breakfast and a meal. Rooms ̲U̲S̲$̲4̲6̲, suites ̲U̲S̲$̲7̲0̲

Casa de Doña Tonita 800m down road to Cerro Cahuí ☏ 5701 7114. Popular gringo hangout and one of the cheapest deals in town. Four basic clapboard rooms, built above the lake, with great views, plus a reasonable six-bed

dorm. There's tasty budget-friendly food in the comedor and the owners look after their guests well. Dorms US$3.50, doubles US$7

★ **Mon Ami** 300m past Doña Tonita's ☎ 7928 8413, ⓦ hotelmonami.com. A wonderful place to stay, this French-owned guesthouse is run by Santiago Billy, a likeable and knowledgeable long-term resident of Petén. This is quite a find, with gorgeous rooms and bungalows scattered around a tranquil, forested plot of land. All the accommodation has style and character, enhanced by the use of local textiles and artistic

flourishes, while the dorm is probably the most attractive in Guatemala. There's excellent swimming from the dock, and be sure to treat yourself to a meal here too. Dorms US$7, doubles US$27

Posada del Cerro 300m past Mon Ami ☎ 5376 8722, ⓦ posadadelcerro.com. Above the lakeshore, this stylish family-owned guesthouse has rooms and apartments that blend modern fittings with natural materials in a jungle setting. Note that some bathrooms are not ensuite. Fine meals are offered, though breakfast is not included. Dorm US$13, rooms US$50, apartments US$70

EATING

You'll find simple comedores in the village centre and most hotels have restaurants.

★ **Restaurant Las Orquideas** 800m along the road to Cerro Cahuí. Superb Italian-owned restaurant, serves fine pizza, pasta, *bruchette* and full meals such as carpaccio and baked lake fish. There's wine by the glass, espresso coffee and your hosts are welcoming, preparing food around an open kitchen. Around US$8–16 a head. Tues–Sun 11am–9.30pm.

Mon Ami 300m past Doña Tonita's ☎ 7928 8413. This charming hotel's lake-facing *palapa* restaurant has excellent French and Italian dishes including magnificent shrimps with garlic and butter (US$15), pasta with pesto (US$3.50) and crêpes. There's a set lunch for US$5, wine and wi-fi. Daily 7.30am–10pm.

Biotopo Cerro Cahuí

Daily 7am–5pm • US$5

On the north shore of the lake, 3km west of the centre of El Remate, the **Biotopo Cerro Cahuí** is a wildlife conservation area comprising lakeshore, ponds and some of the best examples of undisturbed tropical forest in Petén. The smallest and most accessible of Petén's *biotopos*, it boasts a rich diversity of plants and animals, and is highly recommended for birdwatchers. There are two hiking trails, a couple of small ruins and *miradores* on the hill above the lake; pick up maps and information at the gate where you sign in.

Jobompiché

West of Cerro Cahuí along the dirt road that parallels the northern side of the lake, you pass the isolated village of **JOBOMPICHÉ**.

ARRIVAL AND DEPARTURE   JOBOMPICHÉ

By bus Buses (5 daily; 1hr) connect Jobompiché with Santa Elena.

ACCOMMODATION

La Lancha Just west of Jobompiché ☎ 7928 8331, ⓦ lalancha.com. A small rustic-chic hotel, with ten very stylish rooms, that are perched on cliffs above Lago de Petén Itzá – though walls are thin in the cheaper options. The hotel, owned by film director Francis Ford Coppola,

enjoys a peaceful location (apart from the local troop of howler monkeys), has a fine pool and gourmet, if pricey, food. Breakfast is included and mountain bikes and canoes are free for guests, but beware all the extra taxes added to the standard tariffs and seasonal variations. US$150

Laguna Macanché and around

East of the Ixlú junction towards Belize, it's 7km to the village of **MACANCHÉ**, on the shore of **Laguna Macanché**, where a signed track leads north for 1.8km to another wonderfully tranquil place to stay, *Santuario Ecológico El Retiro*. On top of the hill behind the base area lie the stone remains of ancient **Maya residential complexes** – but far more intriguing are the numbers of *chultunes* found here. A *chultún* is a gourd-shaped hole carved out of the bedrock, with a very narrow entrance on top capped by a circular stone; some have side chambers. Their exact use is still unknown, though suggested functions include storage cavities, a refuge or a place to conduct ceremonial or religious rites.

Crocodile sanctuary

El Retiro forms part of an extensive private nature reserve and **crocodile sanctuary** that extends along the lake and into two other lagoons beyond. Several **tours** can be organized here. A superb day-trip (US$30 including lunch) involves a forest hike, boat trip across the lake to the gorgeous neighbouring **Laguneta El Burro**, which is surrounded by thick rainforest dotted with Maya ruins, and on to another lagoon and huge limestone sinkhole. Crocodile-spotting night tours, including dinner, a hike and boat trip cost US$40.

6

ACCOMMODATION	**LAGUNA MACANCHÉ**
Santuario Ecológico El Retiro ☎ 5704 1300, 🌐 retiro -guatemala.com. Set in forested grounds on the north shore of the lake are private bungalows with hot shower and shady porch, as well as spacious tents (US$20/head); you can also camp. There's a good restaurant and a dock for	swimming – and the crocodiles are not usually seen at this end of the lake. In the base area is a serpentarium (guided tours are US$5) with more than twenty species of snake including the deadly fer-de-lance, and a venomous beaded lizard. Volunteer workers are usually welcome. <u>US$60</u>

Tikal

Towering above the rainforest, **Tikal**, 68km from Flores down a smooth paved road, is possibly the most magnificent of all Maya sites. The ruins are dominated by five enormous temples, steep-sided limestone pyramids that rise to more than 60m above the forest floor. Around them are thousands of other structures, many semi-strangled by giant roots and still hidden beneath mounds of earth.

The site itself is surrounded by the **Parque Nacional Tikal**, a protected area of some 576 square kilometres that is on the edge of the much larger Reserva de la Biósfera Maya. The sheer scale of the place is overwhelming, and its atmosphere spellbinding. Whether you can spare as little as a morning or as long as a week, it's always worth the trip.

Dawn and dusk are the best times to see wildlife, when the forest canopy bursts into a frenzy of sound and activity. The air fills with the screech of toucans and the roar of howler monkeys, while flocks of parakeets wheel around the temples, and bats launch themselves into the night. With a bit of luck you might even see a grey fox sneak across one of the plazas.

Brief history: The rise and fall of Tikal

According to recent evidence, the first occupants of Tikal arrived around 900 BC, probably attracted by its position above the surrounding seasonal swamps and by the availability of flint for making tools and weapons. For the next four hundred years there's nothing to suggest that it was anything more than a tiny village of thatched huts. By 500 BC, however, the first steps of a modest astronomical stone temple had been constructed. Tikal remained a minor settlement during the latter years of the Middle Preclassic (1000–400 BC), while 50km to the north, towering temples were being built at **Nakbé**, the first city to emerge from the Petén forest.

In around 250 BC the first significant ceremonial structures emerged. A small pyramid was constructed in the Mundo Perdido, and minor temples were built in the **North Acropolis**, though Tikal was still a peripheral settlement at this stage. Dominating the entire region, formidable **El Mirador** (see p.278) was the first Maya "superpower", controlling trade roots across Mesoamerica.

6

Ruling dynasty established

By the time of Christ, the **Great Plaza** had begun to take shape and Tikal was established as an important site. For the next two centuries, art and architecture became increasingly ornate and sophisticated as the great pyramid was enlarged to over 30m in height, its sides adorned by huge stucco masks. **Yax Ehb' Xok** (First Step Shark) established Tikal's first ruling dynasty around 90 AD: a royal lineage recognized by all 33 (known) subsequent kings, until the record fades in 869 AD.

In the Late Preclassic (400 BC–250 AD) the decline of El Mirador presented an opportunity for Tikal and neighbouring Uaxactún to emerge as substantial centres of trade, science and religion. Less than a day's walk apart, the cities engaged in heated competition, and fought a pivotal battle on January 31, 378 AD, when Tikal's warriors overran Uaxactún. The secret of Tikal's success appears to have been its alliance with Teotihuacán (in today's Mexico) and the introduction of new warfare equipment. Inscriptions attest that it was the arrival of a somewhat mysterious warrior, **Siyak K'ak'** (Fire-Born), armed with the latest weapon – an *atlatl* (a wooden sling capable of firing arrows) – that helped seal the victory. It's probable that Siyak K'ak' ordered the execution of incumbent Tikal ruler Jaguar Paw I, initiating a Mexican-directed takeover, for the next king installed at Tikal, **First Crocodile**, was a son of the Mexican king. First Crocodile married into the Tikal dynasty, and started a new royal lineage, though efforts were made to pay careful reverence to the deposed ruler Jaguar Paw I, and his palace (Structure 5D–46) remained a revered royal residence for the next four centuries.

Tikal: fifth century

The victory over Uaxactún established Tikal as the dominant power in central Petén for much of the next five hundred years. During this time it became one of the most elaborate and magnificent of all Maya city-states, monopolizing the crucial lowland trade routes, its influence reaching as far as Copán in Honduras and Yaxchilán on the Usumacinta. The elite immediately launched an extensive rebuilding programme, including a radical remodelling of the North Acropolis and the renovation of most of the city's finest temples. It's clear that Tikal's alliance with Teotihuacán remained an important part of its continuing power.

Yet as Tikal was expanding during the fifth century, a rival Maya "superpower" – **Calakmul**, or the Kingdom of the Snake – was emerging in the jungles to the north. Through an aggressive series of regional alliances, Calakmul steadily encircled Tikal with enemy cities, including Naranjo and Waka' (see p.288), and was courting a potentially devastating alliance with **Caracol**, a powerful emerging city in today's Belize.

Star war

In an apparent attempt to subdue a potential rival, Wak Chan K'awil, or **Double Bird**, the ruler of Tikal, launched an attack on Caracol in 556 AD, but his strategy was only temporarily successful. In 562 AD, Lord Water of Caracol (backed by Calakmul) hit back in a devastating **star war** (a battle timed to an astronomical event like a solstice), which crushed Tikal. Double Bird was almost certainly sacrificed. The victors stamped their authority over Tikal, smashing stelae, desecrating tombs and destroying written records. The subsequent 130-year period has long been referred to as Tikal's "**hiatus**", but some Mayanists have recently re-evaluated this theory as Temple V was constructed in this era. What is clear is that despite the defeat in 562 AD, Tikal was never broken.

Tikal defeats Calakmul

Towards the end of the seventh century Tikal started to recover its lost power under the formidable leadership of Hasaw Chan K'awil, or **Heavenly Standard Bearer** (682–723 AD). During his reign the main ceremonial areas, the East Plaza and the North Acropolis, were completely remodelled. By 695 AD, Tikal was powerful enough to launch an attack against Calakmul, capturing and executing its king, Yich'aak K'ak' (known as **Fiery Claw** or **Jaguar Paw**). The following year, Hasaw Chan K'awil repeated his astonishing coup by capturing **Split Earth**, the new king of Calakmul, and Tikal regained its position as the dominant city in the Maya World.

Tikal's heyday

Hasaw Chan K'awil's leadership gave birth to a revitalized and powerful ruling dynasty: in the hundred years following his death five of Tikal's main temples were built, and his son, Yik'in Chan K'awil, or **Divine Sunset Lord** (who ascended the throne in 734 AD), had his father's body entombed in the magnificent **Temple I**. He also constructed Temple VI, remodelled the Central Acropolis and principal city causeways, and defeated Waka' and Naranjo in 743 and 744 AD, breaking the ring of hostile cities that encircled Tikal.

Around this time, at the height of the Classic period, Tikal's population had grown to somewhere around one hundred thousand (some Mayanists argue for much more) spread across a central area covering about thirty square kilometres. Its authority also extended to include a series of vassal states – a domain of perhaps five hundred thousand subjects. During this time we know the city was called **Mutul** (or Yax Mutul), a name that could be "Great Green Bundle" or a reference to a knot of hair on Tikal's emblem glyph. (Early explorer Morely coined what's surely the most appropriate name for the site – "Place Where the Gods Speak".)

Crisis and abandonment

By the beginning of the ninth century, severe signs of crisis emerged across the entire Maya region. The exact reasons for the Maya's demise remain unclear but there was a period of climate change, including a catastrophic drought, and recent evidence indicates that this could have led to a revolt against the ruling class.

Population levels at Tikal plummeted, as people fled the area. Tikal's last recorded monument is inscribed on Stela 24, completed in 869 AD. By about 900 AD almost the entire lowland Maya civilization had collapsed, and Tikal was effectively abandoned by the end of the tenth century.

Rediscovery

After its abrupt decline little is known of Tikal until 1695 when a lost priest, Father Avendaño, stumbled upon a "variety of old buildings". The colonial powers were distinctly unimpressed by Petén and for the next 150 years the ruins were left to the jungle. In 1848 they were rediscovered by a government expedition led by Modesto Méndez and Ambrosio Tut. English explorer Alfred Maudslay took the first photographs of the ruins in 1881, showing the temples cloaked in tropical vegetation.

Until 1951 the site could only be reached on horseback. The gargantuan project to excavate and restore the site started in 1956 and involved teams from the University of Pennsylvania in the US and Guatemala's Institute of Anthropology. Much of the major work was completed by 1984, but thousands of minor buildings remain buried by roots, shoots and rubble. There's little doubt that an incredible amount is waiting to be found. In 1996 a workman unearthed a stela (Stela 40, dating from 468 AD) while mowing the grass on the Great Plaza. And in 2003 inscriptions discovered at Temple V have provided convincing evidence that Tikal may not have suffered a Classic-era hiatus at all.

The site museums

Museo Sylvanus Morley Mon–Fri 9am–5pm, Sat & Sun 9am–4pm • US$1.30 **Museo Lítico** Mon–Fri 9am–5pm, Sat & Sun 9am–4pm • US$1.30

An impressive new **Tikal Museum** was under construction at Tikal at the time of research, which should open by late 2012. Funded by the Japanese government, it promises to be one of the finest in the Maya World. The plan is to move many of the treasures presently languishing in the vaults of Guatemala City's archeology museum here, and to include lots of audiovisual displays about Tikal and the Maya.

Museo Sylvanus Morely houses ceramics, obsidian eccentric flints, jade jewellery found in Tumba 116 and the magnificent **Stela 31**, which was inaugurated in 445 AD. This limestone monument shows Tikal ruler Siyah Chan K'awil (Stormy Sky) wearing a jaguar head belt and a jade necklace, flanked by two warriors bearing non-Maya Teotihuacán-style spear throwers and darts. There's also a spectacular reconstruction of the great ruler **Hasaw Chan K'awil's tomb**, complete with 180 worked jade items in the form of bracelets, anklets, necklaces and earplugs, and delicately incised bones, including a famous carving depicting deities paddling a canoe to the underworld.

The **Museo Lítico**, inside the visitor centre (see p.274), holds nineteen more stelae, though they are poorly labelled and there's no supplementary information in English.

The ruins

Daily 4am–8pm • Several ticket options (see p.274)

The sheer scale of the ruins at Tikal can at first seem daunting. The **central area**, with its five main temples, forms by far the most impressive section; if you start to explore beyond this, you can ramble seemingly forever in the maze of smaller, **unrestored structures** and complexes. Compared with the scale and magnificence of the main area, they're not that impressive, but armed with a good **map** (the best is in Coe's guide to the ruins, available in the visitor centre), it can be exciting to search for some of the rarely visited outlying sections. Don't even think about exploring the more distant structures without a map; every year at least one tourist gets lost in the jungle.

Complexes Q and R

From the entrance to the ruins, a path bears to the right from the site **map** towards the prosaically named **Complex Q** and **Complex R**, two of the seven sets of twin pyramids. Commissioned by Yax Ain II, also known as **Chitam**, one of Tikal's last-known rulers, they were built to mark the passing of a *katun* (twenty 360-day years). Twinned pyramids are an architectural feature found only in the Tikal region, with several at the city itself, and a few others found at sites nearby (including Nakúm, Yaxhá and Ixlú).

At Complex Q (inaugurated in 771 AD), the first set you come to, only one of the pyramids has been restored, with the stelae and altars re-erected in front of it. Ceremonies are held here by Maya shamen on auspicious days in the Maya calendar. On the north side is a copy of **Stela 22**, its glyphs recording the ascension to the throne of Chitam II, who is portrayed in full regalia complete with an enormous sweeping headdress and jaguar-skin kilt, holding the staff of authority.

Following the path as it bears around to the left after the twin temples of **Complex R** (built in 790 AD), you approach the back of the North Acropolis and East Plaza.

East Plaza

On the north side of the East Plaza, there's a sauna-style **Sweat House** (similar to those used by highland Maya today). Priests and rulers would have taken a sweat bath in order to cleanse themselves before conducting religious rituals. The central section of this plaza consists of a quadrangle of low structures thought to have been a **marketplace**, and just west of here is a small ball court.

The Great Plaza

From the East Plaza, a few steps bring you (via a second ball court) to the **Great Plaza**, the heart of the ancient city. Surrounded by four massive structures, this was the focus

CUTTING-EDGE ARCHITECTURE

Architecturally, **Temple I** was radically different from anything that had been constructed in the Maya region up to that point – an unequivocal statement of confidence no doubt designed to reassert Tikal's position as a dominant power after a long period in the shadow of rival Calakmul. Comprising a series of nine ascending **platforms**, the style emphasizes the vertical dimensions of the temple and draws the eye to the **roof comb**. To create this soaring effect, hundreds of tons of flint and rubble were poured on top of the completed tomb and the temple was built around this, with a staircase of thick plastered blocks running up the front. The monument is topped by a three-room building and a hollow roof comb originally painted in cream, red and possibly green. On the front of the comb it's just possible to make out a seated figure and a stylized serpent.

6

of ceremonial and religious activity at Tikal for around a thousand years. The earliest part is the North Acropolis; the two great temple-pyramids weren't built until the eighth century. Beneath today's grassy plaza lie four layers of paving, the oldest of which dates from about 150 BC and the most recent from 700 AD. The symmetry of the two temples perfectly reflects the Maya's preoccupation with astronomy – during an **equinox** Temple I's shadow "kisses" the base of Temple II, and later in the day Temple II reciprocates the gesture.

Temple I and the tomb of Hasaw Chan K'awil

Temple I, towering 44m above the plaza, is the hallmark of Tikal – it's also known as the Jaguar Temple because of the jaguar carved in its door lintel, though this is now in a museum in Switzerland. The temple was built as a burial monument to contain the magnificent **tomb of Hasaw Chan K'awil**, one of Tikal's greatest rulers, who ascended the throne in 682 AD (see p.266) and defeated the arch-enemy state of Calakmul. It was constructed shortly after his death in 721 AD, under the direction of his son and successor, Yik'in Chan K'awil. Within the tomb at the temple's core, his remains were found facing north, surrounded by an assortment of jade, pearls, seashells, bone ornaments and stingray spines (used for bloodletting).

Temple II

Standing opposite, like a squatter version of Temple I, is **Temple II**, also known as the Temple of the Masks for the two grotesque masks, now heavily eroded, that flank the central stairway. The two temples were arranged to form a twin pyramid alignment, and their construction marked a seminal change to the ceremonial core of the city. Not only was the sheer size of these new temples a powerful statement, but their position purposely deflected attention away from the adjacent North Acropolis, rising above the monuments where Tikal's elite had been buried for at least five hundred years.

Temple II dates from the beginning of the eighth century, and was built to honour Hasaw Chan K'awil's wife, Lady Twelve Macaw. The structure now stands 38m high, although with its roof comb intact it would have equalled Temple I. It's an easy climb up a wooden staircase to the upper level of the structure, where the echo is fantastically clear and crisp; and the view, almost level with the forest canopy, is incredible, with the Great Plaza spread out below.

The North Acropolis

Occupying the whole of the north side of the plaza, Tikal's **North Acropolis** is one of the most complex structures in the entire Maya World. In traditional Maya style it was built and rebuilt on top of itself, and beneath the twelve temples that can be seen today are the remains of about a hundred other structures. As early as 100 BC the Maya had constructed elaborate temples and tombs here; in about 250 AD the entire thing was

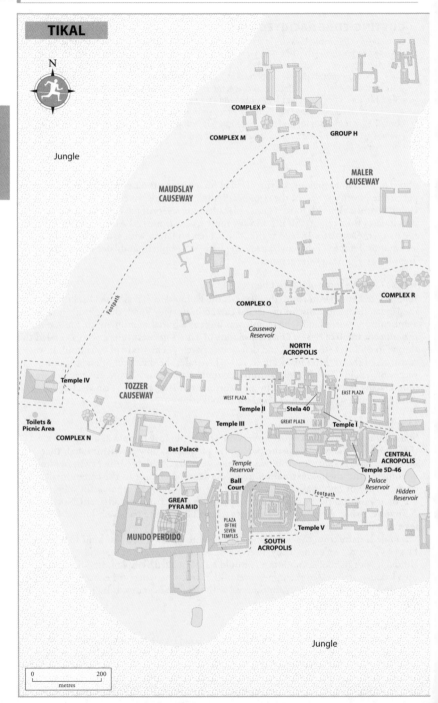

TIKAL

N

Jungle

COMPLEX P

COMPLEX M

GROUP H

MAULER CAUSEWAY

MAUDSLAY CAUSEWAY

Footpath

COMPLEX O

COMPLEX R

Causeway Reservoir

NORTH ACROPOLIS

Temple IV

TOZZER CAUSEWAY

WEST PLAZA

EAST PLAZA

Temple II

Stela 40

GREAT PLAZA

Temple III

Temple I

Toilets & Picnic Area

COMPLEX N

Bat Palace

Temple Reservoir

CENTRAL ACROPOLIS

Temple 5D-46

Palace Reservoir

Hidden Reservoir

Ball Court

Footpath

GREAT PYRAMID

PLAZA OF THE SEVEN TEMPLES

MUNDO PERDIDO

Temple V

SOUTH ACROPOLIS

Jungle

0   200
metres

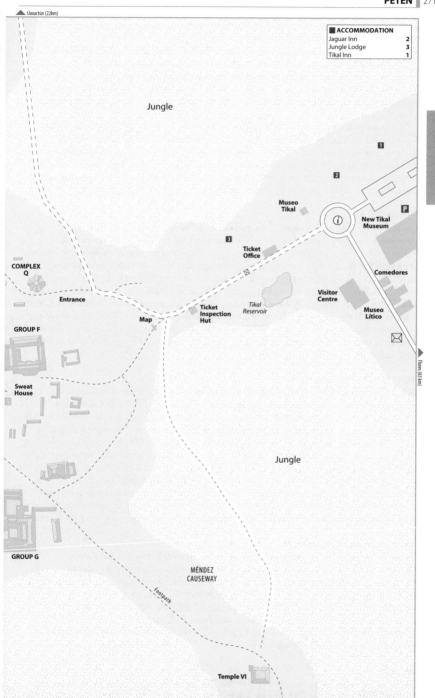

6

torn down and rebuilt as a platform and four vaulted temples, each of which was rebuilt twice during Early Classic times.

Archeologists have removed some of the surface to reveal these earlier structures, including two giant Preclassic stone **masks**, which can be glimpsed under thatched protective roofs; one depicts a hook-nosed god with earplugs wearing a crown-like headdress. Originally these great masks, which adorn many Maya Preclassic temple staircases, would have been finished with a stucco coating of limestone and painted in scarlet and green.

Two lines of **stelae**, carved with images of Tikal's elite, with circular altars at their bases, stand in front of the North Acropolis. These rulers were certainly obsessive in their recording of the city's dynastic sequence, linking it with great historical moments and reaching as far back into the past as possible. Many of the stelae bear the marks of ritual defacement, perpetrated by invaders from Caracol during the Classic era, acts carried out by conquerors as rites of humiliation.

The Central Acropolis

On the other side of the plaza, the **Central Acropolis** is a maze of 45 tiny interconnecting rooms and stairways built around six smallish courtyards. The buildings here are thought to have been palaces, law courts and administrative centres. **Structure 5D-46**, a partly ruined rectangular building with short frontal and rear stone staircases, is particularly intriguing. Dating from around 360 AD, it was the residential home of Chak Tok Ich'aak I (Great Jaguar Paw), and functioned as a royal residence for at least four hundred years. Take a look, too, at the large two-storey building in Court 2 known as **Maler's Palace**, named after the archeologist Teobert Maler who made it his home during expeditions in 1895 and 1904. Behind the acropolis is the palace **reservoir**, one of at least twelve clay-lined pools that were fed by a series of channels with rainwater from all over the city.

West Plaza and Temple III

Behind Temple II is the **West Plaza**, dominated by a large Late Classic palace on the north side, and scattered with various altars and stelae. From here the **Tozzer Causeway** – one of the raised routes that connected the main parts of the city – leads west to the unrestored **Temple III** (60m), covered in jungle vegetation and inaccessible to visitors. A fragment of Stela 24, found at the base of the temple, dates it at June 24, 810 AD, which marked the end of a *katun*. It was customary to construct twin temples to mark this auspicious event, but by this time it's clear that the Classic Maya were in severe difficulties across the region and just raising the manpower necessary to build Temple III would have been quite an achievement. Many Mayanists believe Temple III is a burial monument to **Dark Sun**, the last of Tikal's great rulers, and that it is he depicted as a portly figure wearing a magnificent jaguar costume on the badly eroded lintels that crown the temple's summit.

Bat Palace and Complex N

West of Temple III is a huge residential complex, of which only the **Bat Palace**, characterized by broad staircases, has been restored. Further down the causeway, on the left-hand side, is **Complex N**, another set of Late Classic twin pyramids. Here the superbly carved **Stela 16** shows a flamboyantly dressed Hasaw Chan K'awil, who was buried beneath Temple I, depicted with a huge plumed headdress. **Altar 5** at its base bears a sculpted scene of Hasaw presiding over a sacrificial skull and bones with a lord from Maasal, formerly a vassal state of Calakmul, a clear indicator that Tikal had successfully expanded into the orbit of its bitter rival by 711 AD, when the altar was completed.

Temple IV

At the end of the Tozzer Causeway, **Temple IV** is the tallest of all the Tikal structures at 64.6m (212ft). Built in 741 AD by Yik'in Chan K'awil (Hasaw's son), it is thought by many archeologists to be his burial monument. Ongoing excavations, including the burrowing of five tunnels into the heart of the structure, have failed to find his tomb as yet, though an early pyramid (over which Temple IV was constructed) has been discovered.

Temple IV is most famous for the stunning, carved **wooden lintels**, embellished with images of the victorious king and a riot of glyphs that once adorned its summit. Nowadays you'll have to travel to Switzerland to see them – though you can see an excellent replica of Lintel 3 in Guatemala City's archeological museum.

Twin stairways – one for the ascent, the other for the descent – provide access to the uppermost level of this unrestored temple. Slow and exhausting as the climb is, the finest views of the whole site await. All around you the forest canopy stretches out to the horizon, interrupted only by the great roof-combs of the other temples. Given the vistas, it's not surprising that the sunrise tribe gather here in great numbers, and though the humidity and mist usually shroud the visuals somewhat, the dawn jungle-chorus rarely fails to disappoint.

The Mundo Perdido and the Plaza of the Seven Temples

Southeast of Temple IV are two more important temple complexes. The first of these, the **Mundo Perdido**, or Lost World, form another magical and very distinct section of the site with its own atmosphere and architecture. The main feature here is the **Great Pyramid**, a 32m-high structure whose surface hides four earlier versions, the first an astronomical temple from 500 BC. Very faint remains of sixteen masks, four on each side of the pyramid, can still be made out.

Just east of here, the **Plaza of the Seven Temples** forms part of a complex dating back to before Christ. Archeological digs and restoration work are ongoing here. There's an unusual **triple ball court** on the north side of this plaza, and its eastern flank is formed by the unexcavated South Acropolis.

Temple V

A short trail from the southern part of the Plaza of the Seven Temples leads to the rear of the 58m-high **Temple V**, whose commanding, flared facade has now been fully restored. Recent evidence suggests that this monument, the construction of which took fifty years, was started around 600 AD by the ruler Animal Skull (which would make it the original of Tikal's six great temples) though very little about Temple V is currently known. A vertiginous wooden staircase (closed when it's been raining heavily) attached to the side of the temple rises to a very slender upper level, just beneath the roof comb, from where you get a stomach-churning perspective of the temples of the Great Plaza and an ocean of jungle beyond.

Temple VI

Temple VI, also known as the Temple of the Inscriptions, is a kilometre southeast of the Great Plaza. Only rediscovered in 1957, it's another of Yik'in Chan K'awil's constructions, completed in 766 AD. A medium-sized temple, it's famous for its 12m roof comb, on the back of which is a huge hieroglyphic text, only just visible these days. More than 180 glyphs chart the history of the city from a founding date in 1139 BC (which is close to the first archeological evidence of settlement). Temple VI is another candidate as the burial place of Yik'in Chan K'awil, Tikal's most prodigious monument-builder.

ARRIVAL AND DEPARTURE	TIKAL

From Flores The easiest way to reach the ruins is in one of the tourist minibuses (US$7 return) that meet flights at Flores airport and pick up passengers from every hotel in Flores, Santa Elena and El Remate, starting from 4.30am.

It's wise to arrive early at Tikal when the air is fresh and heat less intense, but note that it's rare to witness an impressive sunrise over the ruins due to mist rising from the humid forest.

From Belize If you're travelling from Belize, change buses at Ixlú, the three-way junction at the eastern end of Lago de Petén Itzá, from where there are plenty of passing minibuses (US$3.50 one-way) all day long.

TICKETS AND INFORMATION

Tikal is open daily 4am–8pm, and has three kinds of entrance tickets. The previous system which allowed you to enter after 3pm and your ticket it was valid for the following day has been dropped. Also those staying at hotels inside the national park have to pay entrance tickets even if you do not enter the ruins area.

TICKETS
Standard ticket The vast majority of visitors choose to buy a standard ticket (US$20, valid 6am–6pm) which will give most people sufficient time at the site.

Sunrise and sunset tickets There are sunrise (4–8am; US$13) and sunset (6–8pm; US$13) tickets for which you have to be accompanied by an official guide, at additional cost. So if you want to arrive at dawn, catch the sunrise and leave at 4pm, you'll need two tickets (US$13 and US$20). Guides can be organized through your hotel, travel agency, or the guide association in Tikal.

INFORMATION
Tourist information Inguat has a desk (6am–4pm) close to the ticket office.

Visitor centre Close to the entrance to the site there's a post office, shops and stalls (which sell souvenirs, hats, sun cream, memory cards for cameras, film, batteries and water) and a visitor centre, where you'll find a café-restaurant, toilets and luggage storage (US$0.15/hr).

Guides There's a licensed guide office in the visitor centre. Guides charge US$50 for up to five people, plus an additional US$8 per extra person for a 4hr tour. Most guides are excellent and very knowledgeable about Tikal's flora and fauna as well as the ruins. Obviously, if you can get a group together, or join others, it doesn't work out to be that expensive.

Publications Three books of note are usually available at the visitor centre: William Coe's *Tikal: A Handbook to the Ancient Maya Ruins*, which is a decent guide to the site, though now a little out of date; *The Birds of Tikal*, by Frank Smythe; and Peter D. Harrison's *The Lords of Tikal*, a very comprehensive and readable account of the city's turbulent history.

Website ⍵tikalpark.com has lots of useful information about the site and the reserve.

ACCOMMODATION

There are three **hotels** at the ruins, all of them fairly expensive and not especially good value. Some visitors find that service standards are not very high here – maybe it's the energy-sapping jungle location. Electricity is sporadic (usually 6–9am and 6–9.30pm), few staff speak much English and credit card surcharges are routinely hefty. That said, spending a night in the forest so close to the ruins is an unforgettable experience.

Campsite Beside new museum. You can camp or sling a hammock at Tikal's basic campsite, complete with rudimentary shower block; hammocks with attached mosquito nets are available for rent (US$5). It's illegal to camp or sleep out among the ruins. U̲S̲$̲4̲

Jaguar Inn ☎7926 0002, ⍵jaguartikal.com. Offers an overpriced choice of thirteen fan-cooled bungalows with small verandas and hammocks, camping, a reasonable restaurant and wi-fi. U̲S̲$̲7̲5̲

Jungle Lodge ☎2476 8775, ⍵junglelodgetikal.com. This attractive lodge offers comfortable bungalows, each with two double beds, a few basic rooms with shared bath and a five-bed dorm (US$10/head) There's also a decent restaurant and a pool. Rooms U̲S̲$̲4̲5̲–̲9̲0̲

Tikal Inn ☎7861 2444, ⍵tikalinn.com. A good choice, offering pleasant thatched bungalows and clean airy rooms all with ceiling fan and hot-water bathrooms, though the decor is a bit dated. There's a great heat-busting swimming pool and restaurant. U̲S̲$̲6̲0̲–̲1̲0̲0̲

EATING AND DRINKING

Several simple but fairly pricey **comedores** are located at the entrance to the site and cold drinks are sold around the ruins by vendors.

Comedor Tikal Fair value with sandwiches for US$2.75 and grilled meats or fish meals for about US$8. Daily 6am–9pm.

Jungle Lodge For a more extensive and expensive menu (US$12 a full meal), head for the restaurant at the *Jungle Lodge* (see above).

Uaxactún and around

Twenty-three kilometres north of Tikal, the adobe and clapboard houses that comprise the friendly village of **UAXACTÚN** are spread out on both sides of an airstrip, as are the ruins of the same name. With a couple of places to stay, a few comedores and daily bus connections from Flores, the village is an ideal jumping-off point for the remote northern ruins of **El Zotz, Naachtún and Río Azul**.

Substantially smaller than Tikal, the site (known as Sia'an K'aan in Maya times) rose to prominence in the Late Preclassic era when it grew to become a major player. Uaxactún developed rivalry with Tikal, which peaked in January 16, 378 AD, when Tikal's warriors conquered Uaxactún armed with the latest high-tech weaponry of the day – spear-throwing slings from Mexico. Uaxactún never recovered from this epochal defeat, and for the remainder of the Classic period was reduced to little more than a provincial backwater.

6

The ruins

Officially US$7.50, but often no fee is collected

Uaxactún **ruins** are not that extensive, and may be a little disappointing after the grandeur of Tikal, but you'll probably have the site to yourself. Village children will offer to guide you around; their charm is irresistible – as are the dolls made from corn husks decorated with beads and dried flowers you'll be implored to buy – though their archeological knowledge is limited. A tip of a quetzal or two is fine.

Group E

The most interesting buildings are in **Group E**, east of the airstrip, where three low, reconstructed temples – Temples E-I, E-II and E-III – built side by side, are arranged to function as an observatory. Viewed from the top of a fourth temple, the sun rises behind the north temple (E-I) on the longest day of the year and behind the southern one (E-III) on the shortest day. This point of observation is above **E-VII sub**, a Preclassic temple with simple staircases on all four sides, the steps flanked by pairs of elaborate **stucco masks** of jaguar and serpent heads. It's clear that this was a sacred monument, a platform for bloodletting and sacrifice, for the jaguar signifies the Jaguar God of the underworld, one of the most powerful deities; the serpent is the fabled "vision serpent".

Groups A and B

On the other side of the airstrip are **Groups A and B**, a series of larger temples and residential compounds, some of them reconstructed, spread out across the high ground. In amongst the structures are some impressive stelae, each sheltered by a small thatched roof, but most lying poignantly broken and supine.

Museum

In the grounds of *El Chiclero* (see p.276) there's a small but interesting **museum** (free), with an astonishing collection of intact vases, plates and other ceramics crammed onto its wooden shelves. Many of the vessels are decorated with glyphs and animal figures, and some have a hole drilled in the centre to ceremonially "kill" the power they contain. Other items include a beautiful necklace and flint axe-heads, polished to a glass-like gleam.

ARRIVAL AND DEPARTURE	UAXACTÚN

By bus Two daily buses (at 2pm & 3pm; 2hr 15min) from Flores pass through Tikal en route for Uaxactún.

ACCOMMODATION

Aldana's No phone. Friendly, family-run place with bare bones wooden rooms and camping (US$2/head). Tours of the region and food are offered. US$5

Campamento Ecológico El Chiclero ☎ 7783 3917, ✉ campamentoelchiclero@gmail.com. Welcoming place offering simple rooms with decent mattresses and nets, camping and hammock space (both US$3.50); bathrooms are shared but kept clean. Owner Antonio Baldizón also organizes 4WD trips (in the dry season Feb–June) to Río Azul and Naachtún. His wife Neria prepares excellent food – large-portioned meals cost US$7. US$16

El Zotz

Twenty-five kilometres southwest of Uaxactún, along a track that's usually passable in the dry season (by 4WD), **El Zotz** is a large Maya site set in its own *biotopo*. Totally unrestored, El Zotz has been systematically looted, although there are guards on duty all year now and there's also a CECON biological station close to the ruins.

The three main temples are smothered in soil and vegetation. Using the workers' scaffold you can climb to the top of the tallest structure, the **devil's pyramid**, from where the roof combs of Tikal can be glimpsed on clear days. A **royal tomb**, dating from around 400 AD, was recently discovered beneath this pyramid, containing the king buried with the tiny corpses of six infants (possibly sacrificial victims).

Zotz means "bat" in Maya and each evening at dusk you'll see tens, perhaps even hundreds of thousands of **bats** of several species emerge from a cave near the campsite. It's especially impressive in the moonlight, the beating wings sounding like a river flowing over rapids – one of the most remarkable natural sights in Petén. Keep an eye out, too, for bat falcons, swooping with talons outstretched in search of their prey.

ARRIVAL AND DEPARTURE   EL ZOTZ

Tours To get there speak to the owners of *El Chiclero* in Uaxactún or the tour operators in Flores (see p.256), who can arrange tours. Three-day trips involving a hike to El Zotz, a day at the ruins and then a hike to Tikal are highly recommended, costing from US$250/head (minimum two people).

Río Azul

US$7.50

The remote site of **Río Azul**, almost on the tripartite border where Guatemala, Belize and Mexico meet, was only rediscovered in 1962. Although almost totally unrestored, the core of the site resembles Tikal in many ways, though it is smaller. The tallest temple (A-III) stands some 47m above the forest floor, poking its head out above the treetops and giving magnificent views across the jungle.

Brief history

Investigations suggest that the site dates back to 900 BC and was an important city until the Middle Classic era. Río Azul prospered as both a trading centre between the Caribbean (where cacao was abundant) and wider Maya World and also as an important agricultural centre. The site's history is deeply intertwined with Tikal and Calakmul, the two superpowers of the era. It's likely that Tikal's ruler Stormy Sky installed one of his sons here as king, but in 530 AD Calakmul overran the city. After this defeat, Río Azul was virtually abandoned, before being occupied again in Late Classic times, only to be sacked again in 830 AD by marauding Puuc Maya from the Yucatán.

The site

Several incredible **tombs** have been unearthed, painted with vivid red glyphs. Tomb 1 is thought to have contained the remains of Stormy Sky's son, while nearby tombs 19 and

23 contained bodies of warriors dressed in clothing typical of the ancient city of Teotihuacán in central Mexico. Many of the finds here are displayed in the archeology museum in Guatemala City (see p.60).

Extensive **looting** occurred after the site's discovery, with a gang of up to eighty men plundering the tombs, and unique treasures (including some incredible green jade masks and pendants) found their way onto the international market. Tombs were stripped bare, and some of the finest murals in the Maya World hacked from walls – though Tomb 1 escaped the worst of the damage.

Today there are two resident guards: the tallest temples are now becoming unsafe to climb, so always heed their advice.

6

ARRIVAL AND DEPARTURE RÍO AZUL

By road The road that connects Tikal and Uaxactún continues for an additional 95km north to Río Azul. This route is only passable in the dry season, and can be covered by 4WDs in as little as 5hr, depending on the conditions.

On foot Walking, or on horseback it's four days each way – three at a push. Trips can be arranged through *El Chiclero* in Uaxactún (see p.276) or through travel agents in Flores (see p.256).

The Mirador Basin

The remains of the first great cities of the Maya are still engulfed by the most extensive forests in the region, an area known as the **Mirador Basin**. The discoveries here in the extreme north of the country have already led to a complete rethink about the origins of the Maya, and it's now clear that this was once the cradle of Maya civilization. The main focus of interest has been the giant site of **El Mirador**, the first Maya "superpower", which is famous for its colossal triadic temple complexes. But neighbouring **Nakbé**, the first city to emerge (around 800 BC), **Wakná** (which was only discovered in 1998) and the massive ruins of **Tintal** (on the scale of Tikal) are just three of the myriad cities that once thrived in this now remotest of regions.

The conditions are very difficult – marshy mosquito-plagued terrain that becomes so saturated that excavations can only be attempted for five months of the year.

THE MIRADOR BASIN UNDER PRESSURE

Undoubtedly the greatest challenge facing the archeologists and Guatemalan authorities is to save the Mirador Basin ruins from the constant threat of encroaching settlers, loggers, drug smugglers, cattle ranchers and tomb looters. Because of this lack of security, environmentalists and Mayanists are lobbying hard to get the entire Mirador region – 2169 square kilometres of jungle stretching from the Mexican border as far south as El Zotz – declared the **Mirador Basin National Park**. President Colom announced in his 2008 inaugural speech that the creation of a national park here was a priority, though this status was not achieved during his four-year tenure. An application is also registered with UNESCO to get Mirador declared a World Heritage Site.

Immediate and effective protection is essential. Successive Guatemalan governments have dithered while neighbouring reserves like Laguna del Tigre have gone up in smoke. Forty armed rangers patrol the Mirador area, otherwise, according to archeologist **Dr Richard Hansen** (who has led the excavations here for decades) "we'd lose the whole city". Hansen sees strictly managed ecotourism, including the construction of a jungle lodge and narrow-gauge railway, as the way to preserve the forest and the dozens of Maya sites in the Mirador Basin. But his vision is not universally shared. Many settlers on the fringes, and inside the reserve, see little future in ecotourism and are lobbying for timber and farming concessions to be allowed. Occasionally these land-hungry campesinos torch a ranger station, and villagers at Dos Aguadas have even been granted a concession to farm inside the Maya Biosphere Reserve. So the choice seems to be fewer trees or more tourists.

Currently only around three thousand people make it to Mirador each year, and archeologists outnumber visitors at any one time. Numbers are tiny because of the effort or expense required to **get to** the ruins (see p.282), which either involves days of hard hiking through dense jungle and swamps or a brief visit as part of a helicopter tour.

El Mirador

6

El Mirador is perhaps the most exotic and mysterious Maya site of all. Encircled by the Petén and Campeche jungles, this massive city surpasses Tikal's scale although we are only now beginning to piece together its history. Mayanists are not even certain of its name – *el mirador* means "the lookout" in Spanish – but it could have been **Ox Te Tun** (Birthplace of the Gods). Until the 1980s, it was assumed Mirador was a city from the Classic era, but this theory has been totally overthrown. We now know that Mirador was a Preclassic capital of unprecedented scale, and its fall around 150 AD was just the first of two catastrophic collapses suffered by the Maya civilization.

The ruins are surrounded by some of the densest tropical forests in the Americas, and you're sure to encounter some spectacular **wildlife**, including the resident troops of howler and spider monkeys, toucans and perhaps even a scarlet macaw. Wildcat numbers in the area are some of the healthiest in Latin America, with an estimated four hundred jaguar, as well as ocelot, *jaguarundi* and puma.

Brief history

The latest research indicates that it was the boggy nature of the Mirador Basin that drew the first settlers here, the richness of its *bajo* mud allowing the early Maya to found villages based on crop cultivation. By 1000 BC (though some ceramic evidence suggests as far back as 1480 BC) these settlements were established and thriving at Mirador. The site chosen for the city itself was a commanding one, on an outcrop of karst (limestone) hills at an altitude of 250m, with swamps providing protection to the east.

By the Middle Preclassic, ceremonial structures were being built, including early temples at Los Monos, El Tigre and the Central Acropolis (generations later these structures would be built over and enlarged to a much grander scale). For centuries Mirador flourished, peaking between 350 BC and 100 AD, when it was home to over one hundred thousand Maya. The city's ruling **Kaan dynasty** were overlords of hundreds of thousands more subjects in the Basin region and overlords of millions in the wider Maya World.

Mirador became a great trading centre as jade and obsidian were brought from the highlands; granite, shells and coral beads imported from the Caribbean and salt carried in from the Yucatán. The city grew to dominate the entire region, and by the time of Christ it must have been something to behold, its emblematic triadic temples painted scarlet with cinnabar and soaring high above the forest canopy, with a web of stone causeways connecting the great capital to dozens of other cities in its empire.

Decline and abandonment

The exact reasons for Mirador's downfall are unclear, but it's probable that a millennium of temple- and empire-building, intensive agriculture and especially forest-burning (to create lime for the thick plaster that covered every building) dried out the swamps and provoked **agricultural and environmental collapse**. Other great cities including Teotihuacán in central Mexico and Tikal were also beginning to flex their muscles by the second century AD.

All the great cities of the Basin faded in the late Preclassic era around 150 AD, but strong evidence indicates that Mirador's inhabitants may have simply upped sticks and shifted 50km to the north, probably because the water supply was better. Here it seems they founded a second superstate, for recently found inscriptions strongly link the ruling Kaan dynasty of Calakmul to Mirador.

Though Mirador's population plummeted, small numbers continued to live in the remains of the great city, for in the late fourth century AD an army from Teotihuacán overwhelmed the few remaining occupants. Mirador was also re-occupied by a small number of settlers in the Late Classic era, who remodelled some monuments before fleeing around 800 AD.

Presently Mayanists are only able to piece together fragments of the history of these empire builders, however, for their story is only just beginning to be told.

6

The ruins

US$8

The **ruins** of El Mirador are still covered in dense jungle, and though many buildings have been stabilized, only a few buildings have been partially reconstructed. In many ways you're experiencing the city the way the great nineteenth-century explorers like Maudslay would have seen Tikal, so you'll have to exercise your imagination to get a vision of its sheer scale and grandeur. But as the **archeological project** here is the largest in the Americas – home to around forty archeologists, dozens of students and around three hundred workers each season – exciting new discoveries are being unearthed all the time.

The centre of the site covers some sixteen square kilometres, stretching between two massive **pyramid groups** facing each other across the forest on an east–west axis. Mirador's **ceremonial core**, sometimes called the West Group, is thought to have been largely the preserve of the elite and high priests and contains hundreds of temple structures and buildings, reservoirs and aqueducts, all ringed by a defensive wall, and probably guarded by gateways.

Tigre Complex

On the western edge of this sacred precinct is the mighty **Tigre Complex**, made up of a huge single pyramid base, and an upper platform with three temples. This triadic temple design, peaking at 55m, is characteristic of El Mirador's architecture (and a model that's replicated at all of the area's Preclassic sites). Tigre's temple base measures 125m by 135m, which is enough to cover around three football fields. Giant stucco **jaguar masks** have been uncovered here, their teeth and claws painted red. Hundreds of obsidian spear points found indicate a major battle in the late fourth century AD, as the forces of Teotihuacán (and possibly Tikal) overran Mirador. At that time this once-omnipotent city would have been a shadow of its former self, a relatively minor settlement.

A staircase has been cut into the side of the Tigre pyramid, and this temple's summit is a favoured spot for sunset (as it's only a 15min walk back to the campsite from here).

THE HERO TWINS PANEL

The Mirador Basin has no rivers (and had a population of hundreds of thousands in the late Preclassic) so the Maya developed extremely efficient water collection systems so that all available rainfall was channelled to huge reservoirs. In 2008, while investigating water channels in the Central Acropolis, archeologists discovered elaborately sculptured panels with scenes from the Maya creation story, the **Popol Vuh**. The two stucco panels, measuring 6m by 8m and still in situ, were carved about 200 BC and show the mythical hero twins swimming into the underworld to retrieve the decapitated head of their father. Dr Richard Hansen described it as like "like finding the Mona Lisa in the sewage system".

6

Structure 34

On the south side of the Tigre complex, **Structure 34** is one of the most studied buildings at El Mirador. This 17m-high pyramid, built around 200 BC, has now been restored and sits under a polycarbonate roof for protection. Giant jaguar claws carved from stucco decorate the facade of the temple, leading archeologists to believe that it was dedicated to ruler Yok'noom Yi'ch'ak K'ak, or "Great Flaming Jaguar Claw".

Structure 34 was actually constructed over the remains of a smaller, earlier temple – exactly like Copan's Rosalila (see p.307). If you tip the guards they might allow you access to a tunnel for a sneaky peek at the original, which has a large stucco mask and red and black paint.

Central Acropolis

In front of the Tigre Complex is El Mirador's sacred hub: the **Central Acropolis**, a long, narrow plaza, where sacrificial ceremonies were performed. A wonderful sculptured panel depicting the Maya creation myth was found here in 2009 (see box, p.279).

Burial chambers unearthed in this central section had been painted with ferric oxide to prevent corrosion and contained the bodies of priests and noblemen surrounded by bloodletting instruments like stingray spines (see p.340). The spilling of blood was seen by the Maya as a method of summoning and sustaining the gods, and was common at all the great ceremonial centres.

South of the Tigre Complex, the **Monos Complex** is another triadic structure (rising to 42m) and plaza, named after the local howler monkeys that roar long into the night and after heavy rainfall. To the north, the **León Pyramid** and the **Cascabel Complex** mark the northern boundaries of the sacred precinct.

Danta Pyramid

Heading away to the east, it's about 1.5km from the Central Acropolis along the Puleston Causeway, past a couple of reservoirs, to the **East Group**, which rises in tiers from the forest floor. The cluster of monumental buildings here all sit on a vast stone base platform that measures 600m by 330m. The trail ascends to a second platform, where you encounter the **Pava temple** group, winding below the jungle-clad Pava pyramid and then climbing up to a third level and then up the flanks of the iconic **Danta Pyramid** itself. Vegetation is steadily being cut from the front of this vast structure, but it's planned to just expose the facade of the pyramid and leave the jungle intact to the rear and sides.

A sturdy wooden staircase leads to the summit of this two thousand-year-old temple, which is 72m above the base platform (and 79m above the forest floor), making it the tallest pre-Columbian structure in the Americas. From the top, high above the jungle canopy, you feel you're at the summit of the Maya World. The hills in the distance are the forest-covered pyramids of other great Maya cities, with the temple tops of Nakbé to the south. On very clear days it's even possible to catch a glimpse of Structure 2 at Calakmul in Mexico, way to the north, a city almost certainly founded by the Kaan Maya from El Mirador.

Around El Mirador

The area **around El Mirador** is riddled with other residential suburbs and smaller Maya sites – you'll pass through about a dozen small ruins if you arrive on foot from Carmelita. Raised **causeways**, ancient trading routes called *sakbe'ob* – some up to 40m wide and 4m in height – connect many of these smaller sites to Mirador. One trail leads south to **La Muerte**, 2km away, where several temples have been restored and some fine tombs and glyphic carvings (now protected by a polycarbonate protective roof) have been uncovered.

Nakbé
Free

About 12km to the southeast of El Mirador down one of the main *sakbé*, **Nakbé** was the first substantial city to emerge in the Maya region. Ruins of the earliest buildings are from around 1000 BC, the community growing to become a city of many thousands by 400 BC, and one of the key centres of Maya culture, calendrics, religion and writing.

Today the site, which has been partially cleared, is virtually unvisited by anyone except archeologists, *xateros* (palm-leaf gatherers) and *chicleros* (rubber tappers). Excavations have revealed that the city had a ceremonial core with **temples**, separated into two groups via a kilometre-long limestone causeway – much like El Mirador. At the eastern end, the temples rise from a platform to peak at 35m, and there are the remains of the earliest ball court ever found in the Maya World, dating back to around 450 BC.

Nakbé's tallest building is in the western group, where **Structure I** reaches 45m; from its summit, La Danta in El Mirador is visible. Archeologists have also found evidence of skilful stucco work – a huge **mask** (measuring 5m by 8m) was found on the side of one of the temples here, though it has since been covered in earth for protection.

Resident guards will show you **chultunes** (storage chambers cut into the limestone bedrock) that you can lower yourself down into – though watch out for snakes and spiders. Nakbé probably has hundreds of outlying structures, including residential complexes grouped around plazas and doubtless many more exciting discoveries will follow.

Tintal

Tintal, another massive site south of El Mirador, is connected by a broad causeway to its giant neighbour. It flourished in Preclassic times and was later reoccupied in the Classic period. The ruins, though severely looted – an estimated two thousand trenches have been cut into the structures here – make an ideal campsite on the route to El Mirador and most hiking trips spend a night here. A defence moat, averaging 25m in width, encircles the ceremonial core.

There are two main temple complexes, both arranged in a **triadic** formation with a central staircase flanked by elaborate stucco masks – some of the earliest examples of Maya sculptural art. Climb to the top of the **Catzin pyramid**, which ascends 50m, for spectacular jungle canopy views, as well as vistas over towards El Mirador.

Wakná

There are over twenty other sites in the Mirador Basin that have barely been touched, including many very early Preclassic settlements. The large site of **Wakná**, or "house of six", was only rediscovered in 1998, after careful analysis of satellite photographs detected temple-like mounds in the jungle. Dr Hansen, accompanied by *chicleros*, led a team to the region and confirmed that the mounds were indeed the remains of a city, later established to be Preclassic in origin. Unfortunately, they weren't the first people to discover the site – a trench cut into one of the temples confirmed that looters had already been active here, and had raided a tomb. Tour operators (see p.256), include Wakná and Nakbé on seven-day trek itineraries to El Mirador.

Naachtún

Recent investigations at extremely remote **Naachtún**, about 25km east of El Mirador and just 1km south of the Mexican border, have revealed it to be a very substantial site. Preclassic in origin, Naachtún is unusual in that it is one of the few ancient cities in the Mirador Basin to survive (and indeed flourish) into the Classic period.

More than forty stelae have been unearthed, and the architecture at the site (perilously located between the two giants of Tikal and Calakmul, and originally called Masuul) reflects styles found in both cities – around its main plaza the temples show strong Tikal influence, while its royal palaces draw on Calakmul design traditions.

ARRIVAL, INFORMATION AND TOURS   THE MIRADOR BASIN

Getting to El Mirador is a substantial undertaking by land. From Santa Elena you first need to get to the isolated village of **Carmelita** (2 daily buses at 5am and 1pm; 3–4hr). Then it's two days of hard **jungle hiking** to the site – most people hire a mule to carry their food and equipment. The journey, impossibly muddy in the rainy season, is best attempted **from mid-January to July** (Feb to April is the driest period). The trip offers an exceptional chance to see virtually untouched forest and perhaps some of the creatures that inhabit it – you're nearly guaranteed to see howler and spider monkeys, bats (including vampires), toucans, pizotes and deer, plenty of bugs, spiders and quite possibly a scorpion or snake.

EQUIPMENT AND COSTS

Whichever way you do it you'll need guides, pack horses or mules, food, water and camping gear. The more people you can gather together, the cheaper the price: a group of four people pay about US$370/head for a five-day trek. Essentials are bug repellent, plasters for blisters, energy snacks and some supplies for the guards, who spend forty days at a time in the forest, largely subsisting on beans and tortillas.

INFORMATION

The websites ⓦ miradorbasin.com and ⓦ miradorpark .com are excellent for information about the site. The highly informative websites ⓦ mostlymaya.com and ⓦ mayaruinsonly.com have more information about organizing the hike, what to take and what to expect. Consult ⓦ elmiradorhike.blogspot.com for the latest news about hiking to Mirador.

TOURS

Tours can be arranged in Flores (*Hostel Los Amigos* is a good place to get a group together and provides excellent information). Tour agencies running trips to Mirador include:
Reino K'an Mirador Tours C 30 de Junio, Flores (☏ 5818 3273 or ☏ 5761 9883, ✉ racsosalas@hotmail.com).

Mayan Lands C Centro América, Flores (☏ 5340 2506, ✉ landsmayan@hotmail.com).
Maya Expeditions in Guatemala City (see p.37). For high-quality trips led by prominent archeologists these are highly recommended.

GUIDES IN CARMELITA

If you speak Spanish, you can also liaise directly with guides in Carmelita, contact either the Guías Comunitarios (☏ 7783 3811 or ☏ 7783 3812 or ☏ 7783 3856) or the Turismo Cooperativa (☏ 5800 0293 or ☏ 7861 0366).

HELICOPTER TOURS

If you'd rather skip the mud and jungle completely, helicopter trips offer a tempting alternative, though you'll only get a fleeting glimpse of the ruins.
Mirador Park ☏ 2367 2837, ⓦ tikalpark.com. Charge US$560/head (minimum four) for a day-trip leaving at 8am from Flores, and returning by 3.30pm. It's also possible to stay overnight and hike back. The owner of this agency, Carla Molina, has been to Mirador many times.
Aerocentro ☏ 2361 5553, ⓦ en.aerocentro.com.gt. Charge US$380 for day-trips.

ACCOMMODATION AND EATING

Comedor Patricia Pinelo Village centre ☏ 7783 3811. Most of the time the menu is simply beans, eggs and tortillas, though if you call ahead some meat can be prepared. They'll organize a bed for the night for you here for very little. Bed <u>US$4</u>

ACCESS ALL AREAS

At the time of research local issues in Carmelita were creating problems for travellers wanting to enter the Mirador Basin. An association of guides, the **Cooperativa Carmelita**, was insisting that all tourists in the entire Basin region (including Nakbé and Tintal) have to be accompanied by guides from their group, paid at their official rates (from US$350/head). Tourists on a helicopter tour at Mirador, and hikers heading to Mirador from Uaxactún have also been charged or turned back. Legal challenges to this action were ongoing. For the latest news consult ⓦ elmiradorhike.blogspot.com.

Sayaxché and around

Southwest of Flores on a lazy bend in the Río de la Pasión, **SAYAXCHÉ** is a fairly rough-and-ready frontier town that's a convenient base for exploring the forests of southern Petén and its huge collection of archeological remains. The complex network of rivers and swamps that cuts through the jungle here has been an important trade route since Maya times. Nearby ruins include **Ceibal**, a compact but beautiful site, while to the south is **Lago de Petexbatún**, a stunning lakeside setting for the Maya sites of **Aguateca** and Punta de Chimino, and the trailhead for the substantial ruins of **Dos Pilas**. A visit to this region offers great opportunities to explore the Petén forest and watch the wildlife, including howler and spider monkeys, crocodiles, iguanas and superb birdlife.

ARRIVAL AND DEPARTURE SAYAXCHÉ

By bus and minibus Getting to Sayaxché from Flores is very straightforward, with minibuses and buses (every 15min) plying the smooth 62km road from Santa Elena to the river bank opposite Sayaxché. A ferry (US$0.30/head) takes you over the Río de la Pasión.
Destinations Buses to Cobán (2 daily; 4hr); Flores (every 15min; 2hr); Raxrujá (every 30min; 2hr 30min).

Boats and tours To get to the ruins, you'll find plenty of boatmen – you'll have to be patient and bargain hard to get a good deal. Try Viajes Don Pedro (☎ 7928 6109) for tours of the area; you'll find their office on the riverfront. The very helpful Julián Mariona, who owns *Posada El Caribe* (see p.285), can also arrange ruins trips and fishing expeditions (both from US$60 a day).

ACCOMMODATION

Hotel Del Río 300m north of the dock ☎ 7928 6138. Efficient, secure hotel with very spacious, clean rooms (some with a/c) and a very friendly host family. US$23–32
Hotel La Pasión 50m up from the dock ☎ 4056 5044. Occupying the upper floors of this red-brick building, rooms are spacious, comfortable and have cable TV, bathrooms and fans. There's free coffee in the pleasant lounge area. US$17

Yaxkín Chel Paraíso Six blocks up and five across (southeast) from the dock ☎ 4053 3484. Rustic bungalows and a restaurant in a verdant garden, where the family grow cocoa, pepper and tropical flowers. It's priced per person, so cheap for single travellers. Owner Chendo can arrange tours and transport. US$13

EATING

Oasis 1km west of town. A slightly bizarre combo, this is part-hardware store, part-civilized, a/c café that serves snacks like hot dogs and nachos. It has the only espresso machine in town. Mon–Sat 7am–6pm.

Restaurant Yaxkín One block up from the dock, on the left. Friendly place that serves up tasty meals and snacks, including good burgers (US$3) and sandwiches. Offers impartial tourist information too. Daily 7am–8pm.

DIRECTORY

Banks Banrural has two branches in town with ATMs, including one opposite the parque central.

Ceibal (Seibal)

Daily 7.30am–5pm • US$8

The minor Maya site of **Ceibal** (sometimes spelt "Seibal"), which you can reach by land or river, is the most accessible ruin near Sayaxché. Surrounded by forest and shaded by huge ceiba trees, **the ruins** are only partially cleared and just a few buildings have been restored. However the mixture of open plazas and untamed jungle is beautiful.

During the Classic period, Ceibal was a relatively minor site, but it grew rapidly between 830 and 910 AD, possibly after falling under the control of Putun colonists from what is now Mexico. Outside influence is clearly visible in some of the carving: speech scrolls, straight noses, waist-length hair and serpent motifs are all decidedly non-Maya. The architecture also differs from other Classic Maya sites, including the round platforms that are usually associated with the Quetzalcoatl cult.

6

The ruins

Ceibal has four main clusters of buildings, all connected by flagstone causeways (*calzadas*) that cut through the forest, and two ball courts. Although most of the largest temples (Structure 10 rises to 28m) lie buried under mounds, Ceibal does have some fine **carving**, superbly preserved due to the use of hard stone. Of the 57 **stelae** found here, the most impressive are in the large Plaza Central (where the surrounding temples are unrestored and still jungle-clad) and in the neighbouring Plaza Sur. The latter plaza's low central temple, **Structure A-3**, has four fine stelae set around its cardinal points and another (Stela 21) in the room at the top of the temple – all were commissioned in 849 AD.

East of the plaza along Calzada I, the crudely carved but unusual monkey-faced Stela 2 is particularly striking, beyond which, straight ahead down the path, lies Stela 14, another impressive sculpture.

Structure 79

If you turn right here along Calzada II and walk for a few minutes, you'll reach the only other restored part, the highly unusual **Structure 79**, a massive circular stone platform superbly set in a clearing in the forest. The exact purpose of this platform, whose foundations date from the Late Preclassic period, is unclear, but it was certainly used for religious ceremonies (a niche where copal resin was burned has been found) and possibly also functioned as an observation deck for astronomy. In front of Structure 79's stairway, a huge, roughly carved **altar**, measuring more than 2m in diameter and bearing the face of a jaguar, is supported by two crouching humanoid figures.

ARRIVAL AND DEPARTURE   CEIBAL

By boat It's around US$70 for a round-trip journey from Sayaxché, including 2hr at the ruins; the hour-long boat trip is followed by a short walk through towering rainforest.
By road Ceibal is just 17km from Sayaxché. Any transport heading south out of town towards Cruce del Pato passes the entrance road to the site, from where it's an 8km walk through the jungle to the ruins. A taxi from Sayaxché, including an hour at the ruins, should cost about US$28.

Lago de Petexbatún

South of Sayaxché, **Lago de Petexbatún** is a spectacular expanse of water ringed by dense forest and containing plentiful supplies of snook, bass, alligator and freshwater turtle. The shores of the lake abound with birdlife and howler monkeys, and there are a number of Maya ruins – the most impressive of which is the partially restored **Aguateca**, suggesting the lake was an important trading centre for the Maya.

Aguateca

Daily 8am–4.30pm • US$7

Aguateca, perched on a high outcrop at the southern tip of the lake, is the site that's furthest away from Sayaxché but the most easily reached, as a boat can get you to within twenty minutes' walk of the ruins. This intriguing site (split in two by a natural chasm) was only rediscovered in 1957 and has undergone recent restoration work. The atmosphere is magical, surrounded by dense tropical forest and with superb views of the lake from two *miradores*. There's a **visitor centre** close to the entrance, where Aguateca's guards are based. The guards always welcome company, and if you want to **stay** they'll find some space for you to sling a hammock or pitch a tent. Bring a mosquito net and food if you wish to stay.

A brief history

Throughout the Late Classic period, Aguateca was closely aligned with (or controlled by) nearby Dos Pilas, the dominant city in the southern Petén, and reached its peak in the eighth century, when Dos Pilas was developing an aggressive policy of expansion. Indeed, Aguateca may have been a twin capital of an ambitious Petexbatún state. Military successes, including a conclusive victory over Ceibal in 735 AD, were celebrated at both sites with remarkably similar stelae – Aguateca's Stela 3 shows Dos Pilas ruler Master Sun Jaguar in full battle regalia, including a Teotihuacán-style face mask. After 761 AD, however, Dos Pilas began to lose control of its empire and the members of the elite moved their headquarters to Aguateca, attracted by its strong defensive position. But despite the construction of 5km of walls around the citadel and its agricultural land, their enemies soon caught up with them, and sometime after 790 AD Aguateca itself was overrun.

6

The ruins

The resident guards will provide you with stout walking sticks – essential as the slippery paths here can be treacherous – before escorting you around the site's steep trails. The tour, which takes a little more than an hour, takes in the palisade defences, temples and palaces (including the residence of Aguateca's last ruler, Tante K'inich) and a barracks. The carving at Aguateca is superbly executed and includes images of hummingbirds, pineapples and pelicans. Its plazas are dotted with stelae, including one on the Plaza Principal depicting Tante K'inich lording it over a ruler from Ceibal, who is shown cowering at his feet, and another that has been shattered by looters who hoped to sell the fragments. Aguateca is also the site of the Maya World's only known **bridge**, which crosses a narrow gash in the hillside, but it's not that impressive in itself.

Punta de Chiminos

Around 4km to the north of Aguateca, jutting out from the west shore of the lake, is a club-shaped peninsula known as **Punta de Chiminos**. This site was the final refuge of the last of the Petexbatún Maya in the Late Classic era, as the region descended into warfare and chaos at the beginning of the ninth century. Here they constructed some formidable defences across the narrow stem of the peninsula, including three rock-hewn trenches and 9m ramparts, which created a man-made citadel. The point is now the spectacular location for the lovely *Chiminos Island Lodge* (see below), though there's very little to see there today.

ARRIVAL AND GETTING AROUND   LAGO DE PETEXBATÚN

By boat It's a 45min speedboat trip from Sayaxché to the northern tip of Lago de Petexbatún.

Tours As it's not feasible to get around the lake independently, it's probably best explored on a tour. Most tour operators in Flores can organize excursions to Aguateca, where prices start at around US$150 for a two-day excursion, though the ideal way to explore this beautiful region is to arrange a boat and guide locally – ask at *Posada El Caribe* or *Chiminos* (see below) to take you on a two- or three-day trip around the lake. There are plenty of options – touring the lake on foot, by boat or on horseback, exploring the jungle, fishing or bathing in the natural warm springs on the lakeshore.

ACCOMMODATION

★ **Chiminos Island Lodge** West side of Lago de Petexbatún ☎ 2335 3506, ⍟ chiminosisland.com. A simply wonderful jungle retreat, with six huge, commodious thatch-roofed bungalows, with stylish bathrooms and private viewing decks above the lake. Bungalow "2 Norte" is the most attractive, with bungalow "1 Norte" second choice. There are some minor ruins in the patch of jungle around the hotel, which is also home to howler monkeys and amazing birdlife. The hotel also has docks for sunbathing and swimming, cooking that's of a very high standard, and attentive and helpful staff. Rates include all meals. <u>US$220</u>

Posada El Caribe Northern tip of Lago de Petexbatún ☎ 7928 6114 or ☎ 5304 1745, ✉ posadacaribe @peten.net. A very friendly and welcoming establishment, run by the Mariona family, with clean, functional screened cabins and good food (US$8–10 a meal). Don Julián, the owner, is a true Petenero and is highly recommended for lake and ruin tours to Aguateca and Dos Pilas; he can arrange horses, 4WD and boat transport, though he speaks very limited English. <u>US$60</u>

Dos Pilas and around

Some 12km west of the northern tip of Lago de Petexbatún, still buried in the jungle, is another virtually unreconstructed site, **Dos Pilas**, which has one of the most fascinating and best-documented histories of any Maya city.

Brief history

Dos Pilas was established around 640 AD by a renegade group of Tikal nobles who fled following the city's defeat by Calakmul. The leader of this breakaway tribe, B'alaj Chan K'awil (Lightning Sky), was clearly a brazen individual, for he swore a treacherous allegiance with Calakmul in 648 AD in an attempt to launch a rival dynasty at Tikal. Dos Pilas clashed with Tikal several times in the years afterwards, as Tikal sought to humble the upstart Dos Pilas ruler. Though B'alaj Chan K'awil ultimately failed in his bid to claim the Tikal lineage, he did repel Tikal in 679 AD, a victory which he celebrated by commissioning several new stelae and launching a substantial reconstruction of the plaza.

Dos Pilas continued to throw its weight around for another century, defeating Ceibal in 735 AD and capturing lords from Yaxchilán and Motul. Monuments including three hieroglyphic stairways were built, though by the latter half of the eighth century the region's instablity was such that the site was completely abandoned.

The ruins

Sadly, the **remains of the city** are less than spectacular, as many temples were partly dismantled during the chaos of the late eighth century. Nevertheless, there's some superb carving to admire, including several wonderful stelae and four small **hieroglyphic stairways**, now protected by thatched shelters grouped around the grassy plaza. On the south side of the plaza are the ruins of a palace, while on the east side a rich tomb was discovered under Temple L-51, probably belonging to the ruler Itzamnaaj K'awiil. Encircling the remains of this ceremonial core, it's still possible to make out the remains of the fortifications, a double defensive wall and stockade that the final occupiers erected.

ARRIVAL AND DEPARTURE	DOS PILAS

Getting to Dos Pilas is not straightforward or cheap. It's best to organize transport in Sayaxché or Flores. Either way you'll have to travel from Sayaxché, and then via a 45min speedboat trip to the *Posada El Caribe* (see p.285), followed by 12km on foot or horseback to the ruins. The hike takes you past the small site of Arroyo de Piedra, with two fairly well-preserved stelae, and the ruins of Tamarindito where another hieroglyphic stairway has been found.

Routes to Mexico

Heading west to Mexico from Petén is fairly straightforward and highly scenic in places, passing remote ruins and patches of dense rainforest. Though the Mexican state of Chiapas has been relatively calm for several years, tensions remain between government and Zapatista-aligned campesinos, and you can expect army security checks every hour or so as you get around. That said, travel is perfectly safe in the region, and the armed forces courteous and polite.

There are two popular **routes**. The first and most scenic involves crossing the Río Usumacinta into Chiapas at **Frontera Corozal**, from either **Bethel**, or a little upstream at **La Técnica** on the Guatemalan bank of the river. This trip enables you to pass the first-class ruins of **Yaxchilán** and Bonampak on the way. Alternatively, it's possible to head northwest **from Flores** to El Naranjo by bus, and cross the border at El Ceibo into the Mexican state of Tabasco.

CROSSING THE BORDER AT BETHEL/LA TÉCNICA

It's a straightforward trip to Mexico via **Bethel**, on the Río Usumacinta, where there's a Guatemalan *migración* post, and a good cheap posada.

By bus and boat Buses (roughly hourly, 5am–3pm; 4hr) leave Santa Elena's Terminal Nuevo for Bethel. At Bethel it's relatively easy to find a shared *lancha* heading downstream (around US$7/head; 30min) to Frontera Corozal.

By bus via La Técnica Alternatively, it's cheaper to get off the bus, obtain your exit stamp in Bethel and continue on the same bus for a further 12km to the tiny settlement of La Técnica, where you can cross the Usumacinta (5min; boats leave when full; US$1.30) to Corozal on the opposite bank. La Técnica lacks accommodation or other facilities.

From Flores Agencies in Flores (see p.256) offer cross-border tickets direct to Palenque using this route (about US$30/head).

Frontera Corozal and Yaxchilán

From the tranquil village of **Frontera Corozal** inside Mexico there's a regular boat service to the spectacular ruins of Yaxchilán. It's usually easy to hook up with other people to share the costs of hiring the boat, a good idea as it's quite steep at around US$140 for up to eight. It's a lovely 45-minute run downstream to the ruins; the banks of the Usumacinta are still covered in thick jungle, particularly on the Guatemalan side and there's plenty of birdlife. Be sure to drop by the little **museum** which has some superb stelae.

ARRIVAL AND DEPARTURE   FRONTERA COROZAL

By taxi and minibus The village is 18km east of the main Palenque–Comitán highway; *colectivo* taxis (US$2.50/head) and minibuses shuttle between the two.

From the highway there are regular minibuses to Palenque (roughly hourly, last around 4pm; 2hr 45min).

ACCOMMODATION

Escudo Jaguar By the riverside ☎ 55 3290 0993, ⓦ escudojaguarhotel.com. Attractive, comfortable rooms and serves meals. U̲S̲$̲1̲8̲–̲5̲4̲

Nueva Alianza Just inland from the dock ☎ 55 5339 0995. Good budget rooms in a large partitioned wooden structure, private cabins and also serves meals. U̲S̲$̲1̲6̲–̲4̲5̲

Piedras Negras

Sixty kilometres downstream from Yaxchilán, the Maya ruins of **Piedras Negras** loom high over the Guatemalan bank of the river. It's one of the most extensive sites in Guatemala, but it's also one of the least accessible. The city was called Yokib' ("the entrance") in Maya times; the Spanish name of Piedras Negras refers to the black stones lining the riverbank. Founded about 300 AD, the city developed an unrelenting rivalry with Yaxchilán for dominance over Usumacinta trade routes, contested by bloody battles and strategic pacts with Calakmul and Tikal. Like its adversary, Piedras Negras is best known for the extraordinary quality of its **carvings**, considered by many to be the finest from the Maya World. Several are in the Museo Nacional de Arqueología in Guatemala City, including a royal throne, exquisitely carved stelae and panels. However, there's still plenty to see here.

The ruins

Upon arrival, the most immediately impressive monument you'll see is a large rock jutting over the river bank with a carving of a seated male figure presenting a bundle to a female figure. This was once surrounded by glyphs, now badly eroded and best seen at night with a torch held at a low angle. As you continue up the hill, across plazas and over the ruins of buildings you get some idea of the city's size. Several buildings are comparatively well preserved, particularly the **sweat baths**, used for ritual purification; the most imposing of all is the **acropolis**, a huge palace complex of rooms, passages and courtyards towering 100m above the river bank. A **megalithic stairway** at one time led down to the river, doubtless a humbling sight to visitors (and captives) before the forest invaded the city.

ARRIVAL AND DEPARTURE PIEDRAS NEGRAS

By boat Getting to Piedras Negras is not straightforward. The perfect way to arrive is by boat along the Usumacinta, following the ancient Maya trade route, though this involves booking an expensive tour – Maya Expeditions are

highly recommended (see p.37) or a long, pricey boat trip from Bethel or Frontera Corozal. Trips from the Mexican bank opposite the ruins are no longer possible.

El Naranjo and Mexican border

This route to Mexico is once again popular with travellers. The river trip is no longer necessary as there's now a paved road right to the Mexican border at **El Ceibo** via the frontier town of **El Naranjo**.

CROSSING THE BORDER AT EL CEIBO

By bus Regular buses connect Santa Elena with El Naranjo (5 daily at 6am, 8am, 10am, noon & 2pm; 4hr), the nearest town in Guatemala to El Ceibo, from where microbuses run to the border post at El Ceibo (every 15min; 15min). If you choose this route note that it is used by Central American

migrants heading to El Norte and there's plenty of military in evidence. Get an early start and avoid getting stuck for the night in El Naranjo, which is a rough place with little to recommend it. On the Mexican side there are bus departures for Tenosique in Tabasco (every 40min; 1hr 15min).

Waka' (El Perú) and the Ruta Guacamaya

To the east of El Naranjo, in the upper reaches of the Río San Pedro, is **Waka'** (also called **El Perú**), a seldom-visited and largely unreconstructed archeological site buried in some of the wildest rainforest in Petén. Waka' ("stood up place") gets its name from its position on a 130m-high escarpment towering above a tributary of the Río San Pedro.

The city grew to become an important middle-ranking Petén settlement in the Late Classic period, controlling important overland and water routes. Despite being the nearest place of any size west of Tikal, it sided with the other great "superpower" – distant Calakmul – in the power politics of the time. Waka' remained under the Calakmul overlordship in the early eighth century, but would later pay for this affiliation when a resurgent Tikal overran the city in 743 AD, after which no monuments were carved here for 47 years.

The ruins

Most of the site's temple mounds are still coated in vegetation, but Waka' is perhaps most famous for its many well-preserved **stelae** and the recent discovery of a fascinating **royal tomb** of a female ruler dating from around 620 AD. This queen was clearly a formidable and highly revered figure as she was buried in a battle helmet with stingray spines for ritual bloodletting – burial customs usually only bestowed on male rulers. The guards here welcome visitors and can act as guides, particularly if you bring along a little spare food.

Wildlife

Close to the site, at the confluence of the San Pedro and Sacluc, there's a biological station at which rangers monitor forests that contain the largest concentrations of **scarlet macaws** in northern Central America. You've also an excellent chance of observing spider and howler monkeys, crocodiles, river turtles and the Petén turkey, and may even see a tapir on the banks of the Sacluc river. The best time to see scarlet macaws is between February and June when they nest in hollows of larger trees, but there are exotic birds in the Waka' region at all times of year.

ARRIVAL AND DEPARTURE **WAKÁ**

Guided tours Tours to Waka', best arranged in Flores (see p.256), are often dubbed La Ruta Guacamaya or "Scarlet Macaw Trail". These exciting two- or three-night trips are by 4WD, pick-up and boat along rivers and through primary forest, staying at the research station or camping at the ruins.

Yaxhá to the Belize border

East of the **Ixlú junction** on the road to Belize, a paved road runs 65km to the Belize border. The main attraction in these parts is **Yaxhá**, a huge Maya city on the fringes of two beautiful lakes: lagunas Yaxhá and Sacnab. The lakes are encircled by the dense jungle, swamps, savannah and wetlands of the **Monumento Natural Yaxhá–Nakúm–Naranjo**, whose 370 square kilometres harbour big cats, two species of crocodile and dozens of other reptiles, as well as prolific birdlife: spoonbills, the giant jabiru stork, eagles and vultures. It's one of the very few places in Guatemala where tapir are known to be breeding. The Postclassic ruins of **Topoxté** are also accessible from Yaxhá, and a third large site, **Nakúm**, is about 18km to the north. Further east, close to the Belize border, a side track leads to the intriguing site of **La Blanca** and its imposing palace.

Holtún

Thirty kilometres from Ixlú there's a sign on the right for the ruins of **Holtún**, a twenty-minute walk from the road. A large site first settled around 850 BC it has tall, unrestored temples adorned with masks, several stelae and altars, and the twinned temples of Pyramid X and Structure 7. On the roadside, look out for the sign put up by Bormán Pérez, who sells good-value wood and ceramic art from his house, and rents bikes and budget rooms.

Yaxhá

Daily 6am–5.30pm • US$10.50

Covering several square kilometres of a limestone ridge overlooking Laguna Yaxhá, **Yaxhá** is a compelling and rewarding Maya site to visit. Its name means "green-blue water", a reference to the wonderful turquoise hue of the lake just below. Of all Guatemala's ruins, only Tikal and El Mirador (and possibly Tintal) can trump the sheer scale and impact of this site, which has forty stelae, numerous altars, nine soaring temple pyramids and two ball courts. The dense jungle and lack of crowds only add to the special atmosphere of the place, and the wildlife is prolific (particularly howler monkeys and toucans).

Brief history

Relatively little is known about the history of Yaxhá, partly due to a relative lack of inscriptions and also because substantial archeological excavations have only recently begun. North of Plaza D the ruins are mostly Preclassic, while the bulk of the large structures in the south of the city date from the Classic era. The sheer size of the city indicates that Yaxhá was undoubtedly an important force in the central Maya region during this era, its influence perhaps only contained by the proximity of the "superstate" Tikal, with which it shares several archeological similarities and close ties. For much of the Classic period, Yaxhá seemed locked in rivalry with the city of Naranjo, about 20km to the northeast, dominating its smaller neighbour for much of this time but suffering a heavy defeat in 799 AD.

The ruins

Restoration work is ongoing at Yaxhá, and most of the buildings have yet to be cleared with many still choked in thick forest. The ruins are spread out over nine plazas, with around five hundred structures having been mapped so far.

6

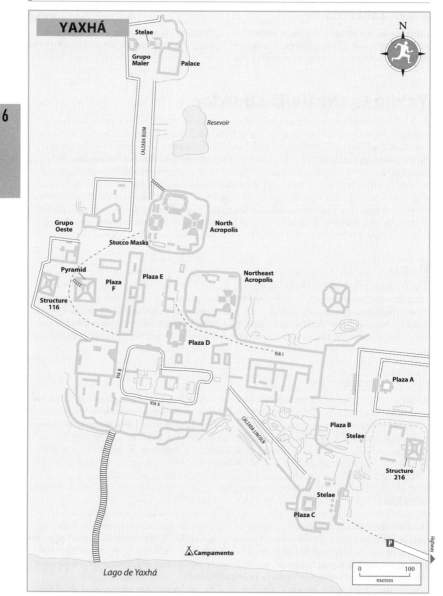

From the entrance you pass through **Plaza C**, where there's a restored pyramid and three stelae on its eastern side. Head northwest up Calzada Lincoln to Plaza D, where there's a ball court, and continue west towards Plaza F. The large **pyramid** here has been fitted with a steep wooden staircase – ascend it for a fine overview of the site, its temple tops and Lago de Yaxhá far below. It's thought this temple functioned as an astronomical observatory.

6

Grupo Maler

Continuing north up Calzada Blom, it's about 750m to the imposing **Grupo Maler** complex (named after the great early twentieth-century Austrian explorer Teobert Maler), where restoration is virtually complete. Here a pair of temples face each other across a grassy plaza in an arrangement that follows the twin-temple alignment tradition established at Tikal. Several weathered stelae stand in front of the ruins of the palace structure as well as the broken remains of a huge circular altar, possibly destroyed by invaders from Naranjo.

Acropolis Norte

South of the Grupo Maler complex, back along Calzada Blom, steps lead up to one of the oldest sections of the city, the Preclassic **Acropolis Norte**, which has been impressively restored. The grassy central plaza here is surrounded by temples on three sides, shaped in a triadic formation that typifies Preclassic Maya architectural design. The large temple on the north side of this acropolis has seven platforms, unusual curved edges and reaches around 22m in height. Steps behind the western temple lead down to a wall decorated with two giant stucco masks, another favoured Preclassic embellishment.

Structure 216

South from the Acropolis Norte you follow a grassy avenue-like trail, its sides overshadowed by soaring unrestored temples, to Plaza D, then east up Vía 1 to Plaza B, an open area bordered by low walls. Steps lead up from here to Plaza A, from where you can scramble up a bank on its south side towards Yaxhá's tallest and most impressive pyramid, the fully restored **Structure 216**. This imposing, Classic Maya temple rises in tiers to a height of more than 30m and has a broad central staircase. There are spectacular vistas over the forest and lakes from its summit – particularly at sunset.

ARRIVAL AND DEPARTURE   YAXHÁ

By road The main Flores–Belize road passes 11km south of the clearly signposted turn-off for Yaxhá. If you're not on a tour, then it's possible to get a ride from the main road as there's regular traffic to La Máquina village, 2km before the lakes.

On a tour Many Flores-based tour operators offer trips to the Yaxhá area; the two-day tours run by Mayan Adventure (see p.256) cost US$195 (minimum four people) and are highly recommended; these also include Nakúm or La Blanca.

ACCOMMODATION

There's a site *campamento* by the lake, below Yaxhá, where you can pitch a tent or sling a hammock beneath a thatched shelter for free.

Campamento Ecológico El Sombrero 2km south of ruins ☎7861 1687 or ☎4147 6830. This fine solar-powered jungle lodge right on the lakeshore has good thatched wooden cabañas (some with private bathroom) and rooms, a campsite, restaurant and a superb library.

There are fair prices for solo travellers. The helpful Italian owner can arrange boat trips on the lagunas, guides and horseriding. A trail from the hotel leads through the forest to other Maya ruins, past *chultunes* and ancient quarries. US$50–65

Topoxté

Topoxté, a much smaller site on an island close to the west shore of Lago de Yaxhá, is best visited as part of a Yaxhá tour. Boat trips from *El Sombrero* or a dock on the south side of Yaxhá ruins are possible too. Large crocodiles inhabit the lake so don't attempt a swim.

This small, unusual site was occupied as late as 1450 AD, making it one of the most substantial Postclassic settlements yet found. The restored temples have upright

---

FIESTAS IN PETÉN

JANUARY
12–15 Flores, the final day is the most dramatic

MARCH
10–19 San José, a small fiesta with parades, fireworks and dances

APRIL
April 27–May 1 Poptún

MAY
1–9 San Benito, sure to be wild and very drunken
15–22 Melchor de Mencos, main day 22nd

23–31 Dolores, main day 28th

JUNE
16 Sayaxché, held in honour of San Antonio de Padua

AUGUST
16–25 San Luis, main day 25th

OCTOBER
1–4 San Francisco
31 San José, a fascinating pagan fiesta (see box, p.261)

NOVEMBER
21–30 San Andrés, main day 30th

---

walls, columns, flat stone roofs and balustraded steps, there are several plazas and the site is riddled with *chultunes*. Seventeen skulls of sacrificed children were found here in one tomb.

Nakúm

The substantial **ruins of Nakúm**, which have been the subject of extensive investigation in the last few years, are 18km north of Lago de Yaxhá. This site now has the second largest number of restored buildings in Guatemala, after Tikal.

It's thought that Nakúm was a trading post in the Tikal empire, funnelling goods to and from the Caribbean coast, a role for which it was ideally situated at the headwaters of the Río Holmul. Settlers first arrived in the Middle Preclassic, but Nakúm rose to prominence in the Late Classic and prospered well into the Terminal Classic period; new buildings were being constructed here as the cities across the rest of the Maya World were collapsing. The city was abandoned around 950 AD.

The ruins

Nakúm's ceremonial centre is split between northern and southern sections, connected by a causeway. The **northern sector** has not been extensively investigated and is largely unrestored but contains a plaza surrounded by low platforms, Structure X (a towering pyramid-temple topped with a building arranged in a triadic pattern) and Structure W (a fourteen-roomed palace).

The **southern section** is highly impressive, and was substantially enlarged in the terminal Classic period – it's here you'll find Nakúm's iconic roof combs. The section contains three large plazas surrounded by temples: thirteen stelae and ten altars dot the Central Plaza. Its grand **acropolis** contains a huge **palace** (Structure D) of 44 rooms and myriad interior patios. Clear evidence of Teotihuacán influence has been found around Patio 1, where Central Mexican green obsidian and *Talud-Tablero* platforms have been unearthed.

ARRIVAL AND DEPARTURE NAKÚM

By road Access from Yaxhá is along a rough track which is usually impassable between July and Jan (unless the road is improved). The rest of the year you'll need a 4WD, though it could still take 1hr 30min to drive).

Tours Two-day horseback tours can be organized by *El Sombrero*; Flores tour operators also run trips here.

La Blanca

This small, unusual site (free) close to the Belize border is primarily of interest because is was occupied much later than most Maya settlements, at least until 1050 AD. Most of the buildings date from the late Classic period. Archeological work is ongoing, so you have the chance to gain direct insight into excavation work.

The entire site is dominated by a huge, ostentatious **palace** of eighteen living quarters built round a square patio. Its intriguing features include a 6m-high arch, some fine murals and also some ancient graffiti.

There's a small **information centre** here with informative panels in English about the site and its history.

6

ARRIVAL AND DEPARTURE   LA BLANCA

Tours La Blanca is 12km south of the Flores-Belize highway, the turn-off is about 10km before Melchor de Mencos; the dirt access road is in good condition. There's very little transport from the highway, so a tour makes sense. Combined trips to La Blanca and Yaxhá are offered by Mayan Adventure in Flores, costing US$55 (minimum four).

Melchor de Mencos and the border

The nondescript but bustling border-town of **MELCHOR DE MENCOS** boasts little of interest for the visitor (though there are a few stelae in the parque). Border formalities are fairly straightforward; you'll probably be asked for a small (illegal) departure tax on leaving Guatemala. **Moneychangers** will pester you on either side of the border – most give fair rates, but there's also an ATM at the Texaco gas station 500m west of the bridge.

CROSSING THE BORDER

On the Guatemalan side Microbuses and buses run between Santa Elena (see p.254) and Melchor (micros every 30min; 2hr 15min). From the border to Tikal taxi drivers charge around US$15/head for a shared ride (they leave when they have four people), or you can do it independently by catching a minibus for Santa Elena (every 30min) and jump off at the Ixlú junction (45 min) and getting another from there.

On the Belize side Buses leave for Belize City every 30min or so (3hr), usually right from the frontier. Shared taxis to Benque Viejo and San Ignacio (US$3/head; 20min) are also possible.

ACCOMMODATION

Río Mopán Lodge Next to immigration on river bank ☏ 7926 5196. Very pleasant option with a small pool and choice of rooms, some with balconies, in verdant grounds. There's a good restaurant and great trips to remote Maya sites are offered. U̲S̲$̲1̲3̲–̲3̲7̲

Into Honduras: Copán and around

COPÁN

Into Honduras: Copán and around

Across the border in Honduras, about five hours by road from Guatemala City, are the ruins of Copán, one of the most magnificent of all Maya sites. While its compact scale is not initially as impressive as Tikal or Mexico's Chichén Itzá, it boasts an astonishing number of decorative carvings, stelae and altars, including a towering hieroglyphic stairway. Throw in a wonderful site museum and the delightful and friendly village of Copán Ruinas, where most people stay, and it's easy to appreciate Copán's appeal.

7

Delightfully located in a sweeping highland valley, the city-state of **Copán** was the southernmost centre of the Maya civilization. The Maya chose a beautiful site on the fertile banks of the Río Copán at a pleasingly temperate altitude of 600m. Today the countryside around Copán is glorious to look at, with green rolling hills of pastureland and tobacco and coffee farms interspersed with patches of pine forest. Though the archeological site is the main attraction, there's plenty more to explore in the surrounding area, with hot springs, fincas and bird reserves close by.

Copán Ruinas

Just 10km east of the Guatemalan border, the small town of **COPÁN RUINAS** is a charming place of steep, cobbled streets and red-tiled roofs set among the lush scenery of Honduras's western highlands. Despite a fast-increasing number of visitors, income from whom now forms the mainstay of the town's economy, it has managed to remain a largely unspoilt and genuinely friendly place. Many travellers are seduced by Copán's delightfully relaxed atmosphere, clean air and rural setting, and end up spending longer here than planned, studying Spanish, eating and drinking well, or exploring the region's other minor sites, hot springs and beautiful countryside.

Parque Central

Half a day is enough to take in virtually all the town's attractions. The **Parque Central** – lined with banks, municipal structures and an attractive, whitewashed Baroque-style church – was designed and built by visiting archeologists Tatiana Proskouriakoff and Gustav Stromsvik. Unfortunately, the simple elegance of the original layout, which followed classical Spanish lines, has been somewhat spoilt by grandiose remodelling initiatives. It does remain a popular place to kill time, however, its benches filled with cowboy-booted farmhands and camera-touting visitors.

HONDURAS BASICS

Getting to Copán is pretty straightforward from Guatemala. There are excellent transport links from Antigua and Guatemala City by direct daily shuttle and luxury buses (see p.81 & p.63), or you can also travel via Chiquimula (see p.215), a longer but cheaper route. The Honduran **currency** is the Lempira; at the time of research the rate was US$1 = L19. Most nationalities (US, Canada, virtually all EU countries, Australia and New Zealand) qualify for a free **thirty-day visa** on arrival, and crossing the border is usually very straightforward. Note that the **country code** for Honduras is 504 and there are no area codes.

SCARLET MACAW

Highlights

❶ Copán Ruinas Combining a delightfully relaxed ambience with a cosmopolitan array of restaurants, bars and boutique hotels, this is a gorgeous little highland town. **See p.296**

❷ Macaw Mountain Bird Park and Nature Reserve This delightful park is a great place to get up front and personal with parrots, birds of prey and rare macaws. **See p.299.**

❸ Hacienda San Lucas One of the finest rural hotels in Central America, it's well worth a visit

for dinner if the rooms tariffs are beyond your budget. **See p.301**

❹ Copán Examine the exquisite carvings and temples at the archeological site dubbed the "Athens of the Maya World". **See p.302**

❺ Finca El Cisne Head to this idyllic farm to experience Honduran hospitality at its best; tours include horseriding and a spa visit. **See p.309**

HIGHLIGHTS ARE MARKED ON THE MAP ON P.298

Museo Regional de Arqueología

Parque Central • Daily 9am–5pm • US$3

On the southwest side of the parque and somewhat eclipsed by the sculpture museum at the site itself is the **Museo Regional de Arqueología**. Inside are some impressive Maya carvings collected from the Copán region, including the glyph-covered Altars T and U; Stela B, depicting the ruler Waxaklajuun Ub'aah K'awiil (Eighteen Rabbit); and some remarkable and intricately detailed **flints** – ornamental oddities with seven interlocking heads carved from obsidian. There are also two remarkable **tombs**. The first contains the remains of a female shaman, complete with jade jewellery and the skulls of a puma, deer and two human sacrificial victims. The other (10J–45), discovered in 1999 during road-building work, was created for an Early Classic–period ruler of Copán during the sixth century and comprises a vaulted burial chamber where the as yet unidentified ruler was buried with numerous ceramics and two large, carved jade pectoral pieces.

Municipalidad

Parque Central • Daily 8am–4pm • Free

Inside the *municipalidad* on the northwest side of the Parque Central is a fantastic permanent **photography exhibition** donated by Harvard University's Peabody Museum, detailing, in beautifully reproduced prints, the first archeological expeditions to Copán at the turn of the twentieth century.

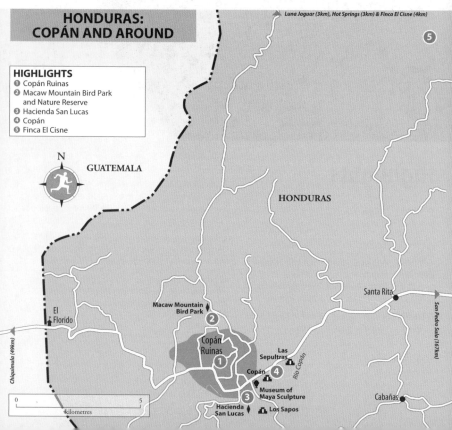

El Cuartel

Av Centro América • Tues–Sun 9am–5pm • US$1 • ☎ 2651 4105

Five blocks north of the parque, **El Cuartel** is an interactive children's learning centre with exhibits about the Maya civilization and a play area. It's located in a renovated army fort and has great views over the town.

Copán's outskirts: the Macaw Mountain Bird Park and Nature Reserve

3km north of parque • Daily 9am–5pm • US$10 • Ⓦ macawmountain.com

The **Macaw Mountain Bird Park and Nature Reserve** has abundant parrots, parakeets, toucans, six species of macaw, grey hawks and a great horned owl and makes a wonderful half-day excursion. Most of the birds have been previously kept as pets and donated to the centre, and breeding programmes have been started for very rare species such as the Buffon macaw and the yellow-lored amazon. There are walk-through aviaries and **nature trails** that wind through a lovely old-growth forest of cedar, mahogany, fig and zapote trees, interspersed with elevated viewing decks. You'll also find a coffee-roasting house and an excellent **café/restaurant** (meals are US$5–12) serving gourmet coffee from the Copán region, as well as an information centre explaining the relationship between the Maya and birds, and a wonderful natural pool for swimming.

ARRIVAL AND DEPARTURE | COPÁN RUINAS

FROM ANTIGUA AND GUATEMALA CITY

Shuttle buses Direct shuttle buses (US$20 one-way) leave Antigua daily at 4am, pausing to pick up passengers in Guatemala City an hour later on demand, and getting to Copán by about 10am; they return to Guatemala at 5.30am and noon. These shuttle buses are operated by several companies in Antigua (see p.81) and Copán including Base Camp (see p.300).

First-class buses Two daily luxury a/c pullman buses (at 3.30am & 6.30am; US$41 one-way) also cover the Antigua–Copán route via Guatemala City, operated by Hedman Alas, based at *Hotel Posada de Don Rodrigo* 5 Av Norte 17 in Antigua; they return from Copán at 2.20pm and 6.30pm. Litegua (see p.63) also operates one daily bus to the El Florido border from Guatemala City at 2.45pm; it returns to Guatemala City from the border at 3am.

FROM CHIQUIMULA VIA EL FLORIDO

You could save a little cash by travelling via the Guatemalan town of Chiquimula, which is regularly served by Rutas Orientales buses from Guatemala City and local buses from Puerto Barrios. From Chiquimula, minibuses leave every 30min (7am–6pm; 1hr 30min) for the border at El Florido, some via the town of Jocotán.

Border formalities are straightforward, though they can be slow – and you'll almost certainly be asked for unofficial US$2–3 taxes to cross here. The Banrural bank (daily 8am–5pm) at the border just inside Guatemala cashes dollars, or you can deal with the ever-present moneychangers who handle dollars, lempiras and quetzals at pretty fair rates.

From El Florido minibuses leave when full (about every 30min until 7pm; US$1.50) to the town of Copán Ruinas, taking around 20min. They arrive and depart from C 18 Conejo, a block or so west of the parque.

TO RÍO DULCE OR LÍVINGSTON

For Río Dulce or Lívingston in Guatemala, it's cheapest to take a minibus to the border at El Florido, then a local bus (every 30min, the last at 6.30pm; US$1.25) to Chiquimula from where there are regular buses to destinations including Puerto Barrios. Shuttle buses (see above) will also drop you off at the El Rancho junction on the Carretera al Atlántico highway, where you can connect with buses heading east.

DRIVING

If you plan to drive inside Honduras, note that you need permission from your Guatemalan rental-car company.

GETTING AROUND

On foot Almost everything of interest is within a few blocks of Copán's Parque Central. Street names have been introduced, though few locals use them.

Tuk-tuks (also called "mototaxis") are plentiful in Copán, and will whisk you around the village or to the ruins for around US$0.50/head a journey.

7

Macaw Mountain Bird Park (3km) & Aguas calientes (22.5km)

ACCOMMODATION
Casa de Café B&B	13
La Casa Rosada	5
Hacienda San Lucas	12
Hotel Calle Real	1
Hotel Don Udo's	11
Hotel Marina Copán	7
Hotel La Posada	6
Hotel Yaragua	8
Iguana Azul	14
Manzana Verde	3
La Posada de Belssy	4
Terramaya	2
Via Via	9
Yat Balam	10

EATING
Café San Rafael	7
Café Via Via	4
Carnitas Nia Lola	8
La Casa de Todo	3
Picame	1
Restaurante La Terraza	2
Twisted Tanya's	6
Vamos a Ver Café	5

DRINKING & NIGHTLIFE
Café Via Via	2
Sol de Copán	1

El Cuartel

Guacamaya Spanish School

Hotel Paty

Casasola Buses

Minibuses to aguas calientes

Quebrada Seesmil

Ruins (2km) & San Pedro Sula (179km)

Minibuses to La Florido border

Palacio Municipal

Parque Central

Market

Museo Regional de Arqueología

Banco Atlántida

Ixbalanque Spanish School

El Florido Border (10km)

Hedman Alas Terminal (200m), B (3km) & Los Sapos (3km)

CALLE DE LA PLAZA

CALLE INDEPENDENCIA

COPÁN RUINAS TOWN

INFORMATION, TOURS AND ACTIVITES

Tourist office C Independencia (daily 8am–7pm; ☎ 2651 3829, ⍟ copanhonduras.org), a block south of the Parque Central. Copán Connections and Base Camp are both excellent sources of information.

Base Camp Inside *Café Vía Vía* ☎ 2651 4695, ⍟ basecamphonduras.com. Tour operator that offers an excellent range of hikes, including an interesting Alternative Copán hike (US$8), full-day walks to Maya Chortí villages (US$35) and trips throughout Honduras.

Copán Connections C Independencia ☎ 2651 4182, ⍟ copanconnections.com. A one-stop source of information on Copán and popular destinations like Lago de Yojoa and the Bay Islands. They also offer canopy tours and trips to hot springs and indigenous villages.

Language schools Copán is an excellent place to study, with two good Spanish schools – four hours of classes plus full family-based accommodation and meals costs US$210–225 a week. Guacamaya (☎ 2651 4360,

ⓦguacamaya.com), two blocks north of the plaza, is the more established; Ixbalanque (☎2651 4432,

ⓦixbalanque.com), southwest of the plaza, is also worth considering.

ACCOMMODATION

Many of the town's older **hotels** have been renovated to attract the ever-expanding organized-tour market, while plenty of stylish new mid-range places have opened in the last few years. Budget options tend to fill up quickly so book ahead.

BUDGET

Hotel Calle Real Av Centro América ☎2651 4230, ⓔhotelcallereal@yahoo.com. Up a steep hill, this place offers tidy, clean accommodation in a leafy, shady garden with hammocks. The rooms, with fan or a/c, are great value. US$21

Iguana Azul Next to Casa de Café B&B, southwest edge of town ☎2651 4620, ⓦiguanaazulcopan.com. Very attractive budget base with four private rooms and two very pleasant dorms (twelve beds in total) all with decent mattresses and shared hot-water bathrooms. Dorms have lockers, there's free purified water, a pretty garden and laundry facilities. Dorms US$7, doubles US$16

Manzana Verde Ⓒ Macanudo ☎2651 4652, ⓦlamanzanaverde.com. The "green apple" is a hostel run by the *Vía Vía* team with a good vibe, three spacious dorms, lockers, kitchen and laundry facilities, a lounge with TV and an information-rich notice board. Dorms US$6

La Posada de Belssy Ⓒ Acrópolis ☎2651 4680, ⓦlaposadadebelssy.com. A good-value choice where the ten rooms (some smallish) have hot-water bathrooms, ceiling fans and cable TV. There's a small pool, nice hangout area at the top of the building, and use of a kitchen. US$16

Vía Vía Ⓒ de la Plaza ☎2651 4652, ⓦviaviacafe.com. Simple, smallish but spotless rooms with en-suite bathrooms at the rear of a popular travellers' café. It can be a tad noisy here at night, but it's decent value and there are nice touches (like a free freshly squeezed juice in the morning). US$16

MODERATE AND EXPENSIVE

★ **Casa de Café B&B** At the southwest edge of town ☎2651 4620, ⓦcasadecafecopan.com. A charming place owned by an American–Honduran couple, with comfortable and airy rooms, all simply yet elegantly presented with wood panelling, desks and private bathrooms with steaming hot water. There's also a fabulous garden where you could lie in a hammock and enjoy the views all day, and a massage pavilion. A substantial breakfast is included. The owners also have two excellent houses for rent opposite that are perfect for families or groups. US$55

La Casa Rosada Northwest of the parque ☎2651 4324, ⓦlacasarosada.com. This attractive B&B has impressive attention to detail with luxury linen and great beds and flat-screen TV. Staff are friendly and accommodating. US$87

★ **Hacienda San Lucas** 4km south of parque ☎2651 4495, ⓦhaciendasanlucas.com. Incredibly classy and atmospheric solar-powered hotel (a converted farmhouse) in the hills south of town, with startling views over the valley. It's an ideal place to relax, with plenty of space – the grounds include the Los Sapos archeological site and a zipline network (see p.308) – and plenty of colonial style. All the spacious rooms have handcrafted, cedar-wood beds and local textile decorations. Gourmet food is served (a five-course dinner is US$30) and horseriding can be arranged. US$140

Hotel Don Udo's Av Mirador ☎2651 4533, ⓦdonudos.com. Classy Dutch–Honduran-owned hotel with sixteen comfortable rooms and suites, most with a/c, set around a garden courtyard. Facilities here include wi-fi, sauna/jacuzzi, sun deck with valley views and a restaurant with good global cuisine. US$68

Hotel Marina Copán Av Centro América ☎2651 4070, ⓦhotelmarinacopan.com. Large luxury hotel right in the heart of town with fine gardens. The stylish rooms, all with a/c, are well presented and spacious, plus there's a small pool, gym and bar. US$110

Hotel La Posada Av Centro América ☎2651 4059, ⓦlaposadacopan.com. Rooms here are a little plain but decent value, with TVs and bathrooms, set off covered walkways with plenty of greenery around. It's a few steps off the plaza. US$41

Hotel Yaragua Ⓒ de la Plaza ☎2651 4050, ⓦyaragua.com. Smallish but comfortable, good-value rooms, set around a little courtyard, with good-quality double beds and cable TVs. US$30

★ **Terramaya** Av Centro América ☎2651 4623, ⓦterramayacopan.com. This boutique hotel features whitewashed walls and wrought-iron metalwork and boasts lots of understated style. Some of the six rooms have generous balconies with hammocks overlooking the Copán valley. There's a massage pavilion outside in the beautiful garden, a wonderful breakfast is included and there's complimentary coffee and iced tea served all day. Service standards are high. US$85

Yat Balam Ⓒ Independencia ☎2651 4338, ⓦyatbalam.com. An excellent boutique-style place with four superb rooms (two have a lounge area and balcony). The design theme combines exposed stone and wood beams with soothing creams. All have fridges, TVs and beautiful bed linen. It's above a few gift shops and a café. US$90

7

EATING

Copán has some superb places to eat and drink, many with an international flavour. Standards are usually very high, with generous portions and good service.

★ **Café San Rafael** Av Centro América ☎ 2651 4546. Deli-café run by a *queso* fanatic who studied cheese-making in California (so you won't go wrong with the cheese sampler platter). Sandwiches are good value, such as the grilled mozzarella and gouda served with plantain chips (US$2.75). Also serves fine coffee, sells good wine and gourmet treats. Free wi-fi. Daily 8am–8pm.

Café Vía Vía C de la Plaza ☎ 2651 4652. This huge, hip Belgian-owned bar-restaurant has a garden terrace at the rear and a real vibe on busy nights. Offers an array of sandwiches (using home-made bread), good breakfasts (US$4), omelettes, set meals (US$5), salads and plenty of veggie options. Daily 6.30am–midnight.

Carnitas Nia Lola Av Centro América ☎ 2651 4196. A quirky alpine lodge lookalike that serves quite pricey but large portions of delicious grilled and barbecued meats, plus some vegetarian dishes. It's also frequented as a drinking venue, with an early evening happy hour and a good mix of locals and visitors. Daily 7am–10pm.

La Casa de Todo C 18 Conejo ⓦ lacasadetodo.com. A lovely garden café with flavoursome, healthy food, lush licuados and coffee. Healthy breakfasts, and for lunch there are home-made soups, sandwiches and pasta, or try the *baleadas* with eggs. The premises also include

Copán's best gift shop, an internet café and laundry. Daily 7am–9pm.

Picame C Acrópolis ⓦ picamecopan.com. Casual, enjoyable Dutch-owned place with gingham tablecloths that's renowned for its spit-roast chicken but also good for an inexpensive breakfast (they serve Nutella baguettes), burrito or baguette. Mon & Wed–Sun 7am–9.30pm.

Restaurante La Terraza C Acrópolis ☎ 2651 4170. In a gorgeous colonial-style building, this café-restaurant serves fine food including breakfasts, waffles, pasta and sandwiches (the pollo wrap is US$7) in an atmospheric setting. Daily 8am–10pm.

Twisted Tanya's Av Mirador and C Independencia ☎ 2651 4182, ⓦ twistedtanya.com. This attractive, upmarket restaurant has an eclectic menu that includes filet mignon with mild jalapeño sauce and four-cheese ravioli with fresh tomato salsa. A three-course meal is US$22, plus there's a daily backpacker menu (4–6pm) for US$6–8. Tanya, a big personality from England, really makes the place. Daily 10am–midnight.

Vamos a Ver Café Av Centro América ☎ 2651 4627. Busy café in a covered patio that offers affordable and delicious home-made soups, sandwiches and snacks. Daily 7am–10pm.

DRINKING

Café Vía Vía C de la Plaza ⓦ viaviacafe.com. The town's number one watering hole, it's packed with travellers most nights. There's salsa on Wednesday (and a teacher present to help you learn those steps) and live music or DJs on weekends. Films are shown on Sunday, Monday and Tuesday. Daily 6.30am–midnight.

Sol de Copán Av Mirador ☎ 2651 4758. Terrific microbrewery-bar run by Thomas, a hospitable German who imports his own hops and ingredients from the homeland to create delicious beers: wheat beers, dark ales and lagers. Also serves tasty grub (around US$5) including sausages and home-made *spätzle* (pasta). Daily 1–11pm.

SHOPPING

La Casa de Todo C 18 Conejo ⓦ lacasadetodo.com. Offers a wonderful selection of handicrafts and souvenirs

including ceramics and jewellery. They also stock books on the ancient Maya. Daily 7am–9pm.

DIRECTORY

Banks Banco Atlántida and two other banks are on the parque; all have ATMs.
Internet *La Casa de Todo* (daily 7am–9pm). Rates are around US$1.25/hr.

Laundry *La Casa de Todo* (see above) charges around US$2.75 for a normal load.
Post office Just off the parque behind the museum.

Copán ruins

Daily 8am–4pm • US$15 including the Las Sepulturas ruins, though access to the archeological tunnels costs an extortionate US$15 extra • Registered guides charge US$30 for up to ten people for a 2–3hr tour

COPÁN RUINS lie 2km east of town, a pleasant fifteen-minute walk along a raised footpath that runs parallel to the highway. Entrance to the site is through the **visitor**

centre on the left-hand side of the car park, where a small exhibition explains Copán's place in the Maya World. Inside the visitor centre there's a ticket office and a desk where you can hire a **guide** – an excellent investment if you really want to get the most out of Copán. On the other side of the car park is a **cafeteria**, serving drinks and reasonable meals, and a small souvenir shop.

Brief history

Archeologists believe that settlers began moving into the Río Copán valley around 1400 BC, taking advantage of the area's rich agricultural potential, although construction of the city is not thought to have begun until around 100 AD. Once the most important **city-state** on the southern fringes of the Maya World, Copán was geographically isolated from the main Maya region, except the city of **Quiriguá**, 64km away to the north. However, despite the distances involved, relations were maintained with other Maya cities, particularly Tikal and Palenque.

Yax K'uk Mo'

Copán remained a small, isolated settlement until the arrival in 426 AD of an outsider, **Yax K'uk Mo'** (Great Sun First Quetzal Macaw), a warrior-shaman who established the basic layout of the city and founded a royal dynasty that lasted for four hundred years. It's unclear whether he was from Teotihuacán, the Mesoamerican superpower, or Tikal (which was under strong Teotihuacán influence at the time). Yax K'uk Mo' became the object of an intense cult of veneration, first established by his son **Popol Hol** and continued by subsequent members of the dynasty over fifteen generations.

Copán's golden era

Little is known about the next seven kings who followed Popol Hol, but in 553 AD, the **golden era** of Copán began with the accession to the throne of **Moon Jaguar**, who constructed the magnificent Rosalila Temple, now buried beneath Temple 16. The city thrived through the reigns of **Smoke Serpent** (578–628 AD), **Smoke Jaguar** (628–695 AD) and **Eighteen Rabbit** (695–738 AD), as the great fertility of the Copán region was exploited and wealth amassed from control of the jade trade along the Río Motagua. These resources and periods of stable government allowed for unprecedented political and social growth, as the population boomed to about 28,000 by 760 AD, the highest urban density in the entire Maya region.

Ambitious rebuilding continued throughout this era, using local andesite, a fine-grained, even-textured volcanic rock that was easily quarried and particularly suited to detailed carving, as well as the substantial local limestone beds, which were ideal for stucco production. The highly artistic carved-relief style for which Copán is famous reached a pinnacle during the reign of Eighteen Rabbit – whose image is depicted on many of the site's magnificent stelae and who also oversaw the construction of the Great Plaza, the final version of the ball court and Temple 22 in the East Court.

Defeat and re-emergence

Following the audacious capture and decapitation of Eighteen Rabbit by Quiriguá's Cauac Sky, construction at Copán came to a complete halt for seventeen years, possibly indicating a period of subjugation by its former vassal state. The royal dynasty subsequently managed to regroup, however, flourishing gloriously, albeit briefly, once more. **Smoke Shell** (749–763 AD) completed the **Hieroglyphic Stairway**, one of the most impressive of all Maya constructions, in an effort designed to symbolize this revival. Optimism continued during the early years of the reign of **Yax Pasaj** (763–820 AD), Smoke Shell's son, who commissioned **Altar Q**, which illustrates the entire dynasty from its beginning, and completed the final version of **Temple 16**, which towers over the site, about 776 AD.

7

Decline

Towards the end of Yax Pasaj's rule, the rot set in: human remains found indicate that the decline was provoked by inadequate food resources created by population pressure, resulting in subsequent environmental collapse. The seventeenth and final ruler, **Ukit Took'**, assumed the throne in 822 AD, but his reign proved miserably inauspicious. Poignantly, the only monument to his reign, Altar L, was never completed, as if the sculptor had downed his tools and walked out on the job.

The nineteenth century

The site was known to the Spanish, although they took little interest in it. Not until the nineteenth century and the publication of *Incidents of Travel in Central America, Chiapas and Yucatán* by **John Lloyd Stephens** and **Frederick Catherwood** did Copán become known to the wider world. Stephens, the then acting US ambassador, succeeded in buying the ruins in 1839 and, accompanied by Catherwood, a British architect and artist, spent several weeks clearing the site and mapping the buildings. Stephens' plans to float Copán's monuments down the Río Copán and on to the US were never realized, but the instant success of the book and the interest it sparked in Mesoamerican culture ensured that Copán became a magnet for explorers.

The twentieth century

British archeologist **Alfred Maudsley** began a full-scale mapping, excavation and reconstruction of the site in 1891. A second major investigation was begun in 1935 by the Carnegie Institution in Washington, during which the Río Copán was diverted to prevent it carving into the site. Since 1977, the Instituto Hondureño de Antropología e Historia has been running a series of projects with the help of archeologists from around the world. Copán is now perhaps the best understood of all Maya cities, and a series of **tunnelling projects** beneath the Acropolis has unearthed remarkable discoveries including, in 1989, the Rosalila Temple, which is now open to the public. In 1993 the Papagayo Temple, built by Popol Hol and dedicated to his father Yax K'uk Mo', was uncovered, and in 1998 further burrowing revealed the tomb of the founder himself.

Museum of Mayan Sculpture

Daily 8am–3.45pm • US$7

Opposite the visitor centre is the terrific **Museum of Mayan Sculpture**, arguably the finest in the entire Maya region, with a tremendous collection of stelae, altars, panels and well-labelled explanations in English. You enter through a dramatic entrance doorway, resembling the jaws of a serpent, and pass through a tunnel (signifying the passage into *Xibalbá*, or the underworld). Dominating the museum is a full-scale, flamboyantly painted replica of the magnificent **Rosalila Temple**, built by Moon Jaguar in 571 and discovered intact under Temple 16. A vast crimson-and-jade-coloured mask of the Sun God, depicted with wings outstretched, forms the main facade of the temple. Other ground-floor exhibits concentrate on aspects of Maya beliefs and cosmology, while the upper floor houses many of the finest original sculptures from the Copán valley, comprehensively displaying the skill of the Maya craftsmen.

Warden's gate

From the museum it's a 200m walk east to the **warden's gate**, the entrance to the site proper, where your ticket will be checked and where there are usually several squabbling **scarlet macaws** to greet your arrival – these are tame and sleep in cages by the gate at night.

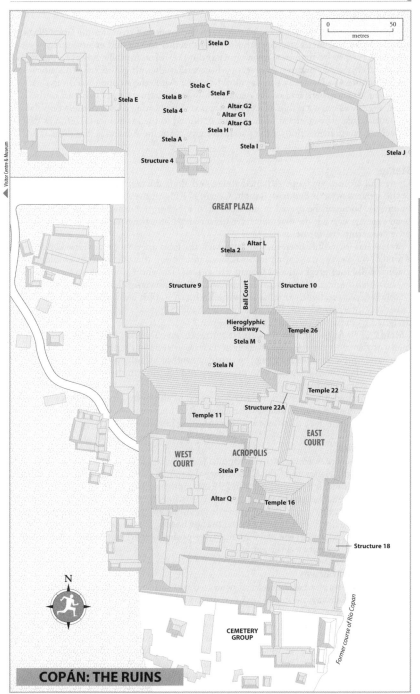

0   50
metres

◄ Visitor Centre & Museum

Stela D

Stela C

Stela B   Stela F

Stela E

Stela 4

Altar G2

Altar G1

Altar G3

Stela H

Stela A

Stela I

Stela J

Structure 4

GREAT PLAZA

7

Altar L

Stela 2

Structure 9

Structure 10

Ball Court

Hieroglyphic
Stairway

Temple 26

Stela M

Stela N

Temple 22

Structure 22A

Temple 11

**EAST
COURT**

**WEST
COURT**

ACROPOLIS

Stela P

Altar Q

Temple 16

Structure 18

N

Former course of Río Copán

**CEMETERY
GROUP**

COPÁN: THE RUINS

The Great Plaza

Straight ahead from the warden's gate through the avenue of trees lies the **Great Plaza**, a large rectangular arena strewn with the magnificently carved and exceptionally well-preserved stelae that are Copán's outstanding features. Initially, however, the visual impact of this grassy expanse may seem a little underwhelming: the first structure you see is **Structure 4**, a modestly sized pyramid-temple, while the stepped buildings bordering the northern end of the plaza are low and unremarkable. This part of the Great Plaza was once a public place, the stepped sides bordered by a densely populated residential area. The grandest buildings are confined to the monumental temples that border the southern section of the plaza, rising to form the Acropolis, the domain of the ruling and religious elite.

Stelae

Dotted all around are Copán's famed **stelae** and altars, made from local andesite. Most of the stelae represent **Eighteen Rabbit**, Copán's "King of the Arts" (stelae A, B, C, D, F, H and 4). Some of the carved monuments here are reproductions, though they have been expertly carved; the originals have been moved into the site museum so they're protected from the elements.

Stela A has incredibly deep carving, although the faces are now eroded; its sides include a total of 52 glyphs, translating into a famous inscription that includes the emblem glyphs of the four great cities of Copán, Palenque, Tikal and Calakmul – a text designed to show that Eighteen Rabbit saw his city as a pivotal power in the Maya World.

Stela B depicts a slightly oriental-looking Eighteen Rabbit wearing a turban-like headdress intertwined with twin macaws; his hands support a bar motif, a symbol designed to show the ruler holding up the sky.

Stela C (730 AD) is one of the earliest stones to have faces on both sides and, like many of the central stelae, has an altar at its base, carved in the shape of a turtle. Two rulers are represented here: facing the turtle (a symbol of longevity) is Eighteen Rabbit's father, Smoke Jaguar, who lived well into his 80s; on the other side is Eighteen Rabbit himself.

Stela H, perhaps the most impressively executed of all the sculptures, shows Eighteen Rabbit wearing the latticed skirt of the Maize God, his wrists weighed down with jewellery, while his face is crowned with a stunning headdress.

The Ball Court

South of Structure 4, towards the Acropolis, is the I-shaped **Ball Court**, one of the largest and most elaborate of the Classic period and one of the few Maya courts still to have a paved floor. It was completed in 738 AD, just four months before Eighteen Rabbit's demise at the hands of Quiriguá; two previous versions lie beneath it. Like its predecessors, the court was dedicated to the great macaw deity, and both sloping sides of the court are lined with three sculpted **macaw heads**. The rooms that line the sides of the court, overlooking the playing area, were probably used by priests and members of the elite as they watched the game.

Hieroglyphic Stairway

Pressed up against the Ball Court and protected by a vast canvas cover is the famed **Hieroglyphic Stairway**, perhaps Copán's most astonishing monument. The stairway, which takes up the entire western face of the Temple 26 pyramid, is made up of some 72 stone steps; every block is carved to form part of the glyphic sequence – around 2200 glyph blocks in all. It forms the longest-known Maya hieroglyphic text, but, unfortunately, attempted reconstruction by early archeologists left the sequence so jumbled that a complete interpretation is still some way off. What is known is that the stairway was initiated to record the dynastic history of the city: some of the lower steps were first put in place by Eighteen Rabbit in 710 AD, while Smoke Shell rearranged and completed most of the sequences in 755 AD as part of his efforts to reassert the city's dignity and strength. At the base of the stairway, the badly weathered **Stela M** depicts Smoke Shell and records a solar eclipse in 756 AD.

Temple 11 and Stela N

Adjacent to the Hierogylphic Stairway, and towering over the extreme southern end of the plaza, are the vertiginous steps of **Temple 11** (also known as the Temple of the Inscriptions). The temple was constructed by Smoke Shell, who is thought to be buried beneath it, though no tomb has yet been found. At its base is another classic piece of Copán carving, **Stela N** (761 AD), representing Smoke Shell, with portraits on the two main faces of the stela and glyphs down the sides. The depth of the relief has protected the nooks and crannies, some of which still bear traces of paint – originally the carvings and buildings would have been painted in a whole range of bright colours, but for some reason only the red has survived.

The Acropolis

From the southwestern corner of the plaza, a trail runs past some original drainage ducts beyond which stone steps climb steeply up the side of Temple 11 to a soaring cluster of temples, dubbed the **Acropolis**. This lofty inner sanctum was the preserve of royalty, nobles and priests; it was the political and ceremonial core where religious rituals were enacted, sacrifices performed and rulers entombed. The whole structure grew in size over four hundred years, the temples growing higher and higher as new structures were built over the remains of earlier buildings. A warren of excavated tunnels, some open to the public, bores through the vast bulk of the Acropolis to the Rosalila Temple and several tombs. From the summit of Temple 11, beside a giant ceiba tree (a tree held sacred by the Maya), there's a panoramic view of the site below, over the Ball Court and Great Plaza to the green hills beyond.

Temple 22

A few metres east of Temple 11 are the **Mat House** (Structure 22A), a governmental building distinguished by its interlocking weave-like patterns, and **Temple 22**, which boasts some superbly intricate stonework around the door frames. Constructed by Eighteen Rabbit, Temple 22 functioned as a "sacred mountain" where the elite performed religious blood-letting ceremonies. Above the door is the carving of a double-headed snake, its heads resting on two figures, which are in turn supported by skulls. The decoration here is unique in the southern Maya region – only Yucatán sites such as Kabáh and Chicanna have carvings of comparable quality.

The East Court

Below Temple 22 are the stepped sides of the **East Court**, a graceful plaza that also bears elaborate carvings, including life-sized jaguar heads with hollow eyes that would have once held pieces of jade or polished obsidian. In the middle of the western staircase, flanked by the jaguars, is a rectangular Venus mask, carved in superb deep relief. Rising over the court and dominating the Acropolis is the tallest structure in Copán, **Temple 16**, a 30m pyramid completed by the city's sixteenth ruler, Yax Pasaj, in 776 AD. To construct the temple Yax Pasaj had to build on top of the **Rosalila Temple**, though it was built with extraordinary care so as not to destroy the earlier temple. The temple served as a centre for worship during the reign of Smoke Serpent, or Butz' Chan (578–628 AD), Copán's eleventh ruler, a period that marked the apogee of the city's political, social and artistic growth – so the discovery of the Rosalila was a very exciting find. You can now view the brilliant original facade of the buried temple by entering through a short **tunnel** – an unforgettable, if costly (US$15), experience. The admission price does at least include access to two further tunnels, which extend below the East Plaza past some early cosmological stucco carvings – including a huge macaw mask – more buried temple facades and crypts including the Galindo tomb.

Structure 18

At the southern end of the East Court, **Structure 18** is a small square building with four carved panels in which Yax Pasaj was buried in 821 AD. The diminutive scale of the structure reveals how quickly decline set in, with the militaristic nature of the panels symptomatic of the troubled times. The tomb was empty when excavated by archeologists and is thought to have been looted. From Structure 18 there's a terrific view of the valley, over the Río Copán, which eroded the eastern buildings of the Acropolis over the centuries until its path was diverted. South of Structure 18, the **Cemetery Group** was once thought to have been a burial site, though it's now known to have been a residential complex and home of the ruling elite.

The West Court

The second plaza of the Acropolis, the **West Court**, is confined by the south side of Temple 11, which has eight small doorways, and Temple 16. **Altar Q**, at the base of Temple 16, is the court's most famous feature and an astonishing example of ancestral symbolism. Carved in 776 AD, it celebrates Yax Pasaj's accession to the throne on July 2, 763 AD. The top of the altar is carved with six hieroglyphic blocks, while the sides are decorated with sixteen cross-legged figures, all seated on cushions, who represent previous rulers of Copán. All are pointing towards a portrait of Yax Pasaj which shows him receiving a ceremonial staff from the city's first ruler Yax K'uk Mo', thereby endorsing Yax Pasaj's right to rule. Behind the altar is a small crypt, discovered to contain the remains of a macaw and fifteen big cats, sacrificed in honour of his ancestors when the altar was inaugurated.

Las Sepulturas

Daily 8am–4pm • Entrance with the same ticket as for Copán.

Two kilometres east of the ruins along a stone pathway is the much smaller site of **Las Sepulturas**, the focus of much archeological interest in recent years because of the information it provides on daily domestic life in Maya times. Eighteen of the forty-odd residential compounds at the site have been excavated, comprising one hundred buildings that would have been inhabited by the elite. Smaller compounds on the edge of the site are thought to have housed young princes, as well as concubines and servants. It was customary to bury the nobility close to their residences, and more than 250 tombs have been excavated around the compounds – given the number of women found in the tombs it seems likely that the local Maya practised polygamy. One of the most interesting finds – the tomb of a priest or shaman, dating from around 450 AD – is on display in the museum in Copán Ruinas town.

Around Copán

The forested, highland region around Copán is very beautiful and loaded with interest including waterfalls, hot springs, a minor archeological site, coffee fincas, ziplines and a spa. Tour operators can set up trips to all these attractions.

Hacienda San Lucas and Los Sapos

4km south of town • Zipline US$35; Los Sapos US$1.50 • ☎ 2651 4495, ⓦ haciendasanlucas.com • A tuk-tuk will cost US$3

The **Hacienda San Lucas** (see p.301) is a lovely rural hotel about 4km south of town, within whose grounds are a couple of interesting attractions. A wonderful sixteen-stage

zipline network has been set up here, with wires commencing in the hills and plunging across the Copán valley, offering a stunning view of the town, then down across the Río Copán and ending up beside the ruins of the Acropolis.

Also in the grounds of the hotel, the ruins of **Los Sapos** date from the same era as Copán. This is a small site whose name derives from a rock carved in the shape of a toad – it's thought to have been a place where Maya women came to bear children, though unfortunately time and weather have eroded much of the carving. You can walk here in around an hour or so from Copán – cross the river after the Hedman Alas bus terminal, bear left and follow the signs.

Santa Rita

Pick-ups leave Copán regularly throughout the day for the peaceful town of **SANTA RITA**, 9km to the northeast. At the river bridge, just before entering the town, a path leads up to **El Rubí**, a pretty double-waterfall on the Río Copán, about 2km away. Organized tours (see p.300) here from Copán are around US$20 per head.

Hot springs

Daily 8am–6pm • US$1.50 • Minibuses (about every 45min; 1hr) head here from the football field west of the parque in Copán

Around 22km north of Copán are some (very) **hot springs**, set in lush highland scenery dotted with coffee fincas and patches of pine forest. You can either wallow around in man-made pools or head to the source via a short trail where cool river water and near boiling-hot spring waters combine.

Luna Jaguar

Daily 8am–5pm • US$10 • ☎ 2651 4746 • Reasonably frequent buses (45min) leave from Hotel Paty, though it's easier to join a trip with Copán's tour operators

On the other side of the river from the hot springs, **Luna Jaguar** is a day-spa set in forested grounds where a stone path connects thirteen different treatment stations (US$30 each) that include natural steam baths, masseurs and a hot spring–fed jacuzzi. It's undoubtedly a lovely natural environment, even if the experience is a little bit themed, and pricey.

Finca El Cisne

Day trip US$70, overnight US$90 (including accommodation, breakfast and dinner) • ☎ 2651 4695, ⊛ fincaelcisne.com

A kilometre or so further north from the spa, 24km from Copán, is the **agroturismo** centre at **Finca El Cisne**, a working finca involved in the production of cardamom, shade-grown coffee, cattle and fruit. Owner Carlos Castejón's family has worked the land here since 1885, and he's a superb host, explaining all about the farm's eco-sensitive agricultural practices. Day-trips include transport from Copán, about three hours of highly scenic horseriding (on well-trained mounts suitable for inexperienced riders), swimming in the Río Blanco and a visit (entrance included) to the Luna Jaguar hot springs. The overnight option gives you time to really enjoy the rural setting and hospitality (Carlos's mother's cooking is legendary). Base Camp tours (see p.300) in Copán, organize the trips here.

7

KEEL-BILLED TOUCAN

Contexts

History

Little is known about the area that is now called Guatemala in the days before the advent of Maya civilization, and even the early origins of the Maya remain fairly mysterious. Today, the Maya world is one of the world's hottest archeological areas, and recent excavations have fostered a greater understanding of the region's history – but also ripped apart many previously accepted theories. Although the historical picture is becoming much clearer, many issues are still subject to ongoing academic polemic.

Prehistory

Opinions differ as to when the first people arrived in the Americas. The established theory is that **Stone Age hunter-gatherers** crossed the Bering land bridge from Siberia to Alaska in several waves beginning about 17,000 years ago, but there's mounting evidence for a much earlier date. Travelling along an ice-free corridor (and possibly in small boats along the coastline) they migrated south into Central America. The first recognizable culture, known as **Clovis**, had emerged by 11,000 BC, and stone tools, including spearpoints, blades and scrapers, dating from 9000 BC have been found in the Guatemalan highlands.

In **Mesoamerica**, an area defined as stretching from north-central Mexico through Central America to Panama, the first settled pattern of development took place around 8000 BC, as a warming climate forced the hunter-gatherers to adapt to a different way of life. The glaciers were in retreat and the big game, upon which the hunters depended, became scarce due to the warmer, drier climate (and possibly over-hunting). This period, in which the hunters turned to more intensive use of plant foods, is known as the **Archaic period** and lasted until about 2000 BC. During this time the food vital to the subsequent development of agriculture, such as corn, beans, peppers, squash and probably maize, were domesticated.

The early Maya

After 2000 BC we move into the **Preclassic** era, a name used by archeologists to describe the earliest developments in the history of the **Maya**. During the **Early Preclassic** (2000–1000 BC), the Maya settled in villages throughout the region, as the foragers became farmers and began making pottery. By 1100 BC, the **Olmec**, often called Mesoamerica's "mother culture", were constructing pyramid-like ceremonial platforms and carving colossal stone heads at San Lorenzo, just to the northwest of the Maya region. Their artistic, polytheistic religious (and almost certainly political) influence spread throughout Maya lands, and Olmec-style carvings have been found at numerous sites along Guatemala's Pacific coast, in El Salvador and at Copán, in

c.11,000 BC	c.8000–2000 BC	3114 BC
Clovis culture. Worked-stone projectile points used for hunting found across Central America.	Archaic period. Villagers farm maize and beans, make pottery and probably spoke a Proto-Maya language.	Mythical start of the Maya Calendar, marking the creation of the present world.

Honduras. The Olmec also developed an early writing system and a calendar known as the "**Long Count**", later adopted by the Maya.

Nakbé and the Middle Preclassic era

The population increased substantially across the Maya region during the **Middle Preclassic** period (1000–400 BC). In northern Petén, **Nakbé** had, by 750 BC, grown to become a substantial settlement, complete with imposing temples and stucco sculptures – evidence that the Maya had progressed far beyond a simple peasant society. By 500 BC other centres – including El Mirador and Cival – were building their first ceremonial structures and astronomical observatories.

It is thought that a common language was spoken throughout the Maya lands, and that a universal belief system, practised from a very early date, may have provided the stimulus and social cohesion to build bigger towns and religious temples. Materials including obsidian and jade from the Guatemalan highlands and granite and salt from Belize were widely traded. Pottery, including red and orange jars and dishes of the **Mamon** style, found at a number of settlements, indicate increasing pan-Maya communication. At the same time, food surpluses and rising prosperity levels gradually enabled some inhabitants to eschew farming duties and become seers, priests and astronomers.

El Mirador and the Late Preclassic

Greater advances in architecture were achieved in the **Late Preclassic** (400 BC–250 AD) as other centres prospered in northern Petén, and the Mirador Basin (see p.277) became the focus of Maya civilization. **El Mirador** expanded to become a massive city, spread over twenty square kilometres, with a population of around one hundred thousand. Taking advantage of the swampland that surrounded their city, Mirador's inhabitants fertilized vast fields of crops using rich **mud** from nearby marshes and seasonal lakes.

Very little is known about the power politics of these times, but the sheer size of El Mirador indicates that the city must have acquired "superstate" status by around 100 BC. Positioned at the heart of a vast trading network, the city was surrounded by hundreds of other settlements like Tintal and Xulnal, all connected by a web of stone causeways, the highways of their day. The La Danta temple complex at Mirador was constructed to a height of 78m – the highest building ever to have been built by a pre-Columbian culture in the Americas – a feat that took an estimated fifteen million days of labour.

Kaminaljuyú

El Mirador's only serious rival during the Late Classic era was located several hundred kilometres to the south, on the site of the modern capital of Guatemala City. **Kaminaljuyú** had established a formidable commercial empire based on the supply of obsidian and jade, and held sway over a string of settlements along the Pacific coast, including Takalik Abaj. It's clear that the southern Maya area was much more influenced by Olmec advances at this time.

Preclassic culture and society

From 1 AD pyramids and temple platforms were emerging at Tikal, Uaxactún and many other sites in Petén, in what amounted to an explosion of **Maya culture**. The

c.1000 BC	750 BC	500 BC
Earliest confirmed settlement in the Mirador Basin and Cival.	Temple complexes constructed at Nakbé. Maya culture eclipses Olmec in Petén.	First evidence of ceremonial buildings at Tikal.

MAYA ARCHEOLOGICAL PERIODS

Maya archeological periods are confusing, not least because when they were established in the mid-twentieth century very little was known about the formative years of Maya civilization. Recent findings have revealed that the Preclassic era was far more advanced than previously thought.

Archeological periods vary according to the source. This guide follows those used in the *Chronicle of the Maya Kings and Queens* by Simon Martin and Nikolai Grube (see p.360).

Pre–2000 BC	Archaic	**600 AD–800 AD**	Late Classic
2000 BC–1000 BC	Early Preclassic	**800 AD–909 AD**	Terminal Classic
1000 BC–400 BC	Middle Preclassic	**909 AD–1200 AD**	Early Postclassic
400 BC–250 AD	Late Preclassic	**1200 AD–Spanish**	
250 AD–600 AD	Early Classic	**Conquest**	Late Postclassic

Maya corbelled arch was developed in this period, and architectural styles became more ambitious. A stratified **Maya society** was also becoming established, the nascent states led by rulers and shamanic priests who presided over religious ceremonies dictated by astronomical and calendrical events. There were specialist craftsmen, architects, scribes and artists capable of creating the exquisite murals of San Bartolo and Popol Vuh stucco sculptures of Mirador (see p.279). Intensive agriculture was also practised using irrigation from vast reservoirs via extensive canal networks.

Drought and disaster

Towards the end of the Late Preclassic period, during the second and third centuries AD, environmental disasters plagued the region. El Mirador and all its satellite cities collapsed by 150 AD, after a long **dry climatic period** and the severe over-exploitation of the forest environment, which severely cut agricultural production.

In the southern region, the eruption of the **Ilopango volcano** in central El Salvador smothered a vast area in ash, probably provoking mass migration from cities including Kaminaljuyú, which was virtually abandoned around 250 AD. Temple building ceased and Pacific trade routes were disrupted. Much of the trade was re-routed to the north, bringing prosperity (but also Central Mexican influence) to the cities of central Petén, including **Tikal**.

The Classic Maya

The development that separates the Late Preclassic from the **Classic period** (250–909 AD) is the introduction of the Long Count calendar and a recognizably Maya form of writing. This occurred by the end of the third century AD and marks the beginning of the greatest phase of Maya achievement.

During the Classic period all the cities we now know as ruined or restored sites were built, almost always over earlier structures. Elaborately carved **stelae**, bearing dates and emblem glyphs, were erected at regular intervals. These tell of actual rulers and of historical events in their lives – battles, marriages, dynastic succession and so on.

300 BC	**200 BC**	**150 BC**
Nakbé temples rebuilt to 45m height; massive building projects commence at El Mirador.	Miraflores culture thrives on Pacific coast and Guatemalan highlands, centred at Kaminaljuyú.	El Mirador enters its greatest era as seventy-metre-high temples are built, giant causeways constructed.

Enter Teotihuacán

Developments in the Maya area during the Early Classic period became increasingly influenced by a giant power to the north – **Teotihuacán**, which dominated Central Mexico and boasted a population of over 150,000. Its **armed merchants**, called *pochteca*, spread the authority of Teotihuacán as far as Petén, the Yucatán and Copán. It's unlikely that Teotihuacán launched an outright military invasion of Maya territory, but the city's influence was strong enough to precipitate fundamental changes. In 378 AD, an armed merchant called **Siyak K'ak** provoked a takeover of Tikal (see p.265), establishing a new dynasty, while at Copán, Yax K'uk Mo' (who was almost certainly from Teotihuacán) founded that city's royal lineage in 426 AD. These Mexicans also brought alternative religious beliefs, and new styles of ceramics, art and architecture – Kaminaljuyú was rebuilt in Teotihuacán style, and Tikal and Copán temples and stelae from the era depict Central Mexican gods.

The Kingdom of the Snake

While Tikal was positioning itself within the Teotihuacán sphere of influence and dominating the Petén, an increasingly precocious rival Maya state was emerging to the north: **Calakmul**, "the kingdom of the snake". From the fifth century, these two states grew to eclipse all other cities in the Maya World, establishing dominion over huge swathes of the region. Each controlling sophisticated trade networks, they jostled for supremacy as Mexican influence waned. Calakmul formed an alliance with **Caracol** (today located in Belize) and defeated Tikal in 562 AD – detailed carvings depict elaborately costumed lords trampling on bound captives. This victory caused a near-hiatus in Tikal's empire building during which there was little new construction at the city or in the smaller centres under its patronage.

Late Classic

The prosperity and grandeur of the **Late Classic** period (600–800 AD) reached across the Maya world: from Palenque in the northwest to Copán in the south and Altun Ha in the east. Bound together by a coherent religion and culture, Maya architecture, astronomy and art reached degrees of sophistication unequalled by any other pre-Columbian society. Trade prospered and populations grew – by 750 AD it's estimated that the region's people numbered around **ten million**. Many Maya states were larger than contemporary western European cities, then in their "Dark Ages".

Masterpieces of painted pottery and carved jade (their most precious material) were created, often for use as funerary offerings. Shell, bone and, occasionally, marble were also exquisitely carved; temples were painted in brilliant colours, inside and out.

In the power politics of the era, Tikal avenged its bitter defeat by overrunning Calakmul in 695 AD and reasserting its influence over its former vassal states of Río Azul and Waka' (El Perú). In a furious epoch of monument building, five of the great temples that define the ceremonial heart of the city were finished between 670 and 810 AD. Elsewhere across Maya lands, cities including Piedras Negras, Yaxhá and Yaxchilán flourished as never before, giving rise to more and more imposing temples and palaces, and unparalleled artistic achievements.

c.1 AD	c.150 AD	292 AD
Emergence of Teotihuacán in Mexico.	El Mirador and other Preclassic cities abandoned, probably due to environmental collapse.	Stela 29 carved at Tikal, with Long Count calendar date.

The Maya in decline

The glory days were not to last very long, however. By 750 AD political and social changes were beginning to be felt; alliances and trade links broke down, wars increased and stelae recording periods of time were carved less frequently.

After 800 AD we move into a period known as the **Terminal Classic** during which the great cities were gradually depopulated, and new construction virtually ceased in the central area after about 830 AD. Bonampak was abandoned before its famous murals could be completed, while many of the great sites along the Usumacinta River were occupied by militaristic outsiders.

Drought and disorder

The reason for the decline of the Maya is not (and may never be) known, though it was probably a result of several factors. It's known that Maya lands were already under severe pressure from deforestation by the late ninth century, when the region was struck by a sustained **drought**. An incredibly high population density put great strains on food production, possibly exhausting the fertility of the soil, and epidemics may have combined to cause the abandonment of city life.

Some Mayanists speculate that there may have been a peasant revolt caused by mass hunger and the demands of an unproductive elite. Whatever the causes, strife and **disorder** appear to have spread throughout Mesoamerica by the end of the Classic period. In the Maya heartland, virtually all the key cities were abandoned, and those few that remained were reduced to a fairly primitive state. Some survived on the periphery, however, particularly in eastern Petén and northern Belize. The settlements of the Yucatán peninsula also struggled on, and though the region escaped the worst of the depopulation, it was conquered by the militaristic **Toltecs** in 987 AD, creating a hybrid of Mexican-Maya culture.

Mass migration

With the decline of Maya civilization in Petén, there was an influx of population into Belize, Yucatán and the south of Guatemala. These areas now contained the last vestiges of Maya culture, and it's at this time that the Guatemala highland area began to take on some of the tribal characteristics still in evidence today. By the end of the Classic period there were small settlements throughout the highlands, usually built on open valley floors and supporting large populations sustained by terraced farming and irrigation. Little was to change in this basic village structure for several hundred years.

Pre-conquest: the highland tribes

Towards the end of the thirteenth century Toltec–Maya invaded the central Guatemalan highlands. Their numbers were probably small but their impact was profound, and following their arrival life in the highlands was radically altered.

Maya society became highly militaristic. The Toltecs were ruthlessly well organized, establishing themselves as a ruling elite over competing tribal empires. The greatest of these were the **K'iche'**, who dominated the central area and established their capital, **K'umarkaaj**. Next in line were the **Kaqchikel** at **Iximché**. On the southern shores of Lago de Atitlán, the **Tz'utujil** had their base on the lower slopes of the San Pedro

378 AD	426 AD	562 AD
Siyak K'ak' leads a Teotihuacán takeover at Tikal and defeats Uaxactún.	Yax K'uk Mo' probably from Teotihuacán, founds dynasty at Copán.	Caracol (in concert with Calakmul) overrun Tikal. Calakmul becomes regional superpower.

volcano. To the west the **Mam** had a fortified capital at **Zaculeu**, while the Cuchumatanes and mountains to the east were home to a collection of groups: the **Chuj, Q'anjob'al, Awakateko, Ixil**, notoriously fierce **Achi** and **Q'eqchi'.** Around the modern-day were **Poqomam**, with their capital at **Mixco Viejo**, while along the Pacific coast were bands of **Pipil**.

The sheer numbers of these tribes give an impression of the extent to which the area was fragmented, and it's these same divisions, now surviving on the basis of language alone, that still shape the highlands today (see map, p.343).

Toltecs

The Toltec rulers probably controlled only the dominant tribes – the K'iche', Mam and Kaqchikel. They brought many northern traditions – elements of a Nahua-based language, new gods and an array of military skills – and fused these with local ideas. Shortly after the Spanish conquest, the K'iche' wrote an account of their history, the **Popol Vuh** (see box, p.104), in which they lay claim to a Toltec pedigree, as do the Kaqchikel.

The Toltec invaders were not content with overpowering just a tribe or two, so under the direction of their new rulers the K'iche' began to expand their empire – between 1400 and 1475 they brought the Kaqchikel, the Mam and several other tribes under their control. At the height of their power, around a million highlanders bowed to the word of the K'iche' king. But in 1475 the man who had masterminded their expansion, the great K'iche' ruler **Quicab**, died, and the empire lost much of its authority.

The Kaqchikel were the first to break from the fold, moving south to a new and fortified capital, Iximché around 1470. Shortly afterwards the other tribes managed to escape the grip of K'iche' control and assert their independence.

Warring highlands

For the next fifty years or so the tribes were in a state of almost perpetual conflict, fighting for access to the inadequate supplies of farmland. The archeological remains from this era give evidence of this instability; gone are the valley-floor centres of pre-Toltec times, and in their place are fortified hilltop sites, surrounded by ravines and man-made ditches.

When the Spanish arrived, the highlands were in crisis. With a growing sense of urgency both the K'iche' and the Kaqchikel had begun to encroach on the lowlands of the Pacific coast. The situation could hardly have been more favourable to the Spanish, who fostered this inter-tribal friction, playing one group off against another.

The Spanish conquest

In 1521, the Spanish conquistadors had captured the Aztec capital at Tenochtitlán and were starting to cast their net further afield. Amidst the horrors of the Conquest there was one man whose ambition, cunning and cruelty stood out above the rest – **Pedro de Alvarado**.

In 1523, conquistador leader Hernán Cortés dispatched Alvarado to Guatemala, entreating him to use the minimum of force "and to preach matters concerning our Holy Faith". His army included 120 horsemen, 173 horses, 300 soldiers and 200

---

c.600 AD

Population density in core Maya region reaches an estimated 965 people per square kilometre. Start of the Late Classic period – two-hundred-year golden age of the Maya, its intellectual and artistic peak.

628 AD

Smoke Imix's (Ruler 12) 67-year reign begins at Copán.

Mexican warriors. Marching south they entered Guatemala along the Pacific coast, where they met and easily defeated a small band of K'iche' warriors. From here Alvarado turned north, entering the Quetzaltenango valley, where they came upon the deserted city of **Xelajú**, a K'iche' outpost.

Battle of Xelajú

Warned of the impending arrival of the Spanish, the K'iche' had struggled to build an alliance with the other tribes, but old rivalries proved too strong and the **K'iche'** army faced the Spaniards alone at Xelajú. Alvarado claimed the invaders were confronted by some thirty thousand K'iche' warriors (though this figure is almost certainly an exaggeration) led by their leader **Tecún Umán** in a headdress of quetzal feathers. Despite the huge disparity in numbers, slingshot and foot soldiers were no match for cavalry and gunpowder, and the Spaniards triumphed. Within days, Alvarado advanced on the K'iche' capital and burnt that to the ground.

Spanish victories

Having dealt with the K'iche', Alvarado turned his attention to the other tribal groups. The **Kaqchikel**, recognizing the military superiority of the Spanish, decided to form some kind of alliance. As a result the Spaniards established their first headquarters, in 1523, alongside the Kaqchikel capital of **Iximché**. From here they ranged far and wide, overpowering the countless smaller tribes. Travelling west, Alvarado's army defeated the **Tz'utujil** on the shores of Lago de Atitlán, aided by Kaqchikel warriors in some three hundred canoes. In 1524, Alvarado sent his brother Gonzalo on an expedition against the **Mam**, who were conquered after a month-long siege. The next year, Alvarado himself set out to take on the **Poqomam** at their capital, **Mixco Viejo** whose forces proved no match for the well-disciplined Spanish ranks.

Despite this string of relatively easy victories, it wasn't until well into the 1530s that Alvarado managed to assert control over the more remote parts of the highlands, including the Cuchumatanes. And then problems also arose at the very heart of the campaign. In 1526, the Kaqchikel revolted against the Spanish, abandoning their capital and moving into the mountains, from where they waged a guerrilla war against their former partners. The Spanish were forced to abandon their base at Iximché, and moved instead to a site near the modern town of Antigua.

Here, on St Cecilia's Day, November 22, 1527, they established their first permanent capital, the city of **Santiago de los Caballeros**. For ten years indigenous labourers toiled in the construction of the new city, neatly sited at the base of the Agua volcano, building a cathedral, a town hall, and a palace for Alvarado.

Verapaz

Meanwhile, one particularly thorny problem for the Spanish was presented by the **Achi** and **Q'eqchi'** Maya, who occupied what are now the Verapaz highlands. Despite all his efforts, Alvarado was unable to conquer either of these tribes. In the end he gave up on trying to control the area, naming it Tierra de Guerra. The situation was eventually resolved by the Church. In 1537, **Fray Bartolomé de Las Casas**, the "protector of the Indians", travelled into the region in a bid to persuade the locals to accept both Christianity and Spanish authority. Within three years the priests had succeeded where

682 AD	695 AD	738 AD
Hasaw Chan K'awil begins 52-year reign at Tikal.	Eighteen Rabbit rules at Copán. Hasaw Chan K'awil of Tikal captures Yich'aak K'ak (Fiery Claw) of Calakmul.	Copán's Waxaklajuun Ub'aah K'awil killed by Cauac Sky of Quiriguá, a subordinate city.

Alvarado's armies had failed, and the last of the highland tribes was brought under colonial control in 1540. Thus did the area earn its name of Verapaz, "true peace".

Alvarado himself grew tired of the Conquest, disappointed by the lack of plunder, and his reputation for brutality began to spread. From 1524 until his death in 1541, Alvarado had ruled Guatemala as a personal fiefdom, desperately seeking adventure and wealth, and enslaving and abusing the local population. By the time of his death all the Maya tribes had been overcome (except for tiny numbers of Itza), although local uprisings had already started to take place.

Colonial rule

The early years of colonial rule were marked by a turmoil of uprisings and political wrangling. When Alvarado's wife Beatriz de la Cueva heard of his death, she plunged the capital into a period of prolonged mourning. She had the entire palace painted black, inside and out, and ordered the city authorities to appoint her as the new governor. Meanwhile, the area was swept by a series of storms, and on the night of September 10, 1541, it was shaken by a massive earthquake. The sides of the Agua volcano shuddered, undermining the walls of the cone and releasing its contents. A great wall of mud and water swept down the side of the peak, burying the city of Santiago and most of its inhabitants.

New capital

The surviving colonial authorities moved up the valley to a new site, where a second **Santiago de los Caballeros** was founded – today known as Antigua. This new city served as the administrative headquarters of the **Audiencia de Guatemala**, which was made up of six provinces: Costa Rica, Nicaragua, San Salvador, Honduras, Guatemala and Chiapas (now part of Mexico). With Alvarado out of the way, the authorities began to build a new society, recreating the splendours of the homeland with a superb array of arts and architecture. By the mid-eighteenth century its population approached eighty thousand. Here colonial society was at its most developed, rigidly structured along racial lines with pure-blood Spaniards at the top, indigenous slaves at the bottom and a host of carefully defined racial strata in between. The city was regularly shaken by scandal and earthquakes, and it was eventually all but destroyed in 1773, after which the capital was moved to its modern site: Guatemala City.

The Catholic Church

Perhaps the greatest power in colonial Central America was the **Church**. The first religious order to reach Guatemala was the Franciscans, who arrived with Alvarado himself, and by 1532 the Mercedarians and Dominicans had followed suit, with the Jesuits arriving shortly after. **Francisco Marroquín**, the country's first bishop, rewarded these early arrivals with huge concessions, including land and indigenous people, which later enabled them to earn tax-free fortunes from sugar, wheat and indigo. In later years a whole range of other orders arrived in Santiago, and religious rivalry became an important shaping force in the colony. Through its wealth and power, the Church fostered the splendour of the colonial capital while ruthlessly exploiting the native people and their land. In Santiago alone there were some eighty churches, and

c.750 AD	800–909 AD	810 AD
Population peaks in central region, total Maya numbers estimated to be around ten million.	Terminal Classic period. Overpopulation and an epochal drought lead to environmental collapse.	Dark Sun builds Temple III, the last of Tikal's great temple pyramids.

alongside these were schools, convents, hospitals, hermitages and colleges. The religious orders became the main benefactors of the arts, amassing a wealth of tapestry, jewels, sculpture and painting, and staging concerts, fiestas and endless religious processions. Religious persecution was at its worst between 1572 and 1580, when the office of the **Inquisition** sought out those who had failed to receive the faith and dealt with them harshly.

By the eighteenth century the power of the Church had started to get out of control, and the Spanish kings began to impose taxes on the religious orders and to limit their power and freedom. The conflict between Church and State came to a head in 1767, when Carlos III banished the Jesuits from the Spanish colonies.

Colonial economy

The Spanish must have been disappointed with their conquest of Central America as it offered little in the way of plunder except meagre amounts of silver around Huehuetenango. In Central America the **colonial economy** was based on agriculture. The coastal area produced cacao, tobacco, cotton and, most valuable of all, indigo; the highlands were grazed with sheep and goats; and cattle were raised on coastal ranches. The jungles of Petén and the lower Motagua valley were largely left unchallenged.

At the heart of the colonial economy was the system of *repartamientos*, whereby the ruling classes were granted the right to extract labour from the indigenous population. It was this that established the system whereby the Maya population was transported to work in the plantations, a pattern – though no longer legally enforced – that remains a tremendous burden today.

Meanwhile, in the capital it was graft and corruption that controlled the movement of money, with titles and appointments sold to the highest bidder. All of the colony's wealth was funnelled through the city, and it was only here that the monetary economy really developed.

Maya society

The impact of the Conquest was perhaps the greatest in the highlands, where the **Maya population** had their lives totally restructured. The first stage in this process was the *reducción*, whereby scattered native communities were combined into new Spanish-style towns and villages. Between 1543 and 1600 some seven hundred new settlements were created, each based around a Catholic church. Ostensibly, the purpose of this was to enable the Church to work on its newfound converts, but it also had the effect of pooling the available labour and making its exploitation (and the demand of tribute) that much easier.

Maya **social structures** were also profoundly altered by post-conquest changes. The great central authorities that had previously dominated were now eradicated, replaced by local structures based in the new villages. *Caciques* (local chiefs) and *alcaldes* (mayors) now held the bulk of local power, which was bestowed on them by the Church. In the distant corners of the highlands, however, priests were few and far between, only visiting the villages from time to time. Those that they left in charge developed not only their own power structures but also their own religion, mixing the new with the old. By the start of the nineteenth century, the Maya population had largely recovered from the initial impact of the Conquest, and in many places these

869 AD	909–1200 AD	c.1250 AD	1450 AD
Last recorded date at Tikal.	Early Postclassic period. Maya collapse sees cities abandoned throughout the region.	Toltec enter Guatemala.	K'iche' state dominates warring highlands.

local structures became increasingly important. In each village *cofradias* (brotherhood groups) were entrusted with the care of saints, while *principales* (village elders) held the bulk of traditional authority, a situation that still persists today. Throughout the highlands, village uprisings became increasingly commonplace as the new indigenous culture became stronger and stronger.

Even more serious for the indigenous population than any social changes were the **diseases** that arrived with the conquistadors. Waves of plague, typhoid and fever swept through a population with no natural resistance. In the worst-hit areas the native population was cut by some ninety percent, and in many parts of the country their numbers were halved.

Impact of colonial rule

Colonial rule totally reshaped the structure of Guatemalan society, giving it new cities, a new religion, a transformed economy and a racist hierarchy. Nevertheless, its **impact** was perhaps less marked than in many other parts of Latin America. Only two sizeable cities had emerged and the outlying areas had received little attention from the colonial authorities. Although the indigenous population had been ruthlessly exploited and suffered enormous losses, its culture was never eradicated. The Maya simply absorbed the symbols and ideas of the Spanish, creating a dynamic synthesis that was neither Maya nor Catholic.

Independence

The apartheid-style nature of colonial rule had given birth to deep dissatisfaction amongst many groups in Central America. Spain's policy was to keep wealth and power in the hands of those born in Spain (*chapetones*), a policy that left growing numbers of Creoles (including those of Spanish with Spanish ancestry born in Guatemala) and *mestizos* (of mixed race) resentful and hungry for power and change. (For the majority of the indigenous people, both power and wealth were way beyond their reach.) As the Spanish departed, Guatemalan politics was dominated by a struggle between **conservatives**, who sided with the Church and the Crown, and **liberals**, who advocated a secular and more egalitarian state.

Moves towards independence

The spark, as throughout Spanish America, was Napoleon's invasion of Spain and the abdication of King Fernando VII. In the chaos that followed, a liberal constitution was imposed on Spain in 1812 and a mood of reform swept through the colonies. At the time, Central America was under the control of **Brigadier Don Gabino Gainza**, the last of the Captains General. His one concern was to maintain the status quo, in which he was strongly backed by the wealthy landowners and the Church hierarchy. Bowing to demands for independence, but still hoping to preserve the power structure, Gainza signed a formal **Act of Independence** on September 15, 1821, enshrining the authority of the Church and seeking to preserve the old order under new leadership. Augustín de Iturbide, the short-lived emperor of newly independent Mexico, promptly sent troops to annex Guatemala to the Mexican empire, a union which was to last less than a year.

1521 AD	1523	1523–40	16th century
Aztec capital of Tenochtitlán falls to Spanish under Cortés.	Alvarado arrives in Guatemala.	Spanish conquest of Guatemala, first Spanish capital founded in 1527.	Antigua capital of Central America; power of the Church grows.

Central America Federation

Through a second Declaration of Independence, in 1823, Guatemala joined the Central American states in a loose **federation**, adopting a constitution modelled on that of the United States, abolishing slavery and advocating **liberal reforms**. These moves were bitterly opposed by the Church and conservatives throughout Central America, and provoked several inter-federation (and internal) conflicts. But in 1830 the political left of Salvador, Honduras and Guatemala united under the leadership of **Francisco Morazán**, a Honduran general, under whom **Mariano Gálvez** became the chief of state in Guatemala: religious orders were abolished, the death penalty done away with, and trial by jury, a general school system, civil marriage and the progressive Lívingston law code were all instituted.

Carrera and the conservative backlash

This liberal era lasted until 1838 when the ailing Central American Federation was dissolved and the reforming Guatemalan administration overthrown by a revolt from the mountains. Seething with discontent, the Maya were united behind an illiterate but charismatic leader, the 23-year-old **Rafael Carrera**, under whose command they marched on Guatemala City. Independence was declared in 1839, with Carrera installed first as a *caudillo* (strongman), and later as president.

Carrera respected no authority other than that of the Church, and his immediate reforms swept aside the changes instituted by the liberal government. The religious orders were restored to their former position and traditional Spanish titles were reinstated. Under Carrera, Guatemala fought a succession of conflicts against liberals in other parts of Central America, and eventually established itself as an independent republic in 1847. Carrera's greatest internal challenge came from the state of **Los Altos**, which included much of the western highlands and proclaimed itself an independent republic. It was a short-lived threat, however, and the would-be state was soon brought back into the republic.

When Carrera died, at the age of 50 in 1865, Guatemala was an impoverished nation (the export of indigo and cochinel had plummeted after the invention of artificial dyes), while its transport network was backward at best. Little was to change under his successor, **Vicente Cerna**, another conservative, who ruled until 1871, but during this period liberal opposition was again gathering momentum, and 1867 saw the first **liberal uprising**, led by **Serpio Cruz**. His bid for power was unsuccessful, but it inspired two young liberals, Justo Rufino Barrios and Francisco Cruz, to follow suit. In the next few years, they mounted several other unsuccessful revolts, and in 1870 Serpio Cruz was captured and hanged.

Rufino Barrios and the coffee boom

The year 1871 marked a major turning-point in Guatemalan politics, for in that year rebels Rufino Barrios and Miguel García Granados entered Guatemala from Mexico with an army of just 45 men. The **liberal revolution** set in motion was an astounding success, the army growing by the day as it approached the capital, which was finally taken on June 30, 1871. Granados took the helm of the new liberal administration but held the presidency for just a few years, surrounding himself with ageing comrades and offering only very limited reforms.

1697	**1773–76**	**1821**
Conquest of the Itza at Tayasal, the last independent Maya tribe falls.	Earthquake destroys Antigua, Guatemala City becomes capital.	Mexico and Central America gain independence from Spain.

Meanwhile, out in the district of Los Altos, **Rufino Barrios**, now a local military commander, was infuriated by the lack of action. In 1872 he marched his troops to the capital, demanded and won elections. Barrios was a charismatic leader with tyrannical tendencies (monuments throughout the country testify to his sense of his own importance) who regarded himself as a great reformer. His most immediate acts were the restructuring of the education system and an attack on the Church – clerics were forbidden to wear the cloth and public religious processions were banned. The Church was outraged and excommunicated Barrios, which prompted him to expel the archbishop in retaliation.

Barrios' liberal perspective was undoubtedly instilled with a deep arrogance, and he would tolerate no political opposition, developing an effective network of secret police and ensuring that the army became an essential part of his political power base.

Barrios also set about reforming agriculture, and he presided over a boom period, largely as a result of the cultivation and export of **coffee**. To foster this expansion Barrios extended the railway network, established a national bank and developed the ports of Champerico, San José and Iztapa. Between 1870 and 1900 the volume of foreign trade increased twenty times.

German immigration

All this had an enormous impact on Guatemalan **society**. Many of the new plantations were owned and run by German immigrants, and the majority of the coffee eventually found its way to Europe. The newcomers soon formed a powerful elite and, although most of the Germans were later forced out of Guatemala (during World War II), their influence can still be felt today in the continuing presence of an extremely powerful political clique. Foreign ideas were deemed superior to indigenous ones, and while European immigrants were welcomed with open arms, the Maya population was still regarded as hopelessly inferior.

Indigenous society was also deeply affected by the needs of the coffee boom, as Barrios instituted a system of **forced labour**. By 1876 up to one quarter of the male Maya population could be dispatched to work on the coffee fincas, often under appalling conditions, while in the highlands landowners continued to employ a system of debt peonage.

As a result of the coffee boom, many Maya lost not only their freedom but also their land, as huge swathes of land were seized. In many areas the villagers rose up in defiance, with significant **revolts** continuing into the twentieth century. Five hundred armed men faced the authorities in Momostenango, only to find their village overrun by troops and their homes burnt to the ground. These land seizures forced the Maya to become dependent on seasonal labour.

Jorge Ubico and the banana empire

Rufino Barrios, who was eventually killed in 1885 while fighting to re-establish a unified Central America, was succeeded by a string of short-lived but like-minded presidents. The next to hold power for any time was **Manuel Estrada Cabrera**, a stern authoritarian who restricted union organization and supported the interests of big business. He ruled from 1898 until he was overthrown in 1920, by which time he was on the verge of insanity.

1847	**1867**	**1872**
Guatemala becomes a republic, independent of Central America, under Rafael Carrera.	First liberal uprising under Serpio Cruz.	Liberal revolution; Justo Rufino Barrios becomes president. Start of coffee boom.

United Fruit Company

Meanwhile, a new and exceptionally powerful player was becoming involved in the country's affairs – the **United Fruit Company**, which would assert its influence over much of Central America until the 1960s. The company moved into Guatemala in 1901, when it bought a small tract of land on which to grow bananas. Three years later, it was awarded a contract to complete the railway from Guatemala City to Puerto Barrios, and in 1912 ownership of the Pacific railway network also fell to the company, giving it a virtual transport monopoly. Large-scale **banana cultivation** really took off, and by 1934 United Fruit controlled a massive amount of land, exporting around 3.5 million bunches of bananas annually and reaping vast profits.

The influence of the United Fruit Company was so pervasive that it earned itself the nickname *El Pulpo*, "the octopus". Control of the transport network brought with it control of the coffee trade: during the 1930s it cost as much to ship coffee from Guatemala to New Orleans as it did from Río de Janeiro to New Orleans.

Against this background the power of the Guatemalan government was severely limited, with the influence of the United States increasing alongside that of the United Fruit Company.

Jorge Ubico

The way became clear for **Jorge Ubico**, a charismatic leader with fascist tendencies and a reputation for efficiency, who was well connected with the ruling and land-owning elite. Guatemala was hit hard by the Depression and Ubico managed to get trade agreements that exempted coffee and bananas from US import duties. Within Guatemala, Ubico steadfastly supported the United Fruit Company. This relationship was of such importance that by 1940 ninety percent of all Guatemalan exports were being sold to the United States.

Internally, Ubico embarked on a radical programme of reform, including a sweeping drive against corruption and a massive road-building effort. But the system of debt peonage continued as a new **vagrancy law** compelled all landless peasants to work 150 days a year for the state or landowners. Not surprisingly, sporadic local protests and revolts against landowners continued in the late 1930s and early 1940s.

Internal security was another Ubico obsession, as he became increasingly paranoid, vainglorious and eccentric. His obsession with Napoleon provoked future Sandinista leader Tomás Borge to describe him "crazier than a half-dozen opium-smoking frogs" while US newspapers dubbed him "the Little Napoleon of the Tropics".

Ubico used a network of informers to unleash waves of repression. But while he tightened his grip on every aspect of government, the rumblings of opposition grew louder. In 1944 discontent erupted in student violence, and Ubico was finally forced to resign after fourteen years of tyrannical rule.

Ten years of "spiritual socialism"

The overthrow of Jorge Ubico released a wave of opposition, with students, professionals and young military officers all demanding democracy and freedom. It was a mood that was to transform Guatemalan politics, one so extreme a contrast to previous transitions of power that the 1944 handover was dubbed **the October revolution.**

1906	1930s	1944–54
Railway to Pacific coast completed.	Jorge Ubico president – banana boom and height of United Fruit Company power.	"Spiritual socialism" presidencies of Arévalo and Árbenz; ended by CIA-backed military coup.

Juan José Arévalo

In the subsequent 1945 elections **Juan José Arévalo**, a teacher, won the presidency with 85 percent of the vote. His political doctrine was dubbed "**spiritual socialism**", and he immediately set about implementing much-needed structural reforms. Under a new budget, a third of the government's income was allocated to social welfare, to be spent on the construction of schools and hospitals, a programme of immunization and a far-reaching literacy campaign. The vagrancy laws were abolished, a national development agency was founded, and in 1947 a labour code was adopted, granting workers the right to strike and union representation.

Some former coffee farms were turned into cooperatives, while new laws protected tenant farmers from eviction. Technical assistance and credit were also made available to peasant farmers.

In Arévalo's final years the pace of reform slackened somewhat as he concentrated on evading various attempts to overthrow him. Despite his popularity, Arévalo was still wary of the traditional elite: Church leaders, old-school army officers and wealthy landowners all resented the new wave of legislation, and repeated coup attempts were made.

Árbenz reforms

Leftist, ex-colonel **Jácobo Árbenz**, one the of leaders of the October revolution, won the 1950 election with ease, and declared that he would transform the country into an independent capitalist nation and raise the standard of living. But the process of overthrowing a feudal society and ending economic dependency led to direct confrontation with the American corporations that still dominated the economy.

Árbenz enlisted the support of the masses, encouraging the participation of peasants in the programme of agrarian reform and inciting the militancy of students and unions. He also attempted to break the great American-owned railway, power and port monopolies and sought to reclaim unpaid taxes from them. Internally, these measures aroused a mood of national pride, but they were strongly resented by the US companies whose empires were under attack.

The situation became even more serious with the **law of agrarian reform** passed in July 1952, which stated that idle and state-owned land would be distributed to the landless, at a fraction of its market value. The new laws outraged landowners. Between 1953 and 1954 around 8840 square kilometres were redistributed to the benefit of some one hundred thousand peasant families – the first time since the arrival of the Spanish that the government had responded to the needs of the indigenous population. The landowner most seriously affected by the reforms was the United Fruit Company (now renamed Chiquito), which lost about half of its property.

As the pace of reform gathered, Árbenz began to take an increasingly radical stance. In 1951, the Communist Party was granted legal status, and in the next election four party members were elected to the legislature, which was staunchly anti-American.

1954 US-backed coup

In the United States the press repeatedly accused the new Guatemalan government of being a communist beachhead in Central America, and the US government attempted to intervene on behalf of the United Fruit Company. Tellingly, Allen Dulles, the new director of the CIA, also happened to be a member of the fruit-company's board.

1954	1960s	1968
Start of military rule and a series of military-backed dictators.	First guerrilla actions, rapidly followed by repressive clampdowns and rise of death squads.	Guatemalan writer Miguel Ángel Asturias wins Nobel Prize for Literature.

CHE GUEVARA IN GUATEMALA

Ernesto "Che" Guevara arrived in Guatemala on New Year's Eve 1953, broke and with no place to stay. He had graduated as a doctor in his native Argentina five months previously, and immediately left to explore Latin America – hitching rides, sleeping rough and cadging meals along the way.

The future *comandante* spent eight months in Guatemala City, living in Zona 1, the historic heart of the capital, in a number of cheap hospedajes. Most of his days were spent in a fruitless search for work as a doctor, surviving on the generosity of the people he met and scratching a meagre income from a series of casual jobs: teaching a few Spanish classes, doing some translation work and peddling encyclopedias and images of the Black Christ of Esquipulas in the capital's streets.

But Guevara had not just come to Guatemala to look for work. In the early 1950s, Guatemala City was a major destination for political idealists, communists and budding revolutionaries from Latin America, all attracted to the country by reformist president **Árbenz** and his party's doctrine of "spiritual socialism". In a letter to his aunt, Guevara wrote of his travels through the region, and avowed his intentions to challenge American hegemony:

Along the way, I had the opportunity to pass through the dominions of the United Fruit … I have sworn before a picture of the old and mourned comrade Stalin that I won't rest until I see these capitalist octopuses annihilated. In Guatemala I will perfect myself and achieve what I need to be an authentic revolutionary.

One of the first people he met in Guatemala was **Hildea Gadea**, a well-connected young Peruvian who later became his first wife. Gadea, an exiled member of Peru's ARPA rebels, introduced Che to a number of other young political activists, including **Rolando Morán**, who was to become the leader of the Guatemalan EGP guerrillas (see p.114). Guevara formed his political consciousness in Guatemala City, his beliefs shaped by hours spent reading Marx, Trotsky and Mao, an instinctive hatred of US imperialism, and marathon theological debates. Of the city's myriad Ladino leftist groups, the Cubans most impressed Che, for they alone had actually launched an armed uprising against a dictatorship (the failed Moncada assault after Batista had cancelled the 1952 Cuban elections). Guevara met **Ñico López**, the Cuban who would later introduce him to **Fidel** and **Raúl Castro**, and with whom he would later regroup in Mexico, set sail for Cuba in 1956 and initiate the revolution.

Guevara remained in Guatemala City throughout the attacks on the capital in June 1954. The young radical wrote to his family denouncing the indecisiveness of the Árbenz government and its inability to organize local militias to defend the country. He swore allegiance to the Soviet Union, and joined the Communist Party while holed up in the Argentine embassy, awaiting deportation after Árbenz had been deposed.

Many of the young Guatemala-based comrades later reassembled in Mexico City where they digested the downfall of Árbenz. Perhaps the biggest lesson Guevara learned was that rather than attempt to negotiate with Washington, it was essential to combat American interference with armed resistance. He was convinced that Guatemala had been betrayed "inside and out", and argued that future revolutionaries must be prepared to establish their internal authority by force and eliminate enemies using repression and firing squads if necessary – "Victory will be conquered with blood and fire, there can be no pardon for the traitors."

In 1953, President Dwight Eisenhower approved plans to overthrow the government and the CIA set up a small military invasion of Guatemala to depose Árbenz. A ragtag army of exiles and mercenaries was put together in Honduras, and on June 18, 1954,

1976	1978
Earthquake leaves 23,000 dead, a million homeless.	Lucas García president; thousands die through repression. US bans arms sales to Guatemala.

Guatemala City was bombed with leaflets demanding the resignation of Árbenz. The Guatemalan president failed to obtain the support of the army, and on the night of June 18, Guatemala was strafed with machine-gun fire while the invading army, described by Árbenz as "a heterogeneous Fruit Company expeditionary force", was getting closer to the city by the hour.

On June 27, Árbenz declared that he was relinquishing the presidency to **Colonel Carlos Enrique Díaz**, the army chief of staff. And on July 3, John Peurifoy, the US ambassador to Guatemala, flew the new government to Guatemala aboard a US Air Force plane. Guatemala's attempt to escape the clutches of outside intervention and bring about social change had been brought to an abrupt end.

Counter-revolution and military rule

Following the overthrow of Árbenz, the army – backed by US aid – rose to fill the power vacuum; it would dominate politics for the next thirty years, propelling the country into a spiral of violence and economic decline.

Carlos Castilo

In 1954 the US ambassador persuaded a provisional government to accept **Carlos Castillo** as the new president, and Castillo wasted no time sweeping away the progressive legislation of the previous ten years. The constitution of 1945 was replaced by a more restrictive version; illiterate people were disenfranchised; left-wing parties were outlawed; and large numbers of unionists and reformers were simply executed. The regime lifted the restrictions that had been placed on foreign investment and returned all the land that had been confiscated to its previous owners, a measure which badly affected the indigenous population. A referendum was rigged to provide a supportive response to Castillo's rule, but his government had only limited backing from the armed forces, and coup rumblings persisted until finally he was shot by his own bodyguard in 1957.

Ydígoras and the 1963 coup

The assassination was followed by several months of political turmoil, out of which **Miguel Ydígoras** emerged as the next president. His disastrous five-year rule was marked by corruption, incompetence, outrageous patronage and economic decline caused by a fall in coffee prices; the formation of the Central American Common Market did help to boost light industry, however. Ydígoras was eventually overthrown when Arévalo threatened to return to Guatemala and contest the 1963 elections, which he might well have won. The possibility of another socialist government sent shock waves through the establishment in both Guatemala and the United States, and President John F. Kennedy gave the go-ahead for another coup. In 1963 the army once more took control, under the leadership of **Enrique Peralta**.

Guerrilla war

Peralta was president for just three years, during which time his authoritarian government was challenged by armed resistance in the highlands of Verapaz and Izabal.

Then, after new president Julio Méndez's offer of amnesty to the guerrillas was rejected, a ruthless counterinsurgency campaign swung into action using US military

1982	1985
Efraín Ríos Montt seizes presidency. Army begins scorched earth campaign in the highlands.	Vinicio Cerezo elected: return to civilian rule though power of military remains great.

advisors, aerial bombardment and napalm. By the end of the decade, the guerrilla movement had been virtually eradicated in the east and its activities, greatly reduced, shifted to Guatemala City, where the US ambassador was assassinated by FAR rebels in 1968.

Political violence became commonplace as **death squads**, backed by the military, operated with impunity, killing anyone they deemed subversive to the state.

Economic decline and political violence

Extreme political violence, economic crises and electoral fraud dominated Guatemala's history between 1970 and the early 1990s. At the heart of the crisis was the injustice and inequality of Guatemalan society: although the country remained fairly prosperous, the benefits of its success never reached the poor, who were denied access to land, education and healthcare.

Rise of the military

The 1970 elections confirmed the power of the military and the far right. **Colonel Carlos Arana**, who had directed the counterinsurgency campaign in the east, was elected president, though only a small percentage of the population was enfranchised.

Once in power he set about eradicating armed opposition, declaring that "If it is necessary to turn the country into a cemetery in order to pacify it, I will not hesitate to do so." The reign of terror reached unprecedented levels, as around 15,000 political killings occurred during the first three years of Arana's rule.

Presidential elections followed in 1974, which were tainted by manipulation and fraud, resulting in the declaration of the right's candidate, **Kjell Laugerud**, as the winner. Laugerud offered limited reforms, allowing greater tolerance towards unions and the cooperative movement, but the army continued to consolidate its authority, spreading its influence across a wider range of business and commercial interests.

The 1976 earthquake and the rise of the Guerrilla Army of the Poor

All of this was interrupted by a massive **earthquake** on February 4, 1976. The quake left around 23,000 dead, 77,000 injured and a million homeless. The poor, their homes built from makeshift materials on unstable ground, suffered the most, and subsistence farmers were caught out just as they were about to plant their corn.

In the wake of the earthquake, during the process of reconstruction, powerful new forces emerged to challenge the status quo. A revived trade-union organization resurfaced, while a new guerrilla organization, the **Guerrilla Army of the Poor** (EGP), set up operations in the Ixil area (see box, p.114). The reaction of the army was brutal. In 1977, US President Jimmy Carter suspended all military aid to Guatemala because of the country's appalling human-rights record.

In the following year, Guatemala's elections were once again dominated by the army, which engineered a victory for **Brigadier General Fernando Lucas García**. Lucas García promised to bring the situation under control, and unleashed a fresh wave of violence. All opposition considered subversive was met with severe repression, while several guerrilla armies developed strongholds in the highlands.

1991	1992
Guatemala recognizes Belizean independence. Peace talks between guerrillas and government.	Rigoberta Menchú wins Nobel Peace Prize.

As chaos threatened, the army resorted to extreme measures, and within a month there was a massacre in **Panzós,** followed by assassinations of Social Democrats and Christian Democrats.

Civil war

The **army** became increasingly powerful and the death toll rose steadily. In rural areas the war against the guerrillas was reaching new heights as army casualties rose to 250 a month, and the demand for conscripts grew rapidly. The four main guerrilla groups had an estimated six thousand combatants and some 250,000 unarmed collaborators.

Under the Lucas García administration the horrors of **repression** were at their most intense. The victims included students, journalists, academics, politicians, priests, lawyers, teachers, unionists and, above all, peasant farmers, massacred in their hundreds. Accurate figures are impossible to calculate but it's estimated that around 35,000 Guatemalans were killed during the four years of the Lucas García regime.

In the field, morale in the Guatemalan military was low. Discontent was growing due to repeated military failures, inefficiency and a shortage of supplies, despite increased military aid and weaponry from Israel.

Ríos Montt

On March 23, 1982, a group of young military officers led a successful coup, which installed **General Efraín Ríos Montt** as the head of a three-member junta.

Ríos Montt was an evangelical Christian, a member of the Iglesia del Verbo, and throughout his rule Sunday-night television was dominated by marathon presidential sermons. He immediately declared his determination to defeat the guerrillas, restore law and order and eradicate corruption. Government officials were issued with identity cards inscribed with the words "I do not steal. I do not lie". A state of siege was declared.

Initially, repression dropped in the cities as corrupt police officers were forced to resign, but in the highlands the war intensified. An **amnesty** was offered, which only a few rebels accepted, and the army set about destroying the guerrillas' infrastructure by undermining their support base.

Montt called his military campaign, "*frijoles y fusiles*" (beans and guns). Villagers were provided with rations and forcibly organized into **civil defence patrols** (PACs), armed with ancient rifles, and ordered to patrol the countryside. Those who refused were denounced as "subversives" and carted off to re-education camps or army-base torture chambers. Campesinos were forced to take sides, caught between the attraction of guerrilla propaganda and the extreme brutality of the armed forces.

Iron-fist policy

Ríos Montt's iron-fist policy was as successful as it was murderous as soldiers swept through the mountains committing massacre after massacre, wiping villages off the map and leaving nothing but scorched earth. Ten of thousands of campesinos fled to safety in Mexico. The guerrillas, their network of support virtually eradicated, were driven into remote corners, and occasionally responded with brutal measures, including the ambush and slaughter of PAC members and villagers. The massacre carried out by EGP guerrillas at the village of Txacal Tze in the Ixil region on June 13, 1982, left an estimated 125 dead.

1996	**1998**
Álvaro Arzú elected. Peace accords signed.	Hurricane Mitch devastates much of Central America; Bishop Juan Geradi assassinated.

By the middle of 1983, Ríos Montt faced growing pressure from all sides, particularly the Catholic Church, which was outraged by the murder of dozens of its priests.

Ríos Montt was pushed aside by yet another military coup in August 1983 (and, nearly thirty years later, was charged with genocide and crimes against humanity).

General Mejía Víctores became president and moves towards democratic elections were implemented. Battles continued in the mountains, but some rehabilitation began as internal refugees were grouped in "**model villages**". Scarcely any money was made available for rebuilding the devastated communities however, and it was often widows and orphans who were left to construct their own homes. In the Ixil region alone the war had displaced sixty thousand people (72 percent of the population). Nationwide more than six hundred villages had been destroyed and around 180,000 had lost their lives.

Human rights groups mobilize

Steadily activists began to mobilize in response. Important grassroots **human rights organizations** began to spring up in this period, including the Mutual Support Group (GAM), comprising families of the disappeared, and the National Commission of Guatemalan Widows (CONAVIGUA), a very significant and largely indigenous group. Though the members of these groups faced routine intimidation and frequent death threats, they marked the emergence of a new period of Maya political activism.

Cerezo and the return to democratic rule

In 1985 presidential elections were held, the first free vote in Guatemala for thirty years. The winner was **Vinicio Cerezo**, a Christian Democrat. His election victory was the result of a sweeping wave of popular support, and in the run-up to the election he offered a programme of reform.

Once in office, however, Cerezo knew that his room for manoeuvre was severely limited. He argued that the army still held 75 percent of power, and declared "I'm a politician not a magician. Why promise what I cannot deliver?" Throughout his six-year rule Cerezo offered a **non-confrontational approach**, seeking above all else to avoid upsetting the powerful alliance of business interests, landowners and generals, and he survived several coup attempts. Political killings dropped in the late 1980s, but the civil war continued in remote parts of the highlands and death squads linked to rogue elements in the military operated in the capital.

The country's leading **human rights organization**, the Mutual Support Group (GAM), hoped that civilian rule would present them with a chance to investigate the fate of the "disappeared" and bring the perpetrators of violence to trial. Cerezo, however, chose to forget the past, and ongoing abuses went largely uninvestigated and unpunished. GAM's leaders, meanwhile, became targeted by hit men.

Nevertheless, a measure of **civilian rule** created a general thaw in the political climate. Real change, however, never materialized. Despite the fact that at least 65 percent of the population still lived below the official poverty line, little was done to meet their needs in terms of education, health, employment, land or tax reform. Acknowledging that his greatest achievement had been to survive, Cerezo organized the country's first civilian transfer of power in decades, in 1990.

2000	2003
FRG's Alfonso Portillo sworn in as president, backed by Ríos Montt.	US decertifies Guatemala as "war on drugs" partner as cocaine-smuggling gangs' influence proliferates.

The Serrano and Carpio administrations

The **1990 elections** were dogged by controversy. Ex-military dictator Ríos Montt was banned from standing as a candidate, but **Jorge Serrano**, a former minister in his government, won (albeit with the support of less than a quarter of the people). An engineer and evangelical with a centre-right economic position, Serrano proved both uninterested and incapable of effecting any real reform or bringing an end to the civil war and the level of human rights abuse remained high.

Maya peasants became increasingly organized and influential, rejecting the presence of the army and the system of civil patrols. The people of Santiago Atitlán expelled the army from their village, after troops shot and killed thirteen people. Matters were brought into sharp focus in 1992 when **Rigoberta Menchú** (see p.348) was awarded the Nobel Peace Prize for her campaigning work on behalf of Guatemala's indigenous population. However, the civil war still rumbled on and the three main guerrilla groups, united as the **URNG**, continued to confront the army.

Small groups of refugees began to return from exile in Mexico. The territorial dispute with **Belize** was officially resolved when the two countries established full diplomatic relations in 1991.

By early 1993, Serrano's reputation had plummeted following a series of **scandals** involving corruption and alleged links with Colombian drug cartels. In May 1993, Serrano pronounced a self-coup, though within days massive demonstrations and the suspension of US aid forced him out.

Ramiro Carpio

Further public protests then blocked an army-backed appointee, and finally **Ramiro Carpio**, the country's human rights ombudsman, was declared the new president. He reshuffled the senior military command, but rejected calls for revenge, declaring that stability was the main goal. Public frustration quickly grew as the new government failed to address fundamental issues, such as crime, land ownership, tax and constitutional reform. Some progress was made in peace negotiations with the URNG guerrilla leadership, however, and the Indigenous Rights Act, passed in 1995, allowed greater constitutional freedom for Guatemala's *indígenas*.

Arzú and the peace accords

Álvaro Arzú of the centre-right PAN party, a former mayor of Guatemala City, was elected president in 1996 with a commitment to private sector-led growth and the free market. He quickly adopted a relatively progressive stance, shaking up the armed forces' power structure and moving quickly to bring an end to the 36-year civil war by meeting guerrilla leaders. The **Peace Accords**, signed on December 29, 1996, concluded almost a decade of talks and terminated a conflict that had claimed two hundred thousand lives. A commitment to investigate wartime human rights violations through a Truth Commission overseen by MINUGUA (the UN mission to Guatemala) was agreed. However progress on development issues was slow. There were token cuts in military numbers, but army officers implicated in orchestrating massacres avoided prosecution – Arzú simply dared not touch them.

2005	2007
CAFTA trade agreement approved by Guatemalan Congress. Land evictions in countryside.	Guatemala named a "failed state" by Foreign Policy magazine.

Murder of Bishop Geradi

In April 1998, two days after the Catholic Church published a human rights report into wartime slaughters that blamed the military for ninety per cent of civil war deaths, one of the investigators, **Bishop Juan Geradi**, was bludgeoned to death. The murder stunned the nation, one newspaper declaring "This wasn't supposed to happen. Not any more."

The acute fragility of the nascent Guatemalan democracy was revealed – most immediately suspected that a vengeful military was responsible for Geradi's assassination. Despite international and domestic outrage – hundreds of thousands attended a silent protest in the capital days after the killing – the perpetrators escaped justice as terrified judges, prosecutors and key witnesses fled abroad following death threats. As Arzú departed in December 1999, Geradi's murderers remained at large.

There was also an alarming upsurge in the crime rate. A new police force, the PNC, quickly gained a reputation as bad as its predecessor for endemic corruption and ineffectualness. But crime and the Geradi case aside, Arzú left office with his reputation as a skilled administrator, who got things done, intact. Huge infrastructure projects, including a massive upgrading of Guatemala's highways, were completed efficiently and to budget. Arzú's good reputation has endured, and he was re-elected mayor of Guatemala City for a fourth term in 2011. Indeed, if the constitution is ever amended to allow second presidential terms, Arzú would have a good shot at re-election.

President Portillo

Former lawyer and professor **Alfonso Portillo** won Guatemala's 1999 presidential elections with a promise to implement the peace accords and tackle crime and gangs. In the grossest of ironies, Portillo confessed to killing two men in Mexico in 1982, declaring, "A man who defends his life will defend the lives of his people". He claimed he had acted in self-defence. But perhaps the most decisive factor in his victory was the support of his political mentor, former general and founder of the right-wing FRG party, Ríos Montt. Throughout Portillo's disastrous term of office Montt was widely perceived to be really in control, pulling all the strings behind the scenes.

Portillo immediately set about attempting to solve the **Geradi case** as three senior military personnel were charged with murder within weeks of his inauguration. Credibly, the military suspects (an intelligence chief and two members of the elite presidential guard) and a priest (who was found guilty of acting as an accomplice) were brought to trial, and found guilty in June 2001 of plotting Geradi's murder.

The Geradi case aside, Portillo lurched from crisis to crisis, and after four years of catastrophic presidency he departed office leaving Guatemala virtually bankrupt. The stench of **corruption** pervaded his entire term as a series of scandals were unearthed and public coffers were emptied. Little or no progress was made on the terms of the peace accords, which included improving indigenous rights.

Crime and hidden powers

Crime levels soared during Portillo's term. Human rights workers, journalists and environmentalists who dared to challenge powerful political and business interests were threatened and killed, while gangs terrorized the city suburbs.

2007–11	2012
Álvaro Colom's presidential term marked by increased gang and narco violence.	Ex-general Otto Pérez begins presidency with iron-fist mandate to tackle crime.

Meanwhile, the **economy** continued to falter, as traditional exports (principally coffee, sugar and bananas) slumped, and low commodity prices affected profitability. Meanwhile, the cocaine trade boomed, as Guatemala became a key transit country. Behind this boom were shadowy **organized crime cartels** – locally known as *poderes ocultos* ("hidden powers") – thought to be headed up by retired generals and including a network of corrupt officials.

Portillo departed leaving Guatemala broke, with an estimated US$1 billion missing from the treasury. Secret bank accounts were discovered in Panama. In 2011, Guatemala's constitutional court ruled that he must be extradited to the United States to face **money laundering** charges.

Óscar Berger

Inaugurated as president in January 2004, Óscar Berger declared that the country was nearly bankrupt and that his goal would be to govern in an austere, cost-conscious manner. Many key positions in his government were filled by members of the Guatemalan elite but he also made several progressive appointments including Rigoberta Menchú (see p.348) as a goodwill ambassador with a brief to implement the peace accords. Significantly, Berger curbed the power of the **armed forces** by slashing military spending: cutting army numbers from 27,000 to 15,500 and closing thirteen military bases.

In the countryside, the issue of **agrarian reform** was combustible. Berger evicted thousands of landless peasants from the fincas they were squatting, a course of action that provoked protests in twenty of the country's 22 departments in July 2004.

As Berger's term neared its end, the key issue for the 2007 election campaign was **crime** (again). With street gangs effectively in control of dozens of poor barrios, a murder rate ten times that in the US, and drug mafias with military links operating with virtual impunity Guatemala had, in the words of the Dutch ambassador, become "a paradise for organized crime". Few in the media, electorate or politics disagreed, and the question was who would best deal with the issue. Social democrat Álvaro Colom advocated "combating violence with intelligence", while his opponent in the presidential run-off Otto Pérez (an ex-military officer, implicated in the Geradi murder) called for an iron-fist approach. Colom narrowly got the nod.

Álvaro Colom

President **Álvaro Colom**, a worthy if slightly uninspiring personality from the centre-left, was a former textile businessman who had also studied Maya religion. His deputy was Rafael Espada, a more flamboyant character, fond of motorbikes who worked as a heart surgeon. Espada described Guatemala as "sick, very sick, in intensive care".

Colom's challenge was to tackle crime and violence, the narco gangs, poverty, land issues, indigenous rights and the environment – without upsetting elements of his coalition, which included representatives from big business and the oligarchy.

Disillusionment set in pretty quickly with Colom's administration, and he developed a slightly bumbling reputation. By contrast, his wife, the ambitious and forceful **Sandra Torres**, was stereotyped as really wearing the trousers – an image which she did little to deter by chairing cabinet meetings and heading a new council of social cohesion with a massive budget. Torres even divorced Colom and attempted to run for the presidency, though this move was ruled out by the constitutional court.

Columnists portrayed Colom as a mild-mannered character who lacked the stomach to fight organized crime and gangs (though seizures of cocaine doubled during his term to a street value of US$10 billion). In one gruesome episode decapitated heads were placed in the grounds of the Congress building and in other landmarks around the capital – an action deemed a warning from the narcos. In another horrific incident, 27 campesinos were butchered in a remote farm. A state of emergency was declared in both Alta Verapaz and Petén.

Unsurprisingly, the Guatemalan population still viewed their nation as being in intensive care as the 2011 elections approached. This time, hardliner Otto Pérez triumphed (though he failed to win any predominantly Maya areas) promising a *mano dura* (iron fist) against crime and the gangs.

Otto Pérez

Assuming office in 2012, President **Otto Pérez** comes from a military background. Chillingly, he was a senior officer in the department of Quiché, including the Ixil region, during the darkest years of the civil war when thousands disappeared and the worst massacres happened. In the early 1990s he was director of Guatemalan military intelligence. Highly respected writer and journalist Francisco Goldman accuses him of being one of the masterminds of the Bishop Geradi murder (see p.331). However, Pérez likes to portray himself as from the moderate wing of the military, who was one of the negotiators who brought about the peace accords.

Not surprisingly, he filled his **cabinet** with ex-military officers – the interior minister was a former Kaibil (implicated in numerous civil war massacres). Accusations of a remilitarization of society were levelled at his administration after the army were ordered to perform highway patrol duties and Pérez wasted no time requesting an increase in military aid from the US.

Other initiatives were a complete surprise, including one totally unexpected proposal to consider legalizing drugs in Guatemala, declaring that it was impossible to fight narco gangs with arms. This brought a predictable condemnation from the US embassy.

State of the nation

Guatemala has many pressing issues. Over forty percent of its people (and more than seventy per cent of the Maya) live in **poverty**. There is wealth, but incomes remain woefully skewed, with taxation accounting for less than ten percent of GDP, the lowest in the western hemisphere. Endemic corruption continues to bleed the nation of much-needed finance. Land reform, another critical issue, has never been tackled in Guatemala. It's generally accepted that seventy percent of the country's agricultural land is owned by just three percent of the population. The squatting of fincas by landless campesinos has proliferated in recent years, and today Guatemala has dozens of potentially incendiary disputes.

Guatemala's **economic performance**, averaging two/three percent GDP growth per year since the mid-1990s, is pretty modest, a little behind most of Latin America, and trailing India, China and most of Southeast Asia by some distance. The country's poor **education system** (thirty percent of adults are illiterate) is a serious handicap, while social instability and crime levels also impact upon international competitiveness and inward investment. **Gang culture** has spread like a cancer throughout the nation: women are targeted with extreme violence (see p.334), and extortion affects everyone from market vendors to bus drivers – over one hundred are murdered each year – who enter gang territory.

Lawlessness also hampers the potential of the nation's **tourism industry**; tourist arrivals dipped 2.8 per cent in 2011 after several years of growth.

Environmental issues

Environmental policy is another critical arena. Contentious **mining** concessions have been granted in indigenous regions, including an open-pit gold mine at Sipacapa in San Marcos, a nickel mine near El Estor and a pit in the department of Santa Rosa. All have been bitterly opposed locally but backed by Otto Pérez. Lago de Atitlán, the crown jewel of Guatemala's tourist industry, is threatened on many fronts (see p.126). Vast tracts of the Petén jungle continue to disappear in smoke as settlers, loggers and

HUMAN RIGHTS IN GUATEMALA TODAY

Guatemala is a poor, troubled country, still scarred by its 36-year civil war (the most bloody in Latin America) with a deeply corrupt justice system. A climate of fear has persisted for decades, and those who dare to challenge the interests of the elite, hidden powers and criminal gangs face intimidation and violence. However, determined activists, lawyers are pressing hard to change the culture of impunity, and in recent years have succeeded in convicting civil war criminals and human rights abusers.

Human Rights Watch's 2012 report on Guatemala concentrated on the high rates of **violent crime** in society and the continuing **culture of impunity**. Campaigning against violent crime or corruption, or challenging the authority of Guatemala's organized crime networks is dangerous work. Every year there are hundred of cases of intimidation and attacks on journalists and human-rights leaders, trade unionists, forensic experts and organizations focusing on economic, social and cultural rights. Death threats are common and families of activists are also targeted. Nineteen human rights defenders were murdered in 2011.

WAR CRIMES IMPUNITY CHALLENGED

One of the most crucial strands of the **Peace Accords** of December 1996 was the establishment of a truth commission, overseen by MINUGUA (the UN mission to Guatemala), to investigate human rights abuses committed during the civil war. Commendably, the culture of impunity that has existed since the end of the civil war is now being challenged. In 2011 charges were issued against senior members of the military and there were several successful prosecutions. Four former army officers responsible for the 1982 Dos Erres massacre and paramilitary chiefs and police agents were given life sentences for "disappearing" people.

Some of the very biggest players were also targeted, including ex-general and former defence minister Héctor López who was charged with ordering twelve massacres between 1978 and 1985. Finally, in January 2012, ex-military dictator **Ríos Montt** was charged with **genocide**, a seminal event witnessed by families of the victims from Ixil, many in traditional dress, who had waited three decades to see this day in court. The case is ongoing.

Strong political backing will be required to continue these cases, and there are dozens more pending prosecutions. Inevitably, human rights campaigners have questioned whether this will be forthcoming given Otto Pérez's military role during the civil war. Credibly, he announced his support of an extension of CICIG (a counter-criminal investigative and prosecuting body) powers until 2015 in his first month in office.

DOMESTIC VIOLENCE AND FEMICIDE

Hundreds of Guatemalan women are murdered each year; in 2011 the official figure was 591. Domestic violence is widespread and until recently there was no effective law against rape. The most disturbing issue of all remains the number of women murdered, many of the victims' bodies showing evidence of torture, mutilation and rape, for apparently motiveless reasons: a sadistic phenomenon known as **femicide**. These deaths were often related to gang violence and territorial disputes, most were killed in street gang initiation rituals.

Greater resources have been now been granted to the UN Commission against Impunity in Guatemala (CICIG) to target the gangs and bring the murderers to justice. Special courts created by the **2008 Law Against Femicide** began to operate in Guatemala City in September 2011. In January 2012 a mass hike up Agua volcano against domestic violence called **Subda por la Vida** (Climb for Life) attracted 12,000 people, including President Otto Pérez.

INFORMATION

For more information on human rights in Guatemala contact either **the Guatemalan Human Rights Commission** – USA (🔾ghrc-usa.org), **Amnesty International** (🔾amnesty.org) or **Human Rights Watch** (🔾hrw.org). These organizations all publish regular bulletins and reports on the current situation in the country.

cattle ranchers have overrun protected reserves including Laguna del Tigre. Some of these invaders have links to drug mafias who clear airstrips in the forest to facilitate the transit of cocaine. The dense forests and ruins of the Mirador Basin (see p.277) remain in peril, where a national park urgently needs to be established.

The Maya achievement

For some three thousand years before the arrival of the Spanish, Maya civilization dominated Mesoamerica, leaving behind some of the most impressive architecture in the entire continent. The scale and grandeur of some Maya cities, such as El Mirador around 100 BC, rivalled their European contemporaries, and the artistry and splendour of Maya civilization at the height of the Classic era arguably eclipsed that in the Old World. Maya culture was complex and sophisticated, fostering the highest standards of engineering, astronomy, stone carving and mathematics, as well as an intricate writing system.

To appreciate all this you have to see for yourself the remains of the great centres. Despite centuries of neglect, abuse and encroaching jungle, they are still astounding – the biggest temple-pyramids tower up to 70m above the forest floor, well above the jungle canopy. Stone monuments, however, leave much of the story untold, and there is still a great deal that we have to learn about Maya civilization. What follows is the briefest of introductions to the subject, hopefully just enough to whet your appetite for the immense volumes that have been written on it.

The Maya society

By the Early Classic period, the Maya cities had become organized into a hierarchy of power, with cities such as Tikal and Calakmul dominating vast areas and controlling the smaller sites through a complex structure of **alliances**. The cities jostled for power and influence, occasionally erupting into open warfare, which was also partly fuelled by the need for sacrificial victims. The distance between the larger sites averaged around 30km, and between these were myriad smaller settlements consisting of religious centres and residential groups. The structure of the alliances can be traced through the use of **emblem glyphs**.

Maya power politics

Only the glyphs of the main centres are used in isolation, while the names of smaller sites are used in conjunction with those of their larger patrons. Of all the myriad Classic cities, the dominant ones were clearly Tikal and Calakmul, with Palenque, Copán, Caracol, Naranjo, Piedras Negras, Yaxhá and Yaxchilán accepting secondary status until the early eighth century AD when the hierarchy began to dismantle. Cancuén, El Pilar, Nakúm, Waka', Dos Pilas and Quiriguá were other key cities, each lording it over, and probably extracting tribute from, many more minor settlements. Trade, marriages and warfare between the large centres were commonplace as the cities were bound up in an endless round of competition and conflict.

Population

By the Late Classic period, **population densities** across a broad swathe of territory in the central area were as high as 965 people per square kilometre – an extraordinarily high figure, equivalent to densities in rural China or Java today – and as many as **ten million** people lived in the wider Maya region. It's thought there were strict divisions between the classes, with perhaps eighty percent being preoccupied with intensive cultivation to feed these vast numbers. The peasant farmers, who were at the bottom of the social scale, also provided the labour necessary to construct monumental ceremonial temples

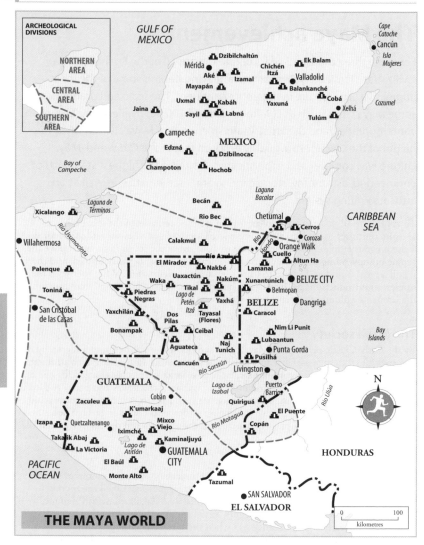

THE MAYA WORLD

(the Maya did not have the wheel) as well as perform regular "military service" duties. Even in the suburbs where the peasants lived, there are complexes of religious structures with simple, small-scale temples where ceremonies took place.

Ordinary Maya

Although the remains of the great Maya sites are a testament to the scale and sophistication of Maya civilization, they offer little insight into daily life in Maya times. To reconstruct the lives of the **ordinary Maya**, archeologists have turned to the smaller residential groups that surround the main sites, littered with the remains of household utensils, pottery, bones and farming tools. These groups are made up of simple structures made of poles and wattle-and-daub, each of which was home to a single

BALL COURTS

Pitz – the Maya **ball game** – was much more than a sport; it represented a battle between the forces of life and death. Though the exact rules are unclear, it's known that the game was between two players (or two teams) who competed on a court by striking a heavy rubber ball with their elbows and hips. Results were sometimes associated with divine judgement and they may have been used to settle conflicts – with the losers being decapitated.

All courts were a similar shape, consisting of a narrow paved playing area flanked by sloping walls, and were usually open-ended. However, they varied greatly in size: most were only 15m or 20m long and around 5m across but the great court of Chichén Itzá measured nearly 100m by 30m. Many courts had stone rings, which the players would attempt to pass the ball through; on others beautifully carved circular stone markers delineated areas of play. Ball courts were a central feature of Maya life, and aside from the ball game were also used for cultural events and rituals. Significant ball courts can be found in Tikal, Copán, Iximché, Mixco Viejo and Zaculeu.

family. The groups as a whole probably housed an **extended family**, who would have farmed and hunted together and may well have specialized in some trade or craft. The people living in these groups were commoners, their lives largely dependent on **farming**. Maize, beans, cacao, squash, chillies and fruit trees were cultivated in raised and irrigated fields, while wild fruits were harvested from the surrounding forest. It's not certain whether the land was privately or communally owned.

Class structure

Until the 1960s, Mayanists had long shared the view that the Maya were ruled by a scholarly **astronomer-priest elite** who were preoccupied with religious devotion and the study of calendrics and the stars. They were thought to be men of reason, with no time for the barbarity of war and conquest, and were often likened to the ancient Greeks. However, this early utopian vision could not have been further from the truth: the decipherment of Maya glyphs has shown that the Maya rulers were primarily concerned with the glories of battle and conquest and the preservation of their royal bloodlines; human sacrifice and bloodletting rituals were also a pivotal part of elite Maya society. The rulers considered themselves to be god–humans and thought that the line of royal accession could only be achieved by sacred validation in the form of human **bloodletting** (see box, p.340).

There were two **elite classes**: *ahau* and *cahal*, who between them probably made up two or three percent of the population. The *ahau* title was reserved exclusively for the ruler and extremely close blood relatives – the top echelon of Maya society; membership could only be inherited. One step down was the *cahal* class, most of whom would have shared bloodlines with the *ahau*. The *cahal* were mainly governors of subsidiary settlements that were under the control of the dominant city-state, and their status was always subordinate to the *ahau*. Although *cahal* lords commissioned their own stelae, the inscriptions always declared loyalty to the regional ruler.

The rulers lived close to the ceremonial centre of the Maya city, in imposing **palaces**, though the rooms were limited in size because the Maya never mastered the use of the arch. Palaces doubled as administrative centres and were used for official receptions for visiting dignitaries, with strategically positioned thrones where the ruler would preside over religious ceremonies.

The "**middle class**" of Maya society consisted of a professional class (*ah na:ab*) of architects, senior scribes (*ah tz'ib*), sculptors, bureaucrats and master artisans, some of whom were also titled, and probably young princes and important court performers. Priests and shamans can also be included in this middle class though, surprisingly, no title for the priesthood has yet been recognized – it's possible that not giving the priests a title may have been a method used by a fearful ruler to limit their influence. Through their knowledge of calendrics and supernatural prophecies, the priests were relied upon to divine the appropriate time to plant and harvest crops.

Role of women

There's no doubt that **women** played an influential role in Maya society, and in the Late Classic period there were even some women rulers – Lady Ahpo Katun at Piedras Negras, Lady Ahpo-Hel at Palenque and a Lady Six Sky at Naranjo. Women also presided at court and were given prestigious titles – Lady Cahal of Bonampak, for example. More frequently, however, as in Europe, dynasties were allied and enhanced by the marriage of royal women between cities. One of the best-documented strategic marriages occurred after the great southern city of Copán had suffered the humiliation of having its leader captured and sacrificed by upstart local rival Quiriguá in 738 AD – a royal marriage was arranged with a noblewoman from Palenque more than 500km away.

Agriculture

Maya **agriculture** adapted to the needs of the developing society, adopting intensive and sophisticated methods from as early as 400 BC when farmers at El Mirador used vast quantities of **swamp mud** to fertilize their crops. Land was terraced, drained or irrigated in order to improve its productivity and ensure that fields didn't have to lie fallow for long periods, and the capture of water became crucial to the success of a site.

The large lowland cities, which are today hemmed in by forest, were once surrounded by open fields, canals and residential compounds, although slash-and-burn was probably practised in marginal and outlying areas. Agriculture became a necessary absorption, with the ordinary Maya trading at least some of their food in markets, although all households still had a kitchen garden where they grew herbs and fruit.

Diet

Maize has always been the basis of the Maya diet, in ancient times as much as it is today. Once harvested it was made into *saka*, a cornmeal gruel that was eaten with chilli as the first meal of the day. During the day labourers ate a mixture of corn dough and water, and we know that *tamales* were also a popular speciality. The main meal, eaten in the evenings, would have been similarly maize-based, although it may well have included meat and vegetables. As a supplement to this simple diet, deer, peccary, wild turkey, duck, pigeon and quail were all hunted with bows and arrows or blowguns. The Maya also made use of dogs, both for hunting and the dinner table. Fish were also eaten, and the remains of fishhooks and nets have been found at some sites, while there is evidence that those living on the coast traded dried fish and salt far inland. The forest provided firewood as well as food, and cotton was cultivated to be dyed with natural colours and then spun into cloth.

Time and the Maya calendar

One of the cornerstones of Maya thinking was an obsession with **time**. For both practical and mystical reasons the Maya developed a highly sophisticated understanding of arithmetic, calendrics and astronomy, all of which they believed gave them the power to understand and predict events. All great occasions were interpreted on the basis of the **Maya calendar**, and it was this precise understanding of time that gave the ruling elite its authority. The majority of the carvings, on temples and stelae, record the exact date at which rulers were born, ascended to power and died.

Calendrical systems

The basis of all Maya **calculation** was the vigesimal counting system, which used multiples of twenty. All figures were written using a combination of three symbols – a shell to denote zero, a dot for one and a bar for five – which you can still see on many stelae. When calculating **calendrical systems**, the Maya used a slightly different notation known as the head-variant system, in which each number from one to twenty was represented by a deity, whose head was used to represent the number.

When it comes to the Maya **calendar** things start to get a little more complicated, as the Maya used a number of different counting systems, depending on the reason the date was being calculated. The basic unit of the Maya calendar was the day, or *kin*, followed by the *uinal*, a group of twenty days roughly equivalent to our month; but at the next level things start to get even more complex as the Maya marked the passing of time in three distinct ways.

The **260-day almanac** was used to calculate the timing of ceremonial events. Each day was associated with a particular deity that had strong influence over those born on that particular day. This calendar wasn't divided into months but had 260 distinct day-names – a system still in use among some Kaqchikel and Mam Maya who name their children according to its structure and celebrate fiestas according to its dictates.

A second calendar, the so-called "**vague year**" or *haab*, was made up of eighteen *uinals* and five *kins*, a total of 365 days, making it a close approximation of the solar year. These two calendars weren't used in isolation but operated in parallel so that once every 52 years the new day of the solar year coincided with the same day in the 260-day almanac, a meeting that was regarded as very powerful and marked the start of a new era.

Finally, the Maya had yet another system, the **Long Count** (see p.350) for marking the passing of history, which was used on dedicatory monuments. In this calendar a great cycle ends on **December 21, 2012**, when there will be huge events across the Maya World (see p.350).

Astronomy

Alongside their fascination with time, the Maya were obsessed with the sky and devoted much time and energy to unravelling its patterns. Observatories were being constructed as early as 500 BC and many sites including Copán, Uaxactún, Tikal, Chichén Itzá and Yaxhá have temples carefully aligned with solar and lunar sequences.

The Maya showed a great understanding of **astronomy**, and with their 365-day "vague year" they were just a quarter of a day out in their calculations of the solar year. At Copán, towards the end of the seventh century AD, Maya astronomers had calculated the lunar cycle at 29.53020 days, not too far off our current estimate of 29.53059. In the Dresden Codex (a copy of which can be found in Guatemala City's Popol Vuh museum), their calculations extend to the 405 lunations over a period of 11,960 days, as part of a pattern that set out to predict eclipses. At the same time, they had calculated with astonishing accuracy the movements of Venus, Mars and perhaps Mercury. Venus was of particular importance to the Maya as they linked its presence with success in war; several stelae record the appearance of Venus prompting the decision to strike at an enemy – an attack known as a "**star war**".

MAYA TIME: THE UNITS

1 *kin* = 24 hours
20 *kins* = 1 *uinal*, or 20 days
18 *uinals* = 1 *tun*, or 360 days
20 *tuns* = 1 *katun*, or 7200 days
20 *katuns* = 1 *baktun*, or 144,000 days
20 *baktuns* = 1 *pictun*, or 2,880,000 days
20 *pictuns* = 1 *calabtun*, or 57,600,000 days
20 *calabtuns* = 1 *kinchiltun*, or 1,152,000,000 days
20 *kinchiltuns* = 1 *alautun*, or 23,040,000,000 days

RITUAL BLOODLETTING AND THE MAYA

Ritual bloodletting was a fundamental part of Maya religious life, practised by all strata of society. It took many forms, from cursory self-inflicted blood offerings to elaborate ceremonies involving the mass sacrifice of captive kings and enemy warriors. The Maya modelled their lives according to a vision of the cosmos, and within this arena, human actions could affect the future, auspiciously or otherwise. Pivotal to this vision was the concept that blood-spilling helped repay man's debt to the gods, who had endowed the gift of life.

First practised by the **Olmec** more than three thousand years ago, bloodletting continued until the arrival of the conquistadors. It's thought ritual blood offerings were initially concerned with renewal and agricultural fertility, and later in the Classic period with warfare and political alliances. The practice grew to apocalyptic degrees of carnage among the **Aztecs**: Spanish chroniclers record the mass sacrifice of eighty thousand victims at the rededication of the Templo Mayor in their capital.

As well as direct representations of the sacrificial act, the Maya developed a symbolic iconography of bloodletting, so that the smallest motif, such as three knotted bands or smoke scrolls, could express blood sacrifice. The fact that depictions of bloodletting were chosen for preservation on **stone**, a costly and laborious medium, confirms its religious, social and political significance.

RITUALS

A common bloodletting ritual may have consisted of cutting earlobes, cheeks or thighs and collecting the blood to burn, or sprinkling it directly on a shrine or idol. Undertaken for numerous reasons – to bless a journey, the planting of crops, or the passing of a family member – these rites may have been accompanied by prayers, the sacrifice of animals and the burning of copal incense.

Elite bloodletting rituals often took place at important or auspicious occasions: during accession ceremonies, at the birth of an heir, to mark the passing of a calendar round, in times of war, drought or disease and to ensure regeneration and prosperity.

There seem to have been two main **auto-sacrificial rituals** practised by the Maya elite. As part of a larger ceremony, the actual act of letting blood may have been preceded by days of preparation, meditation, fasting, sexual abstinence and bodily purification with sweat baths. A male rite was to draw blood by pricking the penis with either a stingray spine, obsidian lancet or flint knife. The second rite – piercing the tongue – was probably performed by both sexes, although it's most famously illustrated by Lady Xoc in the **Yaxchilán lintels** (now housed in the British Museum). The blood offering was then soaked into bark paper and collected in ceremonial bowls to be burnt as a presentation and petition to the gods.

SACRIFICE

The Maya also practised bloodletting in the form of **captive sacrifice**, a highly ceremonial affair in which prolonged death and torture were features – gruesomely depicted in the Bonampak murals. Prisoners then either faced death by decapitation, or by having their hearts removed.

Maya **warfare** often reflected the need for ritual bloodletting, as warriors frequently sought to capture alive rulers of rival cities, who would then be imprisoned and sacrificed at a later date. The soaring temples of the city centre served as ceremonial theatres for elaborate religious rituals, allowing victories to be proclaimed to the entire community. Sacrificial victims would have been especially important to mark the accession of a new ruler, the bloodletting adding legitimacy to the king and affirming his power.   with input from Simone Clifford-Jaeger

Religion

Maya cosmology is far from straightforward as at every stage an idea is balanced by its opposite and each part of the universe is made up of many layers. To the ancient Maya (and many indigenous people today) this is the third version of the earth, the previous two having been destroyed by deluges. The current version is a flat surface, with four corners, each associated with a certain colour: white for north, red for east, yellow for south and black for west, with green at the centre. Above the earth, the sky is supported by four trees, each a different colour and species – these are also sometimes depicted as gods, known as *Bacabs*. At its centre, the sky is supported by a ceiba tree. Above the sky is a heaven of thirteen layers, each of which has its own god, with the very top layer overseen by an owl. Other attested models of the world include that of a turtle (the land) floating on the sea.

Xibalbá

However, it's the underworld, *Xibalbá*, the "Place of Fright", which was of greatest importance to the ancient Maya (and many traditionalists today), as it is in this direction that they pass after death, on their way to the place of rest. The nine layers of hell are guarded by the "Lords of the Night", and deep caves are thought to connect with the underworld.

Gods

The ancient Maya also recognized an incredible array of **gods**, though today this concept of a pantheon is much less common. Every divinity had four manifestations based upon colour and direction, and many also had counterparts in the underworld and consorts of the opposite sex. In addition, the Maya also had an extensive array of patron deities, each associated with a particular trade or particular class, while every activity from suicide to sex had its deity.

Rituals

The combined complexity of the Maya pantheon and calendar gave every day a particular significance, and the ancient Maya were bound up in a demanding **cycle of religious ritual**. The main purpose of ritual was the procurement of success by appealing to the right god at the right time and in the right way. As every event, from planting to childbirth, was associated with a particular divinity, all of the main events in daily life demanded some kind of religious ritual. For the most important of these, the Maya staged elaborate ceremonies.

Although each ceremony had its own format, a certain pattern bound them all. The correct day was carefully chosen by priestly divination, and for several days beforehand the participants fasted and remained abstinent. The main ceremony was dominated by the expulsion of all evil spirits, the burning of incense before the idols, a sacrifice (either animal or human) and **bloodletting** (see box opposite).

Drug and hallucinogenic use

In divination rituals, used to foretell the pattern of future events or account for the cause of past events, the elite used various **drugs** to achieve altered states of consciousness. Perhaps the most obvious of these was alcohol, either made from fermented maize or a combination of honey and the bark of the balnche tree. Wild tobacco, which is considerably stronger than the modern domesticated version, was also smoked. The Maya also used a range of **hallucinogenic mushrooms**, all of which were appropriately named, but none more so than the *xibalbaj obox*, "underworld mushroom", and the *k'aizalah obox*, "lost judgement mushroom".

Indigenous Guatemala

A vital indigenous culture is perhaps Guatemala's most distinctive feature. Although the Maya people may appear quiet and humble, their costumes, fiestas and markets are a riot of colour, creativity and celebration. Most Maya people remain extremely attached to local traditions and values, and regard themselves as *indígenas* first and Guatemalans second.

The indigenous **Maya**, the vast majority of whom live in the western highlands, make up about half of Guatemala's population, although it's hard to define exactly who is Maya. For the sake of the national census, people who consider themselves indigenous are classed as such, regardless of their parentage. And when it comes to defining the Maya as a group, culture is more important than pedigree, as the Maya define themselves through their relationships with their land, gods, villages and families. Holding aloof from the melting pot of modern Guatemalan society, many Maya people adhere instead to their traditional *costumbres*, codes of practice that govern every aspect of life.

As a result, the only way to define Maya culture is by describing its main traits, acknowledging that all indigenous Guatemalans will accept some of these attributes, and accepting that many are neither *indígena* nor ladino, but combine elements of both.

Indigenous culture

When the Spanish set about conquering the Maya tribes of Guatemala they altered every aspect of life for the indigenous people, uprooting their social structures and reshaping their communities. Before the Conquest the bulk of the population had lived scattered in the hills, paying tribute to a tribal elite, and surviving through subsistence farming and hunting. Under Spanish rule they were moved into new **villages** known as *reducciones*, where their homes were clustered around a church. Horizons shrank rapidly as allegiances became localized and the village hierarchies that still dominate the highlands today replaced existing tribal structures.

For almost five hundred years the Maya population has suffered repeated abuse, as the elite has exploited indigenous land and labour, regarding the Maya as an expendable commodity. But within their own communities indigenous Guatemalans were left pretty much to themselves and developed an astoundingly introspective culture that is continually adapting to new threats, reshaping itself for the future. **Village life** has been insulated from the outside world until very recently and in remote areas few women speak much Spanish; 28 native languages and dialects (see map opposite) are still spoken. Today's indigenous culture is a complex synthesis which includes elements of Maya, Spanish and modern American cultures.

Agriculture

The majority of the indigenous population still live by **subsistence agriculture**, their homes either spread across the hills or gathered in small villages. Farmers tend their *milpas*, growing beans, chillies, maize and squash – the staple diet for thousands of years. To the Maya, land is sacred and the need to own and farm it is central to their

Throughout this guide we have used the terms "Maya" or "*indígenas*" to refer to those Guatemalans of Maya origin. You may also hear them called *Índios* (or Indians), though in Guatemala this term has racially pejorative connotations.

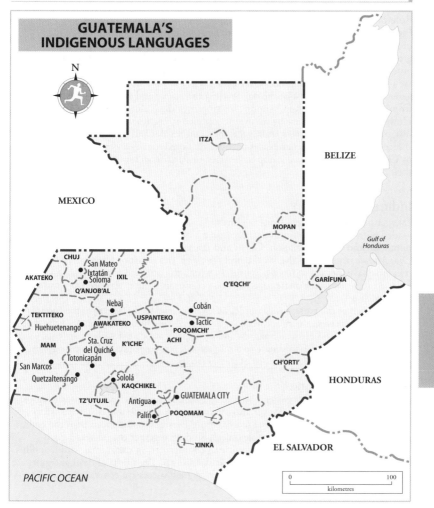

culture, despite the fact that few can survive by farming alone. Some cash crops are also grown – including broccoli, snow peas, fruit and coffee – much of it for export.

Migration

Many Maya migrate to the coast for several months a year, where they often work in appalling conditions on plantations to supplement their income. However, huge numbers are now choosing to head north to the US to work illegally instead, their overseas **remittances** now forming a crucial part of the local economy in virtually every mountain village. Traditional crafts (like rope-making, pottery and textile production) remain important, while cut-flower production for the export market is increasingly profitable. **Tourism** dollars also make a financial impact here and there, particularly around Lago de Atitlán, but also in the Ixil, Alta Verapaz and Quetzaltenango areas, too.

Role of sexes

Family life tends to bow to tradition, with large families very much a part of the indigenous culture. Marriage customs vary from place to place but in general the groom is expected to pay the bride's parents, and the couple may well live with the groom's family. Authority within the village is usually given to men, although women are increasingly involved in decision making. Customs are slowly changing, but generally men spend most of the day tending the *milpas* and vegetable plots, while women are based in the family home, looking after the children, cooking and weaving. However, Maya women are by no means confined to the house and frequently travel to distant markets to sell excess fruit, vegetables and textiles and to buy, or barter for, thread and supplies. In some places particularly noted for their weavings, such as Nebaj or Chajul, whole families decamp to Antigua or Panajachel for three or four days to sell their crafts to tourists.

Indigenous religion

Every aspect of Maya life – from the birth of a child to the planting of corn – is loaded with religious significance, based on a complicated **fusion of the Maya pantheon and Catholic religion**. Christ and the saints have taken their place alongside *Dios Mundo*, the God of the World, and *Hurakan*, the Heart of Heaven. The two religions have merged to form a hybrid, in which the outward forms of Catholicism are used to worship the ancient pantheon, a compromise that was probably fostered by Spanish priests.

The symbol of the **cross**, for example, was well known to the Maya, signifying the four winds of heaven, the four directions and everlasting life. Today many of the deities have both Maya and Hispanic names, and are usually associated with a particular saint. All the deities remain subordinate to a mighty and remote supreme being, and Christ takes a place in the upper echelons of the hierarchy.

God and spiritual world

For the Maya, **God** is everywhere, bound up in the seasons, the mountains, the crops, the soil, the air and the sky. Prayer and offerings mark every important event, with disasters often attributed to divine intervention. Even more numerous than the gods, **spirits** are found in every imaginable object, binding together the universe. Each individual is born with a *nahaul*, or spiritual counterpart, in the animal world, and his or her destiny is bound up with that particular animal. The spirits of dead ancestors are also ever-present and have to be looked after by each successive generation.

Religious hierarchy

Traditionally, a community's **religious hierarchy** organizes its worship. All office-holders are male, and throughout their lives they progress through the system, moving from post to post. The various posts are grouped into *cofradias*, ritual brotherhoods, each of which is responsible for a particular saint. Throughout the year the saint is kept in the home of an elder member, and on the appointed date, in the midst of a fiesta, it's paraded through the streets, to spend the next year somewhere else. The elder responsible for the saint will have to pay for much of the fiesta, including costumes, alcohol and assorted offerings, but it's a responsibility, or *cargo*, that's considered a great honour.

In the traditional village hierarchy, it's these duties that give the elders, known as *principales*, a prominent role in village life and it's through these duties that they exercise their authority, such as the organization of the annual **fiesta**. (In some villages, such as Chichicastenango and Sololá, a *municipalidad indígena*, or indigenous council, operates alongside the *cofradias*, and is similarly hierarchical. As men work their way up through the system they may well alternate between the civil and religious hierarchies.) The *cofradias* don't necessarily confine themselves to the traditional list of saints, and have been known to foster "evil" saints, such as San Simón or **Maximón**, a drinking, smoking ladino figure, sometimes referred to as Judas or Pedro de Alvarado.

Shamanism

On a more superstitious level, native priests (*costumbristas*, or *aj'itz* in K'iche' and Kaqchikel areas) communicate with the gods and spirits to cater to people's personal religious needs. This is usually done on behalf of an individual client who's in search of a blessing, and often takes place at shrines and caves in the mountains, with offerings of copal, a type of incense, and alcohol. The *costumbristas* also make extensive use of old Maya sites, and small burnt patches of grass litter many of the ruins in the highlands. Indigenous priests are also credited with the ability to cast spells, predict the future and communicate with the dead. For specific medical problems, the Maya appeal to *zahorines* who practise traditional medicine with a combination of invocation and herbs, and are closely associated with indigenous religious traditions.

EVANGELISM IN GUATEMALA

One of the greatest surprises awaiting first-time travellers in Guatemala is the number of evangelical churches in the country, with fundamentalist, Pentecostal or neo-Pentecostal services taking place in most towns and villages. Although early Protestant missions came to Guatemala as far back as 1882, the impact of US-based churches remained marginal and largely unnoticed until the 1950s, when **state repression** and the subsequent **guerrilla war** began to weaken the power of the Catholic Church. Up until this time, more than 95 percent of the population was officially Catholic, though the rural Maya had their own hybrid forms of worship that mixed Catholic ceremony with pagan rite.

While the hierarchy of the Catholic Church remained fervently anti-Communist and closely aligned with the economic, political and military elite, during the early 1960s many rural Catholic priests became heavily influenced by liberation theology, supporting peasant leagues and development projects, and some even joined the guerrillas. Subsequently, the ruling class of generals, politicians and big landowners began to consider the Catholic Church as being riddled with communist sympathizers, and targeted perceived troublemakers accordingly. By the early 1980s, so many priests had been murdered by the state-sponsored death squads that the Catholic Church pulled out of the entire department of El Quiché in protest. In contrast, many evangelical missionaries preached the importance of an army victory over the guerrillas and, with their pro-business, anti-communist rhetoric, attracted many converts anxious to avoid suspicion and survive. In addition, the early evangelicals had made it a priority to learn the native Maya languages, and had the Bible translated into K'iche', Mam, Kaqchikel and other tongues.

However, it was the devastating **1976 earthquake** that really sparked the march of US evangelism in Guatemala. Church-backed disaster-relief programmes brought in millions of dollars of medicine, food and toys to those prepared to convert, and shattered villages were rebuilt with new schools and health centres. In the eyes of the impoverished rural villagers, Protestantism became linked with prosperity, and lively evangelical church services, where dancing, music and singing were the norm, quickly gained huge popularity.

The movement received another boost in 1982, when **General Efrían Ríos Montt** seized power in a military coup to become Guatemala's first evangelical leader. The population was treated to Montt's maniacal, marathon Sunday sermons, and a new wave of mission teams entered the country from the southern United States. For many Guatemalans, Ríos Montt represented the best and worst of evangelism: he was frenzied and fanatical, yet also fostered a reputation for strictness and probity (despite the terrible human-rights violations under his brief tenure). Ríos Montt was ousted after just seventeen months in power, though he was to dominate Guatemalan politics through the 1990s and early years of the new millennium together with Alfonso Portillo, another evangelical.

Guatemala is today the least Catholic country in Latin America, with around sixty percent of the population looking to the Vatican for guidance and about forty percent belonging to evangelical churches.

Evangelical Christianity

Until the 1950s, when Catholic **missionaries** became active in the highlands, many indigenous Guatemalans had no idea that there was a gulf between their own religion and orthodox Catholicism. At first, the missionaries drew most of their support from the younger generation, many of whom were frustrated by the rigidity of the village hierarchy. Gradually, this eroded the authority of the traditional religious system: the missions undermined the *cofradias*, disapproved of traditional fiestas, and scorned the work of the native priests. As a part of this, the reforming movement Catholic Action, which combined the drive for orthodoxy with an involvement in social issues, has also had a profound impact.

After the 1976 earthquake, waves of Protestant missionaries, known as *evangélicos*, arrived in Guatemala, and their presence has also accelerated the decline of traditional religion (see box, p.345).

These days there are at least three hundred different **evangelical churches**, backed by a huge injection of money from the US, and offering all sorts of incentives to fresh converts. Most of these churches are fervently against liquor consumption, and as **alcoholism** is a huge issue in indigenous villages, some communities have effectively become dry towns, including Almolonga and Todos Santos Cuchumatán.

Yet despite the efforts of outsiders, the *costumbristas* and *cofradias* are still in business, and many fiestas remain vaguely pagan. Indeed, since the end of the civil war there has been an upsurge in interest in Maya religious practice – the previous president of Guatemala, Álvaro Colom, has studied Maya spiritualism.

Markets and fiestas

At the heart of the indigenous economy is the **weekly market**, which remains central to life in the highlands and provides one of the best opportunities to see Maya life at close quarters. The majority of the indigenous population still lives by subsistence farming but spares a day or two a week to gather together in the nearest village and trade surplus produce. The market is as much a social occasion as an economic one and people come to talk, eat, drink, gossip and have a good time. In some places the action starts the night before with marimba music and heavy drinking.

On market day itself the village is filled by a steady flow of people, arriving by pick-up or bus, on foot or by mule. In no time at all trading gets under way, and the plaza is soon buzzing with activity and humming with conversation, although raised voices are a rarity, with deals struck after protracted, but always polite, negotiations.

The scale and atmosphere of markets varies from place to place. The country's largest is in **San Francisco el Alto**, on Fridays, and draws traders from throughout the country. Other renowned ones are the vegetable market of **Almolonga** and **Sololá**'s huge Tuesday and Friday affairs, but almost every village has its day. **Chichicastenango**'s vast Thursday and Sunday markets are probably Guatemala's most famous, and remain important gatherings for highlanders, though the tourist-orientated souvenir stalls are mushrooming here. But perhaps the most enjoyable of Guatemala's markets are well away from the Carretera Interamericana, in tiny, isolated hamlets. Up high in the folds of the mountains, in places like lonely Chajul or isolated Santa Eulalia, the pleasure is simply soaking up the scene, as traders and villagers barter and banter in the hushed clicks of the local dialect and near-whispers, in the unhurried commercial ritual that so defines Maya highland life.

Maya fiestas

Once a year every village, however small, indulges in an orgy of celebration in honour of its patron saint – you'll find a list of them at the end of each chapter. These **fiestas** are a great swirl of dance, music, religion, endless firecrackers, eating and outrageous drinking, and express the vitality of indigenous culture. Everyone tries to return to their home town at fiesta time, with emigrants journeying from Guatemala City (and even the US) to join in the celebrations. Religious processions are given due importance, as the image of the local patron saint is paraded through the streets, accompanied by the elders of the *cofradía*, who dress in full regalia. The larger fiestas also involve funfairs and week-long markets. Traditional music is played with marimbas, drums and flutes; professional bands also may be hired, blasting out popular tunes through crackling PA systems.

Dance

Dance, too, is very much a part of fiestas, and incorporates routines and ideas that date from ancient Maya times. Dance **costumes** are incredibly elaborate, covered in mirrors and sequins, and have to be rented for the occasion. Despite the high cost, the dancers see their role both as an obligation – to tradition and the community – and an honour.

Most of the dances form an extension of dramatic tradition through which local history was retold in dance dramas. The **Dance of the Conquistadors** is one of the most popular, modelled on the Dance of the Moors and introduced by the Spanish as a re-enactment of the Conquest, although in some cases it's been instilled with a significance that can never have been intended by the invaders. The dancers often see no connection with the Conquest, but dance instead to release the spirits of the dead, a function perhaps closer to Maya religion than Catholicism. The **Palo Volador**, a dramatic spectacle in which men swing perilously to the ground from a 20m pole, certainly dates from the pre-Columbian era (these days you'll only see it in Cubulco, Chichicastenango and Joyabaj), as does the Dance of the Deer, while the Dance of the Bullfight and the Dance of the Volcano relate incidents from the Conquest itself.

Most of the dances do have steps to them, but the dancers are usually blind drunk and sway around as best they can in time to the music, sometimes tumbling over each other or even passing out – so don't expect to see anything too dainty.

In recent years a kitsch amalgamation of traditional and modern dance has evolved. It's quite common to find semi-professional dance troupes of young girls in tight-fitting costumes and fiesta-style masks performing mock-traditional dance steps to marimba with a beat. Purists may condemn this bizarre combination of tradition and vulgarity as a bastardization of centuries-old Mayan custom; many locals find it pretty entertaining.

The Maya today

The Maya were the main victims of the decades-long **civil war**, which not only killed 160,000 highlanders and left a million homeless, but also attacked the very foundation of indigenous culture in Guatemala. The military viewed the Maya as inherently **subversive**, and communities were set against each other as men were conscripted into PAC paramilitary patrols and pressured to betray anyone showing signs of dissidence against the state.

But under civilian rule, a **Maya cultural revival** has steadily matured, as Guatemala's indigenous people have pursued the freedom of organization, protest and participation denied them for centuries. Hundreds of schools have been founded to educate Maya children in their own tongues, increasing numbers of indigenous writers and journalists have emerged, more and more Maya books and magazines are being published and *indígena* radio stations have been set up. The shifting mood has even influenced youth culture, with Maya shamanic courses becoming popular and ladino university students asserting their mixed-race identity and proclaiming a **Maya heritage**. Yet despite these changes Guatemala remains a seismically divided country. **Racism** is endemic and most Maya, still subject to institutionalized discrimination, live in poverty (over seventy percent, according to the government's own figures).

Rigoberta Menchú and the Nobel Peace Prize

In 1992, five hundred years after Columbus reached the Americas, the Nobel committee awarded their Peace Prize to Rigoberta Menchú Tum, a 33-year-old K'iche' Maya woman who had campaigned tirelessly for peace in Guatemala and for the advancement of indigenous people across the world. In their official statement, the Nobel Institute described Menchú as "a vivid symbol of peace and reconciliation across ethnic, cultural and social dividing lines".

Within Guatemala, however, the honour provoked controversy. Few doubted that Menchú had firm connections and deep sympathies with Guatemala's **guerrillas**, although after she was awarded the prize she distanced herself from the armed struggle. Nevertheless, many people argued that her support for armed uprising made her an inappropriate winner of a peace prize. Others feared that the prize would be interpreted as a vindication of the guerrillas and only serve to perpetuate the civil war.

Autobiography

The first volume of Menchú's autobiography, *I, Rigoberta Menchú*, shows her to be essentially a pacifist and suggests that her unspoken support for the guerrillas was very much a last resort. "For us, killing is something monstrous. And that's why we feel so angered by all the repression … Even though the tortures and kidnappings had done our people a lot of harm, we shouldn't lose faith in change. This is when I began working in a peasant organization and went on to another stage of my life. There are other things, other ways."

Menchú's story is undeniably tragic, and her account offers a harrowing look into the darkest years of Guatemalan history and the plight of the nation's indigenous people. However, the accuracy of sizeable parts of her life story, as recounted in her autobiography, were later challenged in *Rigoberta Menchú and the Story of All Poor Guatemalans*, an iconoclastic biography published in 1998 by David Stoll. Stoll concluded that substantial sections of the Menchú legend had been fabricated or greatly exaggerated, and that she had "drastically revised the prewar experience of her village to suit the needs of the revolutionary organization she had joined".

In *I, Rigoberta Menchú*, Menchú describes how the barbaric cruelty of the Guatemalan civil war affected her family, who were political activists, and how they were branded guerrilla sympathizers by the military. Menchú recounts the fight to protect the family farm from greedy ladinos, her family's days working in the plantations of the Pacific coast, and her lack of formal schooling. The deaths of her brother, mother and father at the hands of the armed forces are agonizingly retold. Expanding to cover the wider picture in Guatemala, Menchú condemns the massive disparities between the country's ladino and Maya, and rich and poor. The biography has gone on to sell more than five hundred thousand copies, while Menchú has been invited to speak at events and conferences all over the world. Campaigning for the rights of the Guatemalan Maya and other oppressed minorities from exile in Mexico, she frequently travelled to the United Nations in Geneva and New York to press her case. This period of the Nobel laureate's life is narrated in *Crossing Borders*, the second volume of her autobiography, and an altogether less traumatic and controversial read.

Return from exile

Rigoberta Menchú returned to Guatemala in 1994 as an iconic but divisive figure; in the global arena, however, her reputation was unblemished until the publication of David Stoll's biography. Stoll's book provided compelling evidence that Menchú's family's land dispute was an internecine family feud rather than a racially charged indigenous-ladino altercation; that she never had toiled in the fields of Pacific-coast plantations; and that she had been educated at two private convent schools. He alleged a guerrilla past and questioned the accuracy of her account about the deaths of two of her brothers.

After the biography's publication an international furore ensued, with allegations from *The New York Times* that she had received "a Nobel prize for lying". Menchú evaded responding directly to Stoll's charges, though admitted that she had received some formal education at a convent school in Chiantla. She later sought to distance herself somewhat from *I, Rigoberta Menchú*, and inferred the input of her editor and translator – Arturo Taracena, a guerrilla attaché – had distorted her testimony. Geir Lundestad, director of the Nobel Institute, has expressed support for Menchú, declaring that the decision to give Menchú the award was because of her work on behalf of indigenous people, and not because of her family history.

As the dust settled, a roster of academics lined up to support Menchú's reputation, questioning Stoll's motives and defending the value of her *testimonio* – which, they reasoned, was recounting the civil-war experiences of indigenous Guatemalans as a whole – and followed a tradition of Maya testimonial writing that dated back to the time of the Conquest. No one disputed that her mother, father and brothers died at the hands of the military (with another two hundred thousand Guatemalans), whose extreme brutality has been documented in exhaustive reports compiled by the UN and Catholic Church. Her success bringing global attention to the terrible suffering inflicted on (and continuing repression of) Guatemala's Maya is incontestable, and her work on behalf of the world's indigenous peoples has been unrelenting and highly effective. The two sides of the debate are set out in *The Rigoberta Menchú Controversy* published in 2001, a collection of articles edited by Arturo Arias.

Political career

Today, Menchú is admired by most Guatemalan Maya and the political left, mistrusted by most of the Guatemalan oligarchy, and tends to be despised by the military and those on the right. She was a goodwill ambassador for the Peace Accords in the Berger government, and through her foundation, campaigned for human and indigenous rights in Guatemala, and beyond. Declaring "that there's no peace without justice" she has fought to end the impunity of the armed forces for their civil war atrocities and filed genocide charges in the international courts against the former military rulers.

Menchú contested both the 2007 and 2011 presidential elections, but only polled three percent of the vote on both occasions. She's also campaigned on healthcare issues, with the aim of providing low-cost generic medicines to all. For more information on the Rigoberta Menchú Foundation, consult the website ⓦfrmt.org.

2012

For the time-obsessed Maya, December 21, 2012, is an epochal event. In their Long Count calendar it marks the end of a great cycle, which only occurs every 5125 years. Perhaps because Maya calendars are cyclical, and the date represents the end of an era, all kinds of New Agers and mystic types have got very excited and jumped on the 2012 bandwagon, with wild theories being banded about that this was the day that Maya predicted the world would end. The reality – unless celestial powers prove otherwise – is less cataclysmic, but the date does represent a momentous event in the Maya calendar, particularly for indigenous Guatemalans.

The build-up has been immense. For a decade, tour agencies and tourist boards have been banging the publicity drum about December 21, 2012. Hollywood made a movie (*2012*) predicting a doomsday, with lots of visual thrills and very little in the way of a script. Thousands of articles and books dedicated to the 2012 phenomenon have been written and dozens of documentaries made.

In case you hadn't realized, **December 21, 2012**, is also the winter solstice. The Maya loved to align ceremonial buildings according to their planetary and astronomical knowledge. At many sites, including Tikal, Uaxactún and Chichén Itzá, temple groups were positioned to reflect sunrise on equinoxes and solstices.

Long Count calendar

The ancient Maya used several calendar systems, one of which, the **Long Count**, was based on **great cycles** (a period of 5125 years, made up of thirteen *baktuns*). As the name implies, the Long Count was specifically used to monitor lengthy periods of time. The current great cycle period dates from August 11, 3114 BC (13.0.0.0.0 in the Long Count) and is destined to come to an end on December 21, 2012. So the following day, December 22, is the start of a new cycle and will also be 13.0.0.0.0.

The Long Count system simply records the number of days in the great cycle, a task that calls for five different numbers – recording the equivalent of years, decades, centuries and so on. The thirteen *baktuns* that make up the great cycle are thought to correspond to the thirteen levels in Maya heaven.

In later years, Maya sculptors actually tired of this exhaustive process and opted instead for the Short Count, an abbreviated version.

2012 in Maya inscriptions

For writer John Jenkins the minor Maya site of **Izapa** (in Mexico, just west of the Guatemalan border post of Tecún Umán) is pivotal, as it is here that the Maya inscribed a monument with the date December 21, 2012, and linked it to their knowledge of astronomy. Jenkins believes Stela 25 here maps out the galactic alignment that would mark the end of the Long Count, with an image depicting a creation scene with a bird deity perched atop a cosmic tree, which he says represents the Milky Way. This theory has been disputed by other Mayanists. Additional 2012 inscriptions can be found at **Quiriguá**, where Stela C records a date of 13.0.0.0.0 followed by a reference to the descent of deities. Monument 6 at **Tortuguero** in Mexico also has a similar 13.0.0.0.0 inscription.

READ ALL ABOUT 2012

2012 has seen an explosion of literature about the Maya calendrics, prophesies and so on. Recommended reading includes:

Anthony Aveni *The End of Time: The Maya Mystery of 2012*. Astronomer, professor of anthropology and Native American studies expert, Aveni examines the 2012 theories and evidence with reference to the key Maya scripts and archeology.

Gaspar Pedro González *13 B'aktun: Mayan Visions of 2012 and Beyond*. Written by a Maya novelist, this illuminating book explains Maya concepts of time and spiritual conscientiousness.

John Jenkins *The 2012 Story: The Myths, Fallacies, and Truth Behind the Most Intriguing Date in History*. This author considers that 2012 is all about galactic alignment, explaining his theory with references to Izapa inscriptions.

Mark Van Stone *2012: Science and Prophecy of the Ancient Maya*. The sceptic's guide to 2012, containing a detailed analysis of all the theories.

Doomsayers

Adding further intrigue to the plot, astrophysicists are aware of a black hole at the centre of the Milky Way – called Sagittarius A* – and that in 2012 the sun will align with the plane of the galaxy for the first time in 26,000 years. According to some 2012 doomsayers, at this point Sagittarius A* will disrupt our solar system, creating giant flares on the sun's surface, and ultimately reversing planet earth's magnetic field with cataclysmic consequences. We shall see.

2012 in Guatemala

December 21, 2012, is going to be a huge event in Guatemala. People have been talking about it for years – **over a thousand people** (including academics, ambassadors, historians and 52 Maya spiritual guides) attended a Maya 2012 conference in Antigua as far back 2008. The tourist board Inguat have set up a special 2012 website (ⓦ2012guatemala.com) and is hoping for a record number of visitors.

The date already falls in Guatemala's peak holiday period, so if you're planning on a trip book accommodation and tours well ahead.

Ceremonies involving music, sacred fires, prayers and chanting are planned in Maya sites across the nation. Demonstrations of the Maya ball game will be performed at the big centres. There will be sunrise ceremonies at the ancient observatory of Group E in Uaxactún, whose three temples were constructed to celebrate the equinoxes. Tikal is sure to attract a cast of thousands with Maya-themed events and religious ceremonies.

Landscape and wildlife

Guatemala embraces an astonishingly diverse collection of environments, ranging from the permanently moist rainforests and mangroves of the Caribbean coast to the exposed *altiplano* highlands, where the ground can be hard with frost. Its wildlife is correspondingly varied; undisturbed forests provide a home to both temperate species from the north and tropical ones from the south, as well as a number of indigenous species found nowhere else in the world.

The Pacific coast

Guatemala's **Pacific coastline** is marked by a thin strip of black volcanic sand, pounded by the surf. There are no natural harbours and boats have to take their chances in the breakers or launch from one of the piers (though Puerto Quetzal takes large, ocean-going ships). The sea itself provides a rich natural harvest of shrimp, tuna, snapper and mackerel, most of which go for export. The coastal waters are also ideal for sport-fishing. A couple of kilometres offshore, dorado, which grow to around forty pounds, are plentiful, while farther out marlin, sailfish, wahoo and skipjack ply the waters.

The **beach** itself rises from the water to form a large sandbank, dotted with palm trees, behind which the land drops off into low-lying mangrove swamps and canals. In the east, from San José to the border, the **Chiquimulilla Canal** runs behind the beach for around 100km. For most of the way it's no more than a narrow strip of water, but here and there it fans out into swamps, creating a maze of waterways that are an ideal breeding ground for young fish, waterfowl and a range of small mammals. The sandy shoreline is an ideal nesting site for three species of **sea turtle**, including the giant leatherback (see box, p.189), which periodically emerge from the water, drag themselves up the beach and deposit a clutch of eggs before hauling their weight back into the water. At Monterrico, east of San José, a nature reserve protects a small section of the coastline for the benefit of the turtles, and with luck you might see one here.

The **Reserva Monterrico–Hawaii** is the best place to see wildlife on the Pacific coast, as it includes a superb **mangrove swamp**, which you can easily explore by boat. The mangroves are mixed in with water lilies, bulrushes and tropical hardwoods, amongst which you'll see **herons**, **kingfishers** and an array of **ducks** including **muscovies** and **white whistling ducks**. In the area around Monterrico, flocks of **wood stork** are common, and you might also see the **white ibis** or the occasional **great jabiru**, a massive stork that nests in the area. With real perseverance and a bit of luck you might also catch a glimpse of a **racoon**, **anteater** or **opossum**. You'll also be able to see **alligators** and **iguanas**, if not in the wild then at the reserve headquarters where they are kept in a breeding programme. Other birds you might see almost anywhere along the coast include **plover**, **coot** and **tern**, and a number of winter migrants including **white** and **brown pelican**.

Between the shore and the foothills of the highlands, the **coastal plain** is an intensely fertile and heavily farmed area, where the volcanic and alluvial soils are ideal for sugarcane, cotton, palm oil, banana and rubber plantations and cattle ranches. In recent years soya and sorghum, which require less labour, have been added to this list. Guatemala's coastal **agribusiness** is high cost and high yield: the soils are treated chemically and the crops regularly sprayed with a cocktail of pesticides, herbicides and fertilizers. There's little land that remains untouched by the hand of commercial agriculture so it's hard to imagine what this must once have looked like, but it was almost certainly very similar to Petén, a mixture of savannah and rainforest supporting a rich array of wildlife. These days it's only the swamps, steep hillsides and towering hedges that give any hint of its former glory, although beautiful flocks of white **snowy** and **cattle egret** feed alongside the beef cattle.

Finally, one particularly interesting lowland species is the **oropendola**, a large oriole that builds a long woven nest hanging from trees and telephone wires. They tend to nest in colonies and a single tree might support fifty nests. You'll probably notice the nests more than the birds, which thrive throughout Guatemala and neighbouring countries.

The Boca Costa

Approaching the highlands, the coastal plain starts to slope up towards a string of volcanic cones, and this section of well-drained hillside is known as the **Boca Costa**. The volcanic soils, high rainfall and good drainage combine to make it ideal for growing **coffee**, and it's here that some of Guatemala's best beans are produced, with rows of olive-green bushes ranked beneath shady trees.

Where the land is unsuitable for coffee, lush tropical forest still grows, clinging to the hills. As you head up into the highlands, through deeply cleft valleys, you pass through some of this superb forest, dripping with moss-covered vines, bromeliads and orchids. Close to the most active volcanoes, in areas where farming has not disturbed the environment, are some incredibly rich ecosystems. Around Volcán Santiaguito near Quetzaltenango, more than 120 species of bird have been sighted, including some real rarities such as **solitary eagle**, **quetzal** and **highland guan**. The **azure-rumped tanager**, **maroon-chested ground dove** and **Pacific parakeet** are endemic to this region. The Guatemala Birding Resource Center (Ⓦbirdguatemala.org), a specialist tour operator, runs excellent trips to the Boca Costa region.

The highlands

The highlands proper begin with a chain of **volcanoes**. There are 37 peaks in all, the main backbone ranged in a direct line that runs parallel with the Pacific coastline from the southwestern border with Mexico into El Salvador. (In the eastern highlands, away from the main chain, there's another sprinkling of older, less-spectacular weathered cones.) The highest of the main peaks is **Tajumulco** (4220m), near the Mexican border, while three highly active cones – **Fuego**, **Pacaya** and **Santiaguito** – all belch sulphurous fumes, volcanic ash and the occasional fountain of molten rock. Beneath the surface their subterranean fires heat the bedrock, and in several places hot spring water emerges, offering the luxury of a warm, mineral-rich bath, the best of which is Fuentes Georginas (see p.152).

Highland lakes

On the southern side of the central highlands, volcanic peaks surround two large lakes, Lago de Amatitlán and Lago de Atitlán, both of which are set in superb countryside. South of Guatemala City, **Lago de Amatitlán** has suffered years of environmental mismanagement, and its waters are heavily contaminated and blackened by pollution. The lake remains a popular picnic spot for the capital's not-so-rich.

Farther west, **Lago de Atitlán** is still spectacularly beautiful, with crystal blue water, but increasing tourist development and a population explosion threaten to damage its delicate ecological balance, and a serious **cyanobacteria** explosion affected the lake in 2010 (see p.126).

Central valleys

On the northern side of the volcanic ridge are the **central valleys** of the highlands, a complex mixture of sweeping bowls, steep-sided valleys, open plateaux and jagged peaks. This central area is home to the vast majority of Guatemala's population, and all

---

ATITLÁN'S LOST GREBE

Atitlán's ecosystem was upset as far back as 1958, when **black bass** were introduced in a bid to create sport-fishing. The bass is a rapacious fish and in no time at all its presence had reshaped the food chain. Smaller fish became increasingly rare, as did crabs, frogs, insects and small mammals. The **Atitlán grebe**, a small, flightless water bird unique to the lake, was worst hit. Young grebes were gobbled up by the hungry bass, and by 1965 just eighty of them survived. By 1984, falling water levels, combined with tourist development of the lakeshore, cut their numbers by a further thirty. Today the bird is extinct.

---

the available land is intensely farmed, with hillsides carved into workable terraces and portioned up into a patchwork of small fields. Here the land is farmed by campesinos using techniques that predate the arrival of the Spanish. The *milpa* is the mainstay of Maya farming practices: a field is cleared, usually by slash and burn, and planted with maize as the main crop, with beans, chillies and squash grown as well. Traditionally, the land is rotated between *milpa* and pasture, and also left fallow for a while, but in some areas it's now under constant pressure, the fertility of the soil is virtually exhausted and only with the assistance of fertilizer can it still produce a worthwhile crop. The pressure on land is immense and each generation is forced to farm more marginal territory, planting on steep hillsides where exposed soil is soon washed into the valley below.

Some areas remain off limits to farmers, however, and substantial tracts of the highlands are still **forested**. In the cool valleys of the central highlands, pine trees dominate, intermixed with oak, cedar and fir. To the south, on the volcanic slopes and in the warmth of deep-cut valleys, lush subtropical forest thrives in a world kept permanently moist – similar in many ways to the forest of Verapaz, where constant rain fosters the growth of cloudforest.

Altiplano

Heading on to the north, the land rises to form several **mountain ranges**. The largest of these are the Cuchumatanes, a massive chain of granite peaks that reach a height of 3837m above the town of Huehuetenango. Further to the east there are several smaller ranges such as the Sierra de Chuacús, the Sierra de las Minas and the Sierra de Chamá. The high peaks support stunted trees and open grassland, used for grazing sheep and cattle, but are too cold for maize and most other crops. Guatemalans call this high ground the *altiplano*.

Birdlife

Birdlife is plentiful throughout the highlands; you'll see a variety of **hummingbirds**, flocks of screeching **parakeets**, **swifts**, **egrets** and the ever-present **vultures**. Slightly less commonplace are the **quails** and **wood partridges**, **white-tailed pigeons** and several species of dove including the **little Inca** and the **white-winged dove**. Last but by no means least is the **quetzal**, which has been revered since Maya times. The male quetzal has fantastic green tail-feathers which snake behind it through the air as it flies: these have always been prized by hunters and even today the bird is very rare indeed.

Near Cobán is the **Biotopo del Quetzal** (see p.228), a protected area of **cloudforest** in the department of Baja Verapaz where quetzals breed. You might also try looking for Guatemala's national bird in the remote mountains of the Sierra de Caquipec to the northeast, or in the Chelemhá forest reserve (see p.229) south of Cobán.

The rainforests of Petén

Northeast of the highlands the land drops away into the **rainforests** of Petén, a large chunk of which remains undisturbed, although recent oil finds and a huge influx of cattle ranchers, timber merchants and migrant settlers have cut a swathe through virgin jungle in the past thirty years. The forest of Petén extends across the Mexican border, where it merges with the Lacandón and Campeche rainforests, and into Belize, where it skirts around the lower slopes of the Maya Mountains, reaching to the Caribbean coast.

Today around forty percent of Petén is still covered by **primary forest**, with a canopy that towers between 30m and 50m above the forest floor, made up of hundreds of species of tree, including ceiba, mahogany, aguacate, ebony and sapodilla. The combination of a year-round growing season, plenty of moisture and millions of years of evolution have produced an environment that supports thousands of species of plants and trees. While temperate forests tend to be dominated by a single species – fir, oak or beech, say – it's diversity that characterizes the tropical forest. Each species is specifically adapted to fit into a particular ecological niche, where it receives a precise amount of light and moisture.

This biological storehouse has yielded some astonishing **discoveries**. Steroid hormones, such as cortisone, and diosgenin, the active ingredient in birth-control pills, were developed from wild yams found in these forests, and the highly potent anaesthetic tetrodoxin is derived from a species of Central American frog.

Ecosystem

Despite its size and diversity the forest is surprisingly **fragile**. It forms a closed system in which nutrients are continuously recycled and decaying plant matter fuels new growth. The forest floor is a spongy mass of roots, fungi, mosses, bacteria and micro-organisms, in which nutrients are stored, broken down with the assistance of insects and chemical decay, and gradually released to the waiting roots and fresh seedlings. The thick canopy prevents much light reaching the forest floor, ensuring that the soil remains damp but warm, a hotbed of chemical activity. The death of a large tree prompts a flurry of growth as new light reaches the forest floor, and in no time at all a young tree rises to fill the gap. But once the trees are removed the soil is highly vulnerable, deprived of its main source of fertility. Exposed to the harsh tropical sun and direct rainfall, an area of cleared forest soon becomes prone to flooding and drought. Recently cleared land will contain enough nutrients for four or five years of good growth, but soon afterwards its usefulness declines rapidly and within twenty years it will be almost completely barren. If the trees are stripped from a large area, soil erosion will silt the rivers and parched soils will disrupt local rainfall patterns.

Human influence

Settlement needn't mean the end of the rainforest. Only one small group of Maya, the Lacandones, still farm the forest using traditional methods. They allow the existing trees to point them in the right direction, avoiding areas that support mahogany, as they tend to be too wet, and searching out ceiba and ramón trees, which thrive in rich, well-drained soils. In April a patch of forest is burnt down and then, to prevent soil erosion, planted with fast-growing trees such as banana and papaya, and with root crops to fix the soil. A few weeks later they plant their main crops: maize and a selection of others, from garlic to sweet potatoes. Every inch of the soil is covered in growth, a method that mimics the forest and thereby protects the soil. The same land is cultivated for three or four years and then allowed to return to its wild state – although they continue to harvest from the fruit-bearing plants – and in due course return to the same area. The whole process is in perfect harmony with the forest, extracting only what it can afford to lose and ensuring that it remains fertile. Sadly, the traditional farming methods of the Lacandones are now very rarely practised. New settlers burn the forest and plant grass for cattle pasture, and vast areas of former jungle now have very little biodiversity or fertility.

Wildlife

In its undisturbed state the rainforest is still superbly beautiful and is home to an incredible range of **wildlife**. Amongst the birds, the spectacular scarlet, blue and emerald-green **ocellated turkey**, found only in Petén, is perhaps the most famous. But the forest is also home to three species of **toucan, motmot** (a type of bird of paradise), several species of **parrot** including **Aztec** and **green parakeets** and the endangered **scarlet macaw**, which is said to live to at least fifty. As in the highlands, **hummingbirds, buzzards** and **hawks** are all common. A surprising number of these can be seen fairly easily in the **Parque Nacional Tikal**, particularly if you hang around until sunset.

Although **mammals** are widespread, they are almost always elusive, and your best chance of seeing them is at the bigger reserves and archeological sites, where they may have lost some of their fear of humans. At many forest sites you'll almost certainly see **monkeys**, including the acrobatically agile **spider** and the highly social **howlers**, which emit a chilling, deep-throated roar. The largest land animal in Guatemala is the **tapir** (dante), weighing up to 300kg, and usually found near water. Tapirs are endangered and you're not likely to see one without a guide. Two species of **peccary** (wild pig), the collared and the white-lipped, wander the forest floors in large groups, seeking out roots and palm nuts. The smaller herbivores include the **paca** (also known as the tepescuintle and agouti), a rodent about the size of a piglet, which is hunted everywhere for food. You'll often see **coati** (locally known as *pizotes*), inquisitive and intelligent members of the raccoon family, foraging in the leaf litter around archeological sites with their long snouts, often in family groups of several dozen. Coatis and small **grey foxes** are frequently seen at Tikal, and in many places you can see **opossums** and **armadillos**.

Five species of wild **cat** are found in the region, though most are now rare outside the protected areas. **Jaguars** (called *tigres* in Guatemala) formerly ranged over the whole of the country, but today the densest population is found in the northern Petén, though they are very rarely seen. **Pumas** live in remote forest areas; less rare but still uncommon are the much smaller **ocelot** and the **margay**, which is about the size of a large domestic cat. The **jaguarundi** is the smallest and commonest of the wild cats, and as it hunts during the day you might spot one on a trail.

Take a trip along almost any river in Petén and you've a good chance of seeing **green iguanas, mud turtles** or **Central American river turtles** sunning themselves on logs. **Egrets** and **kingfishers** fish from overhanging branches, while large rivers such as Río de la Pasión and lakes, including Lago de Petexbatún, are also rich, packed with **snook, tarpon** and **mullet**.

Crocodiles are becoming increasingly common in Petén, after previously being hunted almost to extinction, and are now frequently spotted at Lago de Yaxhá and Laguna Perdida. They are not dangerous to humans unless they are very large – at least 3m long – but heed the warnings of locals if they advise against swimming in particular lagoons.

Although there are at least fifty species of **snake** in the region, only a few are venomous and you're unlikely to see any snakes at all. The **boa constrictor** is one of the most common and also is the largest, growing up to 4m, though it poses no threat to humans. Others you might see are **coral snakes** (which are venomous) and **false coral snakes** (which are not); in theory they're easily distinguished by noting the arrangement of adjacent colours in the stripes, but it's best to admire all snakes from a distance unless you're an expert.

At night in the forest, you'll hear the characteristic chorus of frog mating calls, and you'll also frequently find the **red-eyed tree frog** – a beautiful pale-green creature about the size of the top joint of your thumb – in your shower in any rustic cabin. Less appealing perhaps are the giant **marine toads**, weighing in at up to 1kg and growing to more than 20cm. Like most frogs and toads, the marine toad has toxic glands, and its toxin has hallucinogenic properties – an effect put to use in ceremonies by the ancient Maya, who licked the toad's glands and interpreted the resultant visions.

The Caribbean coast

Much of Guatemala's small **Caribbean coastline** is protected as part of the Biotopo Punta del Manabique, a rich wetland habitat, while just inland there are several additional, ecologically diverse reserves around the Río Dulce and Lago de Izabal. This region offers some of the country's finest birdwatching territory.

Immediately inland from the Guatemalan coast, the **littoral forest** is characterized by salt-tolerant plants, often with tough, waxy leaves which help conserve water. Species include red and white **gumbo limbo, black poisonwood, zericote, palmetto** and, of course, the **coconut**, which typifies Caribbean beaches, though it's not actually a native. The littoral forest supports a very high density of fauna, especially **migrating birds**.

Much of the shoreline around Punta del Manabique and Lívingston is still largely covered with **mangroves**, which play an important economic role, not merely as nurseries for commercial fish species but also for their stabilization of the shoreline and their ability to absorb the force of gales and hurricanes. The dominant species of the coastal fringe is the **red mangrove**, although in due course it undermines its own environment by consolidating the sea bed until it becomes more suitable for the less salt-tolerant black and white mangroves. The basis of the shoreline food chain is the nutrient-rich mud, held in place by the mangroves, whose roots are home to **oysters** and **sponges**. In the shallows, "meadows" of **seagrass beds** provide nurseries for many fish and invertebrates, and pasture for conch and turtles.

The coastal zone is home to sparse numbers of the **West Indian manatee**, which can reach 4m in length and weigh up to 450kg. These placid and shy creatures move between freshwater lagoons and the open sea. They were once hunted for their meat but are now protected, and the Biotopo Chocón Machacas has been established in the Golfete region of the Río Dulce as a **manatee sanctuary**. Despite this measure, the manatee remains very rare in Guatemala and you've a much better chance of spotting one in Belize, where their habitat is much less depleted.

CONSERVATION ORGANIZATIONS

Alianza Verde (Green Alliance, Ⓦ alianzaverde.org). Based in Flores, this is a consortium of ecotourism operators and conservation organizations, working closely with Guatemala's National Protected Areas Commission (CONAP) and focusing primarily on sustainable development in the Maya Biosphere Reserve. It's developed the "Green Deal", a code of practice and certification for ecotourism businesses.

Arcas (Ⓦ arcasguatemala.com). Conservation group that provides a refuge for wild animals in Petén (see p.259) and also runs a sea turtle project in the Monterrico–Hawaii area (see p.188).

Centre for Conservation Studies (CECON) A department of Guatemala's University of San Carlos, with head offices at the Botanical Gardens of Guatemala City (see p.59). CECON manages and conducts scientific research in all the nation's *biotopos*. These are often the best-protected areas within reserves, such as Cerro Cahuí in Petén, Monterrico on the Pacific coast and the Biotopo del Quetzal in Baja Verapaz.

Defensores de la Naturaleza (Ⓦ defensores.org.gt). Ecological group that combines conservation with sustainable tourism in the Sierra de las Minas and the Bocas del Polochic reserves (see p.226 & p.212). It also manages the vast Sierra de Lacandón national park in Petén.

Fundary (Ⓦ www.guate.net/fundarymanabique). Working with communities in Punta de Manabique (see p.203) to establish sustainable tourism. Spanish-speaking volunteers, preferably with a background in biology or ecotourism, are sometimes needed to patrol turtle nesting beaches or undertake manatee and dolphin observation.

ProPetén (Ⓦ propeten.org). Petén's largest NGO works on numerous conservation and resource-management projects in the Maya Biosphere Reserve including Las Guacamayas, a biological station near Waka' (El Perú) ruins. Volunteers are needed.

Proyecto Eco-Quetzal (Ⓦ ecoquetzal.org). Long-established NGO (see p.234), with a successful record of protecting the forests around Cobán by offering economic alternatives to indigenous people, including excellent ecotourism projects where visitors stay with Q'eqchi' Maya villagers.

Books

Guatemala has never inspired a great deal of writing until the past few decades, when the civil war and political turmoil has spawned plenty of non-fiction. In recent years, there has also been a boom in titles about contemporary and ancient Maya culture. Yax Te' Books (ⓦyaxtebooks.com) produce a fascinating collection of titles, concentrating on indigenous Maya culture, literature and language. Recently several books about the 2012 phenomenon have been published (see p.351). Titles that we especially recommend are marked with a symbol (★).

TRAVEL

Stephen Connoly Benz *Guatemalan Journey*. Concentrates on the complexities of Guatemalan society and the impact of US culture and evangelism, with informative accounts of life in the capital and the textile-factory businesses.

Peter Canby *Heart of the Sky – Travels Among the Maya*. The author treads a familiar path through the Maya World, encountering an interesting collection of expats, Mayanists, priests, Guatemala City's idle rich and a female shaman. An accessible and informative account.

Anthony Daniels *Sweet Waist of America*. A delight to read. Daniels takes a refreshingly even-handed approach to Guatemala and comes up with a fascinating cocktail of people and politics, discarding the stereotypes that litter most books on Central America.

Thomas Gage *Travels in the New World*. Unusual account of a Dominican friar's travels through Mexico and Central America between 1635 and 1637, including some intriguing insights into colonial life as well as some great attacks on the greed and pomposity of the Catholic Church abroad.

★ **Aldous Huxley** *Beyond the Mexique Bay*. Huxley's travels in 1934 took him from Belize through Guatemala to Mexico, swept on by his fascination for history and religion, and sprouting bizarre theories on the basis of everything he saw. There are some terrific descriptions of Maya sites and indigenous culture, with superb one-liners summing up people and places.

Jonathan Evan Maslow *Bird of Life, Bird of Death*. Maslow sets out in search of the quetzal, using the bird's uncertain future as a metaphor for wartime Guatemala in a work that merges travel and political comment.

Christopher Shaw *Sacred Monkey River: A Canoe Trip with the Gods*. Engaging account of the author's canoe journey along the Usumacinta River that divides Mexico and Guatemala. Nicely crafted prose is enlivened with convincing analysis of ancient Maya cosmology and culture, and the contemporary political and environmental issues affecting the region.

★ **John Lloyd Stephens** *Incidents of Travel in Central America, Chiapas, and Yucatán*. Stephens was a classic nineteenth-century explorer. Acting as US ambassador to Central America, he indulged his own enthusiasm for archeology; while the republics fought it out among themselves, he was wading through the jungle stumbling across ancient cities. His journals, told in a restrained Victorian style punctuated with sudden waves of enthusiasm, make great reading. Some editions include fantastic illustrations by Catherwood of the ruins overgrown with tropical rainforest.

★ **Ronald Wright** *Time Among the Maya*. A vivid and sympathetic account of travels from Belize through Guatemala, Chiapas and Yucatán, meeting the Maya of today and exploring their obsession with time. The book's twin points of interest are the ancient Maya and the civil-war violence. An encyclopedic bibliography offers ideas for exploration in depth, and the author's knowledge is evident in the superb historical insight he imparts through the book. Certainly one of the best travel books on the area.

FICTION, AUTOBIOGRAPHY AND POETRY

★ **Miguel Ángel Asturias** *Hombres de Maíz*. Guatemala's most famous author, Asturias is deeply indebted to Guatemalan history and culture in his work. "Men of Maize" is his masterpiece, classically Latin American in its magic-realist style, and bound up in the complexity of indigenous culture. His other works include *El Señor Presidente*, a grotesque portrayal of social chaos and dictatorial rule; *El* *Papa Verde*, which explores the murky world of the United Fruit Company; and *Weekend in Guatemala*, describing the downfall of the Árbenz government. Asturias won the Nobel Prize for Literature before his death in 1974.

Paul Bowles *Up Above the World*. Bowles is at his chilling, understated best in this novel based on experiences of Guatemala in the late 1930s.

★ **Francisco Goldman** *The Long Night of White Chickens*. Drawing on the stylistic complexity of Latin American fiction, this novel tells the tale of a young Guatemalan orphan who flees to the US and works as a maid. When she finally returns home to her politically turbulent nation, she is murdered. It's an interesting and ambitious story, though its chaotic timeline gives the book a Byzantine intricacy that makes it a dense and laborious read at times.

Norman Lewis *The Volcano Above Us*. Vaguely historical novel published in 1957 that pulls together all the main elements of Guatemala's history. The image that it summons is one of depressing drudgery and eternal conflict, set against a background of repression and racism. In the light of what's happened it has a certain prophetic quality, and remains gripping despite its miserable conclusions.

Kathy Reichs *Grave Secrets*. In this compelling thriller, forensic scientist Tempe Brennon flies to Guatemala to investigate the mass graves of civil-war victims, but is then persuaded to look into the disappearances of four wealthy girls from the capital. Her efforts are thwarted by violence, judicial inadequacies and corruption.

HISTORY, POLITICS AND HUMAN RIGHTS

Tom Barry *Guatemala – A Country Guide*. A concise account of the political, social and economic situation in Guatemala, with a mild left-wing stance. Published in 1990.

Edward F. Fisher and R. McKenna Brown (eds) *Maya Cultural Activism in Guatemala*. Effectual summary of the indigenous movement in Guatemala, with strong chapters on clothing and identity, and the revival of interest in Maya language and hieroglyphic writing.

★ **Francisco Goldman** *The Art of Political Murder*. Investigative journalism at its very best, this is a meticulously researched and passionately told account of the Geradi murder case, and represents the culmination of seven years of reporting. Goldman weaves absorbing profiles of the characters – assassins, military intelligence officers, street kids and Church figures – into the tale to pull off a riveting whodunit. Winner of multiple awards.

Greg Grandin (et al) *The Guatemala Reader: History, Culture, Politics*. Published in late 2011, this is an accessible, up-to-date overview of the nation. Grandin's The *Blood of Guatemala – A History of Race and Nation is* more specialist, a study of Quetzaltenango's elite class of K'iche' Maya and their impact between the mid-eighteenth century and the fall of the Árbenz government in 1954.

★ **Jim Handy** *Gift of the Devil*. Superb history of Guatemala: concise and readable with a sharp focus on the Maya population and the brief period of socialist government. Though written in the mid-1980s, the book nevertheless manages to offer a convincing perspective on the modern Guatemalan state. By no means objective, Handy sets out to expose the development of oppression and point the finger at the oppressors.

Severo Martínez Peláez *La Patria Del Criollo: An Interpretation of Colonial Guatemala*. Superb, damning examination of colonial society in Guatemala and its utter dependence on Maya labour. Written in 1970 by a leading Guatemalan historian and leftist political activist, it remains remarkably relevant today.

★ **Víctor Perera** *Unfinished Conquest*. Superb, extremely readable account of the civil-war tragedy, plus comprehensive attention to the deep inequalities that affect the late author's native country. The book's strength comes from the extensive interviews with both ordinary and influential Guatemalans and incisive analysis of recent history. A great introduction to the subject.

REMHI *Guatemala: Never Again*. Abridged translation of the seminal report published by the Catholic Church of Guatemala into the civil-war atrocities. The investigation contains an excellent historical background to the conflict, harrowing personal testimonies, incisive analysis of military and guerrilla strategies and a chapter devoted to preventing a recurrence.

Victoria Sanford *Buried Secrets: Truth and Human Rights in Guatemala*. A powerful, exhaustively researched investigative study of *la violencia* is based on more than four hundred interviews with massacre survivors, the military and guerrilla forces.

Jennifer Schirmer *The Guatemalan Military Project: A Violence Called Democracy*. Offers an insider's view of the ideology and mentality of the Guatemalan armed forces, based on numerous interviews with senior officers, six ex-defence ministers and three former heads of state.

Stephen Schlesinger and Stephen Kinzer *Bitter Fruit: The Untold Story of the American Coup in Guatemala*. This book traces the US connection in the 1954 coup, delving into the murky water of United Fruit Company politics and showing that the invading army received its orders from the White House.

Jean-Marie Simon *Eternal Spring – Eternal Tyranny*. Highly authoritative photojournalistic study of Guatemala's civil-war period, with crisp text and evocative imagery.

Daniel Wilkinson *Silence on the Mountain: Stories of Betrayal and Forgetting in Guatemala*. Part historical narrative, part personal travelogue and part public testimony, Wilkinson's book gives a voice to those who suffered most during Guatemala's civil war.

INDIGENOUS CULTURE

Krystyna Deuss *Shamans, Witches, and Maya Priests: Native Religion & Ritual in Highland Guatemala*. A unique and fascinating study of Maya customs in the remote Cuchumatanes – in villages where the Maya calendar is still in use – based on decades of research and beautifully illustrated with photographs.

Grant D. Jones *The Conquest of the Maya Kingdom*. A massive academic tome that's also a fascinating history of the Itza Maya and a gripping tale of how the Spanish entered and finally defeated the last independent Maya kingdom, at Tayasal.

⭐ **Rigoberta Menchú** *I, Rigoberta Menchú – An Indian Woman in Guatemala* and *Crossing Borders*. Momentous story of one of Latin America's most remarkable women, Nobel Peace Prize-winner Rigoberta Menchú. The first volume is a horrific account of family life in the Maya highlands, recording how Menchú's family were targeted, terrorized and murdered by the military. The book also reveals much concerning K'iche' Maya cultural traditions and the enormous gulf between the ladino and indigenous societies in Guatemala. The second volume is more optimistic, documenting Menchú's life in exile in Mexico, her work at the United Nations fighting for indigenous people and her return to Guatemala. Although Menchú's courage and determination are undeniable, some, including author David Stoll (see below), have criticized the accuracy of parts of her story.

⭐ **The Popol Vuh** The great K'iche' creation epic, written shortly after the Conquest, is an amazing swirl of mythological characters and their wanderings through the K'iche' highlands, tracing the tribe's ancestry. There are several versions on offer though many of them are half-hearted, including only a few lines from the original. The best is translated by Dennis Tedlock.

⭐ **James D. Sexton** (ed) *Son of Tecún Umán; Campesino; Ignacio* and *Joseño*. Four excellent autobiographical accounts written by a Tz'utujil Maya from Lago de Atitlán. The books give an impression of life inside a modern Maya village, bound up in poverty, local politics and a mixture of Catholicism and superstition, and manage to avoid the stereotyping that usually characterizes descriptions of the indigenous population. Sexton's *Mayan Folktales: Folklore from Lake Atitlán, Guatemala* and *Heart of Heaven, Heart of Earth and other Maya Folktales* unveil a world of wonderfully imaginative fables that underpin a society's strict moral codes and notions of justice and fate.

David Stoll *Rigoberta Menchú and the Story of All Poor Guatemalans*. Iconoclastic biography that delivers a formidable broadside against considerable pieces of the Menchú legend, though some academics have criticized Stoll's literal interpretation of Maya testimonial traditions.

Phillip Werne *The Maya of Guatemala*. A short study of repression and the Maya of Guatemala. The latest edition (published in 1994) is now a little out of date but still interesting.

ARCHEOLOGY

Maya archeology is changing so rapidly that many of the books published even a decade or so back are well out of date with the latest Preclassic research. Dr Richard Hanson's highly anticipated new book on El Mirador, due to be published in late 2012, promises to be a game changer, laying out the latest findings from the great city.

Michael D. Coe *The Maya*. Now in its eighth edition, this clear and comprehensive introduction to Maya archeology is one of the best on offer, though for the latest developments in the Preclassic era you need to look elsewhere. Coe has also written several more weighty, academic volumes. His *Breaking the Maya Code* owes much to the fact that Coe was at many of the most important meetings leading to the breakthrough of glyph-reading. *The Art of the Maya Scribe*, written with Justin Kerr, developer of "rollout" photography – a technique enabling the viewer to see the whole surface of a cylindrical vessel – is a wonderfully illustrated history of Maya writing which also takes the reader on a journey through the Maya universe and mythology via the astonishingly skilful calligraphy of the Maya artists themselves.

⭐ **David Drew** *The Lost Chronicles of the Maya Kings*. Superbly readable and engaging, Drew draws on a wealth of material to deliver an excellent account of ancient Maya political history. The alliances and rivalries between the main cities are skilfully unravelled, and there's a particularly revealing analysis of Late Classic Maya power politics.

Francisco Estrada-Belli *The First Maya Civilization: Ritual and Power Before the Classic Period*. Perhaps the first book to really get to grips with the importance of the Preclassic Maya, this concise and very readable book, published in 2011, is based on recent research from the cities of Cival and Holmul in Petén.

Peter D. Harrison *The Lords of Tikal*. Meticulous study of the Petén metropolis that includes hieroglyphic readings and a tremendous amount of detail about the city's monuments and artefacts and the rulers who commissioned them, Temple V excepted.

⭐ **Simon Martin and Nikolai Grube** *Chronicle of the Maya Kings and Queens*. Published to universal acclaim, this groundbreaking work is based on exhaustive new epigraphic studies, and the re-reading of previously translated glyphic texts. It also includes the historical records of several key Maya cities – including Tikal, Naranjo and Dos Pilas – complete with biographies of 152 kings and four queens, full dynastic sequences and all the key battles. As Michael D. Coe, author of *The Maya*, says: "There's nothing else like this book. It supersedes everything else ever written on Maya history."

Mary Miller and Simon Martin *Courtly Art of the Ancient Maya*. Sumptuously illustrated with images of jade, stucco, stonework and pottery artistry, this book also explains the rituals and customs that defined daily life in the royal courts.

Linda Schele and David Freidel (et al). The authors, in the forefront of "new archeology", have been personally responsible for decoding many Maya glyphs. *A Forest of Kings: The Untold Story of the Ancient Maya*, in conjunction with *The Blood of Kings* by Linda Schele and Mary Miller, shows that, far from being governed by peaceful astronomer-priests, the ancient Maya were ruled by hereditary kings, lived in populous, aggressive city-states and engaged in a continual entanglement of alliances and war. *The Maya Cosmos* by Schele, Freidel and Joy Parker, is perhaps more difficult to read, but it also examines Maya ritual and religion in a unique and far-reaching way. *The Code of Kings*, written in collaboration with Peter Matthews and lavishly illustrated, examines the significance of the monuments at selected Maya sites and is a classic of epigraphic interpretation.

Peter Schmidt, Mercedes de la Garza and Enrique Nalda (eds) *Maya Civilization*. Monumental collaborative effort, with sections written by many prominent Mayanists, lusciously presented with more than six hundred colour images of some breathtaking Maya art. The scholarly text is also impressive, with contributions on the importance of Calakmul to the classic Maya history and detailed essays on the highlands of Guatemala, Maya cosmology and codices.

Robert Sharer *The Ancient Maya*. Classic, comprehensive account of Maya civilization, now in its sixth edition, yet as authoritative as ever. Required reading for archeology students, it provides a fascinating reference for the non-expert, though the latest advances in Preclassic knowledge are excluded.

J. Eric S. Thompson *The Rise and Fall of the Maya Civilization*. A major authority on the ancient Maya, this is an accessible read, though obviously our knowledge has advanced considerably since it was published.

WILDLIFE AND THE ENVIRONMENT

Les Betelsky *Belize and Northern Guatemala*. Other specialist wildlife guides may cover the subject in more detail, but this is a reasonably comprehensive and well-organized single-volume guide to the mammals, birds, reptiles, amphibians and marine life of the region.

Steve Howe and Sophie Webb *The Birds of Mexico and Northern Central America*. A tremendous work, this is the definitive book on the region's birds. Essential for all serious birders.

Thor Janson *In the Land of Green Lightning*. Exquisite photographic collection, concentrating on the diverse wildlife and environment of the Maya region. Includes some astounding images of an exploding Volcán Pacaya.

GUIDES

Elizabeth Bell *Antigua Guatemala: The City and Its Heritage*. The best guide to Antigua, written by a long-term resident and prominent historian. It's available from several shops in Antigua, as is the author's *Lent and Easter Week in Antigua*.

William Coe *Tikal: A Handbook to the Ancient Maya Ruins*. A detailed account of the site, usually available at the ruins, though it does not include the latest findings. The map of the main area is essential for in-depth exploration.

Joyce Kelly *Archaeological Guide to Northern Central America*. Detailed, practical guide to dozens of sites with excellent photographs and accurate maps. This volume covers 38 Maya sites and 25 museums, though it's now a little outdated.

Barbara Balchin de Koose *Antigua for You*. A very comprehensive account of Antigua's colonial architectural wonders, but doesn't offer much else.

Lily de Jongh Osborne *Four Keys to Guatemala*. One of the best guides to Guatemala ever written, including a short piece on every aspect of the country's history and culture. Osborne also wrote a good book on indigenous arts and crafts in Guatemala. Both books are now out of print.

COOKBOOKS

Catalina B. Figueroa *Cocina Guatemalteca: Arte, Sabor y Colorido*. Features a comprehensive range of national dishes and regional specialities, and is available in many bookshops in Antigua.

Copeland Marks *False Tongues and Sunday Bread: A Guatemalan and Maya Cookbook*. If you've travelled widely in Guatemala and suffered an endless onslaught of beans and tortillas, it may be a surprise to find that the country has an established culinary tradition. Marks' book includes many fine Guatemalan recipes like chicken with *mole* sauce as well as the staples like black beans.

Language

Guatemala takes in a bewildering collection of languages, but fortunately for the traveller, Spanish will get you by in all but the most remote areas. Some middle-class Guatemalans speak English, but it's essential to learn at least a few Spanish phrases or you're in for a frustrating time.

The **Spanish** spoken in Guatemala has a strong Latin American flavour to it, and if you're used to the dainty intonation of Madrid then this may come as something of a surprise. If you're new to Spanish it's a lot easier to pick up than the Castilian version. Everywhere you'll find people willing to make an effort to understand you, eager to speak to passing gringos.

The rules of **pronunciation** are pretty straightforward and, once you get to know them, strictly observed. Unless there's an accent, words ending in d, l, r and z are **stressed** on the last syllable, all others on the second last. All **vowels** are pure and short.

A somewhere between the A sound of back and that of father.

E as in get.

I as in police.

O as in hot.

U as in rule.

C is soft before E and I, hard otherwise: cerca is pronounced serka.

G works the same way, a guttural H sound (like the ch in loch) before E or I, a hard G elsewhere – gigante becomes higante.

H is always silent.

J is the same sound as a guttural G: jamón is pronounced hamON.

LL sounds like an English Y: tortilla is pronounced torteeya.

N is as in English unless it has a tilde (accent) over it, when it becomes NY: mañana sounds like manyana.

QU is pronounced like an English K.

R is rolled, RR doubly so.

V sounds more like B, vino becoming beano.

X is slightly softer than in English – sometimes almost SH – Xela is pronounced shela.

Z is the same as a soft C, so cerveza becomes servesa.

Below is a list of a few essential words and phrases, though if you're travelling for any length of time a **dictionary** or **phrase book** is obviously a worthwhile investment. Any good Spanish phrase book or dictionary should see you through in Guatemala, but specific Latin American ones are the most useful. The *University of Chicago Dictionary of Latin-American Spanish* is a good all-rounder, while *Mexican Spanish: A Rough Guide Phrasebook* has a menu reader, rundown of colloquialisms and a number of cultural tips are relevant to many Latin American countries, including Guatemala. If you're using a dictionary, remember that in Spanish, CH, LL and Ñ count as separate letters and are listed after the Cs, Ls and Ns respectively. If you really want to get to grips with Guatemalan slang, swear words and expressions, look out for *¿Qué Onda Vos?* by Juan Carlos Martínez López and Mark Brazaitis, which includes a superb round-up of *guatemaltequismos*. It's available from several bookshops in Antigua.

Maya languages

After years of state-backed *castellanización* programmes when Spanish was the only language of tuition and Maya schoolchildren were left virtual classroom spectators, a network of Maya schools has now been established, with hundreds alone in Q'eqchi' areas of Guatemala. A strong indigenous cultural movement has now developed in the country, intent on preserving the dozens of different Maya languages still spoken (see p.343). Because the Maya birth rate is much higher than the ladino, there is now every chance that the main languages like K'iche', Kaqchikel and Mam will survive, though the fate of the more isolated tongues is far from secure.

If you're planning an extended stay in a remote indigenous region to do development work, it's extremely helpful to learn a little of the local language first. There are a number of language schools where you can **study a Maya language** and pick up the essentials. Cleveland State University's K'inal Winik Cultural Center (ⓦcsuohio.edu /kinalwinik) is devoted to Maya linguistics and culture and publishers of Yax Te' Books, who have several titles on indigenous Guatemalan languages and literature. The Yax Te' Foundation (ⓦyaxtebooks.com), devoted to promoting and supporting Maya culture and language, has some excellent study material and dictionaries.

Maya words do not easily translate into Spanish (or English) so you may see the same place spelt in different ways: *K'umarkaaj* can be spelt *K'umarcaah* or even *Gumarcaj*. Nearly all Maya words are pronounced stressing the final syllable, which is often accented: Atitlán is A-tit-LAN, Wakná is wak-NA.

C is always hard like a K, unlike Spanish.
J is a guttural H, as in Spanish.
U like a W at the beginning of a word and like an OO

in the middle or at the end of a word – Uaxactún is pronounced wash-ak-TOON.
X sounds like SH – Ixcún is pronounced ish-KOON.

SPANISH WORDS AND PHRASES

BASICS

Yes, No	Sí, No
Please, Thank you	Por favor, Gracias
Where?, When?	¿Dónde?, ¿Cuándo?
What?, How much?	¿Qué?, ¿Cuánto?
Here, There	Aquí, Allí
This, That	Este, Eso
Now, Later	Ahora, Más tarde
Open, Closed	Abierto/a, Cerrado/a
With, Without	Con, Sin
Good, Bad	Buen(o)/a, Mal(o)/a
Big, Small	Gran(de), Pequeño/a
More, Less	Más, Menos
Today, Tomorrow	Hoy, Mañana
Yesterday	Ayer

GREETINGS AND RESPONSES

Hello, Goodbye	Hola, Adiós
Good morning	Buenos días
Good afternoon/night	Buenas tardes/noches
See you later	Hasta luego
Sorry	Lo siento/discúlpeme
Excuse me	Con permiso/perdón
How are you?	¿Cómo está (usted)?
I (don't) understand	(No) Entiendo
Could you speak more slowly?	¿Podría hablar más lento?
Not at all/You're welcome	De nada
Do you speak English?	¿Habla (usted) inglés?
I don't speak Spanish	No hablo español
What (did you say)?	¿Mande?
My name is …	Me llamo …
What's your name?	¿Cómo se llama usted?
I am English	Soy inglés(a)
American	americano (a)
Australian	australiano(a)
British	británico(a)
Canadian	canadiense
Dutch	holandés(a)
Irish	irlandés(a)
New Zealander	neocelandés(a)
Scottish	escocés(a)
South African	sudafricano(a)
Welsh	galés(a)

HOTELS AND TRANSPORT

I want	Quiero
I'd like	Quisiera
Do you know …?	¿Sabe …?
I don't know	No sé
There is (is there)?	(¿)Hay(?)
Give me … (one like that)	Deme … (uno así)
Do you have …?	¿Tiene …?
… the time	… la hora
… a room	… un cuarto
… with two beds/ double bed	… con dos camas/ cama matrimonial
It's for one person (two people)	Es para una persona (dos personas)
… for one night (one week)	… para una noche (una semana)
It's fine, how much is it?	¿Está bien, cuánto es?
It's too expensive	Es demasiado caro
Don't you have anything cheaper?	¿No tiene algo más barato?
Can one …?	¿Se puede …?
… camp (near) here?	¿… acampar aquí (cerca)?
Is there a hotel nearby?	¿Hay un hotel aquí cerca?
How do I get to …? is it?	¿Por dónde se va a …?
Left, right, straight on	Izquierda, derecha, derecho
Where is …?	¿Dónde está …?
… the bus station	… el terminal de camionetas

... the nearest bank	... el banco más cercano	30	treinta
... the post office	... el correo/la oficina de correos	31	treinta y uno
		40	cuarenta
... the toilet	... el baño/sanitario	50	cincuenta
Where does the bus to ... leave from?	¿De dónde sale la camioneta para ...?	60	sesenta
		70	setenta
I'd like a (return) ticket to ...	Quisiera un boleto (de ida y vuelta) para ...	80	ochenta
		90	noventa
What time does it leave (arrive in ...)?	¿A qué hora sale (llega en ...)?	100	cien
		101	ciento uno
What is there to eat?	¿Qué hay para comer?	200	doscientos
What's that?	¿Qué es eso?	201	doscientos uno
What's this called in Spanish?	¿Cómo se llama este en español?	500	quinientos
		1000	mil
		2000	dos mil

NUMBERS

		1,000,000	un millión
0	cero	**first**	primero/a
1	un/uno/una	**second**	segundo/a
2	dos	**third**	tercero/a
3	tres	**fourth**	cuarto/a
4	cuatro	**fifth**	quinto/a
5	cinco	**sixth**	sexto/a
6	seis	**seventh**	séptimo/a
7	siete	**eighth**	octavo/a
8	ocho	**ninth**	noveno/a
9	nueve	**tenth**	décimo/a
10	diez		
11	once	**DAYS**	
12	doce	**Monday**	lunes
13	trece	**Tuesday**	martes
14	catorce	**Wednesday**	miércoles
15	quince	**Thursday**	jueves
16	dieciséis	**Friday**	viernes
20	veinte	**Saturday**	sábado
21	veintiuno	**Sunday**	domingo
22	veintidós		

MENU READER

BASICS

Azúcar	Sugar
Carne	Meat
Ensalada	Salad
Huevos	Eggs
Mantequilla	Butter
Pan	Bread
Pescado	Fish
Pimienta	Pepper
Queso	Cheese
Sal	Salt
Salsa	Sauce
Verduras/Legumbres	Vegetables

SOUPS (SOPAS) AND STARTERS

Sopa	Soup
de arroz	with rice
de fideos	with noodles
de lentejas	Lentil
de verduras	Vegetable
Consome	Consomme
Caldo	Broth (usually with meat)
Ceviche	Raw fish salad, marinated in lime juice
Entremeses	Hors d'oeuvres

MEAT (CARNE) AND POULTRY (AVES)

Alambre	Kebab
Bistec	Steak
Cabrito	Kid goat
Carne (de res)	Beef

Carnitas	Stewed chunks of meat
Cerdo	Pork
Chorizo	Sausage
Chuleta	Chop
Codorniz	
Conejo	Rabbit
Cordero	Lamb
Costilla	Rib
Guisado	Stew
Higado	Liver
Lengua	Tongue
Milanesa	Breaded escalope
Pato	Duck
Pavo/Guajalote	Turkey
Pechuga	Breast
Pierna	Leg
Pollo	Chicken
Salchicha	Hot dog or salami
Ternera	Veal
Venado	Venison

SPECIALITIES

Chile relleno	Stuffed pepper
Chuchitos	Stuffed maize dumplings
Enchilada	Flat, crisp tortilla piled with salad or meat
Mosh	Porridge
Pan de banana	Banana bread
Pan de coco	Coconut bread
Quesadilla	Toasted or fried tortillas with cheese
Shuco	Hotdog with trimmings
Taco	Rolled and stuffed tortilla
Tamale	Boiled and stuffed maize pudding
Tapado	Fish stew with plantain and vegetables, served on Caribbean coast

VEGETABLES (LEGUMBRES, VERDURAS)

Aguacate	Avocado
Ajo	Garlic
Casava/Yuca	Potato-like root vegetable
Cebolla	Onion
Col	Cabbage
Elote	Corn on the cob
Frijoles	Beans
Hongos	Mushrooms
Lechuga	Lettuce
Pacaya	Bitter-tasting local vegetable
Papas	Potatoes
Pepino	Cucumber
Plátanos	Plantain
Tomate	Tomato
Zanahoria	Carrot

FRUIT (FRUTAS)

Banana	Banana
Ciruelas	Greengages
Coco	Coconut
Frambuesas	Raspberries
Fresas	Strawberries
Guanabana	Pear-like cactus fruit
Guayaba	Guava
Higos	Figs
Jocote	Small, plum-like fruit
Limón	Lime
Mamey	Pink, sweet, full of pips
Mango	Mango
Melocotón	Peach
Melón	Melon
Naranja	Orange
Papaya	Papaya
Piña	Pineapple
Pitahaya	Sweet, purple fruit
Sandía	Watermelon
Toronja	Grapefruit
Tuna	Cactus fruit
Uvas	Grapes
Zapote	Sweet, pink-fleshed fruit

EGGS (HUEVOS)

a la Mexicana	Scrambled with mild tomato, onion and chilli sauce
con jamón	with ham
con tocino	with bacon
Fritos	Fried
Motuleños	Fried, served on a tortilla with ham, cheese and sauce
Rancheros	Cheese-fried and smothered in hot chilli sauce
Revueltos	Scrambled
Tibios	Lightly boiled

COMMON TERMS

a la parilla	Grilled
al horno	Baked
al mojo de ajo	Fried in garlic and butter
Asado/a	Roast
Empanado/a	Breaded
Picante	Hot and spicy
Recado	A sauce for meat made fromgarlic, tomato and spices

SWEETS (POSTRES)

Crepas	Pancakes
Ensalada de frutas	Fruit salad
Flan	Crème caramel
Helado	Ice cream
Pie de queso	Cheesecake
Plátanos al horno	Baked plantains
Plátanos en Mole	Plantains in chocolate sauce

Glossary of frequently used terms

Aguardiente Raw alcohol made from sugarcane.

Aguas Bottled fizzy drinks such as Coca-Cola or Pepsi.

Alcalde Mayor.

Aldea Small settlement.

Altiplano The highlands of western Guatemala.

Atol Drink usually made from maize dough, cooked with water, salt, sugar and milk. Can also be made from rice.

Ayuntamiento Town hall.

Baleada Stuffed tortilla street-snack (Honduras only).

Barranca Steep-sided ravine.

Barrio Residential district.

Biotopo Protected area of ecological interest, usually with limited tourist access.

Boca Costa Western volcanic slopes of the Guatemalan highlands, prime coffee-growing country.

Brujo Maya shaman.

CAFTA Central American Free Trade Agreement.

CALDH Centre for Legal Action on Human Rights. Pressure group campaigning for justice on behalf of the victims of the civil-war violence.

Calvario Church, often with pagan religious traditions, always located on the western outskirts of a town; also known as the house of the ancestors.

Camioneta Second-class, or "chicken", bus. In other parts of Latin America the same word means a small truck or van.

Campesino Peasant farmer.

Cantina Local hard-drinking bar.

Casita Hut, small house.

Cayuco Canoe.

Chapín Nickname for a citizen of Guatemala.

Chicle Sapodilla tree sap from which chewing gum is made.

Chuj Maya steam sauna.

CICIG Commission with a mandate to investigate, prosecute and dismantle criminal organizations operating in Guatemala.

Classic Period during which ancient Maya civilization was at its height, usually given as 250–909 AD.

Codex Maya manuscript made from the bark of the fig tree and written in hieroglyphs. Most were destroyed by the Spanish, but a copy of the Dresden Codex can be found in the Popol Vuh museum in Guatemala City (see p.60).

Cofradía Religious brotherhood dedicated to the protection of a particular saint. These groups form the basis of religious and civil hierarchy in traditional highland society and combine Catholic and pagan practices.

Comedor Basic Guatemalan restaurant, usually with just one or two things on the menu, and always the cheapest place to eat.

Comida típica Literally "typical food", this indicates a menu of regular Guatemalan-style dishes, nothing fancy but always filling and inexpensive.

CONAVIGUA National Coordination of Guatemalan Widows. Influential, mainly indigenous, pressure group.

Copal Pine-resin incense burned at religious ceremonies.

Corriente Another name for a second-class bus.

Corte Traditional Guatemalan skirt.

Costumbres Guatemalan word for traditional customs of the highland Maya, usually of religious and cultural significance. The word often refers to traditions that owe more to paganism than to Catholicism; practitioners are called costumbristas.

Creole Guatemalan of mixed Afro-Caribbean descent.

Cuadra Street block.

CUC Committee of Peasant Unity.

Cusha Home-brewed liquor.

Don/Doña Sir/Madam. A term of respect mostly used to address a professional person or employer.

Efectivo Cash.

EGP (Ejército Guerrillero de los Pobres) (Guerrilla Army of the Poor). A Guatemalan guerrilla group that operated in the Ixil region and Ixcán areas.

Evangélico Christian evangelist or fundamentalist, often missionaries. Name given to numerous Protestant sects seeking converts in Central America.

FAR (Fuerzas Armadas Rebeldes) (Rebel Armed Forces). Guatemalan guerrilla group that was mainly active in Petén.

Finca Plantation-style farm.

FRG (Frente Republicano Guatemalteco) (Guatemalan Republican Front). Right-wing political party of Ríos Montt and Alfonso Portillo.

GAM (Mutual Support Group). Pressure group campaigning for justice for the families of the "disappeared".

Garífuna Black Carib with a unique language and strong African heritage living in Lívingston and villages along the Caribbean coast between Belize and Nicaragua. See p.206.

Gringo/gringa Any white-skinned foreigner, not necessarily a term of abuse.

Hospedaje Another name for a small, basic hotel.

Huipil Woman's traditional blouse, usually woven or embroidered.

Indígena Indigenous person of Maya descent.

Indio Racially abusive term to describe someone of Maya descent. The word **indito** is equally offensive.

Inguat Guatemalan tourist board.

I.V.A. Guatemalan sales tax of twelve percent.

Ixil Highland tribe grouped around the three towns of the Ixil region – Nebaj, Chajul and San Juan Cotzal.

Kaqchikel (Also spelt "Cakchiquel"). Indigenous highland tribe occupying an area between Guatemala City and Lake Atitlán.

K'iche' (Also spelt "Quiché"). Largest of the highland Maya tribes, centred on the town of Santa Cruz del Quiché.

Ladino A vague term – at its most specific defining someone of mixed Spanish and Maya blood, but more commonly used to describe a person of "Western" culture, or one who dresses in "Western" style, be they pure Maya or of mixed blood.

Legua The distance walked in an hour, used extensively in the highlands.

Leng Slang for **centavo**.

Mam Maya tribe occupying the west of the western highlands, the area around Huehuetenango.

Mara Street gang. Gang members are called mareros.

Mariachi Mexican musical style popular in Guatemala.

Marimba Xylophone-like instrument used in traditional Guatemalan music.

Maya General term for the large tribal group who inhabited Guatemala, southern Mexico, Belize, western Honduras and a slice of El Salvador since the earliest times, and still do.

Mestizo Person of mixed native and Spanish blood, more commonly used in Mexico.

Metate Flat stone for grinding maize into flour.

Milpa Maize field, usually cleared by slash and burn.

MINUGUA United Nations mission, in Guatemala to oversee the peace process.

Narcos Drug-smuggling gangs. There are several in Guatemala including the Mexico-based Zetas. Also Narcotraficante.

Natural Another term for an indigenous person.

PAC Village civil-defence patrols, set up by Ríos Montt in the 1980s. They were responsible for many massacres, and still form a powerful pressure group today.

Palapa Thatched palm-leaf hut.

Parque Town's central plaza; or a park.

Pensión Simple hotel.

Pila Washhouse; sink for washing clothes.

Pipil Indigenous tribal group that occupied much of the Guatemalan Pacific coast at the time of the Conquest. Only their art survives, around the town of Santa Lucía Cotzumalguapa.

Pisto Slang for cash.

Principal village elder.

Pullman Comfortable (ish) bus; basically anything not a chicken bus.

Punta The music of the Garífuna.

Q'eqchi' (Also spelt "Kekchi"). Maya tribal group based around Cobán, the Verapaz highlands, Lago Izabal and the Petén.

REMHI The Catholic Church's Truth Commission, set up to investigate the civil-war atrocities.

Repatriados Guatemalan refugees from the civil war, who have now returned to their country.

Sierra Mountain range.

Tecún Umán Last king of the K'iche' tribe, defeated in battle by Alvarado.

Telgua National telecom company.

Tienda Shop.

Típica Clothes woven from multicoloured textiles, usually geared towards the Western customer.

Traje Traditional Maya costume.

Tzute Headcloth or scarf worn as a part of traditional Maya costume.

Tz'utujil Indigenous tribal group occupying the land to the south of Lake Atitlán.

URNG (Unidad Revolucionaria Nacional Guatemalteca) (Guatemalan National Revolutionary Unity). Umbrella organization of the four former guerrilla groups, now disbanded.

USAC (Universidad de San Carlos) University of San Carlos. Guatemala's national university, formerly a hotbed of political activism.

La Violencia Term often used to describe the bloodiest civil-war years; literally "the violence".

Xate Decorative palm leaves harvested in Petén for export to the US, to be used in flower arrangements.

Xela Another name for the city of Quetzaltenango.

Maya architectural terms

Altar Elaborately carved altars, often of a cylindrical design, were grouped round the fringes of the main plaza. Used to record historical events, they could have also functioned as sacrificial stones. See also **zoomorphs**.

Ball court Narrow, stone-flagged rectangular court with banked sides where the Maya ball game was played. The courts symbolized a stage between the real and supernatural worlds and for the ball players it could be a game of life and death: losers were sometimes sacrificed.

Chultún Underground storage chamber.

Corbel arch "False arch" where each stone slightly overlaps the one below. A relatively primitive technique which severely limits the width of doorways and interiors.

Glyph Element in Maya writing, roughly the equivalent of a letter or phrase; used to record historical events. Some glyphs are phonetic, while others represent an entire description or concept as in Chinese characters. Dominant Classic and Postclassic sites had unique emblem glyphs; some like Copán and Tikal used several.

Lintel Top block of stone or wood above a doorway or window, often carved to record important events and dates.

Palace Maya palaces occupied prominent locations near the ceremonial heart of the city, usually resting on low platforms, and almost certainly housed the royal elite. There are particularly striking palaces at Tikal, Cancuén and La Blanca.

Postclassic Period between the decline of Maya civilization and the arrival of the Spanish, 909–1530 AD.

Preclassic Archeological era now viewed as one of the peaks of Maya civilization, usually given as 2000 BC–250 AD.

Putún Style dominant at Ceibal in central Petén, exhibiting strong Mexican characteristics.

Roof comb Decorative top crest on stone temples, possibly intended to enhance verticality. Originally painted in arresting colours and often framed by giant stucco figures.

Sacbé Paved Maya road or raised causeway. Effective at saving troops, leaders and traders from sloshing through the lowland marshes. Also functioned as trade routes, there are hundreds of kilometres still evident in northern Petén today.

Stela Freestanding, often exquisitely carved, stone monument. Decorating major Maya sites, stelae fulfilled a sacred and political role commemorating historical events. Among the largest and most impressive are the ones at Quiriguá and Copán.

Temple Monumental stone structure of pivotal religious significance built in the ceremonial heart of a city, usually with a pyramid-shaped base and topped with a narrow room or two used for secretive ceremonies and bloody sacrifices. Those at Tikal and El Mirador reach more than 60m.

Toltec Style of the central Mexican tribal group who invaded parts of the Maya region.

Zoomorph Spectacular stone altar intricately carved with animal images and glyphs; there are wonderful examples at Quiriguá.

Small print and index

A ROUGH GUIDE TO ROUGH GUIDES

Published in 1982, the first Rough Guide – to Greece – was a student scheme that became a publishing phenomenon. Mark Ellingham, a recent graduate in English from Bristol University, had been travelling in Greece the previous summer and couldn't find the right guidebook. With a small group of friends he wrote his own guide, combining a highly contemporary, journalistic style with a thoroughly practical approach to travellers' needs.

The immediate success of the book spawned a series that rapidly covered dozens of destinations. And, in addition to impecunious backpackers, Rough Guides soon acquired a much broader readership that relished the guides' wit and inquisitiveness as much as their enthusiastic, critical approach and value-for-money ethos.

These days, Rough Guides include recommendations from budget to luxury and cover more than 200 destinations around the globe, as well as producing an ever-growing range of eBooks and apps.

Visit **roughguides.com** to see our latest publications.

Rough Guide credits

Editor: Alice Park
Layout: Jessica Subramanian
Cartography: Lokamata Sahu
Picture editors: Rhiannon Furbear, Michelle Bhatia
Proofreader: Anita Sach
Managing editor: Mani Ramaswamy
Assistant editor: Jalpreen Kaur Chhatwal
Production: Rebecca Short
Cover design: Nicole Newman, Dan May
Photographer: Tim Draper

Editorial assistant: Eleanor Aldridge
Senior pre-press designer: Dan May
Design director: Scott Stickland
Travel publisher: Joanna Kirby
Digital travel publisher: Peter Buckley
Reference director: Andrew Lockett
Operations coordinator: Becky Doyle
Publishing director (Travel): Clare Currie
Commercial manager: Gino Magnotta
Managing director: John Duhigg

Publishing information

This fifth edition published September 2012 by
Rough Guides Ltd,
80 Strand, London WC2R 0RL
11, Community Centre, Panchsheel Park,
New Delhi 110017, India
Distributed by the Penguin Group
Penguin Books Ltd,
80 Strand, London WC2R 0RL
Penguin Group (USA)
375 Hudson Street, NY 10014, USA
Penguin Group (Australia)
250 Camberwell Road, Camberwell,
Victoria 3124, Australia
Penguin Group (NZ)
67 Apollo Drive, Mairangi Bay, Auckland 1310,
New Zealand
Penguin Group (South Africa)
Block D, Rosebank Office Park, 181 Jan Smuts Avenue,
Parktown North, Gauteng, South Africa 2193
Rough Guides is represented in Canada by Tourmaline
Editions Inc. 662 King Street West, Suite 304, Toronto,
Ontario M5V 1M7
Printed in Singapore by Toppan Security Printing Pte. Ltd.

Help us update

We've gone to a lot of effort to ensure that the fifth edition of **The Rough Guide to Guatemala** is accurate and up-to-date. However, things change – places get "discovered", opening hours are notoriously fickle, restaurants and rooms raise prices or lower standards. If you feel we've got it wrong or left something out, we'd like to know, and if you can remember the address, the price, the hours, the phone number, so much the better.

Please send your comments with the subject line "**Rough Guide Guatemala Update**" to ✉ mail @uk.roughguides.com. We'll credit all contributions and send a copy of the next edition (or any other Rough Guide if you prefer) for the very best emails.

Find more travel information, connect with fellow travellers and book your trip on ⓦ roughguides.com

ABOUT THE AUTHOR

Iain Stewart has been visiting Guatemala since the early 1990s, when he spent an extended stay in the country at the tail end of a round-the-world trip. Since then, he has returned many times, and has written extensively about the country and the Maya region for guidebooks, newspapers and magazines. He knows of no more beautiful place than the Guatemalan highlands, but lives close to the beach in Brighton, England.

Acknowledgements

Iain Stewart: In Guatemala thanks to Inguat for continuing support, thanks particularly to the good-humoured Marlon Laz, with whom I've shared many adventures. In Guatemala City, Lorena and Hank you are fantastic people and do an amazing job, and it's always great to catch up with my mate José. In Antigua, thanks to Michael Tallon, John Rexla and Allyson, all at *Hotel Cirilo*, plus the unique Gloria Villalta. By the lake, cheers to dear friends Deedle and Dave and all the other crew at the Iguana and Isla Verde in Santa Cruz. Tom and Lucas in Xela, it was great to hook up. Elsewhere to Rusty, Chris and Dani down the Río way, in Lanquín to Chris and company, and up in the Petén to Dieter – you are a font of Maya knowledge. At home I couldn't do without the support of my family – Fee, Louis, Monty, Aubs and Susan. And my gratitude to the Rough Guides team, particularly my expert editor Alice Park.

Readers' letters

Thanks to all the readers who have taken the time to write in with comments and suggestions (and apologies if we've inadvertently omitted or misspelt anyone's name):

Thilo Ball; Linda Bratcher; Chris Collington; David Crockett; Mette Filtenborg; David Holloway; Isabel Larios; Adam Mason; Aaldrik Mulder and Sonya Spry; Joe Mulligan; Anne del Oceano; Kim Puccetti; Thomas Schroeder; Marleen ter Haar.

Photo credits

All photos © Rough Guides except the following:
(Key: a-above; b-below/bottom; c-centre; l-left; r-right; t-top)

p.1 AWL Images/Peter Adams
p.2 Robert Harding Picture Library/Ken Welsh
p.4 Getty Images/David Tipling (tl)
p.5 Robert Harding Picture Library/Luca Picciau
p.9 Corbis/Danny Lehman (tr); Richard Maschmeyer/Robert Harding World Imagery (b)
p.11 Getty Images/4 Eyes Photography (br); SuperStock/Martin Engelmann (tr)
p.12 SuperStock/Photononstop
p.13 Alamy/Stefano Paterna (b); Corbis/Glenn Bartley (t)
p.14 Corbis/Daniel LeClair/Reuters (t); Getty Images/Jan Cook (b)
p.15 Corbis/Martin Rietze/Westend61 (t)
p.16 Corbis/Diego Lezama Orezzoli (tr); Getty Images/Jeremy Woodhouse (br)
p.18 Corbis/Colin Brynn/Robert Harding World Imagery (t)
p.19 Corbis/Sergio Pitamitz/Robert Harding World Imagery (t)
p.20 Alamy/Philip Scalia (c); AWL Images/Ivan Vdovin (t)
p.21 Alamy/Maxime Bessieres (tr)

p.48 Corbis/Christian Kober/Robert Harding World Imagery
p.51 Alamy/ Scott B. Rosen
p.61 Corbis/Jorge Silva/Reuters (t)
p.77 Getty Images/Sasha Weleber (t)
p.95 NHPA/Photoshot/Mark Newman/Photo Researchers, Inc.
p.177 Alamy/Michele Falzone
p.197 SuperStock/Photononstop
p.221 NHPA/Photoshot/KEVIN SCHAFER
p.235 Getty Images/Michael Mahovlich/Radius Images (tl); Robert Harding Picture Library/Gg (b)
p.249 Alamy/Jan Csernoch

Front cover Colourful embroidery of Quetzal birds © SuperStock/Travel Library Limited
Back cover Chichicastenango market © Tim Draper/Rough Guides (t); Lago de Atitlán © Corbis/Frank Krahmer (cl); Tree houses at Finca Ixobel © Tim Draper/Rough Guides (cr)

Index

Maps are marked in grey

Map symbols

The symbols below are used on maps throughout the book

✈ International airport	ᵼ Border crossing post	⋀⋀ Mountain range	≍ Bridge
★ Transport stop	♦ Place of interest	▲ Mountain peak	Building
Ⓜ Transmetro	∴ Ruin	◠ Cave	Market
✉ Post office	♯ Castle	Swamp	Church
@ Internet access	∩ Arch	Waterfall	Stadium
ⓘ Information centre	Viewpoint	Gorge	Park
P Parking	Campsite	Volcano	Christian cemetery
Fuel/gas station	Maya ruin	Oasis/palm	Beach
ℂ Telephone office	Archeological site	Electricity tower	

Listings key

- ■ Accommodation
- ● Eating & Drinking
- ■ Nightlife
- ● Shop